Behavioral Intervention

Behavioral Intervention

Principles, Models, and Practices

edited by

Joseph R. Scotti, Ph.D.
West Virginia University

and

Luanna H. Meyer, Ph.D.
Massey University
New Zealand

·P A U L·H·
BROOKES
PUBLISHING Cº

Baltimore • London • Toronto • Sydney

Paul H. Brookes Publishing Co.
Post Office Box 10624
Baltimore, Maryland 21285-0624

www.brookespublishing.com

Typeset by Barton Matheson Willse & Worthington, Baltimore, Maryland.
Manufactured in the United States of America by
The Maple Press Company, York, Pennsylvania.

Most of the case studies that are described in this book represent actual people and circumstances. Selected case studies are composites that are based on the authors' experiences. These case studies do not represent the lives or experiences of specific individuals; any similarity to actual individuals or circumstances is coincidental, and no implications should be inferred. In the case studies that represent real people, the names have been changed to protect identities and written consent has been obtained for their inclusion.

Any information about medical treatments contained herein is in no way meant to substitute for a physician's advice or expert opinion; readers should consult a medical practitioner if they are interested in more information.

Library of Congress Cataloging-in-Publication Data

Behavioral intervention : principles, models, and practices / edited
   by Joseph R. Scotti, Luanna H. Meyer.
       p.   cm.
    Includes bibliographical references and index.
    ISBN 1-55766-294-0 (alk. paper)
    1. Behavior modification.   I. Scotti, Joseph R.   II. Meyer, Luanna H.
BF637.B4B452   1999
153.8'5—dc21
                                                                        99-19479
                                                                        CIP

British Library Cataloguing in Publication data are available from the British Library.

Contents

About the Editors

Joseph R. Scotti, Ph.D., Associate Professor, Department of Psychology, Post Office Box 6040, West Virginia University, Morgantown, West Virginia 26506

Dr. Scotti received his doctorate in clinical psychology at the State University of New York at Binghamton. His research and clinical efforts in the field of developmental disabilities have focused on the development, evaluation, and use of functional assessment technologies in conjunction with positive behavioral support. He has worked in institutional, community, and school settings and frequently conducts training in functional assessment and positive behavioral support through workshops, seminars, and formal university courses. These efforts, as well as part of the work on this book, have been supported by a grant for the School Consultation Project from the West Virginia Developmental Disabilities Planning Council, with additional support from the Monongalia County (WV) Schools. Related areas of research, clinical intervention, and teaching include HIV/AIDS risk reduction in people with developmental disabilities, behavioral assessment, and posttraumatic stress disorder.

Luanna H. Meyer, Ph.D., Professor and Pro Vice-Chancellor, Massey University College of Education, Private Bag 11222, Palmerston North, New Zealand

Dr. Meyer's research and teaching have focused on inclusion, cooperative classroom management, challenging behavior, educational best practices, and multicultural education. She has authored more than 200 books, research articles, and book chapters. In her present role, she administers a College of Education with responsibilities for teaching programs and research and development throughout Aotearoa/New Zealand, including undergraduate through doctoral programs in teacher education, educational psychology, counseling and guidance, educational administration, adult learning, Maori immersion and bilingual education, and policy studies. Part of the work of this book was conducted in her previous position as Professor of Education at Syracuse University, where she directed the Inclusive Elementary and Special Education Program and the national Consortium for Collaborative Research on Social Relationships of Children and Youth with Diverse Abilities.

Contributors

Cynthia M. Anderson, M.A.
Department of Psychology
West Virginia University
Post Office Box 6040
Morgantown, West Virginia 26506

Jennifer M. Asmus, Ph.D.
Assistant Professor
Department of Education Foundations
University of Florida
1403 Norman Hall
Gainesville, Florida 32611

Alisa B. Bahl, M.A.
Department of Psychology
West Virginia University
Post Office Box 6040
Morgantown, West Virginia 26506

Craig Barringer, Ph.D.
Regional Educational Consultant and
    Adjunct Professor
Center for Disabilities and Community Inclusion
University of Vermont
Burlington, Vermont 05403

Wendy K. Berg, M.A.
Senior Research Assistant
The University of Iowa
100 Hawkins Drive, Room 251
Iowa City, Iowa 52242

Karen A. Berkman, Ph.D.
Program Director
Pressley Ridge Schools Autism Program
530 Marshall Avenue
Pittsburgh, Pennsylvania 15214

Denise Berotti, Ph.D.
Psychologist
Developmental Disabilities Institute
Adult Residential Division
99 Hollywood Drive
Smithtown, New York 11787

Terry Chaplin
Clinical Research Psychometrist 2
Penetanguishene Mental Health Centre
500 Church Street
Penetanguishene, Ontario L9M 1G3
CANADA

Douglas Cheney, Ph.D.
Assistant Professor
University of Washington
102 Miller, Box 353600
Seattle, Washington 98193

Daniel W. Close, Ph.D.
Professor
University of Oregon
1235 University of Oregon
Eugene, Oregon 97403

Glen Dunlap, Ph.D.
Professor
University of South Florida
13301 Bruce B. Downs Boulevard
Tampa, Florida 33612

V. Mark Durand, Ph.D.
Professor
Department of Psychology
State University of New York
University at Albany
1400 Washington Avenue
Albany, New York 12222

Kenneth Ervin
Arnold Apartments, Z-1
345 Prospect Street
Morgantown, West Virginia 26505

Ian M. Evans, Ph.D.
Professor
Department of Psychology
Private Bag 3105
University of Waikato
Hamilton
NEW ZEALAND

Judith E. Favell, Ph.D.
Carlton Palms Educational Center
28308 Churchill Smith Lane
Mt. Dora, Florida 32757

Denise Fraser
Florès Rehabilitation Center
185 rue Durand
Saint-Jérôme, Quebec J7Z 2V4
CANADA

Kurt A. Freeman, M.A.
Department of Psychology
West Virginia University
Post Office Box 6040
Morgantown, West Virginia 26506

Barry Glick, Ph.D., N.C.L.
Chief Operations Officer
G & G Consultants
106 Acorn Drive
Scotia, New York 12302

Arnold P. Goldstein, Ph.D.
Professor (retired)
Department of Education
Syracuse University
Syracuse, New York 13210

Jay W. Harding, Ed.S.
University Hospital School
100 Hawkins Drive, Room 251
Iowa City, Iowa 52242

Richard P. Hastings, Ph.D.
Lecturer
Department of Psychology
University of Southampton
Highfield, Southampton
Hampshire SO17 1BJ
UNITED KINGDOM

Robert P. Hawkins, Ph.D.
Professor Emeritus
Department of Psychology
Post Office Box 6040
West Virginia University
Morgantown, West Virginia 26506

Meme Hieneman, Ph.D.
Assistant Professor
University of South Florida
4202 East Fowler Avenue
Tampa, Florida 33620

Dave Hingsburger, M.Ed.
Therapist (Private practice)
33 des Floralies
Eastman, Quebec J0E 1P0
CANADA

Karin Hirstwood
Program Manager
York Support Services Network
152 High Street
Sutton West, Ontario L0E 1R0
CANADA

Robert H. Horner, Ph.D.
Professor
Specialized Training Program
University of Oregon
1235 University of Oregon
Eugene, Oregon 97403

Donald W. Kincaid, Ed.D.
Deputy Director
University Affiliated Center for Developmental
 Disabilities
955 Hartman Run Road
Morgantown, West Virginia 26505

Karen S. Kirk, Ph.D.
Behavior Management Consultant/
 Clinical Psychologist
Department of Defense Dependent Schools (Europe)
PSC 118 Box 644
APO AE 09137

Alex Kopelowicz, M.D.
Assistant Professor
School of Medicine
University of California–Los Angeles
15535 San Fernando Mission Boulevard
Mission Hills, California 91345

Lucien Labbé, M.A.
Clinical Consultant
Florès Rehabilitation Center
185 rue Durand
Saint-Jérôme, Quebec J7Z 2V4
CANADA

Robert Paul Liberman, M.D.
Professor
School of Medicine
University of California–Los Angeles
300 UCLA Medical Plaza
Los Angeles, California 90095

Joseph M. Lucyshyn, Ph.D.
Assistant Professor
Teaching Research Division
Western Oregon University
99 West 10th Avenue, Suite 370
Eugene, Oregon 97401

Nancy B. Meadows, Ed.D.
Associate Professor
Department of Curriculum and Instruction
Texas Christian University
TCU Box 297900
Fort Worth, Texas 76129

Tracy L. Morris, Ph.D.
Assistant Professor
Department of Psychology
West Virginia University
Post Office Box 6040
Morgantown, West Virginia 26506

Kimberly B. Mullen, M.A.
West Virginia University
Post Office Box 6040
Morgantown, West Virginia 26506

Angie Nethercott, M.A.
Coordinator, Special Projects
York Central Hospital
Behaviour Management Services Sexuality Clinic
10 Trench Street
Richmond Hill, Ontario L4C 4Z3
CANADA

Deborah L. Olson, Ph.D.
Assistant Professor
Specialized Training Program
University of Oregon
1235 University of Oregon
Eugene, Oregon 97403

Hyun-Sook Park, Ph.D.
Associate Professor
Education
California State University–Sacramento
6000 J Street
Sacramento, California 95819

Darlene Roberts-Spence
Behavioural Consultant
York Simcoe Brain Injury Services
13 311 Yonge Street, Suite 202
Richmond Hill, Ontario L4E 3L6
CANADA

Sue Tough
York Behaviour Management Services
York Central Hospital
10 Trench Street
Richmond Hill, Ontario L4C 4Z3
CANADA

Glenda L. Vittimberga, Ph.D.
Associate Professor
Division of Administration and Counseling
California State University–Los Angeles
Martin Luther King Hall, Room C-1065
5151 State University Drive
Los Angeles, California 90032

David P. Wacker, Ph.D.
Professor
Special Education
The University of Iowa
100 Hawkins Drive, Room 251
Iowa City, Iowa 52242

Gwendolyn C. Webb-Johnson, Ed.D.
Assistant Professor
Department of Special Education
University of Texas
Sanchez 408A
Austin, Texas 78712

Karen L. Weigle, M.A.
Behavior Analyst Director
East Tennessee
Team Evaluation Center
5908 Lyon's View Drive
Willow Cottage
Knoxville, Tennessee 37919

Foreword

Matt arrived in an alarming condition after a 2-day, nonstop drive from his home state in a van with three staff members. No one had slept; all had bruises and torn clothes. Matt did, too, but he was also in full restraints. He had come to our program "for treatment of multiple, intractable, and very severe behavior disorders: self-injury, property destruction, and aggression." Matt's head was covered with scars and wounds where hair had been; his restraints were in place to prevent him from inserting objects of all manner and size into various orifices; his property destruction was lightning fast and unfailingly effective. Indeed, his records declared that he could destroy a room in 7 minutes— a marvel of measurement. He remained naked much of the time, tearing his clothes and attacking those who attempted to interrupt this or any other act. His behavior was challenging indeed.

We set about our work, first finding Matt under the array of restraints that had been successively and futilely applied to protect him. As these were peeled off, we met a handsome young man of 23, saying nothing vocally but stating his intent with every move. His hands and eyes were in constant motion, scanning the possibilities with an acuteness that belied his label of "profound retardation."

We began the process of getting to know Matt and of understanding his behavior, recording the conditions and contingencies that appeared functional in his life; sampling reinforcers; offering various types and sequences of activities and other environmental rearrangements; searching for alternatives to his current methods of dealing with his world; and exploring means of protecting, interrupting, and consequating his various behavioral challenges.

We were accustomed to dealing with significant challenges, but in Matt's case we were not satisfied with the pace of our discovery or with the potential for helping him change. One day, the start of a solution rode into town. Tom Shea arrived to join our team, sporting two invaluable assets: excellent clinical skills and an outlandish taste in clothes. His red boots and Hawaiian shirt had an effect on Matt that we had not seen: Matt sat motionless, riveted, reverential. Matt had handed us the keys, designating us to help him drive to a better behavioral place.

And so the trip began: brief, then longer periods of participating in activities, learning skills, refraining from problems—all leading to wardrobe changes. Bright ties, wild shirts, Bermuda shorts of every description—all available in Matt's closet for his frequent trips to celebrate his successes. Along the way, only one caveat was introduced: When these garments were sullied (presumably in the interest of hastening a clothing change), Matt experienced a brief but dreadful period of wearing a pinstripe shirt and gray slacks.

Matt's progress was dazzling; few could recognize him as the same individual who had originally come to us. However, this degree and rate of change must be properly credited to Tom's retired mother and her elderly friend, the millionaire, whose death gave Matt a never-ending behavioral life. This gentleman's money, insatiable appetite for clothes, and eye for glitz truly represented a living will for Matt. Tom's mother brought Matt closets full of finery, and through this gift Matt was ensured years of change in his clothes and his behavior.

When visiting with Matt today, one meets an industrious and focused worker, handsome in the afro he had missed years earlier, living amicably with others in a life that he clearly enjoys. He may be wearing a brocade vest, wing tips, and tuxedo pants, but so, too, are half of the men in Florida.

Matt taught us more than we taught him. These lessons, learned many years ago, contributed to the body of experience and literature that is reflected in this book. "Matt's lessons" remind us of how far we have come and gently nudge us toward the lessons that remain.

Lesson 1: The first step in addressing a behavioral challenge is to find the individual of focus. Sometimes, to find the person who is the focus of service, we must search among restraints. More often, we search for the individual among all of the "stakeholders" at the team meeting. As the chapters in this book reflect, *person centered* means a clear and unequivocal emphasis on one person—not the system, not professionals, not other stakeholders whose interests may be well intentioned but inadvertently not contributing to the individual's well-being. If the needs and values of others compete or interfere with those of the individual, then they must be recognized as such and put into their proper, secondary role.

Lesson 2: Methods of analysis and assessment should ask questions, not dictate answers. Functional and structural analysis has represented a giant leap backward to our roots and an equal leap forward to treatment efficacy. As this book reflects, the analysis and assessment of the conditions and contingencies that maintain challenging behavior have steadily advanced and fortunately have become expected practice. Matt's assessments, rare in the days when he began to teach us his "lessons," remind us how essential it is that our assumptions and methods not dictate the answers that we will accept from these analyses.

Matt was an individual whose structural and functional analysis would have been at once clear and less than prescriptive. Though his reinforcers clearly were sensory, literal translations into alternative forms of reinforcement and other aspects of intervention were far less evident. Along came the "red boots," perhaps sensory, certainly a positive reinforcer, but not typically on the list of usual suspects. That type of reinforcer, not necessarily related to or derivable from the assessment methods and results that we had used to that point, made all the difference in terms of efficacious intervention.

Our methods of structural and functional assessment do represent a major advancement, but they are not finished. The benefits of interview methods must be viewed against the poor accuracy of reporting; naturalistic observation is bound by the limitations of the natural environment; analog methods may not manipulate the actual reinforcers at work. These limitations obviously do not mitigate against the use of these methods but rather point to the need to keep our eyes and systems open and our expertise well honed. As methods of functional and structural assessment have become commonly adopted, practitioners may benefit from reminders that the methods are meant to discover, not dictate, answers. Social attention is not the only positive reinforcer that maintains problem behaviors; task demands are not the only "toxic" environmental event that may motivate escape; and setting events may be subtle or apparent only if viewed away from proximal events. Our methods should focus our search for functional events, not blind us to the universe of possibilities. In short, repetition of the mantra of functional analysis should sharpen, not dull, our senses.

Lesson 3: Don't ask the question if you don't want the answer. As this book reflects, the methods of functional and structural analysis are not antithetical but instead have helped to operationalize client-centered services. The locus of control is truly shifting to the individual and away from others who previously assumed expertise, familiarity, or any other basis of imposing the nature and course of supports for the person. From the externally authored, deficit-driven, needs-riddled habilitation plans of the past, the individualized support plans of today are instead oriented to what the individual wants, prefers, indicates a need for—in short, chooses. Though these plans attempt and purport to reflect only the individual's values and wishes, continued evidence of others' imposed values is seen when the individual is said to make "bad choices." This phenomenon is clear when we ask individuals what they want and then devalue their choices. If we ask the questions, then we must be prepared to honor reasonable answers, whether they concern reinforcers or living arrangements. Matt's choices of reinforcers were not unsafe, illegal, or unreasonable; yet some would discredit them as unacceptable on such bases as age inappropriateness, unnaturalness, or social stigmatization. Such critics prefer that we identify more natural or conventional events as reinforcers by sampling more widely or establishing them through "pairing." The shortage of time, functional reinforcers, and research support for the effectiveness of pairing are worthy of discussion at another time. The point here is that Matt had little of the above and had dangerous behavioral issues to address. Under these circumstances, our insistence on "button-down" reinforcers would have served our needs while placing Matt in peril. When we are faced with limitations, conflicting ideas, and competing values, Lesson 3 would direct us back to Lesson 1.

Lesson 4: Principles rule; contingencies count. As the strategies and tactics of addressing challenging behavior have changed over the years, we have seen an increased range and complexity of approaches, evidenced by the rich array described in this book. From the early examples of DROs and time-out procedures applied in relative isolation or precise combinations to treat problems, we now read descriptions of multifaceted life-style approaches to addressing behavioral challenges. In this process, it becomes tempting to forget or to ignore the fundamental principles on which this emergent technology is based. In disregarding the principles that underlie our instructional and therapeutic technology, we are prone to rename our methods or reconceptualize our practices as though they were new and unique and bore no relation to what came before. This tendency encourages the roller coaster ride of "new cures" and discourages the gradual accumulation of a scientifically rigorous and integrated research literature. This literature—as this book makes clear—is the reason and hope for progress on challenging behavior.

A number of years ago, we successfully addressed pica by providing individuals with oral alternatives, principally in the form of popcorn. I laughed when asked about my "popcorn cure for pica" (saying instead that I believed that I had the cure for mental retardation itself), until I reflected on how easily the principles of reinforcement can be lost among "novel" labels and individual techniques. Examples abound. Amid the ecological alterations, instructional approaches, and life-style arrangements that are used to treat challenging behavior, we should not forget that these are rooted in principles of reinforcement and that their success rests directly on their proper adherence to these principles. When we affect behavior by rearranging antecedents, teaching skills, or providing alternative living arrangements, we do so in part by shifting contingencies for behavior. Obvious or not, these principles are at work. We can name these operations what we please, we can distance them from basic principles, we can even announce the demise of contingencies, but without them, meaningful and durable behavior change will not occur. If we do not acknowledge this, then we will lose the best of what has gone before and confuse the rest of what will come. Matt's behavior was not affected by some new or magic formula, though it was tempting to proclaim the new "bootstrap approach to behavior change." The principle and procedure was differential positive reinforcement.

Lesson 5: Labels are best in clothes, not on people. Matt not only wears his clothes, he also enjoys rearranging them by size, color, manufacturer, and type. His use of the labels in his clothes is functional for him. This book attests to the fact that behavioral challenges and their amelioration are not confined to individuals who are "labeled" with developmental disabilities. These chapters elucidate the methods by which successful outcomes can be achieved across diverse people and problems. Through these descriptions, it once again becomes clear that the same principles abide, regardless of the particular techniques and parametric differences that prevail. The universality of the principles of behavior does not imply comparability of therapeutic approaches across problems and people. It does, however, reassure us that we are not starting over each time we attempt to understand and address a behavioral issue.

As a budding young behavioral psychologist in my first job in developmental disabilities, my first assignment from the Chief of Psychiatry was "to stop the facility's pony from biting," the only task that he believed my background in principles of learning and behavior prepared me to do. For many of those early years, we demonstrated that the same principles that accounted for learning in animals applied to humans as well. This agenda has continued with an ever-widening efficacy net to increasingly diverse people and behavioral issues. From the days when we explained that principles such as reinforcement worked for people like Matt—even though he could not understand our explanations—we are demonstrating that these principles work for people who do!

This is a testament to how far we have come in addressing challenging behavior. It is also a tribute to the Matts and the millionaires who contributed to this progress.

Judith E. Favell, Ph.D.
Carlton Palms Educational Center
Mount Dora, Florida

Acknowledgments

This project was not formally supported by any funding sources beyond those that individual chapter authors have acknowledged. We do thank our respective universities and departmental support staff for the time and resources contributed through endless small tasks here and there that add up to a significant effort in the end. From Scotti, thanks go to the Department of Psychology at West Virginia University, Morgantown. From Luanna, thanks to Syracuse University, Syracuse, New York (where she was when the project was initiated), and to Massey University in Aotearoa/New Zealand (where she was when the project concluded).

Many thanks are owed to the fine staff of Paul H. Brookes Publishing Co., especially to Jennifer Kinard, who saw us through the initial stages of the book, and her successor, Christa Horan, who coordinated the final burst of effort and dealt with the attendant multitude of minutia and both minor and major frustrations. There are, of course, many other support staff at Brookes Publishing with whom we had infrequent contact yet owe a share of thanks. We owe a special thank you to Melissa Behm and Paul Brookes for their continued support for this book.

To Kevin Clough
and
Danny,
whose behavior, as the system failed them,
led to their untimely deaths,
alone and without
family or supports

Naked they were blown through the circles of Hell.

Dante, *The Inferno*

To my wife, my mother, and, especially, Lucy Rose:
You are my supports.
JRS

To my family and friends,
who are life's most precious gifts,
and especially to my husband and best friend, Ian,
for sharing his passions for scholarship, commitment, and fun
LHM

Section I

CONTEXT AND CHARACTERISTICS

In planning *Behavioral Intervention: Principles, Models, and Practices,* our explicit intent was to bring together state-of-the-art approaches for intervening with the challenging behavior needs of a wide range of populations and to include contributions from a diverse group of authors, each of whom represent cutting-edge research and development in their respective areas of expertise. Unlike other texts that are available, this book does *not* focus exclusively on *one* diagnostic category or subdiscipline but instead presents a comprehensive overview of recommended practices from each of several areas in which behavior challenges have been addressed. Thus, both established scientist-practitioners and professionals in training can have the benefit of new knowledge in various relevant areas of intervention rather than be restricted to information that focuses only on one population.

The populations and topics that are covered in this book include developmental disabilities, chronic psychiatric disorders, childhood behavior disorders and emotional disturbance, sexual offenders, and street gangs. Separate sections of the book address the current context for behavioral intervention and characteristics of the published literature, model programs based on recommended practices, and extended case studies that allow a full description of the implementation of recommended practices in clinical and community environments. The book concludes with a discussion of critical issues and future directions.

The rich sharing of information represented in this book should be a useful resource for professionals and others who are interested in the individuals who present such different and difficult behavior challenges to the behavioral and mental health system. The book brings up-to-date and synthesizes available information on theory and practice related to behavioral interventions with various needs and populations. Most publications of this nature have been written from either a behavioral psychology perspective or a developmental disability perspective; this book includes a blending of perspectives from both and others.

In the first section, Context and Characteristics, are four chapters that set the occasion for the remainder of the book. In Chapter 1, Evans, Scotti, and Hawkins provide an overview of the past 30 years of the behavioral intervention arena by providing their own personal glimpses of where they—and, by extension, the field—have been and the lessons that they have learned along the way (providing an extended follow-up to Judith Favell's foreword). This chapter may provide a trip down memory lane for some readers who were also "there," but we hope that it will also provide the proper backdrop for newer members of the field who have not witnessed the tremendous changes, improvements, and upheavals since the 1960s. The principles of intervention outlined and utilized in the other chapters of this book come out of the struggles of those years, and it is critical that the antecedents of current activity not be forgotten.

Chapters 2 (Meyer & Park) and 3 (Vittimberga, Scotti, & Weigle) outline the recommended practices that grew out of the period described in Chapter 1. It will immediately become clear to the reader that these two chapters address the issue of recommended practices from two different but wholly complementary perspectives: a more molar social systems view and a more molecular behavior analytic approach.

Some readers will be surprised—pleasantly, we hope—at how well the two perspectives dovetail and even overlap each other to form a single, comprehensive perspective and a continuum from which to address behavior challenges.

Finally, in this section, Chapter 4 (Kirk) presents a detailed analysis of the intervention literature with attention-deficit/hyperactivity disorder. This review makes clear a number of the general deficits in the behavioral intervention literature as a whole that are alluded to in the discussion by Vittimberga and colleagues (Chapter 3).

Chapter 1

Understanding
Where We Are Going by
Looking at Where We Have Been

Ian M. Evans, Joseph R. Scotti, & Robert P. Hawkins

It is hoped that readers will find between the covers of this book a somewhat different point of view of behavioral intervention than that with which they are most familiar and comfortable. The model of intervention that is evident to greater or lesser degrees in each of these chapters moves beyond the largely consequence-oriented approaches—targeting single, isolated behaviors—that have dominated behavior analysis and modification since their inception (Evans & Scotti, 1989; Scotti, Evans, Meyer, & Walker, 1991; Scotti, McMorrow, & Trawitzki, 1993). In reaching the point at which behavioral intervention now is—which includes using functional analysis, focusing on constructional (Evans, 1993; Goldiamond, 1974) or educative (Evans & Meyer, 1985; Meyer & Evans, 1989) procedures, and understanding natural contexts—the field has passed through stages that it should both acknowledge and learn from yet move beyond.

To many readers, both novices and established behavior interventionists, a retrospective look will mean different things. Some will say, "We used to do *that* in the name of behavior modification and analysis? How odd!" Many will ask, "What's *wrong* with that? It's what I learned in graduate school and what I still use."

Some will make the latter statement regardless of when they received their behavioral training: It has been our experience in discussion with colleagues and conducting workshops that "traditional behavior modification" is still the predominant approach to treating behavioral excesses and deficits. These impressions are supported by documentation that the published literature on behavioral intervention in a range of areas—developmental disabilities, chronic psychiatric disorders, attention-deficit/hyperactivity disorder, and conduct disorder—remains rooted in this traditional model (e.g., Carr, Robinson, Taylor, & Carlson, 1990; Lennox, Miltenberger, Spengler, & Erfanian, 1988; Scotti, Evans, Meyer, & Walker, 1991; Scotti et al., 1993; Scotti, Mullen, & Hawkins, 1998; Scotti, Ujcich, Weigle, Holland, & Kirk, 1996; see Chapter 4).

What we present in this chapter is a brief look at where the field has been since the mid-1960s. We highlight the inevitable entanglement of scientific principles and social values, touching on the sociology of ideas and how different emphases in different disciplines can create conflict rather than progress. We argue that applied science cannot afford to retreat behind the mask of disinterested empiricism (Evans, 1997).

We provide some personal glimpses of the work that we did or observed—which was then current and accepted (although some of it clearly violated good practice even by those earlier standards). Some applications look naive or simply incomplete by more recent criteria, and we show through the remainder of this volume what needs to be done to lodge those earlier practices within a larger and more socially relevant context. Behavior analysis, after all, did set out to achieve socially relevant behavior change (Baer, Wolf, & Risley, 1968; Wolf, 1978). It is by stages that we have arrived at the present point, acknowledging that behavior change must be *relevant* and *important* to the person for whom the change is being made and that this might mean changing or creating natural conditions that are more suited to the individual's unique needs.

WHERE WE STARTED

When behavior modification began to emerge as a distinct enterprise, a major component of its evolution was the direct application of principles of operant conditioning. Skinner and his colleagues referred to their research enterprise as the "experimental analysis of behavior," and the application of operant principles was soon labeled "applied behavior analysis." Although some of the pioneers were clinical psychologists who recognized the enormous potential of learning and behavioral principles (e.g., Bijou, Krasner, Lovaas, Staats, Ullmann), many of the other early contributors were experimental psychologists who had worked with animals, sometimes as students or colleagues of Skinner (e.g., Azrin, Foxx, Lindsley, Michael). An important political agenda of the original studies was to demonstrate the potential power of operant principles with people who had been unresponsive to other treatment approaches. As in the basic research laboratory, the scientific agenda was dominated by the demonstration of experimental control and the isolation of particular interventions as the specific independent variables for behavior change.

At about the same time, special education, which until then had been somewhat restricted to the needs of students with relatively mild disabilities, began to attend to the possibility of educating children with more serious developmental delays (Sontag & Haring, 1996). Early work by the Clarkes in Britain (e.g., Clarke & Clarke, 1974) and Gold (1972) in the United States was instrumental in proving that if only students with disabilities would be *taught,* then they could, indeed, learn much more than anticipated. In such a climate, of course, the detailed technology of behavior analysis, based as it was on literally thousands of laboratory studies of simple learning, was a gold mine of ideas and information. If rats and pigeons could be taught elaborate behavioral repertoires by means of reinforcement, shaping, chaining, and stimulus control, then how much more could be taught to children with severe mental retardation? And if persistent behaviors could be reduced through extinction, punishment, and differential reinforcement, then how much more effectively could we eliminate the inappropriate behaviors of children with autism and other behavior disorders?

Special education for students who had mental retardation requiring extensive to pervasive supports and applied behavior analysis rapidly became almost synonymous, with a new, energetic generation of scholars working in this subspecialty, whose original background in education or psychology was irrelevant as long as they were applied behavior analysts: Baer, Guess, Haring, Sailor, Wolf, and many others. There was enormous enthusiasm for direct behavioral data, for single-subject research designs, for the operationalization of intervention strategies, and for the application of very complex principles from the laboratory. Skinner's broad philosophy of science also knitted this diverse group together: a disdain for theory and for hypothetical constructs, eschewing of physiological (and thus medical) principles, and distrust for statistical analysis of group data in favor of the direct manipulation of observable behaviors. How various educational philosophies began to extend and change the links between special education and behavior analysis is examined in greater detail in Chapter 2.

TO BOLDLY GO . . .

It is important to put these pioneering efforts into the social context within which behavior analysis evolved. Demonstrations of the potential of applied behavior analysis were carried out with people for whom there were few alternative treatment services. Behavior modification made a name for itself by intervening with those whom mainstream psychology and psychiatry had left behind as "untreatable": people with mental retardation requiring extensive to pervasive supports, youth who seemed incorrigibly delinquent, and patients with chronic psychosis. As behavior interventionists, we went into places that few cared to look at closely and worked with human beings whom the world had locked away behind high walls. We soon found ourselves within the midst of controversies, however, as society became grudgingly aware of the human rights abuses that were occurring behind those walls—mostly in the name of custodial care, but soon in the name of behavior modification (Cotter, 1967; see Martin, 1975).

Many readers do not remember the career-making exposé of conditions at Willowbrook State School (Staten Island, NY) by then WABC-TV news reporter Geraldo Rivera (1972); and most are unfamiliar with the equally shocking documentation of the conditions at other facilities in New York State (e.g., Blatt, 1973) and across the United States, such as in Peoria (IL) State Hospital (Illinois Legislative Investigating Commission, 1973), Partlow (AL) State School (Beyer, 1983; *Wyatt v. Stickney,* 1971, 1972), and the Pennhurst (PA) State School (Beyer, 1983; *Halderman v. Pennhurst,* 1977). These revelations occurred only in the early to mid-1970s: gross overcrowding, neglect and abuse, filth, and failure to provide any meaningful form of habilitation. The reality remains so shocking that when we show to psychology classes photos from Burton Blatt's *Souls in Extremis* (Blazey, 1973), undergraduates invariably guess that the images are from the early 1900s—they cannot believe that such conditions existed so very recently. But even those who lived through those times and worked in such facilities find it easy—even preferable—to forget.

The upheaval caused by human rights considerations came hand in hand with important analyses of the ethics of treatment and the parameters within which behavioral techniques could be used (Krasner, 1976; Martin, 1975;

Schwitzgebel & Schwitzgebel, 1980). Intemperate usage led to increasing regulation and prohibition of certain procedures by many states and mandated reviews of all behavioral interventions by both human rights and behavior management committees. Even when reviewed and approved, extreme procedures still found their way into intervention plans, often based on the false assertion that all other alternatives had been tried (cf. Berkman & Meyer, 1988). Many behavior analysts resisted attempts to restrict the use of behavioral techniques, arguing that only scientific criteria were valid.

It is within this evolving context that we present some personal glimpses of where the field has been. Current work with the many different groups of people referred to in this text is not context-free. To better move the field forward and to prevent repeating the errors of the past, it helps to look at that context—the setting events, if you will. We do not provide a history of the treatment of mental illness and developmental disabilities (see President's Committee on Mental Retardation, 1977; Scheerenberger, 1987; Trent, 1995) but rather the historical antecedents for three behavior analysts, which suggest how we came to the approaches that we now employ.

A PERSONAL GLIMPSE: HAWKINS

Control of Behavior

When applied behavior analysis began, the mission was to show that behavior analysts could apply a scientific approach to treating problems of human behavior or, more precise, environment–behavior functional relations (cf. Donahoe & Palmer, 1994). First, it was necessary to convince people that behavior was, indeed, what needed to be changed, rather than assumed inner constructs such as ego strength, traits, attitudes, or self-esteem (all of which can be reframed in terms of environment–behavior relations, thus often yielding a clearer insight). Behavior analysts tried to show that the principles of behavior that were already known—mostly discovered in research with other species—were quite potent in achieving such change. This goal of showing that behavior could be strongly influenced was reflected in the main title of a series of three texts by Ulrich, Stachnic, and Mabry (1966, 1970, 1974): *Control of Human Behavior.* The successes often involved individuals with whom other practitioners had failed (e.g., Fuller, 1949; Isaacs, Thomas, & Goldiamond, 1960; Risley & Wolf, 1966; Wolf, Risley, & Mees, 1964), which for me made the demonstrations all the more impressive.

Applied behavior analysts not only were equipped with some powerful principles (e.g., reinforcement, extinction) and procedures (e.g., shaping, fading) but also had research methods with which to demonstrate clearly and scientifically the power of this approach. Thanks largely to Sidman (1960), behavior analysts believed that experiments could be conducted to demonstrate the effectiveness of an intervention with a single subject (cf. Barlow, Hayes, & Nelson, 1984; Kazdin, 1982). This approach to the scientific evaluation of intervention did not require groups of comparable subjects, and the results were obvious *graphically;* a reader did not have to understand inferential statistics to appreciate the speed and magnitude of the effects. Furthermore, the methods of reliably measuring specific behaviors and graphing the data often helped behavior analysts to achieve even more change than could have been obtained otherwise (Hawkins, 1989).

But Which Behavior and How?

As a group, applied behavior analysts generally were not very concerned with issues of *which* behaviors to change. Many were not trained as clinicians and sometimes were not very analytic and sensitive about exactly which behavior should be directly addressed and in which way. If someone in authority said that a particular behavior deficit or, more often, behavior excess was a problem, then behavior analysts were willing to accept that assessment and proceed to modify the identified behavior directly. Furthermore, many behavior analysts were not highly concerned with which behavioral *procedures* were applied to the problem, although the great majority had a bias that favored positive procedures and avoided aversive procedures.

Only gradually did I become aware that some people, in the name of behavior modifi-

cation, were doing things of which I disapproved. For example, one author submitted a manuscript for publication in *School Applications of Learning Theory,* an informal journal that I had begun in 1968, in which the intervention was public humiliation of students who misbehaved in class. I rejected the manuscript in disgust, although it took some effort to explain my reservations when the author responded, "But it worked!"

At one of the Kansas conferences on behavior analysis in education, there was a panel discussion about the training of behavior modifiers. During this panel, Todd Risley described an institution where a doctoral-level psychologist was responsible for a treatment program in which delinquent youth who misbehaved were sent to a ward where "the facilities, food and everything else [were] unsatisfactory" (Michael et al., 1972, p. 27), and they had to earn their way back to a more satisfactory ward; and where anyone who was seen masturbating had to do so in public, with other youth being encouraged to laugh at him (Michael et al., 1972; see also Risley, 1975). In that same discussion, Jon Bailey described an institution in which a professional who claimed to be a behavior modifier implemented procedures such as having a child who stole something wear a sign that read I AM A THIEF and having children who engaged in homosexual acts be forced to re-engage in them in front of staff and other residents. I also heard of abuses that were taking place in some prisons in the name of behavior modification. One might suggest that these professionals were influenced by such writings as that of Baer (1970), who called for more research on punishment, or Kushner (1970), who had considerable success with various aversive procedures; but these practitioners went far beyond the kind of uses that these two researchers were suggesting.

An additional event finally convinced me to speak out. I served on a thesis committee in which the research subject was a young physicist who had just earned his doctorate, but with considerable difficulty. He had accepted a teaching position at a prestigious small college and, during the summer before his first academic year began, developed a debilitating behavior problem. His head became almost constantly turned sharply to one side (torticollis), a condition that would make it quite difficult to perform a teaching job. It seemed apparent to all on the committee that the problem was one of avoiding a frightening task (as he was still readily able to turn his head forward to light a cigarette), although the individual showed no awareness that his behavior was a form of task avoidance. What disturbed me was that the intervention chosen by my colleague (the thesis chair) and his student was to apply escape-avoidance conditioning, whereby the subject would receive a painful electric shock whenever he failed to keep his head turned straight ahead for a certain number of seconds, with that number gradually increasing. The young man cried during the procedure; although he was becoming more and more able to keep his head turned forward, he dropped out of therapy. I do not know what became of him, but it seemed obvious to me that the "treatment" was putting the man in a double escape-avoidance situation: He could avoid the shock, or he could avoid having to teach bright, inquisitive college students. My colleague and his student had chosen an aversive procedure because that was what they were interested in, not because they had analyzed what it might take for the young Ph.D. either to succeed in his new job or to find one that was more fitting. The more I thought about the intervention, the more obvious it became that it not only was inhumane and likely to fail but also that it neglected to make use of a commonsense functional analysis of the individual's problem.

A Humble Confession

I do not claim to be above such errors myself. Beginning in 1966, I was in charge of developing and supervising an in-school treatment program for public school students who were designated as severely "emotionally disturbed." I called it the School Adjustment Program and employed behavioral principles and procedures extensively (Hawkins & Hayes, 1974). The core of the program consisted of several self-contained special education classrooms, although the program did work with other youth in the school (e.g., Schwarz & Hawkins, 1970). In each of the core classrooms, I had constructed lockable isolation booths that were not much larger than telephone booths. Any youth who was particularly disruptive could be placed in the booth as a brief time-out from the availability of reinforcement. I was essentially taking the position that some behaviors simply should be punished. A systematic, consistent effort was not made to functionally analyze every problem so that their unfavorable learning histories could be directly counteracted with more habilitative ones. If an informal functional analysis of the misbehavior did not just happen to occur to either the teachers or myself, then we simply punished the behavior. In defense of the program, I must add that this was in the context of several very positive, constructional practices. For example, the teachers adapted every academic task to each student's current ability to attend and respond correctly; the teachers praised the youth dozens of times per day and often arranged for positive recognition from peers; and a token economy was in constant use whereby the students earned tokens throughout that day for a wide range of desirable academic, social, and personal behaviors, exchanging the tokens for various activities and privileges. Nevertheless, our reaction to misbehavior could have been more humane and effective had we taken the job of functional analysis more seriously.

It should be recognized that, even from the beginning, applied behavior analysts did sometimes base their interventions on a functional analysis of the problem. For example, Zimmerman and Zimmerman (1962) guessed that one child's difficulty with spelling words was due to the extra teacher attention produced by his errors. This led to the use of an extinction technique, which solved the problem. Similarly, Hayes and Hawkins (1970; see also Hawkins & Hayes, 1974) hypothesized that differential teacher attention to errors in reading comprehension was responsible for a girl's high error rate, and changing the balance in favor of correct answers resulted in a comparable increase in correct answers. In a final example—although there were many others—Wolf, Birnbrauer, Lawler, and Williams (1970) hypothesized that the frequent vomiting of a girl with mental retardation in a classroom was being reinforced by her being sent back to her residence hall, so they arranged that the girl would stay in class whenever she vomited (escape extinction), resulting in elimination of that behavior. Although all of these examples illustrate the use of *informal* functional analyses, it should be noted that none of these examples involved rule violations. My impression is that when a problem behavior involved the violation of rules set by authority figures, functional analysis was seldom even considered: Punishment was the immediate solution.

FURTHER PERSONAL REFLECTIONS: SCOTTI

Normalization

What is ironic is that I began my interest in developmental disabilities in the mid-1970s by volunteering at the then-new Syracuse Developmental Center (SDC) as part of an undergraduate class in special education at Syracuse University taught by Burton Blatt, the author of *Souls in Extremis* (1973), referred to previously. The team to which I was assigned—and later hired by as a direct care staff member—was strongly influenced by the works of Wolfensberger, also at Syracuse University, and the concept of normalization (Wolfensberger, 1972). I say that this is ironic because SDC was one of the new institutions built by New York State in response to the Willowbrook scandal and was embracing the then-newest concepts in the treatment of disabilities; for me, however, this was a starting point from which I seemingly was to travel *backward* in time, emerging some years later having seen some of the worst that the field had to offer before fully embracing again the concepts to which I was exposed so early in my professional career.

This is not to say that normalization, as viewed through the eyes of a direct care staff member, was a panacea. It was not. I worked on a unit with 20–25 adults with mental retardation requiring intermittent to pervasive supports. One of the staff members had been at SDC when it was the Syracuse State School and still housed in the original quarters built in the late 1800s when Eduard Seguin and Harvey Wilbur were active in the "educational movement" (which preceded the eugenics movement and the widespread construction of institutions intended to house and segregate thousands of "undesirable"

people). She told stories of how the residents in those days were mostly juvenile delinquents, unwed teenage mothers, and other social rejects—all with supposed "low moral values." One such woman still lived at SDC; she had been institutionalized in the 1930s after one of several pregnancies out of wedlock. I could never understand the diagnosis of mental retardation that she carried, though by the time I worked with her she was more than 70 years old and experiencing senile dementia.

The unit on which I worked, though institutional, was as homelike as possible, with rugs on the floors, cloth-covered chairs (a definite taboo in environments where residents are often incontinent—the mode then was modular, one-piece, plastic furniture), wood-paneled walls, a fake fireplace, and a fish tank and a television—both *without* a protective plexiglass screen. It really resembled the great room of a college dorm more than the day room of an institution. There were normalized daily routines, including riding in a van to an off-grounds worksite where real work for Bell Telephone was done for real pay. We even spent one summer vacation on Cape Cod, and all of the residents and the staff shared a number of cottages at the beach.

Although it was a well-intentioned context, behavior problems (which theoretically were to decrease because the lifestyle had been normalized) occurred, often at high rates and severity. These behaviors included physical and verbal aggression, property destruction, self-injury, public masturbation, and elopement (leaving the grounds without permission), among other problems. We attempted to contain these behaviors when they occurred, but little else was done beyond restricting privileges (for those who were high functioning enough to know that they had lost a privilege) or emergency physical restraint for the most dangerous behavior.

Descent into the Inferno

Then I went back to school for a master's degree and learned about behavior modification and what was beginning to be known as applied behavior analysis. The books from which I learned in my courses included Leitenberg (1976) and Redd, Porterfield, and Anderson (1979). I look back at these now and see the types of procedures recommended for the problem behaviors of people with disabilities: Functional analysis seemed like a theoretical standard that was almost impossible to implement in the cumbersome antecedent-behavior-consequence (A-B-C) format advocated, and the interventions—mostly differential reinforcement, time-out, and overcorrection—were not implemented in a way that took advantage of the obtained function, anyway. As part of finishing the degree program, I completed a 1-year internship on the adolescent inpatient unit at the Galesburg (IL) Mental Health Center. During that time—and the subsequent 2 years as a staff psychologist in the Developmental Disabilities Program—my world view turned upside down. Here was my trip back in time.

Galesburg was a former army barracks and World War II POW camp. By the time I worked in the Developmental Disabilities Program, these aging barracks with their wooden floors were crumbling—not to mention urine soaked, as was all too evident on a hot summer day in those Illinois cornfields. It was as bad structurally and programmatically as anything from Blatt's and Rivera's exposés—*this now being the early 1980s.* With a caseload of more than 110 children and adults in five residential units, the requirement that each individual receive a full psychological evaluation each year consumed about half of the staff's work time. The other half, when not taken up with pointless meetings, was devoted to treatment planning and intervention. It was simply overwhelming, especially because the staff largely were untrained in behavior modification and equally overwhelmed by the task of attempting to keep everyone dressed, clean, fed, and out of harm's way. The most requested treatment plan was an intervention to encourage all of the residents simply to sit quietly in the chairs that lined the walls of the crowded day rooms (my suggesting that individuals should instead be engaged in some meaningful activity was, in that environment, equivalent to high treason!).

In this context, several colleagues and I—replicating the then-current work of Horner (1980), among others—tried to show that the mere introduction of toys (please do not ask whether those toys were even age appropriate!) into this environment decreased behavior problems (see, e.g., Favell, 1973; Pokrzywinski, Scotti, & Hetz, 1982, as described in Scotti, Evans, Meyer, & DiBenedetto, 1991). This simple antecedent intervention was a world-tilting revelation! The very idea that if you give people something fun to do they will not attack each other or engage in stereotypic or self-injurious behavior was totally antithetical to this environment. At the same time, we were implementing such plans as food deprivation for suicidal gestures and dangerous behavior (Scotti, 1983). For example, we adapted an intervention that was recommended to us following a consultation (with a still major behavior research facility) for a young boy with autism who was self-injurious. Nine-year-old "Jaspur" was given five tokens after each meal; one token was removed each time he made a suicidal gesture or engaged in several other dangerous behaviors (including aggression and property destruction). Each token represented one fifth of his next meal; thus, the more threats and gestures, the less of his next meal he received. Typical standards of data graphing showed that the intervention served to reduce the frequency of suicidal threats and dangerous behavior. Although Jaspur was 45 pounds overweight, an elaborate ethics procedure ensured that he would receive a nutritional supplement if he lost an entire meal. During the 8 weeks of the intervention phase, Jaspur actually lost a total of 19 of 224 meals (8.5%), with no more than two complete meals lost consecutively, and he did not lose any weight. This procedure required that the child clearly understand the negative consequences of losing a token, as he had little opportunity to experience those consequences directly. More important than the explanatory mechanism for why this intervention "succeeded," the plan failed to address that his dangerous behavior undoubtedly was motivated by attention in an institutional environment where one literally had to fight to be noticed. Of even greater concern, the plan did not address the disturbing home life to which this adolescent was returned after our "successful" treatment.

Redemption?

After 2 years in this environment, I moved back to New York State to work in another of the new post-Willowbrook institutions. My caseload was smaller by more than half, but now the staff were in a phase of congregating all of the facility's most challenging residents into one unit. The clear but unstated treatment message was that when you learn to behave yourself, you can have all of the niceties that the well-behaved residents have (e.g., an unlocked unit, leisure activities). Although we did not view it this way at the time, it was the ultimate in segregation and congregation of individuals with profound deficits and severe behavior excesses. We viewed it as a handy way to keep everyone else safe and manage the worst behaviors on a set of units with highly trained and motivated staff. To our surprise and frustration at that time, this simply did not work. It was impossible to monitor effectively the wide range of high-frequency behavior excesses, including physical aggression, self-injury, life-threatening pica, feces smearing, property destruction, elopement, public undressing (which we euphemistically called denudative behavior), and whatever else one could dream of.

Functional analyses of the A-B-C type occasionally were conducted, but it really was not necessary because 1) it was clear that most behavior was for attention or escape from demands, and 2) we did not effectively incorporate the functional information into the treatment plans. Consequence-based interventions abounded. On the "positive" side were differential reinforcement programs, but the O or I (for Other or Incompatible behaviors) were never functional or function-based, and neither were the reinforcers (food was the most common reward, but it was unlikely to be the reason that most individuals were "misbehaving"—despite my having ordered cases of cereal and raisins to have on hand for rewards). On the "negative" side, our treatment charts overflowed with time-out, overcorrection, restitution, positive practice, interruption, and physical and mechanical restraint programs. We were overjoyed to see papers being published on the use of restraints (e.g., Silverman, Watanabe, Marshall, & Baer, 1984), the reinforcing value of restraints (e.g., Favell, McGimsey, & Jones, 1978), and the fading of restraints (e.g., Pace, Iwata, Edwards, & McCosh, 1986); and we tried to adhere to what these told

us—never asking why we were using them in the first place.

One of the "treatment" plans that still haunts me was the use of a contingent exercise consequence for the physical aggression of a 6-year-old boy who could not have weighed more than 50 pounds. Whenever he struck a staff member or another resident, we would dutifully, according to the plan, place this boy face down on a mat and sweep the offending arm in an arc from his thigh to over his head (always being careful to keep his arm close to the floor) *non-stop for 15 minutes*. This was in keeping with the burgeoning literature on overcorrection, contingent effort, and related procedures (e.g., Carey & Bucher, 1981; Epstein, Doke, Sajwaj, Sorrell, & Rimmer, 1974; Foxx & Azrin, 1973; Luce, Delquadri, & Hall, 1980), and it even reduced his aggression—*at first*. Gradually, however, the child began to hit us more and more and would even hit us immediately after we released him from the contingent exercise. He would engage in what we called "hit and run," essentially daring us to chase him and do the procedure again—which of course we did because we had to implement the contingencies consistently. The behavior clearly was attention motivated (we even knew that back then), but our intervention did not account for this important fact by teaching other ways of gaining staff attention or exercising some control over his environment.

In the end, I cannot say that I saw many—if any—of our cleverly designed plans have more than a temporary impact on the excess behaviors that we sought to decelerate. After an initial decrease, the behaviors eventually returned to prior levels and we had to revise our interventions (usually in the direction of some nastier consequence), or the topography changed—usually to some more severe behavior. The two plans that, in retrospect, had the greatest impact on excess behaviors were novel (for that time) *antecedent* manipulations. In one, a woman who frequently undressed in public was regularly offered a change of clothing. In another, a man who would severely injure himself and others in his attempts to escape the locked ward so that he could ride the nearby elevator was offered a chance to ride the elevator every so often. The excess behaviors in each of these cases simply ceased under these antecedent manipulations. Although the time and frustration involved in managing these two behaviors decreased dramatically under these interventions, the interventions were not maintained largely because these *proactive* strategies appeared more effortful to staff than the reactive strategies. The overriding philosophy—at both the professional and the paraprofessional levels—was to make behaviors stop through the use of a sufficiently powerful (and generally negative) consequence (see also Chapter 22). Teaching functionally equivalent replacement skills that might render the excess challenging behaviors useless was scoffed at by staff (despite that this even then was a standard of practice [Evans & Meyer, 1985])—largely, I believe, because the state of the mainstream behavioral literature was such that these forms of intervention were not being held up as examples of the best that the field had to offer (see Evans & Scotti, 1989; Scotti, Evans, Meyer, & Walker, 1991; Scotti et al., 1998; Scotti et al., 1996).

SAME DESTINATION, DIFFERENT ROAD: EVANS

My early academic training was in neo-behaviorism, in which the learning theories of Hull, Spence, and Tolman were just as important as Skinner's system. One of the most exciting books to which I was exposed as an undergraduate student was Staats (1963), in which classical and operant conditioning principles were integrated to provide an expanded perspective on human learning, including language, thought, imagery, and the development of complex repertoires. I knew a certain amount about research in operant behavior but was interested in it mostly as a methodology for studying early environmental influences (Evans, 1966). Thus, when I went to the Institute of Psychiatry (Maudsley Hospital, London) to study for my doctoral degree, I was surprised to discover that I was considered something of a Skinnerian.

Shaping New Behaviors

By happy circumstance, fellow graduate student Rosemery Nelson (now Nelson-Grey) and I were given the opportunity to continue some pilot operant work with children in a psychiatric hospital in one of London's outer suburbs (Nelson & Evans, 1968). What was most fortuitous was that although these young children with autism and severe behavior, developmental, and communication disorders had absurdly been removed from their families and placed in a residential environment, the hospital superintendent had the foresight to set up family-style homes rather than a ward environment. This meant that anything that we designed in terms of treatment needed to fit within the ethos of a homelike environment. Full of enthusiasm, I did my best to create a totally artificial operant laboratory in one of the spare bedrooms (Evans, 1970). Only later did I realize that the caring, loving milieu of the Children's Units was a system of significant behavioral influence, although at times its ecology could be better structured to support positive behavior change.

In 1970, I took up my first academic position at the University of Hawaii—Arthur Staats's recent move there piqued my interest. At Hawaii, I was considered not to be a Skinnerian or behavior analyst—I was judged (and appointed for this reason) to be in the Eysenck-Wolpe behavior therapy tradition. After a brief period as an impostor, even my fake union card was taken away. Hawaii, as the most western frontier of the United States, seemed to attract maverick thinkers, and within a few months I was being mentored by Robert Wahler. When he returned to Tennessee shortly thereafter, I inherited his role as trainer in behavior modification at the state's large residential facility, Waimano Training School and Hospital. Situated on magnificent real estate above Pearl City, Waimano was the classic residential institution containing the sights, sounds, and odors already described by my colleagues. But again, thanks to enlightened administrators, my task was to help implement more effective programs by training the direct care staff in behavioral technology.

Over a number of years, I trained in weekly workshops some 300 staff members, helping them understand the conditions under which individuals would learn skills and discard inappropriate tactics of control. Having to problem-solve all manner of difficult behaviors and challenging individuals, I began to realize that the standard strategy of teaching textbook behavioral principles to direct care staff was an enormous waste of time. Only if there were meaningful activities and programs could one expect individuals to make gains. Staats (1975) had begun to discuss the concept of deficit environments that result in deficit repertoires. Behavioral interventions designed largely to control inappropriate behavior could, it became increasingly apparent, do so only when more appropriate alternative behaviors were being developed. But the institution could not possibly sustain ordinary behavior, such as getting a snack, caring for a pet, going out with one's friends, tinkering with old cars, or the myriad of activities taken for granted in the normal world.

Being Shaped Oneself

Although much about the deinstitutionalization movement has already been described by Scotti, a simultaneous movement was equally important. This was the determination of a group of parents that their children with serious disabilities should not be placed in an institution to begin with. This in turn required certain kinds of parenting skills, good family support, and easily accessed school opportunities. I learned a great deal while working with a few determined and dedicated families during the early 1970s. One mother, whose child had autism, a serious seizure disorder, and mental retardation, listened very carefully to my detailed, multifaceted plan for managing her son's disruptive behaviors (tearing everything made of paper, an obsession with wheels and spinning objects, and bolting from the home). As she left my office, she had a curious look on her face, and I stopped her and challenged, "You are not going to follow these suggestions, are you?" She smiled broadly and said, "No, I can't possibly." Marital tensions; the needs of her other children; and her own laid-back, hippie lifestyle together made it inconceivable that she would be able to implement a structured, disciplined, systematic plan. Wahler (1980), in what was one of the most innovative articles to appear in the behavior analysis literature, came to very similar conclusions regarding the ability of "insular mothers" to sustain pro-

grams that these socially isolated, disadvantaged women had initially mastered.

Another mother of a boy with autism—a woman who also was having serious marital difficulties—was determined that her son would attend the same elementary school as her two daughters. I first approached the school to gauge their reaction and talked at length to their special education teacher who was appointed to work with children who had reading difficulties. "But I don't know anything about childhood autism," she argued. "But you do know how to teach," I countered. "How much different can it really be?"—*not knowing the answer myself!* And so Jonathan started at this school, eventually graduating from the high school and subsequently passing a number of community college courses. Soon after, Congress passed the Education for All Handicapped Children Act of 1975 (PL 94-142), and an entirely new era of schooling began. The implications of the developments in special education are discussed in detail in Chapter 2; however, there were certain immediate consequences for my own thinking.

One of the most significant implications came from the presumption that to teach a child new skills it was necessary to follow the steps and sequences of typical development. Not generally being cognizant of issues in curriculum design, skill development programs by applied behavior analysts emphasized the components that were *thought to be* the steppingstones to more complex behaviors. This was manifest in two ways. One was teaching as an early skill a broad response class that appeared to have considerable potential for generalization: Imitation was one of the most popular skills; making eye contact ("look at me") was another. I spent hundreds of hours shaping such responses in children, whose resultant competence was to stare intently at my motor movements and copy them. The second was the task analysis, which had evolved directly from Skinner's success in teaching long chains of behavior to pigeons and rats. The assumption was that everyday behaviors could be broken down into their sequential parts, which could be taught separately, perhaps as a backward chain, but certainly as a series of discrete elements. I also spent many hours designing and implementing detailed programs for teaching, for example, dressing skills, whereby a teacher would deliver many trials giving physical assistance to the child to put on a T-shirt, leaving the final pulling down of the shirt to the child; praise and food treats then were given, the T-shirt was hauled off the child, and the procedure was begun again. Both of these traditions soon were challenged by a compelling body of evidence from special education that instructional strategies following such principles did *not* cause children with severe disabilities to acquire functional skills or competencies that would actually help them in the real world. Lou Brown, probably the most dynamic special educator of the period, used the wonderful aphorism that "pre means never"—indicating that if one tried to teach skills that were supposedly prerequisites to some other, more important behavior, then that final important skill would never emerge.

The Educational Imperative

Lou Brown came to the University of Hawaii as a guest of the Special Education Department, and I went to a number of his seminars as well as to a talk that he gave. He managed to ridicule all of the types of skill development programs that I was implementing; it was difficult not to be defensive. Yet his overall message was captivating, and he created a sense of purpose, a values-based context for what one might do with programs for people with disabilities. Conditions in Hawaii made such ideas possible, thanks to the very rapid implementation of fully integrated education in the statewide school system.

By the end of that decade, Luanna Meyer (Voeltz) and I had a joint research project, designed to investigate the relations among responses that might allow one to target aspects of challenging behavior much more effectively, when good educational practices were in effect. All of our participant children had severe disabilities, and all were in public schools; this fact alone meant that now we had to pay attention to a large range of ecological variables: the teachers' style, judgment, and decision making; the curriculum and the individualized education programs; the other children in the school; and

the attitudes and aspirations of the families. New observational technology allowed us to record, in real time, the occurrence of up to 100 different aspects of atypical behavior, permitting at least five responses to be recorded simultaneously.

Like other technological advances, the capabilities of these recording devices outstripped the theoretical questions that we could address. Using a variety of multivariate clustering techniques, including factor analysis and small space analysis, we looked for consistencies in concomitant responding, in sequences, and in patterns of behavior. The presumption was that by understanding these response relations it would be possible to target elements of the repertoire that could then be diverted to more functional activities. This was behavioral assessment technology taken to its ultimate—but few consistencies emerged. The general principle was correct, and the importance of understanding response relations was clear. It was also apparent that for the first time the human applied technology was far ahead of anything developed in the laboratory. Operant behavior analysts really were not concerned with complex repertoires and their dependence on simple single responses—often consummatory behavior such as lapping at a water spout or pecking at a key. This resulted in little understanding of the way in which behavior was organized, how one behavior might be dependent on or set the occasion for another, or what sequences might exist in more natural environments. This in turn led to a major realization: Decisions about which skill or response to target for treatment were extremely complex. We were particularly impressed by Hawkins's (1975) paper, cleverly entitled "Who Decided *That* Was the Problem?" In the educational context, we investigated these decision processes empirically and suggested some guidelines for teachers (Voeltz, Evans, Freedland, & Donellon, 1982).

The research on response relations had another major professionally interesting consequence. We were able to demonstrate some success in changing undesirable responses, such as self-stimulation and self-injury, through focusing on the teaching of alternative, more adaptive behaviors. Understanding response interrelations (Voeltz & Evans, 1982) thus became the backbone of nonaversive interventions and of helping professionals who work with children with challenging behavior to understand better the kinds of modifications that could be made through normalizing context and lifestyle, teaching positive skills as alternatives (Meyer, Evans, Wuerch, & Brennan, 1985), enriching deficit environments, and creating naturalistic conditions that would support positive behavior change (Meyer & Evans, 1989).

In 1982, I left the University of Hawaii and accepted an appointment at the State University of New York (SUNY) at Binghamton. My emphasis became more on training and consultation, and my direct involvement with individuals with challenging behaviors decreased; one of the doctoral students who was most receptive to this changing view of intervention was Joseph Scotti, who, as he described, was ready to be relieved from direct service in behavioral programming. At SUNY–Binghamton, I continued to conduct related research on what seemed to me to be a similar problem: What was the best way to define competent or independent behavior in people who had limited repertoires? Could behavior be defined as being meaningful by looking at characteristics of behavior other than the rate of occurrence of a specific operant?

This research (Evans, Brown, Weed, Spry, & Owen, 1987) clarified for me even more strongly that the laboratory was not a good source for generating principles of complex behavior. In fact, because of the focus on a particular kind of metric (response rate), the operant laboratory was providing very poor analogs of everyday behavior. Ordinary actions in which people engaged could best be thought of as "routines," to use Neel's term (Neel & Billingsley, 1989). A routine is a sequence of responses that has a distinct beginning (elicited by an appropriate cue) and a defined end (when the purpose of the action has been achieved). Washing the dishes is an example of a complex operant. The routine is initiated when there is a stack of dirty dishes and ends when the dishes are clean. The task itself could be done in a variety of substitutable ways—under a tap, in a dishwasher, in a plastic basin—with some very general and perhaps critical steps (such as some use of dishwashing

material) and could be done cooperatively with others or alone. The reinforcement for such routines is the accomplishment of the critical effect and the opportunity to get on with another routine, and one would not immediately repeat the routine unless one were being paid to wash someone else's dishes. That is called "work"; some people are paid to wash dishes, and the rate of dishwashing undoubtedly is controlled by the payment contingency. Thus, the operant lab has close analogies to work situations but very little to other domains, such as mobility, self-care, or leisure activities (where the critical effect is to "have fun").

Insights

Thinking about these phenomena led me to a few personal conclusions regarding basic science and empirical practice (Evans & Meyer, 1990). One of these is that the fundamental principles of behavior are not incorrect, but they can easily be incorrectly applied. This is because it must be the *principle* that is applied and *not* a literal translation of a laboratory method. It is quite difficult to do this. As Hawkins and Scotti showed previously in this chapter, when a laboratory method, such as a punishment contingency, is applied directly, it has the appearance of being good science, but it can also be a rather naive translation. This then results in behavior analysts' believing that the effectiveness of the translation can be determined empirically, as with an experiment, by demonstrating a change in the target behavior. The *evaluation* of programmatic change (judging its worth or desirability), however, requires knowledge of the social significance of the change, the general benefits to the individual, the durability of the change, and the degree to which the change will lead to continued adaptive behavior in the future. Some of these are the "social validity" criteria that Wolf (1978) articulated so effectively, and Meyer (Voeltz) and I extended the principles to educational contexts (Voeltz & Evans, 1983).

Each of these dimensions is consistent with a variety of behavioral principles; however, I now believe that as the experimental lab does not represent a true sample of the circumstances of everyday life and social interactions, principles derived from the laboratory cannot—alone—

provide a satisfactory basis for analyzing this level of causal influence. Here again Staats has proposed the importance of a multilevel theory in which principles or causal constructs that are used to explain, say, personality may be derivable from more fundamental (molecular) levels of response learning but need to be understood at the molar level. Thus, a clinical construct such as "borderline personality disorder" contains observations about the relations among global characteristics—such as the approach-avoidance conflict experienced over intimate relationships—and these would need to be understood at that level to make any sense of an intervention designed to confound the individual's prediction that people cannot be trusted. *Personality* thus represents characteristic individual differences in the way an individual will respond to the same situation.

WHAT WISDOM HAVE WE ACQUIRED?

Are these personal recollections ("journeys" is a more fashionable descriptor) simply the self-indulgent reflections of two old—and one not so old—guys rocking away on the front porch and sharing stories of the bygone days? We hope not. We have tried to use these professional histories to illustrate the rapidly changing assumptions of a deceptively nonstatic applied behavior analysis. Despite our very different experiences and backgrounds, there are a number of important similarities in how we were influenced and what we have learned, and we think that these have some implications for application in behavioral science.

Role of Theory

It seems necessary to distinguish between aspects of theory that are fundamental tenets of a behavioral philosophy and those that are more "traditions" within a particular approach. Some features of behavior analysis obviously are of the latter variety, and to challenge them is not antibehavioral or an abandonment of certain important general features of the behavioral perspective.

This has had important implications for the development of behavior analysis as there are

hints throughout our personal accounts of how an interest in the metatheory of behaviorism, or in the specific perspective of behavior analysis, sometimes appeared to override the issues being addressed within the theory. To some extent, this was related to the emergence of applied behavior analysis in opposition to established and conventional metatheories, many of which continue to dominate the fields of developmental disabilities and mental health. Behavior analysis is a distinctive way of approaching issues, and this is worth preserving (Hawkins & Forsyth, 1997). But some concepts are dogma rather than matters of principle, and we occasionally have confused the two.

In the past, certain social values that really are entirely compatible with behavior analysis have been resisted. This resistance has been strongest when behavior analysts perceived a threat to current technologies. For instance, the human rights movement, which emphasizes the dignity and humanity of people with severe cognitive disabilities, is perfectly compatible with behavioral metatheory that would avoid categorizing someone on the basis of a psychometric test or limited repertoire of skills. But when the movement appears to challenge the use of procedures that are in the current behavior analysis armamentarium, it seems threatening: the use of deprivation to enhance motivation; the need to control access to material reinforcers; and the intense focus on decelerating the rate of single, isolated target behaviors versus moving people from the highly defined and confining social environment of the institution to the vastly greater variability of a community with different norms for what comprised acceptable treatments and outcomes.

Relevance of Clinical Training

Each of us has explained how the design of *applied* programs seems to require some level of understanding beyond what can be acquired in the laboratory. Again, we are not implying that there really are two types of reality or that the clinical-educational context in any way represents some set of special rules; rather, it is that the real world is complex and that few, if any, professionals can be consistent in the use of fundamental scientific principles to understand it.

As a result, there is a certain kind of knowledge that emerges from experience with individuals in a variety of contexts. This ordinary knowledge—and, in some cases, professional knowledge—is valuable in the design of individually sensitive intervention plans. It reduces the tendency to generalize too narrowly from the laboratory and promotes realization that there are layers of complexity in clinical (which includes educational) situations. Among those that we have encountered are family influences; community contexts (recognizing that we are answerable to community standards—as can be seen in the recent interest in treatment "acceptability"); and broad principles related to freedom from arbitrary control, self-determination, rights, and duties.

We also have a responsibility to the way in which ideas are used. A clinically experienced practitioner might suggest an intervention plan with recognition of its limitations, its temporary nature, or the need to adjust it; but less experienced, less qualified, or less well-trained individuals within what is still a very controlling service delivery system can utilize the same suggestions and ideas to promote management of individuals and their behavior, which is not designed for the benefit of the individual but for the benefit of the service provider. All professionals who work with people with special needs—teachers, nurses, support staff, psychiatrists, psychologists—confront situations, by virtue of the power differential, that they desire to control. To the extent that behavioral procedures can be used to justify tactics that control rather than benefit individuals, behavior analysis is being abused (Donnellan & Cutler, 1991).

Clinicians have an ethical responsibility to understand the implications of changing behavior, as was forcefully demonstrated by Winett and Winkler (1972). The implications of changing one element of a complex system must be considered. When Voeltz and Evans (1982) showed in a literature review that collateral behavior change was the rule not the exception in behavioral intervention (confirmed in later reviews, see Evans, Meyer, Kurkjian, & Kishi, 1988; Scotti, Evans, Meyer, & Walker, 1991), the implications were far-reaching. Although

there could be negative side effects of planned intervention, there also could be extensive benefits in supportive environments. The selection of the focus of treatment becomes still more critical, and many common research designs become untenable, such as the multiple-baseline design, which rests on the assumption that behaviors are independent. The need for a systems perspective—the behavior and the person in natural contexts—is now an accepted standard in applications of behavioral principles.

Moments of Change

A third generalization to emerge from our experiences is that we each experienced critical moments of change when new insights or innovations suddenly emerged to clarify our understanding of our professional activities. In some cases, these were empirical advances. A number have been mentioned, but two can be highlighted:

1. Carr and Durand's demonstration (Carr & Durand, 1985; Durand, 1990) of the importance of the *communicative* function of many excess behaviors clearly has been a turning point in the field. This insight is completely different from the A-B-C type of functional analysis in which antecedents and consequences were thought to explain the controlling variables of behavior. For example, an A-B-C analysis often would reveal that an excess behavior was followed by social attention. This typically resulted in the recommendation to utilize an extinction contingency, whereby social attention would be removed. But what maintains a behavior and what its function is are now recognized to be rather different issues. If the function of the excess behavior is to communicate a complex need or desire, then subjecting it to an extinction procedure likely would *not* be a successful treatment unless the individual could, of his or her own accord, generate a more acceptable alternative way to express a desire in a social environment that was likely to attend to it. Too often, however, we have left it up to the individual to generate that alternative behavior, and he or she either cannot do so or

generates an even more undesirable behavior instead. It is up to us to teach an alternative—to add to the repertoire, not subtract from it.

2. A second empirical revelation was Wahler's (1980) analysis of why mothers who had been trained in behavior management strategies did not continue to implement them, despite their being relatively successful in increasing positive child behaviors. Improved child behaviors simply are not sufficient consequences to sustain highly effortful behavior in a context that otherwise fails to support it. Parents, direct care staff, teachers, whoever are prone to falling into the "coercive traps" that Patterson (1982) described so well, as short-term, low-effort strategies produce immediate but limited results.

Most of the insights into the need to change came from nonempirical sources. Typically, for us, they were commonsense arguments, effectively presented, that what we were doing and accepting as good practice was actually futile, harmful, or demeaning. Too often, behavior analysts have confused these policy arguments with empirical positions. They have challenged policy innovators to produce their data as though one could do a study that could reveal the greater value of an ethical principle. Using age-appropriate materials and procedures in interventions, implementing learning opportunities when they occur naturally rather than in massed or repeated trials, teaching skills that have natural rather than artificial consequences, normalizing people's experiences, being a person rather than a disability, and having a choice of clothes rather than institutional garb are not in and of themselves contributors to criteria of behavior change, but they render the observed behavior change more meaningful. Because it certainly took us time to come to these understandings and to recognize the importance of new ideas, it seems very important to encourage mechanisms whereby good innovations are supported. Apart from anything else, this means that as new standards of practice are accepted, published literature that does not reflect these standards must be rejected.

WHERE TO NOW?

Research Methods

The greatest irony of the changes in values and in policy is that these changes have altered our basic view of research as providing the knowledge base from which effective interventions can be drawn. Single-subject research designs are excellent for demonstrating the influence of a controlling variable. They demonstrate that an effect *can* be achieved in a certain way but not whether it *should* be achieved. Single-subject designs are particularly poor at revealing whether another approach or method would have been preferable. If, for example, an individual is placed under a token economy system whereby demonstrating certain behaviors earns points that can later be traded for material goods, then it would be easy to demonstrate that the procedure controls some behaviors and that the individual's performance is in accordance with the demands of the economy. However, that demonstration does not answer the evaluative questions of whether the individual is best served by such a program, whether it enhances independence or self-determination, and so forth. Thus, we believe that it will be necessary to ensure a variety of methodologies and not to assume that research strategies that are designed to answer questions about direct influences of one variable on another will be able to answer different questions about the relative merits of one intervention strategy as opposed to another.

Choice of dependent variable also is very important. Operant research typically has utilized a specific dimension of behavior, such as rate, to reveal influences of manipulating independent variables; however, in most everyday human contexts, rate as an *outcome* of interest or value is rarely seen. There are many other important dimensions of functional skills, such as fluency, reliability, self-initiation, appropriateness to context, and so forth. Some of these are physically defined (fluency has an ergonomic relation with the type of task being undertaken), but most are socially defined. Social conditions rarely require the repetition of single responses, except, as commented before, in work situations.

If rate is not the behavioral parameter of interest, then data presentation in which rate is expressed over time often is not the most useful format. Applied behavior analysis long ago gave up cumulative records, as these direct rate measures simply are not relevant to nonexperimental environments, but behavior analysts tried to duplicate the concept of rate measurement by reporting the frequency of behavior in a given time unit (e.g., number of aggressive outbursts per hour) and reporting these across days. Thus, the familiar clinical baseline measure has become a ritualistic way of expressing current and changing circumstances for an individual. A fundamental presumption of the interpretation of such designs is that some consistency of performance is achieved under one set of conditions (Sidman's "steady state"); however, this is rarely accomplished in clinical situations because the opportunity to control all of the possibly influential variables is limited. Behavior typically is very variable, and therefore visual inspection of the changes seen when just one set of conditions is changed is likely to be unreliable.

Another presumption of the operant model is that the influence of critical variables on behavior typically is direct and immediate. Altering a reinforcement contingency for a very hungry animal obviously can produce behavior that is highly sensitive to variations in experimental conditions. Thus, the truly causal nature of the independent variable is demonstrated by the fact that its change produces immediate and predictable changes in responding. Clinical interventions, however, virtually never have this quality. We typically have argued that reversal designs are not possible clinically because of *ethical* issues (it would not be fair to an individual who had shown clinical improvement to revert to conditions that resulted in the return to the clinical level of problems); however, the truth is that reversal designs are not possible because the previous conditions cannot be recaptured. For example, if we worked with an individual who had grown up in an institutional environment that denied choice and then we arranged for that individual to have choices, then we may notice some improvements in behavior. If the opportunity to make choices was then removed ("return to baseline"), however, we would not simply have an individual who is experiencing "no choice" as before but rather an individual who is experiencing "denial of the choices that he recently had." The more complex conditions of clinical work and the vastly greater abilities of most individuals (than experimental animals) result in conditions under which clinical interventions are not the manipulation of one external variable but rather the rearrangement of a variety of conditions that all have value and history for the individual. Thus, what is perhaps the most convincing demonstration of behavioral control in the laboratory (the reversal design) has virtually no—or only very limited—application in clinical or applied environments; however, one can think of many books and articles on behavior modification in which these designs are described as *the* proper way to conduct empirical research.

Effective research methods and sound evaluation are crucial if we are going to be able to maximize the impact of changing models, insights, and policies. We have hinted throughout this chapter that demanding "data" is a strategy that has been used in applied behavior analysis to resist values-driven changes. We do need to learn what are researchable questions. For example, "Does inclusion work?" is not a meaningful scientific question, whereas discovering educational strategies that ensure effective social relationships among peers in inclusive classrooms certainly is meaningful. There is a difference between the changing philosophies (described in greater detail in Chapter 2) that are compatible with behavioral metatheory and the fads that so dominate our field and that are compatible with neither.

Theoretical Derivations

In addition to serious empirical issues that the field will have to address, a major realization of our description of changes in the field is that more attention will have to be paid to how theoretical constructs or empirical generalizations are to be used to guide the design of treatment. Probably one of the most important points that we have raised is that trying simply to apply a laboratory procedure in a literal way to a clinical problem has not been very successful. The direct translation of laboratory techniques to the applied arena has resulted in enormously wasteful controversy. The "aversives debate" of the 1980s is perhaps the best example of this. Laboratory research had reasonably demonstrated that one way to reduce the observed frequency of a behavior was to consequate it with an aversive event, but laboratory research also had clearly demonstrated that there were other ways of reducing the frequency of a response, such as extinction. Extinction was a particularly effective procedure for reducing response probability when one knew which reinforcer was maintaining the behavior in the first place, yet another laboratory technique was to reinforce differentially an alternative, physically incompatible behavior—this, too, is effective in reducing the probability of a given response. All three are generalizations from intensive experimental laboratory research. They are reliable phenomena. But when an applied behavior analyst wants to reduce the frequency of a socially undesirable behavior in an individual, how would he or she select one of these principles to use rather than another? There certainly is nothing in behavior analysis, or even in science, that could be used to argue that the first method should be selected over the other two. One could argue that it might produce a more rapid change in behavior, but such comparisons were rarely made and were difficult because the exact parameters of the various conditions could never really be matched. This is even more true with rule-governed behavior in which rapid and stable behavior change can be achieved simply by stating a contingency condition.

In other words, there is little theory about how theory should be applied. In the absence of this critical element of applied behavior analysis, it is difficult to determine whether a theoretical principle has been derived correctly; whether it is then translated correctly; and, having been translated, whether it is applied without other, equally sound principles being violated.

Innovations

Finally, we have a serious problem with the actual movement of basic or experimental understand-ing into clinical practice. We have commented before that one of the ironies of behavior modification and therapy is that accepted practices are somewhat different from what they were in the 1960s; however, these differences are not because of research-based discoveries or findings at the basic level. Although behavior research has continued, virtually all of the principles that are being practiced in applied behavior analysis were known to the field in the 1960s. Although some commentators have bemoaned that contemporary applied behavior analysis largely is out of date and does not incorporate experimentally derived insights from recent laboratory research, most of us are quite happy to rely on our understanding of behavioral principles from our university courses of many years ago.

In applied behavior analysis, there has been some progress in one domain: the role of language in behavioral regulation. What is ironic is that most of the research on stimulus equivalence really has been drawn from applied, or at least human operant (rather than animal), studies. The same might be said of discussions of rule-governed behavior and its clinical relevance. It is not that there have been new discoveries from the operant lab that have influenced applied behavior analysis. These innovations actually have come the other way—from clinical work. As such, they seem to some of us poorly integrated with the essential principles of animal behavior. Here the authors of this chapter respectfully differ in their approach. Hawkins and Scotti have argued that these innovative principles are important additions and need to be understood because they address important concepts such as verbal regulation of behavior and of cognition in a manner that is consistent with radical behavioral metatheory (e.g., Anderson, Hawkins, & Scotti, 1997). As Evans is not a user of such metatheory, the need for theoretical purity is less important to him. He prefers an integrated approach whereby a variety of cognitive principles can simply be added to our basic understanding of behavior, perhaps at a different level of theory. Each of us, however, agrees strongly with Staats's (1990, 1995) suggestion that "bridging" is necessary between approaches and levels of analysis that appear to have incompatible origins or metatheories—but that is an enormous task.

CONCLUSION

It is clear to us that simplistic constructs have outlived their usefulness and need to be expanded. This expansion can be done by greater theoretical innovation, in which the basic tenets of radical or contextual behaviorism are preserved, or it can be achieved by the derivation of other and different principles that will have to be reconciled with radical concepts if both are going to maintain credibility.

In the chapters that follow, a variety of such approaches are explored. Some authors see the need for greater expansion of operant theory; some authors see the need for greater inclusion so that other concepts and eclectic perspectives are added; and some authors see traditional behavior analysis as now being a barrier to progress and in need of major overhaul. Whichever approach the reader ends up favoring, it is clear that behavior analysis, if it does not move forward, is at risk of stagnation. The ethical, values-based, policy, and procedural changes that we have witnessed and documented here clearly show that many variables other than scientific progress have influenced this field. This is a theme taken much further in Chapter 2. Perhaps by understanding these developments better we will be able to make advances in which applied behavior analysis contributes to rather than resists the important changes that are taking place in philosophy, values, policies, and services.

REFERENCES

Anderson, C.M., Hawkins, R.P., & Scotti, J.R. (1997). Private events in behavior analysis: Conceptual basis and clinical relevance. *Behavior Therapy, 28,* 157–179.

Baer, D.M. (1970). A case for the selective reinforcement of punishment. In C. Neuringer & J.L. Michael (Eds.), *Behavior modification in clinical psychology* (pp. 243–249). New York: Appleton-Century-Crofts.

Baer, D.M., Wolf, M.M., & Risley, T.R. (1968). Some current dimensions of applied behavior analysis. *Journal of Applied Behavior Analysis, 1,* 91–97.

Barlow, D.H., Hayes, S.C., & Nelson, R.O. (1984). *The scientist practitioner: Research and account-ability in clinical and educational settings.* New York: Pergamon.

Berkman, K.A., & Meyer, L.H. (1988). Alternative strategies and multiple outcomes in the remediation of severe self-injury: Going "all out" nonaversively. *Journal of The Association for Persons with Severe Handicaps, 13,* 76–86.

Beyer, H.A. (1983). Litigation with the mentally retarded. In J.L. Matson & J.A. Mulick (Eds.), *Handbook of mental retardation* (pp. 79–91). New York: Pergamon.

Blatt, B. (Ed.). (1973). *Souls in extremis: An anthology on victims and victimizers.* Needham Heights, MA: Allyn & Bacon.

Blazey, M. (1973). A photographic essay: 1971. In B. Blatt (Ed.), *Souls in extremis: An anthology on victims and victimizers* (pp. 18–49). Needham Heights, MA: Allyn & Bacon.

Carey, R.G., & Bucher, B. (1981). Identifying the educative and suppressive effects of positive practice and restitutional overcorrection. *Journal of Applied Behavior Analysis, 14,* 71–80.

Carr, E.G., & Durand, V.M. (1985). Reducing behavior problems through functional communication training. *Journal of Applied Behavior Analysis, 18,* 111–126.

Carr, E.G., Robinson, S., Taylor, J.C., & Carlson, J.I. (1990). Positive approaches to the treatment of severe behavior problems in persons with developmental disabilities: A review and analysis of reinforcement and stimulus-based procedures. *Monographs of The Association for Persons with Severe Handicaps, 4.*

Clarke, A.D.B., & Clarke, A.M. (Eds.). (1974). *Mental deficiency: The changing outlook* (3rd ed.). London: Methuen.

Cotter, L.H. (1967). Operant conditioning in a Vietnamese mental hospital. *American Journal of Psychiatry, 124,* 23–28.

Donahoe, J.W., & Palmer, D.C. (1994). *Learning and complex behavior.* Needham Heights, MA: Allyn & Bacon.

Donnellan, A.M., & Cutler, B.C. (1991). A dialogue on power relationships and aversive control. In L.H. Meyer, C.A. Peck, & L. Brown (Eds.), *Critical issues in the lives of people with severe disabilities* (pp. 617–624). Baltimore: Paul H. Brookes Publishing Co.

Durand, V.M. (1990). *Severe behavior problems: A functional communication training approach.* New York: Guilford Press.

Education for All Handicapped Children Act of 1975, PL 94-142, 20 U.S.C. 1400 *et seq.*

Epstein, L.H., Doke, L.A., Sajwaj, T.E., Sorrell, S., & Rimmer, B. (1974). Generality and side effects of overcorrection. *Journal of Applied Behavior Analysis, 7,* 385–390.

Evans, I.M. (1966). *An assessment of visual deprivation effects by the use of operant techniques.* Unpublished honors thesis, Department of Psychology, University of the Witwatersrand, Johannesburg, South Africa.

Evans, I.M. (1970). A modular teaching unit for research and therapy with children. *Journal of Child Psychology and Psychiatry, 11,* 63–67.

Evans, I.M. (1993). Constructional perspectives in clinical assessment. *Psychological Assessment, 5,* 264–272.

Evans, I.M. (1997). The effect of values on scientific and clinical judgment in behavior therapy. *Behavior Therapy, 28,* 483–493.

Evans, I.M., Brown, F.A., Weed, K.A., Spry, K.M., & Owen, V. (1987). The assessment of functional competencies: A behavioral approach to the evaluation of programs for children with disabilities. In R.J. Prinz (Ed.), *Advances in behavioral assessment of children and families* (Vol. 3, pp. 93–121). Greenwich, CT: JAI Press.

Evans, I.M., & Meyer, L.H. (1985). *An educative approach to behavior problems: A practical decision model for intervention with severely handicapped learners.* Baltimore: Paul H. Brookes Publishing Co.

Evans, I.M., & Meyer, L.H. (1990). Toward a science in support of meaningful outcomes: A response to Horner et al. *Journal of The Association for Persons with Severe Handicaps, 15,* 133–135.

Evans, I.M., Meyer, L.H., Kurkjian, J.A., & Kishi, G.S. (1988). An evaluation of behavioral interrelationships in child behavior therapy. In J.C. Witt, S.N. Elliott, & F.N. Gresham (Eds.), *Handbook of behavior therapy in education* (pp. 189–215). New York: Plenum.

Evans, I.M., & Scotti, J.R. (1989). Defining meaningful outcomes for persons with profound disabilities. In F. Brown & D. Lehr (Eds.), *Persons with profound disabilities: Issues and practices* (pp. 83–107). Baltimore: Paul H. Brookes Publishing Co.

Favell, J.E. (1973). Reduction of stereotypies by reinforcement of toy play. *Mental Retardation, 11,* 21–23.

Favell, J.E., McGimsey, J.F., & Jones, M.L. (1978). The use of physical restraint in the treatment of self-injury and as positive reinforcement. *Journal of Applied Behavior Analysis, 11,* 225–241.

Foxx, R.M., & Azrin, N.H. (1973). The elimination of autistic self-stimulatory behavior by overcorrection. *Journal of Applied Behavior Analysis, 6,* 1–14.

Fuller, P.R. (1949). Operant conditioning of a vegetative human organism. *American Journal of Psychology, 62,* 587–590.

Gold, M.W. (1972). Stimulus factors in skill training of retarded adolescents on a complex assembly task: Acquisition, transfer, and retention. *American Journal of Mental Deficiency, 76,* 517–526.

Goldiamond, I. (1974). Toward a constructional approach to social problems: Ethical and constitu-

tional issues raised by applied behavior analysis. *Behaviorism, 2,* 1–79.

Halderman v. Pennhurst, 446 F. Supp. 1295 (E.D. Pa. 1977).

Hawkins, R.P. (1975). Who decided *that* was the problem? Two stages of responsibility for applied behavior analysts. In W.S. Wood (Ed.), *Issues in evaluating behavior modification* (pp. 195–214). Champaign, IL: Research Press.

Hawkins, R.P. (1989). Developing potent behavior-change technologies: An invitation to cognitive behavior therapists. *The Behavior Therapist, 12,* 126–131.

Hawkins, R.P., & Forsyth, J.P. (1997). The behavior analytic perspective: Its nature, prospects, and limitations for behavior therapy. *Journal of Behavior Therapy and Experimental Psychiatry, 28,* 7–16.

Hawkins, R.P., & Hayes, J.E. (1974). The School Adjustment Program: A model program for treatment of severely maladjusted children in the public schools. In R. Ulrich & J. Mabry (Eds.), *Control of human behavior: Vol. III. Behavior modification in education* (pp. 197–208). Glenview, IL: Scott, Foresman.

Hayes, J.E., & Hawkins, R.P. (1970, September). *An analysis of instructional duration as a consequence for correct and incorrect answers.* Paper presented at the annual convention of the American Psychological Association, Miami Beach, FL.

Horner, R. (1980). The effects of an environmental enrichment program on the behavior of institutionalized profoundly retarded children. *Journal of Applied Behavior Analysis, 13,* 473–491.

Illinois Legislative Investigating Commission. (1973). *Three patient deaths at Peoria State Hospital: A report to the Illinois General Assembly.* Chicago: State of Illinois.

Isaacs, W., Thomas, J., & Goldiamond, I. (1960). Application of operant conditioning to reinstate verbal behavior in psychotics. *Journal of Speech and Hearing Disorders, 25,* 8–12.

Kazdin, A.E. (1982). *Single-case research designs: Methods for clinical and applied settings.* New York: Oxford University Press.

Krasner, L. (1976). Behavioral modification: Ethical issues and future trends. In H. Leitenberg (Ed.), *Handbook of behavior modification and behavior therapy* (pp. 627–649). Upper Saddle River, NJ: Prentice-Hall.

Kushner, M. (1970). Faradic aversive controls in clinical practice. In C. Neuringer & J.L. Michael (Eds.), *Behavior modification in clinical psychology* (pp. 26–51). New York: Appleton-Century-Crofts.

Leitenberg, H. (Ed.). (1976). *Handbook of behavior modification and behavior therapy.* Upper Saddle River, NJ: Prentice-Hall.

Lennox, D.B., Miltenberger, R.G., Spengler, P., & Erfanian, N. (1988). Decelerative treatment practices with persons who have mental retardation: A review of five years of the literature. *American Journal on Mental Retardation, 92,* 492–501.

Luce, S.C., Delquadri, J., & Hall, R.V. (1980). Contingent exercise: A mild but powerful procedure for suppressing inappropriate verbal and aggressive behavior. *Journal of Applied Behavior Analysis, 13,* 583–594.

Martin, R. (1975). *Legal challenges to behavior modification: Trends in schools, corrections and mental health.* Champaign, IL: Research Press.

Meyer, L.H., & Evans, I.M. (1989). *Nonaversive intervention for behavior problems: A manual for home and community.* Baltimore: Paul H. Brookes Publishing Co.

Meyer, L.H., Evans, I.M., Wuerch, B.B., & Brennan, J.M. (1985). Monitoring the collateral effects of leisure skills instruction: A case study in multiple-baseline methodology. *Behaviour Research and Therapy, 23,* 127–138.

Michael, J., Bailey, J., Born, D., Day, W., Hawkins, R.P., Sloane, H., & Wood, S. (1972). Training behavior modifiers: Panel discussion. In G. Semb (Ed.), *Behavior analysis and education—1972* (pp. 26–34). Lawrence: University of Kansas Center for Follow Through.

Neel, R.S., & Billingsley, F.F. (1989). *Impact: A functional curriculum handbook for students with moderate to severe disabilities.* Baltimore: Paul H. Brookes Publishing Co.

Nelson, R.O., & Evans, I.M. (1968). The combination of learning principles and speech therapy techniques in the treatment of non-communicating children. *Journal of Child Psychology and Psychiatry, 9,* 111–124.

Pace, G.M., Iwata, B.A., Edwards, G.L., & McCosh, K.C. (1986). Stimulus fading and transfer in the treatment of self-restraint and self-injurious behavior. *Journal of Applied Behavior Analysis, 19,* 381–389.

Patterson, G.R. (1982). *Coercive family process.* Eugene, OR: Castalia.

Pokrzywinski, J., Scotti, J.R., & Hetz, R.N. (1982, May). *Some effects of environmental manipulation on self-stimulatory behavior.* Poster presented at the 8th annual convention of the Association for Behavior Analysis, Milwaukee, WI.

President's Committee on Mental Retardation. (1977). *Mental retardation: Past and present.* Washington, DC: U.S. Government Printing Office.

Redd, W.H., Porterfield, A.L., & Anderson, B.L. (1979). *Behavior modification: Behavioral approaches to human problems.* New York: Random House.

Risley, T.R. (1975). Certify procedures not people. In W.S. Wood (Ed.), *Issues in evaluating behavior modification: Proceedings of the first Drake Conference on Professional Issues in Behavior Analysis, March 1974* (pp. 159–181). Champaign, IL: Research Press.

Risley, T.R., & Wolf, M.M. (1966). Experimental manipulation of autistic behaviors and generalization into the home. In R. Ulrich, T. Stachnic, & J. Mabry (Eds.), *Control of human behavior* (pp. 193–202). Glenview, IL: Scott, Foresman.

Rivera, G. (1972). *Willowbrook: How it is and why it doesn't have to be that way.* New York: Vintage Books.

Scheerenberger, R.C. (1987). *A history of mental retardation: A quarter century of promise.* Baltimore: Paul H. Brookes Publishing Co.

Schwarz, M.L., & Hawkins, R.P. (1970). Application of delayed reinforcement procedures to the behavior problems of an elementary school child. *Journal of Applied Behavior Analysis, 3,* 85–96.

Schwitzgebel, R.L., & Schwitzgebel, R.K. (1980). *Law and psychological practice.* New York: John Wiley & Sons.

Scotti, J.R. (1983, May). *A response-cost program in the treatment of an undersocialized aggressive adolescent.* Poster presented at the 9th annual convention of the Association for Behavior Analysis, Milwaukee, WI.

Scotti, J.R., Evans, I.M., Meyer, L.H., & DiBenedetto, A. (1991). Individual repertoires as behavioral systems: Implications for program design and evaluation. In B. Remington (Ed.), *The challenge of severe mental handicap: A behaviour analytic approach* (pp. 139–163). London: John Wiley & Sons.

Scotti, J.R., Evans, I.M., Meyer, L.H., & Walker, P. (1991). A meta-analysis of intervention research with problem behavior: Treatment validity and standards of practice. *American Journal on Mental Retardation, 96,* 233–256.

Scotti, J.R., McMorrow, M.J., & Trawitzki, A.L. (1993). Behavioral treatment of chronic psychiatric disorders: Publication trends and future directions. *Behavior Therapy, 24,* 527–550.

Scotti, J.R., Mullen, K.B., & Hawkins, R.P. (1998). Child conduct and developmental disabilities: From theory to practice in the treatment of excess behaviors. In J.J. Plaud & G.H. Eifert (Eds.), *From behavior theory to behavior therapy* (pp. 172–202). Needham Heights, MA: Allyn & Bacon.

Scotti, J.R., Ujcich, K.J., Weigle, K.L., Holland, C., & Kirk, K.S. (1996). Interventions with challenging behavior of persons with developmental disabilities: A review of current research practices. *Journal of The Association for Persons with Severe Handicaps, 21,* 123–134.

Sidman, M. (1960). *Tactics of scientific research.* New York: Basic Books.

Silverman, K., Watanabe, K., Marshall, A.M., & Baer, D.M. (1984). Reducing self-injury and corresponding self-restraint through the strategic use of protective clothing. *Journal of Applied Behavior Analysis, 17,* 545–552.

Sontag, E., & Haring, N.G. (1996). The professionalization of teaching and learning for children with severe disabilities: The creation of TASH. *Journal of The Association for Persons with Severe Handicaps, 21,* 39–45.

Staats, A.W. (with contributions by C.K. Staats). (1963). *Complex human behavior.* Austin, TX: Holt, Rinehart & Winston.

Staats, A.W. (1975). *Social behaviorism.* Homewood, IL: Dorsey Press.

Staats, A.W. (1990). Paradigmatic behavior therapy: A unified framework for theory, research, and practice. In G.H. Eifert & I.M. Evans (Eds.), *Unifying behavior therapy: Contributions of paradigmatic behaviorism* (pp. 14–54). New York: Springer.

Staats, A.W. (1995). Paradigmatic behaviorism and paradigmatic behavior therapy. In W. O'Donohue & L. Krasner (Eds.), *Theories of behavior therapy: Exploring behavior change* (pp. 659–693). Washington, DC: American Psychological Association.

Trent, J.W., Jr. (1995). *Inventing the feeble mind: A history of mental retardation in the United States.* Berkeley: University of California Press.

Ulrich, R., Stachnic, T., & Mabry, J. (Eds.). (1966). *Control of human behavior.* Glenview, IL: Scott, Foresman.

Ulrich, R., Stachnic, T., & Mabry, J. (Eds.). (1970). *Control of human behavior: Vol. II. From cure to prevention.* Glenview, IL: Scott, Foresman.

Ulrich, R., Stachnic, T., & Mabry, J. (Eds.). (1974). *Control of human behavior: Vol. III. Behavior modification in education.* Glenview, IL: Scott, Foresman.

Voeltz, L.M., & Evans, I.M. (1982). The assessment of behavioral interrelationships in child behavior therapy. *Behavioral Assessment, 4,* 131–165.

Voeltz, L.M., & Evans, I.M. (1983). Educational validity: Procedures to evaluate outcomes in programs for severely handicapped learners. *Journal of The Association for the Severely Handicapped, 8,* 3–15.

Voeltz, L.M., Evans, I.M., Freedland, K., & Donellon, S. (1982). Teacher decision making in the selection of educational programming priorities for severely handicapped children. *Journal of Special Education, 16,* 179–198.

Wahler, R.G. (1980). The insular mother: Her problems in parent–child treatment. *Journal of Applied Behavior Analysis, 13,* 207–219.

Winett, R.A., & Winkler, R.C. (1972). Current behavior modification in the classroom: Be still, be quiet, be docile. *Journal of Applied Behavior Analysis, 5,* 499–504.

Wolf, M.M. (1978). Social validity: The case for subjective measurement or how applied behavior analysis is finding its heart. *Journal of Applied Behavior Analysis, 11,* 203–214.

Wolf, M.M., Birnbrauer, J.S., Lawler, J., & Williams, T. (1970). The operant extinction, reinstatement, and re-extinction of vomiting behavior in a retarded child. In R. Ulrich, T. Stachnic, & J. Mabry (Eds.), *Control of human behavior: Vol. II. From cure to prevention* (pp. 146–149). Glenview, IL: Scott, Foresman.

Wolf, M.M., Risley, T.R., & Mees, H. (1964). Application of operant conditioning procedures to the behavior problems of an autistic child. *Behaviour Research and Therapy, 1,* 305–312.

Wolfensberger, W. (1972). *The principle of normalization in human services.* Toronto, Ontario, Canada: National Institute on Mental Retardation.

Wyatt v. Stickney, 325 F. Supp. 781, 784 (M.D. Ala. 1971).

Wyatt v. Stickney, 344 F. Supp. 387, 390 (M.D. Ala. 1972).

Zimmerman, E.H., & Zimmerman, J. (1962). The alteration of behavior in a special classroom situation. *Journal of the Experimental Analysis of Behavior, 5,* 59–60.

Chapter 2

Contemporary, Most Promising Practices for People with Disabilities

Luanna H. Meyer & Hyun-Sook Park

Recent years have seen remarkable advances in the achievements of people with disabilities. At the same time, there have been dramatic changes in the nature and the design of services to support those achievements. The word *handicap,* which once was used to describe a characteristic of a person with a disability, is now interpreted as being the consequence of failure by our social institutions and physical infrastructures to accommodate normal human variance. Rather than ascribing *deviance* to any who differ from socially prescribed (and arbitrary) norms of the human condition, society is adopting a more inclusive view of accepting the full range of variance in characteristics. This variance—not deviance—perspective signals a shifting of primary responsibility for adaptation and accommodation from the individual to the "mainstream." New mainstream, or majority, perspectives require an acceptance of divergent points of view and capacities and a commitment to making the necessary adjustments to enable each individual to be a full participant in his or her community. This is quite a different concept from expecting the individual to make all of the necessary changes to fit and adapt—and denying his or her participation until he or she demonstrates a more narrow range of "normal" characteristics and behavior.

This book focuses on behaviors that historically have been judged to go beyond acceptable levels within families, schools, communities, and worksites. The individuals who exhibit such behaviors are judged to represent a challenge to the environment and the people around them. There is no doubt that our social institutions proscribe fairly well-defined behavioral expectations and that individuals who are judged to have behavior problems can be reliably identified by professionals and laypersons alike. Although there have been dramatic changes in attitudes toward people with disabilities over the past decades, the individuals who are the objects of these attitudes continue to be identified as the challenges. Furthermore, most would agree that the individual with behavioral challenges would

Preparation of this chapter was supported in part by Cooperative Agreement No. H086A20003 awarded to Syracuse University by the U.S. Department of Education; however, the opinions expressed herein are not necessarily those of the U.S. Department of Education, and no official endorsement should be inferred. Portions of this work were completed while the first author was affiliated with Syracuse University.

benefit from successful interventions to reduce or eliminate the problem behaviors and their source. What is different today from our approach of a few years ago is how those changes occur. For example, a worker who interacts with the public as part of his or her job might be expected to adhere to a set of social interaction rules reflecting "socially appropriate behavior" in his or her role. If a potential worker regularly breaks those rules, then a traditional behavioral intervention would be to teach him or her mastery of new, appropriate behaviors prior to placement in the job. Alternatively, the workplace could be more accepting of a variety of behaviors provided that those behaviors met certain criteria (e.g., did not represent a threat to self or others) and provided that the person otherwise performed the job well. In another situation, a worker might be cognitively capable of performing four of five expected job rotations at a worksite but evidence persistent difficulty with mastering the fifth routine despite intensive training efforts. Rather than continue to teach indefinitely until mastery is attained, the employer might write a new job description to omit the routine or modify it in ways that will accommodate the abilities (not the disabilities) of the worker. In both instances, others in the environment would be expected to adapt and accommodate. In the first example, both co-workers and the public must become accustomed to a wider range of "socially acceptable behavior." In the second example, one or more co-workers would be assigned the missing routine, and some work responsibilities would be reorganized. The end result for the person with disabilities would be ongoing acceptance and participation. The end result for individuals who do not have disabilities would be to make changes in attitudes and behaviors—perhaps as many as those formerly required for only the person with disabilities. Finally, the end result of a contemporary approach to human variance would be communities that accept all citizens as fully participating members and provide the support needed to ensure that this ideal becomes a reality.

This chapter begins with a brief history of the shift in services for people with significant disabilities through four major phases. The next section highlights key principles of contemporary, most promising practices. Finally, we end with recommendations for criteria to be applied in intervention research to increase the probability that efforts directed to change challenging behavior will be not only effective but also respectful and feasible in typical school and community environments.

STAGES IN HUMAN SERVICES DELIVERY

Changes in human services delivery for people with disabilities can be traced through four major phases (Black, 1996):

1. Custodial care
2. Developmental practice
3. Functionality and integration
4. Self-determination and inclusion

Although these phases are not discrete and do overlap, they capture the major trends in attitudes about and services for people with disabilities. The four phases also differ markedly from one another, although each can be traced in origin from limitations experienced through the application of systems in the previous phase. Furthermore, at any point in time, more than one of these phases exists in either attitudes or practice. This can also be seen in the time lag between research on most promising practices and implementation of innovative practices in existing social institutions, physical environments, and human services delivery patterns.

Custodial Care

Society had little tolerance for people with disabilities in the early 1900s (Black, 1996). The eugenics movement had a major impact on public opinion and reinforced policies and practices of exclusion and isolation of people who were judged to be different and, therefore, inferior. Although there were examples of national genocide against people with disabilities—such as was practiced in Nazi Germany—the more typical response was incarceration and isolation from society along with the prevention of procreation through forced sterilization and gender segregation. Challenging behavior was managed through physical restraint, drugs, radical surgeries, and punishment. Children who were judged to have a disability—mild or severe—were removed from their families and placed outside the home in impersonal congregate care facilities and institutions. As a consequence, family members lost touch with one another. In the aftermath of the deinstitutionalization movement years later as those institutions were closed, there were numerous instances in which it was impossible to return people to their communities because no one knew from whence they came. In some regions, practices were more benign and stressed basic health, safety, cleanliness, and standards of staff–resident ratios intended to reflect humane care while continuing an emphasis on isolation and segregation.

Although it may be impossible to attribute to any one event the reforms that followed, several are notable. Geraldo Rivera's 1972 televised exposé of New York State's Willowbrook shocked the United States, if not the world. Two publications of pictorial essays from inside the institution by Blatt and Kaplan increased the momentum of public concern (Blatt, 1973; Blatt & Kaplan, 1966). Blatt and Kaplan refused to reveal where their photographs had been taken, maintaining steadfastly that it would be wrong to point at only one or even several hospitals: They maintained that the wrongs that they had documented were, in fact, rampant and widespread throughout the system. They insisted that *Christmas in Purgatory* (Blatt & Kaplan, 1966) was not an aberration but was an accurate picture of the mistreatment of people with disabilities across the United States.

During this same time, Nirje (1969) published his treatise on "normalization," describing humane policies and practices for the treatment of people with disabilities; the normalization principle holds that people with disabilities should be afforded conditions that parallel those experienced by other citizens without disabilities as a basic right of the human condition. Wolfensberger (1972) translated Nirje's work into English and began his own long career dedicated to advocacy, staff training, and evaluation of institutional environments following the normalization

principle and practices. Complacency regarding the treatment of people with disabilities clearly had come to an end, although, for the most part, these individuals remained where they were: in institutions and other segregated environments.

Developmental Practice

The next phase in the treatment that was afforded people with disabilities reflected major changes in theories of learning and teaching. Determinism and genetic theories of human capacities were being challenged by learning theory and demonstrations of the effectiveness of applied behavior analysis. Early efforts of applied behavior analysts focused on animals, but several groups of behavioral psychologists in Britain and the United States shifted their attention to a group of children—primarily children with autism but including others with developmental disabilities, as they came to be labeled. People who were previously thought to be ineducable were taught significant functional skills and even communication behaviors using systematic behavioral instruction strategies (e.g., Berkson & Landesman-Dwyer, 1977; Gold, 1968, 1972; Haring & Hayden, 1972; Nelson & Evans, 1968; Risley & Wolf, 1968). Soon after, developmental theorists reinterpreted cognitive discrepancies as developmental delays rather than as fundamental deficits. They hypothesized that people with disabilities might take longer to reach the same levels but could "catch up" to normal development through intensive intervention (Dunst, 1977).

Accompanying this growing professional belief that all children are educable was an international advocacy movement that was probably conceptually driven by the Civil Rights movement. Advocates demanded access to education and therapy services, essential for people with disabilities to reach their full potential. A lengthy civil rights struggle by self-advocates, parents, and professionals resulted in landmark legislation such as Section 504 of the Rehabilitation Act of 1973 (PL 93-112) and the Education for All Handicapped Children Act of 1975 (PL 94-142, later reauthorized and renamed the Individuals with Disabilities Education Act [IDEA] of 1990 [PL 101-476]). Within one generation, virtually all students with disabilities—no matter how severe—were attending school. With rare exception, however, education programs for students with disabilities continued to be segregated from those for students without disabilities. Most often, students with disabilities attended not only separate classrooms but also separate schools. The concept of "mental age" still held sway over the professional and lay community alike, so curricula for students with disabilities were oriented toward what was regarded as their delayed and thus "developmentally young" age. This resulted in education programs that looked quite different from the activities in classrooms for students of similar age without disabilities—thus justifying separate education environments. Separate environments not only were expedient but also, it was argued, offered dedicated opportunity to specifically tailor intensive instruction to the unique needs of students with severe disabilities. The consequence was that students with severe disabilities were provided with educational experiences, but their activities and skill levels increasingly reflected those of much younger children as a function of the opportunities and environments that were made available to them. Thus, even after the school years ended, a young adult with severe disabilities had few of the skills and behaviors that were expected for his or her chronological age—thereby continuing indefinitely his or her unlikelihood of rejoining society as a fully participating member of the community.

Functionality and Integration

Publication of "Criterion of Ultimate Functioning" (Brown, Nietupski, & Hamre-Nietupski, 1976) marked a major turning point in the education of students with disabilities. This important paper rejected the necessity of moving systematically through a series of developmental stages—a *bottom-up* approach to education—and argued that such an approach simply doomed the person with disabilities to a lifetime of falling further and further behind his or her peers. A student with a severe cognitive impairment who was educated according to this bottom-up approach would exit the compulsory school years with the repertoire of a much younger child, which would be of little to no use in real-world families, neighborhoods, and workplaces. Brown and his colleagues presented an alternative, *top-down* approach to curriculum, whereby the desired school-exit (ultimate functioning) skills would become the focus of instruction from early days throughout schooling. If children with severe disabilities learn more slowly than other children and learn fewer skills overall than their peers, then, it stood to reason, wise choices must be made regarding which skills to teach. Brown and his colleagues were confident, again, that any child could learn—given systematic instruction—and constructed their argument on the foundation of the successes of systematic behavioral instruction leading to mastery of a complex array of skills by individuals with the most severe disabilities (Gold, 1968, 1972). Why not, then, concentrate on the important skills—themselves based on the "criterion of ultimate functioning"—that are needed to become a fully participating adult member of one's community? Postschool outcomes became the focus of the education curriculum, and community-based instruction to facilitate mastery of daily living skills resulted in removing children from classrooms for increasing portions of the school day beginning as early as the elementary school years. By high school, employment training was the major emphasis, and adolescents with severe disabilities ideally would have several different job-training experiences by the time they finished school.

During the mid-1970s, the vocational education movement expanded, supported by entitlement legislation throughout the United States. The Association for the Severely Handicapped (TASH; now The Association for Persons with Severe Handicaps) became a major voice in advocating for equitable school and employment opportunities for people with disabilities. A bipartisan movement emerged and enjoyed widespread support regardless of political affiliation, influenced, no doubt, by key policy makers from across the political spectrum who themselves had family members with disabilities. The behavioral technology of systematic instruction continued to develop and produce remarkable achievements as a function of intervention. Finally, advances in technology and increased physical access requirements and provisions across environments supported the concept of full participation and unlimited potential for achievements once thought impossible.

What is ironic, however, is that this was still a model constructed on segregation during the school years and much of the developmental period. Although there were discussions of the importance of "integration," typical peers of similar chronological age were not enrolled in a top-down curriculum, practicing functional skills for adult participation. There were practical barriers to efforts to educate these children side by side. Other problems that emerged seemed quite skill specific and were particularly evident in the employment-training literature. People with disabilities were indeed successful in the actual task-related aspects of the jobs that they were taught, but evidence accumulated that they lacked the social skills to get and keep a job. Students with severe disabilities attended school with other students with severe disabilities; although their community-based instruction and selected mainstreaming activities provided some contact with peers, serious concerns grew about social skills and the absence of meaningful peer interactions (Meyer & Putnam, 1988). Increasingly, arguments appeared that deficits in social skills and loss of social support networks would be the inevitable consequence of educating children with severe disabilities apart from their peers without disabilities. Children with and without disabilities must receive their education side by side, and new structures and curricula must be developed and supported to enable all students to be participating members of every aspect of their communities (Eichinger, Meyer, & D'Aquanni, 1996). By the late 1980s, the call for "full inclusion" had taken hold.

This period also marked major emphasis on the development of new behavioral technologies and positive practices for people who exhibited challenging behaviors. Initially, these developments emerged from the applied behavior analysis community of professionals who had demonstrated the effectiveness of behavioral strategies with a range of challenging be-

havior. For the most part, this work focused on individuals and reported gains over the short term. In their meta-analysis covering the previous 11 years of published intervention reports, Scotti, Evans, Meyer, and Walker (1991) affirmed the short-term success of existing intervention strategies while revealing that little evidence existed in support of long-term behavior change or lifestyle improvements as a result of this work. Concomitantly, a shift was occurring in the literature on interventions with challenging behavior that began planning for the individual by first looking at lifestyle issues and applying "most promising practices" throughout the design of the intervention (Berkman & Meyer, 1988; Horner et al., 1996; Meyer & Evans, 1989; O'Brien, 1987). The ensuing debate regarding the effectiveness of punishment versus positive practices is addressed elsewhere in this book, but what is relevant here is that the argument was neither won nor lost one way or the other. Instead, punishment strategies seemed to fade gradually from the repertoire of interventionists as effective positive practices—seen as more respectful of the person's rights and lifestyle—became widespread and public opinion supported their use.

Self-Determination and Inclusion

Just as significant in driving social change was the continued momentum of the self-advocacy movement by and for people with disabilities (Ward, 1996). Roots of the self-advocacy movement for individuals with disabilities can be traced to 1972 when Nirje extended the normalization principle by teaching self-advocacy skills through adult courses. The movement really began, however, in the late 1980s and early 1990s when people with cognitive disabilities formed self-advocacy groups that were actively engaged in national and regional activities on a variety of issues. In 1988, the Office of Special Education and Rehabilitative Services (OSERS) of the U.S. Department of Education endorsed the Self-Determination Initiative, marking a major shift in the service delivery system. Rather than be passive recipients of programs that often were didactic and controlled by professionals, individuals with disabilities would actively participate in the decision-making process on the programs and services provided for them. Following the OSERS initiative, IDEA and the Rehabilitation Act Amendments of 1992 (PL 102-569) required that educational and rehabilitative programming for people with disabilities be based on a person's choices, preferences, and interests. These legal requirements dramatically changed the relationships between professionals and individuals with disabilities—consumers. Professionals would no longer be viewed as the only experts who control programs and services. Consumers now were partners who would collaborate with professionals in any programming and service delivery efforts. Professionals, furthermore, now were responsible for the empowerment of people with disabilities, encouraging and enabling them to practice self-determination and advocacy skills. Self-advocacy groups made their presence known across the service delivery system, from education during the school years to related adult services including supported living and supported employment (Ward, 1996).

In schools, the segregation of students with significant disabilities in self-contained classrooms and separate buildings continued despite increased advocacy for inclusion and community participation (Meyer, 1991). The professional special education community recommended that these classes be located in age-appropriate, general education schools and that each student participate in part-time integration through negotiation of attendance in nonacademic classes and recess and lunchtime activities; peer tutoring, "Special Friends," or buddy programs; and reverse integration programs whereby students without disabilities would spend time in the special education classrooms (Black, 1996). Both general and special educators justified this pattern of placement in two ways: 1) It was assumed, based on differences in program needs as well as on public opinion about severe disabilities, that students with disabilities could not benefit academically or socially from full-time placement in general education classrooms; and/or 2) it was argued that pull-out programs for students with special needs would allow for specialized, intensive education and related services that would be incompatible with the activ-

ities in the general education classroom. It is somewhat ironic that in the absence of any empirical data to support either separate services or inclusive services, segregated services had become the norm—the default option. Those who advocated inclusive education were expected to demonstrate superior positive outcomes to justify a change in placement pattern (Laski, 1991; Meyer, 1991).

Nevertheless, professionals, parents, and consumers pressed increasingly for systemic education reform in support of inclusive education. This advocacy was supported by information on limited outcomes achieved through partial integration, continued social isolation and stigmatization of students who were "outsiders" in general education environments, and increasing empirical evidence for individual children showing benefits from full inclusion (Ferguson & Ferguson, 1997). Particularly significant was the growing literature on curricula and instructional strategies providing guidance for meeting the individualized education program (IEP) goals of children and youth with severe disabilities within general education classrooms and general education curricular activities (Coots, Bishop, Grenot-Scheyer, & Falvey, 1995; Hunt, Staub, Alwell, & Goetz, 1994) and the growing database that full inclusion was associated with positive social relationships and friendships for students with severe disabilities (Meyer, Park, Grenot-Scheyer, Schwartz, & Harry, 1998a).

Attention to cultural factors represented another major shift in the theory and practice of developmental disabilities. As long as people with disabilities were stereotyped as primarily representatives of particular syndromes, problems, or deficits, the relevance of issues such as culture or gender was ignored or viewed as secondary. In some areas, such as emotional disturbance, learning disabilities, and mental retardation requiring intermittent supports, there was a lengthy and complex literature attempting to call professional attention to racial discrimination, poverty, and ethnocentric service delivery systems as the source of many "handicaps" (Artiles & Trent, 1994; Richardson, 1994). For the most part, however, the mainstream special education literature and professional associations were silent on issues of race and culture. Prior to the 1990s, the literature that focused on individuals with severe developmental delays and behavior problems provided virtually no mention of racial, cultural, or linguistic factors that might be relevant to special education.

Harry's (1992) study of several culturally diverse families and their interactions with the special education system was a critical turning point in highlighting how an ethnocentric service delivery system could effectively disenfranchise people with disabilities and their families. She was able to show, for example, how a highly legal, formal, and Anglocentric approach to due process was disempowering to Latino families whose values and interpersonal social-communication patterns were in conflict with this "entitlement." Consequently, Latino families were increasingly alienated from special education support structures that were culturally incompatible, and children and then adults with disabilities became even more "handicapped" by professional practices that ostensibly were designed to remediate individual needs. Harry and her colleagues (Harry et al., 1995; Harry, Kalyanpur, & Day, 1999; Kalyanpur & Harry, 1999) subsequently have outlined a number of processes for professionals to provide services that would be culturally appropriate and empowering for both the design of special education and family support services, and Meyer, Harry, and Sapon-Shevin (1997) described classroom practices that shifted the focus from a deficit perspective of the child and his or her culture to emphases on the strengths that diverse cultural and personal characteristics can bring to any social structure—including the classroom—reflecting the reality of the population. Chapter 24 provides a contemporary portrait of how racial discrimination contaminates judgments of problem behavior in particular. Webb-Johnson challenges communities to reevaluate practices that accomplish little more than to reinforce existing prejudice and exclusion of individuals from our communities and opportunities for success. Others, such as Hasan (1998) and Townsend (1998), give rich descriptions of the social consequences of those patterns of exclusion across the developmental period.

CONTEMPORARY RECOMMENDED PRACTICES FOR EFFECTIVE INTERVENTIONS

Evans, Scotti, and Hawkins (see Chapter 1) describe the increasing clinical sophistication and environmental sensitivities of the applied behavior analysis movement that parallel in time the growing recognition of the civil rights of people with disabilities in modern society. The historical focus of operant clinical practice on the single target behavior out of context has now shifted dramatically to a universal recognition that successful interventions are seldom so straightforward. Chapter 1 traces the development of a professional and clinical practice that has been increasingly challenged to accommodate complex contexts, multiple intervention components, and longitudinal outcomes in the natural environment.

Learning theory continues to provide the basic principles of establishing new proactive behaviors to replace problem behaviors, of course, but many of the details of those new positive interventions emerged from special education recommended practices that were guided by the normalization principle and other values that are emerging from the disability rights movement. Clinical practice would still be required to demonstrate effective behavior change, but society now expected those practices to withstand scrutiny with respect to human rights and began to demand that effectiveness be far more broadly defined than was first envisioned. The goal of behavioral intervention was now to change people's lives for the better, not manage behavior in the context of unacceptable lifestyles. Interventions would be evaluated against appropriate practices for people who do not have disabilities, with particular reference to peers of similar age, gender, and sociocultural circumstances. Values such as "age-appropriateness" were established based on principles of human dignity and common sense rather than on empirical data. Thus, for example, the early skills replacement toy training program described by Evans et al. in Chapter 1 would be rejected in favor of a skills replacement leisure activities program that was age appropriate (Schleien, Meyer, Heyne, & Brandt, 1995;

Wuerch & Voeltz, 1982). For adults with severe cognitive disabilities, playing with toys that were designed for small children is not necessarily preferable to stereotyped behavior because 1) the image of an adult playing with a toy that is not age appropriate demeans the adult and reinforces stereotypes that someone "has the mental age of a child," 2) evidence was lacking that such toy play would result in meaningful leisure time activity as opposed to simply a new form of stereotyped behavior, and 3) the person with a disability has learned a new skill that does nothing to develop a repertoire that connects him or her with the community or facilitates positive peer relationships (friendships). Thus, the intervention fails a logical requirement to enhance one's quality of life or capacities of the individual to have a better quality of life. Given evidence that one could easily teach an adult with even the most severe cognitive delays how to interact with age-appropriate leisure materials, the logic of applying social values to educational and clinical interventions seems reasonable enough and should offer no threat to scientific rigor or professional practice.

Nevertheless, service delivery reform for people with significant disabilities and challenging behaviors has not been direct, swift, or easy. Support structures institutionalized as physical infrastructures—such as buildings and hierarchical relationships between clinician and client—do not change overnight. The process has been slowed also by the need to demonstrate that people with disabilities would not be harmed by the new practices and that challenging behavior could be addressed effectively without sacrificing recommended practices and principles of human rights. After two decades of this new work, there is now a rich database that illustrates positive outcomes for the range of multiple criteria associated with meaningful lifestyles. The remainder of this chapter describes a set of major principles and practices based on our own work (Berkman & Meyer, 1988; Evans & Meyer, 1985; Hedeen, Ayres, Meyer, & Waite, 1996; Meyer & Evans, 1989; Meyer & Janney, 1992) and that of many colleagues (Carr et al., 1994; Dunlap, Robbins, & Kern, 1994; Durand, 1990; Horner et al., 1990; LaVigna & Donnellan, 1986;

Lovett, 1985, 1996; McGee, Menolascino, Hobbs, & Menousek, 1987). It is essential to understand the progression from our historical focus on intervention with single target behaviors to contemporary interventions involving multiple components in the context of the natural environment (Voeltz & Evans, 1982; see Chapter 1). Furthermore, the "natural environment" for people with significant disabilities now encompasses inclusive schooling, recreation, and even competitive employment training at community worksites (Meyer, 1991). In addition to the dynamics of intervention design that we address here, effective behavioral practice today incorporates team planning, case management, and culturally appropriate family support (Harry, 1992; see Chapter 22).

Communication and Empowerment

The most promising practices for remediating challenging behavior of people with developmental disabilities will almost always include a behavior plan to modify directly the behavior of concern. Although previous practice might have focused on simply eliminating that behavior, more recent practices emphasize an educative approach, which involves teaching the individual one or more replacement skills that 1) are appropriate prosocial behaviors and 2) can perform the same function for the person as the problem behavior (Evans & Meyer, 1985). In the early days, interventions emphasized teaching positive behaviors that filled the time period and/or were physically incompatible with performing the problem behavior; increasingly, the criterion of functional equivalence was advanced. This required a functional analysis of the problem behavior—essential to state-of-the-art behavioral practice and yet not always reported in the intervention literature (Scotti et al., 1991). As clinicians moved away from eliminative programs and began to carry out functional analyses of challenging behaviors, the teaching of communication skills attracted renewed interest. There were very early demonstrations of successful acquisition of communication skills by children with autism taught through operant procedures, but the linking of this instruction with the remediation of problem behavior marked the development of new understandings of the motivations and cognition of people with disabilities.

Communication and Choice

Teaching communication skills to children and adults with disabilities using the principles and practices of applied behavior analysis has changed greatly since the early days of shaping single verbal utterances and then full sentences in laboratory-like environments and contexts. Those early trials were significant in establishing that communication *could* be taught and learned by individuals once labeled uneducable by school and society, but the outcomes reported from this research remained fairly limited. Trained utterances could be dysfunctional (e.g., picture labeling) or functional (e.g., asking to use the toilet, ordering a burger in a fast-food restaurant), but use was restricted to fairly predictable circumstances and set times or events. What was perhaps most interesting about research on communication that was based on operant principles in the 1970s and 1980s was the acknowledgment of a functional relation between communication and behavior (Carr & Durand, 1985; Durand & Carr, 1987). Durand (1990) and later Carr et al. (1994) were instrumental in tying together the multiplicity of research on developing communicative skills in people with autism and other severe disabilities into useful intervention guides that could be used by practitioners in typical schools and communities.

The major emphasis of this work is, of course, that people have a fundamental need to communicate. When individuals lack positive, prosocial communication systems to do so, they will employ whatever alternative strategies are available to them to meet their needs to communicate. For individuals who are nonverbal and have no obvious verbal communication skills, behavior problems might become most functional for meeting basic communicative needs. For some researchers and clinicians, virtually *all* behavior problems were viewed as having communicative functions—leading to the supposition that behavior problems could be eliminated by teaching functional communication as a replacement skill repertoire. Durand's (1988) Mo-

tivation Assessment Scale was more comprehensive as it acknowledged not only behaviors that seemed communicative in function (performing functions such as, "leave me alone," "pay attention to me," and "give me that/something") but also those that did not appear to have a social function (e.g., sensory stimulation, including solitary play). According to this view, problem behavior, such as aggression and self-injury, could be motivated by different social-communicative functions—sometimes motivated by wanting attention and at other times by wanting to be left alone or excused from doing a nonpreferred task or activity. The most lasting intervention would then seem to be one that taught the individual new verbal strategies to attain desired ends and ensured that these new strategies would be at least as effective as the problem behaviors to be extinguished.

This was at one level a simple *replacement skills approach,* but it had a far more profound impact. If new verbal communicative skills were to be at least as effective as the behavior problems that they replaced, then it would be critical that the learner's requests, demands, and wishes have an impact on the environment. Simply learning a prosocial way to request removal of a nonpreferred task or request access to someone or something was not enough. The individual had to experience control over the environment through using the new communicative skill—indeed, the control needed to overshadow a long history of at least partially successful control over the environment using problem behavior. For this to happen, some major parallel changes had to take place:

1. Everyone in the individual's immediate environment had to cooperate in providing access to the desired reinforcers, provided that the new communicative skill was used to gain access to them.
2. Eventually, the rate of access had to be normalized, requiring an extensive fading regimen across a complex array of situations, conditions, and environments but maintaining the "normal" levels of individual compliance/noncompliance allowed to others without disabilities.

3. For any of this to happen, caregivers and professionals had to accede to a major shift in the power relationship between themselves and the individual.

What once seemed like new knowledge affecting only how and what we teach the person with problem behavior now becomes new knowledge requiring major shifts in attitudes and behavior by staff and other caregivers. How does a profession train itself to alter practice fundamentally—not simply incorporate a new behavioral tool in one's clinical repertoire but instead relinquish the professional–client relationship at the most fundamental level? Chapter 22 is a first effort to evaluate a staff training package that would result in staff's not only learning new skills but also accepting and understanding the fundamental principles behind those practices so that they can resist powerful, traditional messages along the lines of, "We know what is best for you," and, "No one can do what he or she wants to do all the time."

Ultimately, the broader emphasis on self-determination has generated a major shift in approaches to working with individuals with disabilities. First, an individual with disabilities is viewed by professionals as an active change agent (Powers et al., 1996). Intervention efforts must not only respect the individual's choices, preferences, and instructional goals but also provide ample opportunities to practice these related self-determination skills. It was helpful that both the ongoing Civil Rights movement on behalf of people with disabilities and the increasing sophistication of behavioral technologies reinforced our service delivery systems and professional community to reflect more respectful intervention and client interactions supporting self-determination. Hedeen et al. (1996) described an intervention plan developed by the education team to remediate the severely disruptive and self-injurious behavior of a 6-year-old boy with autism who was enrolled full time in a general education classroom for the first time in his life. The multiple component program developed for him included trying to understand Shawn's communicative intent, as evidenced by a classroom discussion on his first day in the new school following an incident when Shawn had pulled a classmate's hair:

[The teacher] asked the students if they had any questions about their new classmate; one asked why Shawn made noises and pulled hair. The teacher asked the children what they thought, and many ideas were generated about how he was probably nervous and afraid his first day and how he was excited about PE class and the parachute. They were able to interpret his behavior as his reaction to events and what he was trying to say—in other words, as communication. (Hedeen et al., 1996, p. 144)

Shawn's teacher, other adults at the school, and perhaps most important the other children acknowledged that Shawn had limited understanding about the events and circumstances of a typical day and that it would take time for him to adapt—particularly in the absence of a functional communication system to express his difficulties. Consequently, rather than view his reactions as noncompliance to be modified using a behavioral program, they took a more gradual approach and increased expectations over time:

Other behaviors changed and were allowed to change gradually. For example, Shawn had been in a restraint chair in his old school and at first refused to sit in a chair. He was allowed to stand for activities, and after some time he was more interested in sitting for comfort. . . . Shawn was also allowed to get up from his chair whenever he felt it was necessary; he was never made to sit unwillingly. Within a few weeks, he was sitting through most of the classroom activities . . . he learned incidentally from watching his classmates. (Hedeen et al., 1996, p. 144)

At the same time, systematic instruction in the context of Shawn's day enabled Shawn to acquire new ways of expressing himself:

Finally, Shawn's teachers and parents believed that as he began to communicate more effectively he was less likely to hit himself or pull hair. Even during the remainder of that first year, Shawn learned to respond to choices by pointing to objects or pictures (e.g., what milk to drink, what color to paint with, what center to play at, what student to walk with). He began using a yes/no card and pointing to letters of the alphabet. Shawn's classmates had similar communication cards, so they could ask him questions throughout the day, giving him many opportunities to use his emerging communication skills. (Hedeen et al., 1996, p. 145)

What was also occurring for Shawn was that his communication skills could go beyond functionality: He could have conversations. Communication is valuable because it enables us to have needs and wants met, but it also connects us with one another. Just as learning age-appropriate leisure time activities could enhance a person's access to peers and relationships beyond what can be offered by paid and nonpaid caregivers, it would seem logical that conversational skills could do the same. The development of strategies to teach such conversational skills to even very young children with significant disabilities could have multiple positive outcomes and represents a promising new direction for intervention efforts (Hunt, Alwell, Farron-Davis, & Goetz, 1996).

Empowerment and Professional–Client Relationships

The recognition of the role of self-determination in services for people with disabilities has prompted professionals to rethink traditional roles that entailed control of programs and services to supportive and facilitative relationships. The process of intervention planning has also shifted dramatically from a medical model of diagnosis and prescription by an expert to group decision making, involving the individual with disabilities, family members, and friends as well as the relevant professionals. Examples of such group-planning strategies include Essential Life Style Planning (Smull & Harrison, 1992), Group Action Planning (Turnbull et al., 1996), McGill Action Planning System (MAPS; Vandercook, York, & Forest, 1989), Planning Alternative Tomorrows with Hope (PATH; Falvey, Forest, Pearpoint, & Rosenberg, 1994; see also Chapter 16), Personal Futures Planning (Meyer & Evans, 1989; Mount & Zwernik, 1988; O'Brien, 1987), and a Focus Group Approach (Meyer, Park, Grenot-Scheyer, Schwartz, & Harry, 1998c).

Turnbull, Friesen, and Ramirez (1998) described processes for implementation of a Participatory Action Research (PAR) model for conducting family research. The approach described by Meyer, Park, Grenot-Scheyer, Schwartz, and Harry (1998b) was utilized by Park, Gonsier-Gerden, Hoffman, Whaley, and Yount (1998) in their application of the participatory research process to competitive employment worksites whereby co-workers and employers without disabilities and trainees with disabilities collaborate in the design of interventions. Participatory research approaches fundamentally alter the nature of the consumer–professional relationship throughout the research process; they also have major implications for the design of clinical intervention research with practitioners, families, and other constituent groups. In PAR, the family is empowered to collaborate in planning the clinical intervention with their child. The family and the professional community not only collaborate in the selection of specific evaluation procedures to assess the effectiveness of the intervention but also must reach mutual agreement on the goals of the intervention that are to be assessed. These researchers are candid about the labor-intensive nature of this approach to intervention research but equally optimistic about its potential. Ultimately, the social validity of approaches such as PAR is compelling and may increasingly drive at least some segments of the clinical research community to move in this direction and thus reflect the shift in the balance of power between professionals and families in their work. If some of us, at least, do not attempt this work, then the gap between the literature on recommended practices and new knowledge on the one hand and actual practices in schools and communities on the other is likely to widen even further (Meyer, Park, et al., 1998c).

The focus on self-determination requires improved collaboration among professionals, the family, and the community. As individuals with disabilities are encouraged to practice self-determination skills in different environments and with a variety of program supports and program delivery systems, people who are stakeholders in the well-being of the individuals need to be consistent in their approaches to promoting such efforts. The "interventionist" role is no longer restricted to professional special educators or behavioral psychologists but now includes general education teachers, co-workers, community recreation providers, neighbors, family, and friends. Children, youth, and adults with disabilities have access to full participation in a variety of inclusive environments and programs, and behavioral intervention approaches are now challenged to develop and evaluate procedures that will work in those real-world environments. It should be obvious that these new conditions entail multiple-component interventions and a corresponding decrease in the highly controlled experimental manipulations seen in our literature in the early days of behavioral intervention. But inclusive environments offer unique and powerful opportunities to acquire new prosocial behaviors in environments that model and motivate through social interrelationships that differ greatly from client–professional ones. In the last section of this chapter, we present some ideas for ensuring that intervention plans proposed by interventionists are doable in the real-world environments of schools, homes, and other community environments.

Lifestyle and Environment

Circumstances and situations can be strong predictors of when problem behavior does and does not occur (Berkman & Meyer, 1988; Dunlap & Kern, 1993; Meyer & Evans, 1989). Certain challenging behaviors can be associated reliably with certain events, people, and environments; in at least some of those circumstances, the child may be right to protest and it would be preferable to eliminate the offending event rather than force the child to tolerate an unreasonable situation. At other times, it may not initially seem particularly helpful to identify a functional relation between a problem behavior and a circumstance that is reasonable or cannot be avoided. For example, a functional analysis might reveal a reliable relation between a child's temper tantrums and doing mathematics. If, however, it is judged important for the child to learn at least some mathematics, then the problem cannot be solved by removing the requirement to perform this academic work. Nevertheless, being able to identify precipitating events and problematic circumstances for the child will help to design an intervention to alleviate those problems. Evans and Meyer (1985) described informal hypotheses tests that allow teachers to assess possible functional relations and plan interventions based on that information. In the hypothetical exam-

ple, if aggression is clearly associated with particular academic tasks, then certain principles of applied behavior analysis would offer direction on how to proceed. One might use the "Premack" principle, whereby the student is taught that working on difficult tasks will be followed by the reward of preferred activities. Mathematics instruction might be rescheduled for early in the day when the child is less tired; the teacher might be particularly vigilant during mathematics lessons to watch for signs of frustration and anxiety and to interrupt activities before the child reaches an emotional state in which disruptive behavior becomes almost inevitable in the behavioral chain. Finally, the child might be taught to ask for a break from mathematics— and across his or her lifetime, from other aversive tasks and activities—in a socially appropriate way and, when he or she uses that new skill, be given the kinds of age-appropriate opportunities to pursue interests and avoid personally punishing situations that are widely used by peers without disabilities who have similar challenges. Such principles of functional analysis of problem behavior would be applied in the design of an intervention program, but attention to causal variables has become far broader in shifting from temporal and proximal events to the broader environmental context.

Ecological and Curricular Variables

Brown (1991) was able to demonstrate a reliable relation between severe disruptive behaviors in community residences as a function of changes and transitions in programs. She hypothesized that clients were disruptive because they did not understand and thus could not predict (and prepare themselves) for the impending changes, resulting inevitably in confusion and dysfunctional efforts to adhere to a previously mastered routine. By teaching clients how to use and understand a daily schedule, her agency equipped them with the tools needed to understand changes in routines and schedules. Weeks and Gaylord-Ross (1981) demonstrated that severe behavior problems in children were reliably associated with difficult tasks, and self-injury, aggression, and crying were substantially reduced by errorless learning and ensuring that the task was not too difficult for the child to do. Alternatively, Dunlap, Foster-Johnson, Clarke, Kern, and Childs (1995) demonstrated a decrease in problem behavior during instruction by including elements of a favorite hobby into a 13-year-old student's assignments. In some instances, establishing a functional relation between activities and problem behavior can assist the clinician in identifying preferred activities in which such preferences are central to the goals of instruction. Meyer, Evans, Wuerch, and Brennan (1985) showed clear patterns of excess behavior as a function of interactions with preferred versus nonpreferred leisure activities, thus providing teachers with advice on assessment of preferences for students who are nonverbal. In employment training programs for people with severe disabilities, patterns of problem behavior in a particular environment might be an appropriate indication that a worksite is not a good match for that individual (Park, Meyer, & Grenot-Scheyer, 1993).

Curricular content can play a major role in a student's motivation, learning, and behavior; the general education literature widely acknowledges the difficulties of motivating students who cannot relate curricula to the needs of their daily lives and future interests. In special education, education goals on the IEP are most often selected by the education team (which usually does not include the student), rather than by the student. These goals may therefore be team priorities but not be meaningful to the student. Dunlap, Kern-Dunlap, Clarke, and Robbins (1991) showed how shifting from traditional tasks of completing worksheets and textbook exercises to more engaging instructional activities that were focused on those same academic skills had a dramatic impact on the disruptive behavior of an adolescent with multiple disabilities.

Meyer, Minondo, et al. (1998) reported a series of investigations of the social relationships of adolescents with severe disabilities who were enrolled in inclusive and integrated school environments. This work attempted to relate the behaviors and expectations of peers and adults in school environments to the nature of the social relationships experienced by young people with multiple disabilities and mental retardation

requiring extensive supports. They offered evidence that positive outcomes, such as prosocial behavior, communication, social networks, and community support, are not solely a function of the characteristics of the adolescent with severe disabilities but are influenced by environmental factors, including adult modeling. Georgia, a 15-year-old girl with Rett syndrome, had participated in special education, related services, and general education classes throughout her elementary school years. Georgia experienced some success in acquiring new skills, but the nature of her disability was such that independent access to full participation in inclusive community environments would have been limited. Georgia's mother described opportunities available to Georgia with her adolescent "group" of five to six girlfriends, who called themselves the Supper Club and who were everpresent in her life—not only during the school day but also after school and on weekends:

Georgia is the kind of kid where people make lots of choices for her. This [the Supper Club] is an actual role Georgia chose. Who do you want in the Supper Club, where do you want to go, what clothes do you want to wear, what food do you want to eat? And I just think that must have been so empowering to her to feel like, "I really can say what I want to do with my friends.". . . I must admit it was probably the first time she did anything without us. Up until this time, it was pretty much parent facilitated, parent invited, and this was something Georgia did from school and I was just told when to pick them up and when to drop them off and where.

Another plus is Georgia's self-image in our family. Her sisters were jealous. Who are these kids? Where are you going? I've never been to Sports Star 2000 . . . another thing to talk about, a mutual thing of interest that wasn't there before, where she had always seen them going places and now she was going. That was really great. I think that it really helped her in some of her community skills . . . she had to hold it together— she went to the movies . . . she had to read a menu, she had to make a choice and communicate that to people at the table . . . I think that really, really challenged her to communicate and keep up with some of the skills. (Meyer, Minondo, et al., 1998, p. 220)

Georgia's middle school program was fully inclusive: She spent her entire school day engaged in general education curriculum activities as a member of her middle school team. Her middle school instructional team—which included the traditional subject area teachers along with a special education teacher (and therapists on a less frequent basis)—adapted those curricular activities to meet Georgia's instructional needs, but this did not occur all of the time. Not unlike what happens for middle school students without disabilities, there were times when Georgia was simply part of the group, exposed to "incidental learning" opportunities, which may or may not have been meaningful for her. Nevertheless, this middle school period was associated with significant positive behavior change and, more important for Georgia's family (and her?), meaningful friendships that wove throughout her daily life and were not restricted to school and other activities that were organized by adults. Such inclusive schooling opportunities are becoming increasingly available to students with severe disabilities. Researchers must meet the challenge to document outcomes for students like Georgia in the design of behavioral interventions that are responsive to new, inclusive environments. Although helpful guidance regarding effective interventions is available in the literature, adaptations will be needed to ensure that interventions do not, in the process of addressing one need, disrupt emerging natural support networks that could otherwise extend far beyond services available from paid providers and professional interventionists.

Lifestyle Issues

Berkman and Meyer (1988) detailed a multiple-component intervention program designed to remediate the severely self-injurious behavior of a 44-year-old man who had been institutionalized throughout his lifetime. Their intervention emphasized major lifestyle changes, including moving to an apartment in the community, finding friends and roommates of his choosing, and getting a job. They also implemented various curricular changes that focused on creating a daily schedule of activities that were personally meaningful and that reflected his own control over the environment. Recommended practices were used in the design of new communication, leisure, employment, and community living skills training programs, but Mr. Jordan—as a

man in his 40s—was now given a major say in the specifics of his program.

What was challenging about the Berkman and Meyer (1988) case study was that Mr. Jordan had been confined to increasingly restrictive and punitive procedures designed to control and eliminate his own increasingly negative self-injurious, aggressive, and disruptive behaviors; yet he had successfully resisted nearly 4 decades of behavioral intervention delivered in those restrictive environments. His behavior was regarded as so severe that state agency approval for an intervention plan that would essentially move him to integrated community environments unconditionally was delayed for nearly 1 year at one point because it was considered to be inappropriate (Berkman & Meyer, 1988). Berkman and Meyer believed that nothing short of massive environmental change and maximum individual control over that environment would have an impact on Mr. Jordan's longstanding and dramatic repertoire of negative behaviors. Given the remarkable turnaround in Mr. Jordan's behaviors in the context of a new and more respectful lifestyle, one could retrospectively view his 40 years of disruptive, self-injurious, and aggressive behaviors as a personal protest against unreasonable and inhumane circumstances.

Inclusion

Inclusive schooling, inclusive recreation, and competitive employment in community worksites have become standards of services for people with severe disabilities. Increasingly, educators, recreators, and job coaches are challenged to document that appropriate and respectful environments and programs are in place, and efforts to remediate the individual repertoires of people with severe disabilities should be designed and evaluated in the context of those natural environments. The published literature in each of these areas has grown geometrically, providing rich description of expected program characteristics in each domain (see, e.g., Grenot-Scheyer, Jubala, Coots, & Bishop, 1996, on inclusive schooling; Schleien et al., 1995, on inclusive recreation; and Park, Chadsey-Rusch, & Storey, 1998, on inclusive worksites). The research by Hedeen et al. (1996), described previously, involved the remediation of severe challenging behaviors for two children in the context of inclusive education programs. In one case, this was the child's first inclusive education experience; in the other, previous inclusive education efforts were associated with escalating behavior problems so disruptive and aggressive that the general education school was seeking referral to a more restrictive program. In each case, successful interventions were designed in the context of those general education environments. Hedeen and her colleagues described not only the more traditional behavioral intervention approaches that do focus on target behaviors but also the various systems change modifications that were effected to provide more supportive contexts for the two students. In Chapter 1, Evans, Scotti, and Hawkins trace the development of behavioral interventionists from the laboratory to community environments—not an easy pathway for either the client or the clinician. It appears that with the blending of recommended educational practices and principles of learning, even the most significant behavior challenges can be addressed without fundamental compromise to the lifestyles of people with significant disabilities.

Social Relationships

Social support has been associated with many benefits for the individual and has been consistently positively related to psychological adjustment and well-being and negatively related to psychosocial stress and physical illness (Cassell, 1976; Cobb, 1976; Cohen & Wills, 1985; Gottlieb, 1983). Strully and Strully described the importance of social networks for their daughter, Shawntell, who has severe disabilities:

Relationships, including friendships, are at the very heart of what is needed to ensure a high quality of life for each of us. Friendships help ensure a person's well-being and health, and they help to protect people from exploitation, abuse, and neglect. There was a time when people thought that, for persons with severe disabilities, having friendships was something to explore only after they had reached some level of accomplishment in such areas as skill acquisition and independence, which would make them productive citizens. These aspects of their lives were perceived as more important. . . .

In the 1980s, those functioning in the various capacities of the human services and education systems began to realize that social interaction, specifically having friendships, takes overwhelming precedence over what skills a person needs . . . relationships, including friendships, are at the heart of the matter of having a full life. (1992, pp. 165–166)

There is literature on the potential importance of peer interactions in applied behavior analysis, but the focus of attention is not on the development of social support networks and friendships but on the use of peers as behavior change agents. The extensive literature on peer tutoring in general education is now paralleled by the literature on peer tutoring in special education, with typical children teaching a variety of skills to peers with severe disabilities (e.g., Strain, Kerr, & Ragland, 1979). In our work in inclusive classrooms, we have argued that general education placement makes available to the student with severe disabilities a multitude of positive peer modeling and incidental learning opportunities. For the two children described in Hedeen et al. (1996), we provide numerous examples of severe challenging behaviors that were not specifically "programmed" through behavior-reduction techniques but instead seemed to extinguish naturally over the course of the school year. General education and social inclusion do offer multiple learning opportunities for alternative prosocial behaviors, often guided by direct interventions and social feedback from typical peers. Consequently, Meyer and Evans (1989) maintained, just as segregated environments provide a social context for increasing levels of problem behavior, integrated environments offer new social contexts that discourage challenging behavior and encourage new positive replacement skills as part of the general social interaction patterns in those environments. We have also cautioned against putting children in the position of becoming active behavior change agents: Kishi and Meyer (1994) reported negative memories—6 years later, in older adolescence—revealed in interviews with those young people who recalled being required to manage behaviors of peers with severe disabilities by teachers as part of a peer interaction program. We are unaware of any other research on what could be a significant negative side effect of putting children into the role of behavior change agent, either formally or informally.

Strully and Strully were talking about peers as friends, not as behavior change agents or as positive social models for appropriate behavior. The Strullys viewed friendship with other children as an important outcome for their daughter—not as a means to an end for teaching new skills. They did view friendship as a means to an end in the sense that friendship gives the individual access to other outcomes through social support, and they viewed friendship as an especially empowering process outcome because the selection of at least some future goals is shifted from those that professionals might choose to those that we might choose with our friends.

The Consortium for Collaborative Research on the Social Relationships of Children and Youth with Diverse Abilities carried out a 5-year series of research investigations on social support networks and children's friendships, which has extended further our understanding of the nature and the potential of relationships between young people with and without severe disabilities (Meyer, Park, et al., 1998a). Findings from this research and from colleagues who are working on similar projects include evidence of multiple positive outcomes for peers with and without disabilities, as well as instructive feedback to the professional community about current practices that reinforce barriers rather than facilitate inclusion (Evans, Goldberg-Arnold, & Dickson, 1998; Grenot-Scheyer, Staub, Peck, & Schwartz, 1998; Meyer, Minondo, et al., 1998; Park, Chadsey-Rusch, & Storey, 1998; Salisbury & Palombaro, 1998; Sapon-Shevin, Dobbelaere, Corrigan, Goodman, & Mastin, 1998). We believe that tomorrow's generation of inclusive school graduates with severe disabilities will not evidence anything like the repertoires of challenging behavior of yesterday's generation who spent their lives in segregation and social isolation learning nonpreferred if not outright dysfunctional "skills." Although there will continue to be behavioral challenges, we cannot help but notice in our professional work that there is a marked decrease in extreme cases among the general population of all students with severe

disabilities in so short a period of time. To our knowledge, no research has yet been done to evaluate this issue.

CONCLUSION: THE LIMITS OF INTERVENING

The focus of this book is behavioral intervention in contemporary context. Just as applied behavior analysis has progressed from the laboratory to the community and has been applied to a variety of real-world problems and needs, behavioral interventionists also have been challenged to reframe their efforts within the context of most promising practices and natural supports for people with disabilities. In today's world of self-determination and empowerment, interventions will increasingly be both *by* and *for* people with disabilities. Particularly as natural supports continue to acquire significance based on both theoretical and practical value, the families and other constituencies of people with disabilities will join the professional and the self-advocate in making important decisions about intervention goals and methods. In their outstanding review of the application of scientific knowledge to practice, Hoshmond and Polkinghorne (1992) presented a compelling case for practitioner–researcher collaboration to solve some of the otherwise intractable problems reflected in the gap between typical practices and what we know about recommended practices.

The Consortium for Collaborative Research on the Social Relationships of Children and Youth with Diverse Abilities has carried out extensive collaborative research designed to validate most promising practices designed for implementation in schools and communities rather than remaining confined to research reports—where so many of the most promising practices unfortunately remain once the original experiment has ended. We have delineated a set of criteria demanding more than demonstrations of the effectiveness of interventions under experimental conditions if our research is intended to improve the lives of people with disabilities. The term *naturalistic interventions* (see Chapter 22) might be the best fit for the intentions of this list, but we consider that our work as interven-

tionist researchers must increasingly reflect the following:

1. *Interventions must be doable in context.* To be useful, an experimentally validated intervention must be one that can be implemented in the real world, in typical homes, classrooms, and communities, rather than requiring extraordinary environments.

2. *Interventions must be doable with available resources.* Educational innovations that are likely to outlive the experimental phase are those that use the typical resources that are available in typical social and educational systems, rather than require extraordinary resources that generally are not available.

3. *Interventions must be sustainable over time.* There must be evidence that needed supports are available to ensure that a new intervention approach could be continued over time and will not cease with the departure of selected staff and so forth.

4. *Interventions must be constituency owned and operated.* Those who will be charged to carry out the intervention must believe in it and feel ownership over the strategies and outcomes.

5. *Interventions must be culturally inclusive.* Innovations must be consistent with and respectful of the values, behaviors, and beliefs of a particular learning community and of the people and the families within that community.

6. *Interventions must be intuitively appealing.* Innovations must pass the "grandmother test" (Meyer & Evans, 1989)—that is, be understandable to and seen as sensible not only by those who must use the innovations but also by lay members of a particular community.

As researchers attend to each of these criteria throughout the process of the design and implementation of new approaches, they greatly increase the probability that "recommended and most promising practices" will actually become *practice* and extend beyond the pages of journal articles, book chapters, and final reports and into real-world situations and environments.

REFERENCES

Artiles, A.J., & Trent, S.C. (1994). Overrepresentation of minority students in special education: A continuing debate. *Journal of Special Education, 27,* 410–437.

Berkman, K.A., & Meyer, L.H. (1988). Alternative strategies and multiple outcomes in the remediation of severe self-injury: Going "all out" nonaversively. *Journal of The Association for Persons with Severe Handicaps, 13,* 76–86.

Berkson, G., & Landesman-Dwyer, S. (1977). Behavioral research on severe and profound mental retardation (1955–1974). *American Journal of Mental Deficiency, 81,* 428–454.

Black, J.W. (1996). *Ghost, guest, and classmate: Student membership and teacher decision-making in the design of curricular and instructional adaptations for students with severe disabilities in inclusive classrooms.* Unpublished doctoral dissertation, Syracuse University.

Blatt, B. (Ed.). (1973). *Souls in extremis: An anthology on victims and victimizers.* Needham Heights, MA: Allyn & Bacon.

Blatt, B., & Kaplan, F. (1966). *Christmas in purgatory.* Needham Heights, MA: Allyn & Bacon.

Brown, F. (1991). Creative daily scheduling: A nonintrusive approach to challenging behaviors in community residences. *Journal of The Association for Persons with Severe Handicaps, 16,* 75–84.

Brown, L., Nietupski, J., & Hamre-Nietupski, S. (1976). Criterion of ultimate functioning. In M.A. Thomas (Ed.), *Hey, don't forget about me* (pp. 2–15). Reston, VA: Council for Exceptional Children.

Carr, E.G., & Durand, V.M. (1985). Reducing behavior problems through functional communication training. *Journal of Applied Behavior Analysis, 18,* 111–126.

Carr, E.G., Levin, L., McConnachie, G., Carlson, J.I., Kemp, D.C., & Smith, C.E. (1994). *Communication-based intervention for problem behavior: A user's guide for producing positive change.* Baltimore: Paul H. Brookes Publishing Co.

Cassell, J. (1976). The contribution of the social environment to host resistance. *American Journal of Epidemiology, 104,* 107–123.

Cobb, S. (1976). Social support as a moderator of life stress. *Psychometric Medicine, 38,* 300–312.

Cohen, S., & Wills, T.A. (1985). Stress, social support, and the buffering hypothesis. *Psychological Bulletin, 98,* 310–357.

Coots, J.J., Bishop, K.D., Grenot-Scheyer, M., & Falvey, M.A. (1995). Practices in general education: Past and present. In M.A. Falvey (Ed.), *Inclusive and heterogeneous schooling: Assessment, curriculum, and instruction* (pp. 7–22). Baltimore: Paul H. Brookes Publishing Co.

Dunlap, G., Foster-Johnson, L., Clarke, S., Kern, L., & Childs, K.E. (1995). Modifying activities to produce functional outcomes: Effects on the problem behaviors of students with disabilities. *Journal of The Association for Persons with Severe Handicaps, 20,* 248–258.

Dunlap, G., & Kern, L. (1993). Assessment and intervention for children within the instructional curriculum. In J. Reichle & D. Wacker (Eds.), *Communication and language intervention series: Vol. 3. Communicative alternatives to challenging behavior: Integrating functional assessment and intervention strategies* (pp. 177–203). Baltimore: Paul H. Brookes Publishing Co.

Dunlap, G., Kern-Dunlap, L., Clarke, S., & Robbins, F.R. (1991). Functional assessment, curricular revision, and severe behavior problems. *Journal of Applied Behavior Analysis, 24,* 387–397.

Dunlap, G., Robbins, F.R., & Kern, L. (1994). Some characteristics of nonaversive intervention for severe behavior problems. In E. Schopler & G.B. Mesibov (Eds.), *Behavioral issues in autism* (pp. 227–245). New York: Plenum.

Dunst, C.J. (1977). *An early cognitive-linguistic intervention strategy.* Morganton, NC: Western Carolina Center.

Durand, V.M. (1988). The Motivation Assessment Scale. In M. Hersen & A.S. Bellack (Eds.), *Dictionary of behavioral assessment techniques* (pp. 309–310). New York: Pergamon.

Durand, V.M. (1990). *Severe behavior problems: A functional communication training approach.* New York: Guilford Press.

Durand, V.M., & Carr, E.G. (1987). Social influences on "self-stimulatory" behavior: Analysis and treatment application. *Journal of Applied Behavior Analysis, 20,* 119–132.

Education for All Handicapped Children Act of 1975, PL 94-142, 20 U.S.C. §§ 1400 *et seq.*

Eichinger, J., Meyer, L.H., & D'Aquanni, M. (1996). Evolving best practices for learners with severe disabilities. *Special Education Leadership Review, 3,* 1–13.

Evans, I.M., Goldberg-Arnold, J.S., & Dickson, J.K. (1998). Children's perceptions of equity in peer interactions. In L.H. Meyer, H.-S. Park, M. Grenot-Scheyer, I.S. Schwartz, & B. Harry (Eds.), *Making friends: The influences of culture and development* (pp. 133–147). Baltimore: Paul H. Brookes Publishing Co.

Evans, I.M., & Meyer, L.H. (1985). *An educative approach to behavior problems: A practical decision model for interventions with severely handicapped learners.* Baltimore: Paul H. Brookes Publishing Co.

Falvey, M.A., Forest, M., Pearpoint, J., & Rosenberg, R.L. (1994). Building connections. In J.S. Thousand, R.A. Villa, & A.I. Nevin (Eds.), *Creativity and collaborative learning: A practical guide to empowering students and teachers* (pp. 347–368). Baltimore: Paul H. Brookes Publishing Co.

Ferguson, D.L., & Ferguson, P.M. (1997). Debating inclusion in Schenectady, New York: A response to Gresham and MacMillan. *Review of Educational Research, 67,* 416–420.

Gold, M.W. (1968). Preworkshop skills for the trainable: A sequential technique. *Education and Training of the Mentally Retarded, 3,* 31–37.

Gold, M.W. (1972). Stimulus factors in skill training of retarded adolescents on a complex assembly task: Acquisition, transfer, and retention. *American Journal of Mental Deficiency, 76,* 517–526.

Gottlieb, B.H. (1983). *Social support strategies.* Thousand Oaks, CA: Sage Publications.

Grenot-Scheyer, M., Jubala, K., Coots, J., & Bishop, K. (1996). *Professionals' guide: The inclusive classroom.* Westminster, CA: Teacher Created Materials, Inc.

Grenot-Scheyer, M., Staub, D., Peck, C.A., & Schwartz, I.S. (1998). Reciprocity and friendships: Listening to the voices of children and youth with and without disabilities. In L.H. Meyer, H.-S. Park, M. Grenot-Scheyer, I.S. Schwartz, & B. Harry (Eds.), *Making friends: The influences of culture and development* (pp. 149–167). Baltimore: Paul H. Brookes Publishing Co.

Haring, N.G., & Hayden, A.H. (Eds.). (1972). *The improvement of instruction.* Seattle: Special Child Publications, Inc.

Harry, B. (1992). *Cultural diversity, families, and the special education system: Communication for empowerment.* New York: Teachers College Press.

Harry, B., Grenot-Scheyer, M., Smith-Lewis, M., Park, H.-S., Xin, F., & Schwartz, I. (1995). Developing culturally inclusive services for individuals with severe disabilities. *Journal of The Association for Persons with Severe Handicaps, 20,* 99–109.

Harry, B., Kalyanpur, M., & Day, M. (1999). *Building cultural reciprocity with families: Case studies in special education.* Baltimore: Paul H. Brookes Publishing Co.

Hasan, H.A. (1998). Understanding the gang culture and how it relates to society and school. In L.H. Meyer, H.-S. Park, M. Grenot-Scheyer, I.S. Schwartz, & B. Harry (Eds.), *Making friends: The influences of culture and development* (pp. 263–297). Baltimore: Paul H. Brookes Publishing Co.

Hedeen, D.L., Ayres, B.J., Meyer, L.H., & Waite, J. (1996). Quality inclusive schooling for students with severe behavioral challenges. In D.H. Lehr & F. Brown (Eds.), *People with disabilities who challenge the system* (pp. 127–171). Baltimore: Paul H. Brookes Publishing Co.

Horner, R.H., Close, D.W., Fredericks, H.D.B., O'Neill, R.E., Albin, R.W., Sprague, J.R., Kennedy, C.H., Flannery, K.B., & Heathfield, L.T. (1996). Supported living for people with profound disabilities and severe problem behaviors. In D.H. Lehr & F. Brown (Eds.), *People with disabilities who challenge the system* (pp. 209–240). Baltimore: Paul H. Brookes Publishing Co.

Horner, R.H., Dunlap, G., Koegel, R.I., Carr, E.G., Sailor, W., Anderson, J., Albin, R.W., & O'Neill, R.E. (1990). Toward a technology of "nonaversive" behavioral support. *Journal of The Association for Persons with Severe Handicaps, 15,* 125–132.

Hoshmond, L.T., & Polkinghorne, D.E. (1992). Redefining the science–practice relationships and professional training. *American Psychologist, 47,* 55–66.

Hunt, P., Alwell, M., Farron-Davis, F., & Goetz, L. (1996). Creating socially supportive environments for fully included students who experience multiple disabilities. *Journal of The Association for Persons with Severe Handicaps, 21,* 53–71.

Hunt, P., Staub, D., Alwell, M., & Goetz, L. (1994). Achievement by all students within the context of cooperative learning groups. *Journal of The Association for Persons with Severe Handicaps, 19,* 290–301.

Individuals with Disabilities Education Act (IDEA) of 1990, PL 101-476, 20 U.S.C. §§ 1400 *et seq.*

Kalyanpur, M., & Harry, B. (1999). *Culture in special education: Building reciprocal family–professional relationships.* Baltimore: Paul H. Brookes Publishing Co.

Kishi, G.S., & Meyer, L.H. (1994). What children report and remember: A six year follow-up of the effects of social contact between peers with and without severe disabilities. *Journal of The Association for Persons with Severe Handicaps, 19,* 277–289.

Laski, F.J. (1991). Achieving integration during the second revolution. In L.H. Meyer, C.A. Peck, & L. Brown (Eds.), *Critical issues in the lives of people with severe disabilities* (pp. 409–421). Baltimore: Paul H. Brookes Publishing Co.

LaVigna, G.W., & Donnellan, A.M. (1986). *Alternatives to punishment: Solving behavior problems with non-aversive strategies.* New York: Irvington.

Lovett, H. (1985). *Cognitive counseling and persons with special needs.* New York: Praeger.

Lovett, H. (1996). *Learning to listen: Positive approaches and people with difficult behavior.* Baltimore: Paul H. Brookes Publishing Co.

McGee, J.J., Menolascino, F.J., Hobbs, D.C., & Menousek, P.E. (1987). *Gentle teaching: A nonaversive approach for helping persons with mental retardation.* New York: Human Science Press.

Meyer, L.H. (1991). Advocacy, research, and typical practices: A call for the reduction of discrepancies between what is and what ought to be, and how to get there. In L.H. Meyer, C.A. Peck, & L. Brown (Eds.), *Critical issues in the lives of people with severe disabilities* (pp. 629–649). Baltimore: Paul H. Brookes Publishing Co.

Meyer, L.H., & Evans, I.M. (1989). *Nonaversive intervention for behavior problems: A manual for home and community.* Baltimore: Paul H. Brookes Publishing Co.

Meyer, L.H., Evans, I.M., Wuerch, B.B., & Brennan, J. (1985). Monitoring the collateral effects of leisure skills instruction: A case study in multiple-baseline methodology. *Behaviour Research and Therapy, 23,* 127–138.

Meyer, L.H., Harry, B., & Sapon-Shevin, M. (1997). School inclusion and multiculturalism in special education. In J. Banks & C. McGee Banks (Eds.), *Multicultural education: Issues and perspectives* (3rd ed., pp. 334–360). Needham Heights, MA: Allyn & Bacon.

Meyer, L.H., & Janney, R.E. (1992). School consultation to support students with behavior problems in integrated educational programs. In T.R. Kratochwill, S.N. Elliott, & M. Gettinger (Eds.), *Advances in school psychology* (Vol. 8, pp. 153–193). Mahwah, NJ: Lawrence Erlbaum Associates.

Meyer, L.H., Minondo, S., Fisher, M., Larson, M.J., Dunmore, S., Black, J.W., & D'Aquanni, M. (1998). Frames of friendship: Social relationships among adolescents with diverse abilities. In L.H. Meyer, H.-S. Park, M. Grenot-Scheyer, I.S. Schwartz, & B. Harry (Eds.), *Making friends: The influences of culture and development* (pp. 189–221). Baltimore: Paul H. Brookes Publishing Co.

Meyer, L.H., Park, H.-S., Grenot-Scheyer, M., Schwartz, I.S., & Harry, B. (Eds.). (1998a). *Making friends: The influences of culture and development.* Baltimore: Paul H. Brookes Publishing Co.

Meyer, L.H., Park, H.-S., Grenot-Scheyer, M., Schwartz, I.S., & Harry, B. (1998b). Participatory research approaches for the study of the social relationships of children and youth. In L.H. Meyer, H.-S. Park, M. Grenot-Scheyer, I.S. Schwartz, & B. Harry (Eds.), *Making friends: The influences of culture and development* (pp. 3–29). Baltimore: Paul H. Brookes Publishing Co.

Meyer, L.H., Park, H.-S., Grenot-Scheyer, M., Schwartz, I.S., & Harry, B. (1998c). Participatory research: New approaches to the research to practice dilemma. *Journal of The Association for Persons with Severe Handicaps, 23,* 165–177.

Meyer, L.H., & Putnam, J. (1988). Social integration. In V.B. Van Hasselt, P.S. Strain, & M. Hersen (Eds.), *Handbook of developmental and physical disabilities* (pp. 107–133). New York: Pergamon.

Mount, B., & Zwernik, K. (1988). *It's never too early, it's never too late: A booklet about personal futures planning for persons with developmental disabilities, their families and friends, case managers, service providers, and advocates* (Publication 42-88-109). St. Paul, MN: Governor's Planning Council on Developmental Disabilities.

Nelson, R.O., & Evans, I.M. (1968). The combination of learning principles and speech therapy techniques in the treatment of non-communicating children. *Journal of Child Psychology and Psychiatry, 9,* 111–124.

Nirje, B. (1969). The normalization principle and its human management implications. In R.B. Kugel (Ed.), *Changing patterns in residential services for the mentally retarded* (pp. 179–195). Washington, DC: President's Committee on Mental Retardation.

O'Brien, J. (1987). A guide to life-style planning: Using *The Activities Catalog* to integrate services and natural support systems. In B. Wilcox & G.T. Bellamy (Eds.), *A comprehensive guide to* The Activities Catalog: *An alternative curriculum for youth and adults with severe disabilities* (pp. 175–189). Baltimore: Paul H. Brookes Publishing Co.

Park, H.-S., Chadsey-Rusch, J., & Storey, K. (1998). Social relationships or no relationships: Social experiences at worksites. In L.H. Meyer, H.-S. Park, M. Grenot-Scheyer, I.S. Schwartz, & B. Harry (Eds.), *Making friends: The influences of culture and development* (pp. 317–337). Baltimore: Paul H. Brookes Publishing Co.

Park, H.-S., Gonsier-Gerden, J., Hoffman, S., Whaley, S., & Yount, M. (1998). The application of the participatory research process to the study of the social inclusion of students with severe disabilities working at competitive employment settings. *Journal of The Association for Persons with Severe Handicaps, 23,* 189–202.

Park, H.-S., Meyer, L.H., & Grenot-Scheyer, M. (1993, September). Remember the phrase "All work and no play makes Jack . . ."? Looking for friends on the job. *TASH Newsletter, 19,* 5–6, 8.

Powers, L.E., Wilson, R., Matuszewski, J., Phillips, A., Rein, C., Schumacher, D., & Gensert, J. (1996). Facilitating adolescent self-determination: What does it take? In D.J. Sands & M.L. Wehmeyer (Eds.), *Self-determination across the life span* (pp. 257–284). Baltimore: Paul H. Brookes Publishing Co.

Rehabilitation Act Amendments of 1992, PL 102-569, 29 U.S.C. §§ 701 *et seq.*

Rehabilitation Act of 1973, PL 93-112, 29 U.S.C. §§ 701 *et seq.*

Richardson, J.G. (1994). Common, delinquent, and special: On the formalization of common schooling in the American states. *American Educational Research Journal, 31,* 695–723.

Risley, T., & Wolf, M. (1968). Establishing functional speech in echolalic children. In H.N. Sloane & B.D. MacAulay (Eds.), *Operant procedures in remedial speech and language training* (pp. 157–184). Boston: Houghton Mifflin.

Salisbury, C.L., & Palombaro, M.M. (1998). Friends and acquaintances: Evolving relationships in an inclusive elementary school. In L.H. Meyer, H.-S. Park, M. Grenot-Scheyer, I.S. Schwartz, & B. Harry (Eds.), *Making friends: The influences of culture and development* (pp. 81–104). Baltimore: Paul H. Brookes Publishing Co.

Sapon-Shevin, M., Dobbelaere, A., Corrigan, C.R., Goodman, K., & Mastin, M.C. (1998). Promoting inclusive behavior in inclusive classrooms: "You can't say you can't play." In L.H. Meyer, H.-S. Park, M. Grenot-Scheyer, I.S. Schwartz, & B. Harry (Eds.), *Making friends: The influences of culture and development* (pp. 105–132). Baltimore: Paul H. Brookes Publishing Co.

Schleien, S.J., Meyer, L.H., Heyne, L.A., & Brandt, B.B. (1995). *Lifelong leisure skills and lifestyles for persons with developmental disabilities.* Baltimore: Paul H. Brookes Publishing Co.

Scotti, J.R., Evans, I.M., Meyer, L.H., & Walker, P. (1991). A meta-analysis of intervention research with problem behavior: Treatment validity and standards of practice. *American Journal on Mental Retardation, 96,* 233–256.

Smull, M., & Harrison, S.B. (1992). *Supporting people with severe reputations in the community.* Alexandria, VA: National Association of State Mental Retardation Program Directors.

Strain, P.S., Kerr, M.M., & Ragland, E.U. (1979). Effects of peer-mediated social initiations and prompting/reinforcement procedures on the social behavior of autistic children. *Journal of Autism and Developmental Disorders, 9,* 41–54.

Strully, J.L., & Strully, C.F. (1992). The struggle toward inclusion and the fulfillment of friendship. In J. Nisbet (Ed.), *Natural supports in school, at work, and in the community for people with severe disabilities* (pp. 165–177). Baltimore: Paul H. Brookes Publishing Co.

Townsend, B.L. (1998). Social friendships and networks among African American children and youth. In L.H. Meyer, H.-S. Park, M. Grenot-Scheyer, I.S. Schwartz, & B. Harry (Eds.), *Making friends: The influences of culture and development* (pp. 225–241). Baltimore: Paul H. Brookes Publishing Co.

Turnbull, A.P., Blue-Banning, M.J., Logan Anderson, E., Turnbull, H.R., Seaton, K., & Dinas, P.A. (1996). Enhancing self-determination through group action planning. In D.J. Sands & M.L. Wehmeyer (Eds.), *Self-determination across the life span* (pp. 237–256). Baltimore: Paul H. Brookes Publishing Co.

Turnbull, A.P., Friesen, B.J., & Ramirez, C. (1998). Participatory action research as a model for conducting family research. *Journal of The Association for Persons with Severe Handicaps, 23,* 178–188.

Vandercook, T., York, J., & Forest, M. (1989). The McGill Action Planning System (MAPS): A strategy for building the vision. *Journal of The Association for Persons with Severe Handicaps, 14,* 205–215.

Voeltz, L.M., & Evans, I.M. (1982). The assessment of behavioral interrelationships in child behavior therapy. *Behavioral Assessment, 4,* 131–165.

Ward, M.J. (1996). Coming of age in the age of self-determination: A historical and personal perspective. In D.J. Sands & M.L. Wehmeyer (Eds.), *Self-determination across the life span* (pp. 3–16). Baltimore: Paul H. Brookes Publishing Co.

Weeks, M., & Gaylord-Ross, R. (1981). Task difficulty and aberrant behavior in severely handicapped students. *Journal of Applied Behavior Analysis, 14,* 19–36.

Wolfensberger, W. (1972). *The principle of normalization in human services.* Toronto, Ontario, Canada: National Institute on Mental Retardation.

Wuerch, B.B., & Voeltz, L.M. (1982). *Longitudinal leisure skills for severely handicapped learners: The Ho'onanea curriculum component.* Baltimore: Paul H. Brookes Publishing Co.

Chapter 3

Standards of Practice and Critical Elements in an Educative Approach to Behavioral Intervention

Glenda L. Vittimberga, Joseph R. Scotti, & Karen L. Weigle

The 1980s brought a growing concern over traditional approaches to intervention with the excess behavior of individuals with developmental disabilities (e.g., Carr, Robinson, & Palumbo, 1990; Horner et al., 1990; LaVigna & Donnellan, 1986; Meyer & Evans, 1989; Scotti, Evans, Meyer, & Walker, 1991). Reviews of the developmental disabilities literature indicated that published interventions often lacked adherence to even the most fundamental standards of practice (Carr, Robinson, Taylor, & Carlson, 1990; Lennox, Miltenberger, Spengler, & Erfanian, 1988; Scotti, Evans, Meyer, & Walker, 1991; Scotti, Ujcich, Weigle, Holland, & Kirk, 1996), and an examination of the efficacy of published interventions indicated a general insufficiency in interventions as a whole. This state of affairs was also evident in other literatures, including

chronic psychiatric disorders (Scotti, McMorrow, & Trawitzki, 1993) and childhood behavioral disorders such as conduct disorder (Scotti, Mullen, & Hawkins, 1998) and attention-deficit disorder (see Chapter 4). With increasing professional support for *repertoire-enhancing* interventions, traditional *eliminative* approaches that emphasized the reduction of excess behavior through consequence manipulations became the subject of criticism (Carr, Robinson, Taylor, & Carlson, 1990; Evans & Meyer, 1985; LaVigna & Donnellan, 1986; Meyer & Evans, 1989).

Few would argue that a hallmark of behavior therapy and applied behavior analysis is the reliance on functional analysis (Baer, Wolf, & Risley, 1968; Carr, Robinson, & Palumbo, 1990; Durand, 1987; Evans, 1971; Haynes & O'Brien, 1990). What is surprising is that in a meta-

Support for this work was provided through a grant to Joseph R. Scotti from the West Virginia Developmental Disabilities Planning Council, Charleston, West Virginia, and the Division of Special Education of the Monongalia County Schools, which is gratefully acknowledged. Portions of this work represent the doctoral qualifying examination papers of the first and third authors.

The section "Supporting Recommended Practices in the Educational Environment" (pp. 61–64) has appeared in a previously published article: Weigle, K.L. (1997). Positive behavior support as a model for promoting educational inclusion. *Journal of The Association for Persons with Severe Handicaps, 22*(1), 36–48; reprinted and adapted by permission.

analysis of 403 studies of interventions with behavioral excesses during 1976–1987, Scotti, Evans, Meyer, and Walker (1991) found that only 22% of the interventions reviewed attempted to conduct some form of functional analysis. Those analyses that were reported were primarily anecdotal and not data based. Ethical standards require that the least intrusive intervention be selected, yet this review found examples of the most restrictive interventions being used with the least severe behavior problems. The importance of emphasizing generalization and maintenance of intervention gains has also been elaborated (e.g., Stokes & Baer, 1977), yet only 47% of the studies reviewed reported data on follow-up measures, and a mere 30% attempted any sort of generalization procedures. Perhaps most alarming was that a considerable percentage of the published intervention literature was simply not very effective. Scotti, Meyer, Evans, and Walker (1991) employed statistical metrics designed to assess the efficacy of interventions on two levels: 1) behavioral suppression and 2) degree of behavioral change. Their results indicated that only 44 of the 403 studies reviewed (11%) were judged to be highly effective (judged by degree of behavioral change and suppression), whereas 30%–40% of the studies were judged to be ineffective. Although intrusive interventions were slightly more effective in *suppressing* behavior, there were no differences between the various levels of intrusiveness on degree of behavioral change. This is consistent with the review by Lennox et al. (1988), who found minimal differences in efficacy across levels of intervention intrusiveness (see also Didden, Duker, & Korzilius, 1997).

This growing awareness of the inadequacy of typical interventions for excess behavior has brought the conceptualizations and practices of the eliminative approach under increasing scrutiny. From an eliminative standpoint, excess behaviors (e.g., tantrums, aggression, self-injury, stereotypy) often are conceptualized as "maladaptive." Undoubtedly, such a judgment is due to the vast array of complications that result from such behavior, which may include harm to the individual who is exhibiting the behaviors or to others, disruption of the working or learning environment, or exhibiting bizarre and unusual behavior in public. As a result of this conceptualization, however, the goal of typical, eliminative interventions has been to suppress problem behaviors, primarily by direct consequation of excess behaviors through decelerative techniques. Eliminative interventions also have been criticized as being reactive, overlooking the functions of behavior, and ignoring long-term intervention goals. These criticisms arise from the fact that the eliminative approach suppresses behavior without providing the individual who is exhibiting the behavior with clear behavioral alternatives (Carr, Robinson, & Palumbo, 1990; LaVigna & Donnellan, 1986; Meyer & Evans, 1989), which may then lead to unplanned, collateral behavioral changes (i.e., side effects such as increased aggression or decreased social interaction).

In response to these deficiencies of eliminative strategies, there has been growing support for repertoire-enhancing and functionally based interventions. This approach has been labeled *educative,* to refer to the edifying nature (i.e., the focus on skill-building and proactive supportive strategies) of these interventions (Meyer & Evans, 1989). It recognizes that all behaviors (even problematic topographies) are adaptive, in the sense that they are functional within (or have adapted to) the specific environment in which they occur. Despite the growing popularity of this approach, there remains a shortage of published interventions that systematically identify and utilize the fundamental guidelines of the educative approach as it pertains to the intervention for excess behavior. Reducing this shortage is one purpose of this book; the goal of this chapter is to outline seven critical elements of an educative approach to intervention with excess behavior. Examples of these critical elements come primarily from the developmental disabilities literature, but, as both this chapter and the book show, they apply equally to any intervention literature in which reduction of behavioral excesses typically has been the goal. We begin by first providing a brief description of the educative approach and a discussion of its theoretical basis in behavioral systems theory.

INTRODUCTION TO THE EDUCATIVE APPROACH TO INTERVENTION

The educative philosophy views excess behavior as having adaptive functions yet problematic topographies (Evans & Meyer, 1985; Meyer & Evans, 1989). This premise is based on the view that different behavioral topographies can be functionally related and that altering the rate of one behavior may in turn cause concomitant changes in another response. Educative interventions involve replacing an excess behavior with a response that has a more acceptable topography and that fulfills the same function.

Although there has been increasing support for this intervention philosophy, the basic concepts are not new. For example, Isaacs, Thomas, and Goldiamond (1960) suggested that increasing the rate of acceptable behavior may be an effective option for controlling rates of abnormal behavior. In his discussion of the constructional approach, Goldiamond (1974) suggested that clinical problems are best addressed through the construction of new repertoires. (Hawkins, 1986, has characterized such intervention approaches as "freedom enhancing.") Evans (1971) noted the typical focus on the treatment of behaviors that other people found aversive and suggested instead that generalized changes for both the target individual and his or her social environment be sought as an intrinsic and essential component of intervention.

The educative intervention philosophy is based on theories of behavioral systems that lend themselves to specific intervention practices. The next section briefly reviews behavioral systems theory and its relation to the critical elements of educative intervention.

BEHAVIORAL SYSTEMS THEORY

Historically, the emphasis on demonstration of experimental manipulation and control in behavioral intervention (i.e., behavior modification and behavior analysis) encouraged the selection of discrete and isolated target behaviors (Evans & Scotti, 1989). As a result, the complexity and interrelatedness of behavior was often over-looked during intervention (Evans, Meyer, Kurk-jian, & Kishi, 1988; Scotti, Evans, Meyer, & DiBenedetto, 1991; Scotti et al., 1996; Voeltz & Evans, 1982) and by the experimental designs that typically have been selected to evaluate intervention effectiveness (see Kazdin, 1982; Meyer & Evans, 1993b; Meyer, Evans, Wuerch, & Brennan, 1985; Voeltz & Evans, 1982). Behavioral systems theory is derived from a foundation of empirical evidence suggesting that behavior does not occur in isolation but rather that individual repertoires are complex and interwoven. The implication of this is that interventions that aim to change the rate of a specific behavior may affect other behaviors that are not targeted directly. In fact, Scotti, Evans, Meyer, and Walker (1991) found that 36% of the studies that they reviewed reported collateral behavioral changes (unfortunately, these were rarely data-based reports). The more recent intervention literature includes reports of collateral behavioral change in more than 50% of studies—with an encouraging increase in data-based documentation of those effects (Scotti et al., 1996). Studies are also likely (56% of reports) to discuss the hypothesized organizing principles of behavior, such as response classes, that can account for collateral behavioral changes (Scotti et al., 1996). Unfortunately, data-based reports that document such relations are rare. Because of their importance in the development of educatively based intervention, several of these key organizing principles of behavior are reviewed next.

Response Relations

Some frequently noted organizing principles of behavior are response clusters, response chains, response hierarchies, and response classes. This is by no means an exhaustive list, but these few have been selected as convenient examples for discussion (see Evans et al., 1988; Scotti, Evans, Meyer, & DiBenedetto, 1991; Voeltz & Evans, 1982). *Clusters* refers to discrete behaviors that occur at the same time or in rapid alternation (e.g., concurrent operants). Often, one response within the cluster serves as a *keystone behavior* (Wahler, 1975)—that is, a behavior that is central to other related responses and that sets the occasion for them to occur (Scotti, Evans, Meyer, & DiBenedetto, 1991). The most neutral explanation of the occurrence of response clusters is that they are elicited by the same stimulus; however, the possibility also arises that they are held together by a common function. For example, walking into the bathroom and standing in front of the sink is a sequence of behaviors that are related and are central to the tasks of washing one's hands, brushing one's teeth, and combing one's hair. They also uniquely set the occasion or create the opportunity for hand washing to occur. (Engaging in hand washing without having first arrived at a position in front of a sink would appear abnormal.) Once in front of the sink—a keystone response—multiple behaviors may occur concurrently (e.g., washing one's face while looking in the mirror) or in alternation (e.g., lathering hands and face, then rinsing each, and perhaps repeating this a time or two). Note that the keystone behavior might actually be performed in several ways (e.g., walking unaided, using crutches or a wheelchair) or may even be performed by someone else (e.g., being wheeled into the bathroom, having an aide bring a washing kit to the bedside), all to the same *critical effect* (see Evans, Brown, Weed, Spry, & Owen, 1987; Chapter 1). It is the critical effect of clean hands (the reinforcer or the function) that results in the occurrence of these responses together (it would remain to be demonstrated, however, whether it is the negative reinforcer of removing dirt from one's hands or the positive reinforcer of praise for clean hands—or some combination of these and other effects—that maintains the responses).

The organization of *response chains* is somewhat different. These behaviors reliably occur in succession—typically in a somewhat invariant sequence. It is hypothesized that each response in a chain serves both as the eliciting stimulus for the subsequent behavior and as a reinforcing stimulus for the preceding behavior. Continuing the example of hand washing, one first turns on the faucet, producing the water necessary for the next step of wetting one's hands. Wetting the hands allows lathering with the soap that is then picked up, and so forth. Some steps may be performed slightly out of sequence (e.g., wetting hands before or after picking up

the soap), but the order of other steps is invariant (e.g., turning on the faucet before wetting the hands). Again, the individual steps in this sequence or chain of responses may reinforce or set the occasion for each other, but they also have a common critical effect or function.

Finally, in a *response hierarchy,* a learning history of differential reinforcement is assumed to be related to the relative probability that each behavior will occur in response to a specific stimulus. The implication here is that all behaviors within the hierarchy serve a similar function but with varying degrees of efficiency in producing the critical effect and with differing likelihoods based on the present situation (discriminative stimuli). For example, a child may have several responses that have, historically, resulted in the removal of difficult seatwork in the classroom. The child may, when presented with a math worksheet, whine and squirm in his seat until the teacher removes the work and seats him in a corner (ostensibly for failing to be quiet and sit still). When whining and squirming do not produce this effect, the child may hit a nearby peer, thereby being sent out of the room to see the principal (again producing the critical effect of removing the worksheet). One might inquire why the child does not simply ask for help with the math problems, as not knowing what to do is in part what makes the task so difficult and aversive. Indeed, we might find that the child *will* ask for assistance—and even get it—when a different teacher is present—one who is likely to respond favorably to requests for help. Thus, three responses achieve the same critical effect: removing the difficult task (thus having a common negative reinforcement function). The excess behaviors of whining and squirming are more likely to occur than hitting a peer (which occurs when whining and squirming fail), and both are more likely to occur than asking for help—but this depends on which teacher is present in the room. So, a hierarchy of responses is related by a common function and have different probabilities of occurrence based on certain antecedent stimuli (e.g., the presence of a specific teacher).

Behaviors that have a common function (whether they occur in a response cluster, chain, or hierarchy) are said to be members of a *response class;* that is, they have a common set of reinforcers (positive or negative)—they produce the same critical effect. The previous examples show that a response class consists of multiple behaviors and that they have a variety of different relations with each other. It is essential to recognize, however, that a single response may have *multiple* functions and be a member of *multiple* response classes. Raising one's hand is a single response that has different critical effects depending on the situations in which it occurs, such as seeking help from a teacher, volunteering an answer to a question, requesting to go to the bathroom, hailing a taxi, or voting in a meeting. Imagine the nonverbal child whose self-injurious head hitting similarly serves multiple functions, including escaping physical discomfort (e.g., a sinus headache), seeking teacher assistance, requesting a favorite toy, or removing a task. Each of these may be an outcome that follows the child's head hitting, although they may not be systematic because the function at any one time may not be clear to individuals around the child (i.e., they are merely guessing at his intent and responding through trial and error). Thus, the function of a behavior cannot be determined by observing a single instance and its consequences; multiple observations are required.

Implications of Response Relations

Consider the collateral effects that relations between responses may have. If a keystone behavior sets the occasion for the occurrence of other behaviors within a cluster, then any changes in the frequency of the keystone behavior will be associated with similar rate changes for all of the behaviors in the cluster. Similarly, if a behavior in a chain is eliminated, then this should cause a concomitant decrease in all following behaviors, as well as in the preceding behavior for which the target served as a conditioned reinforcer. In a response hierarchy, if the behavior of highest probability is suppressed, then another behavior within the hierarchy will increase in probability and frequency to fulfill that function (Scotti, Evans, Meyer, & DiBenedetto, 1991).

Consider, then, the implications that such a behavioral systems approach has for interven-

tion. An intervention that is designed to change the rate of one behavior may have an impact—typically, inadvertently—on other behaviors that are not targeted directly. This emphasizes the necessity for monitoring the collateral effects of intervention. Furthermore, if an intervention merely suppresses a response for the individual who is exhibiting the behavior, then another behavior within the individual's repertoire may increase in rate to meet that same function. This suggests the necessity of identifying the functions of behavior *prior to intervention* and planning to teach an appropriate replacement skill to the individual who is exhibiting the undesired behavior. Collateral effects of interventions may be desirable (e.g., increased social interaction), or they may be undesirable and problematic (e.g., increased aggression). When it has provided documentation, the published literature has overwhelmingly indicated positive over negative side effects from intervention, by a ratio of almost 3 to 1 (Scotti et al., 1996); however, the serious lack of data-based monitoring and the low number of studies that monitor *both* positive and negative collateral behaviors make it impossible to determine whether, in fact, interventions primarily have beneficial side effects or there is a bias in reporting positive over negative collateral changes (Scotti et al., 1996). Careful monitoring and advance planning clearly is warranted as ignoring these principles of response organization leaves too much to chance.

Optimally, an intervention will maximize gains by capitalizing on these principles of response relations. The educative approach strives to accomplish this by first conducting a systematic functional assessment to elucidate the maintaining factors of an excess behavior. Information gained from the functional assessment is used to select an appropriate *functional match,* or replacement skill (one that will need to be taught or that exists in the repertoire and needs only to occur more frequently; Durand, 1990; Evans & Meyer, 1985; Meyer & Evans, 1989; Reichle & Wacker, 1993). Providing the individual who is exhibiting the undesired behavior with an effective and functional replacement for the target behavior theoretically should eliminate the necessity for direct consequation of the excess behavior and should promote generalization and maintenance. To evaluate the overall therapeutic gain for the individual, collateral effects are monitored throughout the course of intervention. These implications for practice form the basis of the critical elements for intervention.

CRITICAL ELEMENTS OF EDUCATIVE-BASED INTERVENTION

This section provides an overview of seven critical elements that are fundamental to educative intervention approaches. These critical elements include

1. Appropriately selecting and classifying excess behaviors
2. Conducting a functional assessment of the target behavior as the basis for intervention selection
3. Incorporating skill acquisition and choice making into the intervention
4. Using the least restrictive techniques
5. Monitoring the collateral effects of intervention
6. Employing procedures to enhance maintenance and generalization
7. Producing meaningful outcomes

The presentation of the elements is organized according to the progression that might be followed during intervention. A rationale and illustrative research examples are provided for each element. The goal of this chapter is not to critique or criticize these research examples; they are merely employed as convenient examples and nonexamples of the educative approach. For the most part, they represent the applied behavioral technology of their time.

Appropriately Selecting and Classifying Excess Behaviors

A primary step in intervention is selecting targets for intervention (for more complete discussions, see Hawkins, 1979, 1986; Meyer & Evans, 1989). The implication of response interrelations for the selection of target behaviors is that excess behaviors need *not* be consequated directly to cause a reduction in their rate (Scotti,

Evans, Meyer, & DiBenedetto, 1991; Voeltz & Evans, 1982). The emphasis of the educative approach on providing a functional match makes it possible to reduce excess behaviors through the reinforcement of that functionally equivalent response (e.g., Carr & Durand, 1985a, 1985b; Eason, White, & Newsom, 1982; Horner & Budd, 1985). For example, Carr and Durand (1985a) effectively reduced aggression, tantrums, and self-injury by teaching the participant to produce simple language phrases. These interventions did not require the direct application of consequences to the excess behavior to produce the desired reduction. In applying the educative approach, the principal intervention involves identifying the functional match as the target behavior to increase through skill-building strategies. The excess behavior is monitored as a collateral behavior that likely will decrease once the functionally equivalent skill is taught and reinforced. This is in contrast to eliminative strategies, which directly target the excess behavior. For example, Linscheid, Iwata, Ricketts, Williams, and Griffin (1990) used contingent electric shock with self-injurious hits to the body, and Johnson, Baumeister, Penland, and Inwald (1982) used overcorrection in response to instances of various forms of self-injurious behavior.

Once a behavior has been targeted for modification, the long- and short-term impact of intervention should be assessed (Hawkins, 1986). A cost–benefit analysis can help to determine whether the benefits of the intervention outweigh the potential risks (Meyer & Evans, 1989). The first stage in a cost–benefit analysis is to prioritize the excess behavior for intervention. The classification system devised by Meyer and Evans (1989) incorporates three levels pertaining to the urgency of the behavior. Level I refers to excess behaviors that are urgent or health- and life-threatening, such as severe self-injury and violent aggression. Level II behaviors include those that

1. May be preventing or seriously interfering with learning
2. May eventually become harmful if not treated
3. May present a danger to others

4. Pose a great concern for the individuals in the environment of the individual who is exhibiting the excess behavior

Examples at this level, or severity, include high-frequency stereotypic behaviors (e.g., body rocking, hand waving), disruptive yelling and whining, and mild self-injury that appears to be increasing in intensity. Level III behaviors are targeted for modification for reasons concerning social desirability; they do not otherwise pose a threat of harm or seriously impede the individual's ability to learn new skills, and they may resemble habit behaviors that are seen in the typical population. Examples include distracting hand motions, giggling, inappropriate body posture during social interactions, and nail biting (e.g., Hunt, Alwell, & Goetz, 1988; Mulick, Hoyt, Rojahn, & Schroeder, 1978).

Once the excess behavior has been appropriately classified, consideration should be given to the impact of the intervention on the individual as a whole, not just in terms of the target behavior. With Level I and Level II behaviors, a cost–benefit analysis would consist of generating hypotheses regarding the potential collateral effects of an intervention program. Problem solving must be used to determine which interventions afford the greatest gain with the lowest risk of undesirable collateral effects. The critical nature of Level I behaviors requires immediate intervention, regardless of limitations in staff or program resources. Because of the nonmandatory nature of Level III behaviors, intervention with Level III behaviors may be postponed based on limitations in staff and resources or on the judgment that an intervention may be associated with undesirable changes in collateral behavior.

Conducting a Functional Assessment

To select a replacement behavior that matches the functions of the excess behavior, the functions of the excess behavior first must be systematically assessed. The use of functional analysis is fundamental to behavioral technology (Baer et al., 1968; Carr, Robinson, & Palumbo, 1990; Durand, 1987; Evans, 1971; Haynes & O'Brien, 1990). Unfortunately, multiple reviews of the intervention literature indicate that this important step often is overlooked, in both developmental disabilities (Carr, Robinson, Taylor, & Carlson, 1990; Lennox et al., 1988; Scotti, Evans, Meyer, & Walker, 1991) and chronic psychiatric disorders literature (Scotti et al., 1993) and in other literatures (e.g., Scotti et al., 1998; see Chapter 4). The meta-analysis conducted by Scotti, Evans, Meyer, and Walker (1991) indicated that very few interventions (22%) for individuals with developmental disabilities are based on any form of functional assessment, and even these are primarily of the anecdotal variety (i.e., based on informal observation rather than on data-based techniques). Similarly, Lennox et al. (1988) found that only one third of the studies that they reviewed referred to conducting a functional analysis; and only 17% obtained information from staff, 18% made reference to some form of antecedent-behavior-consequence (A-B-C) analyses (e.g., Bijou, Peterson, & Ault, 1968), and 6% reported a controlled analysis (e.g., Iwata, Dorsey, Slifer, Bauman, & Richman, 1982/1994). The literature on chronic psychiatric disorders is even more dismal on this point: Fewer than one third of some 272 studies over a 26-year period reported even descriptive information about potential controlling variables, and only 3% (9 of 272 studies) reported conducting formal functional analysis procedures prior to intervention. On the positive side, a review by Scotti et al. (1996), which covered developmental disabilities literature from 1988 to 1992, suggested an increase in preintervention functional analyses to 48% (86 of 179) of the studies reviewed. Even more encouraging was the substantial increase in data-based procedures, including direct observation/A-B-C analyses (54%, 33 of 61), experimental analog analyses (38%, 23 of 61), structured interviews (28%, 17 of 61), and standardized questionnaires (10%, 6 of 61). Similarly, Desrochers, Hile, and Williams-Moseley (1997) found in a mail survey of the members of the Psychology Division of the American Association on Mental Retardation that nearly all of their respondents indicated that they "always" (47%) or "often" (46%) base treatment decisions on a functional analysis (however, a majority of these respondents also indicated insufficient time and data collection difficulties as problems when attempting functional assessments).

Functional Analysis versus Assessment

An important issue in the discussion of functional analysis is how it is defined. Skinner (1953) described *functional analysis* as the cause-and-effect relation between independent variables and dependent variables, allowing for prediction and control of a subject's behavior. Based on this definition, an intervention demonstrating the use of contingent electric shock to reduce the rate of self-injurious behavior would fit the definition of a functional analysis; that is, the electric shock was successful in reducing the rate of the self-injurious behavior, demonstrating a relation between this consequence and decreased responding. The function that the self-injurious behavior served, however, was not eliminated or altered. A behavioral systems conceptualization would predict that another behavior may increase in frequency to meet the same function that the self-injury was serving. For example, in one of the cases ("Johnny") described by Linscheid et al. (1990), as self-injurious head hits were reduced through the use of contingent electric shock, the rates of hand posturing, upper-body rocking, and panting increased. One could argue that if a prior functional analysis had established that each of these behaviors was maintained by automatic ("self-stimulatory") reinforcement, then the intervention merely shifted the rates of behaviors within a response class or hierarchy (a formal functional analysis was not reported, but comparative "alone," "demand," and "play" baseline conditions suggest an automatic reinforcement function). Such a pattern of response covariation indicates the need to determine the relations between variables *prior to* intervention, a definition of functional analysis suggested by Hawkins (1986). A useful distinction can be drawn between functional analysis as the demonstration of the control of one variable over another and functional analysis as the identification of factors that are maintaining behavior within an individual repertoire. For clarifi-

cation, the term *functional assessment* is used to refer to analyses of maintaining variables *prior to* the implementation of intervention.

The distinction between functional analysis and functional assessment is illustrated by a study designed to investigate the effects of overcorrection and reinforcement of an alternative behavior. In a study by Johnson et al. (1982), an adult male engaging in self-injurious behavior was required to perform hand movements for 1 minute following instances of self-injury. This intervention was compared with a differential reinforcement of other behavior (DRO) component (pressing a panel for edible reinforcers) and with a combination of overcorrection and DRO. Overcorrection alone was found to be effective in suppressing the self-injurious behavior; thus, the functional relation between the participant's behavior and the intervention components was such that consequating the behavior with overcorrection led to a decrease in rate, whereas food reinforcement for an alternative response did not reduce self-injury. Overcorrection, therefore, appeared to be the effective intervention; however, conducting a prior functional assessment may have helped to identify a functional match to be used as the "other" behavior in the DRO component, perhaps increasing the probability of effectiveness. For example, the self-injurious behavior may have served an escape function. The subject then could have been taught an appropriate manual sign to indicate escape (e.g., STOP), and this could have been negatively reinforced (by allowing escape), resulting in a decrease in self-injury and an increase in appropriate signing. Such an intervention takes advantage of the events (reinforcers) that are maintaining the self-injury and, thus, are demonstrated to be reinforcers. One must therefore ask, "Why use food as the putative reinforcer in this case?" Such a use of food reinforcers (which is quite common in the field) assumes one of two things: 1) that access to food is the reinforcer that is maintaining the excess behavior or 2) that food is equivalent in its reinforcing value to whatever reinforcing consequence (positive or negative) is actually maintaining the self-injurious behavior. It can be seen, then, that the questions that we ask—and when we ask them—can have significant effects on our choice of interventions.

Functional Assessment and Intervention Selection

A variety of techniques have been employed to assess the functions of excess behaviors, ranging from "armchair theorizing" to paper-and-pencil measures, through direct observations and analog manipulations. It is beyond the scope of this chapter to review the various forms of functional assessment that have been developed, which include

- Standardized questionnaires, such as the Motivation Assessment Scale (Durand & Crimmins, 1988; Durand & Kishi, 1987)
- Structured interviews of parents, teachers, staff, and significant others, such as the Functional Analysis Interview (O'Neill, Horner, Albin, & Sprague, 1996; O'Neill, Horner, Albin, Storey, & Sprague, 1990; Willis, La-Vigna, & Donnellan, 1989)
- Descriptive observations, which include what is often known as A-B-C analyses (Bijou et al., 1968; O'Neill et al., 1990; Repp & Karsh, 1990; see also Paul & Lentz, 1977) and scatter plots (Touchette, MacDonald, & Langer, 1985)
- Experimental manipulations or functional analogs (Carr & Newsom, 1985; Carr, Newsom, & Binkoff, 1980; Durand & Carr, 1987; Iwata et al., 1982/1994; Wacker et al., 1990; Weeks & Gaylord-Ross, 1981)

(For overviews and discussions of these procedures, see Lennox & Miltenberger, 1989; O'Neill et al., 1996; O'Neill et al., 1990; and Reichle & Wacker, 1993, as well as a number of examples of applications in many other chapters in this book.)

It is undoubtedly time consuming to conduct a functional assessment, and it is certainly labor intensive—and requires some special training—to conduct direct observations and analog assessments (see Desrochers et al., 1997). When considering the effort involved, one must ask a very basic question: "Does the information obtained from a functional assessment change the intervention that might otherwise have been selected, and does that different intervention result in any greater level of effectiveness with regard to outcome?" A simple real-world example sheds some light on this question. In work conducted by us through the School Consultation Project at West Virginia University, we had the chance to see in a local special education classroom a child ("Jessica") who engaged in several disruptive behaviors (including screaming, falling out of her seat, and hitting and kicking the teacher) that were escalating in frequency. The teacher, who had extensive experience in working with Jessica and similar children (and who was among the better trained teachers with whom we have worked), had identified these excess behaviors as being maintained by attention. Consequently, she employed an intervention whereby Jessica was placed in a time-out area contingent on the occurrence of the behaviors. The behaviors were later assessed by us through several methods, including an analog assessment, and it was determined that the function of Jessica's excess behaviors was to escape difficult academic tasks. The use of contingent time-out by the teacher was—inadvertently—negatively reinforcing her disruptive behaviors and leading to the increase in their frequency. Switching to a functional communication program (Durand, 1990; Reichle & Wacker, 1993), whereby Jessica could obtain brief breaks from tasks by manually signing STOP, resulted in a swift reduction in the rates of excess behavior—and increased time on-task.

It is probable that such errors in the evaluation of function are common in environments where staff are responsible for the behavior of many individuals and they have only a limited amount of time to assess these often elusive maintaining variables, but such assessment does appear to make a difference. Scotti, Evans, Meyer, and Walker (1991) found that the performance of a functional assessment was related to higher effectiveness scores on a measure of behavioral change during the follow-up period, a finding also supported by Didden and colleagues

(1997). In addition, Iwata, Pace, and colleagues (1994) demonstrated—in a summary of 152 single-case analyses of self-injurious behavior—that interventions were more likely to have a positive outcome when they matched the function of the behavior (e.g., use of time-out or ignoring for attention-maintained behavior) than when they did not (e.g., use of time-out for escape-maintained behavior). It is becoming clear that hypothesis-based interventions, in which the intervention is matched to the function of the excess behavior, are an essential component of effective intervention; however, it is equally clear from both the published literature (Scotti et al., 1993; Scotti et al., 1996) and the surveys of practitioners (Anderson et al., 1995; Weigle & Scotti, 1995; see also Chapter 23) that this critical element is not implemented consistently.

Incorporating Skill Acquisition and Choice Making

The information that is gained from a functional assessment should be used to select an acceptable replacement skill for the excess behavior. The behavioral systems rationale for skill acquisition interventions is that the reinforcement of an alternative skill may eliminate the need for the excess behavior (as the function is being met by another response) and subsequently reduce its rate. The skill may be new for the individual, or it may be a behavior that is in the individual's repertoire but occurring at a low rate, presumably because the excess behavior affects the environment more *effectively* (in terms of receiving a higher rate of reinforcement both consistently and more immediately) and *efficiently* (in terms of a lower response effort—that is, the number of responses required and the physical difficulty of the response). The key to an effective intervention, from a systems view, is to make the alternative response more efficient and effective than the excess behavior (Horner & Day, 1991). Such a shift in responding as a result of changes in reinforcer availability is consistent with Herrnstein's (1961) matching law (see Mace & Roberts, 1993), as well as related literature on competing responses (Crosbie, 1993; Dunham, 1972; Dunham & Grantmyre, 1982).

Differential Reinforcement

In a review of the intervention literature by Carr, Robinson, Taylor, and Carlson (1990), skill acquisition strategies were evaluated along with three other categories of positive interventions: DRO, differential reinforcement of incompatible behavior (DRI), and antecedent manipulations. Skill acquisition interventions were the most effective in reducing excess behavior for individuals with developmental disabilities, using a criterion of 90% suppression of the excess behavior (Carr, Robinson, Taylor, & Carlson, 1990). Scotti, Evans, Meyer, and Walker (1991) found skill training interventions to be as effective as a range of other positive and punishment-based strategies, at least in terms of overall behavioral change (but not response suppression). These results from reviews of the literature prior to the 1990s must be interpreted cautiously, however, as it is likely that the skills selected for acquisition in many of the studies that were included in these reviews were *not* functionally equivalent to the targeted excess behaviors.

Being nonaversive does not automatically mean that an intervention is educative. Differential reinforcement methodologies have enjoyed widespread use, but rarely have these interventions been designed to employ "other" or "incompatible" behaviors that are functionally related to the targeted excess behavior or that utilize *function-relevant* reinforcers. New skills often have been taught to serve as responses that are incompatible with excess behaviors, yet the selection of skills typically has not been based on a functional assessment of the factors that had been maintaining the excess behavior. For example, in studies conducted by Eason et al. (1982), Favell (1973), and Mulick et al. (1978), toy-play skills were trained and then subsequently reinforced with the intent of reducing stereotypic behavior. In each of these studies, reinforcing toy play was effective in reducing the stereotypic response; however, there may have been other reasons for these participants not to respond naturally to the presentation of leisure materials other than the simple lack of skill. Functional assessments of the stereotypic behaviors may have revealed other maintaining factors, such as attention or escape—functions that have been documented for stereotypic behavior but that are not commonly thought of as the basis of an intervention (Scotti et al., 1996). Had these other functions been shown to be important maintaining variables for the stereotypic behavior, different skills would have been taught, such as requesting attention or interaction or requesting assistance with or a break from tasks. Skills such as these are not merely incompatible with stereotypic behavior; they may, instead, be functionally equivalent responses that form the basis for increasing repertoires, not merely giving individuals something else to do.

In other interventions that employ DRO, the individual may receive reinforcement merely for the absence of the excess behavior. In these cases, no new behaviors are introduced into the individual's repertoire. For example, in a study conducted by Repp, Deitz, and Deitz (1976), aggressive behavior was effectively reduced through a DRO schedule in which reinforcement was contingent on the absence of the target behavior. Had a functional assessment been conducted to determine the function of the aggressive behavior, an alternative, functionally equivalent response could have been selected. The individual then would have been taught a specific, appropriate skill to replace the aggressive behavior, thus enhancing the repertoire. Instead, such a use of DRO is actually eliminative in that the goal is simply to reduce the target behavior, without targeting any specific skills for increase.

Finally, as noted in a previous section, the reinforcer in typical differential reinforcement programs is all too often nonfunctional. For example, during a recent consultation, we found a DRO program being utilized to reduce aggressive behavior. The reinforcer being delivered—on a rather elaborate schedule—for the absence of aggression was money: Increasing periods without aggression earned an increasing number of dimes. The implicit assumption was that money was a more potent reinforcer than the variables that maintained aggression. When simply asked whether they thought that the individual was being aggressive to gain access to money, the staff responded, "No, he does it when he wants our attention." The "light bulb over the head" then came on, and the plan was quickly revised so that the young man could earn time with staff for periods of no aggression. This was then revised, after a confirming functional assessment, to a plan whereby the young man could actually initiate requests for interaction with staff, which were granted contingent on the absence of aggression for a specified preceding period. Thus, a DRO program was still in effect, but the individual was learning a functional skill and the reinforcer was derived from an analysis of function (i.e., a function-relevant reinforcer).

Choices and Control

Equally critical to providing function-relevant reinforcers and teaching functionally related skills is providing choices among reinforcers and responses. This point strikes to the heart of a major difference between typical, eliminative interventions and educative interventions: the issue of control and who wields it. This issue repeatedly comes up during consultations and continuing education training. If we are to teach new skills to individuals who exhibit excess behaviors, then those skills must be more efficient and effective than the targeted excess behaviors (Horner & Day, 1991). Therefore, individuals must be allowed—even encouraged—to use these replacement skills and must be reinforced for doing so—even if the reinforcer is time spent in a preferred activity or a brief break from a task. Allowing individuals who exhibit excess behaviors to engage in some activity other than what staff and teachers want them to do is apparently a heretical practice, and one that repeatedly meets with the bewildered statement, "But aren't you letting them get what they want?!" The response to this sort of comment should be a simple, "Yup." The reason that individuals engage in excessive and even extreme behaviors is often "to get what they want"; that is, the behavior has a function. All too often, they do get what they want anyway—unfortunately through the extreme means that we seek to control through typically restrictive and punitive means. The educative approach acknowledges the appropriateness of the function of a behavior;

it seeks only to alter the form or topography of the responses that individuals use to meet those functions. If we are to accept the foregoing model of behavioral systems and functional assessment, then we also must accept that reduction of excess behaviors will occur only when we—as care providers and professionals—give up our own excessive need to exercise complete control over the daily lives of individuals with developmental disabilities, chronic psychiatric disorders, and conduct problems.

The ultimate goal is to return to individuals with disabilities the same level of control that any of us has or wants in our own lives. This does not mean that individuals who exhibit excess behaviors—any more than ourselves—are free to do anything they want and at any time they want to do it. But within the constraints of society, laws, the workplace or educational environment, and common civility, there are many choices and options that we exercise but that we fail to allow for our clients and students. Just think how many breaks or pauses you have taken in the course of simply reading this chapter (the "page-turner" that it is, we are not presumptuous enough to think that you have been completely unable to set it down!). Such breaks that are taken by clients and students often are judged to be "off-task behavior," described as "resistant" or "noncompliant," and result in a call for intervention.

What, then, does this mean programmatically? As Durand, Berotti, and Weiner noted, success in teaching communication skills (as the replacement behavior) "relies heavily on allowing individuals to make choices in their daily activities . . . where choice making is discouraged, functional communication training often has limited success" (1993, pp. 332–333). Providing choice is as simple as allowing individuals to select their own activities and reinforcers when this is possible, conducting preference assessments when individuals cannot fully communicate their choices, and allowing individuals to self-initiate and determine their own schedule of activities (Datillo & Rusch, 1985; Fisher & Mazur, 1997; Parsons, Reid, Reynolds, & Bumgarner, 1990). It is also as significant as moving people out of restrictive environments and into the community and allowing self-determination (Guess, Benson, & Siegel-Causey, 1985; Kearney, Durand, & Mindell, 1991; Smull & Bellamy, 1991).

Using the Least Restrictive Techniques

Educative intervention approaches are designed to reduce the need for employing aversive consequence strategies. Although increasing appropriate behaviors should cause a concomitant decrease in excess behavior, it may be necessary to protect the individual from harmful excess behavior prior to the acquisition of the alternative skill. To protect the individual, crisis management techniques, such as brief interruption, brief restraint, and redirection, may be used to stop harmful behavior when it occurs (Azrin, Besalel, & Wisotzek, 1982; Meyer & Evans, 1989; Richman & Bell, 1983). These interventions are intended to interrupt the behavior for the safety of the individual; they are *not* engineered with the specific purpose of causing an overall reduction in a particular challenging behavior (Meyer & Evans, 1989).

Although the use of aversive techniques with individuals who have developmental disabilities has been widely disputed (see Repp & Singh, 1990), the application of aversive techniques is still a common intervention for excess behavior (Scotti et al., 1996). Reviews of the intervention literature indicate that the most intrusive interventions, such as water mist and contingent shock, are used to consequate even mild to moderate excess behaviors, such as stereotypic behaviors (Lennox et al., 1988; Scotti, Evans, Meyer, & Walker, 1991). Although decelerative techniques may successfully suppress behavior (e.g., Linscheid et al., 1990), their use as the exclusive form of intervention violates the educative assumption that the goal of intervention is to expand the individual's repertoire. The interventionist should *not* conceptualize the intervention goal as reducing a challenging behavior and returning the subdued individual to his or her caregivers (Carr, Robinson, & Palumbo, 1990).

A common dictum is that one should follow through a hierarchy of intrusiveness, from least to most, when selecting and attempting interventions. There is little evidence—at least from published studies—that this process is followed consistently. Scotti, Evans, Meyer, and Walker (1991) reported that the current level of intervention intrusiveness was unrelated to the level of any reported prior intervention attempts, noting that most authors failed to report on the history of treatment. These authors also noted that the most intrusive interventions have been applied to the least severe behaviors and that the functional level of the individual also has been a factor in intervention selection: Individuals with more severe disabilities (e.g., profound mental retardation, physical or sensory impairments) were more likely to receive the more intrusive intervention. Some improvement has been noted over time, however. Scotti et al. (1996) noted a decreased use of intrusive interventions in general; when they are utilized, they are much more likely to be employed in combination with procedures such as environmental change, reinforcement-based strategies, and skill training—rather than by themselves. This points to an important trend in the literature toward multicomponent interventions and the realization that it is naive to assume that a single, typically reactive and consequence-based intervention will be sufficient. Interventions must address multiple aspects of an individual's life by altering unsuitable environments, teaching necessary skills, and providing choices—not by simply consequating excess behavior.

Monitoring the Collateral Effects of Intervention

The importance of monitoring collateral effects across the course of intervention has been discussed throughout this chapter. The consistent message is that a wide variety of behaviors should be tracked prior to, during, and following intervention. This point needs no further elaboration. Although historically only a small number of studies reported monitoring collateral changes and the majority of these reports were anecdotal (Scotti, Evans, Meyer, & Walker, 1991), there is a promising trend in the literature toward more data-based evaluations of collateral behaviors (Scotti et al., 1996). The feasibility of

assessing collateral change has been demonstrated (e.g., Johnson et al., 1982; Meyer et al., 1985); it is time to ensure that it becomes a common practice.

One reason to monitor collateral change that has not yet been mentioned is to identify behaviors that are already in the individual's repertoire and that may serve as functional alternatives to the excess behavior. Learning new skills can be effortful for individuals, and they may respond to such instruction as yet another demand. When it is possible to take advantage of existing responses, it behooves us to do so—even if that existing response will eventually require further shaping. In the case of Jessica, discussed previously, observation of her classroom behavior indicated a low rate of finger-pointing behavior. When this behavior was assessed—along with her aggressive behavior—through analog assessment procedures, it was determined that the pointing behavior served an escape function similar to the aggressive and disruptive behavior. Intervention thus consisted of prompting Jessica to use this pointing behavior, rather than the disruptive behavior, to obtain a break from a task. Thus, we were able to quickly reduce the rate of aggression and disruption by shifting reinforcement to an existing response—a response that might have otherwise been viewed only as a collateral and, perhaps, nonfunctional behavior. Eventually, general pointing was shaped into pointing to a STOP sign, and eventually to manually signing STOP.

Employing Procedures to Enhance Maintenance and Generalization

Positive gains that disappear over time and leave the individual to revert to excess behavior are essentially useless. Intervention gains that appear only in the teaching environment are similarly unhelpful. Given this, the most striking point to be conveyed concerning maintenance and generalization research is how little has been done relative to the significance of these issues. The meta-analysis conducted by Scotti, Evans, Meyer, and Walker (1991) indicated that a mere 30% of reported intervention studies addressed issues of generalization in a structured manner. The results were slightly better for maintenance:

47% of the studies reported follow-up data on interventions (half for less than 6 months, and half for more than 6 months). These findings agree with those of Carr, Robinson, Taylor, and Carlson (1990), who reviewed positive intervention studies and found that very few systematically addressed maintenance and generalization. This state of affairs is improving, however; more than half of the studies reported on generalization attempts in the more recent Scotti et al. (1996) review, including generalization across environments, individuals, tasks/activities, and behaviors.

Theoretically, an educative approach should naturally promote generalization and maintenance of intervention gains. Providing an individual with a functional replacement skill should increase the maintenance of intervention gains over time and generalization across environments (Durand, 1987). Placing the newly acquired intervention behaviors into the context of the functional relations that previously maintained the excess behavior should provide the individual with the natural contingencies that Stokes and Baer (1977) suggested are critical to generalization. Even so, it cannot be assumed that generalization will simply occur. Active planning of intervention strategies to promote generalization is necessary. Stokes and Baer (1977) suggested incorporating stimuli and consequences that will be present in the natural environment and direct reinforcement of the behavior when generalization does occur. A focus on the natural environment means living fully inclusive lives in typical environments, with typical peers, and doing typical activities and routines. Deficit environments are associated with deficient repertoires and excess behaviors. Living "ordinary lives" (Emerson, McGill, & Mansell, 1994) is the solution to both and the best step toward planned generalization and maintenance (see also Koegel, Koegel, & Dunlap, 1996; Meyer & Evans, 1989; Reichle & Wacker, 1993).

Producing Meaningful Outcomes

Historically, the outcomes of behavioral interventions were evaluated by a single measure: the frequency of the excess behavior being targeted for reduction. This certainly is an important measure, especially when one seeks to evaluate the utility of a particular intervention. But, as we have noted, interventions themselves primarily focused on single behaviors, with little concern about the relation of that response to others in the repertoire. Once we begin to take a broader, systems view of behavior and intervention, this single outcome measure becomes woefully insufficient. At a minimum, we now need to ask what is happening to the rate of other behaviors—excess and acceptable—in the repertoire and whether the functionally equivalent replacement skill is being learned.

Meyer and Evans (1989, 1993a) provided a hierarchy of behavioral outcome goals and measures that range from the most molecular (the single, isolated target behavior) to more molar constructs of social relationships and support networks. These levels of outcome include

- Improvement in the excess behavior targeted for reduction
- Acquisition of the (functional) replacement skills
- Acquisition of general strategies for self-control (e.g., anger control, relaxation skills, self-monitoring) that support behavioral change
- Increases in positive collateral behaviors ("ripple effects") and decreases in negative collateral behaviors
- Reductions in the need for crisis services and medical management
- Movement to less restrictive placements (residential, employment/educational, and leisure environments) with increased participation and inclusion in those environments
- Subjective improvement in quality of life (e.g., happiness, satisfaction, perceived control)
- Perceived improvement by significant others in the individual's life (e.g., parents, siblings, teachers, staff, community peers)
- Expanded social relationships and support networks

To this comprehensive list we would add 1) decreased negative impact on others and the environment, in terms of injury to others and destruction of property, and 2) improvement on *objective* quality-of-life indicators. We add the last in recognition of the expanding literature that is attempting to identify objective aspects of quality of life, including control over bedtime, meal planning, salary earned through employment, items purchased, transportation, physical access, architectural features of residence, and so forth (Campo, Sharpton, Thompson, & Sexton, 1996; Keith, Schalock, & Hoffman, 1986; Schalock, Keith, Hoffman, & Karan, 1989; Thompson, Robinson, Dietrich, Farris, & Sinclair, 1996).

At one time, behavior analysis was decried as being insensitive and it had to be explicitly stated that social validity was a viable outcome measure (Wolf, 1978). However, despite the vast literature on treatment acceptability (see Miltenberger, 1990, for one review of this literature), we have moved little beyond group studies that ask only the question, "How acceptable is this intervention, applied to this individual, for this particular problem?" We know much about the parameters that seem to affect such ratings (e.g., behavior severity, intervention intrusiveness), but we do not regularly assess the social validity of individual interventions and their outcomes. Even fewer studies gather systematic data on quality of life as an outcome—particularly within comprehensive, multicomponent interventions (e.g., Lucyshyn, Albin, & Nixon, 1997; see Chapter 13). Clearly, it is time that these important outcomes be evaluated and reported with regularity in the published literature. The literature has well established that we can produce reductions in targeted excess behaviors. The important issue now is the difference that this reduction makes in the lives of people with disabilities.

SUMMARY

Reviews of the literature indicate that current treatments for behavioral excesses are not consistently fulfilling the requirements of good practice. As a result, there is growing support for educative approaches to intervention. Educative-based interventions emphasize the functionality of excess behavior and use skill acquisition methodologies to increase the individual's existing repertoire of adaptive, appropriate skills. Educative approaches are based on behavioral systems theory, which emphasizes the behavioral interrelations within response repertoires. This chapter has discussed seven critical elements of educatively based interventions. Consistent use of these elements is essential to effective intervention and evaluation of outcomes. At this point, however, we must ask 1) do practitioners know how to implement these intervention components, and 2) do the environments in which they work support the use of these practices? It is the answers to these questions to which we now turn. In doing so, we focus on teachers and educational environments, as this is the system within which we have been working.

SUPPORTING RECOMMENDED PRACTICES IN THE EDUCATIONAL ENVIRONMENT

A number of reports (Fueyo, 1991; Gleason & Hall, 1991; Merrett & Wheldall, 1993) have indicated that most teacher training programs (for both general and special educators) provide little or no training on classroom control and discipline techniques. The discipline techniques that teachers typically use are learned from anecdotal stories that are shared among teachers (Kampwirth, 1988; Merrett & Wheldall, 1993). In many schools, disciplinary difficulties are hidden as a result of an atmosphere in which teachers are expected to handle whatever problems arise (Miller, 1990). Thus, some teachers may not benefit from collaboration with peers regarding their most challenging situations.

Although special educators typically are thought to have more knowledge of behavioral principles and strategies than general educators, the literature does not necessarily support this assumption. In a study by Weigle and Scotti (1995), special educators reported using common interventions in a blanket form for all students and all excess behaviors, rather than tailoring interventions individually according to the function of the excess behavior. When presented with functional analysis information (i.e., a description of the function of the behavior and antecedents and consequences maintaining the behavior) about a particular behavior in a scenario, the teachers were unable to identify which interventions likely would be effective and which likely would exacerbate the excess behavior.

The self-report of special educators in a study by Ayres, Meyer, Erevelles, and Park-Lee (1994), however, indicated that other factors have impeded the application of recommended practices, regardless of the level of knowledge and skills that the teachers possess. Lack of time for planning and development of interventions greatly deterred the use of skills. Student-to-staff ratio was also reported to be too high to permit the teachers to engage in individual program implementation and recommended instructional practices. Finally, the teachers identified a lack of administrative support for their efforts to include students with severe disabilities into general education. Administrators often had negative attitudes toward such students, which spread to general educators, and did not provide the support staff or time allotments necessary to implement recommended practices successfully (Ayres et al., 1994).

For students with excess, challenging behavior to receive behavioral support from their teachers, the teachers need supports, as well. If teachers are expected to incorporate recommended practices into their daily routines, then the entire system within which schools function must be adapted. (For a model of applying positive behavioral support systems to schools, see Sugai & Horner, 1994.) Such supports will need to be addressed at federal, state, and local government levels (Mansell, 1994). For example, Figure 1 displays an A-B-C comparison of the effects of traditional behavior management versus recommended practices (i.e., positive behavioral support) on teachers' use of skills learned in continuing education courses. As can be seen, in traditional schools, teachers are mandated to obtain a predetermined number of continuing education units (CEUs) to keep their teaching certificates or licensure. With such contingencies in place, teachers typically attend the required courses but infrequently apply the knowledge and skills obtained because there are no contingencies for behavioral change. However, in a system that pro-

vides supports for teachers to apply recommended practices, CEUs are required to retain licensure, but teachers' application of skills will be monitored in the classroom after attending courses. Teachers are also rewarded for correct application of their newly obtained skills with pay/seniority raises. Such contingencies over teacher behavior and supports should lead to improved teacher performance, which may in turn lead to increased job satisfaction and improved student behavior. (For further elaboration on these supports and a model for applying recommended practices, see Weigle, 1997.)

Passing federal and state laws that require some form of inclusion could provide the needed impetus for school system change. Passing state laws and regulations regarding teacher certification, as well as statewide reward systems for exemplary school performance toward meeting inclusion objectives, also could provide motivation for change. The allocation of state funds could be contingent on school and teacher performance toward successfully implementing recommended practices; that is, schools that perform the best could receive the most nonessential, or "extra," funds. Within the schools, that money could be used to reward teachers who demonstrate exemplary skills, or it could be used in ways that teachers and administrators determine as a group. Loucks-Horsley and Roody (1990) explained that although mandates often are necessary to initiate change in schools, supports at the school level are required to ensure successful change.

To modify the organization of schools to one that utilizes recommended practices, the active support of school administrators, particularly school principals, is necessary to keep staff and educators involved and motivated (Ayres et al., 1994; Bickel & Bickel, 1986; Colvin, Kameenui, & Sugai, 1993; Littrell, Billingsley, & Cross, 1994; Miller, 1990; Williams, Fox, Thousand, & Fox, 1990). As Kiracofe (1993) explained, administrative support is necessary to begin a system change process, as well as to maintain the change once it occurs. Kiracofe (1993) outlined a number of steps for initiating system change that may be helpful in implementing recommended practices in schools:

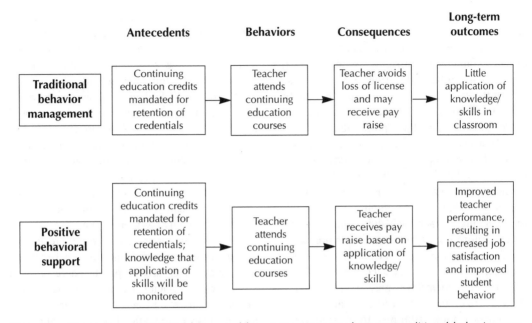

	Antecedents	**Behaviors**	**Consequences**	**Long-term outcomes**
Traditional behavior management	Continuing education credits mandated for retention of credentials	Teacher attends continuing education courses	Teacher avoids loss of license and may receive pay raise	Little application of knowledge/ skills in classroom
Positive behavioral support	Continuing education credits mandated for retention of credentials; knowledge that application of skills will be monitored	Teacher attends continuing education courses	Teacher receives pay raise based on application of knowledge/ skills	Improved teacher performance, resulting in increased job satisfaction and improved student behavior

Figure 1. Comparison of A-B-C relation and long-term outcomes between traditional behavior management and positive behavioral support for teachers attending continuing education classes and applying new skills.

1. Establish commitment from the administrators, teachers, and staff to follow the process.
2. Build ownership of key stakeholders by enlisting those who are most enthusiastic to be the first to be actively involved in implementing recommended practices.
3. Have the key stakeholders begin using recommended practices.
4. Have the key stakeholders reflect on and share their experiences with recommended practices in an ongoing manner.
5. Provide follow-up training and consultation to the key stakeholders and the remaining personnel to begin the process.
6. Analyze outcomes of both targeted students and personnel in training, and analyze the efficacy of current schoolwide discipline programs.
7. Develop action plans to remediate areas of concern.

In addition to enlisting administrative support and motivating key stakeholders, the roles of both special and general educators must be addressed. In an inclusive school, the roles of special and general educators likely will change drastically, for educators will need to share their expertise with one another to address adequately the needs of all students in one classroom (Miller, 1990). This may be accomplished in any number of ways, including

1. Pairing general and special educators and having them share classrooms (e.g., Fuchs & Fuchs, 1994)
2. Having special educators serve as consultants to general educators (e.g., McDonnell, McDonnell, Hardman, & McCune, 1991)
3. Making each teacher responsible for teaching both general and special education students and for consulting with other teachers (Stainback, Stainback, & Jackson, 1992)

This likely will vary by state, perhaps even by county or by school, and may best be an individual district decision based on the expertise and the consultation skills of current staff.

In addition, teachers' schedules will need to be modified to allow for teamwork, data collection, implementation of individual and classroom behavior plans, and intervention planning and evaluation. Lack of time and lack of resources have been identified as leading causes of unsuccessful change processes within schools (Ayres et al., 1994; Miller, 1990; Williams et al., 1990); therefore, the typical school day may be altered, with more shared teaching among teachers, professionals, and paraprofessionals.

To accommodate the changes in teaching, administrative supports will be needed so that teachers can handle the extra work load of implementing recommended practices (Ayres et al., 1994). Administrators might be responsible for arranging teachers' schedules and obtaining coverage for all classrooms and common areas (e.g., lunchroom, playground, halls). If there are insufficient staff to cover such activities, then administrators themselves may need to stand in for teachers on occasion (Littrell et al., 1994).

Furthermore, administrators (including principals and other members of boards of education) will have to maintain the new system within budget restraints and other state-guided limitations. Thus, administrators' jobs will become more difficult until the new systems are in place and functioning semi-independently. However, this work likely will pay off in the long run, as placements outside the public school system will decrease, teacher satisfaction and performance will increase, and student performance and behavior will improve (Mansell, 1994).

CONCLUSION

We have provided in this chapter an overview of standards of practice and the critical elements of an educative approach to behavioral intervention. Undoubtedly, there is much work ahead, and supports are needed not only for individuals who exhibit excess behaviors but also for the professionals and the paraprofessionals who are instrumental in implementing these practices. We have provided a brief overview of a support model for teachers, which could be combined with other practices in staff training and management (see Reid & Parsons, 1995, for a bibliography of this literature, as well as Chapters 22 and 23) and expanded to environments beyond the education system.

This chapter also has provided both a conceptual overview of the strategies involved in the educative approach to behavioral intervention and some of the basic and theoretical underpinnings of that approach (see also Scotti et al., 1998; Chapter 1). Perhaps one caveat concerning the foregoing review should be noted. One could argue that the published literature is *not,* generally, meant to be a model of the recommended practices that clinicians, teachers, and other professionals and paraprofessionals should follow in their own work, rather that published research studies are meant only to demonstrate—under highly controlled and rigorous (i.e., "unnatural") conditions—the effects of certain procedures and variables on particular problem behaviors (e.g., does overcorrection produce a decrease in self-injurious behavior?). Thus, the deficits in the literature that have been noted here are groundless. To this we emphatically counter that practitioners have utilized this literature as a model for their own interventions (sometimes taking procedures too literally and applying them without question), and they will continue to do so. Thus, it behooves the basic researcher and applied clinician-researcher (i.e., scientist-practitioner) to make that published literature more relevant to real-world clinical situations. The time is well past for our field to continue the publication of *only* (or even predominantly) highly controlled "laboratory" demonstrations. We need more studies that adhere to the full range of principles noted here—even if some rigor and adherence to traditional behavior analytic methodologies must be "sacrificed" (see Meyer & Evans, 1993b). In its place, we will have real-world applications that practitioners can more readily emulate and thus are more likely to use in their attempts to effect change in the lives of the individuals with whom they work.

REFERENCES

Anderson, C.M., Mullen, K.B., Freeman, K.A., Lewis, J., Weigle, K., Kirk, K., & Scotti, J.R. (1995, May). *Assessment of a course designed to increase educators' understanding of behavioral principles and functional assessment methodologies.* Poster presented at the 21st annual convention of the Association for Behavior Analysis, Washington, DC.

Ayres, B.J., Meyer, L.H., Erevelles, N., & Park-Lee, S. (1994). Easy for you to say: Teacher perspectives on implementing most promising practices. *Journal of The Association for Persons with Severe Handicaps, 19,* 84–93.

Azrin, N.H., Besalel, V.A., & Wisotzek, I.E. (1982). Treatment of self-injury by a reinforcement and interruption procedure. *Analysis and Intervention in Developmental Disabilities, 2,* 105–113.

Baer, D.M., Wolf, M.M., & Risley, T.R. (1968). Some current dimensions of applied behavior analysis. *Journal of Applied Behavior Analysis, 1,* 91–97.

Bickel, W.E., & Bickel, D.D. (1986). Effective schools, classrooms, and instruction: Implications for special education. *Exceptional Children, 52,* 489–500.

Bijou, S.W., Peterson, R.F., & Ault, M.H. (1968). A method to integrate descriptive and experimental field studies at the level of data and empirical concepts. *Journal of Applied Behavior Analysis, 1,* 175–191.

Campo, S.F., Sharpton, W.R., Thompson, B., & Sexton, D. (1996). Measurement characteristics of the Quality of Life Index when used with adults who have severe mental retardation. *American Journal on Mental Retardation, 100,* 546–550.

Carr, E.G., & Durand, V.M. (1985a). Reducing behavior problems through functional communication training. *Journal of Applied Behavior Analysis, 18,* 111–126.

Carr, E.G., & Durand, V.M. (1985b). The social-communicative basis of severe behavior problems in children. In S. Reiss & R.R. Bootzin (Eds.), *Theoretical issues in behavior therapy* (pp. 219–254). Orlando, FL: Academic Press.

Carr, E.G., & Newsom, C. (1985). Demand-related tantrums: Conceptualization and treatment. *Behavior Modification, 9,* 403–426.

Carr, E.G., Newsom, C.D., & Binkoff, J.A. (1980). Escape as a factor in the aggressive behavior of two retarded children. *Journal of Applied Behavior Analysis, 13,* 101–117.

Carr, E.G., Robinson, S., & Palumbo, L.W. (1990). The wrong issue: Aversive versus nonaversive treatment. The right issue: Functional versus nonfunctional treatment. In A.C. Repp & N.N. Singh (Eds.), *Perspectives on the use of nonaversive and aversive interventions for persons with developmental disabilities* (pp. 361–379). Sycamore, IL: Sycamore Press.

Carr, E.G., Robinson, S., Taylor, J.C., & Carlson, J.I. (1990). Positive approaches to the treatment of severe behavior problems in persons with developmental disabilities: A review and analysis of reinforcement and stimulus-based procedures. *Monographs of The Association for Persons with Severe Handicaps, 4.*

Colvin, G., Kameenui, E.J., & Sugai, G. (1993). Reconceptualizing behavior management and school-side discipline in general education. *Education and Treatment of Children, 16,* 361–381.

Crosbie, J. (1993). The effects of response cost and response restriction on a multiple-response repertoire in humans. *Journal of the Experimental Analysis of Behavior, 59,* 173–192.

Datillo, J., & Rusch, F.R. (1985). Effects of choice on leisure participation for persons with severe handicaps. *Journal of The Association for Persons with Severe Handicaps, 10,* 194–199.

Desrochers, M.N., Hile, M.G., & Williams-Moseley, T.L. (1997). Survey of functional assessment procedures used with individuals who display mental retardation and severe problem behaviors. *American Journal on Mental Retardation, 101,* 535–546.

Didden, R., Duker, P.C., & Korzilius, H. (1997). Meta-analytic study on treatment effectiveness for problem behaviors with individuals who have mental retardation. *American Journal on Mental Retardation, 101,* 387–399.

Dunham, P.J. (1972). Some effects of punishment upon unpunished responding. *Journal of the Experimental Analysis of Behavior, 17,* 443–450.

Dunham, P.J., & Grantmyre, J. (1982). Changes in a multiple-response repertoire during response-contingent punishment and response restriction: Sequential relationships. *Journal of the Experimental Analysis of Behavior, 37,* 123–133.

Durand, V.M. (1987). "Look homeward angel": A call to return to our (functional) roots. *The Behavior Analyst, 10,* 299–302.

Durand, V.M. (1990). *Severe behavior problems: A functional communication training approach.* New York: Guilford Press.

Durand, V.M., Berotti, D., & Weiner, J. (1993). Functional communication training: Factors affecting effectiveness, generalization, and maintenance. In J. Reichle & D.P. Wacker (Eds.), *Communication and language intervention series: Vol. 3. Communicative alternatives to challenging behavior: Integrating functional assessment and intervention strategies* (pp. 317–340). Baltimore: Paul H. Brookes Publishing Co.

Durand, V.M., & Carr, E.G. (1987). Social influences on "self-stimulatory" behavior: Analysis and treatment application. *Journal of Applied Behavior Analysis, 20,* 119–132.

Durand, V.M., & Crimmins, D.B. (1988). Identifying the variables maintaining self-injurious behavior. *Journal of Autism and Developmental Disorders, 18,* 99–117.

Durand, V.M., & Kishi, G. (1987). Reducing severe behavior problems among persons with dual sensory impairments: An evaluation of a technical assistance model. *Journal of The Association for Persons with Severe Handicaps, 12,* 2–10.

Eason, L.J., White, M.J., & Newsom, C. (1982). Generalized reduction of self-stimulatory behavior: An effect of teaching appropriate play to autistic children. *Analysis and Intervention in Developmental Disabilities, 2,* 157–169.

Emerson, E., McGill, P., & Mansell, J. (Eds.). (1994). *Severe learning disabilities and challenging behaviours: Designing high quality services.* London: Chapman & Hall.

Evans, I.M. (1971). Theoretical and experimental aspects of the behavior modification approach to autistic children. In M. Rutter (Ed.), *Infantile autism: Concepts, characteristics and treatment* (pp. 229–251). London: Churchill Livingston.

Evans, I.M., Brown, F.A., Weed, K.A., Spry, K.M., & Owen, V. (1987). The assessment of functional competencies: A behavioral approach to the evaluation of programs for children with disabilities. In R.J. Prinz (Ed.), *Advances in behavioral assessment of children and families* (Vol. 3, pp. 93–121). Greenwich, CT: JAI Press.

Evans, I.M., & Meyer, L.H. (1985). *An educative approach to behavior problems: A practical decision model for interventions with severely handicapped learners.* Baltimore: Paul H. Brookes Publishing Co.

Evans, I.M., Meyer, L.H., Kurkjian, J.A., & Kishi, G.S. (1988). An evaluation of behavioral interrelationships in child behavior therapy. In J.C. Witt, S.N. Elliott, & F.N. Gresham (Eds.), *Handbook of behavior therapy in education* (pp. 189–216). New York: Plenum.

Evans, I.M., & Scotti, J.R. (1989). Defining meaningful outcomes for persons with profound disabilities. In F. Brown & D. Lehr (Eds.), *Persons with profound disabilities: Issues and practices* (pp. 83–107). Baltimore: Paul H. Brookes Publishing Co.

Favell, J.E. (1973). Reduction of stereotypies by reinforcement of toy play. *Mental Retardation, 11,* 21–23.

Fisher, W.W., & Mazur, J.E. (1997). Basic and applied research on choice responding. *Journal of Applied Behavior Analysis, 30,* 387–410.

Fuchs, D., & Fuchs, L.S. (1994). Inclusive schools movement and the radicalization of special education reform. *Exceptional Children, 60,* 294–309.

Fueyo, V. (1991). Implementing a field-based elementary teacher training program. *Education and Treatment of Children, 14,* 280–298.

Gleason, M.M., & Hall, T.E. (1991). Focusing on instructional design to implement a performance-based teacher training program: The University of Oregon Model. *Education and Treatment of Children, 14,* 316–332.

Goldiamond, I. (1974). Toward a constructional approach to social problems: Ethical and constitutional issues raised by applied behavior analysis. *Behaviorism, 2,* 1–85.

Guess, D., Benson, H.A., & Siegel-Causey, E. (1985). Concepts and issues related to choice-making and autonomy among persons with severe disabilities.

Journal of The Association for Persons with Severe Handicaps, 10, 79–86.

Hawkins, R.P. (1979). The functions of assessment: Implications for selection and development of devices for assessing repertoires in clinical, educational, and other settings. *Journal of Applied Behavior Analysis, 12,* 501–526.

Hawkins, R.P. (1986). Selection of target behaviors. In R.O. Nelson & S.C. Hayes (Eds.), *Conceptual foundations of behavioral assessment* (pp. 331–385). New York: Guilford Press.

Haynes, S.H., & O'Brien, W.H. (1990). Functional analysis in behavior therapy. *Clinical Psychology Review, 10,* 649–668.

Herrnstein, R.J. (1961). Relative and absolute strength of response as a function of frequency of reinforcement. *Journal of the Experimental Analysis of Behavior, 4,* 267–272.

Horner, R.H., & Budd, C.M. (1985). Teaching manual sign language to a nonverbal student. *Education and Training of the Mentally Retarded, 20,* 39–47.

Horner, R.H., & Day, M.H. (1991). The effects of response efficiency on functionally equivalent competing behaviors. *Journal of Applied Behavior Analysis, 24,* 719–732.

Horner, R.H., Dunlap, G., Koegel, R.L., Carr, E.G., Sailor, W., Anderson, J., Albin, R.W., & O'Neill, R.E. (1990). Toward a technology of "nonaversive" behavioral support. *Journal of The Association for Persons with Severe Handicaps, 15,* 125–132.

Hunt, P., Alwell, M., & Goetz, L. (1988). Acquisition of conversation skills and the reduction of inappropriate social interaction behaviors. *Journal of The Association for Persons with Severe Handicaps, 13,* 20–27.

Isaacs, W., Thomas, J., & Goldiamond, I. (1960). Application of operant conditioning to reinstate verbal behavior in psychotics. *Journal of Speech and Hearing Disorders, 25,* 8–12.

Iwata, B.A., Dorsey, M.F., Slifer, K.J., Bauman, K.E., & Richman, G.S. (1994). Toward a functional analysis of self-injury. *Journal of Applied Behavior Analysis, 27,* 197–209. (Reprinted from *Analysis and Intervention in Developmental Disabilities, 2,* 3–20, 1982)

Iwata, B.A., Pace, G.M., Dorsey, M.F., Zarcone, J.R., Vollmer, T.R., Smith, R.G., Rodgers, T.A., Lerman, D.C., Shore, B.A., Mazaleski, J.L., Goh, H., Edwards Cowdery, G., Kalsher, M.J., McCosh, K.C., & Willis, K.D. (1994). The functions of self-injurious behavior: An experimental-epidemiological analysis. *Journal of Applied Behavior Analysis, 27,* 215–240.

Johnson, W.L., Baumeister, A.A., Penland, M.J., & Inwald, C. (1982). Experimental analysis of self-injurious, stereotypic, and collateral behavior of retarded persons: Effects of overcorrection and reinforcement of alternative responding. *Analysis and*

Intervention in Developmental Disabilities, 2, 41–66.

Kampwirth, T.J. (1988). Behavior management in the classroom: A self-assessment guide for teachers. *Education and Treatment of Children, 11,* 286–293.

Kazdin, A.E. (1982). Symptom substitution, generalization, and response covariation: Implications for psychotherapy outcome. *Psychological Bulletin, 91,* 349–365.

Kearney, C.A., Durand, V.M., & Mindell, J.A. (1991). *The relationship between choice and adaptive/ maladaptive behavior in persons with severe handicaps: A longitudinal study.* Unpublished manuscript.

Keith, K.D., Schalock, R.L., & Hoffman, K. (1986). *Quality of life: Measurement and programmatic implications.* Lincoln, NE: Region V Mental Retardation Services.

Kiracofe, J. (1993). Strategies to help agencies shift from services to supports. In V.J. Bradley, J.W. Ashbaugh, & B.C. Blaney (Eds.), *Creating individual supports for people with developmental disabilities: A mandate for change at many levels* (pp. 281–298). Baltimore: Paul H. Brookes Publishing Co.

Koegel, L.K., Koegel, R.L., & Dunlap, G. (Eds.). (1996). *Positive behavior support: Including people with difficult behavior in the community.* Baltimore: Paul H. Brookes Publishing Co.

LaVigna, G.W., & Donnellan, A.M. (1986). *Alternatives to punishment: Solving behavior problems with non-aversive strategies.* New York: Irvington.

Lennox, D.B., & Miltenberger, R.G. (1989). Conducting a functional assessment of problem behavior in applied settings. *Journal of The Association for Persons with Severe Handicaps, 14,* 304–311.

Lennox, D.B., Miltenberger, R.G., Spengler, R., & Erfanian, N. (1988). Decelerative treatment practices with persons who have mental retardation: A review of five years of the literature. *American Journal on Mental Retardation, 92,* 492–501.

Linscheid, T.R., Iwata, B.A., Ricketts, R.W., Williams, D.E., & Griffin, J.C. (1990). Clinical evaluation of the Self-Injurious Behavior Inhibiting System (SIBIS). *Journal of Applied Behavior Analysis, 23,* 53–78.

Littrell, P.C., Billingsley, B.S., & Cross, L.H. (1994). The effects of principal support on special and general educators' stress, job satisfaction, school commitment, health, and intent to stay in teaching. *Remedial and Special Education, 15,* 297–310.

Loucks-Horsley, S., & Roody, D.S. (1990). Using what is known about change to inform the Regular Education Initiative. *Remedial and Special Education, 11,* 51–56.

Lucyshyn, J.M., Albin, R.W., & Nixon, C.D. (1997). Embedding comprehensive behavioral support in family ecology: An experimental, single-case analysis. *Journal of Consulting and Clinical Psychology, 65,* 241–251.

Mace, F.C., & Roberts, M.L. (1993). Factors affecting selection of behavioral interventions. In J. Reichle & D.P. Wacker (Eds.), *Communication and language intervention series: Vol. 3. Communicative alternatives to challenging behavior: Integrating functional assessment and intervention strategies* (pp. 113–133). Baltimore: Paul H. Brookes Publishing Co.

Mansell, J. (1994). Policy and policy implications. In E. Emerson, P. McGill, & J. Mansell (Eds.), *Severe learning disabilities and challenging behaviours: Designing high quality services* (pp. 297–313). London: Chapman & Hall.

McDonnell, A., McDonnell, J., Hardman, M., & McCune, G. (1991). Educating students with severe disabilities in their neighborhood school: The Utah elementary integration model. *Remedial and Special Education, 12,* 34–45.

Merrett, F., & Wheldall, K. (1993). How do teachers learn to manage classroom behaviour? A study of teachers' opinions about their initial training with special reference to classroom behaviour management. *Educational Studies, 19,* 91–105.

Meyer, L.H., & Evans, I.M. (1989). *Nonaversive intervention for behavior problems: A manual for home and community.* Baltimore: Paul H. Brookes Publishing Co.

Meyer, L.H., & Evans, I.M. (1993a). Meaningful outcomes on behavioral intervention: Evaluating positive approaches to the remediation of challenging behaviors. In J. Reichle & D.P. Wacker (Eds.), *Communication and language intervention series: Vol. 3. Communicative alternatives to challenging behavior: Integrating functional assessment and intervention strategies* (pp. 407–428). Baltimore: Paul H. Brookes Publishing Co.

Meyer, L.H., & Evans, I.M. (1993b). Science and practice in behavioral intervention: Meaningful outcomes, research validity, and usable knowledge. *Journal of The Association for Persons with Severe Handicaps, 18,* 224–234.

Meyer, L.H., Evans, I.M., Wuerch, B.B., & Brennan, J.M. (1985). Monitoring the collateral effects of leisure skill instruction: A case study in multiple-baseline methodology. *Behaviour Research and Therapy, 23,* 127–138.

Miller, L. (1990). The regular education initiative and school reform: Lessons from the mainstream. *Remedial and Special Education, 11,* 17–22.

Miltenberger, R.G. (1990). Assessment of treatment acceptability: A review of the literature. *Topics in Early Childhood Special Education, 10,* 24–38.

Mulick, J.A., Hoyt, D., Rojahn, J., & Schroeder, S.R. (1978). Reduction of a "nervous habit" in a profoundly retarded youth by increasing toy play. *Journal of Behavior Therapy and Experimental Psychiatry, 9,* 381–385.

O'Neill, R.E., Horner, R.H., Albin, R.W., & Sprague, J.R. (1996). *Functional assessment and program development for problem behavior: A practical handbook.* Pacific Grove, CA: Brooks/Cole.

O'Neill, R.E., Horner, R.H., Albin, R.W., Storey, K., & Sprague, J.R. (1990). *Functional analysis of problem behavior: A practical assessment guide.* Sycamore, IL: Sycamore Publishing.

Parsons, M.B., Reid, D.H., Reynolds, J., & Bumgarner, M. (1990). Effects of chosen versus assigned jobs on the work performance of persons with severe handicaps. *Journal of Applied Behavior Analysis, 23,* 253–258.

Paul, G.L., & Lentz, R.J. (1977). *Psychosocial treatment of chronic mental patients: Milieu versus social-learning programs.* Cambridge, MA: Harvard University Press.

Reichle, J., & Wacker, D.P. (Eds.). (1993). *Communication and language intervention series: Vol. 3. Communicative alternatives to challenging behavior: Integrating functional assessment and intervention strategies.* Baltimore: Paul H. Brookes Publishing Co.

Reid, D.H., & Parsons, M.B. (1995). *Bibliography of organizational behavior management reports in developmental disabilities and related human services.* Morganton, NC: Developmental Disabilities Services Managers, Inc.

Repp, A.C., Deitz, A.M., & Deitz, D.E. (1976). Reducing inappropriate behaviors in classrooms and in individual sessions through DRO schedules of reinforcement. *Mental Retardation, 14,* 11–15.

Repp, A.C., & Karsh, K.G. (1990). A taxonomic approach to the nonaversive treatment of maladaptive behavior of persons with developmental disabilities. In A.C. Repp & N.N. Singh (Eds.), *Perspectives on the use of nonaversive and aversive interventions for persons with developmental disabilities* (pp. 331–347). Sycamore, IL: Sycamore Press.

Repp, A.C., & Singh, N.N. (Eds.). (1990). *Perspectives on the use of nonaversive and aversive interventions for persons with developmental disabilities.* Sycamore, IL: Sycamore Press.

Richman, G., & Bell, J.C. (1983). Analysis of a treatment package to reduce a hand-mouthing stereotypy. *Behavior Therapy, 14,* 576–581.

Schalock, R.L., Keith, K.D., Hoffman, K., & Karan, O.C. (1989). Quality of life: Its measurement and use. *Mental Retardation, 27,* 25–31.

Scotti, J.R., Evans, I.M., Meyer, L.H., & DiBenedetto, A. (1991). Individual repertoires as behavioral systems: Implications for program design and evaluation. In B. Remington (Ed.), *The challenge of severe mental handicap: A behavioral analytic approach* (pp. 139–163). London: Wiley.

Scotti, J.R., Evans, I.M., Meyer, L.H., & Walker, P. (1991). A meta-analysis of intervention research with problem behavior: Treatment validity and standards of practice. *American Journal on Mental Retardation, 96,* 233–256.

Scotti, J.R., McMorrow, M.J., & Trawitzki, A.L. (1993). Behavioral treatment of chronic psychiatric disorders: Publication trends and future directions. *Behavior Therapy, 24,* 527–550.

Scotti, J.R., Mullen, K.B., & Hawkins, R.P. (1998). Child conduct and developmental disabilities: From theory to practice in the treatment of excess behaviors. In J.J. Plaud & G.H. Eifert (Eds.), *From behavior theory to behavior therapy* (pp. 172–202). Needham Heights, MA: Allyn & Bacon.

Scotti, J.R., Ujcich, K.J., Weigle, K.L., Holland, C.M., & Kirk, K.S. (1996). Interventions with challenging behavior of persons with developmental disabilities: A review of current research practices. *Journal of The Association for Persons with Severe Handicaps, 21,* 123–134.

Skinner, B.F. (1953). *Science and human behavior.* New York: Free Press.

Smull, M.W., & Bellamy, G.T. (1991). Community services for adults with disabilities: Policy challenges in the emerging support paradigm. In L.H. Meyer, C.A. Peck, & L. Brown (Eds.), *Critical issues in the lives of people with severe disabilities* (pp. 527–536). Baltimore: Paul H. Brookes Publishing Co.

Stainback, S., Stainback, W., & Jackson, H.J. (1992). Toward inclusive classrooms. In S. Stainback & W. Stainback (Eds.), *Curriculum considerations in inclusive classrooms: Facilitating learning for all students* (pp. 3–17). Baltimore: Paul H. Brookes Publishing Co.

Stokes, T.F., & Baer, D.M. (1977). An implicit technology of generalization. *Journal of Applied Behavior Analysis, 10,* 349–367.

Sugai, G., & Horner, R. (1994). Including students with severe behavior problems in general education settings: Assumptions, challenges, and solutions. In J. Marr, G. Sugai, & G. Tindal (Eds.), *The Oregon Conference Monograph* (Vol. 6, pp. 102–120). Eugene: University of Oregon.

Thompson, T., Robinson, J., Dietrich, M., Farris, M., & Sinclair, V. (1996). Architectural features of community residences for people with mental retardation. *American Journal on Mental Retardation, 101,* 292–313.

Touchette, P.E., MacDonald, R.F., & Langer, S.N. (1985). A scatter plot for identifying stimulus control of problem behavior. *Journal of Applied Behavior Analysis, 18,* 343–351.

Voeltz, L.M., & Evans, I.M. (1982). The assessment of behavioral interrelationships in child behavior therapy. *Behavioral Assessment, 4,* 131–165.

Wacker, D., Steege, M., Northup, J., Reimers, T., Berg, W., & Sasso, G. (1990). Use of functional analysis and acceptability measures to assess and treat severe behavior problems in an outpatient clinic model. In A.C. Repp & N.N. Singh (Eds.), *Perspec-*

tives on the use of nonaversive and aversive inter-ventions for persons with developmental disabilities (pp. 349–359). Sycamore, IL: Sycamore Press.

Wahler, R.G. (1975). Some structural aspects of deviant child behavior. *Journal of Applied Behavior Analysis, 8,* 27–42.

Weeks, M., & Gaylord-Ross, R. (1981). Task difficulty and aberrant behavior in severely handicapped students. *Journal Applied Behavior Analysis, 14,* 449–463.

Weigle, K.L. (1997). Positive behavior support as a model for promoting educational inclusion. *Journal of The Association for Persons with Severe Handicaps, 22,* 36–48.

Weigle, K.L., & Scotti, J.R. (1995, May). *The effects of functional analysis information on ratings of treatment acceptability and effectiveness.* Poster presented at the 21st annual convention of the Association for Behavior Analysis, Washington, DC.

Williams, W., Fox, T.J., Thousand, J., & Fox, W. (1990). Level of acceptance and implementation of best practices in the education of students with severe handicaps in Vermont. *Education and Training in Mental Retardation, 25,* 120–131.

Willis, T.J., LaVigna, G.W., & Donnellan, A.M. (1989). *Behavior assessment guide.* Los Angeles: Institute for Applied Behavior Analysis.

Wolf, M.M. (1978). Social validity: The case for subjective measurement or how applied behavior analysis is finding its heart. *Journal of Applied Behavior Analysis, 11,* 203–214.

Chapter 4

Functional Analysis and Selection of Intervention Strategies for People with Attention-Deficit/Hyperactivity Disorder

Karen S. Kirk

Early in the 20th century, a new concern emerged in the study of psychology regarding functional relations between behaviors and the contexts in which they occur. Influenced by Darwinian principles of adaptability, the "functionalists" rejected the structural approach of Wilhelm Wundt and Edward Titchener, who had attempted to explain human behavior as a series of reactions to physical sensations and "conscious" perceptions (Rachlin, 1970). The emerging line of reasoning suggested that the utility and the context of a given behavior contribute significantly to the behavior's occurrence and that both of these variables should be considered when designing interventions to change a behavior (Boring, 1957). Functionalism also represented a theoretical move in psychology away from an emphasis on structural forms and metaphysical causal mechanisms of problem behaviors toward a concern with the purposes of behaviors and relations among the variables that

predict and control their occurrence (Haynes & O'Brien, 1990).

FUNCTIONAL ANALYSIS OF BEHAVIOR

In 1953, Skinner described the identification of environmental antecedents and consequences of specific target behaviors as one of the basic tools for analyzing and controlling behavior. In the practice of behavior therapy in the 1990s, the assessment component emphasizes the idiographic evaluation of problem behaviors that can be defined objectively. The key feature of behavior analysis is the identification of functional relations between target behaviors and the environmental variables that control and maintain them (Haynes & O'Brien, 1990; O'Leary & Wilson, 1975). Once those relations are established, the importance and the value of this process rest in how the information is used. Whereas

---

Some authors have suggested that the terms *functional analysis* and *functional assessment* refer to different sets of strategies (e.g., DuPaul & Ervin, 1996; Haynes & O'Brien, 1990). However, in this chapter the terms are used interchangeably.

the traditional assessment objective in psychology and medicine is to determine a specific diagnosis based on descriptions of problem behaviors or "symptoms," the purpose of behavioral assessment is to determine the *function(s)* of the identified behavior(s) of concern. That information provides direction as to appropriate intervention strategies for a given individual in his or her idiosyncratic environment (Kanfer & Saslow, 1969; Nelson & Hayes, 1986; Wacker, Northup, & Cooper, 1992). Although a diagnosis sometimes is helpful in terms of communicating about problem areas and gaining access to services, a label for the problem behavior does not indicate an individualized prescription for therapeutic strategies.

In terms of methodology, the traditional diagnostic interview or examination primarily involves a verbal discourse between the evaluator and the individual, whereas a functional assessment of behavior typically includes more active evaluation procedures that build on the information obtained in an interview (Iwata, Vollmer, & Zarcone, 1990; Lennox & Miltenberger, 1989). Functional assessment strategies focus on the identification of environmental variables related to the behaviors of concern and can provide the basis for a more comprehensive understanding and systematic analysis of a specific behavior than is yielded from the customary question-and-answer session (Barrios & Hartmann, 1986; O'Leary & Wilson, 1975). In this chapter, the most common procedures for functionally analyzing behavior are described, and the implications of these assessment procedures are discussed. The utilization of functional analysis strategies in determining appropriate interventions for one clinical population—children with attention-deficit/hyperactivity disorder (ADHD)—is then reviewed, and procedures for conducting functional assessments of the specific target behaviors associated with this diagnosis are proposed.

Methods of Functional Analysis

Various individualized methods for conducting a functional analysis of target behavior have been discussed in the literature (Cone, 1986; Evans, 1985; Iwata et al., 1990), and these assessment techniques have been applied to problem behav-

iors in diverse clinical populations (Haynes & O'Brien, 1990; Scotti, McMorrow, & Trawitzki, 1993). The procedural descriptions and examples provided in this section were drawn predominantly from published research that focused on reducing the challenging behaviors of people with severe developmental disabilities. In the 1980s, the function of behaviors such as self-injury and aggression toward others began to be emphasized because of the potential harmfulness of the behaviors, limited behavior change produced by interventions that focused on the "form" of the behaviors, and practices of using aversive procedures that were increasingly controversial in the context of the disability rights movement (Carr, 1977; Carr & Durand, 1985; Helmstetter & Durand, 1991). Strategies for assessing the functional properties of those types of behaviors varied from relatively informal techniques to controlled experimental analyses.

At the most informal level of analysis, casual observations of an individual's behavior can provide anecdotal information about antecedent and consequent events that might contribute to the occurrence of the behavior (Meyer & Evans, 1989). Reports of such observations over time or across a number of observers can be analyzed to determine patterns of variables related to a specific behavior. Identification of these patterns suggests that a particular behavior is demonstrated *as a function of* certain events in the environment. Another way to express this is that the behavior "serves a certain function" for the individual; typically, that function is either to gain access to or to escape the controlling environmental events or variables (Carr & Durand, 1985; O'Neill, Horner, Albin, Storey, & Sprague, 1990).

Another basic functional assessment strategy involves the determination of current and historical information about the behaviors of concern (Bailey & Pyles, 1989; Edelbrock & Costello, 1988; Groden, 1989). Within the traditional diagnostic interview, the evaluator can identify specific behaviors to target for change, generate an objective definition of each behavior, and determine significant and consistent variables that appear to be related to each behavior (Wacker et al., 1992). For example, descriptions of people, places, events, times, health factors, and the daily schedule of activities in the individual's life and environment can provide the evaluator with clues to patterns of behavior in certain contexts. Additional information that can help the evaluator to generate hypotheses about the function of a target behavior includes examining the outcomes of previous interventions that have been attempted as well as identifying situations in which the target behavior does *not* occur.

Structured interviews are beginning to be designed specifically to address functional aspects of behavior and to focus on the identification of events and situations that are associated consistently with an occurrence of the target behavior, a description of the efficiency and the utility of the behavior, and a determination of naturally occurring consequences for the behavior (O'Neill et al., 1990; Willis, LaVigna, & Donnellan, 1987). These tools focus on more general information about the individual, such as verbal and nonverbal communication strategies and physical abilities and limitations.

The advantages of assessment methods such as reports of casual observations and general or more structured interviews include ease and efficiency of their use. Because the validity and reliability of these procedures are unknown, however, information gathered using anecdotal observations and interviews should be considered only as a starting point. They can be used to generate initial hypotheses regarding the function of a behavior that then can be tested through more formal strategies, including behavior rating scales; direct observation of target behaviors, environmental antecedents, and consequences; and experimental manipulations of environmental variables.

Rating scales should assess not only the occurrence of specific behaviors but also the rater's perceptions of the individual's motivation for performing the behavior (e.g., the Motivation Assessment Scale [MAS; Durand & Crimmins, 1988]). The MAS, designed to identify and determine the purpose of specific self-injurious behavior, assesses four functions:

1. *Tangible*—attempting to obtain desired objects or activities
2. *Attention*—attempting to obtain social reinforcement

3. *Escape*—attempting to avoid an undesired situation or task
4. *Sensory*—attempting to obtain preferred sensory stimulation

Multiple raters can yield a more accurate determination of consistency in behaviors and potentially related variables across settings, people, and time. However, different raters may represent personal or situational biases or actual environmental differences (Luiselli, 1991). If the differences do reveal patterns associated with different settings, then those patterns also could be helpful in determining the motivation behind the behavior.

Another more objective strategy for assessing target behavior is direct observation. To obtain information about a behavior's function, the observer collects data on the occurrence of the target act, the antecedent and consequent events, and general setting variables. A number of measures for conducting systematic behavioral observations have been described in the literature, primarily in research on single-subject experimental designs (for reviews, see Barlow & Hersen, 1984; Tawney & Gast, 1984). An antecedent-behavior-consequence (A-B-C) analysis, for example, involves recording the occurrence of a particular behavior during a specified period of time (e.g., 10 seconds), as well as recording what happens before and after the act (Wahler, House, & Stambaugh, 1976).

O'Neill and his colleagues (1990) developed a Functional Analysis Observation Form to assist the observer in determining the variables related to the target behaviors. The observation system is based on an event-recording procedure that can be used at any time of day and in any setting. The observer records the time and the place in which the specific target behaviors occur, the setting variables and events at the time of the behaviors, the consequences of the behavior, and the perceived function or purpose of the behaviors. On the Summary Form, the observer can interpret the collected data to include an accurate description for each target behavior, prediction of situations in which a particular behavior is likely to occur, and identifying consequences that seem to be maintaining the occurrence of the behavior. From this information, hypotheses about the function of the behavior are formulated and further assessed.

Another procedure, developed by Touchette, MacDonald, and Langer (1985), is a "scatter plot" based on ongoing observations by someone in the person's daily life, such as a parent or a teacher. After recording the time of occurrence of the target behavior along with setting events such as location, current activity, and other individuals present, the observer then can graph the data in a scatter-plot format to identify patterns of a behavior given certain stimulus events. For any of these observational procedures, as patterns of associations between the target behavior and the contextual variables become apparent in the data, a hypothesis about the function of the behavior emerges.

Although objectivity in assessing the behavior of concern is clearly enhanced in observational procedures, there may be logistical obstacles to conducting observations in natural environments (Barkley, 1998). It may be difficult for the clinician to have access to the individual's typical settings, and it may not be possible to train independent observers. Thus, low-rate behavior may not be "captured" in sporadic observations. Furthermore, observational techniques often are cumbersome in identifying and recording environmental events, and the data in a natural setting may be so complex that relations between the behavior and its controlling variables are difficult to extract from multiple confounding variables. To address this problem, Iwata, Dorsey, Slifer, Bauman, and Richman (1982) demonstrated an analog procedure that allows the evaluator to sustain a high degree of control over both the antecedent and the consequent variables of interest, as well as extraneous factors. This process involves exposing the individual to one or more situations that have been identified through initial assessment strategies as predictive of the occurrence of the target behavior, such as an academic setting or a play area. Variables that are hypothesized to contribute to the behavior are then systematically manipulated. For example, to test whether *escape* or *attention* might be motivating the target behavior, two sets of trials are presented: In one set, the individual is allowed to escape con-

tingently from an activity to determine whether the function is to avoid the request or the task; in the second set, the individual is given attention contingent on performing the behavior. Patterns of responding across several trials of these conditions are analyzed to determine the relation between the variable manipulated and the target behavior. Several demonstrations of the validity of this and similar procedures have been reported in the literature (e.g., Anderson, Freeman, & Scotti, in press; Day, Rea, Schussler, Larsen, & Johnson, 1988; Steege, Wacker, Berg, Cigrand, & Cooper, 1989; Sturmey, Carlsen, Crisp, & Newton, 1988).

Reducing the complexity of the natural environment through analog procedures also may reduce the ecological validity of the assessment; thus, the contributions of natural setting events and other variables still may be lost in the process (Barkley, 1991; Scotti, Schulman, & Hojnacki, 1994). To counter this dilemma, Wacker and colleagues examined the possibility of directing parents and teachers in the role of "experimenter" in clinic, school, and home settings (Cooper, Wacker, Sasso, Reimers, & Donn, 1990; Cooper et al., 1992; Ulrich, Wacker, Derby, Asmus, & Berg, 1993). Findings suggest that experimental manipulations conducted by those "front-line providers" reincorporated components of the natural setting and could produce results that were as accurate as clinician-administered analyses. This group also demonstrated that brief experimental analysis sessions (90 minutes versus several days) in natural or clinic settings can provide the necessary information to determine functions and acceptable alternatives to challenging behaviors (Harding, Wacker, Cooper, Millard, & Jensen-Kovalan, 1994; Northup et al., 1991). These "practical" models of experimental, analog analyses should enhance the utility of these procedures in clinic and school settings.

In sum, the functional analysis procedures described in this section can be grouped according to the information obtained. Interview data, rating scales, and direct observations can provide an initial level of "descriptive" information from which target behaviors can be identified and defined, and initial hypotheses about functions of behavior can be generated. Testing of those hypotheses can be accomplished through systematic manipulations of the variables that are thought to be associated with the behaviors of concern. This stage of assessment can be referred to as the "experimental analysis" phase (DuPaul & Ervin, 1996; Kern, Childs, Dunlap, Clarke, & Falk, 1994). The functional analysis process does not end with hypothesis testing, however. The goal is to determine appropriate and effective intervention strategies that can help to replace the challenging behavior with more acceptable alternatives. This final stage of the functional analysis process is described in the next section.

Identification of Effective Alternative Behaviors

It is important to note that it is not the only objective of a functional analysis of behavior to determine the motivation for the target acts so that an appropriate intervention, typically for eliminating the behavior, can be identified. An equally important goal of a functional assessment is to identify effective alternative behaviors that achieve the same outcome as the problem behavior for the individual (Meyer & Evans, 1989; Repp & Karsh, 1990). Alternative behaviors should belong to the same "response class" as the undesirable target behaviors: The function of the behavior is the same, although the form may be quite different (Scotti, Evans, Meyer, & DiBenedetto, 1991). This idea is similar to the notion of "symptom substitution" (Kazdin, 1982), which describes the appearance in an individual's repertoire of another inappropriate behavior when the *form* of the initial target behavior is reduced or eliminated. Appropriate and acceptable behaviors also may covary with the response of concern, in terms of function. Through interview and direct observation assessment methods in particular, behaviors that potentially accomplish the same goals for an individual but that are more desirable and appropriate can be discovered. These acceptable behaviors then can be assessed systematically through experimental manipulations to determine functional equivalence with the behaviors of concern (Anderson et al., in press; Scotti,

Evans, Meyer, & DiBenedetto, 1991; Scotti, Kirk, et al., 1993). The more appropriate behaviors often occur at a low rate at the time of the initial evaluation, but they can immediately become the target for intervention (Anderson et al., in press; Scotti, Evans, Meyer, & DiBenedetto, 1991).

In sum, the outcome of a thorough functional assessment should involve the identification and reinforcement of an appropriate behavioral repertoire rather than simply the elimination of a structurally problematic behavior that actually serves a practical purpose for an individual. Sometimes, however, "problem" behavior occurs because the person has no appropriate alternative strategies (Evans & Meyer, 1985). In these instances, skill instruction is needed, and the social context for the use of new skills being acquired also may need to be ensured (Meyer & Evans, 1989). Recognizing that a person's environment simply may not have provided the opportunities and instruction needed to develop a positive repertoire has been at the core of "educative" approaches such as functional communication training. Such ideas and strategies are in sharp contrast to past practices focused primarily on eliminating or decreasing behavior (e.g., Durand, 1990; see also Chapter 2).

Applications of Functional Analysis in Behavioral Intervention Research

Despite the theoretical underpinnings and potential utility of data-based functional analysis procedures in determining an appropriate intervention strategy, many behavioral researchers still have seemed to rely on "standard practice" for intervention for a given diagnosis (Cone, 1986; O'Neill et al., 1990; Wacker et al., 1990). Although it may be true that such practices originally were derived from etiological hypotheses about a particular disorder or syndrome, that rationale reflects more of a concern for causal mechanisms than a focus on contextual variables and functions of specific problem behaviors. Reviews of behavior therapy literature through the 1980s revealed that systematic functional assessment methods were *not* consistently being applied to identify the most appropriate interventions for individuals and their problem behaviors. For example, in a review of 272 reports of behavioral interventions with individuals with chronic psychiatric disorders in nine journals across 26 years (1963–1988), Scotti, McMorrow, and Trawitzki (1993) found that only 31% of the studies included descriptive information about potential controlling variables, and only 3% conducted formal functional assessments.

Furthermore, although a significant proportion of discussion articles in the field of developmental disabilities has focused on the benefits of conducting functional analyses of target behaviors, three reviews have indicated relatively low rates of implementing these procedures in applied research. In a survey of seven field-related journals from 1981 to 1985, Lennox and his colleagues found that of 162 identified intervention studies for behaviors such as self-injury and self-stimulation, only one third reported that some type of functional analysis of behavior had been conducted prior to selection of an intervention strategy (Lennox, Miltenberger, Spengler, & Erfanian, 1988). Likewise, Scotti and his colleagues found that only 87 of 403 studies (22%) that focused on the same types of behaviors reported some type of functional assessment (Scotti, Evans, Meyer, & Walker, 1991). The latter meta-analysis covered 18 field-related journals, between 1976 and 1987. An update of that review for articles published from 1988 to 1992 (Scotti, Ujcich, Weigle, Holland, & Kirk, 1996) indicated a somewhat higher rate (48% of 179 studies), suggesting an improving trend in the developmental disabilities field for applying functional analysis procedures in assessing problem behaviors.

Nevertheless, across all of these reviews, those studies that did report an attempt to identify controlling variables for target behavior predominantly referred to anecdotal or descriptive accounts of antecedents, behaviors, and consequences, based on interviews and informal observations. Fewer than 20% of the studies that reported some type of functional analysis process actually employed more systematic procedures, such as direct observation/A-B-C analyses and experimental analog methods (Lennox

et al., 1988; Scotti, Evans, Meyer, & Walker, 1991). The Scotti, Ujcich, et al. (1996) review indicated slight improvements on these figures, particularly in terms of higher rates of data-based assessments (34% of 179 studies) and the use of more than one method for identifying functional relations.

As noted in several of the previously mentioned reviews, one of the implications for this limited use of systematic functional assessment procedures was that no clear statement could be made about the relation among identification of behavioral functions, intervention selection, and clinically significant behavior change as a result of intervention (Scotti, Evans, Meyer, & Walker, 1991; Scotti, Ujcich, et al., 1996). A number of studies that reported maintenance of significant intervention effects at follow-up, however, had in fact employed some type of functional assessment procedures (Scotti, Evans, Meyer, & Walker, 1991).

Use of Functional Analysis in Selecting Interventions for ADHD

Not all children and adults with behavior challenges have developmental disabilities. Another group of children and youth who display behaviors that are perceived by parents and teachers as disruptive and distressing (and thus have an urgent need for intervention) have been referred with increasing, if not alarming, frequency in clinical and school settings. Even as early as the 1970s, it was estimated that almost half of all preschool- and school-age children seen in child diagnostic and therapy clinics originally were referred for problems with inattention, overactivity, impulsivity, and/or disruptive behavior (Safer & Allen, 1976). These behaviors have been categorized as the syndrome of attention-deficit/hyperactivity disorder (American Psychiatric Association, 1987, 1994). Epidemiological studies of ADHD have suggested a prevalence rate of 3%–15% of children in community samples (Anderson, Williams, McGee, & Silva, 1987; Whalen, 1989). Barkley (1998) estimated that 3%–5% of the elementary school population demonstrates behaviors consistent with this diagnosis—that is, one to two children in every public school classroom.

The high prevalence of children diagnosed with ADHD has, understandably, resulted in a plethora of research, discussion articles, and monographs regarding issues such as etiology, assessment, and medical treatments and behavioral interventions. The next section reviews some of that published research during the 1989–1993 period to identify whether functional analyses indeed were being included in the assessment of behavior associated with ADHD. Methods for selecting intervention strategies and measuring behavior change were also considered in the review.

INTERVENTION RESEARCH IN ADHD

Studies were included in the review of the published research if they met the following criteria:

1. Involved children in the preschool- and/or elementary school–age range (2–12 years)
2. Described participants as having a clinical diagnosis of ADHD or as having high rates of impulsive, disruptive, off-task, and/or overactive behaviors
3. Did not focus on the behaviors specifically associated with any comorbid diagnoses (e.g., oppositional defiant disorder, conduct disorder, Tourette syndrome)
4. Used behavioral measures as at least one of the outcome variables
5. Had been published in an English-language journal

Furthermore, only studies that investigated medication, behavior, and/or cognitive-behavior therapies were reviewed. Studies that involved medication therapies were included in the review only when a placebo-controlled procedure was used. (For overviews of some of the more "controversial" treatments for children with ADHD and related disorders, such as dietary interventions, megavitamin therapy, applied kinesiology, biofeedback, and optometric visual training, see Goldstein & Ingersoll, 1992, and Silver, 1987.) Computer searches of titles focusing on medical treatments or behavioral therapy for ADHD were conducted through the MEDLINE, PsycLIT, Educational Resource Information Clearing-house, and CINAHL databases. Furthermore, the reference lists of articles identified through those searches were reviewed for additional relevant reports.

Two primary questions were addressed in this review of research. First, methodology was examined in each study to determine whether a functional analysis of the target behaviors' controlling variables had been conducted in the assessment or baseline phase of the investigation and, if so, the type of assessment procedure that was used (e.g., interview, direct observation). Second, the outcomes of interventions in each study were reviewed for reports of clinically significant behavior change, measured by some type of valid, quantitative index of change (e.g., Jacobson & Truax, 1991; see the next section for a more detailed description).

Medication Therapies for ADHD

Medication therapies, particularly stimulant medications, reportedly have been the "mainstay" of treatment for school-age children with ADHD and related difficulties (DuPaul, Barkley, & O'Connor, 1998; Waschbusch, Kipp, & Pelham, 1998). It has been estimated that 2.8% of the school-age population has been prescribed stimulant medications (Safer, Zito, & Fine, 1996). Furthermore, approximately 80%–90% of children with presenting concerns such as overactivity and inattention who are seen by pediatricians have been treated with a stimulant medication at some point (Pelham, 1986; Safer & Krager, 1994). The stimulants include methylphenidate (Ritalin), dextroamphetamine (Dexedrine), magnesium pemoline (Cylert), and Adderall (mixed salts of amphetamine and dextroamphetamine). Other medications, such as antidepressants and antianxiety agents, are most often used in treatment regimens when an individual does not respond well to stimulants (Biederman, Baldessarini, Wright, Knee, & Harmatz, 1989).

Common Practice in Prescribing Medications for ADHD

The origins of stimulant use for children with behavior disorders can be traced to the 1930s, to Bradley's finding that Benzedrine (an amphetamine) was associated with improvements in activity level and school performance among children with significant behavior problems on a psychiatric inpatient ward (Zametkin & Rapoport, 1987). However, little empirical evidence for the effectiveness of stimulants in treating attention problems was presented until the 1960s and 1970s, when rating scales began to be developed (Wilens & Biederman, 1992). These instruments quickly became mechanisms for assessing behavior changes associated with medication trials. In the 1980s, extensive investigations of the efficacy of stimulant medications were conducted. For example, in a MEDLINE search of the years 1983–1991, Wilens and Biederman (1992) identified more than 900 citations on the use of stimulants. Many of those studies noted the safety of the medications, with relatively mild side effects and few atypical responses (DuPaul & Barkley, 1990). Thus, stimulants increasingly were being used for treatment of ADHD symptoms (Frankenberger, Lozar, & Dallas, 1990; Safer & Krager, 1988).

The fact that pediatricians typically are the first professionals to be consulted about children's behavior problems also probably has contributed to the rapid increase in the use of medications (Copeland, Wolraich, Lindgren, Milich, & Woolson, 1987). Unfortunately, the "medical model" has not provided a systematic methodology for diagnosing ADHD or prescribing treatments based on individual needs. For instance, two national surveys of pediatricians and family practitioners in the late 1980s found that physicians' assessment of presenting behavioral concerns (e.g., poor attention, high activity level) involved primarily (more than 90% of survey respondents) parent and teacher anecdotal reports. Standardized rating scales reportedly were used in 75% of cases. Furthermore, the surveys indicated that diagnosis typically was based on definitions of attention and related problems from the pediatric medicine literature (approximately 75% of respondents) rather than on "standard" criteria for attention disorders as indicated in the DSM-III (American Psychiatric Association, 1980) or the DSM-III-R (American Psychiatric Association, 1987; Copeland et al., 1987; Wolraich et al., 1990). Reliance on literature-based definitions of attention deficits is problematic because of inconsistent and unvalidated assertions regarding core and associated features of the disorder (Carlson & Rapport, 1989). Estimates suggest that 25%–50% of children described by pediatricians as having ADHD would *not* have received that diagnosis if DSM criteria were used instead of unstandardized definitions (Jensen, Xenakis, Shervette, Bain, & Davis, 1989; Wolraich et al., 1990). Nevertheless, stimulant medications were prescribed as an initial treatment for more than 80% of the children seen by the pediatricians surveyed; however, very few controlled drug–placebo trials (approximately 5% of cases) were conducted for the treated group.

Two pertinent implications of these diagnosing and medication-prescribing practices can be suggested. First, diagnosis appears to be based primarily on interview report, observations of the child's behavior in the office, and relatively limited use of systematic analyses of behavior. Second, then, treatments (i.e., medications) seem to be selected on the basis of accepted practice for the diagnostic label rather than on a consideration of the functional aspects of the behavior for the individual. Furthermore, inconsistencies in definitions have resulted in a heterogeneous group of individuals described as having ADHD. This significantly compromises comparisons of the efficacy of various treatments and the determination of the most effective treatment for a particular target behavior.

Nonetheless, overall findings of several comprehensive reviews of controlled drug trials provided strong and consistent evidence that stimulants (predominantly methylphenidate, with fewer controlled trials of dextroamphetamine, pemoline, and Adderall) are effective in significantly reducing inattentive, disruptive, overactive, impulsive, and off-task behavior in approximately 70% of children with attention and related problems for at least short periods of time (i.e., 2 weeks to 6 months; Dulcan, 1990; DuPaul et al., 1998; Jacobvitz, Sroufe, Stewart, & Leffert, 1990; Spencer et al., 1996). Placebo response generally has been reported at a rate of 2%–39% of study participants.

Investigating Medication Therapies

Twenty-four studies of controlled medication trials for children with ADHD were identified, according to the inclusion criteria (a full list of these studies is available from the author). By the early 1990s, treatment studies had begun to focus on subtle parameters of behavioral effects, given that the basic clinical efficacy of stimulant medications for individuals with ADHD was no longer in question (Klein, 1987). Thus, in addition to hyperactivity (Tannock, Schachar, Carr, & Logan, 1989) and inattention, investigations addressed aggression (Barkley, McMurray, Edelbrock, & Robbins, 1989) and antisocial behavior (Hinshaw, Heller, & McHale, 1992), noncompliance (Vyse & Rapport, 1989), and organizational skills (Pelham, McBurnett, et al., 1990). A number of studies focused on general behavioral improvement as a function of various preparations of stimulants (Pelham, Greenslade, et al., 1990) and as a function of other drug classes (Biederman et al., 1989; Trott, Friese, Menzel, & Nissen, 1992).

Of the 24 studies identified, *no* indication was found of the use of *any type* of functional assessment procedure in regard to the behavior(s) of concern. It is interesting to speculate that perhaps an emphasis on large sample size in these studies—to obtain appropriate measures of effect size and power—may have precluded a functional assessment of target behavior for individual study participants; none of the investigators mentioned this dilemma, however. In a few articles, the investigators alluded to the hypothesized neurological problem related to the targeted behavior of the group and/or to the associated mechanism of action of the drug being used to point to a specific neurobiological defect or neurochemical dysregulation (e.g., Biederman et al., 1989; Gualtieri, Keenan, & Chandler, 1991; Klorman et al., 1989). These inferences could be viewed as an attempt to identify the physical cause of the problem behavior and to select a medication treatment based on that hypothesis. However, there was no alternative emphasis on contributing environmental factors.

A few general points related to the issue of functional analysis can be drawn from this review of medication therapies, though. First, the finding that a higher rate of parental psychopathology was present in the families of children who demonstrate ADHD *and* concomitant aggressive behavior (e.g., Barkley et al., 1989) is consistent with previous research in this area (Lahey et al., 1988; Schachar & Wachsmuth, 1990) and suggests the need for a comprehensive assessment process. A behavioral evaluation that includes a structured functional analysis interview and direct observation of parent–child interactions should help to determine the many variables, including family issues, that may be controlling or contributing to the target behavior. The poor prognosis for this clinical group in terms of difficulties in social and vocational functioning (Hinshaw, 1991; Weiss & Hechtman, 1986, 1993) implicates the need to identify the most effective ways to intervene on the target behaviors. An appropriate evaluation of presenting problems and related variables should facilitate the selection of effective treatment procedures.

Second, there is some evidence in the reported investigations that methylphenidate suppresses more than just inappropriate behaviors; appropriate alternative actions also may be suppressed (e.g., Buhrmester, Whalen, Henker, MacDonald, & Hinshaw, 1992). Furthermore, the evidence is limited that stimulant medications will be associated automatically with collateral increases in more desirable behaviors, as the treated behaviors of concern decrease (e.g., Hinshaw, Henker, Whalen, Erhardt, & Dunnington, 1989; Pelham, McBurnett, et al., 1990). These findings indicate the need to consider functional response class relations. If two *forms* of responses serve the same *function* for the individual, then they can be described as constituting a response class. Functional analysis procedures could help to determine whether undesirable behaviors that are targeted for decrease are functionally equivalent to acceptable, alternative behaviors. Unfortunately, treatment plans typically seem to neglect specific objectives for increasing those positive alternatives, with the implicit hope that they will "automatically" replace the behaviors targeted for reduction—a false hope (Evans, Meyer, Kurkjian, & Kishi, 1988; Kazdin, 1982; Scotti, Evans, Meyer,

& DiBenedetto, 1991; Voeltz & Evans, 1982). Thus, it appears that in intervention planning, specific procedures for identifying and increasing functionally equivalent, alternative skills must be included. In relation to medication therapies for children with ADHD, perhaps a prudent recommendation is to consider ways to use drugs as a mechanism for improving appropriate skills, such as social interaction behaviors and compliance with requests, rather than to use drugs solely for reducing inappropriate behaviors.

Third, two issues that continue to be controversial in medication therapies for individuals with ADHD are 1) the efficacy of stimulants in treating children with attention problems but without hyperactivity (DuPaul et al., 1998; Rapoport, 1987) and 2) the selection of the appropriate drug and drug preparation (Campbell & Spencer, 1988). In response to the first issue, evidence suggests that inattention and hyperactivity are differentially affected by dosage of methylphenidate (Barkley, DuPaul, & McMurray, 1991; Tannock et al., 1989). One possible reason for these results is that unique environmental (or biological) variables may control the different behaviors (e.g., hyperactivity versus inattention), and those variables need to be identified for an appropriate intervention to be selected. A more functionally oriented assessment procedure could provide crucial information in that regard.

In response to the second issue, a number of studies have examined the effects of various preparations of stimulants and other types of medications on a wide range of behavioral functioning. The general, predominant finding is the idiosyncratic response of each child to various medications and dosing regimens (see also Waschbusch et al., 1998). Elia and her colleagues suggested that flexibility in drug choice and dosage can help to resolve the issues of idiographic responders as well as nonresponders (Elia, Borcherding, Rapoport, & Keysor, 1991). Consistent with this suggestion, a comprehensive functional analysis of behavior could contribute to the selection of an appropriate drug preparation and dosage (if medication therapy is determined to be an effective treatment option). The technology of the 1990s has gradually revealed information about the association between identified behavioral functions and brain mechanisms or receptors, such that function of behavior can perhaps indicate an effective medication treatment (e.g., Rogeness, Javors, & Pliszka, 1992; Zametkin & Rapoport, 1987). This means that a functional analysis of the behavior of concern might yield some valuable information. In fact, a better understanding of behavioral functions may help pharmacologists to identify more effectively the mechanisms of action for drugs, through controlled trials (Schaal & Hackenberg, 1994; see later discussion in this chapter).

Clinical Significance of Treatment Results

Despite the plethora of investigations that report the short-term benefits of stimulants and other medications in reducing a variety of behaviors associated with ADHD, the primary issue that should be addressed is the overall clinical significance of the results of pharmacotherapy over time with children with ADHD. Klein (1987) indicated that methylphenidate-induced behavior improvements frequently have moved children into the "normalized" range of task-related behavior and activity level in the short term, as measured by outcome instruments such as parent and teacher behavior rating scales. Not all problem behaviors, however, reach such a level of clinical significance for every child. Furthermore, there is no consensus as to the operational definition of "normalized" behavior. O'Leary and Pelham (1978), for example, reported that "typical" children in general education classrooms demonstrated off-task behavior at a rate of 25%–30% of responses in a given time interval.

In one controlled study, DuPaul and Rapport (1993) reported that 23 of 31 children (74%) with ADHD were rated in the "normal" range of functioning on standardized measures (teacher rating scales and academic efficiency scores) in terms of levels of attention, academic productivity, and overall classroom conduct, after being treated for several weeks with one of four dosages of methylphenidate (different dosages were effective for different children). These investigators utilized a method suggested by Jacobson and Truax (1991) for determining clinical significance of the treatment effects, which compared posttreatment level of functioning for children during medication conditions with the functioning of the typical control group. When this approach has been applied to data sets, more modest conclusions about therapeutic efficacy have been reported than when statistically significant changes or effects sizes are indicated (Jacobson & Truax, 1991). A reexamination of all of the other studies summarized in this section revealed that only two studies *alluded* to the normalizing effects of medication treatment, in terms of comparisons of therapeutic results among treatment- and control-group participants on behavior rating scales (Hinshaw et al., 1992; Hinshaw, Henker, et al., 1989). *No* other systematic evaluations of clinically significant changes were reported in any of the studies. Thus, there is no clear evidence that the medication therapies investigated in the reviewed articles produced consistent, reliable, and valid short-term changes of behavior in children with ADHD. Furthermore, little empirical support was identified regarding long-term behavior changes associated with medication trials, particularly after medication had been discontinued (i.e., maintenance of behavior improvements). (For further review, see DuPaul et al., 1998, and Schachar & Tannock, 1993.)

A pertinent question, of course, is how to attempt to treat that remaining group—25% in DuPaul and Rapport's (1993) study, for example—who do not move into the typical range of functioning even in short-term analyses of behavior change. For that matter, is the 75% short-term "success rate" acceptable, or do such results suggest the need for each child to receive a more comprehensive, functional assessment of his or her behavior in an effort to determine the most appropriate, effective, and "long-lasting" treatment plan? Researchers who advocate the use of behavior programs in addition to or in place of medication therapies have attempted to address these questions by suggesting a different focus of intervention for the behaviors of children with ADHD. The following review reveals whether these interventions have been associated with more significant behavior change and whether more systematic methods for se-

lecting a specific treatment typically have been employed.

Behavior and Multimodal Therapies for ADHD

Behavior therapies for children with ADHD apparently began to be researched in response to identified limitations of medication as a singular treatment for their diverse problems. The introductory sections of many intervention articles revealed consistent documentation of reasons that behavioral and cognitive-behavioral approaches were increasingly considered as viable alternatives or adjuncts to medication treatments. For example, Horn and his colleagues noted

1. The significant number (approximately 25%–30%) of children who do not respond clinically to drug therapies
2. The number of responders who experience some mild side effects from medication treatments (approximately 60% for the primary side effects of insomnia and decreased appetite; Barkley et al., 1990; DuPaul, Anastopoulos, Kwasnik, Barkley, & McMurray, 1996)
3. The limited improvements in social interactions and academic performance
4. The lack of generalization and maintenance of behavior improvements when medication is withdrawn
5. The inconsistent compliance with administration regimens
6. The possible attributions of an external locus of control for the problems of and solutions to the child's symptoms (Horn, Ialongo, Greenberg, Packard, & Smith-Winberry, 1990; Horn et al., 1991)

Furthermore, as discussed previously, medications primarily seem to be prescribed as a therapeutic technique on the basis of "standard practice" for a particular diagnosis, as opposed to conducting a systematic analysis of presenting behavioral symptoms. One of the purposes of the following summary of behavior therapies for children with ADHD was to determine whether this hallmark of behavioral assessment—the more thorough functional analysis of maintaining variables for the target behavior(s)—has been any more consistently incorporated into those research designs than was reported in the medication literature. The other objective was, again, to examine the efficacy of interventions in terms of clinically significant behavior change.

Investigating Behavioral Therapies

Twenty-seven intervention studies for children with ADHD were identified, according to the inclusion criteria (a full list of these studies is available from the author). The investigations could be divided according to techniques: 1) single behavioral strategies, 2) combined medical and behavioral interventions, 3) parent-training strategies, 4) cognitive-behavioral intervention, and 5) combinations of the four strategies. Of the 27 studies identified between 1989 and 1993, *none* of the investigators actually discussed functional aspects of target behavior, and *none* indicated any specific procedures for conducting a functional analysis. It is interesting to note, however, that a number of studies reported methods of assessment that were fairly "close to the mark." For example, 23 of the studies utilized some type of systematic observational coding scheme to determine frequency counts or rates of targeted behaviors. Most of the coding systems were organized into discrete intervals (i.e., 10–30 seconds); minor adjustments to many of these systems could have provided additional information about environmental variables related to the observed behavior. Furthermore, one study (Horn et al., 1991) used an observational paradigm that involved the creation of an analog setting (i.e., an academic classroom scene); a potential extension of this type of strategy could have involved experimental manipulations of variables hypothesized to be contributing to the behavior(s) of concern.

In addition to strategies for defining target behaviors, some of the explanations for selecting a particular intervention for study, as well as interpretations of results, involved allusions to some of the contextual and interactional aspects of behavior. For example, some of the studies that focused on parent-training procedures suggested that the parents' problems with behavior management had developed in response to the

severity of their children's ADHD-related behaviors. Thus, some of the interactional aspects of parent and child behavior were considered in choosing these treatment strategies.

Findings of this review also raised some particular points about functional analysis. First, a trend in the literature suggests that positive reinforcement of appropriate, alternative behaviors as a singular intervention strategy typically is not efficacious or is at least insufficient for obtaining desired criterion levels of reduction in the core features of ADHD (cf. Pfiffner & O'Leary, 1987). Evidence that contingently delivered positive reinforcement increases arousal, interferes with attention to task, and results in careless task errors has been presented in support of this assertion (Firestone & Douglas, 1975; Hall & Kataria, 1992). A significant factor that has not been addressed, though, is that the two behaviors targeted for change (e.g., off-task versus task-engaged behaviors) may *not,* in fact, be functionally equivalent for a given individual. Unfortunately, no studies attempted to answer this question.

Alternatively, behavioral research has documented that mild punishment contingencies can provide an effective adjunct to positive strategies in treatment plans that are designed to reduce off-task behaviors (Pfiffner & O'Leary, 1987; Rosen, O'Leary, Joyce, Conway, & Pfiffner, 1984; Sherrill, O'Leary, & Kendziora, 1993). In the early 1990s, many studies focused on the types of procedures and contingencies that are "potent" enough to produce and maintain behavior changes (Hoza, Pelham, Sams, & Carlson, 1992). Response cost was the most commonly employed punishment contingency (e.g., Carlson, Pelham, Milich, & Dixon, 1992; DuPaul, Guevremont, & Barkley, 1992; Pelham et al., 1993). The assumption about the efficacy of this strategy is that it increases the salience of the reinforcement contingencies for the positive behaviors (DuPaul et al., 1992; Rapport, Murphy, & Bailey, 1982). Pfiffner and Barkley (1998) also noted that response cost is most effective when *incompatible* appropriate and inappropriate behaviors are targeted for respective increases and decreases. A more accurate statement, however, may be that the procedure's effectiveness depends on whether the alternative behaviors are functionally equivalent.

Second, the emphasis on parent-training interventions is based, in part, on previous research findings that the behavior of children with ADHD often is correlated with ineffective parenting/management strategies (Pisterman et al., 1992; Pisterman et al., 1989; Strayhorn & Weidman, 1989). Indeed, dysfunctional interactions between parents and children have been documented in the ADHD literature (Barkley, 1986; Olson, Bates, & Bayles, 1990), although it is difficult to determine the directionality of influences such as child noncompliance, parental stress, parental depression, and marital conflict (Anastopoulos, Guevremont, Shelton, & DuPaul, 1992). The studies that addressed these issues focused their interventions on changing the parents' behaviors, which reflects an effort to manipulate variables that could be a reaction and/or a contribution to the child's inappropriate behavior. A systematic analysis of hypotheses regarding function and directionality of influences could be conducted through interviews, observation of parent–child interactions (to determine functional relations, not just frequency counts), and experimental manipulations of suspected controlling variables for the child's (and/or the parents') behavior. This information could then be used to help determine an individualized program of therapy for each parent–child dyad or triad.

Third, the origins of research regarding cognitive-behavioral interventions for children with ADHD are interesting to note. In several of the behavior and medication studies discussed in this review, the authors indicated that the therapies under investigation produced behavior change only when they were "in effect"—that is, being implemented (e.g., Erhardt & Baker, 1990; Pelham et al., 1993). Generalization to nontreatment environments and maintenance of treatment effects over time admittedly were poor in most studies, and measures of treatment integrity over time (i.e., into follow-up) rarely were even reported. Cognitive-behavioral researchers used these identified limitations of the "traditional" therapies as a rationale for their approach. The suggestion in this line of investigation is that ad-

equate maintenance and generalization of behavior change can best be achieved when children with ADHD are taught some strategies for self-management of their behavior (Whalen & Henker, 1986). Evidence regarding inappropriate attributions of an external locus of control for one's own behavior, often associated with behavior and medication therapies, is also cited as support for a cognitive-behavioral approach to treatment (Borden & Brown, 1989; Kendall & Braswell, 1985; Whalen, Henker, Hinshaw, Heller, & Huber-Dressler, 1991). The missing component in the treatment of ADHD is presumed to be the internalizing of self-control techniques by the children, to help them overcome their inability to "stop, look, and listen" (Douglas, 1972). Thus, the identified cognitive-behavioral interventions reflected an effort to increase self-monitoring strategies in children with ADHD. An assessment of the functional equivalence of adequate problem-solving skills in relation to behaviors described as impulsive or inattentive likely would contribute additional data to address this issue (for further discussion about the utility of cognitive-behavioral strategies, see also DuPaul & Hoff, 1998).

Finally, it appears that multimodal therapeutic "packages," combining medication, behavioral, and cognitive-behavioral interventions, have become the treatment option of choice for children with ADHD (Arnold et al., 1997; Barkley, 1998). These integrated intervention programs have been shown to achieve greater improvements in appropriate behaviors and more significant decreases in inappropriate actions than any single treatment, through additive or complementary effects (Hinshaw, 1994). Furthermore, the application of multiple strategies reportedly serves to overcome some of the limitations of each type of intervention (Pelham & Murphy, 1986). Nonetheless, the question remains as to what to put "in the package" for an individual treatment plan. Again, it seems that, for an individual child with specific presenting concerns, an idiographic assessment of contributing variables and contextual relations can greatly increase the odds of selecting appropriate techniques to include in an overall therapeutic program.

Clinical Significance of Intervention Results

The issue of normalized or clinically significant behavior change as a result of treatment was addressed in 9 of the 27 identified studies. Seven of those articles indicated that participants' behavior ratings moved into the typical range of functioning (Abramowitz, Eckstrand, O'Leary, & Dulcan, 1992; Donney & Poppen, 1989; Erhardt & Baker, 1990; Fehlings, Roberts, Humphries, & Dawe, 1991; Horn et al., 1990; Horn et al., 1991; Walker & Clement, 1992). Only two studies used a systematic approach to determine clinically significant change or "recovery" (Anastopoulos, Shelton, DuPaul, & Guevremont, 1993; Pelham et al., 1993); again, these investigators employed the procedure described by Jacobson and Truax (1991). (It should be noted that an earlier version of this methodology had been described in 1984 [Jacobson, Follette, & Revenstorf, 1984], thus the recentness of the 1991 publication cannot be cited as a valid reason for not conducting an analysis of meaningful change.) As noted for the medication studies, then, there was limited consistent evidence of reliable behavior change associated with the identified behavioral interventions. Furthermore, only two reports of relatively long-term treatment effects were identified (Ialongo et al., 1993; Strayhorn & Weidman, 1991). These initial findings provided tentative support for greater maintenance of behavior improvements following parent training and self-control training for children than after the termination of a medication therapy conducted in isolation. Clearly, the need for more reports regarding the long-term stability of treatment effects was indicated, particularly given increasing evidence that difficulties associated with ADHD in childhood persist into adolescence and adulthood (Fischer, Barkley, Fletcher, & Smallish, 1993; Gittelman, Mannuzza, Shenker, & Bonagura, 1985; Weiss & Hechtman, 1993).

New Trends in the ADHD Intervention Literature

Despite the relative absence of functional assessment reports in the ADHD intervention literature in the early 1990s, the second half of the decade has been more promising. At least five published investigations have directly addressed the use of functional assessment for behaviors specifically associated with ADHD (Broussard & Northup, 1995; Ervin, DuPaul, Kern, & Friman, 1998; Lewis & Sugai, 1996; Northup et al., 1995; Umbreit, 1995). DuPaul and his colleagues provided comprehensive reviews of these studies (DuPaul, Eckert, & McGoey, 1997; DuPaul & Ervin, 1996).

Several important points can be drawn from these reports. First, all of the studies involved some type of descriptive assessment (e.g., interviews, observations) and development of hypotheses about functional relations between target behaviors and environmental contingencies. Some form of experimental manipulation of those contingencies was then implemented in each study to test the hypotheses. The authors all identified the importance of both phases of the assessment process in determining function versus simple topography of the target behaviors.

Second, all of the assessments suggested behavioral functions that are consistent with those identified in other investigations; that is, children with ADHD seem to be performing behaviors that also serve to help them *escape* undesirable situations, *gain access* to what they prefer (e.g., attention, tangible item or activity), or maintain a desired level of *stimulation* or arousal. These same categories of behavioral functions were identified in previous investigations in the field of developmental disabilities (Durand & Crimmins, 1988; Iwata et al., 1982), suggesting that human behavior, regardless of form or potential etiology of "problems," serves some basic functions for an individual.

Third, two of the five investigations reported a clear implementation of the final phase of functional assessment (Ervin et al., 1998; Umbreit, 1995). Based specifically on the results of the hypothesis-testing process, interventions that addressed alternative ways for the subjects to accomplish their goals (functions) were developed and implemented. In some cases, the intervention involved manipulations of antecedent contingencies; in other cases, changes in consequences for behaviors were implemented. The important factor was that the intervention strategies were clearly related to the identified motivational factors for the individual's behavior, not just to "best practice" for a child with a diagnosis of ADHD.

Finally, an interesting trend in these reported studies was the emphasis on school-based assessments and interventions. Whereas the clinic setting could potentially reduce the ecological validity of functional assessments and proposed intervention strategies, the use of teachers as "experimenters" and providers of descriptive data likely increases the practicality of the process. Furthermore, the contributions of peer interactions and academic demands within school settings also may provide essential information about environmental factors related to behavioral functioning (Northup et al., 1995). Hypotheses can be developed on the basis of more naturally occurring contingencies, and interventions can be identified that are not only relevant to the individual's daily environment but also acceptable to the teacher (Kutsick, Gutkin, & Witt, 1991). Ervin et al. (1998) particularly discussed a model of collaborative consultation that includes educational personnel, who will ultimately be the implementers of most interventions (in addition to parents), in all phases of the assessment. It is prudent to address the treatment acceptability issue because general education teachers, who are the primary service providers for students with ADHD in schools (Reid, Maag, Vasa, & Wright, 1994), typically have had less training in behavior management strategies than specially trained service providers (e.g., special education teachers, school psychologists). The process of functional assessment not only can provide some validation for their input and insights but also can be educational in terms of helping them identify "new" ways of evaluating and managing students' behavior. It is not surprising, then, that most of this newer line of investigations is appearing in the school psychology literature versus more clinically or medically oriented sources.

In terms of clinical significance of the findings in these five studies, none of the authors utilized a specific procedure for analyzing the therapeutic efficacy of the procedures (e.g., the proposed method of Jacobson & Truax, 1991). Thus, questions remain about the potential nor-malizing effects of the hypothesis-driven interventions. Data that support at least the ecological utility of the strategies include measures of procedural integrity by the teachers and satisfaction ratings by students and teachers. Both sets of data ranged from 80% to 100% in terms of positive findings in the Ervin et al. (1998) study, for example. (For further review, see Du-Paul & Eckert's, 1997, meta-analysis of school-based interventions for children with ADHD.)

PROCEDURES FOR CONDUCTING A FUNCTIONAL ANALYSIS OF BEHAVIOR IN ADHD

Though this chapter's review of the treatment literature for children with ADHD is by no means exhaustive, this sampling indicates variable success rates in ameliorating the core and associated features of this disorder. There could be many reasons for these inconsistencies in effectiveness across treatments and across individuals for a specific intervention. As noted throughout the review, one explanation could be the frequent omission of the application of a systematic method for addressing the function, versus the form, of the behavior targeted for reduction. It was quite striking to find that *none* of the studies reviewed prior to the mid-1990s directly addressed the inclusion of a functional analysis of behavior. Some of the earlier behavioral researchers used techniques or interpreted their findings in a way that came close to an analysis of function, but they did not directly discuss functional relations or apply specific assessment strategies that have been presented in the literature. Acknowledging the strategies that more recent investigations have proposed, this section describes specific procedures for conducting a functional assessment of the behavior of children with ADHD, with examples from a typical case.

Functional Analysis Strategies

Pfiffner and Barkley (1998) indicated that the general steps in a functional assessment of target behavior would include the following:

1. Developing an operational definition of the behavior of concern

2. Identifying antecedent events, both proximal and distal, that may be related to the behavior and determining consequences that typically follow and thus seem to maintain the behavior

3. Generating hypotheses about the relations between behavior and setting events

4. Testing the hypotheses through systematic manipulation of antecedents and consequences

5. Intervening with alternative antecedents and/or consequences for the target behavior (see also DuPaul & Eckert, 1997, and Reid & Maag, 1998)

These authors also noted the importance of identifying appropriate, alternative behaviors that can replace the undesirable actions to build the repertoire of the individual rather than simply eliminate behavior(s). They do not, however, address the importance of the functional equivalence of those potential replacement skills with the behavior(s) targeted for reduction.

Luiselli (1991) also addressed the issue of using behavior analysis procedures to select therapeutic interventions for children with disruptive behavior disorders such as ADHD. He described several specific strategies that could be used to conduct a functional analysis, including 1) diagnostic interviewing, 2) behavior checklists, and 3) direct observation of target behavior and the environmental variables related to its occurrence. Luiselli also suggested that assessments of family interactions, parenting behaviors, parental attitudes, and school functioning of the child be included in the overall analysis, although he did not provide examples of particular methods that could be helpful in documenting information about those variables.

Furthermore, Luiselli (1991) also presented a paradigm for applying assessment information in the process of selecting an appropriate treatment strategy. He emphasized that adherence to specific criteria for diagnosis, as from the DSM-IV, need not be the endpoint of assessment (see also Scotti, Morris, McNeil, & Hawkins, 1996). Instead, Luiselli suggested, each behavioral criterion that the child meets should be subsequently analyzed for functional aspects. This proposal is pertinent in terms of pediatricians' typical diagnostic and treatment selection processes (Copeland et al., 1987). It also raises the question of what is the most appropriate setting for initial referrals of children with attention difficulties (e.g., pediatricians in medical settings versus behavioral psychologists in clinical settings).

Identifying Behaviors of Concern

The following suggestions for a comprehensive assessment of behavioral functions in children who are suspected of having ADHD include methods for identifying appropriate, functionally equivalent, alternative behaviors, as well as consideration of how the information gathered in the assessment can be used to determine effective and efficient interventions. The behaviors of concern first must be identified clearly and described objectively. To accomplish this task, one can take advantage of the widespread use of behavior checklists and rating scales for purposes of diagnosing ADHD. Commonly used instruments include the ADHD Rating Scale (DuPaul et al., 1997), the Conners Parent and Teacher Behavior Rating Scales–Revised (Goyette, Conners, & Ulrich, 1978), the IOWA-Conners Teacher Rating Scale (Pelham, Milich, Murphy, & Murphy, 1989), the Home and School Situations Questionnaires (Barkley, 1987), and the parent and teacher report forms of the Child Behavior Checklist (Achenbach, 1991). These scales typically address a number of behaviors demonstrated by children with problems of inattention, overactivity, and impulsivity. Some of them also provide information about topographical features of the behavior, such as frequency, intensity, and/or duration. The Home and School Situations Questionnaires even begin to assess environmental variables that influence the behavior(s) of concern by having the rater identify setting events and antecedent situations. It should be helpful to have several people who are familiar with the child complete two or three different instruments. Then the evaluator can begin to identify the behaviors that should be targeted for intervention. This information also provides a starting point for the interview with the parents and other significant people in the child's life.

Developing Operational Definitions

The interview questions should prompt further description of the behaviors of concern to develop better an operational definition of the presenting symptoms. It is important that specific actions, not simply behavioral traits, be addressed. For example, suppose that 4-year-old Katie, who is being seen for the first time in a mental health clinic, is described by her mother as "hyper," disruptive, and aggressive, with frequent "fits" or temper tantrums. The clinician should try to steer away from using such global descriptors and encourage the mother to report more objectively exactly what Katie does when she is being "disruptive," for example. An objective definition for each target behavior should be agreed on by all people interviewed (preferably including teachers, grandparents, or any other significant people in the child's life) for a consensus in identifying the behavior regardless of the observer or the setting. In Katie's case, the following behaviors of concern might be identified: talking to or yelling at her mother when her mother is engaged in activities, such as cooking or talking on the telephone for more than 2 minutes (disruptive); moving from toy to toy in her preschool classroom rather than focusing on one activity or participating in group activities (disruptive and overactive); and biting her hands and forearms, banging her head on the wall, throwing toys at the wall, talking back to her mother and father (e.g., "Don't tell me no!"), and screaming and spitting on others (i.e., "fit," temper tantrum).

Establishing a History of Behavior

After the target behaviors are identified and clearly described, other topographical parameters and patterns should be examined. The history of each behavior should be assessed through the interview, including a description of the first demonstration of the behavior, if possible, and its course (i.e., severity, frequency, and consistency) over time. Current duration of each episode of the behavior, frequency of episodes, patterns of behavior during each episode, and typical setting events and environmental variables related to the occurrence of the behavior

should be determined. Settings in which or times when the behavior does *not* occur are equally important to identify. Additional information that might contribute to an understanding of the behavior includes documentation of significant personal relationships in the child's life; places that the child goes and what he or she does there; the child's daily schedule of activities; the child's medical history; choices that the child is allowed to make on a daily basis; behavioral strategies that have worked and not worked in the past; and family dynamics, interaction patterns, goals, and priorities (cf. Johnson, 1997). Structured interview guides that can be used or modified to answer these questions include the Functional Analysis Interview (O'Neill et al., 1990) and the Behavior Assessment Guide (Willis et al., 1987). A review of person-centered planning approaches also might be helpful in determining ways to gather this extensive information from a team of individuals who know the child well and are invested in his or her behavior improvement (for a review and procedural description, see Kincaid, 1996). At this stage of the process, it is as important to evaluate the appropriateness of environmental circumstances and behavioral expectations as it is to evaluate the child.

Developing Hypotheses

The next step after determining the history of each behavior is to summarize the information gathered and begin to develop hypotheses about the function of the behavior(s). It is also a good point at which to consider additional assessment strategies for identifying the variables that seem to be controlling and maintaining the target behavior(s). This may include a physical or neuropsychological evaluation, for example, but also should involve direct observation of the target behaviors. The best sources of information regarding the setting events, antecedents, and consequences related to the behaviors of concern are the natural environments of the child and his or her family. In Katie's case, observations in the home, at the school, and at various sites in the community with the family would be a better strategy for identifying the naturally occurring behaviors of the child and others in her environment; observations in the clinic likely would be less helpful (Barkley, 1991).

Using Systematic Observation Techniques

Systematic observation techniques that include the recording of data for events that occur before and after the target behavior, as well as their occurrence, are recommended as superior to casual "watching." As noted previously, a number of observational and behavioral coding systems have been described in the functional assessment and single-subject research design literature. Most of these procedures are time based, such that behaviors of specific individuals in the environment are documented for a certain interval; when the target behavior occurs, the evaluator then can attempt to determine what occurred prior to the behavioral episode as well as the consequent reactions to the behavior (an A-B-C analysis).

Some observational systems have been developed specifically for use with people with ADHD, such as the Structured Observation of Academic and Play Settings (SOAPS; Roberts, Milich, & Loney, 1984). Gordon (1995) also described a less formal observational strategy. Such systems, however, typically provide only a measure of frequency or rate of behavior and are not designed specifically to identify the variables that are related to the target behaviors. It should not be too difficult to revise those coding schemes to include more functional information; an example to follow is the Functional Analysis Observation Form and Observation Summary (see previous description; O'Neill et al., 1990).

Observations of the child's behavior, particularly in naturalistic settings, also can provide information about behaviors in the child's repertoire that seem to serve the same function or purpose as the target behaviors. Often, in initial interviews, parents and teachers do not acknowledge any appropriate, alternative behaviors that might serve the same function for the individual so that these might replace the target behaviors. Careful scrutiny of actual events and the child's interactions with people and the environment, however, typically reveals actions that are present in the child's repertoire and that are func-

tionally related to the behavior of concern. These behaviors often occur at a lower rate or earlier in a chain of behaviors, though. In Katie's case, observations might reveal that she sometimes uses her language to indicate what she wants to do or obtain *prior to* exhibiting such behaviors as yelling at her mother or throwing toys. Those requests, however, probably either do not occur often or typically are ignored or overlooked by Katie's mother or teacher. Such verbalizations early in the behavioral chain may serve the same purpose, though, as the final tantrum-like behavior. As described in the next paragraphs, this hypothesis about functional equivalence can be tested through experimental manipulations.

Testing Hypotheses

Analysis of the data collected from observations should be compared with the interview information. It might be possible to identify the variables that are controlling and maintaining the behavior as well as alternative behaviors that are serving the same function for the individual. If not, then further hypothesis-driven assessment (see Eifert, Evans, & McKendrick, 1990; Evans, 1985; Repp, Karsh, Munk, & Dahlquist, 1995; Scotti et al., 1994) can be conducted—either in the natural environment or in an analog (e.g., clinical) setting. The objective of this process is to manipulate systematically specific antecedent and consequent events, under various conditions, to determine more precisely the variables that are related to the target behaviors (Iwata et al., 1982). In Katie's case, assessment activities might have revealed that her tantrum-like behaviors (e.g., mild self-injury, throwing items, spitting) were part of a chain of behaviors that her mother described as a "fit." These episodes typically began when Katie's mother told Katie "no" after Katie impulsively started to do something or tried to get a particular item that her mother did not want her to do or have. Katie typically either continued to perform the activity or "talked back," which resulted in further reprimands from her mother. Katie then escalated to throwing items, spitting, and/or screaming. When her mother scolded further, Katie sometimes bit herself; when put in her room by herself, Katie typically banged her head on the wall. At this point, her mother would release Katie from the room. Thus, the initial part of this chain of behaviors seemed to serve the function of *escaping* the reprimand to *gain access to what she wanted*. As the chain of behaviors continued to escalate, the end result was that Katie virtually was guaranteed to get what she wanted because her mother always seemed to give in at some point. Similarly, it could be hypothesized that Katie's yelling behavior when her mother was engaged in her own activities served the function of directing the mother's *attention* back to Katie. The behaviors of moving from one activity to another in the classroom may serve the functions of *gaining access to what she wanted* and/or *maintaining a certain level of arousal or stimulation*.

The first hypothesis could be assessed through an experimental (analog) manipulation in the home, wherein the evaluator would set up situations that were likely to result in a tantrum. In one "scene," Katie could escape the negative reprimand because her mother would allow Katie to proceed with what she wanted; if the escape hypothesis were correct, then this likely would stop the tantrum before it escalated. If this condition were repeated, it also would be likely that Katie's attempts to get what she wants might increase in intensity and/or frequency. Alternatively, providing social attention and conversation (from the mother) as a consequence for talking back probably would not deter the tantrum if its true function were to escape. Conversely, attention to Katie when she was disruptive (e.g., when her mother was on the telephone) likely would encourage her inappropriate behavior in subsequent trials of the condition. Data on occurrence (and, as appropriate, intensity and duration) of Katie's responses should be collected across several (e.g., two to five) repetitions of these conditions until a clear pattern of the variables that are maintaining the target behavior becomes evident.

Another manipulation would be to teach Katie, through modeling and reinforcement, a functionally equivalent, alternative way to gain access to the activity or the item that she wanted. It might be acceptable to the mother that Katie get the item or do the activity, as long as she used her language to request it and engaged in a bit of social reciprocity during the process. If Katie's mother attended to Katie's initial appropriate requests and immediately granted Katie's wishes, then the tantrum likely would be averted. This strategy could become an intervention technique, and the following progression of events is likely: After Katie begins to experience some control over her environment via this consequence, her mother probably could begin to increase the amount of time that Katie must wait before she can have the item; eventually, Katie might even take "no" for an answer. In the meantime, Katie is being exposed to multiple opportunities to learn how to delay gratification—surely a valuable life skill for anyone. (For additional examples, see Anderson et al., in press; Nangle, Vittimberga, Miyake, Hammel, & Scotti, 1992; and Scotti et al., 1992.)

Many investigators have documented the value of manipulating antecedent events rather than focusing solely on consequences for inappropriate behaviors (Dunlap & Kern, 1993; DuPaul & Ervin, 1996; Ervin et al., 1998; Martens & Kelly, 1993; Reid & Maag, 1998). The utility of these types of strategies is to reduce effectively the likelihood of the occurrence of the problem behavior. In Katie's case, an example of this strategy is to intervene on her roaming/overactive behavior with one or more antecedent manipulations. For example, play and work times could be structured more effectively so that Katie is provided with clear physical boundaries, highly motivating activities, and social modeling and support so that she can organize her behavior more appropriately. In addition, Katie's schedule of activities may be structured to include many transitions and numerous opportunities for physically stimulating games and tasks. These types of manipulations can function to teach Katie new patterns of responding by altering setting events. Furthermore, the reinforcing "consequences" are built in to the activities. In this example, the inappropriate and appropriate behaviors also can be said to be functionally equivalent because they both still serve the same purpose for the child. Dunlap and Kern (1996) also described strategies for altering curricular components to help prevent inappropriate task-related behaviors.

From Assessment to Intervention

Functional assessment methodology can be applied to a wide range of behaviors exhibited by children who are globally described as "hyper," aggressive, distractible, impulsive, "acting out," and so forth (see Scotti, Mullen, & Hawkins, 1998). The strategies that have been described in this section suggest the utility of functional analysis in guiding the clinician through assessment and initial intervention procedures. These proposals extend the work of investigators who focused on the challenging behaviors of individuals with developmental disabilities (Iwata et al., 1982; Meyer & Evans, 1989) to include another population of children who are frequently referred as a result of problem behavior during their school years. Children with ADHD have been the subject of thousands of diagnostic, assessment, and intervention studies and discussion articles since the late 1970s. However, medical and psychiatric diagnoses that are based on "traditional" assessment strategies often have been presumed to predict appropriate treatment strategies (medical and/or behavioral). Documented limitations of the effectiveness of the most commonly implemented intervention techniques, however, suggested the need for further scrutiny of the assessment and intervention selection processes (Waschbusch et al., 1998). Functional analysis of the behaviors demonstrated by children with ADHD seems to be a viable response to that need. The information presented in this chapter, along with an emerging line of systematic investigations (DuPaul et al., 1997; DuPaul & Ervin, 1996), provides new suggestions to increase the validity and value of assessment procedures and the effectiveness of intervention strategies.

Of course, there are some aspects of the functional analysis process that still may limit its utility. The procedures that are described in this section, for example, can be very time consuming and seemingly impractical in some settings. The line of school-based research that is emerging in the intervention literature has offered some insights into how that problem might be addressed. For example, focusing the assessment process on the school setting seems to be a more efficient use of time because many ADHD-related behavior problems seem to be reported in that "natural" environment. On-site evaluation negates the need in a clinical setting to infer or artificially reproduce hypothesized environmental variables that might be contributing to the target behaviors. Furthermore, briefer versions of systematic manipulations of those associated environmental factors have been found to be as predictive of behavioral functioning as longer, analog procedures (Northup et al., 1991), which helps address the time issue. Finally, involving the front-line personnel (e.g., teachers, parent, peers) in the assessment process helps to increase generalizability, acceptability, and practicality issues.

Barkley (1998) also noted that some assessment strategies that have previously been proposed as part of a comprehensive evaluation of behaviors are not particularly useful in terms of the time–benefits ratio. He advocated for less emphasis on lengthy, time-based sampling of target behavior through direct observation. Indeed, within a functional assessment process, essential information for determining relations between behavior and environmental contingencies likely can be obtained through a number of other, more efficient methods (e.g., interviews across people who interact with the child, rating scales that ask questions about motivations for the behaviors, several brief observations [30 minutes] in the environments in which the target behaviors typically do and do not occur).

Probably the most important limitation that should be acknowledged when analyzing behavior functionally is that the same behaviors often can be motivated by different factors for an individual at different times. That is, if the child had learned a few "powerful" behaviors through environmental contingencies (setting events or consequences), then he or she is likely to demonstrate those actions in a number of situations. Children who demonstrate a high rate of inappropriate behavior often have a limited behavioral repertoire overall. Admittedly, attention or an emotional reaction is sometimes difficult to stifle, particularly for behavior such as spitting or darting into the street. It often is incumbent on the caregiver (teacher or parent) to assess "on the spot" why that behavior occurred. As teachers and parents, as well as clinicians, become more attuned to looking for patterns and reasons for a child's behavior, this process becomes easier. However, when providers and caregivers start realizing why a child's behavior occurs, they will be more likely to change their own behaviors and to manipulate antecedent events to prevent the unacceptable and problem behaviors. Literature from both the developmental disabilities and ADHD fields supports proactive, structured strategies for "managing" problem behavior versus waiting for the behavior to occur and then attempting to alter the consequences (Dunlap & Kern, 1993; Martens & Kelly, 1993). Proactive techniques also provide behaviorally challenged youth with skills-training interventions, which produce increased repertoires of acceptable behaviors. Thus, they can truly benefit from a skills-training intervention package, which seeks to replace undesirable behavior with more effective and acceptable alternatives.

FUNCTIONAL ANALYSIS: IMPLICATIONS FOR RECOMMENDED PRACTICES IN ADHD

Emerging evidence in the ADHD literature indicates that functional assessment of both inappropriate behaviors and alternative, "replacement" behaviors provides a clear and effective direction for intervention. If researchers do not conduct such functional analyses, then intervention efforts are likely to be haphazard and impractical. In many cases, medication and behavioral treatments appear to be conventional choices that are based on "standard," or accepted, practices for a particular diagnosis. An alternative process based on a functional analysis could be useful for both behavioral interventions and medication treatments. Stimulants, for example, initially were used for treating children with ADHD without a comprehensive understanding of how these drugs worked. Furthermore, the neurological or biochemical factors associated with the syndrome were not well understood (Schaal & Hackenberg, 1994). Much pharmacological and neurobiological experimentation has been conducted over the years with a research

population that was already receiving the stimulant medications (DuPaul & Barkley, 1993). This serendipitous experimentation has suggested that those drugs affect certain areas and systems in the brains of individuals who demonstrate problems with attention and overactivity (Hynd, Hern, Voeller, & Marshall, 1991). In some cases, for instance, neurotransmitter activity has been related to specific medications (Rogeness et al., 1992; Zametkin & Rapoport, 1987). As of 1999, however, this work has not resulted in any clear guidelines that clinicians can use to select medication treatments for specific clusters of behaviors.

Pelham (1986) summarized the medication predicament well: The decision of whether to prescribe drugs for a child with ADHD (and which medication and dosage to use) rarely is reached in a systematic way by pediatricians and psychiatrists. Standard practice in pediatric psychopharmacology reportedly is to select a medication based on what is recommended in the literature (i.e., "recommended practice" for a given diagnosis or constellation of behavior) and to adjust the dosage until an optimal response is obtained with no significant side effects, according to reports from parents, teachers, and the child. The problem with this process is, of course, that assessment is not conducted until *after* a chemical substance has been ingested by the individual; children may take these medications for years. Because medication can have a rapid behavioral suppression effect, both clinicians and caregivers likely have overlooked periodic reports of adverse side effects in the short term and ignored the possibility of long-term problems. Furthermore, initial parent and teacher acceptability ratings of medication therapies typically are favorable (Johnston & Fine, 1993; Liu, Robin, Brenner, & Eastman, 1991). Thus, once a medication is prescribed, there seems to be relatively little oversight and virtually no long-term commitment to maintain both intended and unintended effects.

As the discussion in this chapter indicates, however, procedures for identifying appropriate medication therapies, at the initial referral, need to be reevaluated (Vyse & Rapport, 1989). In response to similar issues in selecting drug treatments for people with developmental disabilities, Schaal and Hackenberg (1994) wrote a seminal paper describing the potential use of functional analysis procedures in this determination process. These authors suggested that the effects of medications on behavior are related not only to biochemical factors but also to the environmental variables that are impinging on the individual. The function of neurological anomalies can be interpreted in terms of idiosyncratic relationships between the individual and variables in his or her environment that are controlling behavior. Thus, selection of a medication for treating children with ADHD need not be based solely on the identification of the "causal" physical anomaly. Information obtained from a thorough behavioral assessment can be used to determine the potential effectiveness of a given medication. Knowledge regarding the mechanism of action of each medication can also contribute to the analysis; continued research in behavioral pharmacology and related fields likely will provide more answers in this area.

Overall, the general consensus in the ADHD treatment literature seems to be that multimodal intervention packages, including both medication and behavioral components, will provide the most efficacious and efficient means of changing the behavior of children with ADHD (Nathan, 1992; Richters et al., 1995). This review shows that the choices of interventions that can be included in such a package are numerous and varied. Thus, it is imperative that some sort of systematic method for determining the most appropriate treatments be applied in research and clinical practice. DuPaul and Barkley (1993) advocated for more investigations regarding organismic and environmental variables that might indicate individual responsiveness to multimodal treatment programs. The argument presented in this chapter submits that the appropriate mechanism for accomplishing these objectives is the use of functional analysis to identify the variables that are controlling and maintaining behaviors of concern. This seems to be an essential process for determining the most effective intervention that will help the child develop a more appropriate behavioral repertoire.

CONCLUSION

Given the inconsistent findings of clinically significant effectiveness in the treatment of behaviors that typically are associated with a diagnosis of ADHD, this chapter has discussed the potential advantages of conducting a functional analysis of the presenting problem behaviors. The outcome of a comprehensive, thorough functional assessment should be an indication of a potentially appropriate treatment, including the identification of functionally equivalent alternative skills and behaviors to replace problem behaviors. Continued application of functional assessment procedures throughout treatment also can provide essential information as to the clinical significance of behavior change and the need to alter any aspect of the intervention program. Functional analysis should be considered an integral, dynamic process in treating children with ADHD.

REFERENCES

Abramowitz, A.J., Eckstrand, D., O'Leary, S.G., & Dulcan, M.K. (1992). ADHD children's responses to stimulant medication and two intensities of a behavioral intervention [Special issue: Treatment of children with attention-deficit hyperactivity children]. *Behavior Modification, 16,* 193–203.

Achenbach, T.M. (1991). *Manual for the Child Behavior Checklist and Teacher Report Form.* Burlington, VT: Author.

American Psychiatric Association. (1980). *Diagnostic and statistical manual of mental disorders* (3rd ed.). Washington, DC: Author.

American Psychiatric Association. (1987). *Diagnostic and statistical manual of mental disorders* (3rd ed., rev.). Washington, DC: Author.

American Psychiatric Association. (1994). *Diagnostic and statistical manual of mental disorders* (4th ed.). Washington, DC: Author.

Anastopoulos, A.D., Guevremont, D.C., Shelton, T.L., & DuPaul, G.J. (1992). Parenting stress among families of children with attention deficit hyperactivity disorder. *Journal of Abnormal Child Psychology, 20,* 503–520.

Anastopoulos, A.D., Shelton, T.L., DuPaul, G.J., & Guevremont, D.C. (1993). Parent training for attention-deficit hyperactivity disorder: Its impact on parent functioning. *Journal of Abnormal Child Psychology, 21,* 581–596.

Anderson, C.M., Freeman, K.A., & Scotti, J.R. (in press). Evaluation of the generalizability (reliability and validity) of analog functional assessment methodology. *Behavior Therapy.*

Anderson, J.C., Williams, S., McGee, R., & Silva, P.A. (1987). DSM-III disorders in preadolescent children: Prevalence in a large sample from the general population. *Archives of General Psychiatry, 44,* 69–76.

Arnold, L.E., Abikoff, H.B., Cantwell, D.P., Conners, C.K., Elliott, G., Greenhill, L.L., Hechtman, L., Hinshaw, S.P., Hoza, B., Jensen, P.S., Kraemer, H.C., March, J.S., Newcorn, J.H., Pelham, W.E., Richters, J.E., Schiller, E., Sever, J.B., Swanson, J.M., Vereen, D., & Wells, K.C. (1997). National Institute of Mental Health Collaborative Multimodal Treatment Study of Children with ADHD (The MTA): Design challenges and choices. *Archives of General Psychiatry, 54,* 865–870.

Bailey, J.S., & Pyles, D.A.M. (1989). Behavioral diagnostics. In E. Cipani (Ed.), *The treatment of severe behavior disorders: Behavior analysis approaches* (pp. 85–107). Washington, DC: American Association on Mental Retardation.

Barkley, R.A. (1986). What is the role of group parent training in the treatment of ADD children? *Journal of Children in Contemporary Society, 19,* 143–151.

Barkley, R.A. (1987). *Defiant children: A clinician's manual for parent training.* New York: Guilford Press.

Barkley, R.A. (1991). The ecological validity of laboratory and analogue assessment methods of ADHD symptoms. *Journal of Abnormal Child Psychology, 19,* 149–178.

Barkley, R.A. (1998). *Attention-deficit hyperactivity disorder: A handbook for diagnosis and treatment* (2nd ed.). New York: Guilford Press.

Barkley, R.A., DuPaul, G.J., & McMurray, M.B. (1991). Attention deficit disorder with and without hyperactivity: Clinical response to three dose levels of methylphenidate. *Pediatrics, 87,* 519–531.

Barkley, R.A., McMurray, M.B., Edelbrock, C.S., & Robbins, K. (1989). The response of aggressive and nonaggressive ADHD children to two doses of methylphenidate. *Journal of the American Academy of Child and Adolescent Psychiatry, 28,* 873–881.

Barkley, R.A., McMurray, M.B., Edelbrock, C.S., & Robbins, K. (1990). Side effects of methylphenidate in children with attention deficit hyperactivity disorder: A systemic, placebo-controlled evaluation. *Pediatrics, 86,* 184–192.

Barlow, D.H., & Hersen, M. (1984). *Single case experimental designs: Strategies for studying behavior change* (2nd ed.). New York: Pergamon.

Barrios, B., & Hartmann, D.P. (1986). The contributions of traditional assessment: Concepts, issues, and methodologies. In R.O. Nelson & S.C. Hayes (Eds.), *Conceptual foundations of behavioral assessment* (pp. 81–110). New York: Guilford Press.

Biederman, J., Baldessarini, R.J., Wright, V., Knee, D., & Harmatz, J.S. (1989). A double-blind placebo controlled study of desipramine in the treatment of ADD: I. Efficacy. *Journal of the American Academy of Child and Adolescent Psychiatry, 28,* 777–784.

Borden, K.A., & Brown, R.T. (1989). Attributional outcomes: The subtle messages of treatments for attention deficit disorder. *Cognitive Therapy and Research, 13,* 147–160.

Boring, E.G. (1957). *A history of experimental psychology.* New York: Appleton-Century-Crofts.

Broussard, C.D., & Northup, J. (1995). An approach to functional assessment and analysis of disruptive behavior in regular education classrooms. *School Psychology Quarterly, 10,* 151–164.

Buhrmester, D., Whalen, C.K., Henker, B., MacDonald, V., & Hinshaw, S.P. (1992). Prosocial behavior in hyperactive boys: Effects of stimulant medication and comparison with normal boys. *Journal of Abnormal Child Psychology, 20,* 103–121.

Campbell, M., & Spencer, E.K. (1988). Psychopharmacology in child and adolescent psychiatry: A review of the past five years. *Journal of the American Academy of Child and Adolescent Psychiatry, 27,* 269–279.

Carlson, C.L., Pelham, W.E., Milich, R., & Dixon, J. (1992). Single and combined effects of methylphenidate and behavior therapy on the classroom performance of children with attention-deficit hyperactivity disorder. *Journal of Abnormal Child Psychology, 20,* 213–232.

Carlson, G.A., & Rapport, M.D. (1989). Diagnostic classification issues in attention-deficit hyperactivity disorder. *Psychiatric Annals, 19,* 576–583.

Carr, E.G. (1977). The motivation of self-injurious behavior: A review of some hypotheses. *Psychological Bulletin, 84,* 800–816.

Carr, E.G., & Durand, V.M. (1985). Reducing behavior problems through functional communication training. *Journal of Applied Behavior Analysis, 18,* 111–126.

Cone, J.D. (1986). Idiographic, nomothetic, and related perspectives in behavioral assessment. In R.O. Nelson & S.C. Hayes (Eds.), *Conceptual foundations of behavioral assessment* (pp. 111–128). New York: Guilford Press.

Cooper, L.J., Wacker, D.P., Sasso, G.M., Reimers, T.M., & Donn, L.K. (1990). Using parents as therapists to evaluate appropriate behavior of their children: Application to a tertiary diagnostic clinic. *Journal of Applied Behavior Analysis, 23,* 285–296.

Cooper, L.J., Wacker, D.P., Thursby, D., Plagmann, L.A., Harding, J., Millard, T., & Derby, M. (1992). Analysis of the effects of task preferences, task demands, and adult attention on child behavior in outpatient and classroom settings. *Journal of Applied Behavior Analysis, 25,* 823–840.

Copeland, L., Wolraich, M., Lindgren, S., Milich, R., & Woolson, R. (1987). Pediatricians' reported practices in the assessment and treatment of attention deficit disorders. *Journal of Developmental and Behavioral Pediatrics, 8,* 191–197.

Day, R.M., Rea, J.A., Schussler, N.G., Larsen, S.E., & Johnson, W.L. (1988). A functionally based approach to the treatment of self-injurious behavior. *Behavior Modification, 12,* 565–589.

Donney, V.K., & Poppen, R. (1989). Teaching parents to conduct behavioral relaxation training with their hyperactive children. *Journal of Behavior Therapy and Experimental Psychiatry, 20,* 319–325.

Douglas, V.I. (1972). Stop, look, and listen: The problem of sustained attention and impulse control in hyperactive and normal children. *Canadian Journal of Behavioral Science, 4,* 259–282.

Dulcan, M.K. (1990). Using psychostimulants to treat behavioral disorders of children and adolescents. *Journal of Child and Adolescent Psychopharmacology, 1,* 7–20.

Dunlap, G., & Kern, L. (1993). Assessment and intervention for children within the instructional curriculum. In J. Reichle & D. Wacker (Eds.), *Communication and language intervention series: Vol. 4. Communicative alternatives to challenging behavior: Integrating functional assessment intervention strategies* (pp. 177–203). Baltimore: Paul H. Brookes Publishing Co.

Dunlap G., & Kern, L. (1996). Modifying instructional activities to promote desirable behavior: A conceptual and practical framework. *School Psychology Quarterly, 11,* 297–312.

DuPaul, G.J., Anastopoulos, A.D., Kwasnik, D., Barkley, R.A., & McMurray, M.B. (1996). Methylphenidate effects on children with attention deficit hyperactivity disorder: Self-report of symptoms, side-effects, and self-esteem. *Journal of Attention Disorders, 1,* 3–15.

DuPaul, G.J., & Barkley, R.A. (1990). Medication therapy. In R.A. Barkley (Ed.), *Attention deficit hyperactivity disorder: A handbook for diagnosis and treatment* (pp. 573–612). New York: Guilford Press.

DuPaul, G.J., & Barkley, R.A. (1993). Behavioral contributions to pharmacotherapy: The utility of behavioral methodology in medication treatment of children with attention deficit hyperactivity disorder. *Behavior Therapy, 24,* 47–65.

DuPaul, G.J., Barkley, R.A., & Connor, D.F. (1998). Stimulants. In R.A. Barkley (Ed.), *Attention-deficit hyperactivity disorder: A handbook for diagnosis and treatment* (2nd ed., pp. 510–551). New York: Guilford Press.

DuPaul, G.J., & Eckert, T.L. (1997). The effects of school-based interventions for attention deficit hyperactivity disorder: A meta-analysis. *School Psychology Review, 26,* 5–27.

DuPaul, G.J., Eckert, T.L., & McGoey, K.E. (1997). Interventions for students with attention-deficit/ hyperactivity disorder: One size does not fit all. *School Psychology Review, 26,* 369–381.

DuPaul, G.J., & Ervin, R.A. (1996). Functional assessment of behaviors related to attention-deficit/ hyperactivity disorder: Linking assessment to intervention design. *Behavior Therapy, 27,* 601–622.

DuPaul, G.J., Guevremont, D.C., & Barkley, R.A. (1992). Behavioral treatment of attention-deficit hyperactivity disorder in the classroom: The use of the Attention Training System. *Behavior Modification, 16,* 204–225.

DuPaul, G.J., & Hoff, K.E. (1998). Reducing disruptive behavior in general education classrooms: The use of self-management strategies. *School Psychology Review, 27,* 290–303.

DuPaul, G.J., Power, T.J., Anastopoulos, A.D., Reid, R., McGoey, K.E., & Ikeda, M.J. (1997). Teacher ratings of attention deficit hyperactivity disorder symptoms: Factor structure and normative data. *Psychological Assessment, 9,* 436–444.

DuPaul, G.J., & Rapport, M.D. (1993). Does methylphenidate normalize the classroom performance of children with attention deficit disorder? *Journal of the American Academy of Child and Adolescent Psychiatry, 32,* 190–198.

Durand, V.M. (1990). *Severe behavior problems: A functional communication training approach.* New York: Guilford Press.

Durand, V.M., & Crimmins, D.B. (1988). Identifying the variables maintaining self-injurious behavior. *Journal of Autism and Developmental Disorders, 18,* 99–117.

Edelbrock, C., & Costello, A.J. (1988). Structured psychiatric interviews for children. In M. Rutter, A.H. Tuma, & I.S. Lann (Eds.), *Assessment and diagnosis in child psychopathology* (pp. 87–112). New York: Guilford Press.

Eifert, G.H., Evans, I.M., & McKendrick, V.G. (1990). Matching treatments to client problems not diagnostic labels: A case for paradigmatic behavior therapy. *Journal of Behavior Therapy and Experimental Psychiatry, 21,* 163–172.

Elia, J., Borcherding, B.G., Rapoport, J.L., & Keysor, C.S. (1991). Methylphenidate and dextroamphetamine treatments of hyperactivity: Are there true nonresponders? *Psychiatry Research, 36,* 141–155.

Erhardt, D., & Baker, B.L. (1990). The effects of behavioral parent training on families with young hyperactive children. *Journal of Behavior Therapy and Experimental Psychiatry, 21,* 121–132.

Ervin, R.A., DuPaul, G.J., Kern, L., & Friman, P.C. (1998). Classroom-based functional and adjunctive assessments: Proactive approaches to intervention selection for adolescents with attention deficit hyperactivity disorder. *Journal of Applied Behavior Analysis, 31,* 65–78.

Evans, I.M. (1985). Building systems models as a strategy for target behavior selection in clinical assessment. *Behavioral Assessment, 7,* 21–32.

Evans, I.M., & Meyer, L.H. (1985). *An educative approach to behavior problems: A practical decision model for interventions with severely handicapped learners.* Baltimore: Paul H. Brookes Publishing Co.

Evans, I.M., Meyer, L.H., Kurkjian, J.A., & Kishi, G.S. (1988). An evaluation of behavioral interrelationships in child behavior therapy. In J.C. Witt, S.N. Elliott, & F.N. Gresham (Eds.), *Handbook of behavior therapy in education* (pp. 189–216). New York: Plenum.

Fehlings, D.L., Roberts, W., Humphries, T., & Dawe, G. (1991). Attention deficit hyperactivity disorder: Does cognitive behavioral therapy improve home behavior? *Journal of Developmental and Behavioral Pediatrics, 12,* 223–228.

Firestone, P., & Douglas, V.I. (1975). The effects of reward and punishment on reaction times and automatic activity in hyperactive and normal children. *Journal of Abnormal Child Psychology, 3,* 201–216.

Fischer, M., Barkley, R.A., Fletcher, K.E., & Smallish, L. (1993). The adolescent outcome of hyperactive children: Predictors of psychiatric, academic, social, and emotional adjustment. *Journal of the American Academy of Child and Adolescent Psychiatry, 32,* 324–332.

Frankenberger, W., Lozar, B., & Dallas, P. (1990). The use of stimulant medication to treat attention deficit hyperactive disorder (ADHD) in elementary school children. *Developmental Disabilities Bulletin, 18,* 1–13.

Gittelman, R., Mannuzza, S., Shenker, R., & Bonagura, N. (1985). Hyperactive boys almost grown up. *Archives of General Psychiatry, 42,* 937–947.

Goldstein, S., & Ingersoll, B. (1992, Fall/Winter). Controversial treatments for children with attention deficit hyperactivity disorder. *CHADDER* (Newsletter of the national organization for Children with Attention Deficit Disorders).

Gordon, M. (1995). *How to operate an ADHD clinic or subspecialty practice.* Syracuse, NY: GSI Publications.

Goyette, C.H., Conners, C.K., & Ulrich, R.F. (1978). Normative data for Revised Conners Parent and Teacher Rating Scales. *Journal of Abnormal Child Psychology, 6,* 221–236.

Groden, G. (1989). A guide for conducting a comprehensive behavioral analysis of a target behavior. *Journal of Behavior Therapy and Experimental Psychiatry, 20,* 163–169.

Gualtieri, C.T., Keenan, P.A., & Chandler, M. (1991). Clinical and neuropsychological effects of desipramine in children with attention deficit hyperactivity disorder. *Journal of Clinical Psychopharmacology, 11,* 155–159.

Hall, C.W., & Kataria, S. (1992). Effects of two treatment techniques on delay and vigilance tasks with attention deficit hyperactive disorder (ADHD) children. *Journal of Psychology, 126,* 17–25.

Harding, J., Wacker, D.P., Cooper, L.J., Millard, T., & Jensen-Kovalan, P. (1994). Brief hierarchical assessment of potential treatment components with children in an outpatient clinic. *Journal of Applied Behavior Analysis, 27,* 291–300.

Haynes, S.N., & O'Brien, W.H. (1990). Functional analysis in behavior therapy. *Clinical Psychology Review, 10,* 649–668.

Helmstetter, E., & Durand, V.M. (1991). Nonaversive interventions for severe behavior problems. In L.H. Meyer, C.A. Peck, & L. Brown (Eds.), *Critical issues in the lives of people with severe disabilities* (pp. 559–600). Baltimore: Paul H. Brookes Publishing Co.

Hinshaw, S.P. (1991). Stimulant medication and the treatment of aggression in children with attentional deficits. *Journal of Clinical Child Psychology, 20,* 301–312.

Hinshaw, S.P. (1994). *Attention deficits and hyperactivity in children.* Thousand Oaks, CA: Sage Publications.

Hinshaw, S.P., Heller, T., & McHale, J.P. (1992). Covert antisocial behavior in boys with attention-deficit hyperactivity disorder: External validation and effects of methylphenidate. *Journal of Consulting and Clinical Psychology, 60,* 274–281.

Hinshaw, S.P., Henker, B., Whalen, C.K., Erhardt, D., & Dunnington, R.E. (1989). Aggressive, prosocial, and nonsocial behavior in hyperactive boys: Dose effects of methylphenidate in naturalistic settings. *Journal of Consulting and Clinical Psychology, 57,* 636–643.

Horn, W.F., Ialongo, N., Greenberg, G., Packard, T., & Smith-Winberry, C. (1990). Additive effects of behavioral parent training and self-control therapy with attention deficit hyperactivity disordered children. *Journal of Clinical Child Psychology, 19,* 98–110.

Horn, W.F., Ialongo, N.S., Pascoe, J.M., Greenberg, G., Packard, T., Lopez, M., Wagner, A., & Puttler, L. (1991). Additive effects of psychostimulants, parent training, and self-control therapy with ADHD children. *Journal of the American Academy of Child and Adolescent Psychiatry, 30,* 233–240.

Hoza, B., Pelham, W.E., Sams, S.E., & Carlson, C. (1992). An examination of the "dosage" effects of both behavior therapy and methylphenidate on the classroom performance of two ADHD children. *Behavior Modification, 16,* 164–192.

Hynd, G.W., Hern, K.L., Voeller, K.K., & Marshall, R.M. (1991). Neurobiological basis of attention-deficit hyperactivity disorder (ADHD). *School Psychology Review, 20,* 174–186.

Ialongo, N.S., Horn, W.F., Pascoe, J.M., Greenberg, G., Packard, T., Lopez, M., Wagner, A., & Puttler, L. (1993). The effects of a multimodal intervention with attention-deficit hyperactivity disorder children: A 9-month follow-up. *Journal of the Ameri-*

can *Academy of Child and Adolescent Psychiatry,* *32,* 182–189.

Iwata, B.A., Dorsey, M.F., Slifer, K.J., Bauman, K.E., & Richman, G.S. (1982). Toward a functional analysis of self-injury. *Analysis and Intervention in Developmental Disabilities, 2,* 3–20.

Iwata, B.A., Vollmer, T.R., & Zarcone, J.R. (1990). The experimental (functional) analysis of behavior disorders: Methodology, applications, and limitations. In A.C. Repp & N.N. Singh (Eds.), *Perspectives on the use of nonaversive and aversive interventions for persons with developmental disabilities* (pp. 301–330). Sycamore, IL: Sycamore Publishing.

Jacobson, N.S., Follette, W.C., & Revenstorf, D. (1984). Psychotherapy outcome research: Methods for reporting variability and evaluating clinical significance. *Behavior Therapy, 15,* 336–352.

Jacobson, N.S., & Truax, P. (1991). Clinical significance: A statistical approach to defining meaningful change in psychotherapy research. *Journal of Consulting and Clinical Psychology, 59,* 12–19.

Jacobvitz, D., Sroufe, L.A., Stewart, M., & Leffert, N. (1990). Treatment of attentional and hyperactivity problems in children with sympathomimetic drugs: A comprehensive review. *Journal of the American Academy of Child and Adolescent Psychiatry, 29,* 677–688.

Jensen, P.S., Xenakis, S.N., Shervette, R.E., Bain, M.W., & Davis, H. (1989). Diagnosis and treatment of attention deficit disorder in two general hospital clinics. *Hospital and Community Psychiatry, 40,* 708–712.

Johnson, T.M. (1997). Evaluating the hyperactive child in your office: Is it ADHD? *American Family Physician, 56,* 155–160.

Johnston, C., & Fine, S. (1993). Methods of evaluating methylphenidate in children with attention deficit hyperactivity disorder: Acceptability, satisfaction, and compliance. *Journal of Pediatric Psychology, 18,* 717–730.

Kanfer, F.H., & Saslow, G. (1969). Behavioral diagnosis. In C.M. Franks (Ed.), *Behavior therapy: Appraisal and status* (pp. 417–444). New York: McGraw-Hill.

Kazdin, A.E. (1982). Symptom substitution, generalization, and response covariation: Implications for psychotherapy outcome. *Psychological Bulletin, 91,* 349–365.

Kendall, P.C., & Braswell, L. (1985). *Cognitive-behavioral therapy for impulsive children.* New York: Guilford Press.

Kern, L., Childs, K.E., Dunlap, G., Clarke, S., & Falk, G.D. (1994). Using assessment-based curricular intervention to improve the classroom behavior of a student with emotional and behavioral challenges. *Journal of Applied Behavior Analysis, 27,* 7–19.

Kincaid, D. (1996). Person-centered planning. In L.K. Koegel, R.L. Koegel, & G. Dunlap (Eds.), *Positive behavioral support: Including people with difficult behavior in the community* (pp. 439–465). Baltimore: Paul H. Brookes Publishing Co.

Klein, R.G. (1987). Pharmacotherapy of childhood hyperactivity: An update. In H.Y. Meltzer (Ed.), *Psychopharmacology: The third generation of progress* (pp. 1215–1224). New York: Raven Press.

Klorman, R., Brumaghim, J.T., Salzman, L.F., Strauss, J., Borgstedt, A.D., McBride, M.C., & Loeb, S. (1989). Comparative effects of methylphenidate on attention-deficit hyperactivity disorder with and without aggressive/noncompliant features. *Psychopharmacology Bulletin, 25,* 109–113.

Kutsick, K.A., Gutkin, T.B., & Witt, J.C. (1991). The impact of treatment development process, intervention type, and problem severity on treatment acceptability as judged by classroom teachers. *Psychology in the Schools, 28,* 325–331.

Lahey, B.B., Piacentini, J.C., McBurnett, K., Stone, P., Hartdagen, S., & Hynd, G. (1988). Psychopathology in the parents of children with conduct disorder and hyperactivity. *Journal of the American Academy of Child and Adolescent Psychiatry, 27,* 163–170.

Lennox, D.B., & Miltenberger, R.G. (1989). Conducting a functional analysis of problem behavior in applied settings. *Journal of The Association for Persons with Severe Handicaps, 14,* 304–311.

Lennox, D.B., Miltenberger, R.G., Spengler, P., & Erfanian, N. (1988). Decelerative treatment practices with persons who have mental retardation: A review of five years of the literature. *American Journal on Mental Retardation, 92,* 492–501.

Lewis, T.J., & Sugai, G. (1996). Functional assessment of problem behavior: A pilot investigation of the comparative and interactive effects of teacher and peer social attention on students in general education settings. *School Psychology Quarterly, 11,* 1–19.

Liu, C., Robin, A.L., Brenner, S., & Eastman, J. (1991). Social acceptability of methylphenidate and behavior modification for treating attention deficit hyperactivity disorder. *Pediatrics, 88,* 560–565.

Luiselli, J.K. (1991). Assessment-derived treatment of children's disruptive behavior disorders. *Behavior Modification, 15,* 294–309.

Martens, B.K., & Kelly, S.Q. (1993). A behavior analysis of effective teaching. *School Psychology Quarterly, 8,* 10–26.

McCain, A.P., & Kelley, M.L. (1993). Managing the classroom behavior of an ADHD preschooler: The efficacy of a school–home note intervention. *Child and Family Behavior Therapy, 15,* 33–44.

Meyer, L.H., & Evans, I.M. (1989). *Nonaversive intervention for behavior problems: A manual for home and community.* Baltimore: Paul H. Brookes Publishing Co.

Nangle, D.W., Vittimberga, G.L., Miyake, K., Hammel, D.L., & Scotti, J.R. (1992, May). *A compari-*

son of three functional assessment procedures with a child with developmental disabilities. Paper presented at the 18th annual convention of the Association for Behavior Analysis, San Francisco.

Nathan, W.A. (1992). Integrated multimodal therapy of children with attention-deficit hyperactivity disorder. *Bulletin of the Menninger Clinic, 56,* 283–312.

Nelson, R.O., & Hayes, S.C. (1986). The nature of behavioral assessment. In R.O. Nelson & S.C. Hayes (Eds.), *Conceptual foundations of behavioral assessment* (pp. 3–41). New York: Guilford Press.

Northup, J., Broussard, C., Jones, K., George, T., Vollmer, T.R., & Herring, M. (1995). The differential effects of teacher and peer attention on the disruptive classroom behavior of three children with a diagnosis of attention deficit hyperactivity disorder. *Journal of Applied Behavior Analysis, 28,* 227–228.

Northup, J., Wacker, D., Sasso, G., Steege, M., Cigrand, K., Cook, J., & DeRand, A. (1991). A functional analysis of both aggressive and alternative behavior in an outclinic setting. *Journal of Applied Behavior Analysis, 24,* 509–522.

O'Leary, K.D., & Wilson, G.T. (1975). *Behavior therapy: Application and outcome.* Englewood Cliffs, NJ: Prentice-Hall.

O'Leary, S.G., & Pelham, W.E. (1978). Behavior therapy and withdrawal of stimulant medication in hyperactive children. *Pediatrics, 61,* 211–217.

Olson, S.L., Bates, J.E., & Bayles, K. (1990). Early antecedents of childhood impulsivity: The role of parent–child interaction, cognitive competence, and temperament. *Journal of Abnormal Child Psychology, 18,* 317–334.

O'Neill, R.E., Horner, R.H., Albin, R.W., Storey, K., & Sprague, J.R. (1990). *Functional analysis of problem behavior: A practical assessment guide.* Sycamore, IL: Sycamore Publishing.

Pelham, W.E. (1986). What do we know about the use and effects of CNS stimulants in the treatment of ADD? *Journal of Children in Contemporary Society, 19,* 99–110.

Pelham, W.E., Carlson, C.L., Sams, S.E., Vallano, G., Dixon, M.J., & Hoza, B. (1993). Separate and combined effects of methylphenidate and behavior modification on boys with attention deficit-hyperactivity disorder in the classroom. *Journal of Consulting and Clinical Psychology, 61,* 506–515.

Pelham, W.E., Greenslade, K.E., Vodde-Hamilton, M., Murphy, D.A., Greenstein, J.J., Gnagy, E.M., Guthrie, K.J., Hoover, M.D., & Dahl, R.E. (1990). Relative efficacy of long-acting stimulants on children with attention deficit-hyperactivity disorder: A comparison of standard methylphenidate, sustained-release methylphenidate, sustained-release dextroamphetamine, and pemoline. *Pediatrics, 86,* 226–237.

Pelham, W.E., McBurnett, K., Harper, G.W., Milich, R., Murphy, D.A., Clinton, J., & Thiele, C. (1990). Methylphenidate and baseball playing in ADHD children: Who's on first? *Journal of Consulting and Clinical Psychology, 58,* 130–133.

Pelham, W.E., Milich, R., Murphy, D.A., & Murphy, H.A. (1989). Normative data on the IOWA Conners Teacher Rating Scale. *Journal of Clinical Child Psychology, 18,* 259–262.

Pelham, W.E., & Murphy, H.A. (1986). Attention deficit and conduct disorders. In M. Hersen (Ed.), *Pharmacological and behavioral treatment: An integrative approach* (pp. 108–148). New York: John Wiley & Sons.

Pfiffner, L.J., & Barkley, R.A. (1998). Treatment of ADHD in school settings. In R.A. Barkley (Ed.), *Attention-deficit hyperactivity disorder: A handbook for diagnosis and treatment* (2nd ed., pp. 458–490). New York: Guilford Press.

Pfiffner, L.J., & O'Leary, S.G. (1987). The efficacy of all-positive management as a function of the prior use of negative consequences. *Journal of Applied Behavior Analysis, 20,* 265–271.

Pisterman, S., Firestone, P., McGrath, P., Goodman, J.T., Webster, I., Mallory, R., & Goffin, B. (1992). The role of parent training in treatment of preschoolers with ADHD. *American Journal of Orthopsychiatry, 62,* 397–408.

Pisterman, S., McGrath, P., Firestone, P., Goodman, J.T., Webster, I., & Mallory, R. (1989). Outcome of parent-mediated treatment of preschoolers with attention deficit disorder with hyperactivity. *Journal of Consulting and Clinical Psychology, 57,* 628–635.

Rachlin, H. (1970). *Introduction to modern behaviorism.* San Francisco: W.H. Freeman.

Rapoport, J.L. (1987). Pediatric psychopharmacology: The last decade. In H.Y. Meltzer (Ed.), *Psychopharmacology: The third generation of progress* (pp. 1211–1214). New York: Raven Press.

Rapport, M.D., Murphy, A., & Bailey, J.S. (1982). Ritalin versus response cost in the control of hyperactive children: A within-subject comparison. *Journal of Applied Behavior Analysis, 15,* 205–216.

Reid, R., & Maag, J.W. (1998). Functional assessment: A method for developing classroom-based accommodations and interventions for children with ADHD. *Reading & Writing Quarterly, 14,* 9–42.

Reid, R., Maag, J.W., Vasa, S.F., & Wright, G. (1994). Who are the children with ADHD: A school-based survey. *Journal of Special Education, 28,* 117–137.

Repp, A.C., & Karsh, K.G. (1990). A taxonomic approach to the nonaversive treatment of maladaptive behavior of persons with developmental disabilities. In A.C. Repp & N.N. Singh (Eds.), *Perspectives on the use of nonaversive and aversive interventions for persons with developmental disabilities* (pp. 331–347). Sycamore, IL: Sycamore Publishing.

Repp, A.C., Karsh, K.G., Munk, D., & Dahlquist, C.M. (1995). Hypothesis-based interventions: A theory of clinical decision making. In W. O'Donohue & L. Krasner (Eds.), *Theories of behavior therapy: Ex-*

ploring behavior change (pp. 585–608). Washington, DC: American Psychological Association.

Richters, J.E., Arnold, L.E., Jensen, P.S., Abikoff, H., Conners, C.K., Greenhill, L.L., Hechtman, L., Hinshaw, S.P., Pelham, W.E., & Swanson, J.M. (1995). NIMH collaborative multisite multimodal treatment study of children with ADHD: I. Background and rationale. *Journal of the American Academy of Child and Adolescent Psychiatry, 34,* 987–1000.

Roberts, M.A., Milich, R., & Loney, J. (1984). *Manual for the Structured Observation of Academic and Play Settings.* Iowa City: University of Iowa.

Rogeness, G.A., Javors, M.A., & Pliszka, S.R. (1992). Neurochemistry and child and adolescent psychiatry. *Journal of the American Academy of Child and Adolescent Psychiatry, 31,* 765–781.

Rosen, L.A., O'Leary, S.G., Joyce, S.A., Conway, G., & Pfiffner, L.J. (1984). The importance of prudent negative consequences for maintaining the appropriate behavior of hyperactive students. *Journal of Abnormal Child Psychology, 12,* 581–604.

Safer, D.J., & Allen, R.P. (1976). *Hyperactive children: Diagnosis and management.* Baltimore: University Park Press.

Safer, D.J., & Krager, J.M. (1988). A survey of medication treatment for hyperactive/inattentive students. *Journal of the American Medical Association, 260,* 2256–2258.

Safer, D.J., & Krager, J.M. (1994). The increased rate of stimulant treatment for hyperactive/inattentive students in secondary schools. *Pediatrics, 94,* 462–464.

Safer, D.J., Zito, J.M., & Fine, E.M. (1996). Increased methylphenidate usage for attention deficit disorder in the 1990s. *Pediatrics, 98,* 1084–1088.

Schaal, D.W., & Hackenberg, T. (1994). Toward a functional analysis of drug treatment for behavior problems of people with developmental disabilities. *American Journal on Mental Retardation, 99,* 123–140.

Schachar, R., & Tannock, R. (1993). Childhood hyperactivity and psycholinguistics: A review of extended treatment studies. *Journal of Child and Adolescent Psychopharmacology, 3,* 81–97.

Schachar, R., & Wachsmuth, R. (1990). Hyperactivity and parental psychopathology. *Journal of Child Psychology and Psychiatry and Applied Disciplines, 31,* 381–392.

Scotti, J.R., Evans, I.M., Meyer, L.H., & DiBenedetto, A. (1991). Individual repertoires as behavioral systems: Implications for program design and evaluation. In B. Remington (Ed.), *The challenge of severe mental handicap* (pp. 139–163). New York: John Wiley & Sons.

Scotti, J.R., Evans, I.M., Meyer, L.H., & Walker, P. (1991). A meta-analysis of intervention research with problem behavior: Treatment validity and standards of practice. *American Journal on Mental Retardation, 96,* 233–256.

Scotti, J.R., Kirk, K.S., Weigle, K.L., Cuddihy, K., Lumley, V., Magruda, A., & Rasheed, S. (1993, May). *Analog functional assessments and nonaversive interventions in special education classrooms: A comparison of brief versus extended assessments.* Poster presented at the 19th annual convention of the Association for Behavior Analysis, Chicago.

Scotti, J.R., McMorrow, M.J., & Trawitzki, A.L. (1993). Behavioral treatment of chronic psychiatric disorders: Publication trends and future directions. *Behavior Therapy, 24,* 527–550.

Scotti, J.R., Morris, T.L., McNeil, C.B., & Hawkins, R.P. (1996). DSM-IV and disorders of childhood and adolescence: Can structural criteria be functional? In W. Follette (Ed.), *The DSM-IV [Special issue]. Journal of Consulting and Clinical Psychology, 64,* 1177–1191.

Scotti, J.R., Mullen, K.B., & Hawkins, R.P. (1998). Child conduct and developmental disabilities: From theory to practice in the treatment of excess behaviors. In J.J. Plaud & G.H. Eifert (Eds.), *From behavior theory to behavior therapy* (pp. 172–202). Needham Heights, MA: Allyn & Bacon.

Scotti, J.R., Nangle, D.W., Vittimberga, G.L., Ellis, J.T., Hammel, D.L., Miyake, K., & Zarsadias, A. (1992, May). *Assessment of behavioral systems: I. Excess behaviors and functionally equivalent skills.* Paper presented at the 18th annual convention of the Association for Behavior Analysis, San Francisco.

Scotti, J.R., Schulman, D.E., & Hojnacki, R.M. (1994). Functional analysis and unsuccessful treatment of Tourette's syndrome in a man with profound mental retardation. *Behavior Therapy, 25,* 721–738.

Scotti, J.R., Ujcich, K.J., Weigle, K.L., Holland, C.M., & Kirk, K.S. (1996). Interventions with challenging behavior of persons with developmental disabilities: A review of current research practices. *Journal of The Association for Persons with Severe Handicaps, 21,* 123–134.

Sherrill, J.T., O'Leary, S.G., & Kendziora, K.T. (1993, November). *The effects of reprimand consistency on off-task behavior in the classroom.* Poster presented at the 27th annual meeting of the Association for Advancement of Behavior Therapy, Atlanta.

Silver, L.B. (1987). The "magic cure": A review of the current controversial approaches for treating learning disabilities. *Journal of Learning Disabilities, 20,* 498–512.

Skinner, B.F. (1953). *Science and human behavior.* New York: Free Press.

Spencer, T.J., Biederman, J., Wilens, T., Harding, M., O'Donnell, D., & Griffin, S. (1996). Pharmacology of ADHD across the lifecycle: A literature review. *Journal of the American Academy of Child and Adolescent Psychiatry, 35,* 409–432.

Steege, M.W., Wacker, D.P., Berg, W.K., Cigrand, K.K., & Cooper, L.J. (1989). The use of behavioral assessment to prescribe and evaluate treatments for severely handicapped children. *Journal of Applied Behavior Analysis, 22,* 23–33.

Strayhorn, J.M., & Weidman, C.S. (1989). Reduction of attention deficit and internalizing symptoms in preschoolers through parent–child interaction training. *Journal of the American Academy of Child and Adolescent Psychiatry, 28,* 888–896.

Strayhorn, J.M., & Weidman, C.S. (1991). Follow-up one year after parent–child interaction training: Effects on behavior of preschool children. *Journal of the American Academy of Child and Adolescent Psychiatry, 30,* 138–143.

Sturmey, P., Carlsen, A., Crisp, A.G., & Newton, J.T. (1988). A functional analysis of multiple aberrant responses: A refinement and extension of Iwata et al.'s (1982) methodology. *Journal of Mental Deficiency Research, 32,* 31–49.

Tannock, R., Schachar, R.J., Carr, R.P., & Logan, G.D. (1989). Dose-response effects of methylphenidate on academic performance and overt behavior in hyperactive children. *Pediatrics, 84,* 648–657.

Tawney, J., & Gast, D.L. (1984). *Single subject research in special education.* Columbus, OH: Charles E. Merrill.

Touchette, P.E., MacDonald, R.F., & Langer, S.N. (1985). A scatterplot for identifying stimulus control of problem behavior. *Journal of Applied Behavior Analysis, 18,* 343–351.

Trott, G.E., Friese, H.J., Menzel, M., & Nissen, G. (1992). Use of moclobemide in children with attention deficit hyperactivity disorder. *Psychopharmacology, 106*(Suppl.), 134–136.

Ulrich, S., Wacker, D., Derby, K.M., Asmus, J., & Berg, W. (1993, May). *Using brief functional analyses to identify different functions across settings.* Poster presented at the 19th annual conference of the Association for Behavior Analysis, Chicago.

Umbreit, J. (1995). Functional assessment and intervention in a regular classroom setting for the disruptive behavior of a student with attention deficit hyperactivity disorder. *Behavioral Disorders, 20,* 267–278.

Voeltz, L.M., & Evans, I.M. (1982). The assessment of behavioral interrelationships in child behavior therapy. *Behavioral Assessment, 4,* 131–165.

Vyse, S.A., & Rapport, M.D. (1989). The effects of methylphenidate on learning in children with ADHD: The stimulus equivalence paradigm. *Journal of Consulting and Clinical Psychology, 57,* 425–435.

Wacker, D., Northup, J., & Cooper, L. (1992). Behavioral assessment. In D.E. Greydanus & M.L. Wolraich (Eds.), *Behavioral pediatrics* (pp. 57–68). New York: Springer-Verlag.

Wahler, R.G., House, A.E., & Stambaugh, E.E. (1976). *Ecological assessment of child problem behavior.* New York: Pergamon.

Walker, C.J., & Clement, P.W. (1992). Treating inattentive, impulsive, hyperactive children with self-modeling and stress inoculation training. *Child and Family Behavior Therapy, 14,* 75–85.

Waschbusch, D.A., Kipp, H.L., & Pelham, W.E. (1998). Generalization of behavioral and psychostimulant treatment of attention-deficit/hyperactivity disorder (ADHD): Discussion and examples. *Behaviour Research and Therapy, 36,* 675–694.

Weiss, G., & Hechtman, L. (1986). *Hyperactive children grown up.* New York: Guilford Press.

Weiss, G., & Hechtman, L.T. (1993). *Hyperactive children grown up: ADHD in children, adolescents, and adults* (2nd ed.). New York: Guilford Press.

Whalen, C.K. (1989). Attention deficit and hyperactivity disorders. In T.H. Ollendick & M. Hersen (Eds.), *Handbook of child psychopathology* (2nd ed., pp. 131–169). New York: Plenum.

Whalen, C.K., & Henker, B. (1986). Cognitive behavior therapy for hyperactive children: What do we know? *Journal of Children in Contemporary Society, 19,* 123–141.

Whalen, C.K., Henker, B., Hinshaw, S.P., Heller, T., & Huber-Dressler, A. (1991). Messages of medication: Effects of actual versus informed medication status on hyperactive boys' expectancies and self-evaluation. *Journal of Consulting and Clinical Psychology, 59,* 602–606.

Wilens, T.E., & Biederman, J. (1992). The stimulants. *Psychiatric Clinics of North America, 15,* 191–222.

Willis, T.J., LaVigna, G.W., & Donnellan, A.M. (1987). *Behavior assessment guide.* Los Angeles: Institute for Applied Behavior Analysis.

Wolraich, M.L., Lindgren, S., Stromquist, A., Milich, R., Davis, C., & Watson, D. (1990). Stimulant medication use by primary care physicians in the treatment of attention deficit hyperactivity disorder. *Pediatrics, 86,* 95–101.

Zametkin, A.J., & Rapoport, J.L. (1987). Neurobiology of attention deficit disorder with hyperactivity: Where have we come in 50 years? *Journal of the American Academy of Child and Adolescent Psychiatry, 26,* 676–686.

Section II

MODELS FOR PRACTICE

Section I has provided the background principles for the variety of applications presented in the remainder of this book. We begin the presentation of applications with eight chapters that describe programmatic interventions with a range of populations. Chapter 5 presents the comprehensive biobehavioral treatment and rehabilitation model used by Liberman and Kopelowicz and their colleagues. Readers will find a useful combination of biological and behavioral factors being considered in the development and treatment of serious mental illness and likely will be struck by the high level of involvement of the individual who is the target of intervention in treatment and decision making that is evident in this model program.

Morris and Hawkins (Chapter 6) describe work with children who display behavioral excesses and deficits. Of critical importance in this chapter, which describes interventions for children on two vastly different ends of the continuum, is the application of behavioral interventions in the natural environment and the use of peers and family systems (even when these need to be "created") to both create and support behavior change. This work is followed by the description of Project DESTINY by Cheney and Barringer (Chapter 7) and their work with youth with serious emotional and behavior disorders. These authors describe a comprehensive, school-wide program for keeping children with emo-

tional and behavior disorders in school, with proper supports and interventions adapted to the individual. This theme is echoed by Meadows (Chapter 8) and her work to include students with learning and behavior problems in the general education classroom, presenting a meaningful collaboration between the public school and the university. Glick and Goldstein (Chapter 9) provide the natural extension to the preceding chapters, each of which has dealt with children with behavior disorders. An all-too-natural progression for some children with behavior problems is later conduct disorder and adult antisocial behavior. Glick and Goldstein present their program of Aggression Replacement Training as a means of intervening with these youth when they move into gangs and their aggression escalates to violence and criminal behavior.

Hingsburger and colleagues (Chapter 10) then move the reader in another direction for behavioral intervention by presenting their work in a sexuality clinic for individuals with developmental disabilities. This is a unique area of endeavor, and it is clear through every step of this program that the goal is full community access through a comprehensive program of community supports, advocacy, and clinical intervention. Berotti and Durand (Chapter 11) follow with their own work in the area of developmental disabilities—specifically, a comprehensive program for students with sensory impairments. In addition to extending Durand's functional communication training approach to this population, the chapter is notable for the detail with which the trials and tribulations—and eventual successes—of working with adaptive equipment are described. Close and Horner (Chapter 12) close this section with a unique look at architectural design and its role in positive behavioral support programs, from the perspective of both ensuring safety and intervention success and not creating community residences that appear deviant.

Chapter 5

Biobehavioral Treatment and Rehabilitation of People with Serious Mental Illness

Alex Kopelowicz & Robert Paul Liberman

Based on epidemiological studies, in a 1-year period there are 2 million people in the United States who experience severe and persistent mental illness (i.e., schizophrenic spectrum disorders), representing 1.1% of the population (Regier, Farmer, Lock, Keith, & Rae, 1993). There are more than 300,000 acute episodes of schizophrenia annually in the United States, and the economic cost of this disorder, in terms of treatment and lost income, is more than $30 billion per year (National Institute of Mental Health, 1995). The lifetime loss of income for a male who is diagnosed with schizophrenia late in adolescence has been calculated to be $1,027,000 (Wyatt & Clark, 1987). On any given day, an estimated 100,000 hospital beds are filled with people who are diagnosed with schizophrenia (Rupp & Keith, 1993; Talbott, Goldman, & Ross, 1987).

For the most part, the burden of care for individuals with serious and persisting mental illness falls on the public mental health system. Public mental health systems, however, generally have failed to incorporate the technological advances (e.g., clozapine, psychosocial rehabilitation) that have dramatically improved the treatment of individuals with serious mental illness (Talbott, 1988). These systems have failed

largely because they deliver fragmented—instead of coordinated, comprehensive, and continuous—care. For instance, psychiatrists often medicate individuals without communicating with the person who is providing psychosocial treatment or case management. Pharmacotherapy usually occurs without input from academic medical centers, which validate new drug technologies. This lack of input has resulted in systems that are unable to deliver these new modalities effectively.

The solution to the problem of lack of coordination among systems of care is clear: Develop public mental health systems that focus on providing coordinated, comprehensive care to people with serious mental illness utilizing ongoing assessments of behavioral, functional, and symptomatic states. One such program, the San Fernando Mental Health Center (SFMHC), is a community mental health center located in a suburb of Los Angeles with a predominantly (70%) Latino population. SFMHC provides ongoing treatment to 900 individuals with serious mental illness within a catchment area of approximately 250,000 people. The program is operated and funded directly by the Los Angeles County Department of Mental Health; supplemented financially with Medicaid and Medicare revenues;

and provided with educational, clinical, and research support by the University of California–Los Angeles (UCLA) Department of Psychiatry.

To address the needs of people with serious mental illness, SFMHC has adopted a biobehavioral approach—employing behavioral assessment, social learning principles, and skills training—to amplify the effects of pharmacotherapy. The program's aims include the following:

1. Early detection and treatment of psychotic symptoms
2. Collaboration in managing treatment between caregivers and the individuals receiving treatment
3. Family and social skills training (SST)
4. Teaching of coping skills

When provided concurrently, these four factors have been documented to improve the course and outcome of schizophrenia as measured by symptom recurrence, social functioning, and quality of life (Liberman, 1994). The remainder of this chapter focuses on the principles of biobehavioral treatment and rehabilitation and their applicability to the practices of SFMHC.

VULNERABILITY-STRESS-PROTECTIVE FACTORS MODEL

Schizophrenia can be viewed as a stress-related, neurobiological disorder resulting in disturbances in the form and the content of an individual's thought and perceptual processes, affect, and social and instrumental role behavior. The protean manifestations and variability of schizophrenia—as well as its pervasive disability that places a heavy burden on the individual, family, and society—require a multimodal, individualized, and comprehensive approach to treatment. The goals of treatment and rehabilitation are as follows:

1. Ameliorate positive (e.g., hallucinations) and negative (e.g., withdrawal) symptoms of the disorder.
2. Reduce or delay relapse of psychosis.
3. Strengthen the skills and coping capacities of the individual and caregivers, such as family members.

4. Remove or displace the bizarre and deviant behaviors that are intolerable for the family or the community.
5. Provide social services and community supports that enable the individual to function optimally, despite continuing symptoms and disabilities.

The types of interventions for treating and rehabilitating people with schizophrenia can be guided by a *multidimensional and interactive model* of the disorder that includes *stress, vulnerability,* and *protective factors* (Liberman, Wallace, Vaughn, Snyder, & Rust, 1980; Nuechterlein, 1987). According to this conceptual model, symptoms and their associated social and vocational disabilities are the result of stressors' (e.g., drug use, conflict in the home) impinging on a person's enduring psychobiological vulnerability. The exact nature of the vulnerability is unknown, but it is most likely caused by genetic, congenital, or neurodevelopmental influences and involves abnormalities in neurotransmitter systems. The noxious effects of stress superimposed on this vulnerability can be mediated by protective factors—either acting directly on the individual (e.g., antipsychotic medication, social competence) or on the individual's social environment (e.g., supportive or tolerant family members, responsive community treatment services).

The significance of the multifactorial vulnerability-stress-protective factors model of schizophrenia lies in the guidelines that it offers to clinicians. Medications can buffer the psychobiological vulnerability and underlying biochemical disturbance; training in social and independent living skills confers coping capacities and thereby strengthens the individual's and the caregivers' personal protection against stress and vulnerability; supportive services (e.g., case management, housing, social services entitlements, supported employment) compensate for the individual's residual symptoms and deficits in functioning. Orchestration of these modalities, within a matrix of an effective means of delivering interventions flexibly as individual needs require, can improve the course and outcome of the disorder as well as promote recovery in substantial numbers (Liberman & Mueser, 1989). A case example, which is interwoven throughout the technical aspects of this chapter, assists in demonstrating this process.

When Mr. Gomez first came to the mental health center with his mother, he was unwilling to talk much about his problems. He was a 21-year-old high school graduate who worked part time at the local market. He carried the diagnosis of schizoaffective disorder. He looked sad yet frightened when asked direct questions by the psychiatrist about his symptoms. He spoke quietly and hesitated often but said that his worst problem was that his breath could influence and even endanger people. The voices in his head, which he had heard for the past several years, told him that this would always be true. He was willing to undergo any treatment that would rid him of the torment that he was experiencing.

Mr. Gomez and his psychiatrist decided that an inpatient hospitalization would be necessary. The psychiatrist agreed to follow Mr. Gomez throughout his inpatient stay, maintaining the continuity of care needed for a successful rehabilitation outcome. Over the course of the next several years, Mr. Gomez and a team of biobehavioral rehabilitation practitioners paved a road to recovery that has led to an improved quality of life for Mr. Gomez. The steps on this road are illustrated in a series of vignettes interspersed throughout this chapter.

THE FIRST STEP IN THE BIOBEHAVIORAL TREATMENT PROGRAM: ENGAGEMENT AND RELATED BARRIERS

The successful engagement of an individual in a therapeutic relationship is the first step in the process of biobehavioral treatment and rehabilitation. The terminology used to refer to an individual who is receiving mental health services can affect the engagement process by coloring the relationship and expectations between the practitioner and the individual. Terms can vary depending on the site at which the individual is being treated. For example, the term *patient* may be suitable for inpatients in hospitals; *client* may be used in mental health centers; and *consumers* or *members* may be preferred in outpatient programs or vocational and residential environments. In this chapter, the term *individual* is used interchangeably with all of these terms.

The task for the clinician who is attempting to engage in treating an individual with serious mental illness is to build a *collaborative relationship* with individuals and their families (Corrigan, Liberman, & Engel, 1990; Meichenbaum & Turk, 1987; Minkoff, 1991; Weiden & Havens, 1994). A fruitful collaboration requires that both professionals and patients recognize each other's "agenda" and seek some common ground in developing a comprehensive treatment plan. The inpatient team members agreed that Mr. Gomez needed to be referred to a rehabilitation program to broaden his repertoire of coping skills. Mr. Gomez, however, did not want to lose his part-time morning job at the neighborhood market. Mr. Gomez and the team agreed on his enrolling in an evening rehabilitation program. Neither agenda would have been satisfied if the individual and the treatment team had not worked jointly to identify a mutually satisfying aftercare plan.

The process of engagement is contemporaneous with the setting of overall rehabilitation goals. Helping an individual define his or her desired life roles can be a vehicle for engaging and motivating the individual to participate in a lengthy rehabilitation process. Individuals who actively participate in goal setting are more likely to acknowledge their ownership of the goals, seek reinforcement from significant others when they work toward their goals, and customize or modify their goals as they proceed toward rehabilitation.

Increasingly, individuals with major mental disorders are reluctant to remain in a passive role with their physicians and other service providers. Activating the individual through immersion in a collaborative relationship with a responsible psychiatrist and rehabilitation team is more consistent with the consumer empowerment movement (Zinman, Budd, & Harp, 1987). This movement arose out of a dissatisfaction by many individuals under psychiatric care with the quality of care and respect provided by mental health practitioners to people with severe and persistent mental illness (Anthony, 1993; Deegan, 1992; Fisher, 1994; Unzicker, 1992). From this perspective, patients may be conceived as consumers who, like typical people seeking health care services, want services to address more than one component of their multifaceted lives. Some leaders of the consumer empowerment movement take an "antipsychiatry" position—maintaining that significant growth to fulfill their complex lives is attainable only through self-help, independent of mental health professionals (Chamberlin, 1984). Since the early 1990s, however, the mental health consumer movement has shifted from a radical antipsychiatry viewpoint to a more constructive consumer–professional partnership (Deegan, 1992).

Soon after discharge, Mr. Gomez began to express misgivings about taking medication "for the rest of [his] life." He said that he wished to continue in the rehabilitation program but not if he *had* to take medication. Although the staff were divided on this issue, Mr. Gomez was assured by his psychiatrist that whether he took his medication would have no bearing on his status in the program. However, in the psychiatrist's opinion, stopping the medication at this time would be unwise. Mr. Gomez was gratified that his psychiatrist was offering him a choice tailor-made to his needs, instead of a "take it or leave it" proposition. Mr. Gomez agreed to continue on the medication but hoped to lower his dosage to the least amount necessary to maintain health and promote recovery.

Barriers to the Consumer– Professional Relationship

Failure to educate and engage individuals and their natural caregivers (e.g., family members) in a long-term, collaborative, and informed therapeutic alliance may result in noncompliance with essential antipsychotic medication, psychosocial treatments, and supportive services (Morrison & Bellack, 1984; Van Putten, 1974).

Studies on medication administration have shown that more than three quarters of individuals do not take their medication as prescribed (Boczkowski, Zeichner, & DeSanto, 1985; Kane & Borenstein, 1985; Van Putten, Marder, & May, 1984). The rate of premature dropout from psychiatric rehabilitation programs has been estimated to range from 30% to 40% (Drake, Mueser, Clark, & Wallach, 1996; Falloon, Lindley, McDonald, Vaughn, & Liberman, 1977; Marzillier, Lambert, & Kellett, 1976; Sultan & Johnson, 1985). The importance of identifying the factors that undermine the collaborative relationship has been underscored by the finding from follow-up studies that delaying the initiation of proper treatment is associated with a poorer long-term prognosis in schizophrenia (Wyatt, 1991).

In Table 1, the most common barriers that lie in the path of a therapeutic partnership are divided into five domains (Corrigan et al., 1990). What is interesting is that each domain also reflects what might be an important resource for battling the impact of severe mental illness. The professional needs to be vigilant in looking for and avoiding these potential pitfalls when designing a plan for rehabilitation with an individual.

Treatment-Related Barriers

Many psychiatric and rehabilitative interventions have adverse effects that weaken an individual's resolve to adhere to a treatment plan. For example, individuals who experience dry mouth, akinesia (lack of movement), akathisia (restlessness), dysphoria (state of dissatisfaction, anxiety, and restlessness), or other side effects of antipsychotic medication have been found to deviate from their prescribed drug regimen (Amdur, 1979; Marder & May, 1986; Van Putten & Marder, 1987). Psychosocial treatments also may have noxious effects (Corrigan et al., 1990; Drake & Sederer, 1986). Prolonged and intensive rehabilitation may overstimulate individuals who are exhibiting positive symptoms, thereby exacerbating their psychosis. Another hazard for successful engagement of individuals in treatment can arise when individuals with high levels of negative symptoms are pushed prematurely into social interactions that

Table 1. Barriers to clinician–patient collaboration in treatment and measures to improve collaboration

Barrier	Measure to improve collaboration
Treatment techniques (e.g., side effects of antipsychotic medication)	Educate patient about side effects and their management. Teach patient to keep a diary for tracking side effects.
Patient characteristics (e.g., cognitive deficits)	Use cognitive remediation to improve memory and attention. Develop contingency contracts to promote adherence to medication.
Family characteristics (e.g., unrealistic expectations and emotional overinvolvement)	Encourage family participation in psychoeducation and behavioral family management.
Clinician–patient relationship (e.g., clinician's nihilism and brusque interactions)	Teach patient effective communication and assertive negotiation skills for meetings with psychiatrist. Consult with psychiatrist to improve use of social reinforcement and shaping.
Treatment delivery system (e.g., lack of coordination)	Use outreach case managers and continuous treatment teams to coordinate services. Improve quality of clinic decor and ambience.

exceed their ability or interest. The key to successful titration of treatment—whether pharmacological or psychosocial—is gradualness.

The negative effects of psychopharmacological and rehabilitative interventions can be diminished by titrating the treatment regimen to the comfort, needs, and desires of the individual who is receiving treatment. In terms of rehabilitation, reluctant individuals should be encouraged to attend the rehabilitation program under a diminished schedule. Expectations about participation also are lowered until individuals attain a level of comfort with the interventions. Attendance and participation goals then are increased slowly as the individual reports that he or she is comfortable with the program.

Mr. Gomez reported that he was becoming more agitated and hearing voices again after he began a demanding evening rehabilitation program for 3 hours per night, 5 nights per week. Mr. Gomez was encouraged to attend this partial hospital program only 3 nights per week. He was also permitted to sit unobtrusively in groups until he decided that he was ready to participate.

A second treatment-related factor that may undermine treatment collaboration is the complexity with which the intervention protocol is developed and presented to the individual. Many individuals are unable to understand polydrug protocols, complex rehabilitation schedules, and intricate behavioral contingencies. Problems in communication and comprehension may be exacerbated by the clinician's lexicon. Physicians learn more than 13,000 specialized words during their education and thus may use language that distances the medical practitioner from the public (Blackwell, 1973). If the clinician wants individuals to assume central roles in carrying out their treatment programs, then the program needs to be communicated in simple and straightforward language.

Patient-Related Barriers

A characteristic shared by many individuals with severe mental illness is cognitive disorganization—deficits in short-term memory and sustained attention. These deficits may hamper the ability of some individuals to understand fully and follow their treatment program. This difficulty can be overcome by using environmental prompts such as external, cognitive organizers. For example, light-emitting diodes placed in the cap of a medicine bottle can cue individuals when it is time to take medication (Azrin & Powell, 1969; *Med Tymer,* 1986). Environmental prompts for applying skills learned in psychosocial rehabilitation programs can be provided by third parties (e.g., family members, friends, case managers) by encouraging individuals to complete various independent living skills in their living environment.

Mr. Gomez was unable to understand his homework assignments in the psychosocial rehabilitation program because he was still mildly disorganized after his recent psychotic episode. He was given homework sheets that specified when, where, and with whom he was to practice his newly learned coping skills. He and his therapist made a chart of these coping skills, which Mr. Gomez posted on the kitchen wall of his apartment. Mr. Gomez's therapist telephoned him on the nights when he did not attend the program to remind him to practice these skills at home and gave him positive reinforcement as he reported his progress.

Individuals are unlikely to adhere to treatment programs if they have resigned themselves to fatalistic attitudes about the course of their illness: "Why participate in rehabilitation programs? Nothing will make a difference!" In recognizing the insidious effects of these nihilistic attitudes, some individuals and professionals have started to raise prospects for recovery from schizophrenia (Anthony, 1991, 1993; Kopelowicz & Liberman, 1994). Recovering individuals are those who grasp the stress-related, biomedical nature of their illness; use biopsychosocial treatments to minimize their symptoms, impairments, and disabilities; and work toward actualizing the positive potential of their lives. Professionals may facilitate recovery through integrated and coordinated medication, rehabilitation services, and cognitive remediation (Liberman & Green, 1992). Recovery may also be advanced by the support of peers who have traversed this path successfully (Zinman et al., 1987).

Family-Related Barriers

Although families are an essential resource and support for many individuals who participate in rehabilitation programs (Mueser & Gingerich, 1994), family members may inadvertently un-

dermine an individual's collaboration with the treatment team and participation in the rehabilitation program. Family barriers might arise from overinvolvement in the individual's life or, conversely, detachment and unconcern about the individual's treatment. Individuals often react to overconcern with symptom exacerbation, withdrawal, passivity, or resentment; individuals whose families are detached from them lack vital support from family members.

Clinicians can help family members cope with the burden of caring for an adult with severe mental illness by educating them about the nature and the course of the disorder and by teaching them behavioral strategies for coping and interacting with the family member with mental illness (Anderson, Reiss, & Hogarty, 1986; Falloon, Boyd, & McGill, 1984). *Psychoeducational family intervention* and *behavioral family management* help family members develop problem-solving skills, effective communication methods, and coping strategies that facilitate a working collaboration with their relative or close family member who is experiencing a severe mental illness to manage stress and meet mutual needs. These treatment modalities are discussed more fully later in this chapter.

Mr. Gomez was angry with his mother because she was calling him on the telephone before bedtime to determine whether he had taken his medication and had attended the rehabilitation program that night. Mr. Gomez threatened to quit the program if his mother did not stop pressuring him. Mr. Gomez and his mother were encouraged by the treatment team to utilize the communication skills being taught in behavioral family management to solve the problem. Mr. Gomez proposed calling his mother once per week to tell her about his progress in the program. She agreed, with the proviso that she would ask about his attendance only when she did not receive his weekly call.

Clinician-Related Barriers

Viewing patients and clinicians as *collaborators* is a significant departure from traditional descriptions of the patient's role in treatment (Frank & Gunderson, 1990). For example, proponents of psychodynamic treatments may view an individual's reluctance to pursue a particular treatment goal as *unconscious resistance* on the part of the individual (Alexander, 1963; Basch, 1980) rather than as a lack of collaboration between individual and clinician. Unfortunately, most training programs do not prepare clinicians for competencies required in the rehabilitation of people with severe and persistent mental illnesses (Johnson, 1990; Mirabi, Weinman, Magnero, & Goldsmith, 1978). As a result, clinicians may experience the burden of care that accompanies working with this population as overwhelming, frustrating, and unrewarding. This may lead clinicians to become angry with individuals who are under their care or, conversely, to maintain emotional distance from them while showing signs of burnout, which can significantly undermine collaborative relationships (Corrigan et al., 1994; Maslach & Jackson, 1984).

When Mr. Gomez initially expressed reluctance to attend the rehabilitation program, some members of the treatment team believed that he was trying to avoid the therapeutic expectations of their comprehensive day program. Comments about Mr. Gomez at the staff meeting included how he was "unmotivated," "uncooperative," and "negativistic." Fortunately, one of the staff members knew Mr. Gomez from the market where he worked and was able to help the treatment team formulate an alternative plan that allowed Mr. Gomez to attend the program in the evening and keep working at his job.

The long-term solution to this problem requires educating medical and other professional students about realistic expectations and potent tools for working with individuals with severe mental illness (Moore, Davis, & Mellon, 1985; Stratoudakis, 1990; Wohlford, 1990). This process ideally would begin during graduate education; however, strategies designed to help clinicians who already are in the mental health system are needed as well. For example, practitioners

who develop modest and incremental goals to monitor their patients' progress are less likely to become overwhelmed (Corrigan et al., 1990). This process can be facilitated by supportive supervision by which the supervisor models effective techniques and then reinforces the clinician's efforts to acquire an armamentarium to help individuals to progress toward their incremental goals.

Barriers in the Treatment Delivery System

The manner in which mental health services are delivered may impede the therapeutic process. For example, the conventional "medication call" in hospitals and residential centers, whereby patients are handed their pills in a patronizing manner, offers few opportunities for building positive attitudes toward pharmacotherapy, promoting self-management of medication, or educating individuals regarding the indications and side effects of psychoactive drugs. Similarly, having to wait long to see the therapist or psychiatrist in a mental health center often leads to poor adherence to subsequently prescribed treatments (Craig, Huffine, & Brooks, 1974). Even the unattractive, institutional appearance of many clinics may be aversive and demoralizing to patients and be a barrier to the continuation of treatment (Raynes & Warren, 1971).

Making clinic and mental health center schedules more convenient to individuals and improving the attractiveness of the physical surroundings can help overcome barriers to treatment engagement (Liberman & Davis, 1975). For example, realistic schedules can be created and monitored for compliance; these schedules could be designed to give practitioners enough time to address effectively the needs of the individuals who are under their care. Offering coffee or other refreshments at clinic visits can improve the quality of the treatment experience (Masnik, Olarte, & Rosen, 1981).

Mr. Gomez stopped attending the day treatment program at another facility because groups frequently started late and much of the audiovisual equipment was broken. His favorite aspect of the program that he now attends is the monthly Medication Clinic, which is organized as a social hour in a comfortably furnished room with music playing in the background and cookies served with coffee or tea. The psychiatrist rotates among the patients like a host at a party, observing the patients' behavior, questioning them and their relatives about symptoms and side effects, and noting the need for changes in drug prescriptions, when appropriate. These events also offer Mr. Gomez an excellent opportunity to practice his social skills.

Another set of barriers to efficient use of mental health services relates to patient characteristics, such as socioeconomic status, ethnicity, race, and gender. Despite the fact that ethnic minorities make up about one fourth of the U.S. population and are predicted to outnumber the Caucasian population by the year 2020, research on the use of outpatient mental health services has shown lower rates of utilization by minorities (Wallen, 1992). Financial and acculturation factors may impede access to services (Woodward, Dunnell, & Arons, 1992). A less studied but equally worrisome phenomenon is that although the gender ratio of individuals who are diagnosed with schizophrenia is 1:1, women are *underrepresented* in rehabilitation programs, supportive housing programs, and drug research protocols (Iacono & Beiser, 1992).

Increasingly, the ethnic, racial, and gender characteristics of individuals with severe mental illness are being incorporated into the treatment planning process. The *Diagnostic and Statistical Manual of Mental Disorders, Fourth Edition* (DSM-IV; American Psychiatric Association, 1994) includes an outline for making a cultural formulation, and it contains a glossary of culture-specific disorders. A growing number of municipalities, counties, and states are providing "culturally sensitive" services to a variety of minority groups (Betancourt & Lopez, 1993; O'Sullivan, Peterson, Cox, & Kirkeby, 1989; Rodriguez, Lessinger, & Guarnaccia, 1992; Rogler, Malgady, & Rodriguez, 1989; Tanaka-Matsumi & Higgenbotham, 1994). The National Institutes of Health (NIH; 1994) has issued guidelines encouraging clinical researchers to include minorities and women in treatment protocols. Perhaps the driving force behind this trend is the increasing awareness that providing culturally relevant treatment that is targeted toward increased gender, racial, and ethnic utilization may lead to improved mental health in the population (Hall, 1988; Nuñez-Lopez, 1992).

BIOPSYCHOSOCIAL ASSESSMENT OF CURRENT FUNCTIONAL STATUS

If engagement is the first step on the road to successful biobehavioral rehabilitation, then the assessment process is the road map for that journey. A thorough, carefully conducted assessment pinpoints the areas for rehabilitation and provides a baseline for monitoring its effects. Furthermore, assessment within the framework of biobehavioral rehabilitation with its emphasis on goals and functioning—rather than on illness and symptoms—fosters a collaborative relationship between individual and practitioner that greatly enhances the treatment process.

Of course, assessment is essential for any therapeutic interaction, and some might argue that the clinical sensitivity of an experienced mental health practitioner is all that is needed to conduct an adequate assessment. Indeed, only minimal sensitivity may be needed to detect certain problems (e.g., assaultiveness) that, if present, must be one of the targets of treatment. However, not only may a comprehensive assessment reveal a vast array of factors that subtly influence even the most obvious problems, but it also establishes both the baseline for monitoring the effects of treatment and the collaborative relationship that sustains it. This comprehensive assessment process is illustrated with a battery of integrated and coordinated assessment and treatment planning instruments, developed in 1996, labeled Client Assessment of Strengths, Interests and Goals (CASIG; Wallace, 1996).

Usefulness and Accuracy of Assessment

It is important to note that the value of any assessment depends on the relevance and accuracy of its results. Technically, *relevance* is a synonym for *usefulness* and *validity,* whereas *accu-*

racy is a synonym for *reliability* (Anastasi, 1986, 1993). Clearly, an invalid or unreliable assessment is worthless.

Usefulness

An assessment has validity when the theory on which it is based explains logically what it assesses and describes accurately how the results should be used. The more finely differentiated the theory and the more firmly it is supported by empirical data, the more likely that the relevant variables will be identified and assessed and correct decisions made based on the assessment results. As additional empirical information becomes available, the theory can be modified to incorporate new constructs and eliminate or modify others, and the assessment and decision-making processes can be adjusted similarly—an iterative diagnosis–treatment matching process (see, e.g., Repp, Karsh, Munk, & Dahlquist, 1995; Scotti, Mullen, & Hawkins, 1998).

Table 2 presents the broad goals for the outcomes of biobehavioral rehabilitation, along with the factors that may affect each outcome (and thus must be assessed). The goals are deliberately stated in a broad manner and include those that have been endorsed by various groups, government agencies, and private and public licensing bodies. The goals are to help the individual live in the least restrictive environment,

at the highest level of functioning, with the highest quality of life, and as free of symptoms as possible.

As an example, the four factors that affect an individual's *level of functioning* are shown in the right side of Table 2:

1. The individual's skills
2. The individual's symptoms and signs of mental disorder that can intrude on use of available skills
3. The individual's preferences, desires, and motivations
4. The degree of environmental support

An individual's marginal functioning may be explained by insufficiencies in any one or more of these factors. An individual may lack the requisite skills, be disinterested in functioning better, or live in an environment that neither elicits nor rewards a higher level of functioning. Assessing each of these factors allows the practitioner to determine the possible causes of an individual's marginal functioning and to plan rehabilitation services accordingly.

The factors that affect the remaining areas or domains of goals and outcomes of treatment are also outlined in Table 2. These represent the comprehensive range of domains that must be assessed in the life of an individual if the practi-

Table 2. Outcome goals of psychiatric rehabilitation and factors that affect functioning

Outcome goals	Factors that affect functioning
Highest level of functioning	Individual's skills
	Individual's symptoms
	Individual's preferences, desires, and motivations
	Environmental supports
Highest quality of life	Individual's social network
	Individual's goals, preferences, and desires
	Environmental circumstances
Least restrictive environment	Individual's symptoms
	Performance of unacceptable community behaviors
	Individual's goals, preferences, and desires
	Environmental requirements for acceptable living
As free from symptoms as possible	Prodromal symptoms and warning signs
	Compliance with medication regimen
	Medication side effects

tioner is to be guided in the effective planning of rehabilitation services.

Accuracy

Reliability is built into the assessment process through the consistency with which it is conducted. The more consistent the administration, scoring, and interpretation of the assessment, the more reliable it is. This consistency typically is measured across administrators, across time with the same patient (assuming that no changes have occurred in the interim), and across items used to measure the same construct. Generally, an objective format that elicits limited answers that are scored with a simple categorical system provides a reliable assessment, albeit at the cost of a "rich mine" of raw data. It should be emphasized, however, that regardless of the "richness" of the "mine," inconsistent scoring and interpretation yields inaccurate and useless results.

Client Assessment of Skills, Interests and Goals

CASIG is a set of assessments and forms that help practitioners plan, document, and evaluate biobehavioral rehabilitation. CASIG is based on the model of biobehavioral rehabilitation outcomes and assessment areas presented previously, with the additional assumption that the plan for services must integrate the goals, needs, and constraints of all of the relevant stakeholders: the individual who is getting treatment and his or her significant others, individuals who are in the living environment, and the payor(s).

Master Assessment

The foundation of CASIG is the Master Assessment (MA). The MA assesses performance of functional living skills in 10 areas, subjective quality of life in 11 areas, presence of 5 symptoms and 20 medication side effects, compliance with medication, and performance of 10 unacceptable community behaviors (e.g., assault, alcohol or other drug abuse). The assessment information is collected from the individual during a 60- to 90-minute interview; corroborating information is collected from the individual's significant others and from treatment personnel who know the individual well. In addition, the MA elicits an individual's preferences to change his or her behavior in each of these areas.

Regardless of the area being assessed or the source of the assessment information, the items on the MA all have been designed to achieve several objectives:

1. Reliable administration by any of the paraprofessional and professional staff who typically provide services for individuals
2. Easy incorporation into diverse staffing patterns and clinical responsibilities
3. Inclusion of multiple sources of information so that agreements and disagreements among them can be used to better plan services
4. Bridging of the many facilities in which individuals are served
5. Repeated administration to monitor the progress of individual patient programs and, in the aggregate, monitor the effectiveness and changing characteristics of programs

The assessment results are summarized and then interpreted by comparing them with norms developed from other individuals and with the requirements for successful functioning in various environments. These comparisons, combined with the expectations of the stakeholders, provide the base for treatment planning by the practitioner.

During his CASIG interview, Mr. Gomez was asked about his money management skills. At first, he said that he received a paycheck twice per month and handled the rent and his food purchases well. On further probing, he admitted that frequently he had to borrow money from his mother because of bad budgeting. Although his answers to the scripted CASIG questions may not have pinpointed the problem, the open-ended characteristic of the CASIG interview allowed Mr. Gomez to acknowledge how difficult it was to budget, identify better money management as one of his goals, and plan the appropriate intervention with his caseworker.

Short- and Long-Term Goals Are Keyed to the Phase of Illness

To guard against deviating from the rehabilitation pathway, both the engagement and the assessment processes emphasize the importance of focusing on the rehabilitation goals endorsed and validated by the individual. However, empowering the individual as a full and equal partner in the treatment and rehabilitation process may not always be easy. Negative symptoms, disabilities, intrusive hallucinations, institutionalization, and cognitive dysfunction may impede the individual's ability to participate actively and helpfully in this crucial endeavor. The setting and resetting of short- and long-term goals provide the road markers by which the clinician and the individual can judge whether they are traveling in the right direction.

The clinician and the individual are guided by the continuous interaction of the individual's overall rehabilitation goals with the current stage of the disorder. During the acute, florid stage of the illness, the task for the clinician may be to assist the individual to move from grandiose and unrealistic fantasies to articulating the more proximal and immediate, realistic changes and steps that must be accomplished before the long-term goals can be reached. As the individual's symptoms stabilize and, ideally, ameliorate, the focus shifts to helping the individual define his or her goals in terms of occupational, student, friendship, familial, and residential roles. Still another shift occurs during the late rehabilitation and recovery phase when individuals begin to look for goals that transcend their status as patients *qua* patients. In this phase, the goal is to develop and nurture the *wellness factors* (e.g., hope, courage, self-esteem) that enable individuals not only to manage but sometimes also to overcome the illness.

Logistically, an individual's preferences, desires, and motivations should be operationalized in behavioral terms and divided into long-term and short-term goals. Long-term goals are cast in monthly to yearly time lines and should correlate with overall rehabilitation goals, serving as vehicles for achieving progress toward functional life roles. Long-term goals should be comprehensive in subserving progress in all relevant domains of life functioning (e.g., social/interpersonal, financial, recreational, medical/psychiatric, activities of daily living/independent living skills, vocational/educational, housing/residential). To facilitate accomplishment, an individual should prioritize his or her goals and, when possible, have the goals endorsed by the family, caregivers, and responsible clinicians.

Mr. Gomez found it difficult to formulate long-term goals. He asked, "How can I be certain that I won't end up back in the hospital?" His psychiatrist helped him realize that the premise of that question itself leads to the identification of a long-term goal— namely, to stay out of the hospital. By reworking his fears of failure into desires for success, Mr. Gomez was able to identify several psychosocial areas that he could target for improvement. These included his desire for more friends, his wish for a better relationship with his mother, and his preference for *managing* a convenience store rather than cleaning it. Several sessions were spent assisting Mr. Gomez's efforts to operationalize these goals. He was able to break down the goals into specific behavioral tasks that could be accomplished gradually, given sufficient persistence.

For example, Mr. Gomez expressed the vocational goal of managing a market like the one at which he worked. He noted that the current manager was once the assistant manager and before that, held the job that he— Mr. Gomez—now holds. This insight helped Mr. Gomez recognize the need to "work up the ladder." He identified his short-term goal as asking his supervisor for weekly evaluations of his job performance so as to increase his chances for a promotion. He also acknowledged, however, his difficulty in maintaining conversations with people. He enrolled in a class offered at the rehabilitation program that enabled him to develop basic conversational skills, including how to start, continue, and end a conversation. Utilizing these newly learned skills, Mr. Gomez was able to ask his supervisor for the performance feedback that he wanted and thank him when the supervisor agreed to provide it.

Short-term goals should be cast in daily, weekly, or monthly time lines and should articulate with long-term goals as steppingstones or subgoals. Short-term goals also must be prioritized and endorsed by all parties participating in the rehabilitation. Table 3 illustrates how the biobehavioral treatment and rehabilitation interventions for Mr. Gomez were keyed to the attainment of short- and long-term goals.

FITTING TREATMENT AND REHABILITATION INTERVENTIONS INTO THE GOALS

It is important to move from the identification of symptoms and functional deficits and formulation of positive goals to the delivery of the appropriate biobehavioral treatment modalities. Although setting specific and concrete interpersonal goals is perhaps the most challenging step in an individual's rehabilitation, the failure to reinforce these goals with consistent yet modest accomplishments may lead to discouragement, frustration, and, ultimately, treatment discontinuation. The task for the clinician who is choosing and using the needed interventions is to encourage individuals to reach just beyond their grasp and to facilitate the success of their ef-

forts. The following sections describe such prototypical and essential rehabilitation modalities.

Combining Psychopharmacological and Behavioral Treatments

It has become increasingly clear that the effective treatment of schizophrenia requires individualized pharmacological and psychosocial therapies that are embedded in a comprehensive matrix of rehabilitative services (Vaccaro, Liberman, Friedlob, & Dempsay, 1993). The psychosocial treatments of choice for schizophrenia and other chronic and disabling psychoses are *behavioral* in orientation. These include token economy (Glynn & Mueser, 1992), SST (Liberman et al., 1986), case management (Baker & Intagliata, 1992), vocational rehabilitation (Bond, 1992), and behavioral family therapy (Falloon, 1988).

Optimal control and stabilization of psychotic symptoms is the highest priority in the biobehavioral treatment of people who are experiencing schizophrenia. The treatment of acute and florid psychotic symptoms requires prompt intervention with judicious types and dosages of antipsychotic drugs. This is a prerequisite for psychosocial and behavioral treatments because effective pharmacotherapy removes or ameliorates symptoms (particularly positive symptoms, such as hallucinations and delusions) and improves cognitive functioning, thereby making individuals more responsive to learning from

Table 3. Monitoring progress toward goals

Long-term goals	Short-term goals	Interventions
Vocational		
Manage a market	Ask supervisor for weekly feedback on performance	Conversational skills module
Social		
Have more friends	Ask co-worker to go for a cup of coffee	Successful living group
Psychiatric		
Stay out of hospital	Tell psychiatrist about desire to go off medications because of side effects	Medication and symptom management modules
Family		
Improve relationship with mother	Tell mother that he needs his space	Behavioral family management

their environments (Liberman, Corrigan, & Schade, 1989). In addition, follow-up studies have documented that delaying the initiation of pharmacotherapy is associated with a poorer long-term prognosis in schizophrenia (Wyatt, 1991). Although a substantial minority of people with schizophrenia have proved refractory to antipsychotic drugs alone, many show improvements in their psychotic symptoms when focused, intensive behavior therapy is added to their medication regimens (Glynn & Mueser, 1992; Kuehnel, Liberman, Marshall, & Bowen, 1992; Liberman et al., 1994; Tarrier, Beckett, & Harwood, 1993).

It is becoming increasingly apparent, however, that typical neuroleptics (unlike clozapine and the newer, atypical drugs, such as risperidone) appear to have significant cognitive and behavioral toxicities. At high dosages, these medications can produce marked restlessness, apathy, anhedonia, dysphoria, and Parkinsonism (Van Putten, Marder, & Mintz, 1990). These side effects can *worsen* an individual's ability to attend to a task and have been shown to impair vocational rehabilitation (Hogarty, McEvoy, & Munetz, 1988; Mintz, Mintz, & Phipps, 1992). Researchers have found that neuroleptic medications often have a "therapeutic window"; dosages below or above this window cause an increase in symptoms and a reduced benefit-to-risk ratio (Van Putten, Marder, & Mintz, 1992). This has led to an emphasis on dosage reduction with biobehavioral titration (Van Putten et al., 1993).

Improving Pharmacotherapy with Behavioral Assessment

With pharmacotherapy for psychotic symptoms as a central and priority element in the treatment and rehabilitation of people with schizophrenia and related severe mental illness, the effectiveness of drug treatment depends on the clinician's ability to elicit, rate, and monitor symptoms, leading to appropriate adjustments (or maintenance) of treatment (e.g., medications, crisis services, frequency of visits). Several instruments have been developed to facilitate the detection and monitoring of psychiatric symptoms. The Brief Psychiatric Rating Scale (BPRS; Overall & Gorham, 1988), originally designed for inpatients with an emphasis on the positive symptoms of psychotic disorders (e.g., delusions, hallucinations), has been expanded to 24 items with a companion manual designed to extend its use to outpatients with serious mental disorders (Lukoff, Liberman, & Nuechterlein, 1986; Lukoff, Ventura, Nuechterlein, & Liberman, 1992). The manual provides guidelines for a semistructured interview containing operational definitions for anchor points in each symptom category.

The expanded BPRS assesses many nonpsychotic symptoms that have been found to increase prior to a full-blown relapse (i.e., the prodromal phase), such as anxiety, tension, depression, and emotional withdrawal. Effective treatment with appropriate and judicious use of medication has been demonstrated by titrating dosages against repeated measures of these symptomatic and behavioral benchmarks (Lukoff et al., 1992). The BPRS has been found to be a highly reliable instrument for behavioral assessment when raters underwent a training and quality assurance program (Ventura, Green, Shaner, & Liberman, 1993).

The level or severity of symptoms elicited by the BPRS can be graphed so that changes in baseline levels can be detected and addressed. The graph also serves the dual function of educating the individual about the stress-related nature of the disorder and the effectiveness of medication; for example, symptoms will worsen if antipsychotic medication is discontinued. Finally, mutual monitoring can strengthen the therapeutic alliance between the individual and the clinician.

It is also imperative that clinicians measure an individual's psychosocial functioning on a particular regimen using various informants (e.g., relatives, caregivers, employers) and sources of evaluation for decision making regarding changes in type and dosage of medication. Functional assessment requires that the individual, family, and treaters regularly discuss the individual's social and vocational functioning with the medicating psychiatrist. This approach can result in optimal neuroleptic dosages that maximize functioning and minimize side effects. One should be aware that the individual may continue to experience mild psychotic symptoms while receiving lower dosages of medication and that the complete eradication of these symptoms—at the cost of producing disabling side effects—should *not* be the only goal of treatment, particularly if the symptoms do not substantially intrude on daily functioning.

Social Skills Training

Even with appropriate medication management, yearly relapse rates for people with schizophrenia often are as high as 40%. In addition, many individuals continue to exhibit the "negative" symptoms of schizophrenia (Carpenter, Heinrichs, & Wagman, 1988), which do not respond to neuroleptic medications as well as do the classic "positive" symptoms (Kane & Meyerhoff, 1989). Although various definitions exist, negative symptoms generally include social withdrawal, flat affect, alogia (e.g., poverty of speech), apathy, and anhedonia. In addition, neuroleptics do not improve social skills, which are prerequisites for successful adaptation in the community.

Social skills deficits are assumed to reflect the combined influences of symptoms' intruding on skills, inadequate learning history before the onset of the illness, lack of environmental stimulation, and the loss of skills as a result of prolonged disuse (Liberman, DeRisi, & Mueser, 1989). Thus, an essential component of biobehavioral rehabilitation is SST (Anthony & Nemec, 1984; Liberman, Falloon, & Wallace, 1984; Liberman, King, DeRisi, & McCann, 1975; Liberman et al., 1986). SST is a psychosocial intervention specifically designed to meet the needs of individuals who are socially dysfunctional. SST represents a structured application of behavioral learning principles aimed at helping individuals build a repertoire of skills that improve their ability to function adequately in the community.

With the current ascendance of biological psychiatry, it has been argued that people with schizophrenia cannot learn skills because of their brain disorder, as exemplified by abnormally large cerebral ventricles or a metabolically inactive prefrontal cortex. A large body of research literature, however, supports the effectiveness of structured forms of active-directive training for a wide range of behaviors and skills that are lacking in most individuals with a schizophrenic disorder (Brophy, 1986; Kuehnel & Flanagan, 1984; Liberman, Massel, Mosk, & Wong, 1985; Matarazzo, 1978). In active-directive teaching, trainer and individual together participate in setting precise goals, followed by instructions, modeling with discriminative cuing, behavior rehearsal with prompting and shaping, performance feedback, and generalization and maintenance of skills. (See Liberman, 1988, and Liberman, DeRisi, et al., 1989, for a fuller description of these techniques.)

One concern raised by skeptics about the value of skills training for these individuals is the ability to generalize from the learned material. Despite that people with schizophrenia have serious cognitive problems in information processing and memory (Nuechterlein & Dawson, 1984), two meta-analyses of more than 35 studies of SST with people with schizophrenia found significant effect-sizes on discharge rates from hospitals; relapse rates; acquisition, durability, and generalization of skills; and social adjustment (Benton & Schroeder, 1990; Corrigan, 1991).

Modules for Training Social and Independent Living Skills

Unfortunately, techniques for training social skills are not learned easily by professionals. At least 3–6 months of a training apprenticeship is needed to prepare a psychologist, nurse, social worker, or psychiatrist to use these skills training methods confidently and competently. To overcome this obstacle to widespread dissemination, a step-by-step program of training social and independent living skills was designed to be used more easily by a wider array of mental health professionals and paraprofessionals (Wallace, Boone, Donahoe, & Foy, 1985). Each program, or *module,* includes a *trainer's manual* with step-by-step instructions, a *patient's workbook* with exercises and homework assignments, and a *videocassette* to be shown to the individuals, demonstrating the skills to be learned. Several modules are available: *Medication Management* (including the use of depot neuroleptics), *Recreation for Leisure, Symptom Management, Job Finding, Basic Conversational Skills, Social*

Problem-Solving, Community Re-Entry, Street Smarts, and *Grooming and Self-Care.* Together, the modules form a comprehensive rehabilitation program, but they also can be used selectively to fit the specific needs, interests, and resources of any environment or existing program.

The techniques used to teach the constituent skills of each module include all of the behavioral learning principles known to help people with schizophrenia overcome their learning disabilities: behavior rehearsal, coaching, shaping and fading, modeling, and positive reinforcement. Each module is divided into separate

skill areas that have specific educational objectives. The individuals proceed through each skill area utilizing the eight learning activities outlined in Table 4.

A structured, video-assisted, educational curriculum for teaching medication self-management skills has been validated in controlled clinical trials and field tests (Eckman, Liberman, Phipps, & Blair, 1990; Eckman et al., 1992; Wallace, Liberman, MacKain, Blackwell, & Eckman, 1992). The *Medication Management* module has five skill areas. The first covers how to obtain information about antipsychotic med-

Table 4. Learning activities for each skill area of each module

Learning activity	Tasks for trainer	Purpose
Introduction to skill area	Involve participants in discussion of the skills that will be taught and the benefits of learning them.	To highlight the values and advantages of the training, offsetting the lack of motivation frequently encountered by individuals with schizophrenia
Videotape with questions and answers	Show participants a videotaped demonstration of the skills, and ask questions to be sure that the material is understood and assimilated.	To compensate for cognitive disorganization and psychopathology
Role play	Help participants practice the skills through role plays and coaching.	To compensate for cognitive disorganization and psychopathology
Resource management	Teach participants to identify the resources needed to perform the skills and methods of obtaining these resources.	To help individuals extend their skills into a broader, more flexible problem-solving strategy
Outcome problem solving	Teach participants to solve problems and barriers that might occur when the skills are used in new situations.	To help individuals extend their skills into a broader, more flexible problem-solving strategy
In vivo exercises	Supervise and encourage participants as they perform the skills in new situations with coaching.	To generalize targeted skills into the individual's natural, social environments
Homework assignments	Encourage participants to perform the skills independently in new situations and give reinforcement and feedback for approximations to successful generalization.	To generalize targeted skills into the individual's natural, social environments
Booster sessions	Provide participants with "refresher" training on an as-needed basis.	To maintain skills

ication; the second focuses on learning how to self-administer and self-evaluate the medication correctly; the third emphasizes identifying the side effects of the medication and distinguishing between benign and serious side effects; the fourth provides information to individuals on how to negotiate medication issues with health care providers; and the fifth emphasizes the value and benefits of using long-acting depot neuroleptics.

Breaking this down further, each skill area provides instructions for the trainer to teach specific target behaviors. For example, in the "Negotiating Medication Issues" skill area, there are several requisite behaviors to teach: greeting the health care provider pleasantly; learning to describe specific problems; telling the length of side effect occurrence along with extent of discomfort; requesting action specifically with repetition and clarification, if necessary; asking about the expected time for effect; and thanking the psychiatrist for assistance while using good eye contact, good posture, and clear, audible speech. This module has been demonstrated to help practitioners teach individuals with cognitive impairments how to become informed and reliable consumers of medication (Eckman et al., 1992).

In the *Symptom Management* module, individuals learn how to identify the warning signs of relapse, how to intervene early to prevent relapse once these signs appear, how to cope with the persistent psychotic symptoms that continue despite medications, and how to avoid alcohol and other drugs of abuse. Each skill area can be divided further into target behaviors. In the "Warning Signs" skill area, individuals learn how to discuss warning signs with the doctor and their relatives so that there is agreement on the symptoms that predict relapse (e.g., insomnia, irritability, social withdrawal, ideas of reference). Individuals also are taught to keep a checklist of warning signs to monitor themselves over time. This is designed to help individuals understand the benefits of early intervention and realize when to request help.

These modules were designed to compensate for the cognitive and symptomatic difficulty with learning that is experienced regularly by many individuals with schizophrenia. In one controlled study, 80 individuals with schizophrenia who were receiving constant maintenance neuroleptic therapy were assigned randomly to supportive group therapy or to structured, modularized skills training. The skills training comprised training in medication and symptom self-management using the modules described previously. Individuals in group therapy engaged in an insight-oriented and supportive group process that included education about schizophrenia as an illness and the importance of medication but did not employ behavioral learning techniques. Both treatment conditions involved twice-weekly, 90-minute sessions over the course of 6 months. After 6 months, the individuals who received the skills training program made significant gains in each of the areas taught, whereas those in group therapy did not. These skills, for the most part, were retained 1 year after training was completed (Eckman et al., 1992). Although the data comparing groups for psychopathology were inconclusive, nearly all of the individuals who received skills training systematically and regularly monitored their warning signs throughout the 6-month training period, indicating an increase in the collaborative relationship with the prescribing clinician. Moreover, the individuals who received skills training showed significantly improved social adjustment 2 years after they entered the study (Marder et al., 1996).

Mr. Gomez was encouraged to enroll in the *Medication Management* module because of his history of stopping his medication abruptly. In the group, he said that he discontinued taking his medication because of the inner restlessness that it caused, which disrupted his ability to function on the job. He was surprised to learn that this side effect had a name, *akathisia,* and that it could respond to a variety of treatment strategies.

The modular training taught him how to speak effectively with his psychiatrist about this side effect. When approached by Mr. Gomez, the psychiatrist agreed to decrease the dosage of the antipsychotic medication and to start propranolol, a medication that frequently is helpful to people with akathisia. Mr. Gomez agreed to monitor his symptoms and side effects using the Self-Assessment Rating Sheet located in the Patient Workbook. By keeping a daily log of his symptoms and side effects, Mr. Gomez helped his psychiatrist titrate the medications appropriately.

Behavioral Family Management

Skills training helps the individual and the family or the significant other caregivers become responsible consumers of mental health services, as well as active advocates for their needs in the realm of community support services. Moreover, skills training can equip individuals and their caregivers with the capacity to cope with ambient biopsychosocial stressors (e.g., drugs of abuse, family stress and burden, major life events) to forestall the recurrence of the acute phase of schizophrenia. These findings led to the development of training techniques and educational programs to teach individuals and their families about schizophrenia and its management.

Behavioral family management is most associated with behavioral skills training (Falloon & Liberman, 1983). Training occurs in five stages, with considerable recycling of each stage throughout the therapy. These stages are as follows:

1. Behavioral assessment
2. Education about schizophrenia and its care
3. Communication skills training
4. Problem solving
5. Special problems

The clinical efficacy of this model was systematically evaluated in Los Angeles at the Clinical Research Center for Schizophrenia and Psychiatric Rehabilitation (Falloon et al., 1985; Randolph et al., 1994).

Individuals with schizophrenia who were discharged from psychiatric facilities to stressful home environments were assigned randomly to either 9 months of home-based behavioral family management or equally intensive individual therapy. After 9 months and at the 2-year follow-up, individuals who received the family treatment had fewer hospitalizations, spent less time in the hospital, experienced fewer major exacerbations in psychotic symptoms, and required fewer emergency crisis sessions than did those who received individual therapy. Individuals who received the family intervention also improved more in their social and vocational adjustment and were prescribed—by psychiatrists who were "blind to their treatment condition"—*lower* dosages of neuroleptics to control their symptoms than their compatriots who received individual supportive therapy (Falloon et al., 1985).

Practical programs of skills development for family management of schizophrenia have been replicated with similar results in London (Leff, Kuipers, Berkowitz, Eberlein-Vries, & Sturgeon, 1982), Pittsburgh (Hogarty et al., 1986), Manchester (Tarrier, Barrowclough, & Vaughn, 1988), and New York (MacFarlane, Stastny, & Deakins, 1992). At the West Los Angeles Veterans Affairs Medical Center, behavioral family management was added to customary antipsychotic medication and clinic care. The family management group had a 5% relapse rate after one year, whereas the customary care group had a 30% rate (Randolph et al., 1994).

Mr. Gomez and his mother were in their sixth week of behavioral family management when Mr. Gomez stated that he needed more "space" in their relationship. Although he had previously succeeded in decreasing her telephone calls to "check up on him," he still maintained that the real problem was that she did not trust him. Mrs. Gomez acknowledged his concern but believed that her fears were justified in light of his frequent noncompliance with his medications and subsequent rehospitalizations. Mr. Gomez and his mother were given a chance to reflect on the problem and to contribute to its clarity and specificity. The therapist then asked both of them to generate alternatives for solving the problem. Mrs. Gomez said that she would like to "drop by" Mr. Gomez's apartment weekly to see whether he was okay. Mr. Gomez countered that he would like to invite his mother over for dinner once per month or so because he enjoys her company and would like her to see how well he is doing. Several other alternatives were presented before they evaluated each one and chose a solution.

Personal Effectiveness for Successful Living Group

The Personal Effectiveness for Successful Living approach to equipping individuals with self-advocacy skills was started in 1972 at the Oxnard (CA) Community Mental Health Center and the West Los Angeles Veterans Affairs Medical Center (Hierholzer & Liberman, 1986). In this approach, clinicians use advanced SST principles to teach individuals how to identify and resolve community-based situations, thereby making them somewhat more independent of the mental health system, which, in effect, allows them to act as their own case managers. The foundation of this modality is to utilize a problem-solving approach (Liberman, DeRisi, & Mueser, 1989). People with schizophrenia have been able to learn this method and subsequently apply it competently to meet life difficulties (Liberman et al., 1986; Wallace & Liberman, 1985).

Problem solving in this manner may not be representative of how people deal with most real-life situations (Bellack, Morrison, & Mueser, 1989), but it does afford individuals without the necessary cognitive resources with a method to provide for their biopsychosocial needs. By combining the group process with a problem-solving technique, the group engenders a safe "testing ground" in which members can work through difficulties that they are experiencing in their community adaptation.

Mr. Gomez joined the Personal Effectiveness for Successful Living group to maintain and build on the skills that he learned in the modular groups and to increase his social contacts. One of the group members told Mr. Gomez about a job opening as an assistant manager at a convenience store. Mr. Gomez identified the steps needed to secure that position. In that same session, he and another group member role-played the telephone conversation in which he would engage to get an appointment for an interview. He received constructive feedback from the group members regarding his tone of voice and the appropriate questions to ask.

In the next session, Mr. Gomez announced that he had made the telephone call, scheduling the interview for the following week. He practiced his interview skills with a group member who had experience in job recruitment. Again, the group provided kudos for his eye contact, body language, and attentiveness. The next week, Mr. Gomez was very proud to announce that he had been hired for the position and would start orientation in 3 weeks. He used the 3 weeks to polish his communication skills in the safe environment of the group; members portrayed employees, supervisors, and customers of the store.

COMPREHENSIVE AND COORDINATED SERVICES FOR PEOPLE WITH SERIOUS AND PERSISTENT MENTAL ILLNESS

The empirically validated biobehavioral treatments outlined in this chapter are most efficacious when delivered in a continuous, comprehensive, and well-coordinated manner through a service delivery system (Test, 1992). The cornerstone of this system is the case manager (Baker & Intagliata, 1992; Intagliata, 1982). Soon after the onset of the deinstitutionalization movement, many clinicians realized that to ensure continuity of care for people with severe and persistent mental illness in a system that is complex, fragmented, and frequently inaccessible would require professionals who were trained to navigate the murky waters of social services (Intagliata, 1978). That successful service delivery models with a case management framework have increased the community tenure of previously institutionalized individuals has been empirically validated (Stein & Test, 1978) and replicated in a variety of environments (Test, 1992).

Effective case management can be the vehicle for integrating biopsychosocial treatment and rehabilitation services, as shown in Figure 1. Most individuals with schizophrenia, as part of the nature of their enduring symptomatology, do not readily travel for medical and psychiatric appointments, and they do not eagerly embrace the social contact that is offered by therapeutic services. Instead, it often is necessary to deliver services through a mobile, outreach form of clinical case management.

Although there is little consensus on the role of the case manager (Bachrach, 1989; Kanter, 1989), a case manager in a biobehavioral rehabilitation environment has several specific tasks to perform. These include the following:

1. Assisting individuals to build social networks
2. Facilitating housing and employment
3. Helping individuals interact with the various service organizations to meet ongoing needs
4. Teaching individuals the skills that they require for illness self-management
5. Monitoring the clinical progress of the individuals

6. Undertaking timely clinical interventions when necessary

Each of these tasks requires specific competencies. By acting as the fixed point of responsibility within a continuum of care, case managers have influenced individuals' outcomes toward improved vocational functioning, less social isolation, and more independent living (Goering, Wasylenki, Farkas, Lancee, & Ballantyne, 1988).

After 9 months of working as the assistant manager of the convenience store, Mr. Gomez reported to his case manager that he had received a notice from the Department of Social Services that his Supplemental Security Income (SSI) check was being withheld because he had successfully rejoined the work force. Sensing the anxiety in his voice, the case manager attempted to reassure Mr. Gomez that there were steps that they could take to ease his transition to complete independence. The case manager

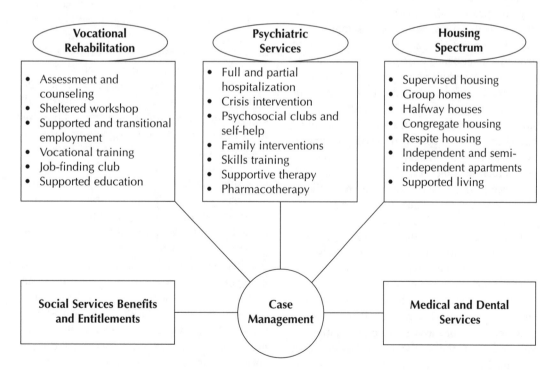

Figure 1. Comprehensive and coordinated services for individuals with serious mental illness.

helped Mr. Gomez write a Plan for Achieving Self Support (PASS), a program established by the Department of Social Services to facilitate this transition process.

The case manager explained how the PASS program was designed to allow Mr. Gomez to set aside income that he earned from his employment for rehabilitative purposes (e.g., tuition for vocational training, putting a security deposit on an apartment). This income would not count against his SSI benefits; thus, he could continue to receive his full SSI check for the life of the PASS. Mr. Gomez decided to write the PASS targeting the purchase of a car. He described in the PASS how a car would allow him to venture beyond his neighborhood, increasing his social functioning and, possibly, providing greater opportunities for job advancement.

MONITORING THE QUALITY OF INTERVENTIONS AND CLINICAL PROGRESS

Biobehavioral assessment and intervention is an ongoing process akin to the psychiatrist who titrates medications based on an individual's fluctuating need. In fact, the effectiveness of drug treatment depends on the clinician's ability to elicit, rate, and monitor symptoms, leading to appropriate adjustments (or maintenance) of treatment (e.g., medications, crisis services, skills training). Instruments such as the BPRS have been utilized by a wide variety of practitioners as sensitive indicators of impending psychotic relapse (Liberman et al., 1993; Subotnik & Nuechterlein, 1988). Behavioral observations, as in time sampling (Paul, 1991) or experience sampling (deVries, 1992), can be even more sensitive indicators of the need for psychiatric intervention than interview-based ratings, but these are more demanding to implement—in terms of both time and expertise.

The CASIG evaluation system was designed with the presumption that treatment planning does not end with the collaborative development of the individual's service plan; treatment consists of continuing cycles of assessment, planning, and service delivery. These cycles reflect the ever-changing nature of treatment; as the services achieve their effects, all of the stakeholders change. In such a fluid environment, treatment cannot be successful unless assessment and services are intertwined components of an ongoing process. New information obtained from an updated assessment infuses new treatment plans, which deliberately make the information obsolete and require yet another assessment. This pattern proceeds through the individual's journey from acute episode to stabilization, rehabilitation, and, if successful, recovery.

Mr. Gomez's case manager was surprised to see Mr. Gomez 2 days in a row at the day treatment program because the staff and Mr. Gomez had agreed several months earlier to decrease Mr. Gomez's attendance gradually to once per month. Although Mr. Gomez denied any problems at first, the case manager sensed that something might be wrong. The case manager asked whether she could conduct a BPRS interview with Mr. Gomez, to which he consented. She discovered significant elevations in depression, anxiety, and hostility, compared with the previous assessment that was conducted 2 months before.

When presented with a graph that illustrated this change, Mr. Gomez acknowledged that his sleep pattern had been disrupted, that his thoughts were confused, and that his mood was sour. On further probing, the case manager found that Mr. Gomez had resumed using marijuana about 6 weeks before. He was sleeping late, arriving to work late, and confused on the job. He became concerned about losing his position after he received a formal warning from his supervisor. He took 2 weeks off from work because he believed that his marijuana use was out of control and hoped that the program could help him. Mr. Gomez and his case manager reformulated his service plan to address his substance abuse. The revised plan called for abstinence, daily 12-step meetings—including a sponsor from the group—and weekly urine drug screenings. Not long thereafter, Mr.

Gomez was able to return to work and function effectively.

CONCLUSION

The results of research studies and clinical trials indicate that people who experience severe mental illness can improve their role functioning, reduce their disabilities, and achieve better quality of life. These positive outcomes, however, are conditional. They are achieved when

1. The methods of teaching role skills are tailored to individuals' cognitive impairments and disabilities
2. There is a partnership between the teaching and the natural environment so that one supports the other
3. The full range of clinical services is provided on a schedule and with an intensity that fits the ongoing course and clinical phases of each individual's illness

There are gaps in the research literature and clinical techniques, however, that should be filled so that biopsychosocial rehabilitation can be even more effective. An understanding of the factors that promote a collaborative relationship between practitioner and patient would contribute to an increase in the number of individuals in active rehabilitation programs. Better methods of assessment would improve both the interpretation of future evaluations and the current clinical practice. Also, because diagnoses predict rehabilitation outcomes only in the broadest terms, far more information is needed about with whom psychosocial rehabilitation is more or less effective (i.e., a treatment-matching approach).

Although we do not need fundamental breakthroughs in the causes and cures of schizophrenia and other mental disorders to make a significant difference in social adaptation and quality of life, technological developments may be integrated with rehabilitation modalities to facilitate the recovery of a greater proportion of patients. For example, although typical antipsychotic medications are thought to impair cognitive functioning, preliminary studies of the effects of risperidone and clozapine on learning and cognitive functioning have been promising (Lee, Thompson, & Meltzer, 1994; McGurk, Green, & Marder, 1994). This finding holds out hope that a synergistic effect with biopsychosocial rehabilitation is possible.

As laboratory studies reveal more about the pathophysiology of schizophrenia and other disabling psychiatric disorders, skills-training techniques can be constructed to remediate directly individuals' problems with attention, memory, and information processing (Green, 1993). The plasticity of the brain may offer many compensatory mechanisms that may be activated by structured and systematic environmental intervention; thus, the biopsychosocial nature of serious mental disorders will illuminate the *bidirectional* pathways among brain–behavior–environment interactions.

Two years after his last hospitalization, Mr. Gomez was still working as an assistant manager at the convenience store. His weekly evaluations were always outstanding, and he believed that his prospects for promotion were good. He lived independently in his apartment but frequently had friends over for coffee. He reported that his relationship with his mother was greatly improved, including having her over for dinner once per month. One month he surprised his mother by also inviting to dinner a woman whom he had just started dating. Despite some anxiety on everyone's part, the evening went very well. He reported only minor symptoms—for example, occasional voices, which he could ignore. No side effects were experienced from his low dosage of antipsychotic medication.

Soon thereafter, Mr. Gomez was asked whether he would be willing to participate in a new program. The mental health department was looking for patients who could work part time as reviewers of mental health facilities. The job consisted of interviewing clients, staff, and administrators of the facilities to get a sense of the overall opinion that people had of the program and then providing feedback as to the benefits and limitations of the program. Because of his experiences with a state-of-the-art biobehavioral rehabilitation program, Mr. Gomez got the job. He has been busy ever since, helping to convince the providers of mental health services to focus on the biopsychosocial needs of people with serious mental illness.

REFERENCES

Alexander, F.M. (1963). *Fundamentals of psychoanalysis.* New York: Norton.

Amdur, M.A. (1979). Medication compliance in outpatient psychiatry. *Comprehensive Psychiatry, 20,* 339–346.

American Psychiatric Association. (1994). *Diagnostic and statistical manual of mental disorders* (4th ed.). Washington, DC: Author.

Anastasi, A. (1986). Evolving concepts of test validation. *Annual Review of Psychology, 37,* 1–15.

Anastasi, A. (1993). A century of psychological testing: Origins, problems and progress. In T.K. Fagan & G.R. VandenBos (Eds.), *Exploring applied psychology: Origins and critical analyses. Master lectures in psychology* (pp. 113–136). Washington, DC: American Psychological Association.

Anderson, C.M., Reiss, D.J., & Hogarty, G.E. (1986). *Schizophrenia and the family.* New York: Guilford Press.

Anthony, W.A. (1991). Recovery from mental illness: The guiding vision of the mental health service system in the 1990's. *Psychosocial Rehabilitation Journal, 16,* 11–23.

Anthony, W.A. (1993). Programs that work: Issues of leadership. *The Journal of the California Alliance of the Mentally Ill, 4,* 51–53.

Anthony, W.A., & Nemec, P.B. (1984). Psychiatric rehabilitation. In A.S. Bellack (Ed.), *Schizophrenia: Treatment, management, and rehabilitation* (pp. 375–413). Orlando, FL: Grune & Stratton.

Azrin, N.H., & Powell, J. (1969). Behavioral engineering: The use of response priming to improve prescribed self-medication. *Journal of Applied Behavior Analysis, 2,* 39–42.

Bachrach, L.L. (1989). The legacy of model programs. *Hospital and Community Psychiatry, 40,* 234–235.

Baker, F., & Intagliata, J. (1992). Case management. In R.P. Liberman (Ed.), *Handbook of psychiatric rehabilitation* (pp. 213–243). New York: Macmillan.

Basch, M.F. (1980). *Doing psychotherapy.* New York: Basic Books.

Bellack, A.S., Morrison, R.L., & Mueser, K.T. (1989). Social problem solving in schizophrenia. *Schizophrenia Bulletin, 15,* 101–116.

Benton, M.K., & Schroeder, H.E. (1990). Social skills training with schizophrenics: A meta-analytic evaluation. *Journal of Consulting and Clinical Psychology, 58,* 741–747.

Betancourt, H., & Lopez, S.R. (1993). The study of culture, ethnicity, and race in American psychology. *American Psychologist, 48,* 629–637.

Blackwell, B. (1973). Treatment adherence. *British Journal of Psychiatry, 129,* 513–531.

Boczkowski, J.A., Zeichner, A., & DeSanto, N. (1985). Neuroleptic compliance among chronic schizophrenic outpatients: An intervention outcome report. *Journal of Consulting and Clinical Psychology, 53,* 666–671.

Bond, G. (1992). Vocational rehabilitation. In R.P. Liberman (Ed.), *Handbook of psychiatric rehabilitation* (pp. 244–275). New York: Macmillan.

Brophy, J. (1986). Teacher influences on student achievement. *American Psychologist, 41,* 1069–1072.

Carpenter, W.T., Heinrichs, D.W., & Wagman, A.M.I. (1988). Deficit and non-deficit forms of schizophrenia: The concept. *American Journal of Psychiatry, 145,* 578–583.

Chamberlin, J. (1984). Speaking for ourselves: An overview of the ex-psychiatric inmates' movement. *Psychosocial Rehabilitation Journal, 3*(2), 56–63.

Corrigan, P.W. (1991). Social skills training in adult psychiatric populations: A meta-analysis. *Journal of Behavior Therapy and Experimental Psychiatry, 22,* 203–210.

Corrigan, P.W., Holmes, E.P., Luchins, D., Parks, J., DeLaney, E., & Kayton-Weinberg, D. (1994). Staff burnout in psychiatric hospitals: A cross-lagged panel design. *Journal of Organizational Behavior, 15,* 65–74.

Corrigan, P.W., Liberman, R.P., & Engel, J. (1990). From noncompliance to collaboration in the treatment of schizophrenia. *Hospital and Community Psychiatry, 41,* 1203–1211.

Craig, T., Huffine, C., & Brooks, M. (1974). Completion of referral to psychiatric services by inner city residents. *Archives of General Psychiatry, 31,* 353–357.

Deegan, P.E. (1992). The independent living movement and people with psychiatric disabilities: Taking back control over our own lives. *Psychosocial Rehabilitation Journal, 15,* 3–19.

deVries, M.W. (1992). *The experience of psychopathology: Investigating mental disorders in their natural settings.* Cambridge, England: Cambridge University Press.

Drake, R.E., Mueser, K.T., Clark, R.E., & Wallach, M.E. (1996). The course, treatment, and outcome of substance disorder in persons with severe mental illness. *American Journal of Orthopsychiatry, 66,* 42–51.

Drake, R.E., & Sederer, L.I. (1986). The adverse effects of intensive treatment of chronic schizophrenia. *Comprehensive Psychiatry, 27,* 313–326.

Eckman, T.A., Liberman, R.P., Phipps, C.C., & Blair, K. (1990). Teaching medication management skills to schizophrenic patients. *Journal of Clinical Psychopharmacology, 10,* 33–38.

Eckman, T.A., Wirshing, W.C., Marder, S.R., Liberman, R.P., Johnston-Cronk, K., Zimmerman, K., & Mintz, J. (1992). Technique for training schizophrenic patients in illness self-management: A controlled trial. *American Journal of Psychiatry, 149,* 1549–1555.

Falloon, I.R.H. (1988). *Handbook of behavioral family therapy.* New York: Guilford Press.

Falloon, I.R.H., Boyd, J., & McGill, C.W. (1984). *Family care of schizophrenia.* New York: Guilford Press.

Falloon, I.R.H., Boyd, J.L., McGill, C.W., Williamson, M., Razani, J., Moss, H.B., Gilderman, A.M., & Simpson, G.M. (1985). Family management in the prevention of morbidity of schizophrenia. *Archives of General Psychiatry, 42,* 887–896.

Falloon, I.R.H., & Liberman, R.P. (1983). Behavioral family interventions in the management of chronic schizophrenia. In W.R. MacFarlane (Ed.), *Family therapy of schizophrenia* (pp. 325–380). New York: Guilford Press.

Falloon, I.R.H., Lindley, P., McDonald, R., Vaughn, C., & Liberman, R.P. (1977). Social skills training of outpatient groups: A controlled study of rehearsal and homework. *British Journal of Psychiatry, 131,* 599–609.

Fisher, D.B. (1994). Health care reform based on an empowerment model of recovery by people with psychiatric disabilities. *Hospital and Community Psychiatry, 45,* 913–915.

Frank, A.F., & Gunderson, J.G. (1990). The role of the therapeutic alliance in the treatment of schizophrenia: Relationship to course and outcome. *Archives of General Psychiatry, 47,* 228–236.

Glynn, S.M., & Mueser, K.T. (1992). Social learning programs. In R.P. Liberman (Ed.), *Handbook of psychiatric rehabilitation* (pp. 127–152). New York: Macmillan.

Goering, P.N., Wasylenki, D.A., Farkas, M., Lancee, W.J., & Ballantyne, R. (1988). What difference does case management make? *Hospital and Community Psychiatry, 39,* 272–276.

Green, M.F. (1993). Cognitive remediation in schizophrenia: Is it time yet? *American Journal of Psychiatry, 150,* 178–187.

Hall, J.K. (1988). Providing culturally relevant mental health services for Central American immigrants. *Hospital and Community Psychiatry, 39,* 1139–1144.

Hierholzer, R.W., & Liberman, R.P. (1986). Successful living: A social skills and problem-solving group for the chronic mentally ill. *Hospital and Community Psychiatry, 37,* 913–918.

Hogarty, G.E., Anderson, C.M., Reiss, D.J., Kornblith, S.J., Greenwald, D.P., Jauna, C.D., & Madania, M.J. (1986). Family education, social skills training and maintenance chemotherapy in aftercare treatment of schizophrenia. *Archives of General Psychiatry, 43,* 633–642.

Hogarty, G.E., McEvoy, J.P., & Munetz, M. (1988). Dose of fluphenazine, familial expressed emotion, and outcome in schizophrenia: Results of a two-year controlled study. *Archives of General Psychiatry, 45,* 797–805.

Iacono, W.G., & Beiser, M. (1992). Where are the women in first-episode studies in schizophrenia? *Schizophrenia Bulletin, 18,* 471–480.

Intagliata, J. (1978). The history and future of associate degree workers in the human services. In K. Nash, M. Lifton, & S. Smith (Eds.), *The paraprofessional: Selected readings* (pp. 206–215). New Haven, CT: Center for Paraprofessional Evaluation and Continuing Education.

Intagliata, J. (1982). Improving the quality of community care for the clinically mentally disabled: The role of case management. *Schizophrenia Bulletin, 8,* 655–674.

Johnson, D.L. (Ed.). (1990). *Service needs of the seriously mentally ill: Training implications for psychology.* Washington, DC: American Psychological Association.

Kane, J.M., & Borenstein, M. (1985). Compliance in the long-term treatment of schizophrenia. *Psychopharmacology Bulletin, 21,* 23–27.

Kane, J.M., & Meyerhoff, D. (1989). Do negative symptoms respond to pharmacological treatment? *British Journal of Psychiatry, 155*(Suppl.), 115–118.

Kanter, J. (1989). Clinical case management: Definition, principles, components. *Hospital and Community Psychiatry, 40,* 361–368.

Kopelowicz, A., & Liberman, R.P. (1994). Self-management approaches for the seriously mentally ill. *Directions in Psychiatry, 14,* 1–7.

Kuehnel, T.G., & Flanagan, S.G. (1984). Training the professionals: Guidelines for effective continuing education workshops. *The Behavior Therapist, 7,* 85–87.

Kuehnel, T.G., Liberman, R.P., Marshall, B.D., & Bowen, L. (1992). Optimal drug and behavior therapy for treatment of refractory institutional schizophrenia. In R.P. Liberman (Ed.), *Effective psychiatric rehabilitation: New directions in mental health services* (pp. 67–77). San Francisco: Jossey-Bass.

Lee, M.A., Thompson, P.A., & Meltzer, H.Y. (1994). Effects of clozapine on cognitive function in schizophrenia. *Journal of Clinical Psychiatry, 55*(9, Suppl. B), 82–87.

Leff, J., Kuipers, L., Berkowitz, R., Eberlein-Vries, R., & Sturgeon, D. (1982). A controlled trial of social intervention in the families of schizophrenic patients: Two-year follow-up. *British Journal of Psychiatry, 146,* 594–600.

Liberman, R.P. (1988). *Psychiatric rehabilitation of the chronic mental patient.* Washington, DC: American Psychiatric Press.

Liberman, R.P. (1994). Psychosocial treatments for schizophrenia. *Psychiatry, 57,* 104–114.

Liberman, R.P., Corrigan, P.W., & Schade, M.L. (1989). Drug and psychosocial treatment interactions in schizophrenia. *International Review of Psychiatry, 1,* 283–295.

Liberman, R.P., & Davis, J. (1975). Drugs and behavior analysis. In M. Hersen, R. Eisler, & P.M. Miller (Eds.), *Progress in behavior modification* (pp. 307–330). New York: Academic Press.

Liberman, R.P., DeRisi, W.J., & Mueser, K.T. (1989). *Social skills training for psychiatric patients.* Elmsford, NY: Pergamon.

Liberman, R.P., Falloon, I.R.H., & Wallace, C.J. (1984). Drug–psychosocial interactions in the treatment of schizophrenia. In M. Mirabi (Ed.), *The chronically mentally ill: Research and services* (pp. 175–212). New York: SP Medical & Scientific Books.

Liberman, R.P., & Green, M.F. (1992). Whither cognitive therapy for schizophrenia? *Schizophrenia Bulletin, 18,* 27–35.

Liberman, R.P., King, L.W., DeRisi, W.J., & McCann, M. (1975). *Personal effectiveness: Guiding people to assert themselves and improve their social skills.* Champaign, IL: Research Press.

Liberman, R.P., Massel, H.K., Mosk, M.D., & Wong, S.E. (1985). Social skills training for chronic mental patients. *Hospital and Community Psychiatry, 36,* 396–403.

Liberman, R.P., & Mueser, K.T. (1989). Psychosocial treatment of schizophrenia. In H. Kaplan & B.J. Sadock (Eds.), *Comprehensive textbook of psychiatry* (5th ed.). Baltimore: Williams & Wilkins.

Liberman, R.P., Mueser, K., Wallace, C.J., Jacobs, H.E., Eckman, T., & Massel, H.K. (1986). Training skills in the psychiatrically disabled: Learning coping and competence. *Schizophrenia Bulletin, 12,* 631–647.

Liberman, R.P., Van Putten, T., Marshall, B.D., Mintz, J., Bowen, L., Kuehnel, T.G., Aravagiri, M., & Marder, S.R. (1994). Optimal drug and behavior therapy for treatment-refractory schizophrenic patients. *American Journal of Psychiatry, 151,* 756–759.

Liberman, R.P., Wallace, C.J., Blackwell, G., Eckman, T.A., Vaccaro, J.V., & Kuehnel, T.G. (1993). Innovations in skills training for the seriously mentally ill: The UCLA social and independent living skills modules. *Innovations and Research, 2,* 43–59.

Liberman, R.P., Wallace, C.J., Vaughn, C.E., Snyder, K.S., & Rust, C. (1980). Social and family factors in the course of schizophrenia: Toward an interpersonal problem-solving method. In J. Strauss, S. Fleck, & M. Bowers (Eds.), *The psychotherapy of schizophrenia* (pp. 227–246). New York: Plenum.

Lukoff, D., Liberman, R.P., & Nuechterlein, K. (1986). Symptom monitoring in schizophrenia. *Schizophrenia Bulletin, 12,* 578–602.

Lukoff, D., Ventura, J., Nuechterlein, K., & Liberman, R.P. (1992). Integrating symptom assessment into psychiatric rehabilitation. In R.P. Liberman (Ed.), *Handbook of psychiatric rehabilitation* (pp. 56–77). New York: Macmillan.

MacFarlane, W.R., Stastny, P., & Deakins, S. (1992). Family-aided assertive community treatment. In R.P. Liberman (Ed.), *Effective psychiatric rehabilitation: New directions for mental health services* (pp. 43–54). San Francisco: Jossey-Bass.

Marder, S.R., & May, P.R.A. (1986). The benefits and limitations of neuroleptics and other forms of treatment in schizophrenia. *American Journal of Psychotherapy, 40,* 357–369.

Marder, S.R., Wirshing, W.C., Mintz, J., McKenzie, J., Johnston, K., Eckman, T.A., Lebell, M., Zimmerman, K., & Liberman, R.P. (1996). Two-year outcome for social skills training and group psychotherapy for outpatients with schizophrenia. *American Journal of Psychiatry, 153,* 1585–1592.

Marzillier, J.S., Lambert, C., & Kellett, J. (1976). A controlled evaluation of systematic desensitization and social skills training for socially inadequate psychiatric patients. *Behaviour Research and Therapy, 14,* 225–238.

Maslach, C., & Jackson, S.E. (1984). Patterns of burnout among a national sample of public contact workers. *Journal of Health and Human Resources Administration, 7,* 189–212.

Masnik, R., Olarte, S.W., & Rosen, A. (1981). Using a PRN list to see appointment-breakers on a walk-in basis. *Hospital and Community Psychiatry, 32,* 635–637.

Matarazzo, R.G. (1978). Research on the teaching and learning of psychotherapeutic skills. In S.L. Garfield & A.E. Bergin (Eds.), *Handbook of psychotherapy and behavior change: An empirical analysis* (2nd ed., pp. 120–145). New York: John Wiley & Sons.

McGurk, S.R., Green, M.F., & Marder, S. (1994). *Spatial memory in treatment resistant schizophrenia.* Coral Gables, FL: Society for Research and Psychopathology.

Med Tymer. (1986). Boston: Boston Research Group.

Meichenbaum, D., & Turk, D.C. (1987). *Facilitating treatment adherence: A practitioner's guidebook.* New York: Plenum.

Minkoff, K. (1991). Program components of a comprehensive integrated care system for serious mentally ill patients with substance disorders. In K. Minkoff & R.E. Drake (Eds.), *Dual diagnosis of major mental illness and substance disorder* (pp. 13–28). San Francisco: Jossey-Bass.

Mintz, J., Mintz, L.I., & Phipps, C.C. (1992). Treatments of mental disorders and the functional capacity to work. In R.P. Liberman (Ed.), *Handbook of psychiatric rehabilitation* (pp. 290–316). New York: Macmillan.

Mirabi, M., Weinman, M.L., Magnero, S.M., & Gold-smith, A.R. (1978). Professional attitudes toward the chronic mentally ill. *Hospital and Community Psychiatry, 36,* 404–405.

Moore, D.J., Davis, M., & Mellon, J. (1985). *Acade-mia's response to state mental health system needs.* Boulder, CO: Western Interstate Commission for Higher Education.

Morrison, R.L., & Bellack, A.S. (1984). Social skills training. In A.S. Bellack (Ed.), *Schizophrenia: Treatment, management, and rehabilitation* (pp. 247–279). New York: Grune & Stratton.

Mueser, K.T., & Gingerich, S. (1994). *Coping with schizophrenia: A guide for families.* Oakland, CA: New Harbinger Publications.

National Institute of Mental Health. (1995). *1995 budget estimate.* Rockville, MD: U.S. Department of Health and Human Services.

National Institutes of Health. (1994, March 9). NIH guidelines for the inclusion of women and minori-ties as subjects in clinical research (59 *FR* 11146–11151). *Federal Register.*

Nuechterlein, K.H. (1987). Vulnerability models of schizophrenia: State of the art. In H. Hafner, W.F. Gattaz, & W. Jangarik (Eds.), *Searches for the causes of schizophrenia* (pp. 212–227). New York: Springer-Verlag.

Nuechterlein, K., & Dawson, M. (1984). A vulnera-bility/stress model of schizophrenic episodes. *Schizophrenia Bulletin, 10,* 300–312.

Nuñez-Lopez, J.A. (1992). Improving and sponsoring mental health research among ethnic minorities. *Outlook, 2,* 1–2. Alexandria, VA: National Association of State Mental Health Program Direc-tors Research Institute.

O'Sullivan, M.J., Peterson, P.D., Cox, G.B., & Kirkeby, J. (1989). Ethnic populations: Community mental health services ten years later. *American Journal of Community Psychology, 17,* 17–30.

Overall, J., & Gorham, D. (1988). The Brief Psychi-atric Rating Scale (BPRS): Recent developments in ascertainment and scaling. *Psychopharmacol-ogy Bulletin, 24,* 97–99.

Paul, G.L. (Ed.). (1991). *Assessment in residential settings.* Champaign, IL: Research Press.

Randolph, E., Eth, S., Glynn, S., Paz, G., Van Vort, W., Shaner, A., & Liberman, R.P. (1994). Efficacy of behavioral family management in reducing re-lapse in veteran schizophrenics. *British Journal of Psychiatry, 164,* 501–506.

Raynes, A.E., & Warren, G. (1971). Some distin-guishing features of patients failing to attend a psy-chiatric clinic after referral. *American Journal of Orthopsychiatry, 41,* 581–588.

Regier, D.A., Farmer, M.E., Lock, B.Z., Keith, S.J., & Rae, D.S. (1993). The de facto US mental and ad-dictive disorders service system. *Archives of Gen-eral Psychiatry, 51,* 492–499.

Repp, A.C., Karsh, K.G., Munk, D., & Dahlquist, C.M. (1995). Hypothesis-based interventions: A theory of clinical decision making. In W. O'Dono-hue & L. Krasner (Eds.), *Theories of behavior ther-apy: Exploring behavior change* (pp. 585–608). Washington, DC: American Psychological Associ-ation.

Rodriguez, O., Lessinger, J., & Guarnaccia, P. (1992). The societal and organizational contexts of cultur-ally sensitive mental health services: Findings from an evaluation of bilingual/bicultural psychiatric programs. *The Journal of Mental Health Adminis-tration, 19,* 213–223.

Rogler, L.H., Malgady, R.G., & Rodriguez, O. (1989). *Hispanics and mental health: A framework for research.* Malabar, FL: Robert E. Krieger.

Rupp, A., & Keith, S.J. (1993). The costs of schizo-phrenia: Assessing the burden. *Psychiatric Clinics of North America, 16,* 413–423.

Scotti, J.R., Mullen, K.B., & Hawkins, R.P. (1998). Child conduct and developmental disabilities: From theory to practice in the treatment of excess behav-iors. In J.J. Plaud & G.H. Eifert (Eds.), *From be-havior theory to behavior therapy* (pp. 172–202). Needham Heights, MA: Allyn & Bacon.

Stein, L.I., & Test, M.A. (Eds.). (1978). *Alternatives to mental hospital treatment.* New York: Plenum.

Stratoudakis, J.P. (1990). Responsibility of states in collaborating with academia to improve the service system. In D.L. Johnson (Ed.), *Service needs of the seriously mentally ill: Training implications for psychology* (pp. 214–231). Washington, DC: American Psychological Association.

Subotnik, K., & Nuechterlein, K.H. (1988). Prodro-mal signs and symptoms of schizophrenic relapse. *Journal of Abnormal Psychology, 97,* 405–412.

Sultan, F.E., & Johnson, P.J. (1985). Characteristics of dropouts, remainers, and refusers at a psychosocial rehabilitation program for the chronically mentally disabled. *Journal of Psychology, 119,* 175–183.

Talbott, J.A. (1988). The chronic patient and public psychiatry. *New Directions for Mental Health Ser-vices, 37,* 105–107.

Talbott, J.A., Goldman, H.H., & Ross, L. (1987). Schizophrenia: An economic perspective. *Psychi-atric Annals, 17,* 577–579.

Tanaka-Matsumi, J., & Higgenbotham, H.N. (1994). Clinical application of behavior therapy across eth-nic and cultural boundaries. *The Behavior Thera-pist, 17,* 123–126.

Tarrier, N., Barrowclough, C., & Vaughn, C.E. (1988). Community management of schizophrenia: A controlled trial of behavioral intervention with families to reduce relapse. *British Journal of Psy-chiatry, 153,* 532–542.

Tarrier, N., Beckett, R., & Harwood, S. (1993). A trial of two cognitive-behavioral methods of treating drug-resistant residual psychotic symptoms in schizophrenia. *British Journal of Psychiatry, 162,* 524–532.

Test, M.A. (1992). Training in community living. In R.P. Liberman (Ed.), *Handbook of psychiatric rehabilitation* (pp. 153–170). New York: Macmillan.

Unzicker, R. (1992). On my own: A personal journey through madness and re-emergence. *Psychosocial Rehabilitation Journal, 3,* 71–77.

Vaccaro, J.V., Liberman, R.P., Friedlob, S., & Dempsay, S. (1993). Challenge and opportunity: Rehabilitating the homeless mentally ill. In H.R. Lamb, L.L. Bachrach, & F.I. Kass (Eds.), *Treating the homeless mentally ill* (pp. 279–297). Washington, DC: American Psychiatric Press.

Van Putten, T. (1974). Why do schizophrenic patients refuse to take their drugs? *Archives of General Psychiatry, 31,* 67–72.

Van Putten, T., & Marder, S.R. (1987). Behavioral toxicity of antipsychotic drugs. *Journal of Clinical Psychiatry, 48,* 13–19.

Van Putten, T., Marder, S.R., & May, P.R.A. (1984). Response to antipsychotic medication: The doctor's and the consumer's view. *American Journal of Psychiatry, 141,* 16–19.

Van Putten, T., Marder, S.R., & Mintz, J. (1990). A controlled dose comparison of haloperidol in newly admitted schizophrenic patients. *Archives of General Psychiatry, 47,* 754–758.

Van Putten, T., Marder, S.R., & Mintz, J. (1992). Haloperidol plasma levels and clinical response: A therapeutic window relationship. *American Journal of Psychiatry, 149,* 500–505.

Van Putten, T., Marshall, B.D., Liberman, R.P., Bowen, L., Marder, S.R., & Mintz, J. (1993). Systematic dosage reduction in treatment resistant schizophrenic patients. *Psychopharmacology Bulletin, 29,* 315–320.

Ventura, J., Green, M.F., Shaner, A., & Liberman, R.P. (1993). Training and quality assurance with the brief psychiatric rating scale. *International Journal of Methods in Psychiatry Research, 3,* 221–224.

Wallace, C.J. (1996). *Client Assessment of Strengths, Interests and Goals.* Camarillo, CA: Psychiatric Rehabilitation Consultants.

Wallace, C.J., Boone, S.E., Donahoe, C.P., & Foy, D.W. (1985). The chronically mentally ill: Independent living skills training. In D. Barlow (Ed.), *Clinical handbook of psychological disorders* (pp. 462–501). New York: Guilford Press.

Wallace, C.J., & Liberman, R.P. (1985). Social skills training for patients with schizophrenia: A controlled clinical trial. *Psychiatry Research, 15,* 239–247.

Wallace, C.J., Liberman, R.P., MacKain, S.J., Blackwell, G., & Eckman, T.A. (1992). Effectiveness and replicability of modules for teaching social and instrumental skills to the severely mentally ill. *American Journal of Psychiatry, 149,* 654–658.

Wallen, J. (1992). Providing culturally appropriate mental health services for minorities. *The Journal of Mental Health Administration, 19,* 288–295.

Weiden, P., & Havens, L. (1994). Psychotherapeutic management techniques in the treatment of outpatients with schizophrenia. *Hospital and Community Psychiatry, 45,* 549–555.

Wohlford, P. (1990). The role of clinical training in psychology to meet the needs of the seriously mentally ill. In D.L. Johnson (Ed.), *Services needs of the seriously mentally ill: Training implications for psychology* (pp. 144–167). Washington, DC: American Psychological Association.

Woodward, A.M., Dunnell, A.D., & Arons, B.S. (1992). Barriers to mental health care for Hispanic Americans: A literature review and discussion. *The Journal of Mental Health Administration, 19,* 224–236.

Wyatt, R.J. (1991). Neuroleptics and the natural course of schizophrenia. *Schizophrenia Bulletin, 17,* 325–351.

Wyatt, R.J., & Clark, K.P. (1987). Calculating the cost of schizophrenia. *Psychiatric Annals, 17,* 586–591.

Zinman, S., Budd, S.U., & Harp, H. (1987). *Reaching across: Mental health clients helping each other.* Riverside: California Network of Mental Health Clients.

Chapter 6

Behavior Excesses and Deficits in Children

Promising Recent Developments

Tracy L. Morris & Robert P. Hawkins

Interventions for children encompass a diverse array of techniques designed to reduce maladaptive or excess behavior and to increase social functioning (cf. Mash & Barkley, 1989). Contemporary intervention strategies are increasingly multidisciplinary in application, involving teachers, social workers, pediatricians, psychiatrists, and child clinical psychologists. This chapter focuses on developments in the field of child behavior therapy since the mid-1980s. Following a discussion of functional assessment and the constructional approach, the chapter presents a brief and selective review of the most promising developments in intervention for conduct problems and social anxiety.

BEHAVIOR EXCESSES AND DEFICITS

In applied behavior analysis of or behavior therapy for clinical problems, the initial assessment process leads to the selection of fairly specific target behaviors (Hawkins, 1979, 1986) or, more proper, specific environment–behavior functional relations (cf. Donahoe & Palmer, 1994). These relations usually can be characterized as either behavior *excesses* or behavior *deficits*. An excess behavior occurs when a person shows a certain class of response too often, too intensely, or in too many stimulus contexts, such as a child's grabbing toys from peers, having tantrums at bedtime, scratching his or her skin, lying, or stealing. It is considered excess because it occurs at a rate or an intensity that is maladaptive in that it is "costly" to the child or to others in the long run (Hawkins, 1986). The cost can be in terms of either lost reinforcers or unnecessary punishers. The behavior may also be viewed as socially maladaptive in that it is atypical and thus may bring about undesirable social consequences (e.g., being teased or ostracized). The behavior is, of course, also adaptive in the sense that it is a product of the learning history that the child's environment has provided (see Meyer & Evans, 1989). A deficit behavior occurs when a person shows a certain class of response at too seldom a rate, at too low an intensity, or in too few stimulus contexts, such as a child's failing to learn to read, infrequently interacting with other children, failing to do homework, talking too quietly, or rarely expressing his or her wishes (i.e., being nonassertive). Again, these are considered deficits only if they are maladaptive in the sense noted above.

Most child clinical referrals emphasize behavior excesses. This is understandable for two reasons. First, because the referral is virtually always initiated by an adult, not by the child, it is the adult's dissatisfaction, not the child's, that begins the process. An adult is far more likely to be dissatisfied by behavior excesses than by behavior deficits, provided that those excesses are costing the adult in some way, such as in terms of discomfort, wasted money, wasted time, embarrassment, inconvenience, danger to someone, or even physical pain. Second, a parent or a teacher more readily notices the presence of some behavior—especially one that is annoying or destructive—than the absence or insufficiency of a behavior, even though that absent behavior is a desirable one.

Regardless of the reasons for such an emphasis on behavior excesses, it creates a significant problem. The natural, immediate reaction to a behavior excess is to try to *eliminate* it. This is not true just of teachers and parents; it is also true of behavioral health professionals—as seen in the history of the field (see Chapters 1 and 3).

SYSTEMIC FUNCTIONAL ASSESSMENT AND SYSTEMIC CONSTRUCTIONAL INTERVENTION

Parents, teachers, and behavioral health professionals are especially likely to try direct elimination of a child's excess behavior when the behavior is an infraction of a rule that has been difficult to enforce or that society views as a moral issue. Consider the following example:

Gary, a 12-year-old boy, is referred to a school psychologist because he is found to have cheated on certain tests repeatedly, despite his teacher's warnings and punishments. The teacher and the parent both give as the referral complaint "cheating on tests."

This referral information immediately suggests as an intervention increasing the surveillance of Gary's work and increasing the magnitude of punishment for further cheating. This is what Goldiamond (1974) would call an *eliminative approach;* it is pathology oriented, meaning that it is oriented toward eliminating the behav-

ior that is considered pathological (see also Evans, 1993; Hawkins, 1986; Meyer & Evans, 1989; Schwartz & Goldiamond, 1975). Although this intervention may succeed in eliminating the problem behavior, the solution is often too simplistic to solve the problem in a way that actually leaves the individual better off.

Goldiamond (1974) contrasted the eliminative approach with what he called a *constructional* one. In a constructional, or an *educative* (Meyer & Evans, 1989), approach, the orientation is toward constructing, not eliminating, repertoires. In such an approach, assessment is designed to discover what the individual might need to learn to *do* rather than what she or he needs to learn *not* to do. Intervention is designed to develop those environment–behavior relations and to expand rather than contract the individual's overall repertoire. It is important to note that constructing further skills tends to increase a child's freedom as well as a child's adjustment in that the child is subsequently capable of doing a greater variety of things to get the reinforcers from his or her environment (Hawkins, 1986). In contrast, eliminative solutions tend to restrict a child's freedom, even when the solutions improve the child's adjustment in a narrower sense.

The simplest constructional solution to Gary's cheating would be to reinforce the direct opposite: his working honestly. This certainly is more constructional and positive than a surveillance-and-punishment strategy; but such a simplistic alternative may be less adequate than it appears. For example, assume that the school psychologist who received the referral goes beyond the simple referral complaint and does some serious assessment, discovering the following additional facts:

1. Gary cheats in only two subjects, not in all subjects.
2. Gary's father beats him when he gets less than a B on a test.
3. The two subjects in which Gary cheats require substantial reading skill, and his reading skill is limited.
4. Gary's limited reading skill is a result of frequent absences from school when he had asthma attacks during grades 1–5, and his

past teachers and administrators were not skillful and motivated enough to make sure that he acquired the skills despite the absences.

5. Gary's present teachers—each of whom has him for only one period per day and thus does not know him well—are mostly unaware of both his asthma and his limited reading skills.

6. The academic subjects in which Gary cheats are taught by rather "cold" teachers who take very little interest in individual children.

This additional assessment information should give the reader a very different interpretation of Gary's cheating and some further ideas for intervention. The prospect of punishing Gary's cheating should seem not only much less humane than it did initially but also unlikely to improve Gary's long-term adjustment—presumably the goal of intervention. This assessment is *systemic* in that it considers various possible sources of the current behavior problem and various resources for alleviating the problem.

The assessment also is *functional* in that it looks for influential variables in the individual's past and present environments rather than at fictional inner causes, such as personality traits, self-efficacy, self-esteem, locus of control, schemas, and so forth. A systemic, functional assessment often will suggest several possible constructional interventions—ones that build skills instead of eliminate behaviors and ones that are both constructional and systemic. They will not necessarily focus on the identified individual; they may focus primarily on other parties. In Gary's case, for example, the school psychologist might work with certain teachers to help them become more sensitive to students' individual life situations, arrange for assessment and remediation of very specific reading skills, and work with Gary's parents to help them arrive at more constructive ways to help Gary progress in school and in life.

DEVELOPMENTAL ISSUES

The chapter authors' approach to behavior excesses is to intervene in *developmentally ap-*

propriate ways, attending to the unique developmental and family factors present. Developmental factors have important implications for behavioral intervention. Age-by-treatment interactions are one example. A common clinical assumption is that intervention tends to be more effective when implemented earlier, as opposed to later, in the individual's life. It is generally held that behavior patterns are less well established in young children and are thus more responsive to change (Mash, 1989). A meta-analysis of the effectiveness of psychotherapy with children and adolescents (Weisz, Weiss, Alicke, & Klotz, 1987) provides indirect support for age-by-treatment interactions—a mean treatment-effect size of .92 was reported for children ages 4–12, whereas the mean treatment-effect size was .58 for children ages 13–18. Although the results of the meta-analysis suggest that positive therapeutic change *in general* may be more rapid with younger individuals, *specific* change strategies may be more effective with older children. Age differences have been reported for the efficacy of self-instructional training across a range of problems (Hobbs, Moguin, Tyroler, & Lahey, 1980). Ability to engage in imagery also has been found to vary as a function of age (Purkel & Bornstein, 1980). Some evidence suggests that the effects of reinforcement and punishment are also a function of age-related factors (Johnson & McGillicuddy-Delisi, 1983).

An integration of classic developmental and behavioral approaches enriches the assessment process and may lead to more effective intervention. Mash (1989) emphasized the importance of identifying specific age-related developmental skills and incorporating those skills into intervention. Undoubtedly, certain approaches will be demonstrated to be more effective within specific age periods than will others. Too often, efforts toward intervention with children have reflected mere downward extensions of work with adults. For example, early work with social skills training (SST) emphasized skills that had been effective in improving the social-interactional performance of adults (e.g., eye contact, formal conversational skills), but those skills were found to be of little consequence in enhancing the performance and social acceptance of children (e.g., Berler, Gross, &

Drabman, 1982; Tiffen & Spence, 1986; White-hill, Hersen, & Bellack, 1980). Identification of developmentally appropriate target goals and modes of behavior change increases the likelihood of intervention success. For example, the peer-pairing approach (Morris, Messer, & Gross, 1995) described later in this chapter utilizes age-appropriate tasks conducted in the natural environment to improve the social interaction and acceptance of primary-grade children.

CONDUCT PROBLEMS AND INTERVENTION IN NATURAL ENVIRONMENTS

In the mid-1960s, behavior analysts began to understand the importance of intervening in an individual's natural environment (e.g., Hawkins, Peterson, Schweid, & Bijou, 1966; Risley & Wolf, 1966; Tharp & Wetzel, 1969). The next section explores the benefits of interventions developed for individuals' natural environments and models for intervention.

The Concept of Intervention in Natural Environments

Behavior analysts' approach of intervention in natural environments grew naturally from the recognition of three basic facts:

1. Individuals learn their adaptive and maladaptive behavior from their natural environment.
2. Behavior remains malleable throughout life.
3. Teaching a person to behave adaptively in a clinic environment does not necessarily produce generalization to natural contexts, which often continue to teach maladaptive behavior.[1]

This leads naturally to the recognition that the same environment could be remodeled to teach more of the adaptive and less of the maladaptive behavior.

Beginning in the late 1960s, there has been an increasing recognition of this notion that intervention should be carried on in the most natural environment feasible. These innovations primarily have been directed at treating conduct problems, whether the youth are formally diagnosed as having conduct disorders (as in the *Diagnostic and Statistical Manual of Mental Disorders, Fourth Edition* [DSM-IV; American Psychiatric Association, 1994]), as being delinquent, or merely as being disturbed (e.g., as in Hobbs, 1966). This population has proved to be especially resistant to intervention, as Kazdin's (1985, 1987) reviews of the relevant research have demonstrated.

The Teaching-Family Model

One of the most exciting innovations was the development of Achievement Place, a group home model for providing interventions for youth with conduct problems (Phillips, 1968; Phillips, Phillips, Fixsen, & Wolf, 1974). The model was developed at the University of Kansas but subsequently has been implemented at many other sites throughout the United States and several other countries. It was eventually named the Teaching-Family Model and became the primary intervention approach of Father Flannagan's Boys' Home (Boys Town), a renowned leader in intervention for such youth.

The general situation used in the model resembles a natural home environment in more respects than the mere fact that it takes place in a family home and involves a maximum of eight youth per home. One of these respects is that the "parents" (called "teaching parents") work 24 hours per day, 7 days per week. The advantages of teaching parents, compared with 8-hour–shift staff—in terms of consistent rules and consequences and in terms of intense commitment to the success of the youth—are obvious. The other ways in which the Teaching-Family Model is innovative are too numerous to present fully; but

---

[1]All learned behavior is adaptive in the sense that it is an adaptation to the contingencies of the environment in which it is learned. That adaptation, however, is often to only the most immediate contingencies, not to the mid- and long-term ones (cf. Donahoe & Palmer, 1994). This results in behavior that, in the long run, is sometimes counterproductive for the individual, for others in her or his environment, or for both. Following Hawkins (1986), this can be called maladaptive or maladjustive.

they can be summarized by the terms *systematic* and *intensive*. To illustrate, six aspects are described as follows:

1. Staff receive intensive training in which they must *demonstrate* and be certified in key skills before taking responsibility for youth; they do not merely learn *about* such skills.
2. After the teaching parents begin serving youth, they are not merely turned loose to implement the system in any way they see fit; they receive consultation, are observed directly at certain intervals, and must meet on-the-job performance criteria.
3. Teaching parents are taught to be both affectionate and firm in their interactions with youth.
4. Every youth is on an extensive point system so that desirable behaviors are consistently reinforced (primarily with commonplace privileges) and undesirable behaviors are consistently punished (with loss of points).
5. The teaching parents are involved with the youth's school in ways that support the teachers' and the youth's academic progress.
6. Although there is a certain set of social, housekeeping, and self-help skills that every youth is taught, there is also considerable individualization based on the youth's needs.

A great deal of research has been conducted on the Teaching-Family Model. Some studies have tested the effects of specific techniques (e.g., Bailey, Wolf, & Phillips, 1970; Braukmann, Maloney, Fixsen, Phillips, & Wolf, 1974; Minkin et al., 1976), whereas other studies evaluated the model as a whole (e.g., Kirigin, Braukmann, Atwater, & Wolf, 1982). The model has had immense influence on numerous other programs, including programs that do not use group homes as a context for intervention.

Foster Family–Based Treatment

One type of intervention that the Teaching-Family Model has influenced is a strategy that is variously called foster family–based treatment (FFBT; see Hawkins, Meadowcroft, Trout, & Luster, 1985), therapeutic foster care, or treat-

ment foster care, among other names (Bryant & Snodgrass, 1990; Hawkins, 1989). In FFBT,

> One recruits couples from the community who are willing to learn a set of treatment procedures, then accept a disturbed or disturbing child or youth into their family who has been removed from her or his own home for one or more reasons. The couples then apply the learned procedures consistently, under supervision, along with just plain good care and parenting. (Hawkins, Luster, & Meadowcroft, 1987, p. 3)

FFBT programs usually are developed as an alternative to institutional placement of youth (Snodgrass & Bryant, 1989), with the goal that the youth will either return to the biological family or, if 18 years old, move on to successful independent living. The intervention may last as little as a few months or as long as several years, depending on the youth's progress and the conditions to which she or he will be discharged. It is the least expensive of all out-of-home intervention strategies (Snodgrass & Bryant, 1989).

Early attempts to start intervention programs that involved foster parents did not consider the foster parent as a primary intervention agent (Bryant & Snodgrass, 1990) and did not have the benefit of behavioral methods. These attempts had very limited success (e.g., DeFries, Jenkins, & Williams, 1970). Nevertheless, several foster parent–based programs were attempted in the 1970s in Canada and the United States (Snodgrass & Bryant, 1989), and several of them survived, although they often were very small. In the 1980s, concerted efforts to develop systematic, behaviorally oriented programs began. Perhaps in part because of the success of these programs, the 1980s saw a burgeoning of FFBT programs all over the United States and Canada. Hawkins (1989) estimated that by 1989 there were approximately 250–500 in Canada and the United States combined, and as of the late 1990s, there may be several times that number. Also in 1989, an international Foster Family-based Treatment Association was organized (Foster Family-based Treatment Association, 1991). The association developed standards of FFBT that are used by member programs for self-assessment, and it publishes a regular newsletter.

Although the Teaching-Family Model influenced several FFBT programs (Meadowcroft & Trout, 1990), such as the ones called PRYDE (Pressley Ridge Youth Development Extension; Hawkins et al., 1985) and People Places (Snodgrass & Campbell, 1981), generally the programs differ in many ways. For example, Snodgrass and Bryant (1989) surveyed FFBT and related programs and found that some of them provided the "intervention parents" with only 1 session of training before they served a youth, whereas others provided as many as 14 sessions. In most programs, preservice training emphasized only knowledge, although 44% did emphasize skills. The staff who worked with the intervention parents had caseloads ranging as high as 31–35 individuals, which precluded any systematic assessment and intervention altogether, and as low as 1–5 individuals, which clearly allowed for genuine individualized intervention. The mode was 6–10 individuals, which still allowed for systematic intervention. Although 82% of the programs had a written intervention plan for each youth, it is not known how individualized, detailed, or constructional those plans were.

To understand FFBT more fully, it is helpful to compare it with two other, very different out-of-home placements: institutions (which typically are called residential treatment centers) and typical foster families (Hawkins, 1989). The similarities to residential intervention are that both it and FFBT

(1) use planned procedures to change behavior and (2) direct those procedures at individually selected goals. The direct treatment personnel (e.g., child care worker), while (3) not normally highly credentialed mental health professionals, are (4) trained and supervised on the job, and (5) apply the planned procedures in approximately the same way to all clients. Further, (6) the procedures are applied throughout the day and night. (Hawkins, 1989, p. 13)

These last four similarities to residential intervention are also differences between FFBT and outpatient, office-based intervention.

The differences between FFBT and residential intervention are that FFBT is more readily individualized because only one or two youth typically live in an intervention home, and FFBT is more personalized and consistent because the intervention personnel do not change every 8 hours and thus are more likely to develop a unique and involved relationship with the youth (Hawkins, 1989).

Similarities between FFBT and foster family care are mostly obvious:

1. The activity takes place in the private home of the substitute family.
2. That family has been evaluated in advance.
3. The family receives some kind of monitoring and assistance.
4. The family is paid.

Differences between the two are that FFBT

1. Applies much higher evaluation criteria
2. Trains the parents in relevant skills
3. Provides much more contact between staff and the intervention parents
4. Pays the parents much better (Hawkins, 1989)

Meadowcroft and Trout (1990) described the procedures used by a few different FFBT programs in carrying out seven of the essential tasks faced by such programs. These tasks are as follows:

1. Recruiting and selecting intervention parents
2. Placing children in specific families
3. Training and supporting intervention parents
4. Serving the children while in the program
5. Serving the biological families of those children
6. Organizing and staffing the program
7. Evaluating the program

To convey an adequate picture of how FFBT functions, the following section briefly describes most of these aspects, plus follow-up procedures used once the child is returned to the biological family.

Recruiting and Selecting Intervention Parents

Recruitment and selection is a constant and challenging task. One does not wish to recruit extensively from families who already provide regular foster care partly because it is a disservice to deplete the ranks of these care providers. Some of the strategies used by various programs include special recruitment campaigns, writing articles for the internal newspapers of industrial plants, addressing PTAs or church groups, paying current intervention parents a "finder's fee" for recruiting successful families, holding Tupperware-type parties for friends and neighbors of current intervention parents, mailing brochures to schools and colleges for placement on bulletin boards, putting brochures in displays of other advertising brochures for tourists, and, of course, advertising in newspapers (Gross & Campbell, 1990).

The recruitment process is selective in itself because the recruited intervention parents are informed of how difficult the youth and the job are. For those who are still interested, the first issue is whether they can meet the state's criteria for licensing as foster families. The next issue is whether they have already demonstrated desired parenting skills, such as holding realistic expectations and being consistent in discipline. Also, they must show a desire to learn new skills and must show resilience because problems will arise repeatedly. Finally, their references must suggest good character (Gross & Campbell, 1990).

Placing Children in Specific Families

Grealish and Meadowcroft (1990) suggested that children be placed in families that are similar to their biological families in socioeconomic status and that the youth have a voice in the selection of the family, just as the family has a voice in selection of a youth. Usually, potential families are given extensive information about the child in advance, followed by two or more preplacement visits; the first visit often is in an office, and the second is in the family's home, perhaps overnight. When all parties agree that a good match has been found, the youth joins the family for the duration of her or his intervention.

Training and Supporting Intervention Parents

Programs vary greatly in both the goals and the methods of training. Among the three behav-

iorally oriented programs described by Meadowcroft and Grealish (1990), the following behaviors were considered crucial for intervention parents:

- Consistently discussing and enforcing rules
- Frequently using reinforcers for good behavior and rarely using punishment
- Nurturing and accepting a child as she or he is
- Giving the child age-appropriate responsibilities
- Modeling adaptive behavior

All three programs required participation in preservice training for 10–24 hours; the training was found to be useful as a screening tool as well. The content of the training differed somewhat across the programs, but all had criteria regarding attendance, homework completion, objective evaluation of the presence of required skills, subjective evaluation by staff, and adherence to state requirements.

Once parents pass the preservice training, they become eligible to serve a child, and the placement process begins. Then, while a child is in the family's home, staff consult with the parents frequently in their home and by telephone. The content of this consultation varies greatly from family to family, program to program, and day to day; but generally it deals with current problems and solutions, use of the procedures taught in preservice training, and record keeping. To continue the professional development of intervention parents, FFBT programs often require participation in the program's in-service training workshops.

FFBT parents typically are paid a per diem fee or a salary that is equivalent to several times what typical foster parents receive. Many programs also provide respite for intervention parents because the job of working with a disturbed youth for 24 hours per day and 7 days per week can be quite stressful.

Serving Children While They Are in the Program

As Meadowcroft, Hawkins, Grealish, and Weaver pointed out, the goal of FFBT is "to bring about changes in socially and personally significant behaviors of troubled and troubling children, and to expand existing and develop new adaptive behaviors" (1990, p. 100). The strategy for achieving this is "to move the child to a home in which the foster parents are skilled and active 'teachers' and have the motivation and support to effect re-education, or treatment" (p. 101). There, the child is exposed to healthy models of all kinds of behavior, ranging from simple housekeeping tasks to difficult social skills, so a wide range of incidental learning occurs. In addition, the intervention parents work specifically on selected target behaviors and use active teaching to develop, increase, or decrease those behaviors. Thus, these parents are the primary intervention agents.

In addition to providing experiences identifiable as intervention, the parents in PRYDE are expected to guide the child's general development, as would any responsible, loving parent. This includes seeing that the child develops some skills of which she or he can be proud, in line with the ReEd principle that "competence makes a difference" (Hobbs, 1966, p. 250). Thus, the planning of intervention includes identifying positive activities that the child and the family like. This can be something that they will do together, something that merely sounds interesting to all of them, or something in which only the youth will engage, with family support. This kind of systemic intervention facilitates the family's development of a positive history together and encourages positive peer relationships, which themselves are a source of valuable development. Finally, it promotes self-esteem.

Different FFBT programs expect different intervention procedures of their parents, but a universal expectation appears to be the extensive use of verbal approval and affection. Many programs, including PRYDE, also employ an individualized token economy motivation system, using a wide variety of individually tailored back-up reinforcers that range from family trips and activities to playthings and edibles for the youth. Furthermore, PRYDE staff establish an arrangement with the youth's school whereby teachers send home a daily report on the child's academic and social behavior so that the parents can provide points and other reinforcers depending on what the report says (cf. Kelley, 1990). In addition, as already mentioned and consistent with Hobbs's (1966) notion that every child should have some skills of which she or he can be proud, PRYDE identifies positive activities that the child—and, often, the family—says that she or he would enjoy and helps the child develop the skills to succeed at those activities.

Like PRYDE, most FFBT programs view the foster parent as the primary agent of intervention, and Chamberlain (1994) gave a particularly cogent analysis of the potential that parents have for influencing a child. In addition to relying on the favorable intervention of trained and supervised foster parents, however, some programs provide a more traditional form of individual therapy by a mental health professional. An excellent example is Chamberlain's (1994) Monitor Program, in which the therapist provides not only weekly individual, office-based sessions but also various other interventions, often outside the office and including the child's intervention parents, school personnel, case manager, or others. Furthermore, either the therapist or the child can initiate telephone contact whenever it seems useful, and the therapist sometimes assumes the role of advocate for the child.

All FFBT programs need to carry out considerable liaison with various agencies and individuals. This includes juvenile court, probation, schools, medical personnel, scouts, Big Brothers, neighbors, and so forth. The liaison can sometimes be conducted by the intervention parent, but much of it falls appropriately to staff.

Working with the Biological Family

The child is not the only one who needs assistance; his or her biological family needs various kinds of assistance as well. Sometimes the family has problems that are so numerous and fundamental that it is difficult to achieve significant gains of any kind. For example, many of the biological parents of youth who are served by PRYDE abuse alcohol or other drugs, and most of the youth have been seriously neglected and sexually abused by someone in their family. Furthermore, the parents often view the problem as their child's, not their own; so the parents are not always interested in making any changes in what they do. Finally, the funding streams that support work with children with severe disturbances are unprepared to reimburse programs at a level that would make it possible to provide all of the family services needed.

In the face of this gloomy picture, it is often amazing how much can be done to help biological families when staff are creative, energetic, and persistent. Most families can make gains that will make it possible for them to accept the child back into their home or at least to have better interactions with the child while she or he lives elsewhere. FFBT programs work with families individually, providing services that range from individual training in the skills of family communication to assistance in finding a job. Sometimes working with biological families in groups can be a useful adjunct to this (Grealish, Hawkins, Meadowcroft, & Lynch, 1990).

Discharge and Follow-Up

When a youth has met her or his goals adequately and the biological family is ready to receive her or him back, the child is discharged to the family. There are, however, numerous exceptions. Sometimes the biological parents are never ready to have the child back and to be even minimally responsible parents. On rare occasions, the family has even moved away and left the child. In such cases, the options range from allowing the intervention parents to adopt the child to reducing services to a level that approximates typical foster care.

Sometimes the youth is close to the age of 18, the age at which reimbursement for services usually must be terminated unless the child is in school. The child then will often remain in the program until age 18 and be discharged to live independently.

Programs differ considerably in how much postdischarge follow-up they do with youth who are former program participants. Because there is no reimbursement for follow-up services, programs have a disincentive to invest much in them. PRYDE and all other Pressley Ridge programs have a commitment to each youth that resembles parents' commitment to their children. The commitment is conveyed in the phrase that staff often utter: "Once a Pressley Ridge kid, always a Pressley Ridge kid." In practice, this means that staff are expected always to be available to and interested in former program partic-

ipants, even if the youth was discharged so long ago that few staff who worked with her or him remain. This may involve merely a 10-minute social conversation with a former participant who walks in unannounced; or it may mean spending several hours helping him or her with some current problem, such as finding a job. It also sometimes means drawing from a special Pressley Ridge fund to help a youth through a difficult but temporary situation. Of course, it does not mean providing long-term housing, food, or other basic support.

Evaluation

There have been few evaluations of FFBT programs. However, a study by Hawkins, Almeida, and Samet (1989) evaluated PRYDE by inspecting the child welfare records of 461 youth who were referred to or accepted by PRYDE. Of these, 341 referrals had been served by other programs in the Pittsburgh area because these programs had spaces for the youth before PRYDE did (a common phenomenon because child welfare typically refers a youth to more than one program at the same time). Thus, the youth who were served by programs other than PRYDE were assumed to be very comparable to PRYDE-served youth, an assumption confirmed by analysis of several demographic variables.

The concept behind the evaluation was that a youth's success after being served by the type of program to which she or he was assigned—called "target programs"—to be evaluated (of which PRYDE was just one) would be reflected in the restrictiveness of the youth's subsequent placements. As the subsequent placement generally reflects the youth's current behavior, the eventual discharge of a youth from a target program to a highly restrictive placement would suggest that the target program had been less successful with the youth than if she or he had been discharged to a less restrictive placement. The authors developed a Restrictiveness of Living Environments Scale (ROLES; Hawkins, Almeida, Fabry, & Reitz, 1992) to assign restrictiveness values to these subsequent placements. The 27 different living environments on the scale ranged from jail (restrictiveness value of 10) to independent living by oneself (restrictiveness of 0.5).

By inspecting records of where the youth went after being discharged from each of the target programs (e.g., residential treatment centers, "intensive treatment units," a therapeutic wilderness camp, group homes, specialized foster care, typical foster care, family home), it was possible to compare the outcomes achieved by various kinds of programs. The authors found that "on the average, PRYDE discharged its client youth to less restrictive placements than did other target programs . . . , significantly less than residential treatment centers and intensive treatment units" (Hawkins et al., 1989, p. 106).

In one of the other analyses, the authors calculated the average restrictiveness of every post-target placement, including all placements after the first one to which the youth was discharged. From their analysis, they concluded that "these data suggest that the youth discharged from PRYDE tend to have equally or less restrictive subsequent placements than youth discharged from other target placements" (Hawkins et al., 1989, p. 107). Because FFBT itself is not nearly as restrictive as were many of the other target placements (5.1 on the ROLES), this result seems to confirm the hypothesis that adequate intervention does not require highly restrictive environments. In addition, PRYDE was found to cost less per day than any of the other types of programs, with the exception of specialized foster care, which is a similar kind of program, and, of course, leaving the child at home.

Two additional studies were conducted by Chamberlain (1994) and her colleagues to evaluate the Monitor Program in Eugene, Oregon. Again, the results suggest that FFBT is as effective or more effective than alternative interventions. Chamberlain also indicated that she has under way a larger, grant-funded, clinical trial study that will yield even further information.

Other Developments Involving Intervention in Natural Environments

There are several other developments in which the education, intervention, and support of both children and adults have moved to more naturalistic environments (e.g., Maybanks & Bryce, 1979). One of these developments typically is

called "family preservation." Although family preservation seems to have begun with the Homebuilders program in Tacoma, Washington (e.g., Haapala & Kinney, 1979; Kinney & Haapala, 1981; Kinney, Madsen, Fleming, & Haapala, 1977), it is now a nationwide movement with many variations on what Homebuilders does. The general notion is that many of the children who are removed from their homes because of neglect, abuse, incorrigibility, and other factors and who are both housed and provided with intervention at great public expense could remain in their homes if their families could be helped to function more adequately. This approach not only saves considerable money, as Kinney et al. (1977) demonstrated, but it also preserves a family integrity that is probably very important to a child's long-term, healthy development.

One family-preservation program that is especially relevant to intervention for children and youth with conduct problems was developed by Henggeler in South Carolina (e.g., Henggeler, Melton, & Smith, 1992; Henggeler et al., 1986). Like Chamberlain's (1994) FFBT program, this program has been shown to be effective in intervening with troubled youth and their families without removing the youth from her or his biological parents. This remarkable achievement promises to lead to more effective methods for intervention both for youth with conduct problems and for their families.

The discussion now turns to the other side of the coin—that is, children with behavior deficits that can significantly affect their social and academic performance. Childhood anxiety (which in itself may be viewed as an excess) is related to—as both cause and effect—significant problems in functioning, particularly social functioning.

BEHAVIORAL INTERVENTION FOR CHILDHOOD ANXIETY

The assessment of and intervention for anxiety and social competence problems in children has a long tradition within the field of behavior therapy. A variety of behavioral intervention modalities have been utilized, including methods grounded in respondent conditioning (Jones, 1924), operant conditioning (Skinner, 1953), and two-factor theory (Mowrer 1947, 1960). The following sections present a brief overview of common behavioral approaches to the management of anxiety. A description of several promising approaches in the intervention for anxiety and social competence deficits follows this overview.

Respondent-Based Procedures

The behavioral intervention for fear and anxiety in children dates to the classic work of Jones (1924) and the elimination of a fear of rabbits in a small boy referred to as "Peter." Intervention consisted of progressively exposing the child to the rabbit while the child was engaged in a pleasurable activity (eating) that was incompatible with fear. Following intervention, Peter's fear dissipated with respect to the rabbit as well as to other, similar objects to which the fear had generalized. The case of Peter typically is presented as an example of "deconditioning" through principles of respondent conditioning.

Systematic Desensitization

Building on Jones's early work, Wolpe (1958) developed a "graduated deconditioning" technique called *systematic desensitization*. The rationale was that anxiety is a set of classically conditioned responses that can be unlearned or counterconditioned through associative pairing with anxiety-incompatible stimuli and responses. In systematic desensitization, anxiety-arousing stimuli are systematically and gradually paired (imaginally or in vivo) with competing stimuli, such as food, praise, imagery, or cues generated from muscular relaxation. Imaginal presentation of fearful stimuli was used predominantly in the initial work with systematic desensitization.

Systematic desensitization with children consists of three basic steps:

1. Training in progressive muscle relaxation
2. Ranking fearful situations from lowest to highest
3. Presenting hierarchical fear stimuli via imagery while the child is in a relaxed state (see Morris & Kratochwill, 1983, for a review of procedures)

Systematic desensitization appears to work well with older children and adolescents (see Barrios & O'Dell, 1989, for a review). Younger children, however, often have difficulty with both obtaining vivid imagery and acquiring the incompatible muscular relaxation response (Ollendick & Cerny, 1981). Strategies such as using developmentally appropriate imagery (Ollendick, 1979) and adjunctive use of workbooks (see Kendall, 1990) may enhance the effectiveness of these procedures with children.

Exposure-Based Interventions

Exposure-based interventions include *flooding* (with response prevention) and *graduated exposure*. These interventions are based on respondent conditioning and the classical extinction paradigm. In the natural environment, individuals typically do not remain in the presence of anxiety-arousing stimuli for a sufficient duration to allow extinction to occur. Moreover, escape and avoidance behaviors are negatively reinforced by removal of the aversive stimuli and cessation of anxiety. Exposure-based procedures require extended presentation of feared stimuli with concurrent prevention of escape and avoidance behaviors for the extinction of the conditioned responses to occur (see Eisen & Kearney, 1995; Morris & Kratochwill, 1983), thus addressing both components of the two-factor model.

Flooding involves sustained exposure (imaginally or in vivo) to feared stimuli—the individual is required to remain in the presence of feared stimuli until his or her self-reported anxiety level dissipates. The term *graduated exposure* refers to progressive in vivo exposure to hierarchically presented fear stimuli. Unlike with systematic desensitization, stimulus presentation generally is not accompanied by progressive muscle relaxation. Reinforced practice often is used in conjunction with graduated exposure whereby positive reinforcement is provided for progressively longer exposure to fear stimuli (Leitenberg & Callahan, 1973). Graduated exposure generally is considered to produce less stress for the individual (and the therapist) and thus often is preferred over the use of flooding with young children.

Operant-Based Contingency Management Procedures

From an operant conditioning perspective, behavior is learned as a function of its consequences. Thus, positive consequences will increase the frequency of a behavior, whereas negative consequences or lack of positive reinforcement (extinction) will decrease the frequency of a behavior. Therefore, all behavior is subject to these contingencies of reinforcement such that inappropriate or maladaptive behaviors will increase when followed by positive consequences or when such behavior results in removal from or termination of an aversive situation (i.e., negative reinforcement).

The use of operant procedures with children who are socially avoidant or anxious requires assessment of the antecedents and consequences that are maintaining the child's fearful behavior. The approach is based on the assumption that these children have not been adequately reinforced for social behavior or have been inadvertently reinforced for nonsocial behavior. Intervention involves arrangement of contingencies in the home, school, or other relevant environments to facilitate social interaction, combined with reinforcement contingent on appropriate social behavior (e.g., Walker, Greenwood, Hops, & Todd, 1979).

Integrating Respondent and Operant Approaches

Two-factor learning theory (Mowrer, 1947, 1960) proposes that both respondent and operant conditioning are involved in the development and maintenance of anxious/avoidant behavior. A concise overview of the two-factor learning theory model has been presented by Lyons and Scotti (1995). Essentially, the theory states that in the face of an aversive event, the organism responds with increased physiological reactivity and subjective distress. These responses become associated with otherwise benign cues that were present at the time of the aversive event. Subsequently, presentation of conditioned stimuli results in physiological reactivity and subjective distress. Escape and/or avoidance of the conditioned stimuli is nega-tively reinforced (through removal of the aversive stimuli). The problem becomes compounded when additional cues lead to increased avoidance over time through the process of stimulus generalization. According to Levis,

Inherent in the development of psychopathology is the learning of two response classes. The first response class involves the conditioning of an aversive emotional state, whereas the second involves learned behavior designed to reduce the negative effects of the first response class. (1985, p. 53)

In the case of social anxiety, a child may have learned to associate social performance situations with increased physiological reactivity (which the child often labels as "fear"). Subsequent avoidance of social performance situations (e.g., refusal to go to a party with peers) results in reduction of aversive physiological arousal, which serves to maintain avoidant behavior. The intervention programs presented next reflect the influence of two-factor theory in their inclusion of both respondent (e.g., graduated exposure) and operant (e.g., skills training) approaches.

INTERVENTION PROGRAMS FOR CHILDREN WITH SOCIAL-INTERACTION SKILLS DEFICITS AND SOCIAL ANXIETY

Peer interaction plays a crucial role in children's social and emotional development. As such, disturbances in peer relationships constitute a risk factor for subsequent psychopathology (Parker & Asher, 1987). Impairment in social functioning may result from a lack of effective social skills, from performance inhibition due to anxiety, or more typically from an interaction of both of these factors (Arkowitz, 1981). Social anxiety and skills deficits may foster withdrawal, restricted peer interaction, and further impairment in social skills and interpersonal relationships (Rubin, LeMare, & Lollis, 1990; Vernberg, Abwender, Ewell, & Beery, 1992). Through this process, a vicious cycle is perpetuated in which the child may become increasingly anxious and ineffective in social situations.

SST programs have been used widely with children who are socially withdrawn to facilitate development of social relationships. In the typical SST program, children are provided with group instruction in the execution of specific behaviors (e.g., play group initiations), group leaders model effective behaviors, and children are given practice opportunities accompanied by feedback and reinforcement. Although SST programs largely have been successful in increasing the specific target behaviors trained, changes in social acceptance by peers typically have *not* followed from traditional SST alone.

Interventions that involve a child's peers (peer mediated) appear to be superior to adult-mediated approaches for remediating social isolation (Strain & Fox, 1981). Typical peer-mediated approaches provide peers with incentives and/or training to increase their rate of positive interaction with target children (e.g., Christopher, Hansen, & MacMillan, 1991; Strain & Odom, 1986). Alternative peer-mediated strategies, however, rely merely on pairing socially isolated children with either "typical" or "popular" status peers in an attempt to provide age-appropriate models of social interaction and opportunities for exposure to social-anxiety provoking stimuli (e.g., Furman, Rahe, & Hartup, 1979; Morris et al., 1995). The inclusion of peers may be a necessary component to effect changes in social acceptance. Although peer-mediated programs have demonstrated efficacy in increasing the social interaction of children with mild to moderate levels of social withdrawal, children with extreme fears and social avoidance may require more intensive and extensive intervention strategies (see the section "Social Effectiveness Therapy for Children"). The following sections describe approaches to the intervention for social anxiety and interaction deficits.

Peer Pairing

In a 1995 study, Morris and colleagues investigated the utility of a peer-pairing procedure in improving the peer acceptance and positive social interaction rate of children who have been neglected by their peers. Children who are peer-neglected are those who are rated as neither liked nor disliked by their peers and who typically are characterized as shy and withdrawn. Children who are peer-neglected have been

found to report higher levels of social anxiety (LaGreca, Dandes, Wick, Shaw, & Stone, 1988) than popular children or children who are rejected by their peers. Conversely, children with an anxiety disorder were more likely to be classified as peer-neglected than were psychiatric and nonpsychiatric controls (Strauss, Lahey, Frick, Frame, & Hynd, 1988).

In the study by Morris et al. (1995), 24 children who were peer-neglected and 24 children who were popular (matched for gender, age, and classroom) were identified through sociometric nominations from an initial pool of 390 first- and second-grade children. Playground observations of social interaction during recess also were obtained (e.g., positive interaction, negative interaction, solitary play). Twelve of the children who were peer-neglected (and their matched popular peers) were assigned at random to the peer-pairing intervention. The remaining children were assigned to a no-treatment, control condition. Peer-pairing consisted of 12 interaction sessions (15–20 minutes each) conducted across a 4-week period; each child who was peer-neglected was paired with a same-gender child who was popular from his or her own classroom. During the peer-pairing sessions, children engaged in joint-task activities (e.g., board games) that required interaction.

Substantial improvements in peer acceptance and positive interaction rates were noted following the peer-pairing intervention. With regard to social status, 75% of target children in the treatment group shifted from the peer-neglected status at pretreatment to average or even popular status posttreatment (only 17% of controls demonstrated improvement in social status). Individual gains in absolute percentage of time spent in positive interaction on the playground during recess ranged from 13% to 45% over baseline levels (average gain of 28%). Prior to intervention, all children who were peer-neglected were found to have positive interaction rates significantly below the mean rates of children with average and popular status. Following the peer-pairing intervention, 50% of the treatment group had positive interaction rates above the mean rate obtained for children with average and popular status. No increase in positive interaction rate was observed for the control group. Gains in peer acceptance and positive social interaction remained constant at a 1-month follow-up.

Peer pairing may be conceptualized as the provision and structuring of a facilitative environment that is conducive to mutually reinforcing social interaction influences. Changes in behavior follow from changes in social reinforcement contingencies. Improvements in observed behavior among children who are peerneglected may be explained by reinforcement mechanisms that operate in the peer-pairing condition. In addition, changes in peer perceptions may derive largely from the altered perceptions and behavior of the peer confederates as a result of social interaction effects. In other words, children in the peer-pairing intervention appeared to enjoy playing together, which may have increased the probability that they would play together at their next regular recess period. Other children could then witness the pair playing together, which may have increased the probability that they, too, would interact with the target child. Such processes may lead children who are peer-neglected to become integrated into the popular peer's social group.

Social Effectiveness Therapy for Children

Social Effectiveness Therapy for Children (SET–C; Beidel, Turner, & Morris, 1994) is a multicomponent behavioral intervention program for childhood social phobia. SET–C is a comprehensive program designed to reduce social anxiety, enhance social skills, increase participation in social activities, and improve selfconfidence. Components of the SET–C program include Parent Education, SST and Peer Generalization, Graduated In Vivo Exposure, and Programmed Practice. The length of the intervention program is 16 weeks. The parent education component consists of one session on the nature of social anxiety and an overview of the intervention program. Subsequent to the parent education component, intervention sessions are held twice weekly for 12 weeks: one small-group session (SST) and one individual session (Graduated In Vivo Exposure). Group sessions are

180 minutes in length (60 minutes of SST and 120 minutes of peer generalization experiences). Strategies used to teach and reinforce appropriate social behavior include instruction, modeling, behavior rehearsal, feedback, and social reinforcement.

SET–C targets five major topic areas:

1. Nonverbal social skills
2. Initiating and maintaining conversations
3. Joining groups of children
4. Establishing and maintaining friendships
5. Positive assertion and negative assertion

A unique and essential component of SET–C is the use of formalized peer interaction experiences to assist in the generalization of social skills to situations outside the clinic. Typical child volunteers are recruited from the community to serve as peer facilitators in the peer generalization experiences (developmentally appropriate group recreational activities, such as roller skating). Following completion of the group SST and individual graduated exposure components, four additional weekly sessions are devoted to programmed practice. Programmed practice consists of individualized therapist-directed exposure activities that the child completes in the natural environment, unaccompanied by the therapist. Although a 3-year National Institutes of Health–funded study is in progress to assess empirically the efficacy of SET–C in intervention for childhood social phobia, initial results have been extremely promising with significant gains demonstrated across several assessment modalities (e.g., self-report, self-monitoring, behavior assessment, parent report).

Cognitive-Behavioral Group Treatment for Adolescent Social Phobia

Cognitive-Behavioral Group Treatment for Adolescent Social Phobia (CBGT–A; Albano, DiBartolo, Heimberg, & Barlow, 1995; Albano, Marten, Holt, Heimberg, & Barlow, 1995) is a 16-session intervention protocol for social phobia in adolescents (for detailed descriptions of the protocol, see Albano & Barlow, 1996, and Albano, DiBartolo, et al., 1995). Designed for adolescents ages 13–17, CBGT–A combines psychoeducation, skills training (cognitive restructuring, problem solving, social and assertiveness skills), and systematic behavioral exposure both within session and in vivo. Therapists utilize modeling, role playing, positive reinforcement, and skill rehearsal. Parents are involved in a limited number of sessions so that the intervention rationale and conceptualization of the disorder can be presented to them and to enlist the parents as coaches to assist with the between-session exposure homework. Results of preliminary studies (Albano & Barlow, 1996; Albano, Marten, et al., 1995) have been promising.

The Family Context

An evaluation of the family context is essential for effective assessment of and intervention for social anxiety and phobia. Patterns of familial aggregation of anxiety disorders have been identified through epidemiological studies (e.g., Turner, Beidel, & Costello, 1987). Higher rates of fears, somatic complaints, school difficulties, and solitary activity have been reported in children of parents with anxiety disorders (Turner et al., 1987).

Retrospectively, adults with anxiety disorders have rated their parents as high on overprotection and low on emotional warmth (Arrindell, Emmelkamp, Monsma, & Brilman, 1983; Morris & Huffman, 1996), as having isolated them from social events, and as expressing excessive social evaluative concerns (Bruch, Heimberg, Berger, & Collins, 1989). Anxious parents may be more likely to model dependency, to reinforce anxious behaviors in their children, and to be socially isolated. In early childhood, opportunities for social interaction must be arranged by the parents. A restrictive family environment may have an adverse impact on the child's development of social proficiency (Daniels & Plomin, 1985; Parke & Bhavnagri, 1989).

Recognizing the impact of anxiety on the family system (see Albano, Chorpita, & Barlow, 1996) and the potential for family members to participate inadvertently in the maintenance of an anxiety disorder, several investigators have developed behavioral intervention protocols that directly incorporate family members in the inter-

vention. For example, Family Anxiety Management (FAM; Heard, Dadds, & Rapee, 1992) is based on behavioral family intervention strategies that have been found to be effective in the intervention for externalizing disorders in youth (Sanders & Dadds, 1992). Following each individual child session, children and their parents participate in a FAM session. Parents are taught reinforcement strategies, with emphasis on differential reinforcement and selective *inattention* to anxious behavior. Contingency management strategies are used to enhance communication and problem-solving skills within the family. The inclusion of FAM sessions has been reported to improve intervention outcomes significantly when compared with individual child intervention alone (Barrett, Dadds, & Rapee, 1996).

CONCLUSION

Contemporary child behavior therapy reflects an awareness of the unique developmental and family contexts that are relevant to the construction and implementation of intervention programs for children, as opposed to mere downward applications of interventions that have been designed for adults. This chapter has discussed functional assessment and the constructional approach to intervention for childhood problems and presented a selective review of promising developments that emphasize a constructional, or educative, approach to intervention for conduct problems and social anxiety and social competence problems. Although considerable advances have been made, continued empirical work is necessary to identify factors that facilitate and that impede successful intervention. Emphasis on the development of *cost-effective* intervention strategies is of particular relevance given the financial climate surrounding mental health–related issues and the increasing need for accountability. Additional areas of concern and needed development with these forms of behavior excesses and deficits include functional diagnostic criteria (Scotti, Morris, McNeil, & Hawkins, 1996) and the further development of functional analysis procedures and their application to various populations (see Scotti, Mullen, & Hawkins, 1998, as well as various other chapters in this book). Finally, the reader should note the important shift in the basic philosophical and conceptual approach to these two clinical areas—a basic paradigm shift that is evident in all of the chapters of this text.

REFERENCES

Albano, A.M., & Barlow, D.H. (1996). Breaking the vicious cycle: Cognitive-behavioral group treatment for adolescent social phobia. In E.D. Hibbs & P. Jensen (Eds.), *Psychosocial treatment research for child and adolescent disorders* (pp. 43–62). Washington, DC: American Psychological Association Press.

Albano, A.M., Chorpita, B.F., & Barlow, D.H. (1996). Childhood anxiety disorders. In E.J. Mash & R.A. Barkley (Eds.), *Child psychopathology* (pp. 196–241). New York: Guilford Press.

Albano, A.M., DiBartolo, P.M., Heimberg, R.G., & Barlow, D.H. (1995). Children and adolescents: Assessment and treatment. In R.G. Heimberg, M.R. Liebowitz, D.A. Hope, & F. Schneier (Eds.), *Social phobia: Diagnosis, assessment, and treatment* (pp. 387–425). New York: Guilford Press.

Albano, A.M., Marten, P.A., Holt, C.S., Heimberg, R.G., & Barlow, D.H. (1995). Cognitive-behavioral group treatment for social phobia in adolescents: A preliminary study. *Journal of Nervous and Mental Disease, 183,* 685–692.

American Psychiatric Association. (1994). *Diagnostic and statistical manual of mental disorders* (4th ed.). Washington, DC: Author.

Arkowitz, H. (1981). Assessment of social skills. In M. Hersen & A.S. Bellack (Eds.), *Behavioral assessment* (pp. 296–327). New York: Pergamon.

Arrindell, W.A., Emmelkamp, P.M.G., Monsma, A., & Brilman, E. (1983). The role of perceived parental rearing practices in the aetiology of phobic disorders: A controlled study. *British Journal of Psychiatry, 155,* 526–535.

Bailey, J.S., Wolf, M.M., & Phillips, E.L. (1970). Home-based reinforcement and the modification of pre-delinquents' classroom behavior. *Journal of Applied Behavior Analysis, 3,* 223–233.

Barrett, P.M., Dadds, M.R., & Rapee, R.M. (1996). Family intervention for childhood anxiety: A controlled trial. *Journal of Consulting and Clinical Psychology, 64,* 333–342.

Barrios, B., & O'Dell, S. (1989). Fears and anxieties. In E.J. Mash & R.A. Barkley (Eds.), *Treatment of childhood disorders* (pp. 167–221). New York: Guilford Press.

Beidel, D.C., Turner, S.M., & Morris, T.L. (1994). *Social effectiveness training for children: Treatment manual.* Unpublished manuscript.

Berler, E.S., Gross, A.M., & Drabman, R.S. (1982). Social skills training with children: Proceed with caution. *Journal of Applied Behavior Analysis, 15,* 151–162.

Braukmann, C.J., Maloney, D.M., Fixsen, D.L., Phillips, E.L., & Wolf, M.M. (1974). Analysis of a selection interview training package. *Criminal Justice and Behavior, 1,* 30–42.

Bruch, M.A., Heimberg, R.G., Berger, P., & Collins, T.M. (1989). Social phobia and perceptions of early parental and personal characteristics. *Anxiety Research, 2/1,* 57–65.

Bryant, B., & Snodgrass, R.D. (1990). Therapeutic foster care: Past and present. In P. Meadowcroft & B.A. Trout (Eds.), *Troubled youth in treatment homes: A handbook of therapeutic foster care* (pp. 1–20). Washington, DC: Child Welfare League of America.

Chamberlain, P. (1994). *Family connections: A treatment foster care model for adolescents with delinquency.* Eugene, OR: Castalia.

Christopher, J.S., Hansen, D.J., & MacMillan, V.M. (1991). Effectiveness of a peer-helper intervention to increase children's social interactions. *Behavior Modification, 15,* 22–50.

Daniels, D., & Plomin, R. (1985). Origins of individual differences in infant shyness. *Developmental Psychology, 21,* 118–121.

DeFries, C., Jenkins, S., & Williams, E.C. (1970). Foster family care for disturbed children: A nonsentimental view. In A. Kadushin (Ed.), *Child welfare services: A sourcebook* (pp. 193–209). London: MacMillan.

Donahoe, J.W., & Palmer, D.C. (1994). *Learning and complex behavior.* Needham Heights, MA: Allyn & Bacon.

Eisen, A.R., & Kearney, C.A. (1995). *Practitioner's guide to treating fear and anxiety in children and adolescents: A cognitive-behavioral approach.* Northvale, NJ: Jason Aronson, Inc.

Evans, I.M. (1993). Constructional perspectives in clinical assessment. *Psychological Assessment, 5,* 264–272.

Foster Family-based Treatment Association. (1991). *Program standards for treatment foster care.* St. Paul, MN: Author.

Furman, W., Rahe, D.F., & Hartup, W.W. (1979). Rehabilitation of socially withdrawn preschool children through mixed-age and same-age socialization. *Child Development, 50,* 915–922.

Goldiamond, I. (1974). Toward a constructional approach to social problems: Ethical and constitutional issues raised by applied behavioral analysis. *Behaviorism, 2,* 1–85.

Grealish, E.M., Hawkins, R.P., Meadowcroft, P., & Lynch, P. (1990). Serving families of children in therapeutic foster care. In P. Meadowcroft & B.A. Trout (Eds.), *Troubled youth in treatment homes: A handbook of therapeutic foster care* (pp. 126–142). Washington, DC: Child Welfare League of America.

Grealish, E.M., & Meadowcroft, P. (1990). Referring to, and placing children in, treatment homes. In P. Meadowcroft & B.A. Trout (Eds.), *Troubled youth in treatment homes: A handbook of therapeutic foster care* (pp. 51–63). Washington, DC: Child Welfare League of America.

Gross, N., & Campbell, P. (1990). Recruiting and selecting treatment parents. In P. Meadowcroft & B.A. Trout (Eds.), *Troubled youth in treatment homes: A handbook of therapeutic foster care* (pp. 33–50). Washington, DC: Child Welfare League of America.

Haapala, D., & Kinney, J. (1979). Homebuilders' approach to the training of in-home therapists. In S. Maybanks & M. Bryce (Eds.), *Home-based services for children and families* (pp. 248–259). Springfield, IL: Charles C Thomas.

Hawkins, R.P. (1979). The functions of assessment: Implications for selection and development of devices for assessing repertoires in clinical, educational, and other settings. *Journal of Applied Behavior Analysis, 12,* 501–516.

Hawkins, R.P. (1986). Selection of target behaviors. In R.O. Nelson & S.C. Hayes (Eds.), *Conceptual foundations of behavioral assessment* (pp. 331–385). New York: Guilford Press.

Hawkins, R.P. (1989). The nature and potential of therapeutic foster care programs. In R.P. Hawkins & J. Breiling (Eds.), *Therapeutic foster care: Critical issues* (pp. 5–36). Washington, DC: Child Welfare League of America.

Hawkins, R.P., Almeida, M.C., Fabry, B., & Reitz, A.L. (1992). A scale to measure restrictiveness of living environments for troubled children and youths. *Hospital and Community Psychiatry, 43,* 54–58.

Hawkins, R.P., Almeida, M.C., & Samet, M. (1989). Comparative evaluation of foster-family–based treatment and five other placement choices: A preliminary report. In A. Algarin, R.M. Friedman, A.J. Duchnowski, K.M. Kutash, S.E. Silver, & M.K. Johnson (Eds.), *Children's mental health services and policy: Building a research base* (pp. 98–119). Tampa: University of South Florida, Florida Mental Health Institute.

Hawkins, R.P., Luster, W.C., & Meadowcroft, P.M. (1987, August). *Foster-family–based treatment: What is it?* Symposium presented at the annual convention of the American Psychological Association, New York.

Hawkins, R.P., Meadowcroft, P., Trout, B.A., & Luster, W.C. (1985). Foster family–based treatment. *Journal of Clinical Child Psychology, 14,* 220–228.

Hawkins, R.P., Peterson, R.F., Schweid, E., & Bijou, S.W. (1966). Behavior therapy in the home: Amelioration of problem parent–child relations with the parent in a therapeutic role. *Journal of Experimental Child Psychology, 4,* 88–107.

Heard, P.M., Dadds, M.R., & Rapee, R.M. (1992, July). *The role of family intervention in the treatment of child anxiety disorders.* Paper presented at the World Congress on Behavioural Therapy, Gold Coast, Australia.

Henggeler, S.W., Melton, G.B., & Smith, L.A. (1992). Family preservation using multisystemic therapy: An effective alternative to incarcerating serious juvenile offenders. *Journal of Consulting and Clinical Psychology, 60,* 953–961.

Henggeler, S.W., Rodick, J.D., Borduin, C.M., Hanson, C.L., Watson, S.M., & Urey, J.R. (1986). Multisystemic treatment of juvenile offenders: Effects on adolescent behavior and family interactions. *Developmental Psychology, 22,* 132–141.

Hobbs, N. (1966). Helping disturbed children: Psychological and ecological strategies. *American Psychologist, 21,* 1105–1115.

Hobbs, S.A., Moguin, L.E., Tyroler, M., & Lahey, B.B. (1980). Cognitive behavior therapy with children: Has clinical utility been demonstrated? *Psychological Bulletin, 87,* 147–165.

Johnson, J.E., & McGillicuddy-Delisi, D.A. (1983). Family environment factors and children's knowledge of rules and conventions. *Child Development, 54,* 218–226.

Jones, M.C. (1924). The elimination of children's fears. *Journal of Experimental Psychology, 7,* 382–390.

Kazdin, A.E. (1985). *Treatment of antisocial behavior in children and adolescents.* Homewood, IL: Dorsey.

Kazdin, A.E. (1987). *Conduct disorders in childhood and adolescence.* Thousand Oaks, CA: Sage Publications.

Kelley, M.L. (1990). *School–home notes: Promoting children's classroom success.* New York: Guilford Press.

Kendall, P.C. (1990). *Coping cat workbook.* (Available from author, 238 Meeting House Lane, Merion Station, PA 19066.)

Kinney, J., & Haapala, D. (1981). Assessment of families in crisis. In M. Bryce & J.C. Lloyd (Eds.), *Treating families in the home* (pp. 50–67). Springfield, IL: Charles C Thomas.

Kinney, J., Madsen, B., Fleming, T., & Haapala, D. (1977). Homebuilders: Keeping families together. *Journal of Consulting and Clinical Psychology, 45,* 667–673.

Kirigin, K.A., Braukmann, C.J., Atwater, J.D., & Wolf, M.M. (1982). An evaluation of Teaching-Family (Achievement Place) group homes for juvenile offenders. *Journal of Applied Behavior Analysis, 15,* 1–16.

LaGreca, A.M., Dandes, S.K., Wick, P., Shaw, K., & Stone, W.L. (1988). Development of the Social Anxiety Scale for Children: Reliability and concurrent validity. *Journal of Clinical Child Psychology, 17,* 84–91.

Leitenberg, H., & Callahan, E. (1973). Reinforced practice and reduction of different kinds of fears in adults and children. *Behaviour Research and Therapy, 11,* 19–30.

Levis, D.J. (1985). Implosive therapy: A comprehensive extension of conditioning theory of fear/anxiety to psychopathology. In S. Reiss & R.R. Bootzin (Eds.), *Theoretical issues in behavior therapy* (pp. 49–82). New York: Academic Press.

Lyons, J.A., & Scotti, J.R. (1995). Behavioral treatment of a motor vehicle accident survivor: An illustrative case of direct therapeutic exposure. *Cognitive and Behavioral Practice, 2,* 343–364.

Mash, E.J. (1989). Treatment of child and family disturbance: A behavioral-systems perspective. In E.J. Mash & R.A. Barkley (Eds.), *Treatment of childhood disorders* (pp. 3–38). New York: Guilford Press.

Mash, E.J., & Barkley, R.A. (Eds.). (1989). *Treatment of childhood disorders.* New York: Guilford Press.

Maybanks, S., & Bryce, M. (1979). *Home-based services for children and families.* Springfield, IL: Charles C Thomas.

Meadowcroft, P., & Grealish, E.M. (1990). Training and supporting treatment parents. In P. Meadowcroft & B.A. Trout (Eds.), *Troubled youth in treatment homes: A handbook of therapeutic foster care* (pp. 64–86). Washington, DC: Child Welfare League of America.

Meadowcroft, P., Hawkins, R.P., Grealish, E.M., & Weaver, P. (1990). Providing services to children in therapeutic foster care. In P. Meadowcroft & B.A. Trout (Eds.), *Troubled youth in treatment homes: A handbook of therapeutic foster care* (pp. 100–125). Washington, DC: Child Welfare League of America.

Meadowcroft, P., & Trout, B.A. (Eds.). (1990). *Troubled youth in treatment homes: A handbook of therapeutic foster care.* Washington, DC: Child Welfare League of America.

Meyer, L.H., & Evans, I.M. (1989). *Nonaversive intervention for behavior problems: A manual for home and community.* Baltimore: Paul H. Brookes Publishing Co.

Minkin, N., Braukmann, C.J., Minkin, B.L., Timbers, G.D., Timbers, B.J., Fixsen, D.L., Phillips, E.L., & Wolf, M.M. (1976). The social validation and training of conversational skills. *Journal of Applied Behavior Analysis, 9,* 127–139.

Morris, R.J., & Kratochwill, T.R. (1983). Childhood fears and phobias. In R.J. Morris & T.R. Kratochwill (Eds.), *The practice of child therapy* (pp. 53–86). New York: Pergamon.

Morris, T.L., & Huffman, D.G. (1996, November). *Influence of parenting style on the development of shyness and social anxiety.* Paper presented at the annual meeting of the Association for Advancement of Behavior Therapy, New York.

Morris, T.L., Messer, S.C., & Gross, A.M. (1995). Enhancement of the social interaction and status of neglected children: A peer-pairing approach. *Journal of Clinical Child Psychology, 24,* 11–20.

Mowrer, O.H. (1947). On the dual nature of learning: A reinterpretation of "conditioning" and "problem-solving." *Harvard Educational Review, 17,* 102–148.

Mowrer, O.H. (1960). *Learning theory and behavior.* New York: John Wiley & Sons.

Ollendick, T.H. (1979). Fear reduction techniques with children. In M. Hersen, R.M. Eisler, & P.M. Miller (Eds.), *Progress in behavior modification* (Vol. 8, pp. 127–168). New York: Academic Press.

Ollendick, T.H., & Cerny, J.A. (1981). *Clinical behavior therapy with children.* New York: Plenum.

Parke, R.D., & Bhavnagri, N.P. (1989). Parents as managers of children's peer relationships. In D. Belle (Ed.), *Children's social networks and social supports* (pp. 241–259). New York: John Wiley & Sons.

Parker, J.G., & Asher, S.R. (1987). Peer relations and later personal adjustment: Are low accepted children at risk? *Psychological Bulletin, 102,* 357–389.

Phillips, E.L. (1968). Achievement Place: Token reinforcement procedures in a home-style rehabilitation setting for "pre-delinquent" boys. *Journal of Applied Behavior Analysis, 1,* 213–223.

Phillips, E.L., Phillips, E.A., Fixsen, D.L., & Wolf, M.M. (1974). *The teaching-family handbook* (rev. ed.). Lawrence: University of Kansas, Achievement Place Project.

Purkel, W., & Bornstein, M.H. (1980). Pictures and imagery both enhance children's short-term and long-term recall. *Developmental Psychology, 16,* 153–154.

Risley, T., & Wolf, M.M. (1966). Experimental manipulation of autistic behaviors and generalization into the home. In R. Ulrich, T. Stachnik, & J. Mabry (Eds.), *Control of human behavior* (pp. 193–198). Glenview, IL: Scott, Foresman.

Rubin, K.H., LeMare, L.J., & Lollis, S. (1990). Social withdrawal in childhood: Developmental pathways to peer rejection. In S.R. Asher & J.D. Coie (Eds.), *Peer rejection in childhood* (pp. 217–249). New York: Cambridge University Press.

Sanders, M., & Dadds, M.R. (1992). *Behavioral family intervention.* New York: Pergamon.

Schwartz, A., & Goldiamond, I. (1975). *Social casework: A behavioral approach.* New York: Columbia University Press.

Scotti, J.R., Morris, T.L., McNeil, C.B., & Hawkins, R.P. (1996). DSM-IV and disorders of childhood and adolescence: Can structural criteria be functional? In W. Follette (Ed.), The DSM-IV [Special Issue]. *Journal of Consulting and Clinical Psychology, 64,* 1177–1191.

Scotti, J.R., Mullen, K.B., & Hawkins, R.P. (1998). Child conduct and developmental disabilities: From theory to practice in the treatment of excess behaviors. In J.J. Plaud & G.H. Eifert (Eds.), *From behavior theory to behavior therapy* (pp. 172–202). New York: Allyn & Bacon.

Skinner, B.F. (1953). *Science and human behavior.* New York: Macmillan.

Snodgrass, R.D., & Bryant, B. (1989). Therapeutic foster care: A national program survey. In R.P. Hawkins & J. Breiling (Eds.), *Therapeutic foster care: Critical issues* (pp. 37–76). Washington, DC: Child Welfare League of America.

Snodgrass, R.D., & Campbell, P. (1981, November). *Specialized foster care: A community alternative to institutional placement.* Paper presented at the Association for Advancement of Behavior Therapy, Toronto, Ontario, Canada.

Strain, P.S., & Fox, J.E. (1981). Peers as therapeutic agents for isolated classmates. In A.E. Kazdin & B.B. Lahey (Eds.), *Advances in child clinical psychology* (Vol. 4, pp. 167–198). New York: Plenum.

Strain, P.S., & Odom, S.L. (1986). Peer social initiations: Effective interventions for social skills development in exceptional children. *Exceptional Children, 52,* 543–551.

Strauss, C.C., Lahey, B.B., Frick, P., Frame, C.L., & Hynd, G.W. (1988). Peer social status of children with anxiety disorders. *Journal of Consulting and Clinical Psychology, 56,* 137–141.

Tharp, R.G., & Wetzel, R.J. (1969). *Behavior modification in the natural environment.* New York: Academic Press.

Tiffen, K., & Spence, S.H. (1986). Responsiveness of isolated versus rejected children to social skills training. *Journal of Child Psychology and Psychiatry, 27,* 343–355.

Turner, S.M., Beidel, D.C., & Costello, A. (1987). Psychopathology in the offspring of anxiety disorders patients. *Journal of Consulting and Clinical Psychology, 55,* 229–235.

Vernberg, E.M., Abwender, D.A., Ewell, K.K., & Beery, S.H. (1992). Social anxiety and peer relationships in early adolescence: A prospective analysis. *Journal of Clinical Child Psychology, 21,* 189–196.

Walker, H.M., Greenwood, C.R., Hops, H., & Todd, N. (1979). Differential effects of reinforcing topographic components of free play social interaction: Analysis and systematic replication. *Behavior Modification, 3,* 291–321.

Weisz, J.R., Weiss, B., Alicke, M.D., & Klotz, M.L. (1987). Effectiveness of psychotherapy with children and adolescents: A meta-analysis for clinicians. *Journal of Consulting and Clinical Psychology, 55,* 542–549.

Whitehill, M.B., Hersen, M., & Bellack, A.S. (1980). Conversational skills training for socially isolated children. *Behaviour Research and Therapy, 18,* 217–225.

Wolpe, J. (1958). *Psychotherapy by reciprocal inhibition.* Stanford, CA: Stanford.

Chapter 7

A Transdisciplinary Model for Students' Social and Emotional Development

Creating a Context for Inclusion

Douglas Cheney & Craig Barringer

"I wish to present a case study in institution building, an account of a planful social invention to meet an acute national problem, the problem of emotional disturbance in children" (Hobbs, 1966, p. 1105). In the mid-1990s, Hobbs's introductory comments to the Seventy-Fourth Annual Convention of the American Psychological Association have as much, if not more, relevance to the introduction of this chapter. Summary data from the Sixteenth Annual Report to Congress (U.S. Department of Education, Office of Special Education Programs, 1994) reinforce the nature of this "national problem" regarding the performance of children and youth with emotional or behavioral disorders (EBD). When reviewed as a group, these students have difficulty meeting academic demands (e.g., low grades, failing classes, more grade retentions); have higher rates of dropping out or aging out of school; are placed in educational or therapeutic environments outside their local schools;

are disproportionately overrepresented by African American children, poor children, and boys; and have higher rates of arrest than either typically developing students or students with other disabilities (U.S. Department of Education, Office of Special Education Programs, 1994). These data suggest that students with EBD continue to present great challenges to schools and communities and require an integrated education program to meet their unique needs.

The purpose of this chapter is to present an approach that addresses programmatic and staff development needs, as well as parent supports, to create the context for students' productive social and emotional development in school and the community. The recommendations in this approach come from the development and implementation of Project DESTINY (**D**esigning **E**ducational **S**upport **T**eams through **In**terdisciplinary **N**etworks for **Y**outh with Emotional or Behavioral Disorders), a research project that

Parts of this chapter are based on two previously published articles: Cheney, Barringer, Upham, and Manning (1996) and Cheney and Muscott (1996). Support for this chapter was in part from Grant No. H237D30012, U.S. Office of Special Education and Rehabilitative Services.

was funded through an initiative for students with serious emotional disturbance, which was authorized in the Individuals with Disabilities Education Act (IDEA) of 1990 (PL 101-476). The initiative is contained in the Programs for Children and Youth with Serious Emotional Disturbance, which is overseen by the U.S. Office of Special Education and Rehabilitative Services (OSERS).

Project DESTINY is based on the theory and practice gained from effective programs for students with EBD that have been implemented since the mid-1960s. For example, as suggested by Rhodes (1963), the general schoolwide curriculum in Project DESTINY relied on individualized learning units, instruction of prosocial skills, and constant feedback to students about their behavior. Furthermore, behavioral interventions similar to those first introduced by Haring and Phillips (1962) and Hewett (1967) were used by classroom teachers to teach and manage desired behaviors of students. Finally, Rhodes's (1967) ecological perspective helped to determine the conditions that lead to the best "fit" between students and classrooms. Values espoused by Hobbs (1966, 1982), emphasizing trust, competence, and affective expression, helped to support strength-based education of youth with EBD.

The work of early pioneers has been enhanced by others to build school-based programs for students with EBD (Jones, 1987, 1992; Peacock Hill Working Group, 1991; Walker et al., 1996). Proven approaches such as ecological assessments of general education classes and teachers' use of effective communication skills and establishment of high expectations have assisted schools in their improvement of services to students with EBD. Consistent use of effective classroom management techniques has provided teachers with strategies to reinforce students positively. Individualized behavior management coupled with social skills instruction for students has created more productive learning environments. Finally, parent education and support programs have strengthened partnerships between schools and families and have led to positive improvements for children (Cheney & Osher, 1997). Schoolwide structures

(e.g., leadership teams, collaborative teaming, co-teaching, home–school partnerships, interagency collaboration) and proven instructional strategies (e.g., social skills training, data-based instruction, behavior plans for skill generalization) serve as the foundation for effective school programs for students with EBD (Muscott, 1995; Peacock Hill Working Group, 1991).

Efforts to design and evaluate programs for students with EBD that expand service models, develop culturally and ethnically sensitive programs, promote parent advocacy, and encourage interagency collaboration now are central to the National Agenda to Improve Outcomes for Children and Youth with EBD (Osher & Hanley, 1996). Collaborative efforts between staff at OSERS and the Chesapeake Institute were successful in creating a national agenda for students with EBD. The agenda was generated through the input of a variety of national stakeholders and includes seven strategic targets for professionals, parents, and students with EBD to

1. Expand positive learning opportunities and results for students
2. Strengthen school and community capacity for working with students
3. Value and address diversity
4. Collaborate with families
5. Promote appropriate assessment
6. Provide ongoing skill development and support to professionals and parents
7. Create comprehensive and collaborative systems (Osher & Hanley, 1996; U.S. Department of Education, Office of Special Education Programs, 1994)

The national agenda is being implemented through a number of discretionary programs that have included research, demonstration, and personnel preparation projects. One of the competitive priorities for these programs has focused on improving the knowledge, skills, and strategies of professionals who work with students with EBD. In addition, this priority emphasized the necessity of collaborative projects that develop working relationships among professionals in education, mental health, social work, and other allied fields and parents of students with EBD. Project DESTINY is 1 of 10 projects funded nationally.

PROJECT DESTINY: DEVELOPING THE CONTEXT FOR THE INCLUSION OF STUDENTS WITH EMOTIONAL OR BEHAVIORAL DISORDERS IN GENERAL EDUCATION PROGRAMS

The staff of Project DESTINY have focused on structures, knowledge, and strategies needed by school and family members to create the context for inclusion of youth with EBD (Cheney, 1994, 1998; Cheney & Barringer, 1995; Cheney, Barringer, Upham, & Manning, 1996). The Project DESTINY model is based on the assumption that inclusion of students with EBD requires full commitment from the faculty, full participation of parents, and dedication of community resources to support the school as the site of integrated and coordinated care. Project DESTINY has consistently used prior theory and research findings to enhance practices in public education. For example, Project DESTINY has emphasized that individual needs of students and families should be used to generate appropriate curriculum for students (Curwin & Mendler, 1988; Glasser, 1965; Neel & Cessna, 1993). This is consistent with Rhodes's (1963) notion that therapeutic work with children and youth should support their goal-driven behavior within the context of interpersonal interactions. Furthermore, this interpersonal behavior must be effective within the context of one's educational program and community (MacFarquhar, Dowrick, & Risley, 1993; Osher & Hanley, 1996; Stroul & Friedman, 1986). Project DESTINY relies on educational practices that are collaborative and problem solving in nature and that involve family members to the maximum extent (Cheney & Osher, 1997; Pugach & Johnson, 1995). Findings from research that recommend grade-level teaming, teacher support, and systematic student services review also have been incorporated (Eber, 1996; Pugach & Johnson, 1995), along with proven strategies such as social skills education, social problem solving, and behavioral contracting (Goldstein, 1988; Rhode, Jenson, & Reavis, 1994; Walker, Colvin, & Ramsey, 1995;

see also Chapter 9). In addition to including families in the educational programs of their children, Project DESTINY has provided important parent support and education programs (Friesen & Osher, 1996; Illback & Nelson, 1996). This effort has therefore attended to important findings from program research and applied them in an approach that is tailored to middle school education.

The Project DESTINY approach addresses four related levels—the individual, the classroom, the school, and the community, including the family—and coordinates 10 components to optimize the social and emotional functioning of students. The goal of the program is to build the capacity of educators, administrators, parents, and other professionals to work more effectively in the public schools with students with EBD. Intensive staff development to enhance the knowledge and strategies of educators has been emphasized throughout this project, along with the creation of new structures for program improvements, school–parent partnerships, and action plans that seek to improve services to students in general education environments. Although differences in training and experience exist among educators, the relationship of a teacher (irrespective of specialty areas) or an administrator to any particular student and family is considered to be paramount in this approach. The model is, therefore, considered to be *transdisciplinary* and involves educators, community professionals, parents, and students in creating a meaningful and successful education program.

The components of Project DESTINY described in this chapter were implemented with teachers, students, parents, and community members at three middle schools in three New Hampshire communities. Specific demographic information on these communities is presented in Table 1. The three middle school sites are attempting to include students with EBD in their general education programs to the greatest extent possible. Project DESTINY provides essential supports to the middle schools to

1. Enhance and expand teachers' knowledge, skills, and strategies for working with students

Table 1. Demographics for community sites

Community	Population of town	Students in middle school	Middle school teachers	Students in Project DESTINY	Families in Project DESTINY
A	75,000	850	60	44	4
B	10,000	520	51	23	7
C	9,400	615	40	33	8

2. Improve collaborative efforts of school teams of four to eight members for working with students in grades 6–8
3. Provide education and support to parents of students with EBD
4. Coordinate service provision for students across a number of community agencies

The first step in Project DESTINY was to present eight in-service training units to faculty of participating schools during 1994–1995. These units were developed to meet the objectives of the project and were derived from empirical findings at the schools regarding teachers' knowledge and skill base and students' functioning in social, affective, and academic areas (Cheney & Barringer, 1995). The training units were presented to the entire school faculty on a monthly basis. Each 90-minute unit was designed to present the requisite knowledge and general awareness for working effectively with students with EBD and their parents. The training units, as described by Cheney and colleagues (1996), are outlined in Table 2.

The second step in Project DESTINY's approach is to apply in a case review format the knowledge, skills, and strategies acquired in the training sessions. Students are scheduled for review, and information concerning their school and community performance is organized on a student services worksheet (Barringer & Hutchens, 1993). The student services worksheet assesses the student's strengths and problems in four areas: biological, interpersonal, cognitive, and affective (discussed later in the section "Increasing Staff Knowledge"). The final approach to assisting teachers with new skills and strategies is to spend time in their classrooms. The purpose of this involvement is to observe the use of new skills by faculty and to coach them in the use of the skills. Coaching has been iden-

tified as a key variable to support teachers' use of effective instructional and management procedures (Gersten & Woodward, 1990).

COMPONENTS OF THE TRANSDISCIPLINARY MODEL

Project DESTINY has promoted 10 components that the chapter authors determined were essential to creating an inclusive school context for students with EBD. *Inclusive context* is defined as a school's capacity to provide appropriate education programs in general education environments through ongoing staff development and commitment of resources. Whereas Project DESTINY's efforts have supported schools with a mission of inclusion, the meaning of inclusion in each school has varied. For example, one school has completely eliminated special education classrooms for students with EBD, another uses a separate problem-solving classroom for students who violate rules in general education classrooms, and the third maintains a modified resource room staffed by a special education teacher to work with students during assigned periods of the day. Across all of these schools, Project DESTINY has worked with faculty, parents, and community professionals to implement the project components. Each component and its implementation in Project DESTINY is described in detail in the sections that follow.

Mission Statement

The chapter authors' observations in schools suggest that there is a great need for school faculty to discuss and review their vision of what can be accomplished for children and youth. In regional and national work, the authors have talked with teachers who were unaware of the rationale, mission, or vision for including students with EBD in general education. The teachers' experiences

Table 2. Staff development topics for Project DESTINY during the 1994–1995 school year

Topic	Topic description
1. Team assessment and program planning for students with emotional or behavioral disabilities (see Eber, 1996; Sugai & Horner, 1994; Walker, Colvin, & Ramsey, 1995)	1. This session focuses on how team members can contribute to understanding students through observations, personal judgments, and archival data. Through the use of the data, team members develop and monitor intervention plans for students.
2. Understanding individual differences of students (see Cicchetti, 1993; Mattison, Lynch, Kales, & Gamble, 1993; Walker & Severson, 1992; Walker, Severson, & Feil, 1995)	2. Project staff prepare descriptions of students from a variety of diagnostic categories. Participants learn defining characteristics of students with different diagnoses and discuss suitable intervention strategies. Distinctions between externalizing and internalizing behaviors are emphasized.
3. Implementing a social skills curriculum (see Goldstein, 1988; Rutherford, Chipman, DiGangi, & Anderson, 1992; Warger & Rutherford, 1996)	3. School faculty review existing social skills approaches. Project staff make suggestions for instructional strategies to teach the skills. School faculty or teams identify social skills to teach, modify curriculum as necessary, design an implementation plan, and teach sets of desirable behaviors in their class-room. Project staff assist the team in monitoring the use of skills by faculty and staff.
4. Crisis prevention and intervention (see Curwin & Mendler, 1988; Goldstein, Palumbo, Striepling, & Voutsinas, 1995; Walker, Colvin, & Ramsey, 1995)	4. Methods for thwarting behavior problems through the development of positive learn-ing environments are discussed. Participants practice the methods to enhance interper-sonal interactions and relationships. In addition, participants develop plans for crisis intervention and identify critical features of a schoolwide plan.
5. Life-space interviews (see Dice, 1993; Wood & Long, 1991)	5. Life-space interviews are one of many problem-solving approaches for students in crisis. They involve six steps: a) identifying incidents, b) getting youth to talk, c) identi-fying central issues and goals, d) choosing youth-valued solutions, e) developing successful plans to use the solutions, and f) preparing to resume classroom activities.
6. Behavioral contracting (see Algozzine, 1992; Rhode, Jenson, & Reavis, 1994; Rockwell, 1993)	6. Contracting allows the youth and the adult to identify specific behaviors of concern and make agreements on performance of accept-able behaviors. Performance of the desired behavior leads to a mutually agreed-on reinforcer. The contract delineates expecta-tions of youth and adults and the time lines, and it is signed by all involved.
7. Collaborative teaming across the disciplines (see Aldinger, Warger, & Eavy, 1991; Pugach & Johnson, 1995)	7. Skills regarding communication, sharing of feelings, problem solving, reaching shared decisions, and monitoring shared goals are discussed. Teams then use the skills to develop interventions for youth.
8. Engaging families as positive partners (see Cheney & Osher, 1997; Friesen & Osher, 1996)	8. The family coordinator presents issues that parents confront while raising their children, as well as issues that they have in dealing with community professionals. The goal is to reach a better understanding of the com-plexities of parenting youth with emotional or behavior disabilities.

Adapted from Cheney, Barringer, Upham, & Manning (1996).

had been that these students needed specialized therapeutic care—care that they felt unable or, sometimes, unwilling to deliver. Some of their students were being reintegrated into their schools and classrooms from residential treatment centers without any schoolwide preparation for the students' return. The teachers' unfortunate conclusion about this situation was that reintegration was the result of a cost-saving move by the central administration.

A growing body of literature suggests that students with disabilities can be integrated into schools when school faculty discuss, create, and implement their vision for educating a diverse group of learners (Harvey, 1994; Keenan, McLaughlin, & Denton, 1994; Muscott, 1995). Diversity includes ethnicity, culture, language, gender, and disability; the challenge to integrate a wide range of student differences has evolved in public schools since the Civil Rights movement began in the 1950s. A remedy for the challenge that is often overlooked is the development of a shared vision and mutual actions. Without a shared vision, institutions are hampered by the illusion that the world is created of separate, unrelated forces (Senge, 1990). Depending on the impact of any single factor, faculty may become divided and unable to build an integrated and forceful educational approach.

Shared visioning has become a common term in corporate and public institutions. Senge (1990) noted that this visioning, or what the organization seeks to create, is met by many individual attitudes in an organization. These attitudes range from commitment to apathy. Organizations that promote their vision typically are successful at explaining why they want to use a particular practice. Successful schools appear to develop shared vision statements and translate them into meaningful actions. Faculty at these schools tend to decrease external blame toward parents and community and increase ownership of the education of a diverse student body. Given the history of discomfort, nonownership, referral to special education, and negative attributions by general educators toward educating students with EBD (Muscott, Morgan, & Meadows, 1996), schools cannot overlook the importance of a unified school mission among all educators.

Finally, a school's or a district's vision and mission statement regarding the context for inclusion of students with EBD need clear, unequivocal administrative support. In the absence of such support, essential structures and strategies are often not given full acknowledgment. The result is that faculty do not receive the necessary time or resources to implement the numerous and essential supports for the students.

In a survey by Cheney (1994), only 20 of the 47 (43%) districts in New Hampshire had a written vision or mission statement for inclusion of students with EBD, even though all indicated that they were implementing an inclusion program. This low percentage suggests that a need exists for schools to develop a collaborative process for educators, parents, and community members to discuss the attitudes, skills, and resources needed to accomplish their vision for inclusive education. For example, the following is part of the mission statement from one school district in which Project DESTINY was implemented:

Inclusion is a system to accept all students as equal members of the school community. Foremost, it is an attitude that embraces the concept that all students are to be valued and provided all opportunities that are offered by the school. It is the recognition that all students are members of the regular education classroom in which they are placed and that all supportive services are secondary only to their classroom placement. The basic assumption to this belief is that all students can be taught by all teachers. (Conval School District, 1993, p. 3)

The remainder of the district's mission statement explains how students will be educated in general education environments with age-appropriate peers in their neighborhood schools. A successful mission statement, therefore, stresses inclusion of all students as equals and is developed by all stakeholders in the school.

Increasing Staff Knowledge

Creating a viable context for including students with EBD in general education requires that staff members have a working knowledge of 1) the typical course of socioemotional development; 2) the multiple factors that affect socioemotional development; and 3) the types of developmental delays or deviations that students demonstrate through their classroom behavior, including psychological disorders of childhood and adolescence. In addition to directing the choice of specific supports for a particular student and facilitating communication among members of the transdisciplinary team, a working knowledge of these issues can influence educators' attributions. These attributions have been found to be important determinants of teachers' interactions with students. Staff members who have a highly differentiated understanding of factors that affect a student's performance are more likely to initiate empathic and supportive interactions with the student (Kauffman, 1989, 1991).

The factors that influence socioemotional development and the various types of developmental problems that occur in the classroom can be grouped within four broad categories: biological, interpersonal (including family), cognitive, and affective (Barringer & Cheney, 1996; Barringer & Hutchens, 1993). Distinctions among these factors are, of course, arbitrary as school or community behavior can result from the interaction of the factors. Project DESTINY has found, however, that gathering information in each of these categories is a convenient way for general education teachers to differentiate among necessary supports for students with EBD. It is, however, beyond the scope of this chapter to consider the myriad developmental differences and formal psychological diagnoses that characterize the heterogeneous group of students classified as having EBD. The manifestation of such difficulties in students' behavior is perhaps best explained using examples of classroom difficulties arising from each developmental factor.

Biological Factors

The influence of biological factors on students' emotions and behavior can limit the effects of environmental interventions used. Psychological disorders that have a biological component will require a complete medical evaluation and typically include medication as part of the intervention strategy. A common example of the influence of biological factors on classroom be-havior is the student with attention-deficit/hyperactivity disorder (DuPaul & Barkley, 1992). Students with severe hyperactive behavior show greater control over their impulsive and socially intrusive behavior when medication is coupled with other forms of intervention (e.g., parent training, behavior management; see Chapter 4). Another biological influence on students' behavior and feelings in the classroom occurs in cases of mood disorders. Although all students experience fluctuating mood, a subset of students appear to have clinical mood disorders as a result of genetically linked, biochemical factors (Gulley & Nemeroff, 1993; Kazdin, 1988; Rende & Plomin, 1990). Indicators of clinically significant mood disorders include agitation, hopelessness, hostility toward others, and rapid mood shifts. The management of these indicators may greatly improve when antidepressant medication is used in combination with cognitive therapy (Brown & Korn, 1989). Knowing the influence of biological factors on students' behavior is helpful when teachers are setting expectations for students with EBD.

Emotional and Interpersonal Factors

The next two categories, emotional and interpersonal functioning, are strongly affected by a student's early attachment to primary caregivers (Ainsworth, Blehar, Waters, & Wall, 1978; Bowlby, 1988; Greenberg, Speltz, & DeKlyen, 1991). *Attachment* refers to the positive feelings and sense of protection and commitment that children experience in their families. Problems with attachment to caregivers have been found to be related to both internalizing behaviors (e.g., social withdrawal, depression, task avoidance) and externalizing behaviors (e.g., defiance, physical aggression, property destruction). For example, Booth, Spieker, Barnard, and Morisset (1992) examined the relation between attachment during infancy and social behavior 4 years later. Compared with their peers, young children whose caregivers were insensitive to their cues (e.g., crying, posturing, reaching) subsequently showed more aggressive interpersonal behavior and negative affect. With respect to behavior problems in classrooms, a student's difficulties in forming affective bonds may extend beyond the family to affect relationships with school staff. These students often present the most disruptive and intransigent of behavior problems (Barringer & Cheney, 1996; Urban & Carlson, 1991). It is, therefore, important for the school staff to understand the nature of attachment to design programs that nurture students' emotional bonds to the staff and the school.

Cognitive Factors

The fourth factor, cognitive development, also has a significant influence on students' classroom behavior. Cognitive development affects students' social adaptation in two primary ways: social cognition and academic skills. Academic skills deficits can be related to feelings of hopelessness, performance anxiety, task avoidance, and withdrawal from group interaction. Likewise, students who display a variety of externalizing behavior problems (e.g., defiance, disruption, complaining) may have academic skills deficits. In either case, academic support and curriculum modification can facilitate plans to influence the student's social behavior.

Problems with social cognition may be related to students' antisocial actions and involve both their levels of moral reasoning (Dodge, 1980; Kohlberg, 1984) and their perceptions of the intentions of others. With respect to moral reasoning, preconventional thinking is characteristic of students who engage in antisocial behavior (e.g., stealing, vandalism). This level of reasoning holds that the right action is the one that protects the individual's self-interests. Using this moral principal to guide their actions, students with EBD often find themselves in violation of classroom rules and ostracized by their peers. Students may also misinterpret their classmates' motives or intentions. Based on their preconventional moral reasoning and faulty social perception, the student may become aggressive because of a belief in justifiable self-defense. When this aggressive behavior is the result of a cognitive deficit, instructional supports are designed to teach the student salient social behaviors of peers, rather than merely punish his or her aggressive behavior (Arbuthnot, 1992).

A Case Illustrating the Four Factors

The following example illustrates how a student's socioemotional adaptation to school is influenced by the four factors. Tommy is a middle school student living with his father, who is an alcoholic. Tommy's father attempts to control Tommy's aggressive behavior with corporal punishment. Tommy's mother, who is chronically depressed and addicted to drugs, left the family when Tommy was a toddler. She returns periodically whenever she needs a place to live. Neither of Tommy's parents completed high school. Despite average cognitive functioning, Tommy's father withdrew from school after numerous discipline problems, failing grades, and reading difficulties.

Tommy refused to participate in classes in two subjects and was in several fights in school. In contrast, Tommy showed no behavior problems in two other subject areas. When Tommy talked with the assistant principal about his behavior problems in the two other classes, he justified his aggression based on his social perception that the teachers did not like him. He also claimed that other students made fun of him. During sessions with the guidance counselor, Tommy arrived consistently and promptly, which suggested that he was seeking a caring relationship. He still, however, appeared to have trouble trusting his counselor and was often hostile or aloof for no apparent reason. In counseling sessions, Tommy occasionally expressed feelings of hopelessness. These feelings centered on his inability to read, his difficulty with writing, and family issues. Finally, Tommy was tired and listless, and he often skipped meals.

Tommy's rule-violating behaviors might appear simple and amenable to typical systems of reinforcement (e.g., grades, school activities) or punishment for negative behavior (e.g., time-out, suspension). When analyzed in terms of biological, interpersonal, cognitive, and affective factors, however, Tommy's behavior and an appropriate intervention are more complex. Considering the impact of all four factors led Tommy's team to a multimodal intervention plan. In addition to manipulating reinforcement contingencies, the plan included the following:

1. Medication to help with moodiness, impulsivity, and concentration (biological)
2. A social skills program to improve his social perceptions and interactions (emotional/interpersonal)
3. A problem-solving intervention to help him understand his role in conflicts (emotional/interpersonal)
4. Academic support and curriculum modifications in language-based subjects (cognitive)
5. Support for Tommy's father to join parenting and substance abuse groups (interpersonal/familial)
6. Outreach services to the family by a community agency (interpersonal/familial)

Development of Social and Emotional Competencies for Students

The previously noted success of behaviorally oriented interventions in modifying student behavior created a reliance on these approaches as a first line of attack against behavior problems in schools (Haring, 1987; Peacock Hill Working Group, 1991). Multimodal approaches have been recommended increasingly in the intervention approaches for nearly all childhood disorders (Conduct Problems Prevention Research Group, 1992; Peacock Hill Working Group, 1991). One aspect of this multimodal approach should assist students with understanding and managing their emotions and the impact of their emotions on their social behavior and thought processes (Jones, 1992). In addition, attachment to individuals in the school and community develops in a similar manner as attachment to family members (Hawkins et al., 1992; Hawkins, Doueck, & Lishner, 1988). This suggests that school staff need to attend to attachment as a vital piece of a student's social and emotional development. Thus, socioemotional objectives must be as central to a school curriculum as are academic competencies.

This type of curriculum not only supports the social and emotional development of students with EBD but also acknowledges the importance of social and emotional growth for *all* students. The New Hampshire Department of Education (1991) recognized the importance of students' socioemotional development and responded by producing a Comprehensive Guidance and Counseling Program that included competencies for students and classroom activities for counselors and teachers to meet the developmental needs of students. The student competencies provide teachers and counselors with direction as they broaden their educational curriculum for students. Table 3 provides examples of these competencies and activities for students in each of three developmental periods (elementary, middle, and secondary). Program guidelines suggest that this curriculum requires the leadership of the school counselor, the cooperation of the school's classroom teachers, and action by the school principal to provide scheduled time to implement the curriculum on a regular basis. This is a clear example of how collaboration across the disciplines within the school is essential for effective program implementation to occur.

This competency-based approach is fully implemented when classroom teachers provide regularly scheduled lessons that are matched to lead students toward mastery of the competencies. In all classrooms, three areas are emphasized during instructional activities: 1) emotional expression, 2) the relation between emotions and behavior, and 3) the connection between affect and cognition. As is the case with academic instruction, the socioemotional component of the teacher's lesson plan must be consistent with and based on a careful assessment of the student's existing socioemotional competencies. Lessons that go too far beyond the student's current competencies will be either too frustrating with respect to emotional factors or irrelevant with respect to cognitive factors. In either case, an inability of students to learn or increase their socioemotional competence may be falsely attributed to a lack of motivation rather than to instructional techniques.

Transdisciplinary Planning and Intervention Team

The central strategy for improving educational services for all children has been collaboration

Table 3. Social and emotional competencies of students and activities by grade

Competency	Elementary school age (grades K–5)	Middle school age (grades 6–8)	High school age (grades 9–12)
Students will describe feelings toward other people in their daily lives.	Students are given social situations: 1) receiving a birthday present, 2) losing a coat, and 3) arguing with a friend. Students discuss the range of feelings and write them on a bulletin board.		Students work in teams and draw or paint a picture of how they feel about other people in class. Students write a one-page paper interpreting their artwork. Short stories that match these feelings are read.
Students will explain how their feelings, values, and attitudes reflect those of the social group to which they belong.		A class is divided into two groups or societies (10–15 per group). Each group makes up three rules by which their society lives (e.g., people wearing glasses take them off when speaking). A moderator helps members from each society observe and determine rules of the other society. Members discuss their observations and determine whether they should adopt or reject the rule. Societies debate the importance of their rules.	

among professionals (Cheney et al., 1996). *Collaboration* has been defined by Bruner (1991) as a process that leads to the attainment of goals that cannot efficiently be reached by any single agent. At the school level, collaborative efforts have had an effective impact on problems related to student behavior, attendance, and achievement (Kretovics, Farber, & Armaline, 1991). Small cluster teams of teachers working across content areas have improved their instructional strategies, have solved problems regarding structural issues, and have used research findings to improve the academic performance, attendance, and motivation of students.

Collaboration typically is considered to be a process that brings educators together to change attitudes, skills, and knowledge. From a special education perspective, collaboration most frequently has been used to bring teachers together in teams (e.g., teacher assistance teams, mainstream assistance teams, prereferral teams) to discuss formally or informally student performance problems and to determine appropriate interventions (Chalfant, Pysh, & Moultrie, 1979; Fuchs, Fuchs, & Bahr, 1990; Graden, 1989; Pugach & Johnson, 1988). Collaboration is believed to have an indirect influence on student performance (Idol & West,

1991). Creating the context for an inclusive school environment involves expanding the collaborative process by developing transdisciplinary teams. These teams include faculty, students, parents, and community members. Ongoing team meetings clarify mental health issues, review complex situations, and assist in the understanding of diverse cultural behavior. This information is used for decision-making purposes and to allocate resources as recommended by the team.

In the Project DESTINY Training Model, transdisciplinary teams use the developmental model to formulate student programs in inclusive environments. Transdisciplinary teams in Project DESTINY function like behavioral support teams (Colvin, Kameenui, & Sugai, 1993), offering ongoing consultation concerning developmental problems. Teams meet weekly to analyze a student's strengths and needs, plan programs, make referrals to community services, and evaluate progress. A program coordinator or advisor is assigned to each student and is responsible for coordinating the activities of the team as well as the student's individualized program. With the help of other team members, the advisor monitors both the implementation of the student's program and the effect of the program on the student's performance. Once a program is implemented, the advisor is responsible for scheduling periodic follow-up meetings with the student, family, and team. These follow-up meetings have proved to be critical to the success of the student's program and typically occur once or twice monthly.

The principals in Project DESTINY's schools have provided the leadership required to implement and maintain this team approach. They have assured team members and scheduled time for daily team meetings, some of which focus on students of concern. Teachers also have been willing to use their planning time for discussing the socioemotional development of students. Parents have taken time from their work or home schedules to attend these meetings. Finally, students, although sometimes reluctant, became involved participants in these meetings. Everyone involved has recognized the extra effort required to try new approaches, assess outcomes of program modifications, and interact frequently with other team members.

Annual Group Screening Program for Early Identification of Students with Emotional or Behavioral Problems

Since the mid-1980s, user-friendly screening approaches have been researched and published in packages such as the Systematic Screening for Behavior Disorders (SSBD; Walker & Fabre, 1987; Walker & Severson, 1992) and the Early Screening Project (Walker, Severson, & Feil, 1995). These packages are valid and reliable for identifying students of concern on the basis of externalizing and internalizing behaviors. *Externalizing behaviors* are those that students demonstrate toward people or objects in their environment, whereas *internalizing behaviors* are those directed inwardly toward oneself. These two dimensions have proved to be reliable in a number of studies and help teachers understand behavioral differences of students (Achenbach, 1991; Campbell, 1990).

These screening approaches ask teachers to complete three steps. First, they categorize students in their class as having either internalizing or externalizing behavior. Next, teachers complete rating scales on the top three students of concern (internalizing and externalizing). Third, students who exceed normative or standardized criteria on the rating scales are observed in both academic and social situations to determine whether they need increased levels of support. For some students who pass through all three stages of the SSBD, prompt referral to the school's transdisciplinary team is warranted. These students would be referred as a result of the observation of extremely frequent or intense externalizing or internalizing behavior.

When nominating students of concern, sixth- and seventh-grade teachers in the project have indicated that they find the distinction between externalizing and internalizing behavior helpful. Project DESTINY has therefore concluded that the context for inclusive schooling should include this yearly screening process. Using this approach, school faculty become more efficient and *proactive* in monitoring and planning interventions for students who are at risk for developing EBD.

Necessary Resources Are Allocated in Schools to Implement Identified Services for Students

The inclusive education literature has consistently recommended that classrooms require all of the necessary supports, adaptations, and modifications to meet the objectives listed in students' individualized education programs (Pearpoint, Forest, & Snow, 1992; Porter & Collicott, 1993; Stainback & Stainback, 1992; Tashie et al., 1993). Acquiring necessary resources is perhaps one of the most difficult challenges to meet, as many of the supports and resources in public school environments are not consistent with those that are available in day and residential treatment programs for students with EBD. This lack of supports may account for an overemphasis on academics in schools at the expense of social and emotional goals and objectives (Knitzer, 1993; Knitzer, Steinberg, & Fleisch, 1990).

Which resources should be dedicated to the effort to create the context for inclusion? It appears that time, space, materials, and equipment are the most critical resources in the lives of educators. These resources can be considered at many levels within the classroom, building, and community. Obviously, as this model is implemented across communities it would demand more resources than when it is implemented within a single classroom. Schools that are moving away from self-contained classrooms to community-based models that draw together agencies and families face these resource challenges.

Some communities have been able to implement more comprehensive and inclusive environments for students with EBD. For example, the LaGrange Area Department of Special Education has developed a functional school-based interagency team with flexible funds to implement an array of interventions (Eber, 1994; Eber, Nelson, & Miles, 1997). Mental health workers help teachers implement social and emotional curricula across the district. Teachers receive additional training in effective social problem solving, and a schoolwide social skills curric-

ulum could be supported. Equipment such as carrels, bookcases, and computers can also be shared across schools and agencies. Finally, additional instructional assistants are sometimes needed to support students' social and emotional development.

Many schools throughout the United States, though, are battling loss of resources and are being required to do more with less. In these more typical cases, faculty can adopt practices, such as social problem solving and social skills instruction, to move in the direction of increased support for themselves and for their students. For a minimal expenditure, a problem-solving curriculum can be adopted and the time allocated for staff to plan and implement it. Experience in Project DESTINY indicates that schools need to devote 10 hours initially to receive specific training around schoolwide curriculum intervention. They then need approximately 2 hours per month to review their progress. Weekly updates and questions might occupy 10–20 minutes in faculty meetings. There is no denying that even this level of involvement requires a substantial commitment in schools.

Effective Schoolwide Strategies Are Used Proactively and Consistently

In work with project schools, the Project DESTINY team members are constantly impressed by the progress that schools make when they commit essential resources to improving educational programs. Conversely, when schools do not commit these resources, team members hear of ongoing problems and regressive practices. For example, social problem solving long has been suggested as an effective method for helping students identify alternative prosocial behaviors in problematic social situations (Cheney, Greenberg, & Kusche, 1991; Conduct Problems Prevention Research Group, 1992; Pellegrini & Urbain, 1985). Likewise, social skills training programs have been successful at teaching specific social behaviors to students (Goldstein, Sprafkin, Gershaw, & Klein, 1980; Walker, Todis, Holmes, & Horton, 1988). What has not been successful is the instruction of social skills in isolated classrooms in the absence of a plan that helps students *generalize* skills throughout the school or the community. Project DESTINY has, therefore, promoted the use of the following five schoolwide strategies to assist teachers in supporting students' new social skills:

1. A schoolwide social skills curriculum
2. An interpersonal problem-solving process
3. An in-school counseling program
4. A crisis intervention program
5. Clearly stated behavioral expectations for students

In Project DESTINY's project schools, these approaches work interactively to promote prosocial behavior of middle school students. While these approaches provide support for the performance of students with EBD, the strategies also help teachers to manage the behavior of all students. The following example explains how three of the strategies have been used in one of the project schools.

The first step toward an effective schoolwide strategy is to assist school staff in the identification of their schoolwide behavioral expectations and goals for socioemotional development. All schools seem quite adept at identifying unacceptable school behaviors and punitive consequences for students who are tardy, destroy property, or use abusive language. When asked to generate schoolwide prosocial behavior, school staff have mentioned four broad areas: 1) respecting and complying with teachers, 2) respecting and cooperating with peers, 3) taking care of property, and 4) doing one's best academic work. Coincidentally, these are similar domains found in many social skills programs.

Project DESTINY's next step has been to explain how social skills programs can be used to teach desired behaviors in these four domains. For example, respect for teachers was stated as following directions, asking questions, and stating personal opinions in the classroom. Cooperating with peers was specified as working together, discussing one's position on assignments, and helping one another in the classroom. This specification of positive social behavior encouraged the faculty to use common language when teaching social behavior across various environments in the school.

Finally, teachers needed a corrective process to use with students who violated school and classroom rules. A five-step problem-solving approach has been useful for teachers in Project DESTINY's demonstration schools. Teachers discuss rule violations with students by asking the student five questions (Mendler, 1992; Villa, Udis, & Thousand, 1994):

1. What are you doing?
2. Is it against the rules?
3. What can you do instead?
4. When will you begin?
5. How long can you do it (the alternative behavior)?

Teachers use this approach to problem-solve rule violations with students immediately and orally. When oral discussion is unsuccessful, students are asked to sit down and write a plan, responding to the same five questions. If the student is still uncooperative, then he or she is told to write a plan with a teacher or an assistant in another room.

Project DESTINY recommends that the problem-solving assistant *not* be the principal or the vice principal so that teachers teach and students learn responsible behavior throughout the school. The student should be provided opportunities to self-correct his or her behavior before any further consequences are invoked. Students who threaten the safety of themselves or others are excluded from this process and receive immediate crisis intervention. Safety should always be preserved, and students who threaten the safety of others typically are referred to community team meetings that include parents.

Parent and Family Programs Develop Partnerships Between Educators and Families

One major change in comprehensive programs for students with EBD has been the inclusion of parents and family members as therapeutic members of teams. This inclusion of families stands in contrast to past approaches of treating parents as yet another client when the student received services (Collins & Collins, 1990). Previous lack of support for parents was based on a belief that the child's disability was a result of inadequate or inappropriate parenting (Caplan & Hall-McCorquodale, 1985). As discussed previously, childhood disorders are a result of several factors that include biological, interpersonal, cognitive, and affective components (Campbell, 1990; Friesen & Koroloff, 1990).

Considering the many influences on a child's development, it is essential to determine a functional role for parents in their child's education (Chesapeake Institute, 1994; Knitzer, 1993). Developing an array of family supports is just beginning to be translated into practice, and some of the new roles for parents include education, support, and advocacy (Friesen & Koroloff, 1990; Friesen & Osher, 1996). As parents' roles in education and intervention change, it is essential that parents' perceptions be monitored and assessed frequently (Soderlund, Epstein, Quinn, Cumblad, & Petersen, 1995). Initial evaluation of a survey of 121 parents involved in a comprehensive service-delivery program suggested that parents are favorable toward comprehensive services and appreciate being included in the planning process. They also, however, find services to be inconveniently located, narrowly defined, and expensive (Soderlund et al., 1995).

In the Project DESTINY model, it is a priority to include parents and family members of youth with EBD in planning and implementing education and related services. This has been accomplished by having a family services coordinator meet with all parents/guardians and invite them to attend twice-monthly support meetings. Across the project schools, 60% (18 of 30) of the parents of students with EBD consistently participated in the group meetings (Cheney et al., 1996).

During the 1994–1995 school year, these support groups developed five major goals:

1. Understanding emotional and behavioral disorders
2. Understanding the impact of the disorder on their family
3. Practicing communication skills
4. Using the new skills with school personnel
5. Understanding community resources

The groups have had a major impact on the ability of parents to share the impact of their children's disabilities on other family members. During group meetings, members have explored their own cultural differences, personal values, and expectations for their children and for themselves. Finally, they have identified ways to gain access to new community resources.

An initial evaluation of these family support groups indicated that families were positive about the meetings, reported improvements in their children's behavior, and individually attended more than 75% of the sessions. The parents reported many specific changes that they experienced, including (Cheney et al., 1996)

1. Support from others who share common life experiences
2. Increased understanding of teachers' feelings and experiences with their children
3. Learning about community resources for their son or daughter
4. Increased skill at meeting with the teachers to develop mutually beneficial goals

These positive results are similar to those of other supportive programs that focus on building positive home–school partnerships (Evans, Okifuji, & Thomas, 1995; Friesen & Osher, 1996).

Individual Adaptations Are Developed When Schoolwide Programs Do Not Meet Students' Needs

Even when intensive services are provided, a small group of students whose socioemotional difficulties are of high intensity (e.g., assaultive behavior, destruction of property) or of low frequency (e.g., psychosis) will need individual adaptations. Examples of individual adaptations include altering classroom rules, adjusting time constraints for academic tasks, and modifying homework requirements (Villa et al., 1994). Consistency across students is traded for a rule of fairness. The rule of fairness suggests that teachers should attempt to meet individual students' needs rather than treat all students the same (Mendler, 1992). This notion appears to be more readily accepted by students who have cognitive or physical disabilities but poses difficulties for some teachers when applied with students with EBD.

To make program modifications for individual students, the transdisciplinary team must consider each student's unique needs. Project DESTINY's initial findings have suggested that general education teachers do not feel competent in their skills for managing individual students with EBD. In particular, teachers in Project DESTINY initially rated themselves as having little or only some competence in promoting social development, teaching social skills, using strategies to reduce aggression, counseling or problem-solving social issues with students, and developing crisis prevention plans (Cheney & Barringer, 1995).

To improve teachers' skills in individual modifications, a student services format was included in the Project DESTINY model. Using a student services format, team members gathered data relevant to the four developmental factors and synthesized these data at team meetings to develop action plans. The action plan was based on consensual agreement and focused on student strengths in response to identified problems.

Example of the Process: John

The following is an example of the student services process that was used with "John," a sixth-grade student with a long history of emotional and behavioral problems. The transdisciplinary team that worked with John had several concerns about his performance. He was disruptive in class and did not complete assignments or homework on time. The disruptions involved noncompliance with the teacher's directions, talking out, and distracting classmates from their work. John had a short attention span, and the teachers could not leave him unsupervised.

Because John's teachers lacked theoretical knowledge regarding emotional or behavioral disorders, they were unable to interpret or respond adequately to John's behavior. It was nearly impossible for them to distinguish between behavioral manifestations of John's disability and common classroom misbehavior (e.g., inattention, restlessness, incomplete assignments). Usually, John was able to choose to arrive to class on time or complete his work, but more frequently his distractibility, aggression, and mood shifts were manifestations of his emotional disability.

This situation was complicated further by the fact that common age-appropriate behavior and behaviors associated with an emotional disability are not mutually exclusive. For example, some nights John would just decide to "blow off" homework, whereas other nights his clinical depression would make it impossible for him to concentrate on work. In the absence of specific knowledge about causal mechanisms of EBD, general educators have little choice but to respond to all students with the same techniques; that is, when a student's homework is not completed and the reasons for noncompletion are inconsequential, the standard classroom consequences accrue regardless of cause. Thus, teachers often apply and reapply ineffectively to the most complex students in a classroom (in terms of their behavior) the same management techniques that are applied to any other student in the class. As discussed next, teachers were assisted by the Project DESTINY transdisciplinary team to learn an ever-expanding repertoire of strategies to meet John's educational needs.

At the first team meeting, team members were concerned about John's sloppy handwriting, disorganized math worksheets, math errors, and impulsive behavior. He would grab materials from other group members and refuse to do his share of the work. Team members had said that they had tried everything in an attempt to improve his behavior and academic performance to his classmates' level. They reprimanded John constantly, frequently reviewed classroom rules, used time-out in the classroom, and sent him to the vice principal for consequences. Team members were frustrated, and several members discussed losing their temper with John. All of the teachers stated that they were still committed to helping John through individual adaptations, but they did not know what new adaptations to try.

At their second meeting, the team brought an action plan. The plan consisted of a behavioral contract that specified that John would be given two chances to "respond to adult requests in a timely manner." The contract stated that John would lose points each time he did not respond in a timely manner. The contract did not mention instruction of new skills necessary to respond promptly to the teachers' requests, such as looking, listening, and having materials prepared. Teachers thought this instruction of new skills was unnecessary for a sixth grader such as John, even though the teachers considered his classroom performance to be a manifestation of his emotional disability. All of the teachers believed that they did not have sufficient experience or training to educate a student with serious emotional disturbance.

In their third meeting, the team completed a questionnaire that was composed of items concerning each of the four developmental factors that were influencing John's behavior: biological, interpersonal/familial, cognitive, and affective. Based on this questionnaire, the team compiled a list of strengths and problems for John.

After considering the developmental factors that were influencing John's behavior, the team reconceptualized his problem and developed more relevant solutions. When viewed within this developmental context, John's behavior was seen to be purposeful and related to specific problems in all four areas. His repeated attempts to gain teacher attention, for example, were seen as efforts to control the relationship and gain physical proximity. Teacher proximity appeared to be reassuring to John, despite his academic, affective, and interpersonal problems. John's strengths, problems, and resultant action plan are outlined in Table 4.

After implementing the action plan, the tone of the student–teacher interactions and of the teachers' comments about John changed to supportive and analytical. John began meeting with his faculty mentor each afternoon to discuss the day or a topic of interest. John's disruptive behavior and academic difficulties continued but at a reduced level. Having conceptualized John's problem behavior as the result of longstanding developmental problems, team members were more tolerant of his slow rate of change, and they agreed to look at long-term as opposed to short-term improvements for John.

Student- and Family-Centered Services Are Developed to Coordinate Interagency Community Efforts

The essence of the community-based mental health movement for children and youth has been to coordinate systems of care in their communities and to avoid sending them to residential programs in distant communities. Systems of care are intended to be child and family centered, as opposed to agency centered, and coordinated across agencies to become more user friendly for families. Agencies that lacked the history or mechanism to work in a coordinated fashion (e.g., juvenile justice, children and youth services, recreation, vocational rehabilitation) are drawn together to work with families in developing child-centered, community-based treatment plans (Nelson & Pearson, 1991; Stroul & Friedman, 1986). The guiding principles of this system emphasize least restrictive, normative environments; family participation in service delivery; service coordination; and sensitive, nondiscriminatory services to individuals. Families and their children, who previously were involved with multiple agencies for service delivery, began to receive coordinated and integrated care.

Since 1990, the Mental Health Services Program for Youth (MHSPY) has funded interagency demonstration projects in states. The focus of the MHSPY has been to create systems of care for families who have children or youth with EBD. The programs were started in eight states and emphasize community-based care in normative environments, use of effective clinical practices, integration of financial and clinical decision making across agencies and families, and accountability for outcomes (Cole & Poe, 1993). Concurrently, state and federal departments of education have cooperated with mental health and juvenile justice departments to fund additional projects. Reviews of many of these programs can be found elsewhere (Carter, 1994b; Cole & Poe, 1993; Nelson & Pearson, 1991).

Excellent examples of interagency, community-based systems of care are found in Carter's (1994b) review of 26 model programs

Table 4. Strengths, problems, and actions for John

Strengths	Problems	Actions
Biological		
1. Student is in good health	1. Born addicted to cocaine 2. Predisposition to depression and drug addiction in family	1. Support mother in obtaining medication evaluation for John from a child psychiatrist.
Interpersonal/Familial		
1. Interacts with peers and staff 2. Displays good social skills at times 3. Mother provides close supervision 4. Mother has conferences with teachers, is cooperative, and wants to support John in school	1. Disruptive in groups 2. Very few friends 3. Erratic caregiving during infancy due to maternal drug addiction 4. Possible problems in early attachments	1. Provide guided practice in completing a cooperative project with at least two classmates before involving in cooperative learning group. 2. Attempt to build relationships with peers through structured play. John should be allowed to associate with younger students if he makes the choice. 3. Establish schedule of monthly meetings with John, mother, and John's faculty mentor.
Cognitive		
1. Student is of average intelligence 2. Short-term memory seems average for age	1. Very short attention span 2. Reading achievement score at third-grade level	1. Consider additional classification of having a learning disability to gain maximum academic support; modify grade 6 curriculum to be consistent with John's current functioning. 2. Provide John with specific, written guidelines concerning the daily schedule and review throughout the day.
Affective		
1. Shows a wide range of emotions 2. Calms down quickly when removed from group	1. Frequently in a bad mood for no apparent reason 2. Overreacts to minor conflicts or disappointments	1. Schedule predictable one-to-one social interactions between John and his teacher/mentor at least once each day. 2. Avoid placing John in overstimulating situations "where he is known to become excited to the point of violating school rules."

for youth with EBD and their families. The prototype programs of the Alaska Youth Initiative, Ventura County Program, and Kentucky Impact have been frequently reviewed as progressive and effective; the following section highlights innovative work by a newer program, Project WRAP.

Project WRAP is a school-based systems change program in Illinois (Eber, 1994, 1996). The goal of Project WRAP is to "wrap" supportive community services around youth with EBD and their families and to retrain service providers to facilitate innovative approaches. Service coordination is conducted at the community level and at the school level to promote inclusive education of youth with EBD. Furthermore, parent networks are developed for advocacy, support, and resource development. There is also an emphasis on changing traditional roles to more functional contemporary roles. For example, special educators become facilitators of inclusion and work schoolwide to assist teachers with strategies to assist students in classrooms. In addition, social workers work as family coordinators to assist parents in developing support networks and brokering necessary services identified by parents.

Work with Project DESTINY supports the preceding suggestions that interagency teams must have a local administrative body to review policy issues and to oversee flexible funds for providing supports to families. Project DESTINY has also found that these policy teams need to be linked to school-level coordinating teams to monitor student progress effectively. Finally, the school-based coordinating team must meet regularly at a parent-accessible site (e.g., school, home, other community location) for parents and professionals to coordinate student and family services.

CASE STUDY OF ONE SCHOOL IN PROJECT DESTINY

The process of program development at one of the Project DESTINY middle schools exemplifies how the 10 principles of the Project DESTINY Transdisciplinary Model can be applied to school improvement efforts. The initiative to improve the quality of the school began when the superintendent of the school district mandated that each school faculty and administration identify goals for the year 2000. This process was guided by the vision and mission statement, provided in Figure 1, that was developed and agreed on by community members, the board of education, school administrators, and faculty members. The commitment within the mission statement was consistent with the full inclusion of all disability groups throughout the school district. Thus, rather than be developed in isolation by the special education department, the program for students with EBD was tied conceptually to the districtwide plan for improving the overall quality of education. The program development necessary to achieve this goal at the middle school also included input from the school's principal, the entire school faculty, and concerned members of the community.

Preparing today's students to create tomorrow's opportunities

Vision
This district's vision is of a school and community that work in harmony
to prepare students to be lifelong learners capable of successfully meeting the challenges
of living and working in the 21st century.

Mission
Our mission is a commitment, in concert with the entire community,
to provide quality services to each student, parent, and resident through planned, focused,
and continuous improvement of our educational programs and practices.

Figure 1.   Mission statement.

The faculty were quite concerned about the dramatic increase in behavior problems at the middle school and therefore created a transdisciplinary Respect and Responsibility Team. This team was formed specifically to explore strategies and solutions to decrease the frequency and intensity of students' behavior problems. When interviewed about this situation, the principal described the problems addressed by this team in the following manner:

A few students were starting to take over the school. No matter what we tried, it didn't work. Detentions, in-school suspension, and out-of-school suspension just weren't working with most of these kids. We also tried a lot of behavior modification—like token economies, contingency management, and rewarding good behavior. Some of the good kids said, "I should misbehave too, so that I can go out and play basketball." We agreed to try anything and everything that would make things better within the building.

We decided that we wanted to teach responsibility, not just continually try to control behavior. We sent teams to a number of workshops and analyzed possibilities for our school. As a result of researching various possibilities, the Respect and Responsibility Team found a problem-solving approach called the planning process. The team even recommended the hiring of a person to monitor the room. The board approved the approach, but the community did not support additional funding for a new position. The school, therefore, used the supervisor of special education in the middle school because it figured that most of the students using the planning room would be students in special education.

Having identified a strategy, the school hired an educational consultant who was known throughout the region to be skilled in school-wide social problem solving (referred to as the planning process). The consultant presented an overview of the process to the school's staff and interested parents. The process was then adopted by the faculty, and the first people to receive the planning process training were the members of the school's Responsibility and Respect Team. The members of this team then served as liaisons and trainers for the rest of the faculty. Teams at each grade level were responsible for identifying instances of rule-violating behavior that warranted removal from the classroom.

The planning process appealed to the staff primarily because it involved instruction and discipline rather than punishment and control. Part of the instruction involved establishing consistent expectations for performance across the teachers involved with any student. Teams at each grade level agreed to socioemotional competencies for all of the students in the school, and these competencies were translated into rules that were consistent across classrooms. To ensure further fairness and consistency, each teacher was provided with a short script concerning what would be said to students who violated school rules. The steps were as follows (successful completion of any step results in returning to classroom):

1. Ask student to describe his or her behavior and identify the classroom rule violated.
2. Ask student to make an oral plan to replace the rule-violating behavior with a behavior that was consistent with the rules.
3. Ask student who could not make an oral plan to write a plan specifying how long he or she would commit to acceptable behavior.
4. Send student to a Planning Room if the student did not follow the plan successfully; in Planning Room, have student develop plan to return to classroom.
5. Ask student who violates Planning Room rules to write a plan concerning how he or she would modify behavior to remain in the Planning Room. (Failure to write a plan to stay in the Planning Room results in immediate referral to the principal's office.)
6. Give student the choice of either writing a plan to return to the Planning Room or going home; if he or she chooses to go home, then he or she returns to the principal's office the following day and begins the problem-solving sequence again.

During a common planning time, grade-level teams identified a small group of students who would be eligible to participate in the Planning Room program. They also informed parents that their son or daughter would be involved in the program. Finally, they developed a process for monitoring the progress of all participating students. Before implementing the planning process, the school faculty adopted a method for evaluating the effectiveness of the planning process at the student and school levels. The Planning Room staff kept student records, which were graphed and reviewed weekly, concerning the frequency and duration of visits to the Planning Room, the number of referrals to the principal's office, and the frequency of students' choosing to go home. In addition, improvements in the quality of students' written plans were noted. The Planning Room staff recorded the frequency of referrals during particular times of the day and which teachers made the most referrals to the Planning Room.

Students who participated in the program generally have shown a rapid decline in both the frequency of visits to the Planning Room and the duration of each visit. For several of the students participating in the program, one visit to the Planning Room was sufficient to prevent further incidents of rule-violating behavior. The principal reported that the number of behavioral incidents requiring his involvement was reduced by more than half. Parents have responded favorably to the planning process because of the reduction in behavioral incidents in school and the numerous efforts to teach responsibility.

The components of the Project DESTINY Training Model discussed previously have supported the school's efforts to become a completely inclusive, developmental context for students with EBD. The initial screening has been useful for faculty to identify in a systematic manner students with internalizing and externalizing behaviors. Teachers, administrators, and counselors attended monthly presentations by the Project DESTINY staff and learned essential knowledge on topics in the area of EBD. During twice-monthly student services reviews, the Project DESTINY staff have also helped the grade-level teams to develop individual adaptations for students with unique needs using the developmental perspective.

Finally, and perhaps most important, the family coordinator from Project DESTINY conducted a series of support groups for parents whose children were involved with the Planning Room program. Support groups have provided an opportunity for parents to share their frustrations and successes with one another. The Project DESTINY staff led discussions and information

groups concerning the role of the family in EBD, behavior management techniques, and working with the school within special education guidelines. These support groups have been very successful and have been recognized by the faculty and administration as a crucial component of the school program. The grade-level teams and the principal in one school continued to provide support services to parents after federal funding for the project ended in 1996. The district provided funds to hire the family services coordinator.

VISUAL REPRESENTATION OF THE TRANSDISCIPLINARY MODEL

Figure 2 provides a visual representation of how the transdisciplinary model works in school practice. There are three broad factors within which the model's components cluster; the factors cover the areas of planning and development, school implementation, and community involvement. The logical and linear implementation of the model suggests that planning leads to school implementation and is followed by community involvement. Project DESTINY's experience has demonstrated, however, that linear development and logical progression do not always prevail. Thus, Figure 2 suggests that pathways of implementation can occur in several directions.

In Project DESTINY's experience, one school began the search for strategies to use in the model and created its own teams. This led to influencing the district's strategic plan and included community constituents as involved members. A second school started with community involvement and developed a functional interagency team while creating a vision and a mission for inclusive schooling. These factors then led the middle school staff to review their practice; develop grade-level, transdisciplinary teams; and implement the model. The point is that each school, district, and community has its own unique approach to addressing these factors and taking the necessary steps to implement the model.

Although the model has proved to have a high degree of utility and effectiveness in addressing the social and emotional development of students in middle schools, it is not a panacea for the complex issues of students with EBD. It

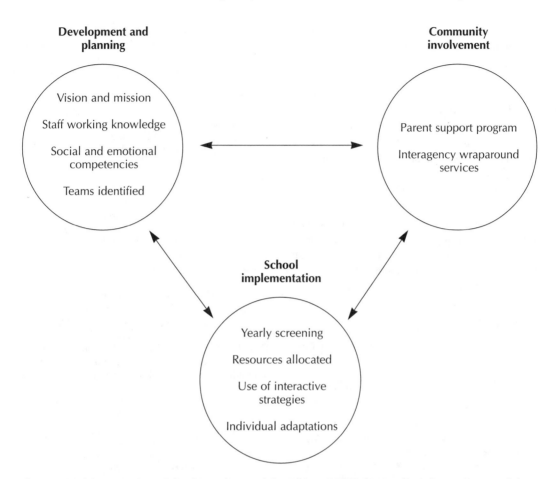

Figure 2. The interaction of the three phases of the Project DESTINY transdisciplinary team model.

is a working model that addresses the needs of students, teachers, and parents and that requires the active participation of all involved.

CONCLUSION

This chapter has proposed 10 components that have been found to be essential in the creation of inclusive school environments for middle school students with EBD. The components were identified and used in Project DESTINY, a federally funded research project implemented at three middle schools in New Hampshire. To date, initial findings, both qualitative and quantitative, have supported the utility of this transdisciplinary approach.

The components in this approach are not unique to Project DESTINY, and they are not suggested for use only with students with EBD. Instead, the authors of this chapter believe that the components are necessary elements for supporting the socioemotional development of all middle school youth. Youth in middle schools typically span age ranges from 11 to 15 years and undergo dramatic changes in their biological, interpersonal, cognitive, and affective development. Schools must play a critical role in helping these students develop the skills to prepare them for adolescence and further secondary education. As Ames and Miller (1994) outlined in their book on middle school reform, there are several principles in changing middle schools that are needed to support both systemic and student changes. Some of the principles that Ames and Miller emphasized were personalizing relationships among adults and students; clear visions; careful planning; close links among school, home, and community; and multifaceted intervention strategies. The authors of this chapter cannot agree more fully with these principles. The Project DESTINY model includes several specific recommendations to make deeper, more enduring structural changes in schools. These structures must be fully supported and deeply committed to by students, faculty, and parents. Students with EBD will always require extensive and daily support to help them with their social and emotional development. Project DESTINY's experience and findings suggest that those who want to take the steps to allocate the resources to implement the transdisciplinary model can transform and enhance the context for the social and emotional development of their students.

REFERENCES

Achenbach, T. (1991). *Manual for the Teacher's Report Form.* Burlington: University of Vermont Department of Psychiatry.

Ainsworth, M.D.S., Blehar, M.C., Waters, E., & Wall, S. (1978). *Patterns of attachment.* Mahwah, NJ: Lawrence Erlbaum Associates.

Aldinger, L.E., Warger, C.L., & Eavy, P. (1991). *Strategies for teacher collaboration.* Ann Arbor, MI: Exceptional Innovations.

Algozzine, B. (1992). *Problem behavior management: Educator's resource service* (2nd ed.). Gaithersburg, MD: Aspen Publishers, Inc.

Ames, N.L., & Miller, E. (1994). *Changing middle schools: How to make schools work for young adolescents.* San Francisco: Jossey-Bass.

Arbuthnot, J. (1992). Sociomoral reasoning in behavior-disordered adolescents: Cognitive and behavioral change. In J. McCord & R.E. Tremblay (Eds.), *Preventing antisocial behavior: Interventions from birth through adolescence* (pp. 283–310). New York: Guilford Press.

Barringer, C., & Cheney, D. (1996). Facilitating the social/emotional development of middle school students: A model for improving school-based collaboration. *The Eighth Annual Research Conference Proceedings: A System of Care for Children's Mental Health. Expanding the Research Base* (pp. 135–142). Tampa: University of South Florida, Florida Mental Health Institute, Research and Training Center for Children's Mental Health.

Barringer, C., & Hutchens, M. (1993). *Developmental checklist for students with emotional/behavioral disorders.* Unpublished manuscript.

Booth, C.L., Spieker, S.J., Barnard, K.E., & Morisset, C.E. (1992). Infants at risk: The role of preventa-

tive intervention in deflecting a maladaptive developmental trajectory. In J. McCord & R.E. Tremblay (Eds.), *Preventing antisocial behavior: Interventions from birth through adolescence* (pp. 21–42). New York: Guilford Press.

Bowlby, J. (1988). *A secure base: Parent–child attachment and healthy human development.* New York: Basic Books.

Brown, S.L., & Korn, M.L. (1989). Somatic and psychological treatments of depression [Special issue]. *Psychiatric Annals, 19,* 388–393.

Bruner, C. (1991). *Thinking collaboratively: Ten questions and answers to help policy makers improve children's services.* Washington, DC: The Education and Human Services Consortium.

Campbell, S.B. (1990). *Behavior problems in preschool children.* New York: Guilford Press.

Caplan, P.J., & Hall-McCorquodale, I. (1985). Mother blaming in major clinical journals. *American Journal of Orthopsychiatry, 55,* 345–353.

Carter, J. (1994). *Organizing systems to support competent social behavior in children and youth: Model programs and services.* Eugene, OR: Western Regional Resource Center.

Chalfant, J.C., Pysh, M.V.D., & Moultrie, R. (1979). Teacher assistance teams: A model for within-building problem solving. *Learning Disability Quarterly, 2,* 85–96.

Cheney, D. (1994). Inclusion of students with emotional and behavioral disorders in general education programs: Definition, history and recommendations. In L.M. Bullock & R.A. Gable (Eds.), *Monograph of the Council for Children with Behavior Disorders' second forum on inclusion* (pp. 1–5). Reston, VA: Council for Exceptional Children.

Cheney, D. (1998). Using action research as a collaborative process to enhance educators' and families' knowledge and skills for youth with emotional or behavioral disorders. *Preventing School Failure, 42,* 88–93.

Cheney, D., & Barringer, C. (1995). Teacher competence, student diversity and staff training for the inclusion of middle school students with emotional and behavioral disorders. *Journal of Emotional and Behavioral Disorders, 3*(3), 174–182.

Cheney, D., Barringer, C., Upham, D., & Manning, B. (1996). Project DESTINY: A model for developing educational support teams through interagency networks for youth with emotional or behavioral disorders. In R.J. Illback & C.M. Nelson (Eds.), *Emerging school-based approaches for children with emotional or behavioral problems: Research and practice in service integration* (pp. 59–76). Binghamton, NY: Haworth Press.

Cheney, D., Greenberg, M., & Kusche, C. (1991). Teacher effectiveness with PATHS: A social-cognitive curriculum for elementary students. *The Oregon Conference Monograph, 3,* 81–85.

Cheney, D., & Muscott, H. (1996). Preventing school failure for students with emotional and behavioral disabilities through responsible inclusion. *Preventing School Failure, 40*(3), 109–116.

Cheney, D., & Osher, T. (1997). Collaborating with families. *Journal of Emotional and Behavioral Disorders, 5,* 36–44.

Chesapeake Institute. (1994). *National agenda for achieving better results for children and youth with serious emotional disturbance.* Washington, DC: Author.

Cicchetti, D. (1993). Developmental psychopathology: Reactions, reflections, projections. *Developmental Review, 13,* 471–502.

Cole, R.F., & Poe, S.L. (1993). *Partnerships for care: Systems of care for children with serious emotional disturbances and their families.* Washington, DC: Washington Business Group on Health.

Collins, B., & Collins, T. (1990). Parent–professional relationships in the treatment of seriously emotionally disturbed children and adolescents. *Social Work, 35,* 522–527.

Colvin, G., Kameenui, E.J., & Sugai, G. (1993). Reconceptualizing behavior management and schoolwide discipline in general education. *Education and Treatment of Children, 16,* 361–381.

Conduct Problems Prevention Research Group. (1992). A developmental and clinical model for the prevention of conduct disorder: The FAST Track Program. *Development and Psychopathology, 4,* 509–528.

Conval School District. (1993, October). *Statement of inclusive education.* (Available from J. Lory, Conval School District, Peterborough, NH 03458.)

Curwin, R.L., & Mendler, A.N. (1988). *Discipline with dignity.* Alexandria, VA: Association for Supervision and Curriculum Development.

Dice, M. (1993). *Intervention strategies for children with emotional or behavioral disorders.* San Diego: Singular Publishing.

Dodge, K.A. (1980). Social cognition and children's aggressive behavior. *Child Development, 51,* 162–170.

DuPaul, G.J., & Barkley, R.A. (1992). Social interaction of children with attention deficit hyperactivity disorder: Effects of methylphenidate. In J. McCord & R.E. Tremblay (Eds.), *Preventing antisocial behavior: Interventions from birth through adolescence* (pp. 86–116). New York: Guilford Press.

Eber, L. (1994, March). *Bringing the wraparound approach to school: A model for inclusion.* Paper presented at the meeting of the Research Conference for Children's Mental Health, Tampa, FL.

Eber, L. (1996). Restructuring schools through the wraparound approach: The LADSE experiences. In R.J. Illback & C.M. Nelson (Eds.), *Emerging school-based approaches for children with emotional or behavioral problems: Research and practice in service integration* (pp. 135–150). Binghamton, NY: Haworth Press.

Eber, L., Nelson, C.M., & Miles, P. (1997). School-based wraparound for students with emotional and behavioral challenges. *Exceptional Children, 63,* 539–555.

Evans, I.M., Okifuji, A., & Thomas, A.D. (1995). Home–school partnerships: Involving families in the educational process. In I.M. Evans, T. Cicchelli, M. Cohen, & N.P. Shapiro (Eds.), *Staying in school: Partnerships for educational change* (pp. 23–40). Baltimore: Paul H. Brookes Publishing Co.

Friesen, B., & Koroloff, N. (1990). Family-centered services: Implications for mental health administration and research. *The Journal of Mental Health Administration, 17*(1), 13–25.

Friesen, B., & Osher, T. (1996). Involving families in change: Challenges and opportunities. In R.J. Illback & C.M. Nelson (Eds.), *Emerging school-based approaches for children with emotional or behavioral problems: Research and practice in service integration* (pp. 187–208). Binghamton, NY: Haworth Press.

Fuchs, D., Fuchs, L., & Bahr, M. (1990). Mainstream assistance teams: A scientific basis for the art of consultation. *Exceptional Children, 57,* 128–139.

Gersten, R., & Woodward, J. (1990). Rethinking the regular education initiative: Focus on the classroom teacher. *Remedial and Special Education, 11*(3), 7–16.

Glasser, W. (1965). *Reality therapy.* New York: Harper & Row.

Goldstein, A.P. (1988). *The Prepare Curriculum: Teaching prosocial competencies.* Champaign, IL: Research Press.

Goldstein, A.P., Palumbo, J., Striepling, S., & Voutsinas, A.M. (1995). *Break it up: A teacher's guide to managing student aggression.* Champaign, IL: Research Press.

Goldstein, A.P., Sprafkin, R.P., Gershaw, N.J., & Klein, P. (1980). *Skillstreaming the adolescent.* Champaign, IL: Research Press.

Graden, J. (1989). Redefining "prereferral" intervention as intervention assistance: Collaboration between general and special education. *Exceptional Children, 56,* 227–231.

Greenberg, M.T., Speltz, M.L., & DeKlyen, M. (1991). Attachment security in preschoolers with and without externalizing behavior problems: A replication [Special issue]. *Development and Psychopathology, 3,* 413–430.

Gulley, L.R., & Nemeroff, C.B. (1993). The neurobiological basis of mixed depression-anxiety states. *Journal of Clinical Psychiatry, 54,* 9–16.

Hallahan, D.P., Keller, C.E., McKinney, J.D., Lloyd, J.W., & Bryan, T. (1988). Examining the research base of the Regular Education Initiative: Efficacy studies and the adaptive learning environments model. *Journal of Learning Disabilities, 21,* 29–35.

Haring, N.G. (1987). *Assessing and managing behavior disabilities.* Seattle: University of Washington.

Haring, N.G., & Phillips, E. (1962). *Educating emotionally disturbed children.* New York: McGraw-Hill.

Harvey, V.S. (1994). A practitioner's viewpoint: Inclusion of students with emotional and behavioral disorders. In L.M. Bullock & R.A. Gable (Eds.), *Monograph of the Council for Children with Behavior Disorders' second forum on inclusion* (pp. 10–15). Reston, VA: Council for Exceptional Children.

Hawkins, J.D., Catalano, R.F., Morrison, D.M., O'Donnell, J., Abbott, R.D., & Day, L.E. (1992). The Seattle social development project: Effects of the first four years on protective factors and problem behaviors. In J. McCord & R.E. Tremblay (Eds.), *Preventing antisocial behavior: Interventions from birth through adolescence* (pp. 139–161). New York: Guilford Press.

Hawkins, J.D., Doueck, H., & Lishner, D.M. (1988). Changing teaching practices in mainstream classrooms to improve bonding and behavior of low achievers. *American Educational Research Journal, 25,* 31–50.

Hewett, F. (1967). Educational engineering with emotionally disturbed children. *Exceptional Children, 33,* 459–467.

Hewett, F.M., & Forness, S.R. (1977). *Education of exceptional learners.* Needham Heights, MA: Allyn & Bacon.

Hobbs, N. (1966). Helping disturbed children: Psychological and ecological strategies. *American Psychologist, 21,* 1105–1115.

Hobbs, N. (1982). *The troubled and troubling child.* San Francisco: Jossey-Bass.

Idol, L., & West, J.F. (1991). Educational collaboration: A catalyst for effective schooling. *Intervention in School and Clinic, 27*(2), 70–78.

Illback, R., & Nelson, C.M. (1996). School-based integrated service programs: Toward more effective service delivery for children and youth with emotional and behavioral disorders. In R.J. Illback & C.M. Nelson (Eds.), *Emerging school-based approaches for children with emotional or behavioral problems: Research and practice in service integration* (pp. 1–6). Binghamton, NY: Haworth Press.

Individuals with Disabilities Education Act (IDEA) of 1990, PL 101-476, 20 U.S.C. §§ 1400 *et seq.*

Jones, V.F. (1987). Major components in a comprehensive program for seriously emotionally disturbed children and youth. In R. Rutherford, Jr., C. Nelson, & S. Forness (Eds.), *Severe behavior disorders of children and youth* (Vol. 9, pp. 94–121). Austin, TX: PRO-ED.

Jones, V.F. (1992). Integrating behavioral and insight-oriented treatment in school based programs for seriously emotionally disturbed students. *Behavioral Disorders, 17,* 225–236.

Kauffman, J.M. (1989). *Characteristics of behavior disorders of children and youth.* Columbus, OH: Charles E. Merrill.

Kauffman, J.M. (1991). Effective teachers of students with behavior disorders: Are generic teaching skills enough? *Behavior Disorders, 16,* 225–237.

Kazdin, A.E. (1988). Childhood depression. In E.J. Mash & L.G. Terdal (Eds.), *Behavioral assessment of childhood disorders* (2nd ed., pp. 157–195). New York: Guilford Press.

Keenan, S., McLaughlin, S., & Denton, M. (1994). Planning for inclusion: Program elements that support teachers and students with emotional/behavioral disorders. In L.M. Bullock & R.A. Gable (Eds.), *Monograph of the Council for Children with Behavior Disorders' second forum on inclusion* (pp. 6–10). Reston, VA: Council for Exceptional Children.

Knitzer, J. (1993). Children's mental health policy: Challenging the future. *Journal of Emotional and Behavioral Disorders, 1*(1), 8–16.

Knitzer, J., Steinberg, Z., & Fleisch, B. (1990). *At the school house door: An examination of programs and policies for children with behavioral and emotional problems.* New York: Bank Street College of Education.

Kohlberg, L. (1984). *Essays on moral development: Vol. 2. The psychology of moral development.* San Francisco: Harper & Row.

Kretovics, J., Farber, K., & Armaline, W. (1991). Reform from the bottom up: Empowering teachers to transform schools. *Phi Delta Kappan, 73,* 295–299.

MacFarquhar, K.W., Dowrick, P.W., & Risley, T.R. (1993). Individualizing services for seriously emotionally disturbed youth: A national survey. *Administration and Policy in Mental Health, 2*(3), 165–174.

Mattison, R.E., Lynch, J.C., Kales, H., & Gamble, A.D. (1993). Checklist identification of elementary schoolboys for clinical referral or evaluation of eligibility for special education. *Behavioral Disorders, 18,* 218–227.

Mendler, A. (1992). *What do I do when . . . ? How to achieve discipline with dignity in the classroom.* Bloomington, IN: National Educational Services.

Muscott, H. (1995). A process for facilitating the appropriate inclusion of students with emotional/behavioral disorders. *Education and Treatment of Children, 18,* 369–386.

Muscott, H., Morgan, D., & Meadows, N. (1996). Planning and implementing effective programs for school-aged children and youth with emotional and behavioral disorders within inclusive schools. In *Mini-Library Series on Emotional/Behavioral Disorders* (pp. 1–42). Reston, VA: Council for Children with Behavioral Disorders.

Neel, R., & Cessna, K. (1993). Behavioral intent: Instructional content for students with behavior disorders. In K. Cessna (Ed.), *Instructionally differentiated programming: A needs based approach for students with behavior disorders* (pp. 31–40). Denver: Colorado Department of Education.

Nelson, C.M., & Pearson, C.A. (1991). *Integrating services for children and youth with emotional or behavioral disorders.* Reston, VA: Council for Exceptional Children.

New Hampshire Department of Education. (1991). *New Hampshire comprehensive guidance and counseling program.* Concord: Author.

Osher, D., & Hanley, T.V. (1996). Implications of the national agenda to improve results for children and youth with or at risk of serious emotional disturbance. In R.J. Illback & C.M. Nelson (Eds.), *Emerging school-based approaches for children with emotional or behavioral problems: Research and practice in service integration* (pp. 7–36). Binghamton, NY: Haworth Press.

Peacock Hill Working Group. (1991). Problems and promises in special education and related services for children and youth with emotional or behavioral disorders. *Behavioral Disorders, 16,* 299–313.

Pearpoint, J., Forest, M., & Snow, J. (1992). *The inclusion papers: Strategies to make inclusion work.* Toronto, Ontario, Canada: Inclusion Press.

Pellegrini, D.S., & Urbain, E.S. (1985). An evaluation of interpersonal cognitive problem solving training with children. *Journal of Child Psychology and Psychiatry, 26,* 17–41.

Porter, G., & Collicott, J. (1993). New Brunswick School Districts 28 and 29: Mandates and strategies that promote inclusive schooling. In R.A. Villa, J.S. Thousand, W. Stainback, & S. Stainback (Eds.), *Restructuring for caring and effective education: An administrative guide to creating heterogeneous schools* (pp. 187–200). Baltimore: Paul H. Brookes Publishing Co.

Pugach, M.C., & Johnson, L.J. (1988). Rethinking the relationship between consultation and collaborative problem-solving. *Focus on Exceptional Children, 21*(4), 1–14.

Pugach, M.C., & Johnson, L.J. (1995). *Collaborative practitioners, collaborative schools.* Denver: Love Publishing.

Rende, R.D., & Plomin, R. (1990). Quantitative genetics and developmental psychopathology: Contributions to understanding normal development. *Development and Psychopathology, 2,* 393–407.

Rhode, G., Jenson, W.R., & Reavis, H.D. (1994). *The tough kid book.* Longmont, CO: Sopris West.

Rhodes, W.C. (1963). Curriculum and disordered behavior. *Exceptional Children, 30,* 61–66.

Rhodes, W.C. (1967). The disturbing child: A problem of ecological management. *Exceptional Children, 33,* 449–455.

Roach, V. (1995). Supporting inclusion: Beyond the rhetoric. *Phi Delta Kappan, 97*(4), 295–299.

Rockwell, S. (1993). *Tough to reach: Tough to teach.* Reston, VA: Council for Exceptional Children.

Rutherford, R., Chipman, J., DiGangi, S., & Anderson, K. (1992). *Teaching social skills: A practical instructional approach.* Ann Arbor, MI: Exceptional Innovations.

Senge, P.F. (1990). *The fifth discipline: The art and practice of the learning organization.* New York: Bantam Doubleday.

Skiba, R., Polsgrove, L., & Nasstrom, K. (1996). Developing a system of care: Interagency collaboration for students with emotional/behavioral disorders. In *Mini-Library Series on Emotional/Behavioral Disorders* (pp. 1–38). Reston, VA: The Council for Children with Behavioral Disorders.

Soderlund, J., Epstein, M.H., Quinn, K.P., Cumblad, C., & Petersen, S. (1995). Parental perspectives on comprehensive services for children and youth with emotional and behavioral disorders. *Behavioral Disorders, 20,* 157–170.

Stainback, S., & Stainback, W. (Eds.). (1992). *Curriculum considerations in inclusive classrooms: Facilitating learning for all students.* Baltimore: Paul H. Brookes Publishing Co.

Stroul, B.A., & Friedman, R.M. (1986). *A system of care for severely emotionally disturbed children and youth.* Washington, DC: CASSP Technical Assistance Center at Georgetown University.

Sugai, G., & Horner, R. (1994). Including students with severe behavior problems in general education settings: Assumptions, challenges, and solutions. *The Oregon Conference Monograph, 6,* 109–120.

Tashie, C., Shapiro-Barnard, S., Dillon, A., Schuh, M., Jorgensen, C., & Nisbet, J. (1993). *The status of integrated educational services for students with severe disabilities in New Hampshire.* Durham: University of New Hampshire, Institute on Disability.

Urban, J., & Carlson, E. (1991). Patterns of individual adaptation across childhood [Special issue]. *Development and Psychopathology, 3,* 445–460.

U.S. Department of Education, Office of Special Education Programs. (1994). *Sixteenth annual report to Congress on the implementation of the Individuals with Disabilities Education Act.* Washington, DC: Author.

Villa, R.A., Udis, J., & Thousand, J.S. (1994). Responses for children experiencing behavioral and emotional challenges. In J.S. Thousand, R.A. Villa, & A.I. Nevin (Eds.), *Creativity and collaborative learning: A practical guide to empowering students and teachers* (pp. 369–390). Baltimore: Paul H. Brookes Publishing Co.

Walker, H., Colvin, G., & Ramsey, E. (1995). *Antisocial behavior in school: Strategies and best practices.* Pacific Grove, CA: Brooks/Cole.

Walker, H., & Fabre, T. (1987). Assessment of behavior disorders in the school setting: Issues, problems, and strategies. In N. Haring (Ed.), *Assessing and managing behavior disabilities* (pp. 198–234). Seattle: University of Washington Press.

Walker, H.M., Horner, R.H., Sugai, G., Bullis, M., Sprague, J.R., Bricker, D., & Kaufman, M.J. (1996). Integrated approaches to preventing antisocial behavior patterns among school-age children and youth. *Journal of Emotional and Behavioral Disorders, 4,* 194–209.

Walker, H., & Severson, H.H. (1992). *Systematic screening for behavior disorders.* Longmont, CO: Sopris West.

Walker, H.M., Severson, H., & Feil, E. (1995). *The Early Screening Project.* Longmont, CO: Sopris West.

Walker, H.M., Todis, B.J., Holmes, D., & Horton, G. (1988). *The Walker social skills curriculum: The ACCESS adolescent curriculum for communication and effective social skills.* Austin, TX: PRO-ED.

Warger, C., & Rutherford, R. (1996). *Social skills instruction: A collaborative approach.* Ann Arbor, MI: Exceptional Innovations.

Wood, M.M., & Long, N.J. (1991). *Life space intervention: Talking with children and youth in crisis.* Austin, TX: PRO-ED.

Chapter 8

A University–Public School Collaborative Project for Including Students with Learning and Behavior Problems in General Education Classrooms

Nancy B. Meadows

Overall, fewer students with emotional and behavior disorders (EBD) are served in general education classrooms (16%) than are students with other disabilities (35%). Furthermore, 56.4% of all students with EBD are placed in self-contained classrooms or separate facilities (Office of Special Education Programs, 1994). Such placement trends are not surprising given that the traditional *cascade-of-services model* suggests that as intensity of need becomes greater, more restrictive placements are necessary. Cessna and Skiba (1996) explained clearly that when students with EBD are viewed as having severe needs that require a wide variety and intense level of services, they are placed in more restrictive environments in which such services and resources should be available. It has been argued, however, that *placement* has become confused with *treatment,* that placement should be based on the individual needs of students and *not* on the availability of resources or services in a particular environment, and that intensity of need does not have to be equated with more restrictive placement (Cessna &

Skiba, 1996; Knitzer, 1993; Muscott, Morgan, & Meadows, 1996; Neel & Cessna, 1993). Proponents of this argument support a *needs-based model* whereby services are determined by both the academic and the behavioral needs of the student (Cessna & Skiba, 1996; Neel & Cessna, 1993). In a needs-based model, there are no assumptions as to *where* those services will be delivered; rather, it is assumed that schools will serve as communities of learning, that services will be delivered throughout the school in a variety of environments, and that all educators will teach all students.

A needs-based model of services has several implications for inclusion of students with EBD in general education classrooms. First, the variability and the severity of the needs of students with EBD can be met in general education classrooms when resources and services are channeled in that direction. Level and intensity of need become predictors for increased resources, not for placement (Cessna & Skiba, 1996). Second, collaboration among all *stakeholders* in the inclusion process is essential if needs-based programming is to be implemented successfully. Third, educators must be prepared and prerequisites must be in place at all levels, which will lead to a process of responsible inclusion, thereby guarding against the possibility of simply "dumping" students into general education environments.

Given these considerations, the focus of this chapter is on the Hubbard Project, a collaborative university–public school project that was designed from a needs-based perspective to meet the needs of elementary school students with learning disabilities (LD) and EBD in their general education classrooms. The chapter is divided into four sections. First is a brief discussion of the several needs that students with EBD typically have and that present challenges to both educators and parents. Once identified, these challenges served as a basis for many of the discussions underlying the development of the needs-based project. This section is followed by an overview of the Hubbard Project as it was implemented during the 1995–1996 academic year. The third section of the chapter focuses on Charlie, an 8-year-old boy with EBD, whose story provides an in-depth case example and highlights the needs-based services and collaboration that define the Hubbard Project. Finally, as no project is perfect and few projects involving students with EBD ever truly "end," the chapter concludes with a discussion of some of the questions raised during the school year and describes directions for the future.

CHALLENGES PRESENTED BY STUDENTS WITH EBD

Students with EBD often exhibit disruptive behaviors and poor social skills and typically have academic difficulties that stretch the resources of general and special educators (Cessna & Skiba, 1996; Kauffman & Pullen, 1989). The challenges that these students present often are viewed by teachers and administrators as barriers to inclusion in general education classes. This is not surprising, as students with EBD challenge the ways in which teachers are prepared to teach, the discipline policies of most schools and school districts, the curriculum

implemented in general education classrooms, and the need for extensive services beyond what schools traditionally offer students. The challenges outlined in this section were originally discussed by Muscott et al. (1996); readers are referred to that resource for a more detailed discussion.

The First Challenge: Owning the "Problem"

The educational reform movement has emphasized the attitude that "it takes a whole village to educate a child" (Betances, 1993). Classroom teachers and school administrators, however, often believe that the responsibility for teaching students with special education labels belongs solely to the special education teacher (Meadows & Ellis, 1994). This is especially true for students with EBD, whose behavior both challenges and disrupts the educational environment (see Heflin, Boreson, Grossman, Huette, & Iigen, 1993; Muscott, 1994). As one secondary teacher for students with EBD stated, "I was told that as long as I kept my kids in my classroom, the door on the hinges, and blood shed to a minimum, my program would be considered successful" (Meadows & Cavin, 1996, p. 22).

History has taught Hubbard Project participants that although some students with EBD have been educated in general education classrooms, most have not. Walker and Bullis (1990) noted that when students with EBD have been included in general education classes the results often have been disastrous. As a result, students with EBD, particularly those who exhibit aggressive and disruptive behavior, typically are the first group to leave the general education classroom and the last group to return. Once referred for evaluation, they typically are removed from the general education classroom and educated in separate placements. Attitudinal research reveals that students with EBD experience the highest peer rejection rates of any students with disabilities in the field and are the least acceptable candidates for reintegration into general education among all students with disabilities (Braaten, Kauffman, Braaten, Polsgrove, & Nelson, 1988; Downing, Simpson, & Miles, 1990; Landrum & Kauffman, 1992).

The Second Challenge: Preparing Teachers

As a group, classroom teachers have felt both ill equipped and unwilling to handle the variability and intensity of challenging behavior that students with EBD have exhibited (Martin, Lloyd, Kauffman, & Coyne, 1995). Indeed, some students with EBD have posed risks to other students in general education classrooms in which necessary supports were absent. Furthermore, some students' needs are so intense that there is an increased likelihood of injury when adults lack the necessary skills and intervention strategies to build relationships with these students and to deescalate intensifying patterns of behavior (Walker, Colvin, & Ramsey, 1995; Wood & Long, 1991). Studies show that fewer than half of general education teachers have received any coursework dealing with specialized instruction (Brown, Gable, Hendrickson, & Algozzine, in press). In one survey of inclusive practices, special education administrators rated ineffective teacher skills as the second most significant barrier to the inclusion of students with EBD (Cheney, 1994). In a related study, general and special education teachers in elementary schools across Pennsylvania who had experience with inclusion indicated the need for training and at the same time reported such training unavailable (Wolery, Gessler, Caldwell, Snyder, & Lisowski, 1995). Considering these facts, it is no wonder that many general education teachers feel insufficiently prepared to cope with the demands imposed on them by students with EBD. Quality preservice and in-service training that focuses on attitudes and effective methodology is necessary if administrators, teachers, and support personnel are to meet the challenge of educating these students successfully *and* feel competent in the process.

The Third Challenge: Providing Resources to Meet Support Needs

There is evidence that the availability and quality of services for students with EBD varies greatly from state to state and from locality to locality (Muscott, 1988; Wood & Smith, 1986) and that the availability of resources often drives a student's placement decision rather than his or her actual academic and/or behavioral needs (Cessna & Adams, 1993). In many places, students with EBD are unnecessarily relegated to more restrictive environments. In other places, students with EBD are "dumped" into general education classrooms with few if any supports for either the student or the teacher. Research on the cascade-of-services model has demonstrated consistently that the severity of behavior problems cannot account for the differences in the placement of students along the continuum of services (Bullock, Zager, Donohoe, & Pelton, 1985; Muscott, 1994; Peterson, Zabel, Smith, & White, 1983). Muscott, for example, reported considerable overlap in the severity of maladaptive behavior exhibited by students in resource rooms, special classes, special schools, and residential treatment centers, particularly at the level of secondary school placements.

Surveys of teachers reveal discrepancies between teachers' perceived needs and the availability of resources for inclusive practices (Martin et al., 1995; Wolery et al., 1995). For example, one group of surveyed teachers reported that they were frustrated by the lack of services and financial resources available to meet the needs of students with EBD (Martin et al., 1995). Practitioners who came together in Dallas, Texas, for a Working Forum on Inclusion reported that lack of financial resources was a problem but lack of time in their day to deal with the "extra" work involved with having students with EBD in their classrooms was an even greater problem (Meadows & Ellis, 1994).

The Fourth Challenge: Developing Differentiated Programming to Meet the Needs of Students with EBD

Developing differentiated curricula that meet the diverse needs of students with EBD is always a challenge. This becomes an even greater challenge when full-time general education placements are considered for these students. Students with EBD who remain in self-contained classrooms all day have been shown to demonstrate greater extremes in behavior, either by being more aggressive and unable to demonstrate self-control or by being more introverted and withdrawn (Meadows, Neel, Scott, & Parker, 1994). It is not surprising that children with more extreme educational needs would be the last to be included in general education classrooms. It does, however, pose a serious problem for schools as they move toward more inclusive placements for these students. If children with less extreme educational needs are not doing well in inclusive environments (Gable, Laycock, Maroney, & Smith, 1991), then major modifications will need to be made if children and youth with more serious educational needs are to succeed there.

Unfortunately, some studies suggest that the instructional modifications that might be necessary to support successful inclusion are not commonplace. Studies (Meadows et al., 1994; Ysseldyke, Thurlow, Wotruba, & Nania, 1990) have indicated that teachers seldom make academic or social changes to accommodate the needs of students with learning and behavior problems; teachers rely on traditional management strategies and classroom rules to reduce inappropriate behaviors, seldom teaching *new* behaviors. When teachers perceive the problem as being within the child, many would prefer to have the child removed from the classroom than to adapt instruction. Idol and West (1987) reported that such resistance is a major barrier to the efficacy of consultation services.

The Fifth Challenge: Reintegrating and Including Students Who Were Previously Excluded

Prior to attending special education environments, the majority of students with EBD have failed—either academically or behaviorally—in traditional classrooms; they are also the least likely to experience success once they are returned to general education. Given the well-documented problems that students with EBD have in general education classrooms, many educators have argued that systematic models for reintegration and inclusion are needed to improve the poor success rates of these students as they return to general education programs (Gable et al., 1991; Laycock & Tonelson, 1985; Lloyd, Kauffman, & Kupersmidt, 1988; Muscott & Bond, 1986; Muscott et al., 1996). In a na-

tional survey of educational programs for adolescents with EBD, however, Epstein, Foley, and Cullinan (1992) found that although mainstreaming was the most commonly listed program feature, only one third of the programs actually emphasized inclusion-related skills and procedures.

Parents and educators also believe that the development of peer support and friendships is a key to successful inclusion of all students with disabilities in general education environments and is the component most often overlooked in the reintegration process (Stainback, Stainback, & Wilkinson, 1992). Getting along with peers, making friends, and maintaining relationships often are difficult processes for students with EBD, and these students are particularly at risk for social failure when they are returning to be with peers who have previously rejected them. Students with EBD not only need the skills to make and maintain friends, but they also need to be provided with structures in their environments that maximize their chances for success. Within these environments, they need access to potential friends, encouragement for interaction, and continuity of relationships across environments (Searcy, 1996).

The Sixth Challenge: Providing Wraparound Services and a Coordinated Service Delivery Plan

Students with EBD and their families often have needs that extend beyond the school. It is critical that services for these students be comprehensive and the result of collaborative efforts on the part of educators, family, and the various agencies and community services involved. Because students with EBD often are regarded more negatively than students with other disabilities, it frequently is difficult to obtain sustained involvement from the various stakeholders. For example, interactions between parents and educators often are fraught with issues of blame and guilt (Coleman, 1992). When planning an inclusive program, parents and educators might also have differing goals for the children. Many students with EBD require social services, such as social-welfare services, juvenile justice/correctional services, and mental health services. If a need for these services is indicated, then it is the responsibility of the educators involved with the student to ensure that these agencies are represented on the child study team. It is also important for parents to be aware of these services. In a follow-up study of adolescents with EBD, Neel, Meadows, Levine, and Edgar (1988) found that parents often were unaware of services that were available for their child. Planning wraparound services for students with EBD may also require multiple committees. For example, the student may need to have access to the following (Guetzloe, 1994):

1. Interagency councils of service providers
2. Building teams, such as crisis management or the child study team
3. Content area teams (secondary) or grade-level teams (elementary)
4. Co-teaching or collaborative teaching teams

Some committees may be needed for long-term services, whereas access to others may be intermittent or used to meet short-term goals.

AN OVERVIEW OF THE HUBBARD PROJECT

The Hubbard Project is a research collaboration between Texas Christian University (TCU) and Hubbard Heights Elementary School. Hubbard Heights Elementary School is an urban public school with grade levels from prekindergarten through fifth grade. The school has a total of 762 students—709 general education students and 53 students qualifying for special education services (e.g., with LD, serious emotional disturbances, speech-language impairments, other health impairments). The special education services are primarily delivered via pull-out resources. There are 34 general education classroom teachers and 3 special education teachers. Demographically, Hubbard Heights is in a low-income area of Fort Worth, Texas; approximately 75% of students qualify for the free or reduced-cost lunch program. The ethnic breakdown of the school is 79% Hispanic, 15% Caucasian, and 6% other (African American, Asian, Middle Eastern, and Native American).

TCU is a private university in Fort Worth with a total student body of 6,000; 430 students are enrolled in the School of Education, and 60 of those students are majoring in special education. During the 1995–1996 academic year, 15 special education undergraduate students at the junior and senior levels participated in this project as university mentors. The project coordinator was a faculty member whose area of emphasis is behavior disorders and LD. The inclusion facilitator was a graduate student majoring in educational administration with extensive teaching experience and experience with adapting and modifying curricula for students with learning difficulties.

The focus of the Hubbard Project was to meet students' academic, behavioral, and social needs in general education classrooms and to prepare the teachers at Hubbard for the increased inclusion of students with learning and behavior problems in their classrooms. The project arose from conversations among university faculty and public school personnel concerning the lack of ownership that general education teachers had for the teaching and learning of students with learning and behavior problems. Informal observations by the special education teachers, principals, and university faculty indicated that many students with disabilities, when not working with the special education teacher, were left to their own devices in their general education classrooms. Although the principals and teachers at Hubbard had adopted the attitude that "all teachers teach all students," this sense of community and ownership of all students seldom crossed the special education/general education boundaries.

Initial discussions among TCU and Hubbard participants uncovered several needs, including the following:

1. Knowledge of teachers' attitudes toward the special education students in their classes, how those students functioned on a daily basis, and the types of accommodations typically made for them
2. Intense study of students' academic and social needs, along with an in-depth look at how teachers could adapt, modify, and re-

structure their instruction in an effort to meet these needs

3. Professional and staff development and the resources necessary to meet and maintain the needs of the school community as a whole

4. The development of a structure that would mutually benefit both the Hubbard Heights Elementary School community and the TCU faculty and students

The Hubbard Project's first priority was to gather as much information as possible to determine which students and teachers had the greatest instructional needs so that the Hubbard Project would be able to develop appropriate needs-based interventions and assign available resources accordingly. The project began by having the inclusion facilitator (IF) and the lead resource teacher observe the special education students in their general education classrooms. Observations focused on the following: 1) the degree to which the students participated in day-to-day academic instruction in the classroom and 2) any accommodations that were made to facilitate their participation. Each classroom was observed for a minimum of 2 hours. There were several classrooms in which teachers made modifications where and when necessary (e.g., shortened tasks, more flexible time limits), and special education students seemed to blend in with their peers. There were other classrooms, especially those with a disproportionately high number of students with disabilities, in which the special education students were often given the same work as the rest of their classmates; work that they seldom understood and, therefore, work in which they seldom were engaged. Because the special education students were coming and going from the classroom and often were disruptive, many of them were seated together at the back of the classroom.

The Hubbard Project's next step was to gain some knowledge of the teachers' perspectives. Teachers were asked to complete a 12-item survey about their attitudes toward inclusion of students with mild disabilities in their classrooms and the curricular modifications and teaching adaptations that they typically made for these students. Results indicated that the majority of teachers believed that providing individualized instruction according to student needs helps the students and that using individualized criteria for grading assignments and tests is important. When asked to rate their actual classroom practices, however, teachers reported that they only occasionally used individualized education programs (IEPs) as a resource in planning and only occasionally adapted their instructional planning or provided daily, individualized instruction for the special education students in their classes. Teachers indicated that they would welcome some technical assistance in academic areas, but most believed that they did not need help with classroom management or dealing with children with behavior problems. Several teachers expressed in written comments that the help that they needed was to have the children with "more serious learning and behavior problems" removed from their classrooms for longer periods of the day.

In addition to these surveys, the Hubbard Project staff informally interviewed each teacher. From these interviews, a clearer picture emerged of what teachers perceived as their own needs as well as their perceptions of their students' needs. Quite often, interviewers heard comments such as, "I need help if Charlie is going to be in my class all day." Or perhaps more important, "Charlie can't be in my class all day because he is a resource student." When asked about specific children and how they performed in class, teachers expressed such thoughts as, "I don't expect him to do as much," or, "He just does what he can." The interviews also confirmed what the Hubbard Project staff had already learned from the surveys. Of the 34 teachers with whom Hubbard Project staff talked, only 3 said that they regularly and systematically modified instruction for their students with disabilities.

Next, the Hubbard Project staff reviewed all students' IEPs to determine their specific academic goals and objectives and the adaptations and modifications, if any, that were required by the students' Admission Review Dismissal (ARD) teams. Most students had academic IEP objectives for reading and language arts only ($n = 32$), 1 student had IEP objectives for only math skills, and 18 students had IEP objectives for both reading and language arts and math.

The Hubbard Project staff found no specific goals or objectives directed toward improving students' behavior or increasing their social competence. The Hubbard Project staff were very curious about this and on further inquiry learned that ARD teams in this district seldom included behavioral goals unless students were taught in self-contained or more restrictive environments. Two of the students who were reviewed by the Hubbard Project staff had "monitor only" status, and their IEP objectives were directed toward successful participation in their general education classrooms.

After reviewing and discussing all of the information and data that the Hubbard Project staff had collected, the team decided that in some classes there was less individualization of instruction and more isolation of special education students from their peers. Special education students in these classes were considered to need an intervention resembling "triage," in which their needs could be prioritized in terms of behavioral interventions and modified instruction, especially in reading, language arts, and content areas such as science and social studies. Some students and teachers were doing so well overall that the Hubbard Project staff decided that their needs would be met best if the special education teacher worked in the classroom as a "collaborator" with the general education teachers. The overall objectives for the Hubbard Project became as follows:

1. To provide ongoing monitoring of students' academic, behavioral, and social needs
2. To develop a user-friendly system that would enable teachers to adapt, modify, and restructure their instruction to meet students' needs
3. To facilitate professional and staff development and the resources necessary to meet and maintain the needs of the school community as a whole
4. To develop a structure that would mutually benefit the elementary school and university faculty and students

Collaborative Activities

Each of the activities described in this section is a result of the Hubbard Project staff's initial needs assessment as well as of ongoing monitoring and discussions that occurred on a regular basis throughout the school year. The activities were developed to give all participants an opportunity to gain some insights and understanding of children with learning problems as well as to meet specific needs exhibited by students. In addition, the Hubbard Project strove to create structures that faculty and students at Hubbard and at TCU found mutually beneficial.

Inclusion Facilitator

The IF was a TCU-funded departmental graduate assistant assigned to work 20 hours per week with the TCU professor who initiated the Hubbard Project. Her role in this project was critical because she acted as a liaison between both campuses as well as among the general and special education teachers and students at Hubbard. She was the common communication source among all project participants. Her responsibilities included the following:

1. Ongoing monitoring of students' and teachers' needs through anecdotal observations and informal interviews of students and teachers
2. Developing a resource file to assist teachers in adapting and modifying their instruction
3. Participating in grade-level planning periods to help teachers identify and meet students' needs
4. Assisting in the classroom with small-group instruction, often modeling modified instructional practices for teachers
5. Obtaining outside resources and wraparound services, as needed
6. Always serving as a warm and caring support person and problem solver for teachers and students

More specific examples of the pivotal role that she played in the success of this project appear in the case descriptions later in this chapter.

On-Site University Course

During the spring semester, an undergraduate special education seminar with an enrollment of 12 students was taught 2 days per week in one of the resource classrooms at Hubbard. Each TCU student was placed with one of the classes that the Hubbard Project staff's initial needs assessment had determined needed triage. They worked 3 hours each week in the classroom, taught students individually and in small groups, kept a journal of their experiences, and collected work samples throughout the semester. The issues discussed in class arose from their field experiences and reflections. For example, many of the TCU students worked with children in special education classes who were receiving medication for hyperactivity. Consequently, the students read articles and discussed the effects of medication and the implications for treatment of attention-deficit/hyperactivity disorder (ADHD). Inclusion was a natural topic for the course and was discussed from the perspective of the various stakeholders in the inclusion process, as was the issue of "responsible" inclusion. In addition, because the course was taught on the Hubbard campus, the lead resource teacher was available to talk with TCU students and share her professional expertise and perspective on several of the issues discussed in class.

TCU students were responsible for assisting teachers in planning curricular adaptations and modifications in assignments for their assigned students. They were also strongly encouraged to make suggestions about instruction and implement their own ideas. For example, Miss Richards (a TCU student) was asked to assist Cathryn, a second-grade student, with her writing. Cathryn did not like to write and had refused to participate in a writing workshop or in any journal-writing activities. When Miss Richards met with Cathryn about this, Cathryn explained that her "fingers didn't go fast enough." Miss Richards then began to teach Cathryn keyboarding and word-processing skills. As a culminating activity, Miss Richards and Cathryn wrote, illustrated graphically, and "published" a book about dinosaurs. In another example, Charlie, a second-grade boy who is labeled as having LD and serious emotional disturbances, and Mrs. King developed a "book-on-tape" project with accompanying illustrations. Miss Harris discovered that several of her students who were labeled as gifted appeared less than motivated. She recruited three TCU students through an-

other class that she was taking, negotiated with the professor for them to be given extra credit, and created a 4-week Inquiry unit in which the Hubbard and the TCU students worked together on a science project.

TCU students also experienced many frustrations when they encountered the teachers' normal demands for autonomy and ownership of their classroom. For example, some teachers were very restrictive in what they would allow TCU students to do in their classrooms. One teacher insisted that the TCU student sit in a specific place and provide very limited assistance to the student with whom she was working. Another teacher repeatedly left the classroom when the TCU student arrived, leaving the TCU student to act as substitute teacher. The Hubbard Project staff met regularly with the TCU students to problem-solve regarding such situations; however, these situations and students' frustrations remained relatively the same throughout the course of the year.

Academic Modifications and Adaptations

Developing a curriculum to meet the needs of students with learning problems in general education classrooms is often problematic because general and special education operate from different perspectives. General educators develop curricula for groups of students and base the curricula on the scope and the sequence of particular content area skills and information. Special educators are trained to develop curricula based on individual needs of students. The Hubbard Project advocated an "expanded curriculum" that would allow teachers to discuss both the individual and the group and to discuss both the students' needs and the curriculum (Cessna & Adams, 1993; Muscott et al., 1996). The Hubbard Project's goal was to develop an expanded curriculum that would effectively meet the needs of individual students as well as the larger group and that could be integrated with the more traditional curriculum of the inclusive classroom. The Hubbard Project staff believed that such a differentiated academic curriculum was critical to the project's success with teachers as well as with students.

The Hubbard Project actually operated at two levels. At a more general level, "resource files" were introduced to the Hubbard teachers. These were large file boxes that were divided into sections according to academic areas and that contained a variety of suggestions for adapting curricula and modifying academic tasks. Some suggestions were quite simple (e.g., recording books on tape, highlighting texts, shortening assignments, allowing more time to complete work, folding worksheets in half, providing page numbers next to study guide questions). Some ideas in the file were more complex (e.g., how to develop a peer tutoring program, how to implement cooperative learning groups, explanations of various collaborative teaching strategies). Each box also included a section on behavior management strategies and provided teachers with suggestions for meeting specific needs that were identified in the grade-level team meetings. The resource file was placed in the teachers' planning room in which grade-level teams met weekly for lesson planning.

On a more specific level, the Hubbard Project created adaptations based on individual students' needs. For example, second-grade students spent 45 minutes per week in a computer-based "newspaper" class. Students chose topics, wrote stories on the computer, and added graphics to enhance the stories. The students with reading and writing difficulties were constantly asking for help with ideas and with spelling, so these students were given the task of writing a creative sentence with each of their weekly spelling words and illustrating the sentence graphically. As they became more proficient at this, they moved on to writing and illustrating a silly story with their spelling words. Not only did the students gain computer and keyboarding practice, but also the teacher reported that their spelling grades improved.

One critical area that the Hubbard Project staff believed needed to be addressed was what to do about the special education students during the many times that other students were preparing for the state-mandated achievement test, the Texas Assessment of Academic Skills (TAAS). A teacher began to send her special education students to the resource room during

unscheduled times and for extended periods of time because she believed that the TAAS practice would be inappropriate for students in special education. After further investigation, the Hubbard Project found that other teachers were doing this as well. While the general education students practiced for TAAS, the special education students either had "free time" or were sent to the resource room.

The IF and the lead special education teacher asked for copies of the TAAS mathematics problems to modify for the special education students. They asked a mathematics instructor from TCU to help with the modifications. This instructor had never done this sort of task before, so the Hubbard Project staff combined her mathematics talents with the teachers' knowledge of the students, their disabilities, and which modifications worked best with them. The group came up with a set of mathematics problems that were very similar to the original problems. The modifications used similar mathematics questions but adjusted the level and the amount of reading necessary and incorporated words that the students would recognize from their special education reading program. Geometric designs that were a part of the problem were enlarged to allow students to cut them out, hold them, and piece together the answers. Manipulatives—specifically "rods" of different colors—also were used to help the students further visualize the problems.

Because the TAAS practice was supposed to be implemented in small groups, it was relatively easy for the IF and the lead resource teacher to work with the special education students in the classroom during the regularly scheduled instructional time. Teachers began to realize that the special education students also could participate in TAAS practice sessions and work on similar concepts as the rest of the class. The special education students did not have to endure the embarrassment of segregation from their peers because they were no longer labeled as being exempt from taking the TAAS.

Co-teaching Strategies

Co-teaching refers to the collaboration between general and special educators who plan, teach, and evaluate instruction together. The lead resource teacher and two fifth-grade teachers formed a co-teaching team. These teachers taught together 2 days per week in 2-hour blocks of time. Although they planned together, the fifth-grade teachers took the "lead" in instruction and the resource teacher acted more as an instructional assistant and provided back-up and support during planned instruction. This is not the ideal co-teaching situation; however, it did allow the special education teacher to monitor the progress of the special education students and to provide respite for the teachers when difficult situations arose. (See the Summer 1993 issue of the journal *Preventing School Failure* [Volume 37, Number 4] for an excellent review of co-teaching strategies and their implications for the merger of general and special education programs.)

Wraparound Services

Several of the special education students at Hubbard had needs that extended beyond the school environment. Parents often were unaware of the services that were available or felt unable to gain access to the services once they were informed of them. The Hubbard Project staff believed that it was critical that services for these students be as comprehensive as possible and that they be the result of collaborative efforts on the parts of TCU and Hubbard educators, families, and the various agencies and community services. Entering the classroom offered opportunities to discover some wraparound needs requiring such mutual support.

Hubbard qualifies for many social services, including a hospital van that provides medical care, prescriptions, and immunizations. The school also has parenting classes, courses that teach English to adults, and general equivalency diploma courses. Administrators and staff have learned to take advantage of what the community offers, and the school provides many services to their students and families. What the Hubbard Project staff noticed by working closely with the special education teachers and students was that some children were still quite needy even with services provided through the school.

A very evident and critical need was clothing. As the weather became colder, the Hubbard Project staff noticed that students were coming to school without warm clothing and coats. Hubbard Project staff believed that part of their sup-

port should be to obtain clothing donations. The special education teachers took the responsibility for identifying children who needed a coat, a sweater, or shoes; and TCU students, the IF, and the professor solicited donations. In addition to clothing, some children were supposed to be wearing glasses but were not. The IF put the school nurse in touch with an agency that would provide and replace glasses free of charge to the children who needed them.

Laura, a child with developmental disabilities, illustrates how wraparound services were provided. Laura is incontinent; she wets her pants a little at a time throughout the day. As a result, she smells of urine, and the other children in her class do not want to be around her. Sending Laura to the restroom more often helped, but it was not sufficient. Laura needed help with developing social skills and making friends. To address this situation, the Hubbard Project staff decided to provide the nurse with a supply of Pull-Ups. This involved having the child go to the nurse first thing in the morning, put on the Pull-Ups, and wear them all day. This worked rather well. She still needed frequent bathroom breaks, but the problem became more manageable for Laura and her peers and teachers.

Professional and Staff Development

As a group, many general education teachers feel poorly equipped to handle the needs of students with learning and behavior problems in their classroom. As studies show that fewer than half of general education teachers have received any coursework dealing with specialized instruction (Brown et al., in press), professional and staff development was an important component of this project. The Hubbard Project focused on small-group (grade-level teams) and individual instruction rather than relying on whole-school in-service sessions. Professional development topics were chosen as needs arose. For example, strategies to deal with noncompliance were addressed when Paul, a fourth-grade student, consistently refused to do any work except in the resource room. Teaching students self-management and organizational skills was chosen as a topic for second-grade teachers because some students were having difficulty with keeping track of papers, books, and other belongings when they moved from one classroom to another. These students also were reluctant to begin working independently.

As a group, however, the members of the Hubbard Project believed that professional and staff development was the weakest component and the one that needed the most development during the next school year. The Hubbard Project staff believed that the premise was good— that is, to develop in-services based on students' and teachers' needs. But, because the Hubbard Project tried to integrate staff development topics into regularly scheduled planning time, it turned out that there was rarely time to cover topics, and there was little time for follow-up. Using teacher planning time also seemed to generate a "Band-Aid" approach in which each problem was handled in a superficial manner.

CHARLIE: A CASE STUDY

The following discussion of Charlie, a boy with EBD, highlights several key points made in this chapter. Charlie's story does not represent an ideal model of inclusionary practices; rather, it brings into focus many of the issues that surround the inclusion of students with EBD in general education classrooms. A number of Charlie's needs resulted in his requiring a variety of educational and wraparound services. Charlie's problems certainly were not unique; however, Charlie presented some difficult challenges for the general education teachers and administrators, who had little or no experience working with children with EBD. The discussion focuses on 1) an analysis of the educational system and Charlie's needs and 2) interventions that were put in place in response to those needs.

Charlie's Story

Charlie was labeled as having EBD and LD. He also received medication for ADHD. He began the school year (1995–1996) as a new second-grade student at Hubbard Heights. Charlie lived with his mother and his older sister; his parents were divorced. Charlie's older brother was in prison. Both Charlie and his sister participated in the free lunch program at school. During a potentially harmful cold spell in the month of January, Charlie and his mother and sister spent 2 weeks in a homeless shelter because they had been evicted from their home. During this time, however, the mother always managed to get the children to school even though the shelter was not near the school and she had to drive them to school rather than rely on the school bus. While Charlie was living in the shelter, he had some very difficult days at school. Quite understandable, he became very possessive of his backpack and his belongings and was ready to fight anyone who came near him or his possessions.

Charlie had a negative self-concept and a history of anger and aggression toward himself and others and was frustrated easily. His relationships with other children were much poorer than with adults, and he had great trouble making friends. His behavior problems included fighting, explosive episodes, sudden mood changes, and self-injurious behavior. On one occasion, he pierced his hand with a pair of scissors and claimed that another child had hurt him. On many occasions, he claimed that his classmates had stolen from him. In each case, he was found to have actually "stolen" the item in question. He had negative feelings toward his classmates. Charlie became very angry when someone violated his space or so much as brushed up against him, and he was frequently sent to the office because of fighting. Charlie was also quite manipulative and attempted to deceive teachers without remorse. His problems were apparent both in and out of school.

Anecdotal observations were corroborated by the results from the Achenbach Teacher Report Form (TRF; Achenbach, 1991b) and the Child Behavior Checklist (CBCL; Achenbach, 1991a). The TRF showed significant problems in both Internalizing and Externalizing areas with significant elevations in Anxious/Depressed, Social Problems, and Aggressive Behavior and borderline significance in Delinquent Behavior. Charlie was described as being nervous, suspicious, hurt by criticism, and expressing feelings of worthlessness. He was viewed as lying, cheating, using bad language, arguing, disturbing the classroom, fighting, showing explosiveness, and evidencing sudden mood changes. Results of the CBCL indicated significant scores for Obsessive-Compulsive, Somatic Complaints, Social Withdrawal, and Aggressive Behavior. He was described as evidencing nightmares, having poor peer relationships, being disliked by other children, being hyperactive, showing cruelty to others, fighting, using bad language, and attacking people.

Charlie was functioning approximately 1 year below his second-grade level placement in math and reading. His Wechsler Intelligence Scale for Children–III (Wechsler, 1991) scores indicated intelligence in the normal range of functioning (Verbal IQ = 97; Performance IQ = 104; Full Scale IQ = 100). Charlie's second-grade teacher reported that he was unable to keep up with the rest of the students and that she had to place him at the back of the classroom facing the wall because he was so disruptive. The special education teacher reported that he was learning to read, but slowly. When given unstructured free time in the classroom, Charlie typically chose to put together puzzles or to draw.

At the beginning of the 1995–1996 academic year, recommendations for Charlie from the ARD committee included the following:

1. A behavior management plan stressing favorable results for cooperative behavior and consistent consequences for inappropriate behavior
2. Counseling and/or play therapy through school and/or an outside agency with the parent being responsible for obtaining outside agency help
3. Reevaluation of medical management with consideration given to alleviating depressive and/or aggressive symptoms
4. Placement in Big Brothers and/or the Independent School District Growth Center Project (a special program within the school district that offered mentoring services)
5. Simultaneous recognition of attention difficulties, emotional problems, and manipulative tendencies
6. Placement in a general education classroom with support from special education staff

An Analysis of the System and Student Needs

Charlie initially was placed in an inclusive second-grade classroom. At first, he received 1 hour of reading and language arts support from the resource room teacher and 1 hour of counseling per week from the school counselor. As Yell and Shriner (1996) pointed out, it was Charlie's "presumptive right" to have an inclusive education. The general education environment clearly was the preferred placement, or least restrictive environment, and the resource teacher and the counselor should have provided supplementary aids and services. As Yell and Shriner also indicated, however, Charlie's unique educational needs should have been the ultimate consideration in determining placement and services. In Charlie's case, his needs and the environment in which he was placed were often in direct conflict, and problems occurred in rapid succession. By the end of the first month of school, Charlie's teacher had moved his desk to the back of the room facing the wall, he was sullen and angry, his general education teacher avoided contact with him as much as possible, his peers were afraid of him, he was no longer allowed recess privileges, and he was made to eat lunch alone in the resource room or the principal's office. Charlie spent large portions of his day in a "time-out" mode and was no longer receiving an appropriate education based on his academic and social needs.

There were several factors that had a great impact on the initial success or failure for Charlie and his teachers and peers. According to Cheney and Muscott (1996; see also Chapter 7), responsible inclusion requires many changes in the way in which schools are organized and instruction is delivered. In Cheney and Muscott's (1996) seven-step process model of inclusion, the first step requires the school to gain support for the concept of inclusion and have a commitment to provide the time and the resources to make inclusion successful. Once faculty have agreed that inclusion is the ultimate goal, they work to reconceptualize and reorganize school structures to support the inclusion process. In Charlie's elementary school, the commitment to inclusion was primarily from administrators and special education faculty. General education teachers had agreed that inclusion was an important goal, but most had not realized that inclusion meant that they were responsible for the educational needs and instructional planning for the students with disabilities in their classroom. In Charlie's case, his teacher relied heavily on the special education teacher for support and planning. If the special education teacher was not directly involved, then Charlie received very little classroom instruction. Administrators and faculty had some support structures in place (e.g., instructional aide in the classroom, university tutors, team planning meetings), but they were inadequate for the unique and intense challenges that Charlie presented. Thus, teachers and administrators moved into Phase Two, Program Redevelopment and Reimplementation, in a default mode. That is, it was not well thought out and planned but rather a reaction to the daily "curriculum of the moment" (Meadows, Melloy, & Yell, 1996) events that Charlie generated.

Charlie brought his teachers and support staff face to face with two uncomfortable truths. First, because Charlie was a difficult child with disruptive behavior, academic difficulties, and poor social skills, he stretched the abilities and resources of general and special educators. Second, the system that Charlie was in was not well-suited to handling these difficulties in behavior. At the outset, Charlie and his teachers were caught between the proverbial rock and a hard place: The need to educate Charlie in the appropriate least restrictive environment was paramount, yet he presented such challenges to the general education environment that the initial results were disastrous, both for the general education classroom teachers and students and for Charlie.

Student need commonly is associated with restrictiveness of placement—the more intense the student's needs are, the more restricted the placement is. When a needs-based approach is applied, however, the intensity of need is associated not with restrictiveness of placement but with a corresponding need for increased resources. For Charlie to remain in the general education classroom, he needed more resources that would meet his needs. Charlie's needs required a needs-based system in which there would be a shared responsibility to meet the needs of the whole child (Cessna & Skiba, 1996).

In December, a multidisciplinary team met to reevaluate Charlie's needs and his placement.

Some of Charlie's more apparent needs included learning appropriate ways to handle anger and aggression, problem-solving skills, feedback for appropriate behaviors, a structured and supportive classroom environment, a behavior management plan that encourages cooperation and positive peer interactions, friendship skills and opportunities to develop friends, and academic modifications consistent with his behavioral and attention problems.

Interventions

Based on Charlie's identified needs, several changes were made in Charlie's educational program. The remainder of this section contains brief descriptions of interventions that were implemented for Charlie. These interventions complied with legal and policy implications; were based on a process model of intervention; and were driven by Charlie's academic, social, and behavioral needs. People involved in the interventions included general and special education teachers, school principal and vice principal, school counselor, school psychologist, two TCU faculty members, and a class of 12 undergraduate special education majors. Some of the interventions were developed specifically for Charlie, whereas others were part of the Hubbard Project as described previously in this chapter.

Professional Development

Hubbard had weekly grade-level planning sessions of approximately 3 hours in duration. During the time that teachers were planning, their students were eating lunch; having recess; and participating in physical education, music, and computer lab. These planning meetings originally were developed 3 years earlier for the purpose of providing time for reflective and collaborative planning among the teachers in the same grade. They also were used as informal professional development sessions; student and teacher needs determined the topics discussed. Charlie's behaviors and needs were the topic of several of these sessions, which led the second-grade team to focus on learning behavior management techniques and appropriate academic modifications. Regardless of the intervention being discussed, the students' needs served as the reference point for discussion.

Daily Class Structure

Charlie's second-grade teachers used a team approach to instruction; that is, one teacher taught math, another taught reading and language arts, and a third taught science and social studies. They coordinated their teaching around specific units of interest. For Charlie, changing classes was a nightmare. He had a difficult time settling into each new environment. Even more difficult than his daily schedule was the weekly teacher planning time when he had to move among lunch, recess, physical education, music, and computer lab with very little consistent supervision. Thus, Charlie's daily schedule was readjusted so that he could stay with the same teacher for longer periods of time.

Differentiated Curriculum for Social Skills

Charlie had very few positive peer relationships. He was verbally and physically aggressive with his peers, and, as a consequence, children avoided him when possible. Developing and implementing formal and informal social skills curricula for Charlie was imperative. Formally, teachers used Skillstreaming the Elementary School Child (McGinnis & Goldstein, 1984) and Interpersonal Cognitive Problem Solving (Spivack & Shure, 1985). An informal social skills curriculum was developed based on the social task model of social competence (Meadows & Cavin, 1996; Neel & Meadows, 1991). Instructional strategies included modeling, role playing, and feedback and involved such skills as accepting criticism, using self-control, staying out of fights, solving problems, expressing anger appropriately, and dealing with frustration. Plans to help Charlie make friends also were included in the differentiated curriculum area of social competence (Searcy, 1996).

Academic Modifications

Charlie's academic needs were considered as they related to his social and behavioral needs. For example, Charlie had a difficult time beginning tasks; once a task was started, he became

easily distracted. His assignments, therefore, were broken down into smaller chunks. His organizational skills were poor, so the Hubbard Project staff developed an organizational system that included a three-ring binder with pocket dividers to keep his work together and organized. Charlie also was frustrated easily and became angry when he was unable to understand or complete an assignment. He began keeping "extra" work and "fun" worksheets in his binder and learned to move to a new task when he became frustrated and teacher assistance was not readily available. Other modifications included books and texts on tape, math manipulatives, visual drawings and pictures to assist with math word problems, shortened assignments, and shortened periods of time that Charlie was expected to do seatwork.

Behavior Plan

School faculty developed for Charlie a behavior plan that incorporated teaching him new behaviors to meet his identified social needs and included a traditional behavioral contract that utilized a token economy. During the 2 weeks in January when Charlie and his family lived in a shelter for homeless people, Charlie "earned" various types of snack foods, which he and his sister could eat in the evening. Food rewards were replaced gradually by activity rewards, such as one-to-one time spent with his teacher or a TCU mentor. Understandably, during the time when Charlie lived in the homeless shelter, his need to be in control of situations escalated. He also became very attached to his backpack as it was his only personal possession allowed in the shelter. His behavior plan during that time focused on providing him with choices so as to increase the control that he felt in certain situations and also to teach him skills that would allow him to escape adverse situations in more appropriate ways.

Crisis Management

School faculty developed for Charlie a crisis management plan that included his teachers, peers, the principal and vice principal, counselor, university mentor, and his mother (who brought him to school each day). Teachers attempted to intervene before the situations elevated to crisis levels. A typical crisis for Charlie began with the need to escape. When he was pressed to do something that he either did not want to do or believed that he could not do, he quickly became agitated; this was usually followed by short bursts of verbal aggression and then threats of physical violence. At that point, when he felt "cornered," Charlie carried out his threats of physical violence or ran away. The crisis plan for Charlie included having other students vacate the room while one student was assigned to get help from the office. The teacher remained calm and gave Charlie the previously taught "calming down" message. Following the quiet time, the teacher began a discussion with Charlie about what had just happened. He was reinforced for staying calm and talking matter-of-factly about the situation. Once the crisis was past, Charlie and his teacher made plans for his returning to the classroom (Meadows et al., 1996).

Collaboration

There were several levels of collaboration operating simultaneously in Charlie's case. First, there was collaboration among general and special education teachers. Charlie's academic and social instruction was carefully orchestrated by all involved. There also was collaboration among the public school and the university. In addition, Charlie's mother was actively involved and supportive, which the Hubbard Project staff believed was critical for Charlie's success. As several others in the field of EBD have pointed out, consistency among all of the collaborators is essential (Mostert, 1996; Nelson & Pearson, 1991).

University Mentors

Charlie was paired with a university mentor—an undergraduate student who was majoring in special education—who worked with him twice per week. Activities typically were multi-academic in nature; however, school work was not precluded from the plan. Interactions with his mentor focused on building social and problem-solving skills and providing opportunities for getting along with others.

As Charlie's story illustrates, the needs of a student with EBD are complex and challenging. There is a high probability that, at some time in

a special educator's career, he or she has heard a phrase similar to, "Oh, you must be so patient to work with those children." It is true that patience is a highly regarded characteristic of teachers who work with students with EBD. Such patience, however, is not reserved just for students; teachers of EBD students may need even more patience in dealing with the educational and other support systems. A needs-based system is bottom-up; that is, the students' needs serve as the driver of the system. Although traditional educational systems recognize the individual needs of children, the Hubbard Project tries to meet these needs within a system that is operationally a top-down system. For children with needs similar to Charlie's, the educational response must be well integrated and comprehensive, which will require the full cooperation and coordination of the entire educational community (see Weigle, 1997, for a behavioral support model for *teachers*).

IMPLICATIONS FOR FURTHER COLLABORATIVE ACTIVITIES

On the basis of the original goals and objectives for the Hubbard Project and the participants' experiences during the first year, several additional collaborative activities were identified for the 1996–1997 school year, as well as ways to expand some of the project's activities.

Increased Opportunities for Professional Development

Teachers in inclusive classrooms must have current knowledge of appropriate academic modifications, effective instructional and behavior management, and positive behavioral support strategies. When staff development in these areas is effective, it helps replenish teachers' skills and energy levels (Cheney, 1994; Muscott et al., 1996). One objective during the first year of this project was to make in-services an integral part of weekly planning sessions because the Hubbard Project staff believed that training that occurred in schools with teams that naturally work together had the potential to be more effective. The members of the Hubbard Project still think that is true; during the second project year, however, there were plans to make several changes in the approach. First, the Hubbard Project staff scheduled several schoolwide in-service sessions, with follow-ups to occur during the weekly planning sessions. Although "one-shot" workshops may not be effective in and of themselves, they are a useful beginning. Also, by implementing schoolwide in-service sessions, teachers had information prior to their planning sessions and were able to use the information as a basis for problem solving.

Increased Ownership of Special Education Students by General Education Teachers

It is important for general education teachers to believe that they are the primary educators of all children in their classes, including the special education students. The members of the Hubbard Project believe that progress was made toward this goal; however, the project still has a long way to go. This is an attitude shift that may occur more naturally as opportunities for professional development increase. However, in the second year of the project, as part of the teachers' yearly evaluation, administrators looked at the degree to which teachers made adaptations and modifications for their special education students. The team is hopeful that this will provide both contingency plans and feedback to teachers, thereby increasing their active role in the planning of programs for special education students.

Increased Special–General Education Collaborative Teaching

Co-teaching refers to the collaboration between general and special educators who plan, teach, and evaluate instruction together. The Hubbard Project staff believe that co-teaching benefits students and that it also increases opportunities for collecting data, monitoring student progress, and providing respite for teachers when difficult situations arise. This occurred on a limited basis during the first project year. During the second year, however, there were two co-teaching teams—one at the prekindergarten level and one at the fifth-grade level. Results from these experiences are under review for publication. To summarize briefly, however, prekindergarten teach-

ers, school administrators, and parents indicated a high level of satisfaction with the program. Results from fifth-grade participants were less positive and indicated that the co-teaching situation was actually more of a teacher and teacher aide relationship, with the special education teacher serving as the paraprofessional.

Implementation of a Prereferral Team

The Hubbard Project proposed that a schoolwide *prereferral* team be created during the second project year. The primary purpose of this team is to assist teachers with behavior and academic modifications, as well as to provide interventions and suggestions *prior* to a student's being referred for special education services. The Hubbard Project staff decided that the team would be representative of all school staff (i.e., general and special educators, support staff, and administration) with one teacher from each grade level and that members would be selected using a combination of voluntary and appointed options (Walker et al., 1995). Once formed, the prereferral team consisted of two administrators (the vice principal and a school district special education specialist), two special education teachers (prekindergarten and resource), and five general education teachers (K-1, 2, 3, 4, and 5). The team met biweekly throughout the school year. It is interesting to note that special education referrals decreased only slightly. Team members, however, reported a high degree of satisfaction with the prereferral processing and believed that the team provided support both for themselves and for the other teachers in the school. Toward the end of the year, team members indicated that most meetings focused on academic and behavior problems of students already in special education rather than on prereferral students.

Social Skills Instruction

During the first project year, the primary focus was to meet the academic needs of students. Many of the special education students in this project, however, also have problems with social skills and making friends. Teaching social skills requires formal and informal instructional methods as an integral component of the total curriculum. During the second project year, the Hubbard Project staff implemented curriculum materials to address the interrelated issues of affect, overt behavior, and problem solving. Informally, the Hubbard Project taught within the context of the "curriculum of the moment." For example, if a child is frustrated easily, then the teacher would teach new social skills for dealing with frustration, which might include asking for help or taking a brief time-out from the situation. Or, the teacher might take a literature-based approach to instruction, which might include using books and stories in which the characters model the new social skill being taught. The underlying premise of both formal and informal social skills instruction is that it needs to be relevant to the child, incorporating skills that the child will actually use in everyday situations.

CONCLUSIONS

Collaborative university and public school relationships have the potential for making significant improvements in a short period of time. These changes, however, require a willingness to ask questions about old habits and new trends and to suggest different ways of reaching old and new goals. Collaborative projects are excellent vehicles for change; they are, however, easier to plan, coordinate, and implement once university participants are established at the school. This requires not only time and effort but also tolerance by everyone involved for a variety of teaching philosophies and methods and a belief that the relationships established are of mutual benefit. From the university perspective, the Hubbard Project has provided students and faculty with invaluable opportunities to share in the lives of children and, in some cases, their families. Hubbard Heights teachers willingly have offered their professional expertise to the TCU students. In addition, Hubbard benefited from the many hours that TCU students contributed, both in and out of the classroom. There have been exceptions, such as times when TCU students have observed attitudes and teaching strategies that have been less than perfect and times when TCU students have been less than enthusi-

astic or less than prepared. Those situations have provided a different type of learning experience for all involved. Overall, the mutual benefits of this project have far exceeded the problems that the Hubbard Project has faced, and with ongoing, collaborative efforts, the project will continue to grow and change in the future.

REFERENCES

Achenbach, T.M. (1991a). *Manual for the Child Behavior Checklist/4–18 and 1991 profile*. Burlington: University of Vermont, Department of Psychiatry.

Achenbach, T.M. (1991b). *Manual for the Teacher's Report Form and 1991 profile*. Burlington: University of Vermont, Department of Psychiatry.

Betances, S. (1993). *It takes a whole village to educate a child*. Paper presented at the National Education Association conference series, Tampa, FL.

Braaten, S., Kauffman, J., Braaten, B., Polsgrove, L., & Nelson, C.M. (1988). The regular education initiative: Patent medicine for behavioral disorders. *Exceptional Children, 55,* 21–27.

Brown, J., Gable, R.A., Hendrickson, J.M., & Algozzine, B. (in press). Prereferral practices of regular teachers: Implications for regular and special education teacher preparation. *Teacher Education and Special Education.*

Bullock, L.M., Zager, E.L., Donohoe, C.A., & Pelton, G.B. (1985). Teachers' perceptions of behaviorally disordered students in a variety of settings. *Exceptional Children, 52,* 123–130.

Cessna, K.K., & Adams, L. (1993). Implications of a needs-based philosophy. In K.K. Cessna (Ed.), *Instructionally differentiated programming: A needs-based approach for students with behavior disorders* (pp. 7–18). Denver: Colorado Department of Education.

Cessna, K.K., & Skiba, R.J. (1996). Needs-based services: A responsible approach to inclusion. *Preventing School Failure, 40*(3), 117–123.

Cheney, D. (1994). Inclusion of students with emotional and behavioral disorders in general education programs: Definition, history, and recommendations. In L.M. Bullock & R.A. Gable (Eds.), *Monograph on inclusion: Ensuring appropriate services to children and youth with emotional/behavioral disorders. II* (pp. 1–5). Reston, VA: The Council for Children with Behavioral Disorders.

Cheney, D., & Muscott, H.S. (1996). Preventing school failure for students with emotional and behavioral disabilities through responsible inclusion. *Preventing School Failure, 40*(3), 109–116.

Coleman, M.C. (1992). *Behavior disorders: Theory and practice*. Needham Heights, MA: Allyn & Bacon.

Downing, J.A., Simpson, R.L., & Miles, B.S. (1990). Regular and special educators' perception of nonacademic skills needed by mainstreamed students with behavioral disorders and learning disabilities. *Behavioral Disorders, 15,* 217–226.

Epstein, M.H., Foley, R.M., & Cullinan, D. (1992). National survey of educational programs for adolescents with serious emotional disturbance. *Behavioral Disorders, 17,* 202–210.

Gable, R.A., Laycock, V.K., Maroney, S.A., & Smith, C.R. (Eds.). (1991). *Preparing to integrate students with behavioral disorders.* Reston, VA: Council for Exceptional Children.

Guetzloe, E. (1994). Inclusion of students with emotional/behavioral disorders: The issues, the barriers, the possible solutions. In L.M. Bullock & R.A. Gable (Eds.), *Monograph on inclusion: Ensuring appropriate services to children and youth with emotional/behavioral disorders. II* (pp. 21–24). Reston, VA: The Council for Children with Behavioral Disorders.

Heflin, L.J., Boreson, L., Grossman, M.A., Huette, J., & Iigen, J. (1993). Advocate, not abdicate. In L.M. Bullock & R.A. Gable (Eds.), *Monograph on inclusion: Ensuring appropriate services to children and youth with emotional/behavioral disorders. I* (pp. 17–20). Reston, VA: The Council for Children with Behavioral Disorders.

Idol, L., & West, J.F. (1987). Consultation in special education: Part II. Training. *Journal of Learning Disabilities, 20,* 474–494.

Kauffman, J.M., & Pullen, P.L. (1989). An historical perspective: A personal perspective on our history of service to mildly handicapped and at-risk students. *Remedial and Special Education, 10*(6), 12–14.

Knitzer, J. (1993). Children's mental health policy: Challenging the future. *Journal of Emotional and Behavioral Disorders, 1,* 8–16.

Landrum, T.J., & Kauffman, J.M. (1992). Reflections on characteristics of general education teachers perceived as effective by their peers: Implications for the inclusion of children with learning and behavioral disorders. *Exceptionality: A Research Journal, 3*(3), 185–188.

Laycock, V.K., & Tonelson, S.W. (1985). Preparing emotionally disturbed adolescents for the mainstream: An analysis of current practices. In S. Braaten, R.B. Rutherford, Jr., & W. Evans (Eds.), *Programming for adolescents with behavioral disorders* (Vol. 2, pp. 63–73). Reston, VA: Council for Exceptional Children.

Lloyd, J.W., Kauffman, J.M., & Kupersmidt, J.B. (1988). Success of students with behavior disorders in regular education environments: A review of research and a systemic model for development of interventions. In K. Gadow (Ed.), *Advances in learning and behavioral disabilities* (Vol. 8, pp. 225–264). Greenwich, CT: JAI Press.

Martin, K.F., Lloyd, J.W., Kauffman, J.M., & Coyne, M. (1995). Teachers' perceptions of educational placement decisions for pupils with emotional or behavioral disorders. *Behavioral Disorders, 20,* 106–117.

McGinnis, E., & Goldstein, A.P. (1984). *Skillstreaming the elementary school child.* Champaign, IL: Research Press.

Meadows, N.B., & Cavin, D.C. (1996). Teaching social skills to adolescents with behavior disorders: A social task approach. *Beyond Behavior, 7*(2), 22–25.

Meadows, N.B., & Ellis, L. (1994). Inclusion: Another option along the continuum of services for students with emotional/behavioral disorders. *Monograph: Designing Effective Programs for Students with Emotional/Behavioral Disorders.* Denton: University of North Texas.

Meadows, N.B., Melloy, K.J., & Yell, M.L. (1996). Behavior management as a curriculum for students with emotional and behavioral disorders. *Preventing School Failure, 40*(3), 124–130.

Meadows, N.B., Neel, R.S., Scott, C.M., & Parker, G.M. (1994). Academic performance, social competence, and mainstream accommodations: A look at mainstreamed and non-mainstreamed students with behavior disorders. *Behavior Disorders, 19*(3), 170–180.

Mostert, M.P. (1996). Interprofessional collaboration in schools: Benefits and barriers in practice. *Preventing School Failure, 40*(3), 135–138.

Muscott, H.S. (1988). The cascade of services model for behaviorally disordered students from residential treatment centers to public school program. In M.K. Zabel (Ed.), *TEACHING: Behaviorally disordered youth* (Vol. 2, pp. 33–43). Reston, VA: Council for Exceptional Children.

Muscott, H.S. (1994). Creating more inclusive schools for students with emotional/behavioral disorders: Issues, structures and strategies. In L.M. Bullock & R.A. Gable (Eds.), *Monograph on inclusion: Ensuring appropriate services to children and youth with emotional/behavioral disorders. II* (pp. 42–47). Reston, VA: The Council for Children with Behavioral Disorders.

Muscott, H.S., & Bond, R. (1986). A transitional education model for reintegrating behaviorally disordered students from residential treatment centers to public school programs. *Teaching Behaviorally Disordered Youth, 2,* 33–43.

Muscott, H.S., Morgan, D., & Meadows, N.B. (1996). *Planning and implementing effective programs for school-aged children and youth with emotional/behavioral disorders within inclusive schools.* Reston, VA: The Council for Children with Behavioral Disorders.

Neel, R.S., & Cessna, K.K. (1993). Instructional themes: A pragmatic response to complexity. In K.K. Cessna (Ed.), *Instructionally differentiated programming: A needs-based approach for students with behavior disorders* (pp. 41–52). Denver: Colorado Department of Education.

Neel, R.S., & Meadows, N.B. (1991). Determining social tasks: A preliminary report. *Monograph in behavioral disorders: Severe behavior disorders of children and youth* (Vol. 13, pp. 38–46). Reston, VA: The Council for Children with Behavioral Disorders.

Neel, R.S., Meadows, N.B., Levine, P., & Edgar, E.B. (1988). What happens after special education? A statewide follow-up study of secondary students who have behavioral disorders. *Behavioral Disorders, 13,* 209–216.

Nelson, C.M., & Pearson, C. (1991). *Integrating services for children and youth with emotional and behavioral disorders.* Reston, VA: Council for Exceptional Children.

Office of Special Education Programs. (1994). *Sixteenth annual report to Congress on the implementation of the Individuals with Disabilities Education Act.* Washington, DC: U.S. Department of Education.

Peterson, R.L., Zabel, R.H., Smith, C.R., & White, M.A. (1983). Cascade of services model and emotionally disturbed students. *Exceptional Children, 49,* 404–408.

Searcy, S. (1996). Friendship interventions for the integration of children and youth with learning and behavior problems. *Preventing School Failure, 40*(3), 131–134.

Spivack, G., & Shure, N.B. (1985). *Alternate solutions and instruction for testing and scoring children's interpersonal problem solving.* San Francisco: Jossey-Bass.

Stainback, W., Stainback, S., & Wilkinson, A. (1992). Encouraging peer supports and friendships. *Teaching Exceptional Children, 24*(2), 6–11.

Walker, H.M., & Bullis, M. (1990). Behavior disorders and the social context of regular class integration: A conceptual dilemma? In J.W. Lloyd, A.C. Repp, & N.N. Singh (Eds.), *The regular education initiative: Alternative perspectives on concepts, issues, and models* (pp. 75–93). Sycamore, IL: Sycamore Press.

Walker, H.M., Colvin, G., & Ramsey, E. (1995). *Antisocial behavior in school: Strategies and best practices.* Pacific Grove, CA: Brooks/Cole.

Wechsler, D. (1991). *Wechsler Intelligence Scale for Children* (3rd ed.). San Antonio, TX: The Psychological Corporation.

Weigle, K.L. (1997). Positive behavior support as a model for inclusion: Theoretical and procedural considerations. *Journal of The Association for Persons with Severe Handicaps, 22*(1), 36–48.

Wolery, M., Gessler, M., Caldwell, N.K., Snyder, E.D., & Lisowski, L. (1995). Experienced teachers' perceptions of resources and supports for inclusion. *Education and Training in Mental Retardation and Developmental Disabilities, 30,* 15–26.

Wood, F.H., & Smith, C.R. (1986). Issues in the identification and placement of behaviorally disordered students. *Behavioral Disorders, 10,* 219–228.

Wood, M.M., & Long, N.J. (1991). *Life space intervention: Talking with children and youth in crisis.* Austin, TX: PRO-ED.

Yell, M.L., & Shriner, J.G. (1996). Inclusive education: Legal and policy implications. *Preventing School Failure, 40*(3), 101–108.

Ysseldyke, J.E., Thurlow, M.L., Wotruba, J.W., & Nania, P.A. (1990). Instructional arrangements: Perceptions from general education. *Teaching Exceptional Children, 22*(4), 4–8.

Chapter 9

Aggression Replacement Training

A Comprehensive Approach
for Assaultive, Violent, and Ganging Youth

Barry Glick & Arnold P. Goldstein

We live in a world in which aggression is richly rewarded: immediately, effectively, and efficiently. We teach children to be aggressive at a very early age. We teach it in our homes, schools, churches, and communities. By the time children reach adolescence, they have been desensitized to the aggression and hostility that surrounds them by the multitude of violent acts that inundate them through television and other media—to the point that they no longer value what is just, fair, and right in their world.

Juvenile crime statistics have indicated that there is more crime committed by adolescents, more violence perpetrated on people and property by people younger than 18, and more youth being incarcerated in both the juvenile and adult justice systems than ever before. The rates of juvenile offenses have increased by as much as 23% (from the 1980s to the early 1990s), depending on the survey and manner of calculation and the type of offense (Howell, 1997). Juvenile delinquency, especially aggressive behavior, violent acts, and homicide, affects every part of society, infiltrating families, schools, and communities. Aggression and violence among young people cross all socioeconomic, cultural, and religious boundaries.

Most troubling is the dramatic rise in the rates of homicides by and against juveniles. This increase is in part attributed to the increasing access and lethality of weapons—particularly firearms—but mostly to the out-of-control growth of youth gangs and associated violence (Howell, 1997). The growth in the number of youth gangs is staggering. In 1980, it was estimated that 286 cities were experiencing problems from an estimated 2,000 gangs with approximately 100,000 members (Miller, 1982, cited in Howell, 1997). In 1995, it was estimated that 2,000 cities, towns, and counties were plagued by more than 25,000 gangs with more than 650,000 members (National Youth Gang Center, in press, cited in Howell, 1997). Such numbers clearly provide more than a sufficient number of models for aggressive and violent behavior and for the opportunity to be victimized by and desensitized to violence. To paraphrase Attorney General Janet Reno, "America must not only take better care of its children before they get into trouble, but also not abandon them once they are in trouble" (Allen-Hagen, 1993, as cited in Howell, 1997, p. 2).

PSYCHOLOGY OF
ADOLESCENT AGGRESSION

Because aggression is learned at a very early age and is richly and immediately rewarded, effectively and efficiently, by the time a child reaches adolescence, there are explicit and tangible characteristics of aggressive youth:

1. *Verbal and physical aggression:* Quay (1983) studied behaviors of children and adolescents and used a multivariate analysis to develop a classification for aggressive youth. He found that aggressive children could be identified by such behaviors as fighting, disruptiveness, profanity, irritability, quarrelsomeness, defiance of authority, irresponsibility, high levels of attention seeking, and low levels of guilt feelings or remorse. Quay observed active antisocial aggression that resulted in conflict with authority figures, especially parents, teachers, social institutions, and sometimes peers.
2. *Skill deficiencies:* Most aggressive adolescents have skill deficiencies. They have not developed the social competencies necessary to negotiate their environments successfully. As such, they more often use inappropriate, reactionary behaviors to deal with anger-producing situations.
3. *Immaturity:* Young people who tend to be aggressive also exhibit behaviors that include short attention span, clumsiness, preference to play and associate with younger children, passivity, daydreaming, and incompetence. These immature behaviors often lead to alienation from peers. These behaviors represent patterns that are more appropriate at earlier stages of development but unacceptable during adolescence. In the case of conduct disorders, immaturity leads to attacks on others or withdrawal (as seen in personality disorders).
4. *Withdrawal:* Patterson, Reid, Jones, and Conger (1975) labeled withdrawal behaviors as a "personality problem," whereas Quay (1983) labeled these behaviors as "disturbed neurotic" and "overinhibited." These patterns of behavior are characterized by depression, feelings of inferiority, self-

consciousness, shyness, anxiety, hypersensitivity, seclusiveness, and timidity. Withdrawal ordinarily is not associated with aggression, but it certainly is thought to be one precursor of the aggressive adolescent; and it is often clinically diagnosed as a component of the passive-aggressive personality.

From our own work, as well as that of Bandura (1973), Fehrenbach and Thelen (1982), and Feindler, Marriott, and Iwata (1984), among others, there is strong agreement that certain conditions promote aggression among adolescents:

1. Weak familial or social bonds
2. Being the target of aggression
3. Frequently observing successful aggression
4. Being reinforced (positively and negatively) for aggression
5. Information-processing skills deficits
6. Deficient moral reasoning
7. Deficits in prosocial skills

Although no one of these is more critical than another, aggressive young people either exhibit a number of these attributes or experience many of these conditions. These deficit environments, deficient prosocial skills and problem-solving strategies, and models of—and reinforcement for—aggressive behaviors insidiously combine to produce aggressive youth. An intervention program must address each of these critical factors if there is to be any chance of lasting success.

AGGRESSION
REPLACEMENT TRAINING

Origin and
Psychological Foundations

Until the early 1970s, there existed three major psychological approaches that clinicians used to alter the behavior of aggressive, ineffective, unhappy, or disturbed people. These psychotherapeutic treatment approaches were applied to programs for aggressive youth and include the following:

1. The psychodynamic approach, which includes psychoanalytically oriented, individ-

ual psychotherapy (Guttman, 1970); activity group therapy (Slavson, 1964); and the varied array of treatment approaches posited by Redl and Wineman (1957)

2. The humanistic, or client-centered, approach exemplified by the individual and group psychotherapy of Rogers (1957, 1970), the alternative educational programs offered by Gold (1978), and the approach to school discipline developed by Dreikurs, Grunwald, and Pepper (1971)

3. The behavior modification approach, which includes a wide variety of interventions that reflect the systematic use of contingency management, behavioral contracting, the training of teachers and parents as managers of behavior change, and related techniques (O'Leary, O'Leary, & Becker, 1967; Patterson, Cobb, & Ray, 1973)

Each of these three therapeutic philosophies differs from the others in several fundamental aspects. However, one significant similarity is the assumption that individuals have somewhere within themselves, as yet unexpressed, the effective, satisfying, nonaggressive, or healthy behaviors whose expression is the goal of therapy and the clinician. This latent potential in all three approaches is realized by the client if the clinician is sufficiently skilled in reducing or removing the obstacles to learning insights and in teaching the individual the appropriate social skills.

In the early 1970s, an important new approach to intervention, the psychosocial-educational approach, began to emerge. Under this approach, the individual is viewed in educational, pedagogical terms rather than as a "patient" in need of "therapy." The trainer of psychological skills assumes that he or she is dealing with an individual who is lacking, deficient, or at best weak in the skills necessary for effective and satisfying interpersonal functioning. The task of the trainer becomes the active and deliberate teaching of desirable behaviors rather than interpretation, reflection, or reinforcement. Psychotherapy between a patient and a psychotherapist developed into proactive training of psychological skills between a trainee and a trainer.

However, the inadequacy of prompting and shaping and related simplistic applications of operant procedures to add new behavior to an individual's repertoire was becoming increasingly apparent. Coupled with the widespread deinstitutionalization of approximately 400,000 people during the 1970s—the majority of whom were substantially deficient in important skills for daily functioning—it had become apparent that the American mental health movement had little of therapeutic value to offer.

These factors, relevant supportive research, the incompleteness of the operant approach, large numbers of individuals with major skill deficiencies, and the paucity of useful interventions for a large segment of American society—all in the context of historically supportive roots in both education and psychology—demanded a new intervention, something prescriptively responsive to an individual's needs. The intervention that was proposed as a response was psychological skills training.

The psychological skills training movement began in the early 1970s. As our research program progressed and we achieved skill enhancements for our clients (Goldstein, 1981; Goldstein, Sherman, Gershaw, Sprafkin, & Glick, 1978), we shifted our focus from teaching a broad array of interpersonal and daily living skills to adult, psychiatric inpatients to a more explicit concern with skills training for aggressive young people. As many writers had demonstrated, delinquent and other aggressive youth displayed widespread deficiencies in interpersonal, planning, aggression management, and other psychological skills (Conger, Miller, & Walsmith, 1965; Freedman, Rosenthal, Donahoe, Schbundy, & McFall, 1978; Mussen, Conger, Kagan, & Gerwitz, 1979; Patterson et al., 1975; Spence, 1981). Our approach, then, was to remediate these deficits through skills training.

Philosophical Foundations

Aggression Replacement Training (ART), like any other intervention program, is based on a set of philosophical principles and theoretical constructs. It is important to understand these tenets if the program is to be understood and implemented with integrity.

Habilitation versus Rehabilitation

ART is a habilitative treatment program. *Habilitation* is teaching something that has not previously been learned, whereas *rehabilitation* is an attempt to reinstate previously learned skills, qualities, or behaviors now in disuse. We know from our own research and experience that many of the young people who exhibit aggressive and violent behaviors do not have the appropriate skills to do otherwise. They have never learned the skills necessary to keep them from harm's way and, therefore, require *habilitation.* Unfortunately, many of the programs and services provided to these aggressive young people are based on *rehabilitative* principles, which assume that the youth have skills that merely need to be relearned or reinstated. Youth, therefore, are often frustrated and impatient with such programs. These conditions often increase the very aggression and violence that we seek to reduce.

Differential and Prescriptive Programming

Programs for adolescents, especially aggressive and hostile children and youth, need to be within the context of differential programming if they are to be effective. *Differential programming* simply means that there is an array of programs and services that are available to the youth based on each young person's individual needs. Differential programming should not be confused with quantity in that such a precept may operate within a small, community-based organization that has only one program, or it may operate within a large services system—such as a state agency—that includes many programs and services. The principle is the same in that differential programming means that each of the programs, or services within one overarching program, are well defined, are clearly distinct from one another, and together form a continuum of care (an array of services or programs) from which the provider may select appropriate interventions for the individual youth.

Concurrent with differential programming, programs should be *prescriptive;* not in the sense that the medical model views prescriptiveness but from the standpoint that prescriptive programs ensure that *different juveniles will respond to different change agents.* As such, each and every professional who deals with a young person always must ask the following series of questions (see also Paul, 1969) and know the answers to each *before* any program or service is delivered: 1) which types of youth 2) meeting which types of change agents 3) for which types of interventions 4) will yield the optimum results (outcomes)?

It is on these two philosophical foundations—that is, differential programming and prescriptive programming—that we have developed and designed all of our youth interventions, especially ART.

Program Design and Development

Clinicians and others who deal with aggressive adolescents or juvenile delinquents understand that these youth often have developed acting-out behaviors in combination with substandard and deficient alternative prosocial conduct. Many of these young people are skilled in fighting, bullying, intimidating, harassing, or manipulating others. However, they are inadequate in more socially desirable behaviors, such as negotiating differences; dealing appropriately with accusations; and responding effectively to failure, teasing, rejection, and anger, among the other skills.

ART, our response to this skills deficit perspective, is a multimodal, psychosocial-educational intervention. It is specifically, differentially, and prescriptively designed to deal with aggression and violence in young people—a complex repertoire of interrelated behaviors, hence, the need for a multimodal intervention. The primary ART clinicians for these youth are the counselors, teachers, child care workers, and others who have direct care responsibilities for young people commonly labeled as juvenile delinquent, aggressive, and hostile. The intervention is composed of three distinct yet integrated components, each with a 10-week curriculum, in which groups of youth participate. Typically, each individual attends each component once per week, for a total of 3 hours of involvement with ART per week.

COMPONENTS OF AGGRESSION REPLACEMENT TRAINING

Structured Learning Training

Structured Learning Training (SLT), the *behavioral* component of ART, is designed to teach aggressive and hostile youth prosocial skills to use in anger-producing situations. These skills include the following:

1. Basic social skills (e.g., listening, conversation, extending compliments)
2. Advanced social skills (e.g., seeking assistance, giving instructions, apologizing)
3. Expressing and responding to feelings (self and others)
4. Alternatives to aggression (e.g., negotiation, self-control, assertiveness)
5. Managing stress (e.g., peer pressure, sportsmanship, dealing with failure)
6. Planning (e.g., deciding on a course of action, goal setting, information gathering)

Structured learning has its roots in the early 1970s, being greatly influenced by the social learning theorists, in particular the work of Bandura:

The method that has yielded the most impressive results with diverse problems contains three major components. First, alternative modes of response are repeatedly modeled, preferably by several people who demonstrate how the new style of behavior can be used in dealing with a variety of situations. Second, learners are provided with guidance and ample opportunities to practice the modeled behavior under favorable conditions until they perform it skillfully and spontaneously. The latter procedures are ideally suited for developing new social skills, but they are unlikely to be adopted unless they produce rewarding consequences. Arrangement of success experiences, particularly the initial efforts at behaving differently, constitute the third component in this powerful composite method. . . . Given adequate demonstration, guided practice, and success experiences, this method is almost certain to produce favorable results. (1973, p. 253)

At that time and for several years thereafter, Goldstein's studies were conducted in public mental health hospitals, with long-term, highly skill-deficient, chronic patients (Gold-stein, 1981). By 1973, the skills training approach was applied to emotionally disturbed, aggressive adolescents in a private child care institution and then within institutions for juvenile delinquents (Glick & Goldstein, 1987; Goldstein et al., 1978).

Simultaneously, other research groups applied prosocial skills training approaches to adolescent trainees. Fleming (1976), for example, studied peer influences and demonstrated that gains in negotiating skills are as great when the social skills group leader is a respected peer as when the leader is an adult. Litwack (1976), building on transfer of skill enhancements, demonstrated that adolescents who anticipate later serving as a peer leader have increased levels of skill acquisition; that is, when adolescents expect to teach others a skill, their own level of skill acquisition benefits, a finding clearly supportive of Reissman's (1965) helper therapy principle. Trief (1976) found that successful use of social skills training to increase perspective taking (seeing situations from the other person's viewpoint) also leads to significant increases in cooperative behavior. These findings, along with our own research and that of Golden (1975), Litwack (1976), and Raleigh (1977), have considerable implications for planning further research on transfer enhancement for social skills training.

Yet other areas of research influenced the design and development of SLT. As with adults, the value of teaching certain skill combinations to adolescents was examined. The literature is replete with information about aggressive adolescents who get into trouble when they respond with overt hostility to authority figures with whom they disagree. Golden (1975) responded to this type of event by teaching young people skills in which they reflected on the feeling of the authority figure while expressing their own assertiveness (i.e., forthright but nonaggressive statements of their own position). Jennings (1975) was able to use prosocial skills training successfully to teach adolescents several of the verbal skills necessary to participate in more traditional, insight-oriented psychotherapy; and Guzetta (1974) was successful in providing empathic skills to parents, thus closing the gap between them and their children.

All of these historical antecedents support our own research and findings in two very significant areas for our own social skills training program, SLT. The first area is *skill acquisition.* Across diverse trainee populations (including aggressive and hostile adolescents in urban secondary schools and juvenile delinquency institutions) and target skills, skill acquisition is a reliable training outcome, occurring in more than 90% of SLT trainees. It is acknowledged that gains that are demonstrable in the training context are rather easily accomplished, given the potency, support, encouragement, and low threat value of trainers and procedures in that context. The more consequential outcome question—by far—pertains to trainee skill performance in real-world contexts (i.e., skill transfer). The second area of importance thus is *skill transfer.* Across diverse trainee populations, target skills, and applied ("real world") environments, skill transfer occurs with approximately 45%–50% of the SLT trainees. Goldstein and Kanfer (1979), as well as Karoly and Steffan (1980), indicated that across several dozen types of psychotherapy involving many different types of psychopathology, the average transfer rate on follow-up is between 15% and 20% of patients. The 45%–50% rate consequent to SLT thus is a significant improvement on this collective base rate. It must be underscored that this cumulative average for transfer also means that the gains shown by half of the trainees were limited to in-session acquisition. Of special note, however, is that skill transfer is a function of the explicit laboratory-derived transfer-enhancing techniques that were developed as part of the ART program.

SLT groups are composed of between six and eight chronically aggressive young people who have common cognitive skills deficits. The room is set up like a classroom, in which the young people sit at tables with a flipchart and an overhead projector at the front of the classroom. The trainer begins by defining the skill to be taught that week and then modeling the skill for the group. After the modeling display is completed, the trainer discusses with the group the current need that each trainee has for the skill; it is critical that each young person see the relevance of the skill to his or her own situation. The trainer then selects one group member to role-play his or her particular situation. This individual is the *main actor* for this particular vignette. The trainer facilitates the setting up of the role play, setting the stage and the particulars of the scene. The role play then is conducted. After the role play, the group provides feedback to the main actor. A specific order is used to ensure that the feedback is *positive* and *targeted.* The co-actor (another group member) is asked to provide feedback about his or her own participation and how it felt to participate in the role play; then the other group members are asked to provide their comments, each of whom had been assigned to look for a particular learning point of the skill. Then the trainers and, finally, the main actor give their impressions. "Homework" then is assigned to the main actor, which essentially is a contract to practice a specific skill and its component steps sometime before the next class, indicating where and with whom this will be done. This is called *transfer training.* The review of the homework report (what was done, how it went, what could have been done instead, etc.) constitutes the first 5 minutes of the next week's class. The next role player is selected, and the SLT class is conducted in this manner until each group member has the opportunity to role-play the skill of the week.

The process to conduct an SLT class may be summarized as follows:

1. Define the skill.
2. Model the skill.
3. Discuss the trainee's current need for the skill.
4. Select the role player (main actor).
5. Set up the role play.
6. Conduct the role play.
7. Provide feedback.
8. Assign homework.
9. Select the next role player.

Each of these functions—modeling, role-playing, performance feedback, and transfer training—is geared toward enhancing acquisition of prosocial skills, which the young person may use in anger-provoking situations. The group facilitator needs to ensure that each of these functions is implemented correctly, using appropriate training techniques. It is critical to understand these four concepts and the techniques utilized because the method is the same for both the SLT and the Anger Control Training (ACT) component of ART.

Anger Control Training

Even though aggressive youth learn appropriate prosocial skills to use in anger-provoking situations, they very often are unable to use their newly acquired skills. Aggressive adolescents identify anger as the emotion that they most often experience and that interferes with their ability to use the skills that they have learned. As such, ACT is the affective component in ART. This second part of ART is designed to teach young people about the nature of anger, the specific signs and behaviors that they may exhibit, and techniques to reduce their anger before they lose control and react only to their emotions.

ACT is based on work by Feindler et al. (1984) and on the earlier anger control and stress inoculation research of Meichenbaum (1977) and Novaco (1975). The goal is to teach aggressive youth the inhibition of violent responses and how to control their own levels of anger-related arousal. We designed ACT so that the same procedures that are used to teach skills in SLT are used in this component, as well, namely modeling, role playing, performance feedback, and transfer training. For example, as homework is assigned in SLT, *Hassle Logs* are used to help generalize what is learned by the youth in class to their real-world situations. These Hassle Logs are completed by each youth during the week and reflect actual provocations that the youth had experienced. The Hassle Log is an easily completed checklist for the youth to indicate

1. Where the youth was (e.g., class, job, movie)
2. What happened (e.g., was insulted, property was taken)
3. Who the offending person was (e.g., friend, teacher, parent)
4. What the youth did in response (e.g., hit, walked away, ignored)
5. How the situation was handled (rated from "poor" to "great")

6. How angry the youth felt (rated from "burning mad" to "not at all")

The logs are kept in a loose-leaf binder and are used for role-play material during the ACT session.

ACT is based on a simple model of conflict resolution called the *A-B-C Model of Conflict Situations.* In the very first ACT session, this model is introduced and defined. "A" stands for *antecedents,* or what led up to the conflict situation; "B" stands for *behavior,* or what the individual did; and "C" stands for *consequences,* or the results of the individual's behavior in this situation. During each of the 10 weeks of training, participating youth learn a series of links in a chain of anger-control responsiveness. The first link, *triggers,* is external events and internal conditions (self-statements) that give rise to anger and angry feelings: what actually provokes the young person. Once this initial concept is introduced, the group members turn their attention to identifying the particular physiological and kinesthetic *cues* that let each individual know that it is *anger*—and not fear, anxiety, or some other affect—that they are experiencing. Cues of anger include, for example, tensed biceps, clenched teeth, flushed cheeks, hair on neck standing erect, sinking stomach reaction, increased heart rate, and pounding chest.

Once the triggers and cues are identified, youth are taught a series of effective anger-reducing techniques: 1) deep breathing, 2) counting backward, and 3) pleasant imagery (i.e., imagining a peaceful scene). During succeeding weeks, each link of the chain is taught, including contemplating the long-term consequences of alternative behaviors to the anger being experienced, and the use of reminders. *Reminders* are like internal triggers in that they are explanations, instructions, or self-statements; however, reminders are designed to *lower* anger arousal. Some reminders are generic and may be used widely, such as "chill out," "calm down," and "cool off"; others are situation-specific such as, "That guy didn't cut me off on purpose, he probably had an emergency and needed to get off at this hospital exit."

If the trainees properly use what is learned thus far, they may reward themselves through self-evaluation techniques that are taught in the fifth week of the curriculum. By the sixth or seventh week, the young person has learned a sufficient number of social skills to be able to complete the role playing of an anger-lowering response to a provocation by showing the group the correct behaviors to use instead of aggression, namely a prosocial skill. Thus, an aggressive adolescent who is prone to violence is taught to respond to provocation (others' and his or her own) less impulsively, more reflectively, and with less likelihood of acting out negatively.

Moral Education

Even though a youth knows an appropriate skill to use in an anger-producing, antisocial situation and is able to control his or her angry feelings, that young person still may choose not to use the skills that he or she has. That is why Moral Education (ME) is the third component to ART. ME is the *cognitive* component that teaches young people a process of moral reasoning so that they learn to view their world in a more fair, just, and equitable manner.

Moral reasoning is based on the work of Kohlberg (1969), whose Theory of Moral Development posits that there are six stages of development to how individuals come to view their world. Although not everyone needs to develop through all six stages, many do function at the higher levels. Briefly, Kohlberg's six stages of moral judgment fall within three levels (McGraw, 1987):

Preconventional
Stage 1: Heteronomous morality
Stage 2: Individualism, instrumental purpose, and exchange
Conventional
Stage 3: Mutual interpersonal expectations, relationships, and interpersonal conformity
Stage 4: Social system and conscience
Postconventional or Principled
Stage 5: Social contract or utility and individual rights
Stage 6: Universal ethical principles

As a person moves through these levels and stages, his or her sociomoral perspective changes from concern about concrete rules and immediate punishment and reward to the more abstract rules, duties, and laws of the social system and finally to a concern for universal values and principles (McGraw, 1987).

In a long and pioneering series of investigations, Kohlberg (1969, 1973) demonstrated that exposing young people to a series of moral dilemmas (e.g., in a discussion-group context that includes youth reasoning at different levels and stages of moral thinking) arouses cognitive conflict that frequently advances young people who are reasoning at lower stages of moral development to that of the higher-level peers in the group. Ideally, the dilemmas employed are interesting; relevant to the adolescents' world; and involved with issues of fairness, justice, or the needs or rights of others.

Arousing the cognitive conflict and the perspective taking that are necessary for the enhancement of moral reasoning is most likely to occur when a range of reasoning levels are present in the discussion groups. For that reason, the ME groups usually consist of 12 young people and 2 trainers, in contrast to the 6- to 8-member SLT and ACT groups. Once the groups are formed, trainers choose and prepare the moral dilemmas, create a proper environment and attitude for the discussion to take place, initiate the discussion, guide the discussion, and then end the discussion. Facilitators are trained to accomplish each of the procedural steps outlined next:

1. *Choose and prepare a dilemma:* First, the trainers should anticipate how the participants will reason at each stage. Second, the trainers should prepare elaborations to generate disagreements for each dilemma. Third, the trainers should prepare at least two counter-arguments for how to deal with the dilemma.

2. *Create the proper environment and attitude:* The facilitators should ensure that the group is physically and psychologically safe and secure enough for the participants to share ideas and beliefs openly and freely. The facilitators then should identify the goals of the

group. Once the goals have been articulated (i.e., provide explanations for the purpose of the ME group, the group format, members' role, leaders' role, and group norms), the trainers should establish group norms to be followed and invite group members to identify norms that they want to follow.

3. *Initiate the discussion:* The facilitators distribute copies of a moral dilemma and read or have a group member read the dilemma to the group. The major points of the dilemma then are summarized through brief group discussion. The trainers should encourage the group to ask questions that help make the dilemma more clear. The facilitators then should clarify questions, problems, or misconceptions about the dilemma.

4. *Guide the group discussion:* The leaders begin the ME discussion by obtaining initial opinions from each member and his or her rationale for the positions that he or she takes. Keeping this part of the discussion brief, the trainer then rephrases or paraphrases each member's rationale, writes a short summary of initial statements on newsprint or a chalk board, and conducts a "differing opinions" debate.

5. *End the discussion:* The facilitators then summarize the debates and present an argument at one stage higher than the most sophisticated or abstract argument presented. Because there are no right or wrong answers in the debate discussion, the objective of the ME sequence is to expose individuals to higher-order levels of moral reasoning.

AGGRESSION REPLACEMENT TRAINING RESEARCH AND EFFICACY EVALUATIONS

This section presents and examines a series of program evaluations and research efficacy studies of ART. Some of these investigations were conducted by our own research group; a number were the efforts of others. We now have more than a decade of research and experience with ART as an intervention for aggressive and violent youth. The assessments that follow report the impact of ART, ART's apparent strengths and weaknesses, and what may be gleaned for further research and development in this area.

Annsville Youth Center Project

The first ART program evaluation was conducted at the Annsville Youth Center, where the program was first developed, designed, and implemented. Sixty young men between the ages of 14 and 17 years were incarcerated in this noncommunity residential facility for such crimes as burglary, robbery, assault, and various drug offenses. Twenty-four of the youth participated in the 10-week ART program. Each resident attended three sessions per week, one each of SLT, ACT, and ME. A second group of 24 youth were assigned to a Brief Instruction Control Group that did not utilize the ART program. This condition was included in the research plan to control for any apparent ART-derived gains in skills that did not directly result from ART and to control for the cases in which 1) the young men already possessed the skills and were not using them, 2) they simply were motivated to display already acquired skills, or 3) they acquired the skills as a result of maturation. A third, more traditional No-Treatment Control Group consisted of 12 youth who did not participate in ART or in the Brief Instruction groups.

The evaluation goals of this project were to study the effectiveness of ART with specific reference to

1. *Skill acquisition:* Did the youth learn the 10 prosocial skills in the ART curriculum?

2. *Minimal skill transfer:* Could the youth perform the skills in response to a new situation, similar in format to those in which they were trained?

3. *Extended skill transfer:* Could the youth perform the skills in response to new situations, dissimilar in format and more like real life than those in which they were trained?

4. *Anger-control enhancement:* Would the youth actually exhibit fewer altercations or other acting-out behaviors, as reflected in weekly behavior incident reports completed on all participating youth by Annsville staff?

5. *Impulse reduction:* Were the youth rated to be less impulsive and more reflective

and self-controlled in their interpersonal behavior?

Analyses of data revealed that youth undergoing ART, compared with both control groups, acquired and transferred (both minimal and extended) 4 of the 10 social skills: 1) expressing a complaint, 2) preparing for a stressful conversation, 3) responding to anger, and 4) dealing with group pressure. In addition, there were significant differences between the ART groups and the control groups on both the number and the intensity of in-facility acting-out behaviors, as well as on staff-rated impulsiveness.

After the posttest was completed, new ART groups were formed in Week 11 for the 36 youth in the two control groups. This phase essentially replicated all of the procedures that were conducted during the first 10 weeks of the ART group. Sessions again were held three times per week for 10 weeks. The research methodology in this second phase was an "own-control" test for the efficacy of ART, with particular attention to discerning possible reductions in acting-out behaviors by comparing the number of incident reports during Weeks 11–20 (while in ART) with the number during the initial phase (Weeks 1–10) when these 36 youth were participating in their respective control groups. Both statistical comparisons, for number and severity, conducted to test for replication effects yielded significant positive improvements.

During the Annsville project, 54 residents were released from the facility and returned to communities. The hope was that ART might serve as a sufficiently powerful inoculation such that moderate carryover of in-facility ART learning to the community would occur. Seventeen of the released youth had received the ART program; 37 had not. We contacted each youth's aftercare worker (similar to a parole officer responsible for community supervision) throughout New York State, and—without informing the worker whether the youth had or had not received ART—requested that the worker complete the global rating measure on each of his or her Annsville residents who were discharged during that time period. In four of the six areas rated (home and family, peer, legal, and overall, but not

school or work), ART youth were significantly superior in rated in-community functioning than were the young men who had not received ART. We were intrigued by the results of this informal assessment as there very often is considerable difficulty with this population with successfully transferring acquired skills to community environments from the more protective institutional environment. Many times, it is the family and the peers who serve as reinforcers of antisocial behaviors, ignoring or even punishing constructive alternative actions. Such indifference or overt hostility from these real-world significant others served as information that would prove beneficial in some later community-based projects.

MacCormick Youth Center Project

The second efficacy evaluation of ART was conducted at the MacCormick Secure Center, a New York State Division for Youth maximum security facility for male juvenile offenders between the ages of 13 and 21 years. Crimes committed by these young men included murder, manslaughter, rape, sodomy, attempted murder, armed assault, and armed robbery. Our second project sought both to replicate the exact procedures and findings of the Annsville Project and to extend them to youth who are incarcerated for substantially more serious, heinous felonies. Fifty-one youth participated in this study, which employed the same preparatory activities, materials, ART curriculum, testing, staff training, resident training, supervision, and data analysis methodology as the Annsville Project.

Data indicated significant acquisition and/ or transfer of training on 5 of the 10 prosocial skills. These findings, as well as the skill deficits that were identified, essentially replicated the Annsville SLT results. In contrast to the Annsville results, the MacCormick data also yielded a significant result on the Sociomoral Reflections Measure, which was used to assess levels of moral development. At MacCormick but not at Annsville, youth who participated in the ME sessions progressed significantly in their stage of moral reasoning during the 10-week intervention period.

With respect to overt, in-facility behaviors, youth who received ART, compared with those who did not, increased significantly over their base rates in constructive, prosocial behaviors (e.g., offering or accepting criticism appropriately, employing self-control when provoked) and decreased significantly in their staff-rated levels of impulsiveness. In contrast to the Annsville findings, MacCormick youth who received ART did not differ from controls in either the number or the intensity of acting-out behaviors. These findings appear to be explained largely by the substantial differences in potential for such behaviors between the two institutions. Annsville is not a locked, closed facility. The 60 young people at Annsville live in one dormitory, in contrast to the locked, single-room sleeping quarters at MacCormick. MacCormick, a higher security facility, also had an enriched staffing pattern, more than 2:1 over Annsville's; and MacCormick operated under different regulations, which allowed for a stricter system of sanctions and controls. Therefore, it appears that the opportunity to engage in acting-out behaviors was less across all conditions at MacCormick as compared with Annsville. Thus, a *floor effect* seems to be extant, which makes the possibility of decreases in acting-out behavior as a result of ART participation at MacCormick numerically more difficult than at Annsville. At Annsville, such behaviors were contextually more possible at baseline and thus could—and did—decrease over the intervention period. At MacCormick, all young men started low and—likely for these same contextual reasons (sanctions, controls, richer staffing)—remained low. The use of prosocial behaviors by the MacCormick youth— with regard to which no floor or ceiling effect influences are relevant—did increase differentially as a function of the ART intervention.

Community-Based (Aftercare) Project

The findings of the first two research efforts show that ART is a multimodal, habilitative intervention of considerable potency with incarcerated, aggressive, and violent adolescents and young men. ART enhances prosocial skill competency and overt prosocial behaviors, reduces the level of rated impulsiveness, and—in one of the two samples studied—both decreases the

frequency and the intensity of acting-out behaviors and enhances the participants' levels of moral reasoning. Furthermore, some moderately substantial evidence, provided independently, reveals that ART leads to valuable changes in community functioning.

The third efficacy study of ART sought to ascertain the value of ART when provided to youth who were already in aftercare, living in their community. Eighty-four young people participated in this project. Because of the influence that significant others could have on this population, ART was offered not only to the youth but also to their parents and other family members.

Participating youth were assigned to intervention conditions on a random basis (with departures from randomization only to accommodate the rigors of the five-city, multisite, time-extended nature of the project): 1) providing ART to youth and their parents or other family members, 2) providing ART to youth only, and 3) a No-ART control group. The community-based ART program was designed to last for 3 months, during which the youth attended meetings twice per week, for a planned total of approximately 25 sessions. Each meeting lasted approximately 2 hours, during which the participants first discussed current life events and experienced difficulties while in aftercare; then SLT was conducted (usually for a skill that was relevant to the life events and/or experienced difficulties); and then, on an alternating session basis, either ACT or ME was conducted. An ART session was held for the parents and other family members each week to demonstrate the skills that were offered to the young men. When family members were unable to attend the weekly meeting, they were provided ART in a modified form via a weekly home visit or telephone visit.

Because each of these youth had previously been involved in the ART program while in a residential facility, the two groups that continued ART in the community environment each chose, in consultation with their trainers, which of the 50 prosocial skills in the full curriculum they would learn. Hence, different groups learned different, if not overlapping, sets of skills. Therefore, participant change on *individual* skills was not examined in the statistical analyses but rather the total skill change for youth who participated in the two ART conditions, as compared with each other and the No-ART control group.

The results indicated that although the two ART groups did not differ significantly from each other, they both showed significant increases in overall interpersonal skill competencies as compared with the No-ART control group. A significant outcome emerged for all three groups for decreases in self-reported levels of anger in response to mild (e.g., seeing others abused, minor nuisance, unfair treatment) but not severe (e.g., betrayal of trust, control or coercion, physical abuse) anger-provoking situations.

Recidivism is considered by juvenile justice authorities to be a particularly critical evaluation criterion to indicate success within juvenile justice interventions. Research (Maltz, 1984) indicates that the vast majority of young people who return to their communities from incarceration and recidivate do so within the first 6 months after release. Thus, for the purposes of this effort, *recidivism* was defined as those youth who were rearrested within the first 6 months following release to their communities. The young men were tracked for a 6-month period, during which they participated in the ART program for the first 3 months only (the control group, of course, did not receive ART at all during the 6-month tracking period).

Analyses of the frequency of rearrest by condition showed a significant effect for youth who participated in ART: Both ART groups were rearrested significantly less than were youth in the No-ART control group (43% recidivism, or 14 of 32 participants). When the two ART conditions were compared, there was a substantial decrease in the percentage of rearrests when the families of the youth participated simultaneously in their own ART groups (15% recidivism, or 2 of 13 participants), as compared with the group in which only the youth participated in ART (30% recidivism, or 6 of 20 participants). The family groups were taught reciprocal (to what the youth were learning) prosocial skills, as well as anger-control techniques. This may have provided for the delinquent youth a more responsive and prosocial real-world environment (i.e., providing a context in which the newly acquired skills were reinforced and praised rather than ridiculed).

The Pro-Social Gang Project

The final effort to evaluate the efficacy of the ART intervention was based, in part, on the belief that aggressive and violent youth are most influenced by their own peers. As such, those peer groups that exerted the most control, power, and authority over their members were sought. Thus, the investigation studied 10 gangs in Brooklyn, New York, over a 2-year period. The intervention was conducted at two private, not-for-profit, community-based organizations: the Brownsville Neighborhood Youth Action Center, which served young people in the Crown Heights and Brownsville neighborhoods, and Youth Dares, which served the youth of the Sheepshead Bay neighborhood. Crown Heights is predominantly African American, whereas the Sheepshead Bay neighborhood is predominantly Caucasian and Italian American.

Managing this multisite, multigang project required diverse planning, training, supervision, data collection, data analysis, budget management, and resource coordination efforts. The fundamental strategies to ensure accomplishment of the evaluation goals were *consultation* and *negotiation*. We conducted frequent, honest, and open communication with the agencies. Staff input was used in program design, planning, and implementation. We continued this participatory process throughout the project to its completion, providing training, supervision, and project monitoring on a frequent (at least weekly) and regular basis.

We conducted a quantitative appraisal of the project. As in the three previous evaluations, both proximal and distal criteria were examined. The proximal criteria included skill acquisition and anger reduction. The distal criteria included participant-rated performance in a variety of areas of functioning in the community and whether the gang member was rearrested during an 8-month period consisting of 4 months of the ART sequence and 4 months of follow-up.

The assessment used for SLT was The Skill Checklist (Goldstein, Glick, Irwin, Pask-

McCartney, & Rubama, 1989; Goldstein, Sprafkin, Gershaw, & Klein, 1980). This checklist consists of brief descriptions of the 50 prosocial skills that compose the SLT. The rater indicates the frequency with which he or she believes the youth uses each skill. The assessment for the ACT component was The Anger Control Inventory (ACI; Hoshmand & Austin, 1987; Hoshmand, Austin, & Appell, 1981). This inventory is a 66-item questionnaire completed by the youth themselves (as are all of the assessments, on a pre- and posttest basis). The instrument is designed to assess both the young person's overall level of self-reported anger arousal and the degree of anger aroused in the individual as a function of several different types of potentially provocative situations. The 11 subscales of the inventory include Seeing Others Abused, Intrusion, Personal Devaluation, Betrayal of Trust, Minor Nuisance, Control/Coercion, Verbal Abuse, Physical Abuse, Unfair Treatment, Goal Blocking, and Neutral. The Community Adjustment Rating Scale (Goldstein & Glick, 1987) was used to measure postintervention community function. This scale affords the rater (the staff trainers in this project) the opportunity to rate each gang member on the following dimensions: Home and Family Adjustment, School Adjustment, Work Adjustment, Peer Adjustment, and Legal System Adjustment.

Essentially all of the young people who participated in this project had been arrested at least once and often several times. The gang members were tracked for 8 months, again using rearrest as the criterion index of recidivism (Farrington, Ohlin, & Wilson, 1986).

The results were encouraging. Repeated measures analysis of variance, crossing project condition (ART versus control) with time of measurement (pretest versus posttest), revealed a significant interaction effect favoring ART participants for each of the following seven skill categories: Beginning Social Skills, Advanced Social Skills, Feelings, Relevant Skills, Aggression Management Skills, Stress Management Skills, and Planning Skills, as well as a Total Skills score. None of the resultant comparisons on the ACI yielded significant group differences. It is noteworthy, however, that on all ACI subscales, those youth who received ART demonstrated greater gain in anger control than did control-group youth. As such, the magnitude of between-condition differences is not significant; however, its uniform direction may suggest a trend toward the impact of ART on participant anger control.

Of the five community functioning domains rated by group leaders using the Community Adjustment Rating Scale, only Work Adjustment resulted in a significant difference between groups. Peer Adjustment showed a marginally significant difference between the groups ($p < .07$), as did a weighted total score on the Community Adjustment Rating Scale ($p < .06$). The direction of these results all favored ART over the control-group participants. For example, in the months immediately following their ART sequence, the majority of the participating Lo Lives (a Crown Heights gang) left their gang and took jobs in retail businesses. At an analogous point in time, a substantial number of the Baby Wolfpack (another Crown Heights gang) obtained employment in the construction trades, rebuilding much of the neighborhood that they themselves had ravaged.

Arrest data for the youth who participated in the first two ART sequences, as compared with their respective control groups, indicated that 5 of 38 ART participants (13%) and 14 of 27 control-group members (52%) were rearrested during the 8-month tracking period, a statistically significant difference. The primary rationale for working with intact gangs in this project was the opportunity afforded by such a strategy to capture a major feature of the environment and turn it in prosocial directions. Once the youth learned specific prosocial behaviors, they were able to transfer and maintain them (or be discouraged from using them) by the people with whom these youth interacted regularly. The favorable outcome, as indicated by rearrest rates, implies the possibility that such a harmonious and prosocially conducive post-ART peer environment may have been created.

Other Efficacy Evaluations

The research efforts described thus far provided a series of encouraging findings with respect to the effectiveness of ART, proximal both to the ART procedures (i.e., skill acquisition, anger control, enhanced moral reasoning) and to distal effects (i.e., reduced rearrest; enhanced community functioning; less hostility, violence, and volatility). Summarized next are the findings from other, independent research efforts.

Curulla (1990) compared the following three groups in her study of 67 young adult offenders in a Seattle, Washington, community environment: 1) a 14-week standard ART program, 2) ART without the ME component, and 3) a No-ART control group. Curulla reported the following:

Tendency towards recidivism and actual recidivism were compared among the three groups. Tendency towards recidivism, as measured by the Weekly Activity Record, was significantly reduced in the dilemma group [standard ART]. The nondilemma [ART without ME] and control [No-ART] groups showed no significant reduction. The dilemma group also had the lowest frequency of subsequent offense. . . . However, the difference in actual recidivism among the three groups did not reach statistical significance due to the low incidence of recorded changes during the 6-month follow up. (1990, pp. 1–2)

Curulla corroborated the previously described results in that overt acting-out behaviors were significantly reduced with ART participation. However, unlike the previous findings, post-ART recidivism was *not* reduced.

Jones compared ART with ME and a No-Treatment control group, using highly aggressive male students in a Brisbane, Australia, high school. Her results were positive and consistent with findings already cited:

Compared to the two control conditions, students completing the ART program showed a significant decrease in aggressive incidents, a significant increase in coping incidents, and acquired more social skills. Students in Condition I [the ART Program] also improved on . . . self-control and impulsivity . . . ART appears to be an effective intervention for aggressive youth within a high school setting. (1990, p. 1)

Coleman, Pfeiffer, and Oakland (1991) evaluated the effectiveness of a 10-week ART program with adolescents with behavior disor-

ders in a Texas residential treatment center. Results indicated improved participant skill knowledge but not actual overt skill-related behaviors. Coleman et al. commented, "The current study thus provides additional support for the contention that although cognitive gains can be demonstrated, the link to actual behavior is tenuous, especially with disturbed populations" (1991, p. 14).

It appears, however, that the likelihood of overt behavioral expression (i.e., performance) of newly acquired skills is less a function of the degree of trainee emotional disturbance and more a matter of trainee motivation to perform, as well as the perceived likelihood that staff or other significant people will reward such overt behaviors. Coleman et al. continued,

Of the 10 social skills that were taught, 3 accounted for the improvement in social skills knowledge: keeping out of fights, dealing with group pressure, and expressing a complaint. The fact that Goldstein and Glick (1987) also found these same skills to be improved in two separate studies suggests that these skills may be the most responsive to intervention. One plausible explanation is that these three skills may be construed as contributing to self-preservation, especially within the context of residential or institutional living. (1991, p. 15)

One final investigation, also affirming the efficacy of ART, applies the intervention in yet another environment and a new direction. Gibbs (1986) and his co-workers in the Ohio Department of Youth Services had for some years employed and evaluated a Positive Peer Culture treatment approach in their work with delinquents. This small-group approach, which they described as being guided by adults but run by the youth, places on the young people most of the responsibility for the management of their living environment, as well as for the change in their own behaviors. Gibbs's rationale for this approach was based on his experience that although youth were highly motivated to conduct their own governance, they often lacked the skills and anger control to do so. Gibbs and his colleagues combined Positive Peer Culture with ART to yield a motivation plus skills-oriented intervention that they named EQUIP, as the program provides youth with the means—or equipment—to help themselves.

These investigators conducted an efficacy evaluation of EQUIP at a medium security institution for juvenile felony offenders, the Buckeye Youth Center, in Ohio. Three conditions were implemented: EQUIP, a motivational control group, and a No-Treatment control group. Outcome results were significant and supportive of the EQUIP intervention on both proximal and distal criteria. Gibbs and his research group commented, "Institutional conduct improvements were highly significant for the EQUIP relative to the control groups in terms of self-reported misconduct, staff-filed incident reports, and unexcused absences from school" (1986, p. 18).

Interestingly, whereas the recidivism rate of EQUIP subjects was low (15%) at both 6 and 12 months following release, the control group rates worsened from 6 to 12 months (25%–35% for the motivational control; 30%–40% for the simple passage of time control). This pattern suggests that the treatment result is maintained as a stable effect. (Gibbs, 1986, p. 19)

These other efficacy evaluations combine to suggest that ART is a significant treatment intervention. With considerable reliability, ART appears to promote skill acquisition and performance, improve anger control, and decrease the frequency of acting-out behaviors. Beyond institutional and residential walls, the effects of ART persist, however, less fully perhaps than when the youth is in a controlled environment with support and persistent reinforcement.

CONCLUSION

ART is indicated to be a viable treatment intervention to mitigate the violence and hostility exhibited by adolescents, especially those who are placed within juvenile or adult corrections systems. The basis of ART is not to assume that aggressive youth have the skills (both cognitive and behavioral) that they need to succeed in the greater society and that they simply are not motivated to exhibit these skills. Rather, the assumption is that deficit environments, combined with models for and reinforcement of aggressive behavior, in addition to a failure to have learned

prosocial skills, result in the aggressive behavior of these youth. Thus, an answer to the present predicament is to teach behavioral skills and cognitive strategies, involve real-life significant others in the maintenance of those skills, and arrange conditions that make those newly acquired skills effective and functional for the youth. Although there are no quick "cure-alls" that resolve the violence now widely evident in society, the repertoire-enhancing program of ART may be used prescriptively and differentially as a multimodal intervention to deal with the complex nature of aggression—a behavior that in society is richly rewarded: immediately, effectively, and efficiently.

REFERENCES

Bandura, A. (1973). *Aggression: A social learning analysis.* Upper Saddle River, NJ: Prentice-Hall.

Coleman, M., Pfeiffer, S., & Oakland, T. (1991). *Aggression replacement training with behavior disordered adolescents.* Unpublished manuscript, University of Texas, Austin.

Conger, J.J., Miller, W.C., & Walsmith, C.R. (1965). Antecedents of delinquency, personality, social class and intelligence. In P.H. Mussen, J.J. Conger, & J. Kagan (Eds.), *Readings in child development and personality* (pp. 442–468). New York: Harper & Row.

Curulla, V.L. (1990). *Aggression replacement training in the community for adult learning disabled offenders.* Unpublished manuscript, University of Washington, Seattle.

Dreikurs, R., Grunwald, B.B., & Pepper, F.C. (1971). *Maintaining sanity in the classroom.* New York: Harper & Row.

Farrington, D.P., Ohlin, L.E., & Wilson, J.Q. (1986). *Understanding and controlling crime.* New York: Springer-Verlag.

Fehrenbach, P.A., & Thelen, M.H. (1982). Behavioral approaches to the treatment of aggressive disorders. *Behavior Modification, 6,* 465–467.

Feindler, E.L., Marriott, S.A., & Iwata, M. (1984). Group anger control for junior high school delinquents. *Cognitive Therapy Research, 8,* 299–311.

Fleming, D. (1976). *Teaching negotiation skills to pre-adolescents.* Unpublished doctoral dissertation, Syracuse University, Syracuse, NY.

Freedman, B.J., Rosenthal, R., Donahoe, C.P., Schbundy, D.G., & McFall, R.M. (1978). A social behavioral analysis of skill deficits in delinquent and nondelinquent adolescent boys. *Journal of Consulting and Clinical Psychology, 46,* 1448–1462.

Gibbs, J.C. (1986). *Small group sociomoral treatment programs: Dilemmas for use with conduct-disordered or antisocial adolescents or preadolescents.* Unpublished manuscript.

Glick, B., & Goldstein, A.P. (1987). Aggression replacement training: An intervention for counselors. *Journal of Counseling Development, 65,* 356–362.

Gold, M. (1978). Scholastic experiences, self-esteem, and delinquent behavior: A theory for alternative schools. *Crime and Delinquency, 17,* 290–309.

Golden, R. (1975). *Teaching resistance-reducing behavior to high school students.* Unpublished doctoral dissertation, Syracuse University, Syracuse, NY.

Goldstein, A.P. (1981). *Psychological skills training.* Elmsford, NY: Pergamon.

Goldstein, A.P., & Glick, B. (1987). *Aggression replacement training: A comprehensive intervention for aggressive youth.* Champaign, IL: Research Press.

Goldstein, A.P., Glick, B., Irwin, M., Pask-McCartney, C., & Rubama, I. (1989). *Reducing delinquency: Intervention in the community.* Elmsford, NY: Pergamon.

Goldstein, A.P., & Kanfer, F.H. (1979). *Maximizing treatment gains: Transfer enhancement in psychotherapy.* New York: Academic Press.

Goldstein, A.P., Sherman, M., Gershaw, N.J., Sprafkin, R.P., & Glick, B. (1978). Training aggressive adolescents in prosocial behavior. *Journal of Youth and Adolescents, 7,* 73–92.

Goldstein, A.P., Sprafkin, R.P., Gershaw, N.J., & Klein, P. (1980). *Skillstreaming the adolescent.* Champaign, IL: Research Press.

Guttman, E.S. (1970). Effects of short-term psychiatric treatment for boys in two California youth authority institutions. In D.C. Gibbons (Ed.), *Delinquent behavior* (pp. 126–139). Upper Saddle River, NJ: Prentice-Hall.

Guzzetta, R.A. (1974). *Acquisition and transfer of empathy by parents of early adolescents through structured learning training.* Unpublished doctoral dissertation, Syracuse University, Syracuse, NY.

Hoshmand, L.T., & Austin, G.W. (1987). Validation studies of a multifactor cognitive-behavioral Anger Control Inventory. *Journal of Personality Assessment, 51,* 417–432.

Hoshmand, L.T., Austin, G.W., & Appell, J. (1981, August). *The diagnosis and assessment of anger control problems.* Paper presented at the annual meeting of the American Psychological Association, Los Angeles.

Howell, J.C. (1997). *Juvenile justice and youth violence.* Thousand Oaks, CA: Sage Publications.

Jennings, R.L. (1975). *The use of structured learning techniques to teach attraction enhancing skills to residentially hospitalized lower socioeconomic emotionally disturbed children and adolescents: A psychotherapy analogue investigation.* Unpublished doctoral dissertation, University of Iowa, Iowa City.

Jones, Y. (1990). *Aggression replacement training in a high school setting.* Unpublished manuscript.

Karoly, P., & Steffen, J.J. (Eds.). (1980). *Improving the long-term effects of psychology.* New York: Gardner.

Kohlberg, L. (1969). Stage and sequence: The cognitive-developmental approach to socialization. In D.A. Goslin (Ed.), *Handbook of socialization theory and research* (pp. 347–480). Chicago: Rand McNally.

Kohlberg, L. (1973). *Collected papers on moral development and moral education.* Cambridge, MA: Harvard University, Center for Moral Education.

Litwack, S.E. (1976). *The use of the helper therapy principle to increase therapeutic effectiveness and reduce therapeutic resistance: Structured learning therapy with resistant adolescents.* Unpublished doctoral dissertation, Syracuse University, Syracuse, NY.

Maltz, D. (1984). *Recidivism.* New York: Academic Press.

McGraw, K.O. (1987). *Developmental psychology.* New York: Harcourt, Brace, Jovanovich.

Meichenbaum, D. (1977). *Cognitive behavior modification: An integrative approach.* New York: Plenum.

Mussen, P.H., Conger, J.J., Kagan, J., & Gerwitz, J. (1979). *Psychological development: A life-span approach.* New York: Harper & Row.

Novaco, R.W. (1975). *Anger control: The development and evaluation of an experimental treatment.* Lexington, MA: D.C. Health.

O'Leary, K.D., O'Leary, S., & Becker, W.C. (1967). Modification of a deviant sibling interaction pattern in the home. *Behaviour Research and Therapy, 5,* 113–120.

Patterson, G.R., Cobb, J.A., & Ray, R.S. (1973). A social engineering technology for retraining the families of aggressive boys. In H.E. Adams & I.P. Unikel (Eds.), *Issues and trends in behavior therapy* (pp. 139–224). Springfield, IL: Charles C Thomas.

Patterson, G.R., Reid, J.G., Jones, R.R., & Conger, R.E. (1975). *A social learning approach to family intervention* (Vol. 1). Eugene, OR: Catalese.

Paul, G.L. (1969). Behavior modification research: Design and tactics. In C.M. Franks (Ed.), *Behavior therapy: Appraisal and status* (pp. 29–62). New York: McGraw-Hill.

Quay, H.C. (1983). *Technical manual for the behavioral classification system for adult offenders* (Grant # FB-6). Washington, DC: National Institute of Corrections.

Raleigh, R. (1977). *Individual versus group structured learning therapy for assertiveness training with senior and junior high school students.* Unpublished doctoral dissertation, Syracuse University, Syracuse, NY.

Redl, F., & Wineman, D. (1957). *The aggressive child.* New York: Free Press.

Reissman, F. (1965). The helper therapy principle. *Social Work, 10,* 27–32.

Rogers, C.R. (1957). The necessary and sufficient conditions of therapeutic personality change. *Journal of Consulting Psychology, 21,* 95–103.

Rogers, C.R. (1970). *Carl Rogers on encounter groups.* New York: Harper & Row.

Slavson, S.R. (1964). *A textbook in analytic group psychotherapy.* New York: International Universities Press.

Spence, S.H. (1981). Differences in social skills performance between institutional juvenile male offenders and a comparable group of boys without offense records. *British Journal of Clinical Psychology, 20,* 163–171.

Trief, P. (1976). *The reduction of egocentrism in acting-out adolescents by structured learning therapy.* Unpublished doctoral dissertation, Syracuse University, Syracuse, NY.

Chapter 10

Intervening with Sexually Problematic Behavior in Community Environments

Dave Hingsburger, Terry Chaplin, Karin Hirstwood,
Sue Tough, Angie Nethercott, & Darlene Roberts-Spence

"He did what?!"

This question, asked by a shocked behavior therapist in 1983, led to the creation of a sexuality clinic to serve people with developmental disabilities.

Working with individuals with disabilities who exhibit problem behaviors is difficult. One tries to prepare for the worst while hoping for the best. Sometimes, there is no preparation that can help. The Sexuality Clinic, which serves people with developmental disabilities, grew out of work with one such individual (Griffiths, Hingsburger, & Christian, 1985; Griffiths, Quinsey, & Hingsburger, 1989). When working with a young man who had been recently integrated into a school environment, service providers faced all of the issues that could be expected. He needed to learn to control his temper, attend to tasks, and follow simple instructions. The primary objective, however, had been to teach him that turning over his teacher's desk when he was frustrated was unacceptable. The team was nearly through with the training programs and was gratified that the young man responded to a positive-based behavior program—in this case, a token

economy. The telephone call then came as a shock. His mother, understandably upset, was telling the young man's behavioral consultant that the young man had been charged with sexually molesting a neighbor's child. The staff had been ready to discharge him, and now this had happened. What, his mother wanted to know, were the staff going to do?

More and more literature addresses intervention options for people with developmental disabilities who engage in sexually offensive behavior (Demetral, 1994; Haaven, Little, & Petre-Miller, 1990; Knopp & Lakey, 1987; Myers, 1991; Parsons, 1989; Ward et al., 1992). In 1984, when faced with devising intervention for the young man described previously, the staff of the Sexuality Clinic found that there was no such richness of resources; a cursory search of the literature revealed that very little had been written regarding sex offenders with developmental disabilities. There were articles that addressed sexually offensive behaviors, such as public disrobing (Durana & Cuvo, 1980) and public masturbation (Cook, Altman, Shaw, & Blaylock, 1978), and there were articles that discussed the issue of sexuality and disability (Johnson &

Johnson, 1982; West, 1979); but little had looked specifically at working with individuals with disabilities who engaged in deviant sexual behaviors, such as pedophilia (i.e., child molestation) or biastophilia (i.e., rape; Love, 1992). Moreover, the exclusive aim of the literature seemed to be the reduction of problematic sexual behavior; little was discussed about teaching an individual how to express sexuality in healthful ways.

It did not take long to learn that the problem for most agencies in the 1980s (and for many in the 1990s) was *not* sexually *inappropriate* behavior but *sexuality* (Fegan & Rauch, 1993; Hingsburger & Griffiths, 1986). The clinic had to develop a means of understanding and interpreting sexual behavior as it occurred and to develop a reason that it was a problem. In many cases, the problem was that neither individuals with disabilities nor the agencies that provided their housing had "figure-ground discrimination abilities" (Hingsburger, 1994); that is, they could not distinguish between what is healthy sexual expression and what is problematic sexual expression. When, for example, a consenting couple (heterosexual or homosexual) was found in a private place engaging in mutually agreed-on behavior, the response by an agency was not much different from when an adult with a disability was found attempting to solicit sex from a minor. One of the original individuals being helped by the clinic asked, "What difference does it make who I touch? People get mad." His question was in response to a naive therapist's attempting to discuss "appropriate sexual expression." It was realized early that only part of the work of a clinic that served people with developmental disabilities would be in actual treatment of or intervention for sexually inappropriate or deviant behavior. The other part of the work—and often the most onerous—would be to work with agencies and organizations to develop healthful environments in which adults could live (Brown, Carney, Cortis, Metz, & Petrie, 1994).

At the start of the clinic, an advisory committee was established. This advisory committee was constructed such that a variety of perspectives would be brought to the discussion of service provision to individuals with developmental disabilities who had engaged in sexually offensive behavior. The five perspectives brought together on a quarterly basis are as follows:

1. *Community perspective:* Invited are representatives whose views can reflect the perspective of the community at large and the interests of potential victims as well as those whose interests need representation.

   Also invited are representatives of agencies and schools that provide residential, vocational, or educational support to individuals served by the clinic; probation system representatives (if appropriate); and the funding body for such agencies.

2. *Advocacy perspective:* Invited are representatives who can provide community advocacy and the perspective of the individual who is being served. As needed, representatives who can bring a legal perspective are invited.

3. *Clinical perspective:* The consulting psychologist of the intervention team is invited to represent the clinical views under consideration. Other clinical staff or clinical experts may be asked to attend meetings.

4. *Agency perspective:* The chief executive officer or delegate and the coordinator of the clinic are invited to represent the perspective of the sponsoring agency.

5. *Individual perspective:* Staff from the intervention team, from the community agencies, and from service coordination attend as needed to share perspectives on the treatment and/or intervention needs with regard to a specific individual. Because of issues of confidentiality, only those staff who are involved with an individual may be guests for the pertinent portion of the meeting.

The committee provides external reviews of both the individual and the intervention issues and ensures that legal, clinical, advocacy, or community issues are considered. Out of the advisory committee has grown a general consensus regarding the rights of individuals with disabilities to intervention as well as the right to live in environments that foster appropriate sexual expression. Developing within agencies policy that reflects the philosophy of the clinic is a major issue. The committee supports the clinic in its work both with individuals who are receiving intervention—who need effective and humane policies—and with agencies that support them—which sometimes need guidance in developing these policies. The advisory committee is invaluable in building a community consensus and recognizing that intervention that is designed solely to suppress sexuality is a violation of individual rights and is procedurally unethical.

In working with the advisory committee, the clinic presents difficulties in intervention areas that are specific to individuals or to staff or agencies that refuse to acknowledge the adulthood of the individuals whom they serve. The clinic cannot work with an individual who has engaged in a serious sexual offense unless the agency that provides his or her housing has a policy that states a definition for appropriate sexual expression. Similarly, for individuals who have not sexually offended but who have been referred for sex education or relationship training, it is unethical to teach about relationships or intercourse if they will be punished for either. Because the advisory committee comprises housing, education, and vocational services agencies, it has developed a regionwide sensitivity to the problems of policy, education, and sexual health. The clinic's efforts also have been facilitated by broader social change regarding people with disabilities. Since the clinic's inception, much more work has been published to substantiate the need for the development of appropriate environments for people with developmental disabilities (Hingsburger, 1990; Kempton, 1993; Monat-Haller, 1992; Rowe & Savage, 1987). Others have emphasized the need for attitude change from systems and society (Coleman & Murphy, 1980; Gochros, Gochros, & Fischer, 1986; Hingsburger, 1993; Lusthaus, 1991; Morris, 1991).

INITIAL CONTEXTUAL ASSESSMENT

Given that the clinic was founded in a behavioral unit and that behaviorists strive to understand behavior in context, the founders of the clinic agreed that behavior skills would be of paramount importance in both the assessment of and the intervention for people with disabilities who engage in problematic sexual behaviors. The concept of *counterfeit deviance* was developed as a means of guiding therapists through a complex assessment regarding the behavior of the referred individual (Hingsburger, Griffiths, & Quinsey, 1991). In effect, counterfeit deviance (see Table 1) attempts to place the behavior into a context that can lead to both an understanding of the behavior and a determination of how to proceed with intervention. There are five contexts that are evaluated to determine whether a person has a real or a counterfeit deviance.

Historical Context

Many people with disabilities have lived and continue to live in nonnormative environments, and it is important to understand the values that an individual has learned while growing up in these environments. It is perhaps best to conceptualize living in an environment such as an institution as living in a different culture (Hingsburger, 1985). It is odd that society expects people who lived for decades in an institutional environment to learn community norms and values *instantaneously* when they are suddenly deinstitutionalized. It is almost as if society expects community norms to pop into a person's head on the bus ride from the institution to the community.

An individual who was referred as an "exhibitionist" and a "potential rapist" had recently moved from an institution to a community environment. In the institution, he had lived on an all-male ward with several beds per room. He was used to going to the bathroom in full view of others and being nude around both other men with disabilities and female staff. When he moved to the group home, he did not understand doors, walls, private places, or private spaces. He would get up in the morning, walk nude with an erection through the house, and go into women's bedrooms to watch them get dressed. It is not surprising that the agency personnel panicked (i.e., they considered him an exhibitionist and potential rapist), but it was necessary to emphasize a number of issues. In his previous culture, nudity was a given and people walked in on

Table 1. Counterfeit deviance

Structural
The behavior occurs because of the environment in which the person lives.
Modeling
The behavior occurs as a result of learning inappropriate social behaviors from models in the home environment.
Behavioral
The behavior occurs as a means of seeking attention or avoiding a task.
Partner selection
The behavior occurs as an attempt to form a sexual relationship of any kind.
Inappropriate courtship
The behavior occurs as an attempt to communicate sexual interest in another person.
Sexual knowledge
The behavior occurs as a result of lack of sexual information.
Perpetual arousal
The behavior occurs as a result of the inability or unwillingness to complete a sexual behavior, such as masturbation.
Learning history
The behavior occurs as a result of the individual's having lived in a nonnormative environment.
Moral vacuum
The behavior occurs as a result of a lack of understanding of cultural mores.
Medical
The behavior occurs as a result of a medical problem.
Medication side effects
The behavior occurs as a result of problems caused by medications.

others frequently. Even without considering institutionalization, all-male environments (or all-female environments) have different privacy rules from those that operate in mixed-gender environments. This man did not understand privacy or the invasion of privacy. Having an erect penis in the morning does not necessarily indicate anything more than the need to urinate or the presence of a typical physiological cycle; for the individual, it may have had nothing to do with sexual desire. His behavior is understood easily when it is considered in a historical, social context.

The other historical factor that must be considered is abuse and assault. The statistics on abuse of people with disabilities is staggering. Many first sexual experiences of people with disabilities are rape or molestation (Hingsburger, 1995b; Senn, 1988; Sobsey, 1994; Sobsey, Wells, Lucardie, & Mansell, 1995; Stimpson & Best, 1991). That people with disabilities learn inappropriate lessons from sexual victimization cannot be overstated. Clinicians who conduct assessments regarding sexual acting-out behavior need to be prepared to learn of past or present

abuse. It also is imperative that the learning of past abuse does not become an *excuse* for the individual to offend against others. The importance of past abuse, clinically, is in determining how that abuse affected the individual's understanding of sexuality and his or her own sexual behavior. This knowledge can be of tremendous importance in building an intervention plan.

In working with a middle-age man with a developmental disability who had been referred for coercing a woman with a disability to have sex with him, the clinician noted that the man showed genuine confusion regarding the issue of consent and force. In therapy, it was discovered that he had been sexually assaulted quite regularly by a male staff member in a large institution. He stated that he did not like the assault and that he did not like to be forced. Even so, he acknowledged that sometimes he felt pleasure in his body. It was critical then to learn that he, like many survivors of sexual assault, had difficulty understanding that although he did not like the assault, his body felt some pleasure (Danica, 1990; Everstine & Everstine, 1989). For many survivors of sexual assault who do not have disabilities, the existence of pleasure during assault is a confusing issue and one that needs to be addressed with therapeutic caution. However, in this example, the man with cognitive impairments had simplified the situation and determined that force leads to pleasure, and pleasure negates the force. He believed that although the woman did not want to have sex with him, she would like some of the feelings that she would have in her body if he forced her, and those feelings would make his behavior acceptable. Faulty reasoning was based on his own experiences; knowing the information and his reactions, the clinic staff then had a good foundation for teaching this man about relationships and consent.

Situational Context

It is impossible to assess the sexual behaviors of an individual with a developmental disability without understanding the system in which he or she lives. Systemic or situational analysis requires the therapist to develop a sense of how the system itself views people with disabilities and their sexuality. This gives the therapist a means of understanding an individual's responses and an individual's perceptions of his or her behavior.

"Inappropriate" Becomes "Appropriate"

Standardized sexual knowledge assessment tools, such as the Socio-Sexual Knowledge and Attitude Test (SSKAT; Wish, McCombs, & Edmonson, 1980), are helpful tools for understanding what an individual with a disability knows and believes about sexuality; however, use of such a tool without an understanding of the situational context of a response can lead to false assumptions about an individual's abilities and an individual's interpretations of his or her own behavior and living situations. For example, one of the questions on the SSKAT asks an individual to point to places in which it is appropriate to have sex. In scoring the test, one is to mark as correct an answer that indicates that the bedroom is an appropriate place to have sex and to mark as incorrect the public park as an appropriate place to have sex. Although this is an understandable scoring system, it also can be considered simplistic. For an individual who lives in a system that has determined that no sexual behavior is allowed on site, the answer of "park" as an appropriate place to have sex is much more accurate than is "bedroom." Without this knowledge, the therapist can be fooled into thinking that the problem is inherent in the individual's understanding or misunderstanding of appropriate sexual behaviors, when in reality the individual is making very astute observations of a current environment and the appropriateness of "inappropriate" behaviors.

"Inappropriate Works"

In environments in which there are limited staffing and little stimulation, an individual with a disability can learn by accident that touching one's genitalia is an effective means of garnering much wanted attention or, better still, redirection to much wanted activities. In this way, the genitals can be seen as an odd "nurse call button." It also has been noted that individuals have attempted to perform masturbatory behaviors as a means of getting out of unwanted tasks (Hingsburger, 1995a). Engaging in public masturbation in the workshop may be an effective way of getting out of boring or otherwise aversive routine tasks or contracts.

"Appropriate" Is "Inappropriate"

When an individual learns—usually quickly and usually after being caught only once—that appropriate sexual expression is harshly punished, other avenues for expressing sexuality are sought. Quick, furtive sexual acts in the back of a sheltered industry are "safe sex" in environments that frown on and actively punish the building of loving relationships. In working with people with disabilities, the clinic has noted that a form of erotophobia (i.e., "a persistent and general tendency to respond to sexual cues with negative emotions" [Hingsburger, 1992, p. 31]) is developed through consistent exposure to negative attitudes toward sexuality (Hingsburger, 1992; Hingsburger & Tough, 1993; Hutchinson, 1990).

Educational Context

Sex education as provided to large numbers of people with developmental disabilities began in the late 1980s. There is an increasing number of curricula available, and these curricula address a number of areas regarding sexuality and sexual behaviors, from sexual (biological) facts (Kempton, 1988) to "safer sex" and HIV/AIDS risk reduction (Scotti, Speaks, Masia, Boggess, & Drabman, 1996; Scotti et al., 1997) to building boundaries (Champagne & Walker-Hirsch, 1981, 1986, 1988) to becoming a sexual self-advocate (Hingsburger & Ludwig, 1993). Moreover, there are curricula that address topics in sexuality for individuals with hearing impairments (Edwards, Wapnick, Mock, & Whitson, 1982) and for people who use alternative communication strategies (Ludwig & Hingsburger, 1993). There are slide programs (Kempton, 1988), explicit videotapes and drawings (Azzopardi, Horsely, & Pietsch, 1990), and exact replicas of genitalia (Jackson, 1988) as well as programs for young adolescents (Stangle, 1991) and programs that are suitable for adults (Kempton, 1988). There are films that address subjects such as masturbation (Hingsburger, 1995a; Hingsburger & Woods, 1995) and programs and study guides for staff (Kempton, 1993; Scotti, Ujcich, et al., 1996). The proliferation of sex education packages is a good sign, but the dates on these programs also tell us that individuals with disabilities who are older than 40 years could not have benefited from the increasing awareness of the importance of sexuality training.

The lack of training leads not only to confused understanding about sexuality but also to frustration and sexual acting out. One of the men served by the clinic was alone in the community for the first time after having been taught to travel from his home to work at a sheltered industry, and he began to sexually offend women at the bus stop. Although the behavior was called "assault" by the authorities, he was simply pulling up dresses and pulling down panties. It is not our intent either to infantilize this fellow or minimize the emotional trauma of the victims, but it is not difficult to see the similarity between these actions and those of young children performing precisely the same behavior. When children engage in this behavior, it is perceived as a means of satisfying curiosity. In looking through this man's file, the clinic staff

noted that he never had received any form of sex education; interviews with staff and family revealed that all were certain that the man had never had sex education, nor had he ever asked any sexual questions. Everyone had assumed that he never asked because he had a disability and therefore was nonsexual; it is more often the case that because he had no sex education he would have no *language* to ask basic questions. Given this information, the clinic staff hypothesized that the lifting of a woman's dress might be considered a *behavioral question* that deserved an answer. It was gratifying to discover that a single sex education class that allowed him to learn about the female body and to see what it looked like while emphasizing body privacy "cured" his sexually offensive behavior.

It also is important to note that whereas people without disabilities who are not given sex education through the family or the school learn from their peers, people with disabilities do not have this opportunity (Kempton, 1993). Individuals with disabilities, like their peers without disabilities, typically do not learn about sexuality from their parents, but unlike their peers they also do not learn from friends. Their primary sex educator is the television. One young woman who developed a crush on one of her male instructors at the sheltered industry did not accept that because he was married her crush on him was unacceptable behavior. In an interview, she stated that married people on television have sex with other people all the time.

Medical Context

Many people with disabilities take a variety of medications that can affect sexual functioning (Long & Rybacki, 1995). When bizarre forms of masturbation manifest, it should be routine to check medications to determine whether they could be responsible for the person's sexual functioning. Although a woman's masturbation using a wire brush might be conceptualized as genital self-injury, determining that she is taking a medication that causes a numbing of the genitals can make her behavior more understandable. Rather than interpreting the behavior as self-injury, staff then would be more likely to view it as a strategy to increase the stimulation to the clitoris to compensate for the numbing effect of the medication.

In addition, people with disabilities experience sexuality—similar to people without disabilities—in their bodies. Issues that cause difficulties, such as prostate problems, need to be diagnosed for the person to function well. Along with this, there needs to be an understanding that the genitals have a dual purpose and that issues that are genitally based but not sexually based need to be investigated. The discomfort and itching of a urinary tract infection or a yeast infection can lead to behaviors that look a great deal like public masturbation or "excessive" masturbation.

Sexual Context

Although there are many reasons other than sexual deviance that a person with a disability might sexually offend, it would be unwise to assume that the presence of a disability makes the person *unable* to be sexually deviant. In the clinic's history, most of the referred individuals do not have a *clinical deviance*. If one includes general consultation and sex education, then fewer than 5% of the individuals referred for sexually inappropriate behavior are actually clinically deviant. The clinic's success rate is evidenced by its having had only five recidivistic acts in the more than 300 individuals whom the clinic has served since the mid-1980s. It also is significant to note that each act of recidivism occurred during intervention, and none have occurred postintervention. Furthermore, those who reoffended did so only once. When looking at the individuals who have reoffended, 100% of them tested as clinically deviant. Intervention can still be effective for those who are clinically deviant. In any case, a good assessment is necessary to determine the appropriate course of treatment.

It is clear that a clinician cannot tell simply by the topography of a behavior whether someone is clinically deviant. An objective measure needs to be taken to give the clinician a means of determining whether the intervention should be educational, attitudinal, or situational or whether the intervention should focus on changing arousal patterns.

OBJECTIVE BASELINES

The contextual assessment, as its name implies, gives the therapist a context in which to place the behavior. Intervention is guided by this context, and each of the intervention strategies is aimed at giving individuals a new context in which to conceptualize sexuality in general and their own sexual behavior specifically. Clinicians use a number of objective measures to assist with intervention because measurement of intervention success is more than a subjective sense that everything is going well. Likewise, it is dangerous to operate on a therapist's or an agency's intuitions rather than on objective data about an individual's progress and the individual's probability of reoffending.

Laboratory Assessment of Sexual Arousal

Phallometric assessment has been used since the early 1970s in the assessment of men who have committed sexual offenses against children and adults for several years (Quinsey, Chaplin, & Varney, 1981). The procedures have been performed in a similar manner by several laboratories, although they have not been completely standardized across all laboratories (Law & Osbourn, 1983). The Sexuality Clinic's phallometric assessment uses a computer to monitor a man's sexual arousal while he attends to audio and/or visual stimuli in the privacy of a sound-attenuated room. The man to be assessed places a mercury-in-rubber strain gauge around the shaft of his penis. This gauge is connected to a plethysmograph, which allows a computer to monitor the degree of sexual arousal exhibited during any given time period.

Phallometric assessment of sexual preference is an effective way to determine whether an individual's arousal pattern is one of several possible factors that may help explain why he engaged in inappropriate sexual behavior. It should *not* be used as a measure of a person's guilt or innocence in reference to a particular allegation.

When considering the appropriateness of phallometric testing for a particular individual, several considerations should be made. First, match the individual's offense history or self-disclosed problem with an appropriate set of assessment stimuli. Second, ensure that the individual is able to comprehend the relevant cues in any audiotaped stimuli, or ensure that he or she has the visual acuity to perceive the visual stimuli. In addition, he or she should be able to concentrate for the duration of a session, which usually lasts approximately 1 hour. Third, ensure that an individual is not exposed to degrees of deviance much beyond those expressed by him in behavior or fantasy. The commercially available stimuli often used in research on and intervention for other groups of individuals are *inappropriate* for use in many cases. In view of these concerns, the clinic continues to develop specialized stimulus sets that target particular groups. For example, the clinic has a set of audiotaped stimuli that are written in very simple language, which unambiguously target behavior that is more typical among individuals who have developmental disabilities.

The results of the phallometric assessment are graphed, giving the therapist a clear indication of whether the individual has real or counterfeit deviance. The results in Figures 1 and 2 show how a typical heterosexual male responds to the slide and audio stimuli. In these graphs, it is possible to see that the person tested responded most strongly to slides and stories of adults, and arousal dropped off fairly dramatically to the child stimuli. Figures 3 and 4 show a pedophilic response to the same stimuli. Here the response to slides of children or stories of sexual behavior with children either competes with or is equal to the response to those presenting age-appropriate stimuli. The slide categories can be more specific to age, whereas the audiotaped stimuli can measure response to stories depicting direct sexual action to individuals in the broader categories.

Throughout the course of intervention, the baseline phallometric measure is used to determine progress toward changing arousal patterns. This result alone, however, is no guarantee that the person will not reoffend. Systemic issues remain a concern throughout intervention. For example, an individual who is clinically diagnosed as a pedophile may, through therapy, change his arousal pattern to become attracted to adults. This change, though gratifying, is helpful only if the individual lives within a system that allows appropriate sexual expression. If the individual lives in a system that will punish him for the new and appropriate sexual interest, then all is lost. In effect, the original offense at the time of referral

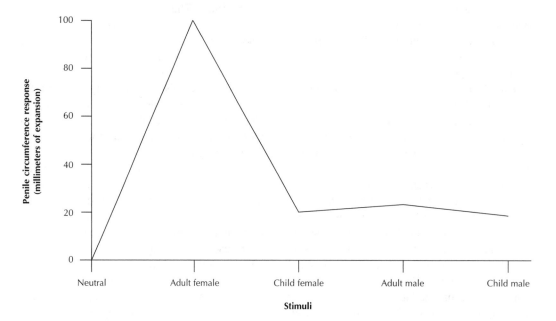

Figure 1.   Phallometric assessment results for a heterosexual male, with audiotaped stimuli.

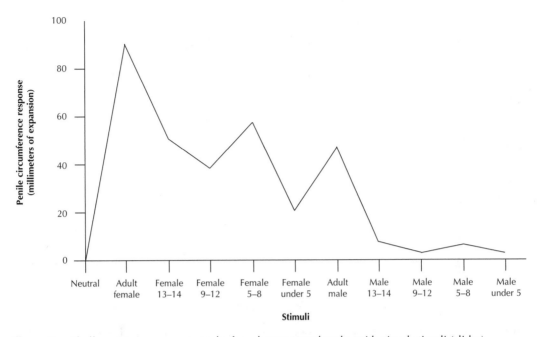

Figure 2. Phallometric assessment results for a heterosexual male, with visual stimuli (slides).

may be due to deviant sexual interest, whereas subsequent offenses could be due to counterfeit deviance after intervention. In addition to a change in phallometric measures, successful intervention for clinical deviance must be documented by accompanying behavior change. The behavior change should be recorded in the natural environment or by other evidence of learning to cope with the deviant arousal and using relapse prevention skills to reduce risk of reoffending.

The Socio-sexual Skills and Attitude Inventory

The SSKAT, developed by Wish and colleagues (1980), is one of the few tests that have been standardized for people with developmental disabilities. Its usage allows the therapist to determine what the individual knows about sexuality and how the individual feels about what he or she knows. It is not uncommon for the therapist to discover, for example, that the individual knows everything that there is to know about masturbation but believes that it is 100% inappropriate and that the people who do it should go to jail. This test, then, allows a determination of which individuals require what emphasis in

sex education and whether the emphasis in sex education should be informational or attitudinal.

This assessment is often one of the first tools used wherein the individual and the therapist begin working together. As such, this tool is viewed as the beginning of therapy rather than as an assessment separate from the therapeutic process. The therapist is to take great pains to develop therapeutic rapport and to ensure that the individual learns that there are rights within the intervention process. The assessment often is very stressful for the individual. It is important to remember that the individual is undergoing this process because of a serious behavior problem; usually the referring person (i.e., parent/agency representative/probation officer) has stated in very strong terms that the individual is in serious trouble. The individual often determines that sex got him or her in trouble, and now having to discuss sexual issues—when all that he or she wants to do is state that it will never happen again and have things go back to normal—is difficult. To get an accurate reading of the individual's knowledge and attitudes, the SSKAT is given over a period of time and individuals are told that they can stop the test if they become uncomfortable or upset. This ensures

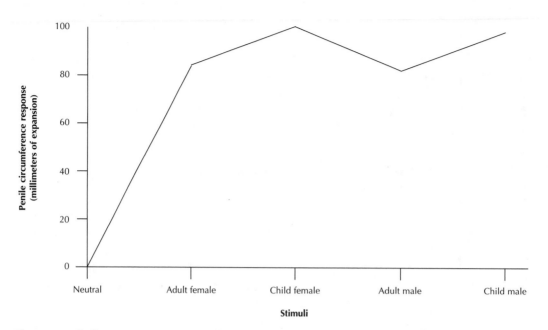

Figure 3. Phallometric assessment results for a male pedophile, with audiotaped stimuli.

that the therapist is viewed as helping and understanding rather than as another person in a long line of staff who make the individual do what the individual does not want to do. It also ensures that the therapist gets a more accurate measure of the individual's actual knowledge and attitudes.

The SSKAT also probes for past sexual abuse. The questions are vague enough not to be leading but are specific enough to encourage re-

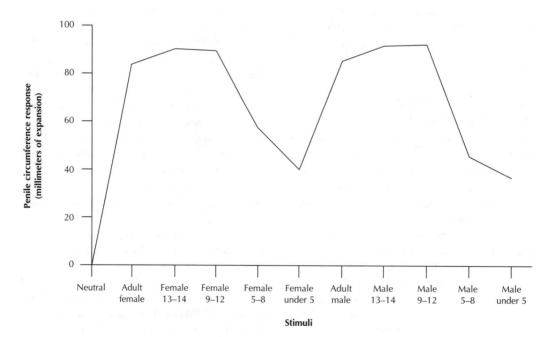

Figure 4. Phallometric assessment results for a male pedophile, with visual stimuli (slides).

porting. The therapist has to be prepared to hear reports of past or present sexual victimization and to know the process that must be followed should abuse be reported.

Used as a pre- and posttest of sexual knowledge, the SSKAT allows the therapist to report real changes that occur regarding the individual's sexual knowledge. This ensures a measure of real learning after a sex education class or sex education through individual sessions with the therapist. More than that, as the test measures attitudes, the therapist has an objective measure of the effects of sex education or counseling on the individual's perception of sexual behaviors ranging from hand holding to intercourse.

Age-Discrimination Card Sort Test

The clinic created a card sort test to be used in establishing a baseline for each individual's knowledge about secondary sexual characteristics and his or her ability to determine age by looking at magazine pictures. The clinic team cuts out current magazine pictures of males and females in the age categories of adult, adolescent, child, and infant. These pictures then are circulated to at least 10 staff members, who are asked to determine which pictures belong in which age category. Those pictures with 100% agreement as to age category are then included in the Age-Discrimination Card Sort Test.

During the age-discrimination test, an individual is asked to look at each picture and then assess by age each person pictured. Once the individual has made that determination, his or her answer is not questioned but the test giver does ask how the determination was made. The therapist wants to determine which social or physical cues are being used to determine the age of the individual. It is not unusual for an individual to reveal that height is the salient cue signaling adulthood rather than secondary sexual characteristics.

Although this is not a standardized test, it does give the therapist a baseline measure against which progress can be determined. If the person does not recognize secondary sexual characteristics as a determination of adulthood, then a further test that examines more specifically the individual's knowledge about adulthood is administered. In this test—again not standardized— the therapist draws an outline of two bodies of

equal size. The individual then is asked to draw more detail on each of the bodies to make them into an adult woman and into an adult man or to tell the therapist what to draw on the bodies. The individual typically begins with nonstressful body parts, such as eyes, nose, and mouth; as the individual continues, the therapist listens for the language that is used to describe genitalia and to see whether and where body hair is placed on the outlines. Second, the individual is given a tall outline and a short outline and asked to draw or to instruct the therapist to draw the body parts of an adult and a child. Both male and female drawings are done.

The intervention strategies that arise from this exercise are specifically aimed at increasing the individual's ability to assess age accurately and thereby become more competent in both phallometric measures and understanding the therapeutic intervention. It is essential that the therapist know what the individual means when he states that he is "masturbating while thinking about *girls.*" To ensure accuracy of results, the therapist teaches the use of age-appropriate and descriptive language while teaching about the names and functions of body parts. When the individual can accurately use words such as woman, man, boy, and girl, the therapist has a much better understanding of the individual's self-reports.

Preference of Sexual Partner Card Sort

Using the same cards as in the Age-Discrimination Card Sort Test, an individual is presented with a variety of pictures of people of different ages and asked to select who would be a good person with whom to go on a date. The individual's gender and age preferences are noted as the presenter asks the individual why he or she would like to date the person in the picture. In general, the answers fall into one of two categories— physical reasons and social reasons. The physical reasons relate to the attractiveness of the person in the picture, such as, "She is pretty," or, "He looks nice." These physical descriptors tend not to vary based on the age of the person pictured. The social reasons may vary based on age. When looking at a picture of an adult male wearing a baseball cap, the individual may say, "He looks as if he likes baseball and so do I."

When looking at a child, the individual may say that he or she would like to date this person "because she would have to do what I tell her" or "he is just a boy so he wouldn't tease me." This helps to discriminate why, for example, he may have been approaching children as potential sexual partners even though his phallometric measure is that of a typical adult male.

SETTING THE STAGE
FOR INTERVENTION

The authors of this chapter believe that part of the reason for the success of the Sexuality Clinic's intervention package is that the therapists are given "room" to do the assessment and to develop an intervention plan. Unlike those who work with sexual offenders without disabilities, the therapists at the clinic have the luxury of working with a well-established system that is set up to support people with disabilities. Those who work with sex offenders without disabilities often are at a loss to provide effective on-site supervision and to monitor relapse carefully by utilizing the skills of the staff who are assigned to their care. When first beginning to develop an intervention plan, the therapists determine the level of support that the person is presently receiving. In general, the clinic finds two widely different scenarios.

The most common scenario is that the person, because of the nature of his or her disability, is living in a supervised or semisupervised situation. In this case, it is relatively easy for a clinician to pull together a team to support the individual through the initial stage of intervention and to supervise the gradual transition to maximum community access as intervention continues. With the individual's permission, the clinician meets with the support team and outlines the kind of supervision that is necessary and the planned relapse-prevention strategy. In these meetings, it is not necessary to discuss the individual specifically because the staff members are being informed generally about how to support someone who has engaged in a sexual offense.

The more difficult scenario is that of an individual with disabilities who is not being supported in a system and who has little in the way of a support circle. For individuals who are living on their own in the community and who have come to the attention of service professionals only because of an offense, it is very difficult to pull the support team together. In these situations, the clinic has attempted to include families; social workers; probation officers; and, in some cases, landlords, spouses, and friendly neighbors as part of the support circle. It is not uncommon for the individual with the disability to prefer that these people not know the specifics of the problem. In reality, however, most of them probably know of the offense through local media reports or through neighborhood gossip. Even so, the clinic maintains individual wishes for confidentiality while it still attempts to have the individual connect more closely with a network for support.

There are several people of primary importance who have roles on the intervention team; each of these people is part of the social network and has opportunities not only for supervision but also to help the individual generalize work done with the therapist to more natural environments. Although the primary player is the clinician, who meets frequently with members of the team, there are regular meetings of the team wherein progress is noted and goals are established. These meetings typically are called and facilitated by the individual's advocate and ensure that there are regular reviews of the intervention, progress on goals, and the rationale for any restricted access to the community.

Direct Care Staff

The individual is encouraged to choose a direct care staff member as a "safe person" who can be contacted when the individual who is receiving treatment recognizes that he or she is engaging in prerelapse behavior. For example, two individuals used this opportunity to say that they were having sexual thoughts that were bothersome. The contact can be made by the individual even if it is just to chat or to ask questions regarding basic sexuality issues. Once chosen, this safe person is educated specifically about the concerns with the individual. This person also is instructed in how to determine when relapse may be occurring and the information that needs to be passed on to the clinical team.

Management Representative: Housing Agency

Before any therapeutic intervention is begun, it is necessary for the housing agency and the intervention agency to agree on general intervention goals. These goals are determined in a meeting among the clinician, the individual's advocate, and a senior management representative who has the power to speak for the agency. There must be a commitment on the part of both the intervention team and the housing agency that success in intervention will be reflected in changes in the living style or supervision level. The management representative, who has the ultimate liability for the individual, has a right to expect to receive evidence that the intervention is progressing and documentation that there have been real behavior or clinical changes on which the therapist is basing his or her opinion that the individual is progressing.

Individual's Advocate

The individual has a right to an advocate who is not tied either to the housing agency or to the intervention agency. Given that some of the assessments can be considered intrusive and that the intervention can be long and arduous, the individual needs independent advice and advocacy throughout the process. A housing agency or intervention agency that attempts to secure individual consent to intervention is in an obvious conflict of interest. It is clear that the housing representative and the intervention representative have a vested interest in the individual's entering and continuing intervention. The role of the individual's advocate is to assess the individual's real willingness to undergo assessments (e.g., the phallometric measure) and to continue with intervention. The Sexuality Clinic has established a long-held policy that it is a voluntary service; individuals can terminate therapy any time that they so choose, and they can refuse any aspect of intervention that they choose (refusal, however, may result in termination). Even with the use of advocates, only two individuals have refused intervention since the clinic has been operating. This likely is because individuals see the benefits of intervention, including increased com-

munity access, better relationships with a support system, and a sense of personal self-control.

Clinician

The clinician provides service both to the individual and to the system in which the individual lives. The clinician is responsible for coordinating the assessment, from determining the necessity of phallometric measurement to performing a contextual analysis of the behavior. During this time, the clinician develops the social framework and puts necessary supports into place. From the contextual analysis, the clinician develops an intervention hypothesis and writes a report outlining the intervention and the objective measure that will be used to determine success.

Consulting Psychologist

The clinic consults a number of psychologists with a variety of specialties; these psychologists oversee the intervention approaches in the clinic and are available to help build intervention plans and to troubleshoot regarding intervention problems. The consulting psychologist sits on the advisory committee and helps to formulate clinic policy and procedures. The person in this role also serves to explain and endorse intervention strategies as they are determined for each individual.

Advisory Committee

The role of the advisory committee to build a general consensus and a philosophical framework has already been discussed. The advisory committee also is a forum for therapists to present specific cases. Given that the advisory committee represents a broad range of expertise—from clinical to legal—the therapist can draw from a number of suggestions on individual cases. The advisory committee's role is to advise, not to supervise; therefore, it is not uncommon to have arise out of a case discussion a variety of suggestions that will give a therapist new avenues to pursue.

GOALS OF INTERVENTION

The primary goal of intervention is to ensure that the individual does not reoffend. This goal pervades intervention strategies and is a concern from assessment, during intervention, and after intervention. Unlike with many other problem behaviors that a behavior therapist expects will reduce in frequency and severity through the program history, there is little room for error in work with sexual offenders. Clinically, any individual who has offended is regarded as very seriously at risk to reoffend. One of the hazards of relying on the phallometric measure and its determination regarding whether an individual is clinically deviant or his or her behavior is from counterfeit deviance is the tendency to take behaviors that result from clinical deviance much more seriously than those that arise from, say, poor sex education. It needs to be acknowledged that, similar to the victim, the therapist does not care what motivated the behavior. What is important is that the behavior occurred and, without intervention, is likely to recur. Although it is true that counterfeit deviance may be more responsive to intervention than clinical deviance, the behavior is equally serious and the ramifications equally damaging for the victim.

As the therapeutic process in working with offenders is long, complex, and highly intrusive in the life of the individual, it is important to look at the goals of intervention from the perspective of the offending individual. For the therapist, there is the goal of establishing appropriate sexual behaviors and decreasing the probability of reoffense; for the individual, the goal usually is greater access to the community. There is an assumption, then, that the individual's access to the community is or has been curtailed as a result of the sexual offense. In fact, for many individuals, the home support agency has responded quickly and severely to the sexual acting-out behavior. Often, individuals have been put under house arrest as the agency goes through the trauma of determining how to react institutionally to the behavior.

For individuals whose freedom has been curtailed as a result of their behavior, there is motivation for undergoing intervention: If they can reestablish trust with the agency, then they can begin a process of regaining the personal freedoms that they had lost. This is the best scenario for intervention. Everyone has a goal wherein there is a payoff. For the therapist, the goal is to increase competence and decrease the probability of reoffense (true for either real or counterfeit deviance). For the agency, the goal is to provide a safe environment for people with disabilities while protecting the community from further assault. For the individual, the goal is to regain personal freedom.

For individuals who have sexually offended but have not lost community access because they never had it in the first place, the process is quite different. Some individuals, because of their disability rather than their sexual offense, require a great deal of supervision in both community and segregated environments. In these situations, typically the individual has offended when the staff are said to have "turned their backs for just a second." Here, the clinician has to ask some difficult questions. First, is the behavior a result of counterfeit deviance, and is the individual capable of undergoing an educative approach? If so, then education is appropriate. Second, is the behavior a result of a clinical deviance? If so, then is long, arduous therapy applicable? Often it is found that by training the staff on how to "do" supervision and what the potential dangers are that might trigger a reoffense, the individual's quality of life is returned to its state before the offense. Actual therapy regarding the deviance, then, is not pursued, and the goal has changed to staff training rather than individual intervention.

COMPONENTS OF INTERVENTION

The assessment process is invaluable in determining the course of action for a particular individual. It is important to remember that individuals who are clinically deviant often need intervention strategies that are similar to those of individuals who have a counterfeit deviance. It may be tempting to focus on the deviance and forget that the individual has not had sex education or has poor social skills. When determining which intervention components need to be employed in specific situations, the clinician needs to ensure that all avenues of intervention that may lead to reduced risk of reoffense have been considered.

Social Skills Training

Many people with developmental disabilities do not have the social skills necessary to form healthy, reciprocal relationships with other people. Without these relationships, people are at risk for difficulties with emotional adjustment, community integration, appropriate expression of sexuality, and vulnerability to sexual abuse (Smith, Valenti-Hein, & Hellar, 1985). York Behaviour Management Services developed the Social LIFE (Learning In a Functional Environment) game as a means of teaching social skills to people with developmental disabilities (Griffiths et al., 1989). The process first was used in a prison and showed promise for use with individuals with cognitive impairments (Quinsey & Varney, 1977). The game is played by three participants and one mediator. Prior to playing the first game, two goals are determined for each of the participants. For example, someone's goal may be to learn how to greet people when meeting them for the first time. Based on the individual goals, question cards are written.

There are four categories of cards (Give and Take, Choices, Fill-In, and Play a Role) from which participants answer questions by landing on a color-coded square. The game board is modeled after the Monopoly game. Throughout the game, participants also are taught a four-step, problem-solving approach (Stop, Think, Act, Check It Out). After the participant chooses a question card from the appropriate deck, he or she is asked to use the problem-solving approach to determine a response to the question. Participants win money, which they can use to purchase a social reinforcer for themselves and the entire group. Participants learn to generalize the skills learned in the game to other environments through homework assignments that focus on their individual goals. The game has been found to be very successful in teaching both social skills and problem-solving skills as a result of its individualized approach.

For individuals with disabilities who have sexually offended, the game provides an opportunity to learn in a group and get feedback from group members regarding a variety of responses. Because of the chance nature of the game, the individual has only a one-in-four chance of selecting one of his or her own cards. This same chance allows one to see other players respond to question cards that target their own skill impairment. Here the individual can learn from a model, and reinforcement also can be provided for that player using the skill. Part of the work of the game is learning to respect the other players and hearing their reactions to social mistakes.

Video Self-Modeling

Video self-modeling is a positive self-modeling technique that enhances self-esteem while helping a person learn how to use the strategies being taught (Ward et al., 1992). The person is videotaped while dealing successfully with a situation that typically is problematic. This method has been used for a variety of target behaviors, including sociosexual training and anger management training (Benson, 1995). It has been effective when used with individuals with poor impulse control and poor self-visualization. As a technique, it is very helpful in the cognitive restructuring process because the person is provided with an image of future potential successful behavior (Ward et al., 1992).

The steps involved in using the video self-modeling procedure are similar to those used in making a movie:

1. The script is written by involving the individual in the process and using that person's language in the script as in the following example:
   Jack [introduction to the movie]: Hi, my name is Jack, and I am going to watch myself ask my housemate to have sex with me.
   Jack: I'm starting to feel good.
   Housemate: That's nice.
   Jack: Do you want to come up to my bedroom and touch me?
   Housemate: No, not right now.
   Jack [taped self-talk]: I'm feeling horny, but he doesn't want to have sex with me. I can either go to my bedroom and masturbate, or I can stay here and watch television.
   Jack [summary to movie]: I did a good job. I asked my housemate to have sex with

me. He said no. I decided to go to my bedroom by myself.

2. The lines are practiced.
3. An audiotape is made for the sections of the
   scenarios that involve self-talk.
4. Arrangements are made for the videotaping
   of other people required in the movie.
5. Appropriate settings and locations are established for the videotaping.

During the videotaping, the majority of the
camera angles focus on the main person involved, who is made to feel like the "star" of the
movie. After videotaping, the video is edited to
create a polished finished product that allows
the individual to see him- or herself following a
set pattern of behavior in response to a situation.

The person initially watches the videotape
no more than once per day. Once the person is
familiar with the movie, viewings are decreased
to less frequent intervals until it is used only occasionally as a refresher. This approach helps to
avoid satiation that occurs when the individual
is no longer interested in viewing the movie. It
is important to maintain interest in the videotape
for a long enough period to allow a regular reminder of the new skills while they are initially
being applied in the individual's life. The success of the entire process depends on a positive
and fun atmosphere while making the video and
a reinforcing approach to viewing the video.

This approach is an excellent addition to
the counseling sessions because the therapist
can provide a direct, concrete, and very personal
model for the individual regarding behaviors that
seem abstract when they are explained. Individuals can begin to see themselves as successful
people who are capable of handling the stressors
that come their way. By creating scripts that apply directly to the area of referral, the individual
regularly can see cues that typically would lead
to relapse but instead lead to successful resolution. Given the nature of sexuality, this may be
the only way to influence directly the behaviors
that occur in private places.

Sex Education

One of the cornerstones of intervention is sex
education. For almost all individuals referred to

the clinic, sex education is necessary either to
provide information or to change attitudes toward
sexuality. Part of the difficulty with providing
sex education is that when the clinic becomes
involved, the individual is usually an adult and
has had a lifetime of negative sexual messages,
sexual victimization, and punishment for appropriate sexual behavior. It would be naive to begin
intervention by seating this individual in front of
sexually explicit slides about the basics of the
body. Successful sex education must deal with
any erotophobia that has been developed during
the individual's lifetime. In the administering of
the SSKAT, the therapist looks for evidence of
erotophobia and begins to desensitize the individual to the discussion of sexuality. Erotophobia, as it applies to people with developmental
disabilities, is expressed in a number of ways, as
follows (Hingsburger & Tough, 1993):

- The person has an extreme fear of his or her
  own genitalia.
- The person has extreme panic reactions to
  benign pictures of nudity.
- The person states that all sexual behavior is
  bad.
- The person views all sociosexual behavior as
  wrong.
- The person denies his or her own adulthood
  or sexuality.
- The person is angry at his or her own body
  for signs of sexual development.
- The person engages in ritualistic or self-
  punishing behavior following normal sexual
  behavior.
- The person destroys evidence of sexual
  behavior.
- The person threatens consenting sexual partners not to tell other people about their sexual activity.
- The person exhibits selective negative knowledge about sexuality.

When this information is not taken into
consideration, the therapist becomes yet another
person who forces an individual through a clinical procedure or program "for his or her own
good." For the individual to learn, he or she must
be prepared and be able to cope emotionally with

the curriculum. It may be considered cruel to show sexually explicit material or present sexually liberal attitudes to an individual who has been taught that sexuality is always wrong, that sexual body parts are disgusting or dirty, and that sexual activity is sinful.

Sex education, then, begins with the development of a safe environment and is considered by the clinical staff as a therapeutic process more than as an educative process. Sex education begins not with discussion of ovaries and testicles but with a development of openness and trust within the group (or between therapist and individual); as such, it starts with less stressful subjects. The first two pieces in the sex education process are Feelings Education (Ludwig, 1991; Ludwig & Hingsburger, 1989) and Self-Concept/Assertiveness Training (Stangle, 1991). Feelings Education aims to teach individuals with disabilities about the acceptability of all feelings and the need to express those feelings. One particularly important aspect of the curriculum is teaching that suppressed feelings lead to dangerous behaviors. This concept is of great importance for sex offenders, many of whom offend when they are angry or frustrated. To demonstrate the effect of suppressed feelings, the instructor holds a balloon and then asks the participants to talk about what makes them angry. At each example of things that make people angry, the instructor blows a puff of air into the balloon. Soon the balloon is close to bursting. The participants are asked what will happen if more air is added to the balloon. They all are aware that it will burst, so they are asked to suggest ideas for letting air out of the balloon. For each suggestion, some air is released from the balloon until it is deflated.

This example, obviously, is about more than anger; it is about building a group process and developing group cooperation. The participants learn to work together and share aspects of their lives and feelings in an atmosphere that encourages participation and listening. During the first few classes, related but nonsexual issues are discussed, and there is the opportunity for the establishment of a group that supports and understands anxiety, anger, and fear. This is the kind of environment in which sex education can be offered. It is important to remember that sex education done well changes attitudes, increases knowledge, and develops confidence. These outcomes can be accomplished only by recognizing the confusing and conflicting emotional responses that people whose experiences of sexuality have been either victimization or punishment will have when presented positive sexual messages. The *process* is more important than the curriculum. A variety of curricula have been mentioned, and most are quite thorough in their presentation of sexual information. There are, however, a few areas that often need much more work for healthy attitudes to develop.

Masturbation

The most problematic subject for an individual to learn new attitudes about may be masturbation. Almost all offenders—deviant or not—have negative attitudes toward masturbation when they are first referred to the clinic. Beyond the typical myths about blindness, deafness, and baldness as a result of masturbation, many have been told that the behavior will lead to jail, loss of services, and family disappointment. The threats are numerous and often have had devastating results on the individuals' behavior. From bizarre masturbatory habits to "humping" against furniture or other people (as a result of having learned not to touch the genitals) to genital self-injury, individuals have attempted to follow the "rule" of not touching the genitals and yet deal with the sexual drive.

Using pictures of masturbation from the various curricula is often effective in introducing the subject but may not help the individual to accept the behavior as typical and valuable. Reluctance to accept masturbation as a healthy alternative to sexual intercourse is very problematic for individuals with a clinical deviance, as masturbatory reconditioning and fantasy training are a major part of arousal-change programming; without acceptance of masturbation, this intervention will be impossible. One of the intervention aids developed through the clinic is a videotape of a man masturbating (Hingsburger & Woods, 1995). This videotape is different from others that are available in that the model discusses myths about masturbation, talks about the realities of sharing space with others, emphasizes privacy, and demonstrates gentle masturbation through to completion. This videotape has shown immediate results in giving new attitudinal information regarding masturbation. It is one thing for a therapist to sit in an office and say that masturbation is acceptable and another for a person to watch someone talk about masturbation and demonstrate how it is done in a gentle and fulfilling manner.

Homosexuality

Given the long history of institutionalization of people who have disabilities, a frank and honest presentation about homosexuality is mandatory. The fact is that even in community agencies, the individual has a greater opportunity to engage in homosexual behavior than in heterosexual behavior. Harsh or negative attitudes toward sexuality that lead to sex segregation have not led to a cessation of sexual behavior; instead they have led to increased prevalence of homosexual behavior.

In work regarding homosexuality, a distinction is made between homosexuality and homosexual behavior. What separates the two is that homosexual behavior is accompanied by heterosexual fantasy, whereas sexually expressed homosexuality is accompanied by homosexual fantasy. This may seem confusing, and indeed it is. The clinic's therapist does not accept a history of homosexual behavior or even a stated homosexual orientation as necessarily the individual's "natural" orientation. Although the clinic accepts homosexuality as a valued form of sexual expression, therapists need to be careful in making assumptions regarding the individual's opportunities to be heterosexual.

Should a person be homosexual, he or she will be exposed to the same degree of homophobic attitudes as gay people in the larger society. As a result, he or she may develop self-hatred as a response to a barrage of hateful messages about homosexuality (Hingsburger, 1999). Part of the clinician's work is to help the individual come to terms with his or her sexuality and to express it in appropriate ways (Schneider, 1988). Through the advisory committee, the clinic has received instruction to allow people with developmental disabilities who are gay to receive peer counseling through organizations that serve the gay community. From gaining access to a minister from Metropolitan Community Church (a gay-positive church) to getting counseling from the AIDS Committee of Toronto, people with developmental disabilities who are gay, like other people who are gay, have opportunities to be served in an accepting environment.

Arousal Change

When the clinic began, arousal reduction for inappropriate sexual interest was conducted using punishment-based therapeutic techniques. Covert sensitization with olfactory aversion was a standard part of the intervention (Barlow, 1977). This required the individual to imagine an inappropriate sexual fantasy to create a state of sexual arousal. When aroused, the individual was to signal the therapist, who would present the aversive odor until the individual reported that the inappropriate fantasy had ceased and the arousal was gone. Because individuals might have difficulty with the cognitive and self-reporting demands of this procedure, the clinic changed this procedure somewhat: The individual would be presented with a deviant fantasy, and the odor would be presented at the first offense in the fantasy. For example, if the fantasy involved walking along the beach and seeing lots of children in small swimsuits, the odor would not be presented until the fantasy reached a point at which the individual first approaches a child with intent to molest. Again, it was difficult to measure whether the individual was engaged cognitively in the procedure, and there were no signs that the procedure was working—either by behavior change or as measured on the phallometric test. Because of these factors, olfactory aversion has not been used in the clinic since the mid-1980s. Not only has the cessation of punishment not increased relapse, but also other, more positive techniques have made greater impact on behavior change. Positive intervention strategies have shown success in changing individuals' arousal patterns as indicated on a phallometric test.

Masturbatory Reconditioning and Fantasy Training

A great deal of work is done to teach people with disabilities to use appropriate fantasy during masturbation. When individuals whose test results indicate deviant sexual arousal come to the clinic, part of the assessment interview is to determine offense history as it relates to places where offenses have occurred along with details regarding the choice of victim. These verbal reports are compared with information from the phallometric measure; there seldom has been variance between the subjective reports and the objective tests. In doing this interview, the therapist gains as much information as possible about masturbatory habits. Of primary interest is how often the person masturbates and the nature of the fantasy material used.

Although some individuals report that they masturbate only to "pictures in their head," more common is that they have put together some kind of masturbatory material. Pedophiles may have large stashes of pictures of young children gleaned from magazines and newspapers. Some of these have been found in wallets and are used as masturbatory materials in the workplace, bus stations, and other public places. Individuals who are aroused by sexual violence may rent movies that focus on sexually violent acts. Still others use telephone sex lines that tell stories about violence, rape, and child sex. For all of these individuals, the accessibility of deviant materials is much greater than accessibility of nonviolent, age-appropriate erotica. Because of the nature of deviance, materials that others may find sexually neutral, such as television shows that portray violence or that have children responding with "cute" but "coquettish" mannerisms, often are very arousing to those who have a clinical deviance. Thus, those who do exhibit deviant arousal are able to find "erotically charged" material in catalogs, in television programs, and even on the covers of children's magazines (Money, Wainwright, & Hingsburger, 1991).

Part of the work of the clinician is to teach the individual to find age-appropriate materials that are interesting and sexually stimulating. Usually, a contract is made between the therapist and the individual: The individual agrees to relinquish all materials currently used for masturbation, and the therapist agrees to provide other, appropriate explicit materials. The therapist works very closely with the individual to find materials that are potentially arousing (Jehu, 1979). Some of the strategies used are described in the next sections. It is important to note, though, that these procedures are used only with those who are already using deviant pictures, telephone sex lines, and pornographic videotapes of questionable content. These procedures are not used with all who come into treatment, and the use of these procedures is reviewed carefully.

Masturbation Boards

The individual and the therapist look through erotic magazines (the clinic does not use materials showing sexual intercourse; the magazines that the clinic uses have pictures of nude models), and the individual points to pictures of people whom he or she finds "handsome" or "pretty." If these models clearly are adults, then they are cut from the magazines and taped or glued to a small piece of bristol board. Pictures are chosen until there are a number of appropriate stimuli on the board. This board then can be used by the individual in a private place in his or her home. Prior to implementing this strategy, the therapist should ensure that the individual has a private place at home to masturbate and to store masturbatory materials.

Censored Magazines

For some individuals who prefer to use magazines, the clinic purchases magazines and then censors all pictures that may have models who look very young and all cartoons and stories with questionable content. The individual can turn in these magazines for new magazines.

Erotic Audiotapes

Some individuals prefer auditory stimuli (often, these are individuals who have huge telephone bills from telephone sex lines), and they work with their therapist to note which kind of "stories" they like. Audiotapes then are made by a clinic representative who does not work with the person in treatment. The therapist's voice should not be used on the erotic tapes as this may create unwanted boundary issues and promote inappropriate behavior in therapeutic sessions. The audiotapes give the individuals a strong erotic story that uses content that they have indicated is arousing but that clearly is appropriate.

Selected Videotapes

If the individual is renting erotic videotapes from a local video store, then an agreement is reached to allow the therapist the opportunity either to preview the videotapes or to provide videotapes that have only appropriate images on them.

Reasons for Masturbatory Reconditioning and Fantasy Training

The previously described procedures do a number of things. First, they give the therapist a great deal of control over the masturbatory fantasies used. Again it must be stated that these procedures are used for individuals who are clinically deviant and whose behavior has injured others. For these individuals, learning to become aroused by sexual material that is appropriate is an important clinical goal. First, it can be assumed that if they are deviant, then either they are using deviant fantasies to become aroused or they are using materials that feed the deviance. If this is the case, then therapeutic control over masturbatory material is not as Draconian as it may seem. Second, the actual work of creating new materials communicates a great deal of acceptance of sexuality and gives the clear message that the individual is not being asked to stop having sexual feelings. Instead, the individual has clear, physical evidence of acceptance of his or her sexuality, within appropriate bounds. Third, the presence of the material in the individual's home also communicates that, in addition to the therapist, the home environment welcomes an appropriate sexual outlet. This message may be the most important, as the individual's history within housing agencies might have been quite different.

Covert Sensitization

Covert sensitization is still used, but the olfactory aversion component is no longer part of the process. In the form used at the clinic, covert sensitization is conducted using stories in which behaviors lead to punishment and stories in which behaviors are entirely positive and acceptable. In the clinic's punishment scenarios, the therapist presents a fantasy. At first point of offense, instead of olfactory aversion, the therapist changes his or her voice to describe strongly the individual as being caught, punished, and sent to jail. Individuals often report that the story of being caught and going to jail is more punishing than any smell that has ever been presented. It may be that the use of a punishing consequence in the story is educational because the individual learns that his or her behavior has real consequences that are quite painful. It also may be that the individual never before has understood the consequences of acting on his or her deviant sexual fantasy.

Anti-androgen Medication

The clinic has never recognized anti-androgen medication as a therapy per se; instead, it considers the use of this medication as an adjunct to therapy. When a person first comes to the clinic and is being assessed, anti-androgen medication may be used as a means of giving some control over the inappropriate behavior. During therapy, a goal is to reduce and discontinue the medication as the individual learns other ways to cope with the deviant arousal.

MEASURING INTERVENTION SUCCESS

Given that objective measures are used in the intervention process, success is measured by comparing pre- and posttesting in sex education, card sort tests, and phallometric measures. Although these are important, they should not be considered as the sole measure of success. A person in intervention is deemed to be successful if he or she gains greater access to the community, demonstrates and reports use of relapse strategies, and remains offense-free.

Individual Gains Greater Access to the Community

If during and after intervention the individual has earned greater access to the community and if quality of life has returned to equal to or greater than what it was at the time of the offense, then the intervention is deemed successful. It must be recognized that there needs to be a process that enables the individual to earn greater access to the community (Hingsburger, Nethercott, Naylor, Hillis-Ormested, & Tough, 1994). This process typically begins with the individual's choosing a place that he or she would like to go unaccompanied in the community, and this is achieved through a simple task analysis program. The community spot (e.g., convenience store, bank, post office) is checked to ensure that it is not in a high-risk area (e.g., near a park, school, or playground), and then the route is mapped.

Each step of the outing is broken into steps, and clearly set criteria are drawn so that the individual knows which behaviors are acceptable. Staff accompany the person on the trip, reinforce all appropriate social behaviors, and document the individual's responses to people met on the outing. This is done even if the individual had full community access prior to the offense. This process gives the clinic documented evidence that the behavior was taken seriously and that attempts were made to ensure that the community was kept safe. As the individual proceeds through the task analysis, the criteria for success of each step are increased as the individual is allowed longer and longer periods of time out of sight of a supervising staff member. At the final step, the individual knows that he or she is being watched at least during 1 in 10 trips to that particular spot in the community. Once successful, other community outings are targeted. This process gives the individual hope and an understanding that there is a point to the therapy and education. It also allows the clinic a means of coming to trust the individual in the community again.

Individual Demonstrates and Reports Use of Relapse Strategies

If an individual is caught in a high-risk situation on an outing to the community or in a social event, then the intervention is considered to be successful when the strategies learned to remove oneself from the situation are used. The clinic encourages individuals to admit that they were in a risky situation and report how it was handled. Life comes with risk, and individuals who are pedophiles are going to find themselves in contact with children no matter how much planning is done. One individual happily reported that at a Christmas party, a child approached him for a hug, and he redirected the hug to a handshake and then directed the child back to his parents. The individual was rightly proud of his behavior, and his ability to report the occurrence showed that he understood risk and how to handle it.

Individual Remains Offense-Free

It may be tempting to measure success by whether there are charges against the individual who is living in the community. This is naive. Many individuals came to the clinic because the agencies became aware of an offense but the legal establishment did not decide to press charges. In two situations, the clinic has had individuals who reoffended but were not charged. The offense rate—not the charge rate—determines success.

CONCLUSION

The clinic's success rate in working with people with disabilities who have sexually offended is very high. This is because many of the individuals were not clinically deviant, and therefore systemic or educational changes could and would make a great deal of difference in their ability to live successfully and offense-free in community environments. This is important to note and should be a caveat to agencies that try to sidestep the sexuality of those in their care through restricting access to sexual opportunities; writing negative policies; or attempting to punish, medicate, or program away sexual impulses. This has not worked; in fact, this may cause offenses to occur. Human beings are sexual. That statement, although obvious, has not been fully accepted by those who provide human services to people with disabilities. Until it is, agencies that attempt to repress and oppress the sexuality of those whom they serve may be in part responsible for victimization of community members by the very people whom the agencies are supposed to help.

REFERENCES

Azzopardi, S., Horsely, P., & Pietsch, D. (1990). *So you won't get AIDS . . . STD/AIDS prevention education for people with intellectual disabilities.* Victoria, British Columbia, Canada: Family Planning Association of Victoria.

Barlow, D.H. (1977). Assessment of sexual behavior. In A.R. Ciminero, K.S. Calhoun, & H.E. Adams (Eds.), *Handbook of behavioral assessment* (pp. 461–509). New York: Wiley-Interscience.

Benson, B.A. (1995). Psychosocial interventions update. *Habilitative Mental Healthcare Newsletter, 14,* 110–113.

Brown, G.T., Carney, P., Cortis, J.M., Metz, L.L., & Petrie, A.M. (1994). *Human sexuality handbook: Guiding people towards positive expressions of sexuality.* Springfield, MA: The Association for Community Living.

Champagne, E., & Walker-Hirsch, L. (1981). *Circles 1: Intimacy and relationships.* Santa Barbara, CA: James Stanfield Associates.

Champagne, E., & Walker-Hirsch, L. (1986). *Circles 2: Stop abuse.* Santa Barbara, CA: James Stanfield Associates.

Champagne, E., & Walker-Hirsch, L. (1988). *Circles 3: Safer ways.* Santa Barbara, CA: James Stanfield Associates.

Coleman, E.M., & Murphy, W.D. (1980). A survey of sexual attitudes and sex education programs among facilities for the mentally retarded. *Applied Research in Mental Retardation, 1,* 269–276.

Cook, J.W., Altman, K., Shaw, J., & Blaylock, M. (1978). Use of contingent lemon juice to eliminate public masturbation by a severely retarded boy. *Behaviour Research and Therapy, 16,* 131–134.

Danica, E. (1990). *Don't: A woman's word.* Toronto, Ontario, Canada: McLelland and Stewart.

Demetral, G. (1994). A training methodology for establishing reliable self-monitoring with the sex offender who is developmentally disabled. *Habilitative Mental Healthcare Newsletter, 13,* 57–60.

Durana, I.L., & Cuvo, A.J. (1980). A comparison of procedures for decreasing public disrobing of an institutionalized profoundly mentally retarded woman. *Mental Retardation, 18,* 185–188.

Edwards, J., Wapnick, S., Mock, P., & Whitson, L. (1982). *Feeling free.* Portland, OR: Ednick Communications.

Everstine, D.S., & Everstine, L. (1989). *Sexual trauma in children and adolescents: Dynamics and treatment.* New York: Brunner/Mazel.

Fegan, L., & Rauch, A. (with McCarthy, W.). (1993). *Sexuality and people with intellectual disability* (2nd ed.). Baltimore: Paul H. Brookes Publishing Co.

Gochros, H.L., Gochros, J.S., & Fischer, J. (1986). *Helping the sexually oppressed.* Upper Saddle River, NJ: Prentice-Hall.

Griffiths, D., Hingsburger, D., & Christian, R. (1985). Treating developmentally handicapped sexual offenders: The York Behaviour Management Services Treatment Program. *Psychiatric Aspects of Mental Retardation Reviews, 4*(12), 49–52.

Griffiths, D.M., Quinsey, V.L., & Hingsburger, D. (1989). *Changing inappropriate sexual behavior: A community-based approach for persons with developmental disabilities.* Baltimore: Paul H. Brookes Publishing Co.

Haaven, J., Little, R., & Petre-Miller, D. (1990). *Treating intellectually disabled sex offenders: A model residential program.* Orwell, VT: Safer Society.

Hingsburger, D. (1985). From culture to culture: Issues in deinstitutionalization. *Journal of Practical Approaches to Developmental Handicap, 9*(1), 8–11.

Hingsburger, D. (1990). *I contact: Sexuality and people with developmental disabilities.* Mountville, PA: Vida Publishing.

Hingsburger, D. (1992). Erotophobic behavior in people with developmental disabilities. *The Habilitative Mental Healthcare Newsletter, 11*(5), 31–35.

Hingsburger, D. (1993). Staff attitudes, homosexuality and developmental disabilities: A minority within a minority. *The Canadian Journal of Human Sexuality, 2,* 199–222.

Hingsburger, D. (1994). The ring of safety: Teaching people with disabilities to be their own first line of defense. *Developmental Disabilities Bulletin, 22*(2), 72–79.

Hingsburger, D. (1995a). *Hand made love: A guide for teaching about male masturbation through understanding and video.* Eastman, Québec, Canada: Diverse City Press.

Hingsburger, D. (1995b). *Just say know! Understanding and reducing the risk of sexual victimization of people with developmental disabilities.* Eastman, Québec, Canada: Diverse City Press.

Hingsburger, D. (1999). *A real nice but: Articles that inform, inspire and infuriate.* Eastman, Québec, Canada: Diverse City Press.

Hingsburger, D., & Griffiths, D. (1986). Dealing with sexuality in a community residential service. *Psychiatric Aspects of Mental Retardation, 5*(12), 63–68.

Hingsburger, D., Griffiths, D., & Quinsey, V. (1991). Detecting counterfeit deviance: Differentiating sexual deviance from sexual inappropriateness. *The Habilitative Mental Healthcare Newsletter, 10*(9), 51–54.

Hingsburger, D., & Ludwig, S. (1993). *Sexual self advocacy.* East York, Ontario, Canada: SIECCAN.

Hingsburger, D., Nethercott, A., Naylor, D., Hillis-Ormested, T., & Tough, S. (1994). Community access for sex offenders with developmental disabilities: A process for dealing with trust, risk and responsibilities. *The Habilitative Mental Healthcare Newsletter, 13*(6), 98–100.

Hingsburger, D., & Tough, S. (1993). Treating erotophobic behaviour in people with developmental disabilities: A case history and therapeutic model. *The Habilitative Mental Healthcare Newsletter, 12*(3), 33–36.

Hingsburger, D., & Woods, S. (1995). *Hand made love: An instructional video on male masturbation.* Eastman, Québec, Canada: Diverse City Press.

Hutchinson, M. (1990). *The anatomy of sex and power.* New York: William Morrow and Company.

Jackson, J. (1988). *Jim Jackson's model of human genital anatomy.* Cambridge, MA: Jim Jackson and Company.

Jehu, D. (1979). *Sexual dysfunction: A behavioural approach to causation, assessment, and treatment.* New York: John Wiley & Sons.

Johnson, D.M., & Johnson, W.R. (1982). Sexuality and the mentally retarded adolescent. *Pediatric Annual, 11,* 847–853.

Kempton, W. (1988). *Life horizons: 1 and 2. The physiological emotional aspects of being male and female for persons with developmental and learning disabilities* [Slides and teacher's guide]. Santa Monica, CA: Stanfield Film Associates.

Kempton, W. (1993). *Socialization and sexuality: A comprehensive training guide for professionals helping people with disabilities that hinder learning.* Haverford, MA: Kempton.

Knopp, F.H., & Lakey, L.B. (1987). *Sexual offenders identified as intellectually disabled: A summary of data from 40 treatment providers.* Orwell, VT: Safer Society.

Law, D.R., & Osbourn, C.A. (1983). How to build and operate a behavioral laboratory to evaluate and treat sexual deviance. In J.G. Greer & I.R. Stuart (Eds.), *The sexual aggressor: Current perspectives on treatment* (pp. 293–335). New York: VanNostrand Reinhold.

Long, J.W., & Rybacki, J.J. (1995). *The essential guide to prescription drugs: Everything you need to know for safe drug use.* New York: HarperCollins.

Love, B. (1992). *Encyclopedia of unusual sex practices.* Fort Lee, NJ: Barricade Books.

Ludwig, S. (1991). *Sexuality: A curriculum for individuals who have difficulty with traditional learning methods.* York, Ontario, Canada: York Public Health.

Ludwig, S., & Hingsburger, D. (1989). Preparation for counseling and psychotherapy: Teaching about feelings. *Psychiatric Aspects of Mental Retardation Reviews, 8*(1), 1–7.

Ludwig, S., & Hingsburger, D. (1993). *Being sexual.* East York, Ontario, Canada: SIECCAN.

Lusthaus, E.W. (1991). Drastic actions: The results of viewing people as less than human. *Developmental Disabilities, 19,* 28–48.

Monat-Haller, R.K. (1992). *Understanding and expressing sexuality: Responsible choices for individuals with developmental disabilities.* Baltimore: Paul H. Brookes Publishing Co.

Money, J., Wainwright, G., & Hingsburger, D. (1991). *The breathless orgasm: A lovemap biography of asphyxiophilia.* Buffalo, NY: Prometheus Press.

Morris, J. (1991). *Pride against prejudice: Transforming attitudes to disability.* Philadelphia: New Society Publishers.

Myers, B.A. (1991). Treatment of sexual offenses by persons with developmental disabilities. *American Journal on Mental Retardation, 95,* 563–568.

Parsons, H. (1989). *Intellectually handicapped sex offender.* Mystic, PA: Ross, Loss & Associates.

Quinsey, V.L., Chaplin, T.C., & Varney, G.W. (1981). A comparison of rapists' and non sex offenders' sexual preferences for mutually consenting sex, rape and physical abuse of women. *Behavioral Assessment, 3,* 127–135.

Quinsey, V.L., & Varney, G.W. (1977). Social skills game: A general method for modeling and practice of adaptive behavior. *Behavior Therapy, 8,* 279–281.

Rowe, W.S., & Savage, S. (1987). *Sexuality and the developmentally handicapped: A guidebook for health care professionals.* Queenston, NY: Edwin Mellen Press.

Schneider, M.S. (1988). *Often invisible: Counseling gay and lesbian youth.* Toronto, Ontario, Canada: Central Toronto Youth Services.

Scotti, J.R., Nangle, D.W., Masia, C.L., Ellis, J.T., Ujcich, K.J., Giacoletti, A.M., Vittimberga, G.L., & Carr-Nangle, R. (1997). Providing an AIDS education and skills training program to persons with mild developmental disabilities. *Education and Training in Mental Retardation and Developmental Disabilities, 32,* 113–128.

Scotti, J.R., Speaks, L.V., Masia, C.L., Boggess, J.T., & Drabman, R. (1996). The educational effects of providing AIDS-risk information to persons with developmental disabilities: An exploratory study. *Education and Training in Mental Retardation and Developmental Disabilities, 31,* 115–122.

Scotti, J.R., Ujcich, K.J., Nangle, D.W., Weigle, K.L., Ellis, J.T., Kirk, K.S., Vittimberga, G.L., Giacoletti, A.M., & Carr-Nangle, R. (1996). Evaluation of an HIV-AIDS education program for family-based foster care providers. *Mental Retardation, 34,* 75–82.

Senn, C.Y. (1988). *Vulnerable: Sexual abuse and people with an intellectual handicap.* Downsview, Ontario, Canada: G. Allan Roeher Institute.

Smith, D., Valenti-Hein, D.C., & Hellar, T. (1985). Interpersonal competencies of retarded adults: Implications for social, vocational and sexual adjustment. In M. Signma (Ed.), *Children with dual diagnosis: Mental retardation and mental illness* (pp. 72–79). New York: Grune & Stratton.

Sobsey, D. (1994). *Violence and abuse in the lives of people with developmental disabilities: The end of silent acceptance?* Baltimore: Paul H. Brookes Publishing Co.

Sobsey, D., Wells, D., Lucardie, R., & Mansell, S. (1995). *Violence and disability: An annotated bibliography.* Baltimore: Paul H. Brookes Publishing Co.

Stangle, J. (1991). *Special education: Secondary family life and sexual health: A curriculum for grades 7–12.* Seattle: Seattle Public Schools.

Stimpson, L., & Best, M.C. (1991). *Courage above all: Sexual assault against women with disabilities.* Toronto, Ontario, Canada: DisAbled Women's Network.

Ward, K.M., Heffern, S.J., Wilcox, D.A., McElwee, D., Dowrick, P., Brown, T.D., Jones, M.J., & Johnson, C.L. (1992). *Managing inappropriate sexual behavior: Supporting individuals with developmental disabilities in the community.* Anchorage, AK: ASET.

West, R.R. (1979). The sexual behaviour of the institutionalized severely retarded. *Australian Journal of Mental Retardation, 5,* 11–13.

Wish, J., McCombs, K., & Edmonson, B. (1980). *Socio-sexual Knowledge and Attitude Test.* Chicago: Stoelting.

Chapter 11

Communication-Based Interventions for Students with Sensory Impairments and Challenging Behavior

Denise Berotti & V. Mark Durand

The assessment of and intervention for severe challenging behavior, such as self-injury and aggression, continue to be major concerns for those who work with individuals with developmental disabilities. Fortunately, developments in the understanding of the nature and function of challenging behavior have been made (e.g., Carr, 1977; Durand, 1987; Iwata, Dorsey, Slifer, Bauman, & Richman, 1982). These advances have resulted in the development of interventions that are based on the notion that challenging behaviors often serve a meaningful purpose or function for individuals. Successful interventions for individuals who engage in challenging behavior to obtain attention, for example, have included noncontingent presentation of attention (Vollmer, Iwata, Zarcone, Smith, & Mazaleski, 1993), presentation of attention contingent on the nonoccurrence of challenging behavior (Vollmer et al., 1993), and the presentation of attention contingent on the occurrence of an alternative behavior (Durand, Crimmins, Caulfield, &

Taylor, 1989; Vollmer, Iwata, Smith, & Rodgers, 1992). All of these interventions provide the individual with the variable that is maintaining the problem behavior (i.e., attention) so that he or she no longer needs to rely on challenging behavior to obtain the attention. Similar interventions for behavior problems maintained by escape from work and access to tangible items also have been demonstrated to be successful (e.g., Kennedy & Haring, 1993; Kennedy & Itkonen, 1993).

A related intervention that is based on the assessment of the function of the problem behavior and that has generated a great deal of empirical support is *functional communication training* (Carr et al., 1994; Durand, 1990). The goal of this intervention is to identify the specific purpose of the challenging behavior and then to teach the individual a new communicative response that serves the same function as the problem behavior. For example, an individual who engages in aggression to escape from a

This work was supported in part by the U.S. Department of Education Office of Special Education and Rehabilitative Services (Grant No. H086G00005); however, the opinions expressed here do not necessarily reflect the policy of the U.S. Department of Education, and no official endorsement should be inferred.

task might be taught to request a brief break from this work.

Functional communication training occasionally has been implemented by teaching individuals to request verbally the variables that are maintaining their problem behavior (e.g., Carr & Durand, 1985; Durand & Carr, 1992; Mace & Lalli, 1991). This approach, however, has been limited to individuals who have adequate verbal skills. Attempts to teach individuals with severe communication deficits to request verbally the variables that previously were obtained by challenging behavior will fail if their speech is difficult to understand (Carr et al., 1994).

To address this problem, alternatives to verbal speech have been used to teach individuals with severe communication deficits to make requests and, thus, reduce the occurrence of the targeted excess behavior. People have been taught to make requests by using sign language (e.g., Bird, Dores, Moniz, & Robinson, 1989; Durand & Kishi, 1987; Horner & Budd, 1985), gestures (Carr & Kemp, 1989; Carr et al., 1994), and communication books (Hunt, Alwell, & Goetz, 1988).

Despite these positive outcomes, however, the literature on augmentative communication suggests that silent communication systems, such as picture books and signing, that are used to teach nonverbal individuals to communicate may have some significant limitations. Problems may occur if, for example, individuals are taught to use communication systems with which most people are not familiar (e.g., sign language [Bryen & Joyce, 1986; Mirenda, Iacono, & Williams, 1990; Rotholz, Berkowitz, & Burberry, 1989]). An individual who uses such a system would continue to be unable to communicate with untrained people, and presumably challenging behavior would continue in their presence (Durand, Berotti, & Weiner, 1993). Even people who are familiar with sign language may have difficulty responding to communication attempts if the individual has motor deficits that interfere with intelligible signing (Bryen, Goldman, & Quinlisk-Gill, 1988; Bryen & Joyce, 1986; Rotholz et al., 1989).

Another problem with silent communication systems is that they have the potential to be ignored, particularly when the listener is not oriented toward the speaker at the time of the communication attempt (Calculator & Dollaghan, 1982; Steege et al., 1990). Unless the individual is taught how to get the attention of the listener before he or she makes a statement or request, the communicative attempt likely will fail (Doss & Reichle, 1989). In sum, the effects of functional communication training are limited to the extent that people in the environment are able to understand and respond to a speaker's requests in an appropriate manner. If people in the speaker's environment are unable to respond to communication, then individuals will be likely to continue to rely on problem behavior to express their wants—and they will remain dependent on others to interact with untrained people.

One solution to these problems is to teach students to request the variables that are maintaining their challenging behavior through the use of vocal-output devices that emit clear, spoken English when activated (Durand, 1993; Steege et al., 1990; Wacker et al., 1990). Work by our research group was designed to replicate and extend this work by evaluating the long-term maintenance of functional communication training as an intervention for severe behavior problems displayed by students with multiple disabilities. Advantages of vocal-output devices include the following:

1. Listeners do not require training to be able to understand the messages.
2. Adaptive equipment can be used to make communicating easy even for individuals with the most severe physical disabilities.
3. The vocal output allows the person to get the attention of a listener, even when the listener is not oriented toward the individual.

Individuals who use these devices should be able to communicate successfully both to trained staff and to untrained community members.

Described in this chapter are research efforts with a group of individuals who have significant sensory impairments in addition to challenging behavior. In this research program, students were taught to use commercially available vocal-output devices (Speak Easy, Voicemate, Parrot, Wolf communication board, or Introtalker) to elicit the variables that were maintaining their challenging behavior in the classroom. The students were also taught to use their devices with untrained people in the community. The research program was developed to address the needs of students in inner-city New York public schools who have multiple disabilities and engage in challenging behavior.

PARTICIPANTS

Twenty-two students from six inner-city public schools participated in the program. Descriptive information for each student who was involved in the program is displayed in Table 1. Students were between 6 and 18 years of age. All students were diagnosed with multiple disabilities. More specific, each student was diagnosed with a sensory impairment (hearing or visual impairments) and mental retardation requiring limited to extensive supports. Several of the students had additional diagnoses, including cerebral palsy and autism. Finally, all students engaged in challenging behavior, such as self-injury, tantrums, and aggression.

THE PROGRAM

The program was implemented over a 3-year period (1990–1993). Each year, approximately seven new students joined the project. There were several goals for the program:

1. To educate and train professionals and paraprofessionals in the assessment and intervention of challenging behavior

Table 1. Descriptive data

Name	Chronological age (years)	Mental age (months)	Diagnoses
Art	9	9	Severe mental retardation (MR), hearing and visual impairments
Carol	16	No testing	Severe MR, visual impairment
Bob	16	No testing	Severe MR, cerebral palsy, visual impairment
Donna	18	24	Severe MR, visual and hearing impairments
Jane	10	No testing	Severe MR, visual and hearing impairments
John	17	No testing	Severe MR, visual impairment
Mary	8	No testing	Severe MR, hearing impairment, blindness, cerebral palsy
Nat	12	7	Severe/profound MR, hearing and visual impairments
Rose	6	No testing	Severe MR, cerebral palsy, visual impairment
Kathy	11	18	Severe MR, visual impairment
Nancy	9	18	Moderate/severe MR, hearing impairment
Rob	15	24	Profound MR, visual impairment
Rick	7	18	Profound MR, blindness, cerebral palsy
David	6	No testing	Severe/profound MR, visual impairment
Teri	18	No testing	Severe MR, visual impairment
Sam	13	9	Profound MR, visual impairment
Jim	15	18	Autistic disorder, severe/profound MR, hearing impairment
Lisa	6	18	Severe MR, visual impairment
Juan	7	16	Moderate/severe MR, hearing impairment, peripheral retinal deficits
Kate	7	No testing	Severe MR, hearing impairment
Ray	12	No testing	Severe MR, hearing impairment
Chris	10	No testing	Severe/profound MR, bilateral ear tubes

2. To assess the variables that were maintaining the students' challenging behavior
3. To develop and implement communication-based interventions for the students' challenging behavior
4. To assess the generalization and maintenance of these interventions

For each of the 3 years of the program, representatives from the board of education identified the public schools that had the greatest need of support for students with multiple disabilities and severe challenging behavior. The principals of these schools were asked to nominate students who displayed each of the following characteristics:

1. Severe developmental disabilities
2. Hearing or visual impairments
3. Limited communicative abilities
4. Challenging behavior

All identified students for whom parental permission was received were included in the program.

STAFF TRAINING

A major goal of this program was to educate and train individuals who worked with the students on a daily basis in the assessment and intervention of challenging behavior. This was done in two ways. First, all teachers and assistant teachers attended an all-day workshop on the assessment of and intervention for challenging behavior. Staff were taught to implement functional communication training (Durand, 1990). More specific, they were taught how to identify the variables that were maintaining their students' challenging behavior by using various assessment methods and to replace the challenging behavior with functionally equivalent communicative responses. In addition, all staff received ongoing training in the classroom for up to 3 years, as needed.

Teachers were asked to identify their students' behaviors that they believed were the most problematic in terms of harm to the student or to others (e.g., self-injury, aggression) or in terms

of interfering with educational goals (e.g., frequent crying). Teachers identified one behavior or more for each student.

Self-injurious behavior (e.g., hand biting, head banging) was identified for 12 of the students (55%), aggressive behavior (e.g., scratches others, bites others) was identified for 8 of the students (36%), and having a tantrum (e.g., screaming, crying) was identified for 6 of the students (27%). Hand waving, noncompliance, and property destruction each were identified for 1 student.

FUNCTIONAL ASSESSMENT

It is widely agreed that interventions for challenging behavior should be based on an assessment of the variables that are controlling the targeted behavior (e.g., Carr et al., 1994; Durand, 1990; O'Neill, Horner, Albin, Storey, & Sprague, 1990). To assess the function of a problem behavior, the antecedents and the consequences of that behavior need to be identified. Challenging behaviors are often found to serve one or more of the following functions:

1. To avoid or escape nonpreferred stimuli (e.g., difficult demands, nonpreferred staff)
2. To gain access to preferred stimuli (e.g., toys, attention)
3. To increase sensory stimulation

Once the purpose of a targeted behavior is understood, individuals can be taught to request appropriately those variables that previously were obtained by the challenging behavior.

To conduct a functional assessment, it is recommended that at least two assessment methods be conducted (Durand, 1990). If two assessment methods agree, then there is greater confidence in the accuracy of the assessment. Consistent with this, a multicomponent assessment was employed. The first component of the functional assessment was the *teacher interview.* Teachers were questioned about the antecedents and the consequences of a student's challenging behavior and were asked to identify the situation in which the student was most likely to exhibit the targeted behavior. The teachers were asked whether the challenging behavior was more frequent during specific situations (e.g., during demands, while alone, during transitions, while waiting, when the student saw something that he or she wanted) or seemed to occur regardless of what was going on around the student. Similarly, the teachers were asked to discuss how other people responded to the occurrence of challenging behavior (e.g., attend to the student, remove demands, provide a favorite item) to identify a consistent pattern of consequent events that might be maintaining the target behavior.

The teacher interviews resulted in initial hypotheses concerning the variables that might be maintaining the challenging behaviors of the students. To increase the probability of an accurate assessment, the Motivation Assessment Scale (MAS; Durand & Crimmins, 1992) was also used to identify the variables that were maintaining the challenging behavior. The MAS consists of 16 questions concerning how an individual would behave in a variety of situations. Raters are asked to indicate how likely, ranging from "never" to "always" on a seven-point, Likert-type scale, a student would be to display a specific problem behavior in each of several situations. The items are organized into four factors, allowing for an assessment of the relative influence that sensory stimulation, escape from demands, social attention, and access to tangibles have on the problem behavior. The MAS has been determined to have adequate interrater and test-retest reliability (Bihm, Kienlen, Ness, & Poindexter, 1991; Durand & Crimmins, 1988; Kearney, 1994). The MAS also has been determined to be valid in terms of predicting how participants would behave in analog situations (Durand & Crimmins, 1988).

The primary teacher and an assistant teacher for each student were asked to complete an MAS for each identified behavior. Teachers were asked to define the identified behavior in specific and observable terms and to indicate the specific environment in which the behavior occurred. The teacher and assistant teacher then independently answered the 16 questions of the MAS. The average score for each of the four factors was calculated, and the rank order of the factors was determined. The factor with the highest

mean score was considered to be the most important variable that was maintaining the problem behavior. If two or more of the factors had equally high scores (within .50 points of each other), then the behavior was considered to be multiply motivated.

The MAS was completed for the 22 students on 29 different behaviors. The teachers identified one problem behavior for 15 of the students, two problem behaviors for 6 students, and three problem behaviors for 1 student. Eighteen of the behaviors (64%) were determined to be either primarily or partially maintained by escape from demands; 13 of the behaviors (46%) were determined to be either primarily or partially maintained by access to tangibles; 13 of the behaviors (46%) were determined to be either primarily or partially maintained by sensory stimulation; and 8 of the behaviors (29%) were determined to be either primarily or partially maintained by social attention. Seventeen of the 29 identified behaviors were considered to be multiply motivated. It should be noted that a form, or topography, of behavior was as likely to serve one function as another.

A final assessment method, employed with most of the students, was direct manipulation of the student's environment to assess for concomitant changes in the rate of challenging behavior. The students were observed during the situation that was suggested by the interview and by the MAS to be very likely to elicit the problem behavior, as well as during a second situation that was believed to be *unlikely* to elicit the challenging behavior. Each situation was presented to the student at least three times across several visits. The sessions were videotaped and scored for the frequency of challenging behavior.

This direct manipulation of situations was conducted for 14 of the 22 students. The functional assessment for the other eight students comprised the teacher interview and the MAS only. For 11 of the students for whom a functional analysis was conducted, a clear distinction in the rate of challenging behavior was observed between the two situations. One of the other students, Jim, engaged in very infrequent yet serious property destruction that could not be easily captured on videotape during the time limits of the sessions. The other two students, Kathy and Nancy, engaged in very high rates of challenging behavior during both situations; all three forms of assessments agreed that their challenging behaviors were multiply motivated.

ILLUSTRATION OF THE FUNCTIONAL ASSESSMENT PROCESS

The evaluation of Lisa's tantrums illustrates the functional assessment process that was used in the program. Lisa was 6 years old when she joined the program, and she had a visual impairment and mental retardation requiring extensive supports. She was referred to the program because of frequent tantrums during which she would drop to the floor and scream. According to her teacher, this behavior interfered a great deal with Lisa's education; in fact, because of her tantrums, the teachers rarely tried to work with her at all. The teacher and the assistant teacher agreed that Lisa most frequently displayed tantrums when demands were made of her and that the tantrums successfully terminated work sessions—suggesting that the tantrums may have been maintained by escape from demands. The MAS was completed by both Lisa's teacher and one of her assistant teachers, and the results were consistent with the teacher interviews: The highest scores on the MAS were accrued on the scale assessing escape from demands.

Finally, Lisa was observed and videotaped during two situations. Each situation was repeated three times. During the first situation, Lisa's teacher was directed to ask Lisa to engage in a task, with frequent demands being made. During the second situation, Lisa was left alone and no one interacted with her. The 10-minute sessions were divided into 10-second intervals for scoring purposes. When directed to work, Lisa engaged in tantrums during an average of 16% of the 10-second intervals, compared with 0% of the intervals when she was left alone.

Taken together, the assessment methods suggested that Lisa's tantrums were maintained by escape from demands. These converging results provided increased confidence in the accuracy of the assessment. For some students, however, the three forms of functional assessment

did not always agree. In these cases, data continued to be collected (i.e., interviews and observations continued) until agreement was reached. Results of the functional assessment then were used to design the most appropriate intervention.

INTERVENTION

Functional Communication Training

Once the presumed variable or variables that were maintaining the targeted behaviors were identified for each student, the students each were provided with a vocal-output device that was programmed to emit one or more phrases that were related to the identified function of their challenging behavior. Because the parents of several of the students, as well as many of the assistant teachers, spoke only Spanish, several of the communication boards were programmed to emit requests in both English and Spanish. This allowed the students to be able to communicate with all of the significant people in their lives, regardless of their primary language.

The students were provided with a variety of communication devices. Vocal messages were programmed or recorded on these devices, and the messages were activated when the student touched the appropriate area of the device. All of the devices had the capability of emitting numerous messages; however, the students in this program were taught to use only from one to six messages, depending on their needs and abilities.

Following distribution of the communication devices, the teachers and the assistant teachers participated in a series of in-class training sessions. The goal of this training was for the teachers to learn how to implement functional communication training with the assistance of the vocal-output devices (see Durand, 1990, for a complete description of the general procedures). The initial training session with the students was conducted by project staff from the University at Albany. Following the initial demonstration of functional communication training, all subsequent training sessions with the students were conducted by the teachers and assistant teachers. Teachers were provided with step-by-step instructions on the specific procedures of functional communication training, including the criteria for gradually fading physical and verbal prompts. The role of the university staff throughout the program was as consultants, visiting approximately once per month to demonstrate procedures, answer questions, provide feedback, modify the intervention if necessary, and videotape the progress of the students.

Training sessions were conducted during the situation in which the student displayed the most frequent problem behavior. For example, one 9-year-old boy named Art was observed to engage in head hitting when he had nothing to do. The results of the teacher interview and the MAS suggested that this behavior was maintained by sensory stimulation. Thus, intervention for Art began by briefly leaving him alone without providing him with any activities. In a similar fashion, intervention for students who engaged in problem behavior to obtain their favorite tangible item began by displaying that item to the students yet keeping it out of their reach, and intervention for students who engaged in problem behavior to obtain social attention began by having a favorite person nearby but not paying attention to the student. Finally, students who engaged in challenging behavior during demand situations were asked to complete a small amount of work.

Once the students had spent a *brief* amount of time in the situation that elicited their problem behavior, they were prompted to use their communication devices to request the variable that was maintaining their targeted behavior. Art, for example, was physically and verbally prompted to activate his Wolf communication board, which was programmed with the phrase, "May I have the light box?" This prompt occurred *prior to* any sign that Art was becoming distressed in that situation. The light box was Art's favorite toy and apparently provided him with an alternative form of sensory stimulation. A student's request was quickly granted, and the procedure was repeated. As the students began to activate the boards more independently, verbal and physical prompts were faded. Students who engaged in challenging behavior that was assessed to be multiply motivated were then taught to make requests in the additional relevant situations. Table 2 displays each student's primary challenging be-

havior, the primary motivation of that behavior, and the first functionally equivalent request that they were taught in the program. (Several students were taught to make additional requests after they mastered the first request.)

Adaptive Modifications to the Communication Devices

The students in this program all had sensory impairments and required special efforts to help them use their communication devices effectively. Seventeen of the 22 students who participated in the program had visual impairments. These students needed help with finding their boards and learning how to activate them. By attaching various fabrics to the communication devices, the students could learn to search for their boards and to find the area of the device that needed to be pressed to activate the appropriate message.

Rob, for example, had a severe visual impairment and appeared to be unable to see his communication board. Rob engaged in frequent aggression that was determined to be maintained by escape from demands and access to favorite foods. Intervention began by teaching Rob to request a break from work. When Rob touched the left side of his communication board, it emitted the phrase, "May I have a break?" To teach Rob where he needed to apply pressure, the left side of the board was covered with a thin piece of corduroy. Eventually, Rob learned to search his desktop for the corduroy and request a break. After Rob became proficient at this response, a second phrase was added to his board. The right side of his board was now covered with a thin piece of fine sandpaper, and the board was programmed to emit the phrase, "May I have something to eat, please?" With frequent training sessions, Rob learned to associate the corduroy with a break and the sandpaper with food.

Hearing impairments also may have made learning to use the communication devices a little more difficult for some students. Although the primary function of the vocal output was to get the listener's attention and to make a clear request of the listener, sound also appears to provide useful feedback that may help students learn to use vocal-output devices (Locke & Mi-

Table 2. Primary challenging behavior, function, and functionally equivalent communication responses

Name	Challenging behavior	Primary function	First functionally equivalent response taught
Art	Head hitting	Sensory	"May I have the light box?"
Carol	Hand biting	Escape and tangibles	"I'd like to listen to music."
Bob	Pushing others	Escape	"Music, please."
Donna	Scratching others	Tangibles	"I'd like something to do."
Jane	Eye poking	Sensory	"I'm bored."
John	Head hitting	Escape	"May I have a break?"
Mary	Hand biting	Escape	"May I have a break?"
Nat	Scratching others	Escape	"May I have a break?"
Rose	Head banging	Escape	"May I have a break?"
Kathy	Hand biting	Attention	"Please come here."
Nancy	Head banging	Attention	"Please come here."
Rob	Scratching others	Escape	"May I have a break?"
Rick	Hand biting	Escape	"May I have a break?"
David	Screaming	Tangibles	"May I have that back?"
Teri	Tantrums	Escape	"May I have a break?"
Sam	Face slapping	Escape	"May I have a break?"
Jim	Throwing objects	Tangibles	"May I have that?"
Lisa	Tantrums	Escape	"May I have a break?"
Juan	Tantrums	Tangibles	"May I have that?"
Kate	Tantrums	Tangibles	"May I have something else?"
Ray	Face slapping	Tangibles	"May I get some water?"
Chris	Tantrums	Escape	"May I have a break?"

renda, 1988). The vocal output emitted from the devices provides students with feedback indicating that they were successful in activating the message. Ten of the students who participated in the program could not benefit fully from that contingent feedback because of hearing impairments; therefore, the devices of those students who were identified as having some level of hearing impairment were adjusted to the maximum volume in hopes of providing the students with some degree of auditory feedback upon activating the board. Several students, however, appeared not to be able to hear any sounds. To provide those students who had severe hearing impairments but not severe visual impairments with a stimulus to associate with their message, colorful pictures that represented the target phrase were placed on their devices.

Nancy, for example, engaged in frequent tantrums and occasional head banging when her favorite teacher walked out of the room. Her device, therefore, was programmed to emit the phrase, "Please come here." Nancy appeared to be unable to hear her device, although she could see well. To assist Nancy with learning to use her communication board, a photograph of her favorite teacher was taped over the part of the board that needed to be pressed to activate the message requesting attention from her teacher. Nancy quickly learned to associate pressing the picture with the presence of the teacher. Later, Nancy was similarly taught to request a soda and to request a break from work. Our observations were consistent with the finding that textured communication systems are useful for students with visual impairments (Murray-Branch, Udavari-Solner, & Bailey, 1991).

CURRICULUM MODIFICATION

The primary emphasis of this program was to teach the students to request with the communication devices the variables that were maintaining their problem behaviors; however, recommendations occasionally were made concerning the curriculum being offered. Several authors have described individuals whose challenging behaviors occurred in the presence of certain stimuli (e.g., certain instructional programs, certain staff) and how these behaviors have been reduced by modifying those stimuli or removing them altogether from the individual's environment (e.g., Dunlap & Kern, 1993; Dunlap, Kern-Dunlap, Clarke, & Robbins, 1991; Kennedy & Itkonen, 1993; Touchette, MacDonald, & Langer, 1985). Therefore, when students who participated in this program were observed to exhibit problem behavior when directed to engage in nonfunctional or age-inappropriate activities (e.g., stringing beads), it was recommended that students not be required to perform such tasks.

The recommendations made concerning the curriculum of one young boy, David, illustrate how curriculum modification was used in this program. David was 6 years old when he was referred to the program for his frequent, intense screaming. Several situations appeared to elicit David's screaming, including being directed to dress a doll. Instead of teaching David to request a break from this activity, it was suggested that David be required to practice buttoning his own shirt instead of the doll's clothing. David seemed pleased with this modification and was not observed to scream while he practiced buttoning his own shirt. At this point, functional communication training was implemented with David to address his screaming when someone took something away from him. He was taught to use his communication device to say, "May I have that back?"

INTERVENTION RESULTS AND MAINTENANCE

All of the baseline and intervention sessions were videotaped for later scoring of the frequency of challenging behavior. Three of the 22 students engaged in very low rates of problem behavior, but they were extremely disruptive when these behaviors did occur. Their progress was evaluated via teacher reports, as the low rates of behavior did not allow them to be easily captured on videotape. For the other 19 students, progress

was assessed by scoring the videotaped baseline and intervention sessions for the percentage of intervals of challenging behavior. A multiple baseline across students design was used to evaluate the efficacy of the interventions.

Data were collected for 6 of the 19 students for 1 year or longer. An examination of the mean percentage of intervals of challenging behavior before and after intervention demonstrated that the intervention led to a reduction of challenging behavior for all of the students and continued for more than 1 year for several students. (Data are available from the second author.)

GENERALIZATION ACROSS UNTRAINED PEOPLE

In addition to the maintenance of the intervention effects, the program aimed to determine whether the students could successfully use their devices and communicative responses with untrained members of the community. Because the students were taught to use vocal-output devices that communicated in clear, spoken English and Spanish, it was believed that untrained people would be able to understand and respond to the students in the desired manner (Schepis & Reid, 1995).

Before intervention began, several students were observed in community environments, such as malls, restaurants, and a bowling alley. Challenging behaviors were nearly nonexistent during baseline in the community. This appeared to be related to several factors: Demands were few, attention was high, they all had something to do, and the purpose of the outings often was to eat lunch. In other words, when in the community, the students rarely experienced the situations that elicited their challenging behavior in the classroom; however, they remained entirely dependent on their teachers to interact with community members for them. For example, on a typical lunch outing, the students and several teachers would sit at a table while one teacher went to order all of the meals. The vocal-output devices were programmed with a phrase that would allow the students to make requests independently (e.g., "May I have a hamburger kid's meal, please?"). The students were taught to use their devices to order their own drinks, snacks, and meals and to request participation in carnival games.

To assess the generalization of communication skills, the dependent variable that was recorded during community sessions was whether untrained community members would respond appropriately to the students' requests. An appropriate response occurred when the untrained community member granted a student's request without any assistance from a teacher. For example, if a student used his or her device to order a cheeseburger and a small Coke, then an appropriate response was scored when the child received that meal without the community member's having to ask a teacher for assistance to understand what the student wanted.

Assessment of the effects of training in the community for some students was difficult because some schools rarely organized trips into the community. This was often related to the high crime rate around many of these schools, busing problems, and low teacher–student ratios. Ten of the students, however, were able to go into the community on a regular basis, and generalization was assessed for these students. Both trained and untrained people were able to understand and respond to the students' requests at a high rate, often more than 90% of the time.

DIFFICULTIES
DURING THE RESEARCH

Despite the positive outcomes that were generated by this program, a number of problems did arise and required changes in aspects of the program. Often, the students did not appear to use the communication devices as planned, and modifications needed to be made to their communication plans. The problems encountered while conducting this program are discussed next along with the resolutions reached.

Several of the problems that were encountered during this program were related to the vocal-output devices. Problems occasionally occurred when students were not matched with the right type of augmentative equipment. When deciding who should get which type of device, program staff needed to consider several student attributes, such as physical strength, mobility,

type of sensory impairment, and fine motor control (Mirenda et al., 1990). Students with severe physical disabilities, for example, required special consideration when they were being provided with communication devices. Four of the students in the program had an additional diagnosis of cerebral palsy and were nonambulatory. These students had difficulties with reaching and activating their devices, and additional adaptive equipment was necessary. Two students were able to reach for and place their hands on the communication devices, but they did not have enough strength to activate them; therefore, their original communication boards needed to be supplemented with a light-touch activator. Two other students could not control their hands well enough to place them on the communication board and, therefore, required a mounting system that could be attached to their wheelchair. The mounting system positioned the light-touch activators by the students' heads, allowing them to activate the message by moving their heads slightly in one direction.

Mary appeared to benefit from this type of adaptive equipment. Mary was 8 years old when she first became involved in the program. She was diagnosed with mental retardation requiring extensive supports, blindness, a hearing impairment, and cerebral palsy, and she was nonambulatory. When directed to complete school work, Mary frequently bit her hand. She was provided with a device that was programmed to say, "May I have a break?" During the initial sessions, it became obvious that because of spasticity, Mary was not going to be able to reach the communication device that was placed on her wheelchair tray. In addition, she did not have the strength to activate the device when her hand was guided to it by her teachers. Initial attempts to teach Mary to communicate failed. To help Mary communicate independently, program staff provided her with a very sensitive activator, called a leaf switch, and a wheelchair mounting device that positioned the leaf switch by Mary's head. To activate the message, Mary needed to apply only 2 ounces of pressure with her head. With training, Mary learned to move her head slightly to the left to activate her device and receive a break.

Another problem that became obvious when using certain communication devices was that many were too large and cumbersome for the students to carry with them. This was not a problem for individuals who used a wheelchair because the devices were simply attached to their trays and neither the students nor the teachers had to worry about carrying the devices from place to place. For other students who were ambulatory and active, however, the larger devices occasionally presented a problem. When the students remained in one place (e.g., eating lunch, doing desk work, brushing their hair), the devices were simply placed within reach. When the students moved around, however, they had to learn to go back to where their board was placed to communicate (rarely were students willing to carry their boards with them). This proved to be very difficult for some students (especially those with visual impairments) and to be a very inefficient form of communication.

This latter issue of response efficiency is of great concern, with important implications for the intervention for challenging behavior. Research has demonstrated that the efficiency of a new, functionally equivalent response is critical in the efficacy of functional communication training (Horner & Day, 1991; Horner, Sprague, O'Brien, & Heathfield, 1990). If the new, appropriate response is less efficient to emit in terms of physical effort, time delay, and schedule of reinforcement as compared with the challenging behavior, then the student will continue to rely on the challenging behavior to effect change in his or her environment.

John's intervention illustrates the potential problems associated with some of the larger communication devices. John was a 17-year-old student with a visual impairment who occasionally engaged in severe head hitting. The results of interviews and the MAS each suggested that John's head hitting was maintained by escape from demands. Intervention for John consisted of teaching him to use his device to request a break from work. Teachers reported that he did learn to use the device successfully and that he engaged in less head hitting while working in his seat. Several of John's tasks, however, required him to work while standing up. It was

John's job, for example, to sweep the work area. John understandably was unwilling to carry his device while engaged in such work, and his teachers noted that he was just as likely to engage in head hitting during these tasks as he was before intervention began.

It became apparent that while John was standing away from his device, head hitting was a more efficient way to get out of work than going over to the desk, finding the board, and pressing the appropriate key. To address this problem, John's device was replaced with a smaller one that he could wear on his belt. John learned to activate this device when he wanted a break, regardless of where he was or what he was doing. This, in turn, resulted in decreased challenging behavior.

Another factor to consider when providing the students with vocal-output devices was the intelligibility of the devices. The first several boards provided to students in this program used synthetic, computerized speech, which can be difficult to understand (Hoover, Reichle, Van Tasell, & Cole, 1987). Some teachers and assistant teachers required experience with the devices before they could understand the students' messages. Furthermore, teachers believed that the voice sounded too much like a robot. This is a common complaint by staff working with students who use devices with synthesized voice output (Schepis & Reid, 1995). Thus, it seemed likely that these devices would have limited use with untrained teachers and community members. Fortunately, during the period that the program was in effect, many advances were made in vocal-output devices. The second group of students who joined the program were provided with devices that used digitized speech that had recordings of actual voices on them. In addition, several of the students who had been provided with the original boards had their old devices replaced with the new recordable ones. In other words, rather than the artificial sounding output, these devices could be made to sound like a student with similar demographics as the student using the device. For example, a 9-year-old boy without disabilities recorded all of the messages for the boys in the program, and an adult male did so for the adolescent males. Similar efforts were directed toward providing the females with devices with appropriate voices recorded on them.

CONCLUSION

Overall, this program suggests that using vocal-output devices for functional communication training has the potential for reducing the challenging behavior of students with multiple disabilities. An important area of future research is matching students with the most appropriate device and device modifications as there are few guidelines concerning how to choose a communication system for a given individual (Mirenda et al., 1990). Although the program described in this chapter did not directly compare the differential success that students had with various devices, clinical work with these students did result in some preliminary suggestions for matching individuals with multiple disabilities with the most appropriate vocal-output devices:

1. Consider the students' strengths as well as the advantages and limitations of the devices.
2. For students with auditory impairments, provide devices that have volume controls to allow them to hear the feedback of the vocal output. Provide colorful pictures for students who are completely deaf so that they have a stimulus that will assist them in associating messages with outcomes.
3. Consider the difficulty level of activating the communication device. For students with motor difficulties, provide light-touch activators and head switches.
4. Consider the portability of the device and the activity level of the student. For active students, provide small devices that can be worn on their belts.

In sum, vocal-output devices are seen as being particularly valuable for individuals with multiple disabilities. This and previous research efforts (e.g., Durand, 1993; Durand & Kishi, 1987) support attempts to provide effective interventions for the challenging behaviors of individuals with sensory impairments. The communication training strategy used in this series of studies was effective despite a long history of a lack of success in teaching formal communication skills to these students. This experience should serve as incentive to workers in this area to pursue constructive skills training approaches with these individuals, even in the face of previous unsuccessful efforts.

REFERENCES

Bihm, E.M., Kienlen, T.L., Ness, M.E., & Poindexter, A.R. (1991). Factor structure of the Motivation Assessment Scale for persons with mental retardation. *Psychological Reports, 68,* 1235–1238.

Bird, F., Dores, P.A., Moniz, D., & Robinson, J. (1989). Reducing severe aggressive and self-injurious behaviors with functional communication training: Direct, collateral and generalized results. *American Journal on Mental Retardation, 94,* 37–48.

Bryen, D.N., Goldman, A.S., & Quinlisk-Gill, S. (1988). Sign language with students with severe/profound mental retardation: How effective is it? *Education and Training in Mental Retardation, 23,* 129–137.

Bryen, D.N., & Joyce, D.G. (1986). Sign language and the severely handicapped. *The Journal of Special Education, 20,* 183–194.

Calculator, S., & Dollaghan, C. (1982). The use of communication boards in residential settings. *Journal of Speech and Hearing Disorders, 14,* 281–287.

Carr, E.G. (1977). The motivation of self-injurious behavior: A review of some hypotheses. *Psychological Bulletin, 84,* 800–816.

Carr, E.G., & Durand, V.M. (1985). Reducing behavior problems through functional communication training. *Journal of Applied Behavior Analysis, 18,* 111–126.

Carr, E.G., & Kemp, D.C. (1989). Functional equivalence of autistic leading and communicative pointing: Analysis and treatment. *Journal of Autism and Developmental Disorders, 19,* 561–578.

Carr, E.G., Levin, L., McConnachie, G., Carlson, J.I., Kemp, D.C., & Smith, C.E. (1994). *Communication-based intervention for problem behavior: A user's guide for producing positive change.* Baltimore: Paul H. Brookes Publishing Co.

Doss, S., & Reichle, J. (1989). Establishing communicative alternatives to the emission of socially motivated excess behavior: A review. *Journal of The Association for Persons with Severe Handicaps, 14,* 101–112.

Dunlap, G., & Kern, L. (1993). Assessment and intervention for children within the instructional curriculum. In J. Reichle & D.P. Wacker (Eds.), *Communication and language intervention series: Vol. 3. Communicative alternatives to challenging behavior: Integrating functional assessment and intervention strategies* (pp. 177–203). Baltimore: Paul H. Brookes Publishing Co.

Dunlap, G., Kern-Dunlap, L., Clarke, S., & Robbins, F.R. (1991). Functional assessment, curricular revisions, and severe behavior problems. *Journal of Applied Behavior Analysis, 24,* 387–397.

Durand, V.M. (1987). "Look homeward angel": A call to return to our (functional) roots. *The Behavior Analyst, 10,* 299–302.

Durand, V.M. (1990). *Severe behavior problems: A functional communication approach.* New York: Guilford Press.

Durand, V.M. (1993). Functional communication training using assistive devices: Effects on challenging behavior and affect. *Augmentative and Alternative Communication, 9,* 168–176.

Durand, V.M., Berotti, D., & Weiner, J. (1993). Functional communication training: Factors affecting effectiveness, generalization, and maintenance. In J. Reichle & D.P. Wacker (Eds.), *Communication and language intervention series: Vol. 3. Communicative alternatives to challenging behavior: Integrating functional assessment and intervention strategies* (pp. 317–340). Baltimore: Paul H. Brookes Publishing Co.

Durand, V.M., & Carr, E.G. (1992). An analysis of maintenance following functional communication training. *Journal of Applied Behavior Analysis, 25,* 777–794.

Durand, V.M., & Crimmins, D.B. (1988). Identifying the variables maintaining self-injurious behavior. *Journal of Autism and Developmental Disorders, 18,* 99–117.

Durand, V.M., & Crimmins, D.B. (1992). *The Motivation Assessment Scale (MAS) administration guide.* Topeka, KS: Monaco & Associates.

Durand, V.M., Crimmins, D.B., Caulfield, M., & Taylor, J. (1989). Reinforcer assessment: I. Using problem behavior to select reinforcers. *Journal of The Association for Persons with Severe Handicaps, 14,* 113–126.

Durand, V.M., & Kishi, G. (1987). Reducing severe behavior problems among persons with dual sensory impairments: An evaluation of a technical assistance model. *Journal of The Association for Persons with Severe Handicaps, 12,* 2–10.

Hoover, J., Reichle, J., Van Tasell, D.J., & Cole, D. (1987). The intelligibility of synthesized speech: ECHO II versus VOTRAX. *Journal of Speech and Hearing Research, 30,* 425–431.

Horner, R.H., & Budd, C.M. (1985). Teaching manual sign language to a nonverbal student: Generalization of sign use and collateral reduction of maladaptive behavior. *Education and Training of the Mentally Retarded, 20,* 39–47.

Horner, R.H., & Day, H.M. (1991). The effects of response efficiency on functionally equivalent competing behavior. *Journal of Applied Behavior Analysis, 24,* 719–732.

Horner, R.H., Sprague, J.R., O'Brien, M., & Heathfield, L.T. (1990). The role of response efficiency in the reduction of problem behaviors through functional equivalence training: A case study. *Journal of The Association for Persons with Severe Handicaps, 15,* 91–97.

Hunt, P., Alwell, M., & Goetz, L. (1988). Acquisition of conversation skills and the reduction of inappropriate social interaction behavior. *Journal of The Association for Persons with Severe Handicaps, 13,* 20–27.

Iwata, B.A., Dorsey, M.F., Slifer, K.J., Bauman, K.W., & Richman, G.S. (1982). Toward a functional analysis of self injury. *Analysis and Intervention in Developmental Disabilities, 2,* 3–20.

Kearney, C.A. (1994). Interrater reliability of the Motivation Assessment Scale: Another, closer look. *Journal of The Association for Persons with Severe Handicaps, 19,* 139–142.

Kennedy, C.H., & Haring, T.G. (1993). Combining reward and escape DRO to reduce the problem behavior of students with severe disabilities. *Journal of The Association for Persons with Severe Handicaps, 18,* 85–92.

Kennedy, C.H., & Itkonen, T. (1993). Effects of setting events on the problem behavior of students with severe disabilities. *Journal of Applied Behavior Analysis, 26,* 321–327.

Locke, P.A., & Mirenda, P. (1988). A computer-supported communication approach for a child with severe communication, visual and cognitive impairments: A case study. *Augmentative and Alternative Communication, 4,* 15–22.

Mace, F.C., & Lalli, J.S. (1991). Linking descriptive and experimental analysis in the treatment of bizarre speech. *Journal of Applied Behavior Analysis, 24,* 553–562.

Mirenda, P., Iacono, T., & Williams, R. (1990). Communication options for persons with severe and profound disabilities: State of the art and future directions. *Journal of The Association for Persons with Severe Handicaps, 15,* 3–21.

Murray-Branch, J., Udavari-Solner, A., & Bailey, B. (1991). Textured communication systems for individuals with severe intellectual and dual sensory impairments. *Language, Speech and Hearing in the Schools, 22,* 260–268.

O'Neill, R.E., Horner, R.H., Albin, R.W., Storey, K., & Sprague, J.R. (1990). *Functional analysis of problem behavior: A practical assessment guide.* Sycamore, IL: Sycamore Publishing.

Rotholz, D.A., Berkowitz, S.F., & Burberry, J. (1989). Functionality of two modes of communication in the community by students with developmental disabilities: A comparison of signing and communication books. *Journal of The Association for Persons with Severe Handicaps, 14,* 227–233.

Schepis, M.M., & Reid, D.H. (1995). Effects of a voice output communication aid on interactions between support personnel and an individual with multiple disabilities. *Journal of Applied Behavior Analysis, 28,* 73–77.

Steege, M.W., Wacker, D.P., Cigrand, K.C., Berg, W.K., Novak, C.G., Reimers, T.M., Sasso, G.M., & DeRaad, A. (1990). Use of negative reinforcement in the treatment of self-injurious behavior. *Journal of Applied Behavior Analysis, 23,* 459–467.

Touchette, P.E., MacDonald, R.F., & Langer, S.N. (1985). A scatter plot for identifying stimulus control of problem behavior. *Journal of Applied Behavior Analysis, 18,* 343–351.

Vollmer, T.R., Iwata, B.A., Smith, R.G., & Rodgers, T.A. (1992). Reduction of multiple aberrant behaviors and concurrent development of self-care skills with differential reinforcement. *Research in Developmental Disabilities, 13,* 287–299.

Vollmer, T.R., Iwata, B.A., Zarcone, J.R., Smith, R.G., & Mazaleski, J.L. (1993). The role of attention in the treatment of attention-maintained self-injurious behavior: Noncontingent reinforcement and differential reinforcement of other behavior. *Journal of Applied Behavior Analysis, 26,* 9–21.

Wacker, D.P., Steege, M.W., Northup, J., Sasso, G., Berg, W., Reimers, T., Cooper, L., Cigrand, K., & Donn, L. (1990). A component analysis of functional communication training across three topographies of severe behavior problems. *Journal of Applied Behavior Analysis, 23,* 417–429.

Chapter 12

Architectural Design in Positive Behavioral Support

Daniel W. Close & Robert H. Horner

The goal of this chapter is to emphasize the role that architectural variables play in the effective support of people with problem behaviors. Our interest in this topic is the result of work from 1991 to 1998 in supporting people with severe cognitive disabilities who have histories of extreme problem behavior and who moved from state institutions to local communities. The process has impressed on us the need for attention to detail and for thoughtful design of individualized supports. Now is an important time to attend to factors such as architecture. We are in the midst of a structural change in our definition of support for people with disabilities. Social values, professional technology, and public policy are converging on a new vision of residential support—a vision in which people with disabilities live rich lives and are fully included in the communities, schools, workplaces, families, and social networks that compose society (Kleinfield, 1997). This vision is a dramatic reversal of our expectations of just a few decades ago, and it presents an array of significant challenges. Among the foremost challenges is whether this inclusive vision extends to individuals with disabilities who engage in severe problem behaviors. Are

we prepared to support as valued members of our society people who engage in self-injury, severe aggression, property destruction, and pica? We believe that the answer is "yes" but only if we can deliver the supports that both provide reasonable safety for all involved and result in a lifestyle that is complete, personalized, and of high quality. A growing number of demonstration projects report on people with histories of extreme problem behavior who are supported successfully in community environments (Berkman & Meyer, 1988; Horner et al., 1996; Lehr & Brown, 1996; Lucyshyn, Olsen, & Horner, 1995; see Chapter 13). In each case, it is clear that success was not the result of a single instructional or behavioral "intervention" but the integration of social values, enlightened public policy, and comprehensive behavioral support. We believe that an important element of this process is detailed attention to the physical features of living, working, and transportation contexts.

Our message is twofold. First, attention to the physical features of an environment can influence behavior. Architectural variables can affect 1) the behavior of the person who is residing in that environment, 2) the behavior of the

The activity that is the subject of this chapter was supported in whole or in part by the U.S. Department of Education, Grant No. H133B2004; however, the opinions expressed herein do not necessarily reflect the position or policy of the U.S. Department of Education, and no official endorsement should be inferred.

staff who deliver support, and 3) the expectations of family and nonpaid members of the community (Rotegard, Hill, & Bruininks, 1983). Second, there is no simple list of architectural factors that are universally appropriate for all people based on their diagnostic label or type of problem behavior; rather, important architectural features must be defined for each individual based on a functional assessment of his or her problem behaviors, as well as on his or her preferences and activity patterns. Taking the time to consider and to attend to architectural variables can have a dramatic effect both on the type and the intensity of support and on the outcomes of that support (Thompson, Robinson, Graff, & Ingenmey, 1990). The need to attend to architectural factors is grounded in two major developments that have occurred since the late 1970s: a social commitment to the inclusion of all people with disabilities and the growing development of a comprehensive behavioral support technology.

IMPLICATIONS OF INCLUSION

Inclusion of people with disabilities refers to the full embedding of people in the social and functional life of their community. At work, at home, at school, and in the community, the notion of inclusion emphasizes that people with disabilities not only are physically present but also are accepted and recognized as belonging in the environment (Meyer, Peck, & Brown, 1991). People who are included in a context have natural roles, functions, and responsibilities. They are part of the process rather than an appendage or an addendum.

People who violate social norms traditionally have been excluded from rather than included in the ongoing life of communities. For people with severe disabilities, this segregation took the form of state institutions, special schools, and hospitals. A dramatic shift in social policy since the 1950s has been the effort first to *integrate* and then to *include* people with severe disabilities in society. Lakin, Prouty, Braddock, and Anderson (1997) documented that the number of people with disabilities in state institutions has decreased from 150,000 in the 1970s to 58,000 in 1996. There is every reason to believe that this process will continue.

Institutional care is becoming prohibitively expensive (Braddock, 1994; Prouty & Lakin, 1995). A wider array of community support options are being developed, and the social values that support public policy emphasize the need for building the capacity of local communities to include and support all members (Prouty & Lakin, 1995). Finances, values, and technology all suggest that the challenge for the future will be to determine how communities can be enhanced so that people with disabilities who once were viewed as outcasts can live as valued, contributing members (Singh, 1995). A piece of that process is a serious reexamination of the role that architectural variables play in the support of individuals with histories of severe problem behavior.

AN EMERGING TECHNOLOGY OF BEHAVIORAL SUPPORT

A second development that increases the need to attend to architectural variables is the emergence of a broadened technology of behavioral support (Carr et al., 1997; Carr et al., 1994; Durand, 1990; Horner et al., 1990; Meyer & Evans, 1989; Repp & Singh, 1990; Scotti, Ujcich, Weigle, Holland, & Kirk, 1996). Conventional behavior management procedures only targeted strategies for reducing problem behaviors. The emerging technology of behavioral support also emphasizes attention to all social, physical, structural, and instructional variables that affect how a person lives (Evans & Meyer, 1985; Horner & Carr, 1997; Koegel, Koegel, & Dunlap, 1996). As Risley (1994, 1996) framed this approach, "We begin by getting the person a life, then we look for ways to reduce problem behaviors" (1996, p. 426).

In many ways, applied behavior analysis is the use of behavioral principles to design and construct *effective* environments. A classroom, workplace, community environment, and home are effective to the extent that problem behaviors are minimized, people are safe and healthy, adaptive behaviors are being learned, and the activities that people perform reflect their personal preferences. To the extent that architectural factors influence behavior, health and safety, patterns of activities, and social interactions, they are an integral part of positive behavioral support technology. To emphasize this point, consider just a few of the important ways that the technology of behavioral support is changing.

Change in the Outcomes

The measure of "success" for a behavioral intervention has changed. Successful behavioral support alters not only the likelihood that the problem behaviors will occur but also the full range of behavior patterns that lead to a stable, functional life. To reduce problem behaviors yet leave an individual in a barren, boring environment is unacceptable. Problem behaviors are barriers to social contact, activities, and societal rewards. The reduction of problem behaviors should be accompanied by access to opportunities that make life interesting and enjoyable. Effective behavioral support leads to rich patterns of living, in addition to a reduction in problem behavior.

Functional Assessment

Among the most important advances in behavioral technology is the reemergence of behavioral assessment procedures (Carr, 1977; Iwata, Dorsey, Slifer, Bauman, & Richman, 1982; Iwata & Fisher, 1994; Mace, Lalli, Pinter-Lalli, & Shea, 1993; O'Neill et al., 1997; Repp, Felce, & Barton, 1988; Wacker et al., 1990). It is an expected professional practice in many parts of the country to conduct a functional assessment prior to designing behavioral support. A functional assessment involves interviews, direct observations, and in some cases experimental manipulations to identify the specific behaviors that are a problem, the situations (contexts) in which these behaviors occur and do not occur, and the consequences that maintain the problem behaviors (Carr et al., 1994; Durand, 1990; Horner & Carr, 1997; O'Neill et al., 1997).

From a scientific perspective, the reemergence of functional assessment is a reemphasis on the practical use of principles of behavior. It is a move away from a medical model in which documentation of a problem behavior led to a "behavioral prescription." Because different people engage in loud screaming under different situations and the screams of the two people are maintained by different reinforcers, it is reasonable to expect that the procedures used for be-

havioral support will be different. This requires the individualized construction of behavioral interventions based on our scientific understanding of behavior rather than reliance on prepackaged procedures that are administered based on diagnostic label or simply on the topography of the behavior (Carr, Robinson, & Palumbo, 1990).

The advent of functional assessment is more than a technical advance, however. In a very practical manner, functional assessment is a method of treating people with dignity and respect. Taking the time to understand the individual functions of problem behaviors is both technically sound and philosophically respectful.

Behavioral interventions are being developed based on the information obtained from functional assessments. This approach to understanding behavior problems and to organizing support is changing the very structure of behavioral intervention procedures. One central change is the move from the use of single procedures to the application of "multicomponent" interventions.

Multicomponent Interventions

Multicomponent interventions involve the manipulation of many different parts of an environment to obtain desired changes. Instead of simply using reprimands to decrease aggression, a multicomponent strategy may involve redesigning activities to increase physical exertion, teaching communication skills that serve the same function as aggression, and using systematic rewards to increase the use of communication rather than aggression. The point is that in a multicomponent format the support personnel rely on information from the functional assessment to engineer many elements in an environment to make that environment effective for the individual. As part of this process, additional attention should be given to the role of architectural variables.

ARCHITECTURAL VARIABLES IN BEHAVIORAL SUPPORT

Terms such as *behavioral, architectural,* and *environmental psychology* have been developed to describe the relation between the design of environments and human effectiveness (Friedman,

Zimring, & Zube, 1978). Frank Lloyd Wright, the great architect of the early 20th century, often described architecture as "art with a purpose" (Wright, 1920). Despite the great potential for environments to meet specific human needs, many buildings simply do not "work." Indeed, for individuals with severe behavior challenges, many of the buildings designed on their behalf contribute to their destructive behaviors rather than foster competence and personal growth.

A central purpose of this chapter is to describe a process that was used to make physical environments work better for individuals with severe challenging behaviors. Traditional notions of environmental design were married with detailed behavioral information about the individuals who would be living in a particular home. It is important to note that each of the individuals from whom we have learned had unique behavior challenges. Although information on basic design feature is presented, it is crucial to emphasize that many of the individuals required simple yet highly individualized physical design changes to adapt to their new homes. Stated otherwise, no "cookie cutter" designs were utilized for the project; each person's unique needs were considered in the design of his or her home.

The following section presents a process for identifying architectural features associated with the behavioral support that we developed with individuals who moved from one state institution to several community environments. The individuals who participated in this process were selected by the staff of a 1,100-person institution as among the 25 most behaviorally challenging residents. Each of the people who moved was 18 years of age or older, had hospitalized him- or herself or someone else on multiple occasions, and had at least a 10-year history of severe problem behavior. A more complete description of the individuals and their overall support structure has been provided elsewhere (Horner et al., 1996; Knobbe, Carey, Rhodes, & Horner, 1995; Lucyshyn et al., 1995). To provide a context for the process for identifying architectural changes, brief case study descriptions are provided of the types of challenges that individual residents posed.

It is 6:12 A.M., and Carl is lying on his back on the floor moaning and waving his fingers in front of his face to cast shadows from the overhead light. Both of his feet are propped on the edge of an opened steel door. Every 15 seconds or so, he violently pushes the door with both feet in an attempt to close it. This violent pushing back and forth lasts 20–30 seconds. The metal door closer prevents Carl from slamming the door shut. Carl continues this routine for approximately 2–3 hours. He finally gives up his attempt to slam the door and eats breakfast.

Following breakfast, Carl once again assumes his position in front of the open door. He now screams loudly as he violently pushes the door with his feet. The door fails to close. This process is repeated for another 2–3 hours until staff coax him into a break for lunch.

Following several days of 8–12 hours of door pushing, Carl finally stops pushing against the door. Staff have calmly told Carl throughout the episode, "The door will close by itself. Let the door close by itself." Although the door-closing mechanism has prevented the door from being slammed shut, Carl has succeeded in tearing the door frame from the steel bolts that were welded into the wall to stabilize the unit.

It is 3:00 P.M. on a warm summer day. Harry has been on a community outing to the annual county fair a few blocks from his home. The street in front of his two-bedroom, wooden-frame house is filled with cars from the visitors to the fair. As Harry's car approaches the driveway to the house, he begins to strike the plexiglass barrier that separates him from the driver in the front seat. As soon as the driver stops the car, Harry quickly opens the back seat door and runs to the front porch. The screen on the front door flaps as Harry flings it open and enters the house. Harry quickly moves through the living room, pounding on the walls as he passes. Once in his bedroom, he falls on the bed and just as quickly pounds on the walls and door frame as he returns to the living room. Harry twirls around in the living room and falls to his knees on the wooden floor. He quickly bounces up from his knees and heads to the kitchen, pounding the walls and door frame as he passes. He opens the small refrigerator and locates a bottle of fruit juice, which he guzzles while standing. He throws the empty container into the kitchen sink and wipes his hands on his T-shirt.

During this 90-second move about the house, staff attempt to slow Harry enough to encourage him to use the schedule to start him on a new routine. Harry moves so quickly that staff are unable to communicate any meaningful instructions or suggestions to him. Harry now leaves the kitchen and goes to the living room window and gently taps the glass. Staff immediately say, "No, Harry, don't hit the glass." Harry looks at the staff and hits the glass a bit harder. Staff attempt to prevent Harry from further touching the glass but to no avail. A final hit to the glass breaks the pane. Harry runs to his bedroom, closes the door, and lies on his bed in a fetal position.

Art is 25 years old. For the past 6 years, he has lived in a specially designed home that is part of a duplex apartment building. His side of the duplex has one bedroom with a living room, dining room, and bathroom. He shares a kitchen with two men, who live in the two-bedroom unit on the other side of the duplex. The three also share a large backyard. Art has a long history of leaving his home without supervision. On numerous occasions when he has left without supervision, he has run through streets without regard to common safety practices, including running in front of moving cars, trucks, and bicycles.

Art's destination on these excursions usually is a local grocery store, convenience store, or fast-food outlet. Prior to entering the state institution, Art frequently left his group home to visit one such store. Art's primary mode of operation once in the store is to locate the cold beverage area and select a favored soda pop. He then immediately consumes the drink and searches for other favored items in the store. He will then exit the store without paying for the items.

The staff of the store that he frequented when living in the group home typically would see Art enter the store and inform the staff at the group home of his presence. The staff then would come to the store, pay the bill, and escort Art home. On one occasion that significantly contributed to his institutional placement, Art pulled over an entire refrigerator full of drinks onto the floor of the store.

Critical Architectural Features Interview Process

Synthesizing the functional assessment approach to problem behaviors and the process used by architects in designing and building living spaces was an exciting and challenging endeavor. The goal of this integrated process was to design individualized living spaces for 25 individuals with developmental disabilities and severe problem behaviors. The objectives were to decrease the incidence of severe problem behaviors and to offer a reasonable lifestyle for the individuals.

The research literature on the relation between physical environmental features and problem behaviors is not well defined or particularly extensive. Our research and demonstration efforts, however, have convinced us of the pivotal role that architecture plays in both the development and the prevention of severe problem behaviors. In the following section, the process used to design and maintain living spaces for 25 individuals with severe problem behaviors is described. This discussion details both the successes and the failures.

Archival Records Review

The first step in the process of developing individualized living spaces was an extensive review of all relevant personal and historical records. In the case of the majority of the individuals for whom we designed support, there were extensive records available at the institution in which they lived. Archival review involved building a history of where the individual had lived; identifying people who were important to the individual, or at least people with whom he or she had spent time; and placing within a time frame the major medical, behavioral, and social events of the individual's life. The first goal of the archival review was to build a picture of the life that the individual had experienced. The second goal was to use the clinical information in the file to understand the way that others had interpreted the challenges that that individual presented and the strategies that had been employed (successfully and unsuccessfully) to address those challenges.

Interview with Family and Significant Others

Information was obtained from family members and important, nonpaid "others" in an effort to identify critical features of living space that would facilitate success. The goal was to talk to people who had a long history with the individual to find out which features of living, working, and transportation spaces created problems and which features seemed desirable for the individual. We assumed that all problem behaviors that had occurred in the past likely would be seen again in the future, although we recognized that the behaviors seen in one environment would not necessarily be predictive of behaviors in a different environment. We also assumed that people who had a long history with the individual would have seen him or her in different environments and would have a wider range of experiences from which to draw. The goal was to frame a series of questions that would identify the specific features of living, working, and travel contexts that would minimize problem behaviors and maximize prosocial behaviors. We organized the interview around five central questions.

Critical Features of the Living Space

Family members were asked to identify specific features of a living environment that would be critical and desirable for success. This question led to discussion of such items as the type of lighting that was used, the materials used for windows, the coverings for windows, the features of the shower, the presence of carpeting, door frame construction, and how to make the environment "homelike." In several cases, family members had difficulty with this question. Four sets of parents had been forced to seek out-of-home placement for their child because of the high degree of property damage that occurred when the child was in the family home. Dave's father remarked, in a comment that related several family members' thoughts on the subject,

There is no way you are going to make this unit homelike. When Dave lived with us, our home was like an armed camp. Every door was locked. We had no pictures on the walls. Our walls had plywood covering the holes that Dave made when he would throw things or run his fist through the wall. We had broken windows, and we couldn't keep curtains or screens. Our kitchen cupboard, the refridge, and all drawers were under lock and key. I'm not exaggerating. Our lives were all directed at protecting the younger kids and keeping Dave from destroying the house. So in all due respect, I just hope you can make the house safe for him and the staff to live in.

Another parent approached the question from a different perspective by emphasizing that her son always liked to sit in the sun. She noted that the home should have lots of windows and even requested that her son have a "wooden bench that is located near an open window so that he can see me drive up when I visit."

Potential Housemates

The physical features of a living environment are affected by the total number of people in the environment and the needs for privacy, cooperation, visual monitoring of events at home, and so forth. As such, an important part of any interview focused on housemates (how many, if any, etc.). This question was critical because in many respects all of the individuals for whom we were designing living spaces had extensive histories of conflict with others. Given the nature of the effort, there were significant pressures to design the optimal yet fiscally responsible living space. Several family members had very strong feelings that their son or daughter would benefit from the "right housemate," whereas others strongly suggested that their child live alone. Still other families identified specific individuals with whom their son or daughter had fought in the past or for whom their son or daughter had expressed intense dislike in the current living unit in the institution. Eric's mother summarized the responses of several family members when she exclaimed,

Just don't put him with another person who screams. He can't stand screaming, and he always seems to be in a unit with someone who screams. He is very sensitive and will definitely abuse himself and the staff if he has to live with another screamer.

Walt's Mom also noted, "Walt does not like living with other people who he perceives to be disabled. I suggest you develop a place for him where he can live alone with staff support."

Health and Safety

We found that although family members would identify certain types of issues when asked to describe generally the critical physical features, they added more features when asked to focus specifically on aspects of the living environment that would be necessary for safety. Much valuable information was gleaned from this part of the interview and formed the basis for many of the accommodations in each home. Regarding health and safety features, Harry's mother was concerned about his bathroom and bedroom. She emphasized,

Harry has lots of problems in the bathroom. He gets really hot and thirsty, so he needs lots of water. I don't want him drinking from the toilet; I want him drinking healthful juices. He also makes a big mess in the bathtub. Getting him into the shower is not easy. He likes baths. When he is in the bathtub, he will splash water all over the floor. The staff at the group home know how hard it is to get Harry in the shower. One staff person was really hurt trying to get him in the shower. I think he needs a bathroom that will let him get a bath without hurting him or the staff. The floor needs to be as slip-proof as possible. Harry has fallen, and so have staff. It gets really wet sometimes.

Carl's parents focused their attention on the kitchen. They noted,

Carl likes to help out in the kitchen. The only problem is that he will break or destroy everything in the process. We know. He's done it countless times at home. Also, the kitchen will have to be organized so that he knows where everything is stored. Carl does not like things out of order. You should be sure that all pans, pots, and dishes are durable, or they will be broken. You also should not have things like plastic bags, small objects, or food like dry beans, popcorn, or anything that he can choke on. Also, don't let other clients in the kitchen or dining room when Carl is there. He will attack them or attack staff. Carl likes to

be by himself or with staff. Also, Carl will throw food; heck, he'll throw anything. He even throws things he likes if he thinks it will keep people away. Also, Carl will help you clean, but be sure he is well supervised. Carl does things really fast and doesn't always finish what he starts.

Tim's mother and grandmother were especially concerned about the sharp corners and other obstacles in the home for their son, who both is blind and engages in high rates of self-injurious behavior. They noted,

Tim has lived in a large hospital since he was a little boy. He's always had big rooms, big hallways, and lots of people around. We're concerned that a little house will not work for Tim. He's blind and can't see things in his way. If he gets scared to move around, he'll just sit there and cry. His feet are also very curled up and sore. He wears special shoes, and he could hurt his feet on the corners of the bed or on chairs. Tim will need to have a ramp going up to his home because he can't climb stairs. We haven't seen Tim climb stairs since he was a little boy. He'll hit his face if he is scared. We want to see this home before he moves in, and we want to approve it before he moves in. He also hits his head in the bathroom sometimes when he sits on the toilet. He'll do this if he's constipated. What can you do to make sure he doesn't get hurt on the toilet?

Neighborhood

Families were asked, "What type of neighborhood would best meet your son's or daughter's lifestyle and safety needs? Please focus on urban versus rural, quiet or busy, near businesses or shopping centers, near other families." This question addressed an issue to which family members found it difficult to respond. Many of the family members themselves lived in rural areas and were ambivalent about this issue. On the one hand, they recognized that their son or daughter required extensive medical, behavioral, and other support services that typically would be associated with an urban or a suburban environment. On the other hand, many of the families were genuinely concerned about the crime, traffic, and crowded nature of the urban sites of Eugene, Corvallis, and Salem, Oregon. In addition, families were concerned about the time and distance that it would take to travel to visit their child.

The following are examples of responses from both rural and urban family members. Charley's family lives in a small town in southern Oregon. Their foremost concerns were crime and the perceived "counter culture" environment of Eugene. His mother said,

Charley can't tell the difference between right and wrong. He needs to be protected from all the people out there who are not Christian. We couldn't handle Charley at home because evil people were always getting him to do bad things. In Eugene, you have lots of people who take drugs, listen to satanic music, and do evil things. I [prefer that] he not live in Eugene. Salem seems fine to me even though it will take us an extra hour to come visit him. Every time I come to Eugene, I see the worst kind of people. I don't want my son exposed to these people.

Bill's father lives in Portland, the most densely populated area of Oregon. During the interview, he noted,

I want what's right for Bill. He's lived in Salem for 25 years, so I guess you could say it is his home. I visit him every month or so, and I know how tough he can be. When he lived at home with the family, he really enjoyed the out-of-doors. I would hope that he would have a house with a big yard. You have to keep Bill busy or he'll drive you crazy. Bill has lots of energy, and getting him outside will be helpful. As for neighbors, I don't think he'll pay much attention to them. He can be a handful if he wants something the neighbors own. I don't think he should live on a busy street because he's never learned to cross streets or stay on sidewalks. If Bill gets away, I don't know what he'll do. I'll visit him regularly wherever he lives.

Carl's mother expressed great concern about the neighborhood. She noted,

Carl should live in a place where if he gets out he can't get hurt. I'm not saying he should live out in the country, but he cannot live on another busy street. I would hope that you could find a place that would give him some open spaces in case he gets out.

Transportation

Families were asked, "What important features of a vehicle would best meet your child's transportation needs? Please focus on safety concerns for your child, other passengers, and the driver." This question both addressed the most optimistic features of the proposed plan and broached another of the family members' greatest fears. Many family members had not transported their son or daughter in a vehicle for many years. Visits to their son or daughter occurred at the institution with no travel away from the facility. Other family members had fresh memories of disastrous events associated with travel and attempted to communicate this in the interview. Many family members expressed disbelief that their son or daughter could be transported safely in any manner. Only one family member mentioned using the city bus.

Interview with Direct Services Staff

The architectural features of a home, workplace, or vehicle need to accommodate the kinds of activities that will occur there, the kinds of problems that have been noted in the past, and the kinds of features that the individual finds desirable. We learned about these features first through observation and conversation (when possible) with the individuals with disabilities themselves. We learned about these features from the families and close friends of the individuals, and we learned a tremendous amount from the direct services staff who worked daily with the individuals. To a great extent, we asked staff the same types of questions that we asked the family members: "What are critical features that would make the home safe, responsive, and individually appropriate?" We asked about the physical features, the neighborhood, housemates, daily routines, toileting and grooming routines, travel, diet, the pace of activities, personal dislikes and dangers, and open-ended questions about "other" issues. From these questions, we formed individualized pictures of the features of an environment that would be important for safety, for preferred activities, and for reduced problem behavior. In most cases, there was strong agreement between the staff and the families about the needed architectural features.

Architectural Design Features

Assessment information from the different sources (residents, family, friends, support staff, and medical personnel) was integrated into specific recommendations for the physical environments. Recommendations about the features of a physical environment that would affect health and safety, effective mobility, and personal preference became part of each individual's personal plan of support. The architectural recommendations were blended within a comprehensive support plan that also focused on the activity patterns, social options, communication skills, living skills, and detailed procedures for preventing and responding to severe problem behaviors. Of the 12 homes with which we helped, 9 involved moderate to significant renovation and 3 were homes that were new construction, which gave us the opportunity to introduce information that was gathered from the assessments as the home was built. Across the different homes, a small set of basic principles served us well:

1. When a feature of a home has a history of being damaged, eliminate it or make it durable (e.g., windows, door frames, toilets, faucets, walls).
2. Design spaces to accommodate a resident *and* support staff (special attention is needed in the design of kitchens, utility rooms, and bathrooms, where space often is designed for use by one person at a time).
3. Include design features that are particularly valued by the people who live there (e.g., shower, closet space).
4. The external design should blend in with the community and look homelike and attractive.

We were impressed by the individual nature of the architectural changes that were made across houses. There was not a single list of architectural modifications for certain types of challenges but rather an ever-growing list of individualized features that changed from house to house. Some of the changes that we believe were most important or most common are described in more detail next. Our effort has been to provide an index of those architectural changes that seemed most significant and to describe the kinds of ongoing architectural modifications that have been needed since the homes were built.

Electrical and Plumbing Features

Each of the homes had simple health and safety features built into their design. For example, all homes were equipped with sensitive "ground fault interruption" (GFI) circuits. These devices function to terminate a circuit immediately when a minor fluctuation in the electrical current occurs, and they are far more sensitive than traditional electric circuit breakers. The GFI circuits prevent injury to residents or staff who may place a foreign object or body part in an electrical outlet. In addition, plastic plating was installed over electrical plugs and outlets to prevent accidental electrocution.

The plumbing systems were installed with scald valves on each faucet (sink and tub/shower) in the kitchen and the bathroom. This device automatically adjusts the warmth of the water in a faucet to a preset temperature of 120 degrees, preventing individuals from being scalded by water that is too hot yet providing for sufficient warmth to conduct personal hygiene and other household cleaning tasks. Each kitchen sink garbage disposal was equipped with a "batch-style" safety device, which is a long metal device that is placed into the garbage disposal to activate and turn off the appliance. The device prevents individuals from placing their hands in the garbage disposal while it is operating.

Bathroom Features

Bathrooms are dangerous places. They often are hard; angular; small; wet; slippery; and full of protruding bars, counters, tubs, and fixtures. We learned to view bathrooms in a new light as plans of support were developed to balance personal dignity, choice, and independence with safety, hygiene needs, and ongoing needs for direct staff support. This balance was especially important for individuals with physical disabilities as well as cognitive and behavior challenges. Special attention was given to showers, grab bars, and physical space in bathrooms. Bathrooms often were equipped with 5-foot-wide walk-in showers. These showers were chosen because many injuries occur both to individuals and to staff during the showering process. These attractive, preformed fixtures were installed flush with the bathroom floor surface to eliminate the need to step up into the shower. In addition, the showers were large enough that staff could assist individuals in the shower if showers were difficult or dangerous for an individual.

All of the bathrooms were equipped with heavy-duty grab bars to assist individuals with getting on and off the toilet and for stability and ease of mobility on the wet bathroom floor surface. In Darin's case, the grab bar near the toilet became a target for self-injury even though he needed the grab bar to get up from the toilet. His functional assessment indicated that his self-injury was maintained by escape from the bathroom. He was willing to be in the bathroom for short periods, but not for extended intervals. In response to this situation, he was taught to signal when he wanted to leave the bathroom, and a plastic foam material similar to the covering used for bicycle handle bars was placed on the grab bar to minimize the danger of hitting his head on the grab bar. This combined strategy proved both safe and effective.

The bathroom in Joe's home was small, efficient, and useful for many functions. An important architectural feature recommended by the staff who knew him best was access to a bathtub. Joe was used to soaking in a tub each day, and his functional assessment data suggested that bathing was both very enjoyable and followed by calm periods without problem behavior. Both personal preference and proactive behavioral support arguments supported the need to add a tub. In this case, a utility space next to the bathroom was adapted to house a tub, and regular opportunities to soak in the tub were built into Joe's daily routine (and communication system). When Joe moved to his new home, the tub was a major focus of his attention for many months. The exact impact of having a tub on his problem behavior cannot be determined, but his level of self-injury has declined over time; he has become more involved in the local community; and, after 2 years of living in his home, he was able, with the help of staff and friends, to buy a hot tub. The personal hot tub has become the preferred focus, but the original tub continues to be used in periods of inclement weather or when the hot tub is not working.

Floor Covering

A variety of floor coverings were installed in the homes, depending on the assessed needs of the individuals. The general rule for the houses was hardwood floors with large area rugs in the living and bedroom areas and vinyl floors in the kitchen and the bathroom. Hardwood floors were chosen because of the high rate of urination and defecation that occurred in the living and bedroom areas at the institution. A hardwood floor has an easy maintenance feature and is viewed as attractive and homelike. In contrast, carpets retain the smell of urine and quickly contribute to a foul odor in the home. It is important to note that hardwood floors will buckle if liquid is not immediately removed. In addition, hardwood floors need to be reinforced with a durable polyurethane covering every 3–4 months in homes with heavy usage.

In Joe's home, a hardwood floor was not appropriate because of his high rate of self-injurious head banging on the floor. Thus, it was necessary to provide extensive padding for the floor and, at the same time, deal with the fact that both Joe and his roommate were at times incontinent. This challenge was indeed complex, and a variety of plastic foam, synthetic, and "safety turf" pads were researched. Unfortunately, the retention of liquid was a problem with all of the plastic and synthetic pads. The solution came with the installation of a $\frac{1}{2}$-inch-thick horsehair pad encased with a plastic coating that prevented penetration of liquid yet softened the floor surface to protect Joe's head. A "liquid-resistant" carpet was placed over the horsehair pad in both the living room and Joe's bedroom. The carpet requires regular cleaning with an industrial-rated carpet cleaner.

An exception to the vinyl floor covering in the bathroom was made in Harry's house. Harry's bathroom was equipped with a 5-foot-wide walk-in shower. Harry takes several showers each day, and large volumes of water cover the floor. In spite of the industrial-strength vinyl that originally covered the floor, the floor continued to buckle and heave. Thus, an epoxy with natural sand floor was installed to provide both safety from falling on a wet surface and the durability needed to withstand constant water on the floor.

A final variation in floor covering was the floor in Brett's bedroom. The functional assessment information indicated that Brett engaged in "knee bouncing," which involves his bouncing up and down on his knees as a form of both relaxation and stress reduction. Brett's knees, shins, ankles, and feet all had been injured by this behavior, and it was important to minimize harm by providing him with a soft surface on his bedroom floor. This situation was resolved by placing a 6-foot by 8-foot section of 1-inch-thick rubber mat (typically used in the sport of wrestling) on his bedroom floor.

Wall Coverings and Other Surfaces

In the home that was renovated for Amy and her roommates, the primary concern was to remove all of the toxic lead-based paint that had accumulated over the years. This lead-based paint abatement process included the removal of paint from the exterior and interior surfaces. (The exterior paint removal was required by local guidelines that prevented aluminum or plaster siding from being placed on homes deemed of historic significance.) After the lead-based paint was removed, all of the exterior and interior wall surfaces were covered with lead-free paint.

In the homes that were built for Carl and Harry, special attention was given to the construction to prevent damage to the individuals and to the walls. The walls in their homes were constructed with a high-density particle board that traditionally is used in cabinetry. This particle board was placed over the 2-inch by 4-inch framing studs in the walls and then plastered with a high-density plastic covering. Finally, the plastic covering was painted with white interior latex. The net effect of this combination of wall coverings was a durable wall that did not bruise or dimple like traditional sheet rock, while the plastic coating softened the surface. Hitting or kicking the wall damaged neither the wall nor the individual. The result has been brief, initial bouts of wall hitting, followed by years without kicking or hitting the walls.

Fencing

Another controversial issue in the design of the homes was fencing around the property. Many of the parents and a few of the state officials feared that a traditional 6-foot fence would not provide the necessary security to prevent the individual from leaving the facility. Another major concern was that debris from the street and from people passing the homes could find its way onto the property, thereby providing unwanted material for potential pica, self-injury, or property destruction. Furthermore, many neighbors and local building officials insisted that any fences be consistent with neighborhood standards and local zoning ordinances. Finally, concern was expressed that materials provide a fence that was attractive and that would not become a focus for pica behavior. Given these concerns, it was necessary to design a range of fences to meet individual needs.

Amy and her roommates each had undergone surgery to remove intestinal obstructions as a result of pica while living in the institution. The medical officials at the institution believed that the next intestinal obstruction could be fatal for Amy or her roommates. Amy frequently attempted to leave her living unit at the institution, preferring to be outside. Unfortunately, much material was available for her to ingest in the yard; hence, her access was restricted. Functional assessment information indicated that Amy enjoyed spending time outside and especially enjoyed flowers, plants, and trees. She would approach, touch, and look at flowers and plants in a very appropriate manner. To ensure access to her yard yet maintain safety from the dangers of pica, a fence was designed to provide a barrier to street debris, and her yard was redesigned to contain preferred plants—but not items associated with pica. To keep material from coming into the yard from the busy street, a 6-foot wooden fence with a 1-foot wooden lattice extension was constructed. The fence design was selected because several other fences in the neighborhood had a similar design. In addition, the design was compatible with the local building code, and it was physically attractive. Another feature of this fence was that the inside surfaces were smooth; there were no foot- or handholds on the inside surface. Furthermore, the inside surface was sanded and coated to minimize the splintering of the wood. The fence provided a clear physical barrier that was sturdy, secure, and aesthetically pleasing.

Art's fence presented the greatest design challenge. In contrast to Amy and her roommates, Art was athletic and could easily scale a

6-foot fence with a 1-foot lattice extension. All of the people involved in the design of his living space were adamant that a fence be used to "slow him down long enough so that staff can know if he has left the property." The neighborhood around Art's house had many different fence designs, including a wooden fence with a plant arbor.

The fence design ultimately chosen for Art was a 6-foot wooden fence with a 1-foot wire lattice extension attached to a wooden beam. The wire lattice was positioned at a 90-degree angle to the fence so that it would be more difficult for Art to hold onto the wire and swing himself over the fence. Shrubbery was planted so that it would grow between the wire lattice to form a natural arbor. Unfortunately, this design was not adequate to keep Art from exiting the yard. After a brief period of analysis, Art found that he could spread the wire lattice apart and wriggle his way to the top of the beam and over the fence. Art also found that the place at which the fence met the side of the house provided the handholds and leverage needed to work his way up and over the fence.

During a 2-year period, different fence designs were developed in response to Art's innovative efforts, and ongoing behavioral support was implemented to minimize Art's unaccompanied outings. At this point, the fence makes leaving difficult but not impossible and, coupled with other communication, choice, and predictability support, has provided many escape-free months.

The fence design for Harry's house was a 6-foot wooden structure without lattice. In Harry's case, the problem was not going *over* the fence but breaking the boards on the fence and going *through* it. During a 2- to 3-year period, the maintenance staff repaired more than 30 feet of fence boards. Once a board was loosened by Harry's kicking, he would target the board until it was destroyed. Harry was not interested in leaving the home, only removing imperfections on the fence. After much cost and labor to fix the boards on Harry's fence, a plan was devised to strengthen the entire structure. Multiple sheets of 4-foot by 8-foot, $\frac{1}{2}$-inch-thick plywood were screwed onto the boards of the fence to reinforce the structure. This dramatically strengthened the fence while maintaining a pleasant appearance. Harry initially attempted to weaken individual boards without success, but he no longer targets the fence for destruction.

Egress from House into the Yard

A major goal of the design of all of the living spaces was to provide immediate egress from bedrooms and the living room into the yard. The architects described their approach as "layers of freedom" (G. Braddock, personal communication, August 28, 1989). The essential features of these layers of freedom to egress is that the individuals have a variety of ways to move out of a given space within the house without leaving the larger facility. The main purpose of security within the facility is to alert staff that someone has left the living space and is either on the porch or in the yard. This increase in personal choice is complementary to the overall community activity orientation of the agency.

In Amy's house, for example, Amy and her roommates have complete access to the living room, kitchen, and their individual bedrooms. When they leave the living space to enter the covered porch or the yard, a small buzzer alerts staff that they are out of the home. Another example of this approach is Harry's home. Harry has immediate access to all areas of the home except the kitchen. He also has immediate access to the fenced yard from his bedroom. This ease of exiting living space appears to be an important feature for decreasing Harry's destructive behavior.

Security Measures

Although the layers-of-freedom approach to egress within the living space was designed into each building, detailed security measures also were a prominent feature in each of the homes. Given the potential for significant compromises of health and safety, these security measures were deemed important by family members, state officials, and project planners. Conversely, given local zoning regulations, state fire marshall regulations, and the values of the field of developmental disabilities, these security issues are some of the most controversial features of the living spaces.

At the strong recommendation of those who knew Amy well, every closet, drawer, cupboard, and non–living space door in Amy's home was locked. A total of 14 flush, embedded locks were installed in the kitchen alone. Consistent with the layers-of-freedom approach to security, the belief was that the locks would be used for safety purposes until Amy and her housemates became accustomed to being in the home and therefore were not interested in targeting the objects in the closets, drawers, or cupboards. This approach proved cumbersome and unworkable for Amy, Amy's housemates, and those providing support. The risk of damage to drawers and ingestion of objects in closets and drawers may have been overstated. Within a month, Amy had developed an extensive pattern of activities in her new neighborhood. She had a supported job, a regular coffee house routine, and a series of places to go and people to see. Her initial testing of access to drawers and closets quickly stopped; within 2 months, the support staff members stopped locking the drawers and cupboards. In fact, training efforts shifted to helping Amy and her housemates use the cupboards and drawers independently. As part of this training effort, the kitchen became the center of the home for Amy and her housemates. Each of them had multiple food items available to them in the refrigerator and the cupboards. The housemates all participated in food preparation activities, including making coffee; baking muffins and biscuits; using the stove; mixing fruit drinks; and chopping carrots, celery, oranges, and bananas into bite-size chunks for snacking. In the several years that Amy and her housemates have lived in the community, there has not been a behavioral incident reported that concerned kitchen objects, utensils, or supplies. With training and regular access to drawers and cupboards, the locks proved unnecessary.

IMPACT OF ARCHITECTURAL VARIABLES

Our experience leaves us with a strong impression that architectural variables are a central part of effective behavioral support. We believe that research is needed to understand more fully the impact of architectural variables on community support, especially in three main areas:

1. Impact on the behavior of people with disabilities
2. Impact on the behavior of support personnel
3. Impact on the behavior of others who visit (or have contact with) the home

Impact on the Behavior of People with Disabilities

The focus of this chapter has been on the extent to which architectural analysis can reduce the natural contingencies associated with certain undesirable behaviors. The central message is that in some cases we create physical spaces that inadvertently set the occasion for problem behaviors or systematically reward problem behaviors. Altering the physical features of the environment often will be more effective at reducing problem behaviors than building a dramatic behavioral intervention. Research is needed, however, on how best to identify architectural variables associated with problem behavior and to document unequivocally the link between these variables and behavior reduction.

Impact on the Behavior of Support Personnel

All too often, residential support for individuals with problem behavior places people with disabilities in dysfunctional physical spaces. Their behavior may actually deteriorate in response to the space features, and staff are asked to engage in dramatic intervention efforts. An extremely important feature of effective architectural intervention is that it can reduce the need for staff to use extreme measures. The role of direct care staff in the support of an individual who has a history of breaking windows is very different if the individual lives in an environment where the glass windows have been replaced by a less breakable material. Too often we use physical intervention by staff to compensate for vulnerable features of a physical environment. Given the strong need for staff to build positive rapport with an individual in order to focus on teaching the individual new skills, this shift away from needing to protect the physical environment can

make a huge difference in the quality of interactions between a person with disabilities and
those providing support.

Impact on the Behavior of Others

One of the key reasons for providing support in
typical communities is to take advantage of the
proximity to others: family, friends, and supportive communities. The value of this proximity is
placed at risk, however, when the physical features of a home suggest deviance, institutionalization, or a place of work. We find that families
are more inclined to visit their family member
when the home is small, comfortable, and accessible. We find nonpaid friends more likely to
visit when the environment is inviting, homelike, and easy to reach. Social relationships are
an important part of a rich life in the community. The architectural features of a home (both
inside and outside) appear to affect the social
behaviors of family and friends. We have far too
little research to document the full range of critical variables that affect the social behaviors of
others, but initial work in this area supports the
contention that architectural variables are worthy of careful analysis (e.g., Thompson, Robinson, Dietrich, Ferris, & Sinclair, 1996).

BUILDING SUPPORT ECOLOGIES

Effective behavioral support for individuals with
histories of extreme problem behavior is a process of designing environments that "work." We
do not "fix" people but rather reorganize contexts so that people can be successful. We create
contexts in which new skills can be learned; old,
antisocial habits prove ineffective; and personal
success is commonplace. Contexts that build on
success, social support, and safety to gradually
achieve adaptation to the local community are
the goal of positive behavioral support.

Effective environments are individualized,
involve careful attention to activity patterns, include well-trained professional personnel, employ functional instructional systems, deliver
systematic contingencies of reinforcement, facilitate social contacts, and include detailed attention to architectural factors. At this point in
our development of effective behavioral sup-

port, too little attention has been paid to the important contribution of the physical environment
in the lives and behavior patterns of individuals
who receive community support.

CONCLUSION

The goal of this chapter has been to emphasize
the need for a better understanding of the link
among architectural variables, problem behavior,
and behavioral support strategies. Our experience in designing support for a group of individuals with histories of extreme problem behavior
has convinced us that architectural factors are
central to effective support. We have described
the variables that have been most dominant in
our efforts and the process that we used to
embed architectural design in both the assessment and the clinical support plans. Although
each of these individuals now has an active life
in his or her community and although each person has demonstrated important reductions in
problem behavior, we cannot draw a direct link
between our efforts at architectural modifications and these clinical gains.

It is important to recognize that architectural
design was not *the* behavioral intervention but
simply one part of a comprehensive, multicomponent intervention. As with all elements of comprehensive support, the architectural changes for
each person were guided by the functional assessment of when, where, how, and why problem behaviors occurred. The architectural elements of support were combined with changes
in activity patterns, social network development,
instruction on new communication skills, and
careful attention to the consequences for appropriate and problem behaviors. Although considerable effort was given to anticipating the architectural variables that would be important for
each person, our experience has promoted hu-
mility: We have learned that only so much can
be anticipated, that people change and grow, and
that effective behavioral support may involve
ongoing alterations of physical space. We have
learned that architectural support for people with
severe problem behaviors is much more than
simply hardening walls and windows; it is carefully building physical designs that promote suc-

cessful accomplishments (e.g., bathing, cooking, choice in movement). We have also learned that more than minimal effort is needed to build architectural supports that both improve safety *and* retain positive aesthetic appearance. Appearance is important. The appearance of an environment sends an important message to the people who live in a home, to the people who provide support in that home, and for families and friends who visit the home (Thompson et al., 1996). By including those who live, work in, and visit a home in the decisions about how the home would be physically altered, we learned the importance of attending to small things that can deliver unintended messages.

REFERENCES

Berkman, K.S., & Meyer, L.H. (1988). Alternative strategies and multiple outcomes in the remediation of severe self-injury: Going "all out" nonaversively. *Journal of The Association for Persons with Severe Handicaps, 13,* 76–86.

Braddock, D. (1994). Presidential address 1994: New frontiers in mental retardation. *Mental Retardation, 32,* 434–443.

Carr, E.G. (1977). The motivation of self-injurious behavior: A review of some hypotheses. *Psychological Bulletin, 8,* 800–816.

Carr, E.G., Horner, R.H., Turnbull, A., Magito-McLaughlin, D., McAtee, M., Smith, C.E., Ryan, K.A., Marquis, J., & Doolabb, A. (in press). Positive behavior support: A research synthesis. *Monograph of the American Association on Mental Retardation.*

Carr, E.G., Levin, L., McConnachie, G., Carlson, J.I., Kemp, D.C., & Smith, C.E. (1994). *Communication-based intervention for problem behavior.* Baltimore: Paul H. Brookes Publishing Co.

Carr, E.G., Robinson, S., & Palumbo, L.W. (1990). The wrong issue: Aversive vs. nonaversive treatment. The right issue: Functional vs. nonfunctional treatment. In A.C. Repp & N.N. Singh (Eds.), *Perspectives on the use of nonaversive and aversive interventions for persons with developmental disabilities* (pp. 361–379). DeKalb, IL: Sycamore Press.

Durand, V.M. (1990). *Severe behavior problems: A functional communication training approach.* New York: Guilford Press.

Evans, I.M., & Meyer, L.H. (1985). *An educative approach to behavior problems: A practical decision model for interventions with severely handicapped learners.* Baltimore: Paul H. Brookes Publishing Co.

Friedman, A., Zimring, C., & Zube, E. (1978). *Environmental design evaluation.* New York: Plenum.

Horner, R.H., & Carr, E.G. (1997). Behavioral support for students with severe disabilities: Functional assessment and comprehensive intervention. *The Journal of Special Education, 31,* 84–104.

Horner, R.H., Close, D.W., Fredericks, H.D.B., O'Neill, R.E., Albin, R.W., Sprague, J.R., Kennedy, C.H., Flannery, K.B., & Heathfield, L.T. (1996). Supported living for people with profound disabilities and severe problem behaviors. In D.H. Lehr & F. Brown (Eds.), *People with disabilities who challenge the system* (pp. 209–240). Baltimore: Paul H. Brookes Publishing Co.

Horner, R.H., Dunlap, G., Koegel, R.L., Carr, E.G., Sailor, W., Anderson, J., Albin, R.W., & O'Neill, R.E. (1990). In support of integration for people with severe problem behaviors: A response to four commentaries. *Journal of The Association for Persons with Severe Handicaps, 15,* 145–147.

Iwata, B.A., Dorsey, M.F., Slifer, K.J., Bauman, K.E., & Richman, G.S. (1982). Toward a functional analysis of self-injury. *Analysis and Intervention in Developmental Disabilities, 2,* 1–20.

Iwata, B.A., & Fisher, W. (Eds.). (1994). Functional analysis approaches to behavioral assessment and treatment [Special issue]. *Journal of Applied Behavior Analysis, 27*(2).

Kleinfield, N.R. (1997, June 22). A room of his own. *The New York Times,* p. l.

Knobbe, C.A., Carey, S.P., Rhodes, L., & Horner, R.H. (1995). Benefit–cost analysis of community, residential and institutional services for eleven adults with severe mental retardation who exhibit challenging behaviors. *American Journal on Mental Retardation, 99,* 533–541.

Koegel, L.K., Koegel, R.L., & Dunlap, G. (1996). *Positive behavioral support: Including people with difficult behavior in the community.* Baltimore: Paul H. Brookes Publishing Co.

Lakin, C., Prouty, B., Braddock, D., & Anderson, L. (1997). State institution populations smaller, older, more impaired. *Mental Retardation, 35,* 231–235.

Lehr, D.H., & Brown, F. (Eds.). (1996). *People with disabilities who challenge the system.* Baltimore: Paul H. Brookes Publishing Co.

Lucyshyn, J.M., Olson, D., & Horner, R.H. (1995). Building an ecology of support: A case study of one young woman with severe problem behaviors living in the community. *Journal of The Association for Persons with Severe Handicaps, 20,* 16–30.

Mace, F.C., Lalli, J.S., Pinter-Lalli, E.P., & Shea, M.C. (1993). Functional analysis and treatment of aberrant behavior. In R. Van Houten & S. Axelrod (Eds.), *Behavior analysis and treatment* (pp. 75–99). New York: Plenum.

Meyer, L.H., & Evans, I.M. (1989). *Nonaversive intervention for behavior problems: A manual for home and community.* Baltimore: Paul H. Brookes Publishing Co.

Meyer, L.H., Peck, C.A., & Brown, L. (Eds.). (1991). *Critical issues in the lives of people with severe disabilities.* Baltimore: Paul H. Brookes Publishing Co.

O'Neill, R.E., Horner, R.H., Albin, R.W., Storey, K., Sprague, J.R., & Newton, J.S. (1997). *Functional assessment of problem behavior: A practical assessment guide* (2nd ed.). Pacific Grove, CA: Brooks/Cole.

Prouty, R., & Lakin, K.C. (1995). *Residential services for persons with developmental disabilities: Status and trends through 1994.* Minneapolis: University of Minnesota, Research and Training Center on Community Living.

Repp, A.C., Felce, D., & Barton, L.E. (1988). Basing the treatment of stereotypic and self-injurious behaviors on hypothesis of their causes. *Journal of Applied Behavior Analysis, 21,* 281–289.

Repp, A.C., & Singh, N.N. (Eds.). (1990). *Perspectives on the use of nonaversive and aversive interventions for persons with developmental disabilities.* Sycamore, IL: Sycamore Press.

Risley, T. (1994, September). *Getting a life.* Presentation at the National Conference on Positive Behavioral Support, Santa Barbara, CA.

Risley, T. (1996). Get a life: Positive behavioral intervention for challenging behavior through life arrangement and life coaching. In L.K. Koegel, R.L. Koegel, & G. Dunlap (Eds.), *Positive behavioral support: Including people with difficult behavior in the community* (pp. 425–437). Baltimore: Paul H. Brookes Publishing Co.

Rotegard, L.L., Hill, B.K., & Bruininks, R.H. (1983). Environmental characteristics of residential facilities for mentally retarded persons in the United States. *American Journal on Mental Deficiency, 88,* 49–56.

Scotti, J.R., Ujcich, K.J., Weigle, K.L., Holland, C.M., & Kirk, K.S. (1996). Interventions with challenging behavior of persons with developmental disabilities: A review of current research practices. *Journal of The Association for Persons with Severe Handicaps, 21,* 123–134.

Singh, N.N. (1995). Moving beyond institutional care for individuals with developmental disabilities. *Journal of Child and Family Studies, 4,* 129–145.

Thompson, T., Robinson, J., Dietrich, M., Ferris, M., & Sinclair, V. (1996). Architectural features and perceptions of community residences for people with mental retardation. *American Journal on Mental Retardation, 101,* 292–313.

Thompson, T., Robinson, J., Graff, M., & Ingenmey, R. (1990). Home-like architectural features of residential environments. *American Journal on Mental Retardation, 95,* 328–341.

Wacker, D.P., Steege, M.W., Northup, J., Sasso, G., Berg, W., Reimers, T., Cooper, L., Cigrand, K., & Donn, L. (1990). A component analysis of functional communication training across three topographies of severe behavior problems. *Journal of Applied Behavior Analysis, 23,* 417–429.

Wright, F.L. (1920). *Environmental science.* Chicago: University of Chicago Press.

Section III

EXTENDED CASE STUDIES

Whereas Section II provided models for practice by describing overall programs of intervention, this section focuses on individual cases. Here are a number of extended case descriptions that provide readers with the nuts-and-bolts details of intervention. In each of these case descriptions, the lack of immediate success in the "real world," as compared with outcomes that we typically read about in journal articles, is particularly noteworthy. These are realistic cases in which we have encouraged the authors to describe the problems, setbacks, and failures, as well as the successes. In this way, we hope that practitioners have a model for problem solving when (not if) things do not go perfectly smoothly in their own attempts at intervention.

The section begins with detailed case descriptions by Lucyshyn, Olson, and Horner (Chapter 13), Fraser and Labbé (Chapter 14), and Berkman (Chapter 15). In each of these cases, a young adult with developmental disabilities and severe challenging behavior was successfully integrated—to varying degrees—into the community. Each of these efforts varies in the rigor of data keeping and presentation and in the style of recounting the journeys that they describe; but each presents a comprehensive, person-centered effort that did not always go according to plan.

Anderson, Freeman, Mullen, and Scotti (Chapter 16) then present their efforts to take

behavioral intervention "on the road" by describing their process of consultation in communities around West Virginia. Of note here is the decision-making process and accommodations that must be made when conducting functional assessments outside highly controlled environments. Berotti and Durand (Chapter 17) then describe the functional assessment and intervention for a young woman—also during an on-the-road consultation. This extended case provides a good glimpse into the details of implementing the functional communication training program that was described in Chapter 11. Berg, Wacker, Harding, and Asmus (Chapter 18) then recount the details of their functional assessments and communication intervention with a 3-year-old girl with mental retardation. This case provides the reader with many of the fine-grained details that need to be attended to when conducting functional assessments and skills-training interventions.

Hieneman and Dunlap (Chapter 19), using two case examples, provide a discussion of the issues—and frustrations—that surround the development and conduct of comprehensive positive behavioral support plans in the community. Sometimes, a major challenge to intervention is the stakeholders and community agencies with which one needs to collaborate for a plan to succeed. These authors describe their conceptualization of team-based support and how they have attempted to bring the members together.

Finally, lest the reader begin to think that comprehensive, positive behavioral support is only for individuals with developmental disabilities, Anderson, Bahl, and Kincaid (Chapter 20) describe their application of person-centered planning with a 14-year-old girl who had a history of parental physical abuse and was residing in a group home. The case illustrates well the application of the principles outlined previously in this book to yet another population with serious behavior challenges.

Chapter 13

Building an Ecology of Support for a Young Woman with Severe Problem Behaviors Living in the Community

Joseph M. Lucyshyn, Deborah L. Olson, & Robert H. Horner

Adults with developmental disabilities are relocating from large institutions to local communities (Hill, Lakin, & Bruininks, 1988). Individuals with developmental disabilities who engage in problem behaviors, however, continue to represent a large percentage of individuals who remain in institutional settings (Cunningham & Mueller, 1991; Lakin & Bruininks, 1985). In fact, problem behaviors are the most common reason cited for new admission or reentry to institutions (Bromley & Blacher, 1991; Hill & Bruininks, 1984). The presumption has been that problem behaviors should be reduced before a person

moves from the institution—an "eliminative" approach (Meyer & Evans, 1989) to intervention (Foxx, Bechtel, Bird, Livesay, & Bittle, 1986; Skodak-Crissey & Rosen, 1986; Zigler, Hodapp, & Edison, 1990). An alternative view that a regular lifestyle is the foundation for reducing problem behaviors is offered by proponents of 1) supported living for people with severe disabilities (Boles, Horner, & Bellamy, 1988; Howe, Horner, & Newton, 1998; Taylor, Biklen, & Knoll, 1987) and 2) positive behavioral support (Carr, Robinson, Taylor, & Carlson, 1990; Durand, 1990b; Horner et al., 1990; Koegel, Koegel, & Dunlap,

Preparation of this chapter was supported in part by the U.S. Department of Education (Cooperative Agreement No. H133B20004 and Grant No. H133C20114). The opinions expressed herein, however, do not necessarily reflect the position or policy of the U.S. Department of Education, and no official endorsement should be inferred.

This chapter is partially adapted from Lucyshyn, J.M., Olson, D., & Horner, R.H. (1995). Building an ecology of support: A case study of one young woman with severe problem behaviors living in the community. *Journal of The Association for Persons with Severe Handicaps, 20,* 16–30. Copyright 1995 by The Association for Persons with Severe Handicaps; reprinted and adapted by permission.

The authors thank Dr. Philip M. Ferguson for his assistance with the design of the qualitative methodology, Dr. Robert E. O'Neill for his help with the summary of behavioral and lifestyle data, and Dr. Richard W. Albin for his suggestions related to the clinical time-series data. They also thank Jane Bell for her computer skills; Kate Werner for her early assistance with qualitative data collection and analysis; Smita Shukla, Alan Surratt, and Julie Rychards for their assistance with quantitative data collection; and Dr. Bonnie Todis for her helpful comments on the qualitative data analysis. Finally, they thank family members, staff, and friends of Emma who contributed their time and effort to make this study possible.

1996; Meyer & Evans, 1989). Although there is some empirical evidence for supporting individuals with problem behaviors in the community (Berkman & Meyer, 1988; Horner et al., 1996), the database remains small. In addition, the complexities and potential richness of community life suggest the value of supplementing quantitative measures of resident behavior and lifestyle with qualitative descriptions and analysis (Kaiser, 1993; Meyer & Evans, 1993a, 1993b; Nisbet, Clark, & Covert, 1991; Repp & Singh, 1990; Taylor & Bogdan, 1981).

The broad purpose of the case study in this chapter is to provide a comprehensive description of the behavioral support and lifestyle outcomes experienced by one woman with a history of life-threatening, self-injurious behaviors during her move from a large public institution to the community. Within this broad purpose, there are three goals. The first goal is to provide an in-depth picture of community-based support for a person with severe problem behaviors by describing 30 months of data and by employing both *quantitative* and *qualitative* research methods. The second goal is to provide an example of using lifestyle measures and problem behavior measures to index the outcomes of behavioral support. The third goal is to illustrate the link between a functional assessment and the design and continual adaptation of a multi-element support plan (Carr, Robinson, & Palumbo, 1990; Horner & Carr, 1997).

METHOD

Focus Participant

At the time of the study, Emma was a 26-year-old woman with the diagnosis of autism, mild to moderate mental retardation, and hyperactivity. She was physically capable and often communicated her interests and desires verbally. During the study, she was taking between 125 and 675 milligrams (mg) of chlorpromazine per day. Before moving to the community, Emma lived for $7\frac{1}{2}$ years in a residential institution for individuals with developmental disabilities. Severe problem behaviors, including intense self-injury, were the primary reason for institutional placement.

Psychologist and family reports indicated that Emma continued to engage in intense self-injurious behaviors while residing in the institution. These behaviors resulted in significant tissue damage and multiple hospitalizations. Emma would bite her hands and arms, forcefully bang her head against objects and corners, pull out her hair, or pound her face with her fist. In addition, she engaged in aggressive behaviors toward staff, including scratching their hands, arms, and face; pulling their hair; or striking them with her protective helmet. Previously unsuccessful treatments included high dosages of psychotropic medication (e.g., 1,000 mg/day of chlorpromazine), contingent aversive stimulation (e.g., water mist, electric shock), and environmental enrichment (e.g., differential reinforcement, a social "bonding" program modeled after Gentle Teaching procedures [McGee, Menousek, Hobbs, & Menousek, 1987]).

Setting and Program Description

Emma lived in a small, three-bedroom house in a middle-income neighborhood one third of a mile from the downtown district of a moderate-size city in the Pacific Northwest. She lived with one housemate, Carol, a 37-year-old woman with mental retardation requiring pervasive supports. The house in which Emma lived was operated by a nonprofit residential service program for people with severe cognitive disabilities and a history of extreme problem behaviors (Horner et al., 1992). Emma received one-to-one staff support during the day; an awake staff person was present to support Emma and her housemate at night. Emma also received assistance with her job as a produce sorter at an organic foods warehouse, where she worked for 4 hours per week. A local supported employment organization obtained this job for Emma and provided a job coach to support her during her work hours.

Design of a Competent Environment

Seven months before Emma moved into the community, a series of assessments were conducted. A functional assessment of Emma's problem behaviors was completed using procedures recommended by O'Neill et al. (1997). This assessment indicated that Emma's self-injury and aggression were multiply maintained by avoidance of aversive situations, access to preferred objects, and attention from preferred people. In addition, medical support needs were identified; critical features interviews were conducted with her staff and family to identify the characteristics of a community living situation that would be safe, responsive, and individually appropriate (Horner et al., 1992); and a futures planning meeting was held to identify Emma's preferences, her family's visions for the future, and the initial members of Emma's support network (Kincaid, 1996; O'Brien, 1987).

Based on the assessment information, renovations were made to Emma's new home, her housemate was identified, staff were hired and trained, and a behavioral support plan was developed. During Emma's first year in the community, this support plan was revised frequently based on new information from repeated func-

tional assessments. The initial plan included a large number of features; a synthesis of the main features is provided in Table 1.

Quantitative Measurement

Quantitative measurement focused on six variables of interest:

1. The frequency of self-injurious behavior per week
2. The frequency of aggression toward others per week
3. Activities performed in the community
4. Social integration (social network and socially integrated activities)
5. Staff changes per week
6. Medication taken per week

Table 1. Emma's initial positive behavioral support plan

Lifestyle/Ecological Interventions

1. Provide opportunities for frequent home and community activities on a daily basis (20 community activities per week).
2. Support Emma's contact with family and/or friends at least four times per week.
3. Offer Emma choices for interaction, activity, possessions, foods, and snack items.
4. Give Emma control over her passive restraints. She may wear her helmet and arm and ankle guards at all times, but she will be given 10–20 opportunities per day to remove them. If she removes a restraint, then she may have it back at any point by asking.

Antecedent Interventions

1. Increase predictability about staff schedules and activity patterns by providing Emma with a weekly staff schedule picture calendar.
2. When Emma repeats or becomes anxious about an issue, write or draw a "promise card" that gives her the relevant answer or information. Place the card in her "promise book," and refer her to the proper card in her book when she next raises the issue.
3. Provide Emma with at least 50 positive social interactions each day.

Teaching New Behaviors

1. Teach Emma to communicate *verbally* her need for assistance, desire for attention, need for information or reassurance, and refusal to do a task or activity, and honor these communications.
2. Teach Emma to do deep breathing as a self-control strategy to reduce her anxiety.

Reinforcement Strategies

1. Use positive contingency contracts to motivate Emma to participate in tasks and activities (e.g., getting up and dressed in the morning).
2. Praise Emma often for verbally communicating her wants and needs, remaining calm, and actively participating in tasks or activities.

De-escalation Procedures

1. Physically block attempts at self-injury or aggression (e.g., place your arm between Emma's fist and head when she attempts to strike herself), redirect, and verbally reassure her.

Emergency Procedures

1. Physically restrain Emma, using approved procedures, when she engages in intense self-injury or aggression and cannot otherwise be blocked or redirected, so as to prevent injury to herself and others—not as a programmed consequence.

Data were collected during an 8-month period prior to Emma's move to the community (August 1988 through March 1989) for some variables and across the 30 months following her move (April 1989 through September 1991).

Self-Injurious Behavior

Self-injurious behavior was defined as Emma's hitting her head against a surface, biting herself, pulling out her hair, hitting herself with her fist, kicking herself on her shins, and pinching herself. Data were collected 24 hours per day by the community program staff using the Functional Assessment Observation Form described by O'Neill et al. (1997). Data were recorded as "events" of self-injury. An event was the occurrence of one or more self-injurious responses in rapid succession; a period of at least 30 seconds without self-injury was required before a new event was recorded. Data were tallied and reviewed by support staff at weekly staff meetings.

Aggression Toward Others

Aggression was defined as Emma's striking others with her helmet, scratching others, hitting others with objects or with her fist, and pulling others' hair. Measurement and review procedures for aggression were the same as for self-injurious behavior. The results provided a weekly count of the number of events with one or more instances of aggression.

Activities Performed in the Community

Data on the frequency of activities in the community were collected in two ways. The first was indirect measurement via the Resident Lifestyle Inventory (RLI; Kennedy, Horner, Newton, & Kanda, 1990). This questionnaire provides a list of 144 activities and was completed by program staff who participated regularly in activities with Emma. For each activity, staff rated 1) whether the activity occurred during the preceding 30 days, 2) the frequency of its occurrence, and 3) whether it typically occurred in the community or in the home. The RLI has been demonstrated by Kennedy and colleagues (Kennedy, Horner, Newton, & Kanda, 1990) to have acceptable congruent validity (.81) and test-retest reli-

ability (.83). The social validity of the RLI also was demonstrated by Kennedy, Horner, Newton, and Kanda (1990) wherein more than 70% of direct services staff reported that use of the RLI improved their effectiveness. RLI data were collected twice in the institution prior to Emma's move and once each year during the 3 years following her move.

The second measure of activity patterns was collected through direct observation by the program staff on a 24-hour basis using the Valued Outcomes Information System (VOIS; Newton et al., 1988). Staff completed a small "tag" for each activity performed in the community. An event was scored as a "community activity" if it lasted for at least 15 minutes and was performed outside the property boundary of the home. This system produced a frequency count of the number of community activities performed each week. This count also was tallied and reviewed by support staff at weekly staff meetings.

The RLI also was used to measure Emma's activity preferences. For each activity listed on the RLI that support staff had done with Emma, a rating of "preferred," "not preferred," or "unclear" was provided to indicate Emma's preference for that activity. Newton, Ard, and Horner (1993) demonstrated that staff assessment of resident preference using this system agreed with resident choice behavior with 92% accuracy.

Social Integration

Emma's social life was measured quantitatively in two ways. The first way was through an index of her social network, and the second way was through direct observation of activities performed with others. Emma's social network was measured using the Social Network Analysis Form (SNAF; Kennedy, Horner, & Newton, 1990). This interview was completed on each SNAF administration by Emma and two staff members who had worked for at least 3 months with Emma and who provided a list of people perceived as socially important to Emma under the headings of 1) family, 2) friends, 3) people paid to provide support, and 4) co-workers and housemates. The SNAF was administered twice before Emma moved from the institution and four times after she moved into the community.

The second empirical index of Emma's social life was obtained via the VOIS direct observation system. The same activity tags used to record physical integration had space on them to indicate whether the activity was socially integrated. To be recorded as socially integrated, the activity needed to involve a minimum of 15 minutes of socially reciprocated interaction with a person who was neither paid to provide support nor a housemate (Newton et al., 1988). These data were collected only after Emma moved to the community, and the data resulted in a count of socially integrated activities that was reviewed weekly by program staff.

Staff Changes

Functional assessment interviews with staff in the institution suggested that staff turnover was a significant setting event related to the frequency and intensity of Emma's problem behavior. As such, staff changes in the community were monitored carefully using the personnel records of the support agency. Changes were defined as new staff starting, staff making significant changes in hours of employment (e.g., full time to relief, relief to part time), and staff terminating employment. The frequency of these changes was tallied and summarized as a cumulative frequency per week.

Medication

The type and the amount of medication that Emma took each day were recorded by medical and support staff following procedures mandated by the Oregon Administrative Rules. From these records, the weekly dosage level of chlorpromazine, in milligrams, was summarized.

Reliability and Validity

Because interobserver agreement scores were not gathered for weekly behavioral and lifestyle data, alternative strategies were employed to strengthen the reliability and validity of these data. The reliability and the accuracy of weekly time-series data (e.g., aggression, community integration) were enhanced through initial and ongoing training in data collection for all staff supporting Emma, weekly data review meetings led by a program manager, and the omission of weekly data judged to be inaccurate. The convergent validity of lifestyle data was strengthened by the use of multiple quantitative measurement strategies (e.g., time-series weekly frequency data, empirically validated lifestyle assessment instruments; Campbell & Fiske, 1959; McGrew & Bruininks, 1994; Widaman, Stacy, & Borthwick-Duffy, 1993). Finally, the convergent validity of behavioral and lifestyle data was strengthened further by the use of *triangulation* across research methods (Patton, 1990). Qualitative interviews and participant observations, in addition to providing an indepth description and interpretation of Emma's life in the community, served to support the quantitative results.

Qualitative Measurement

Interviews and participant observations were completed over a 7-month period by the chapter's first author beginning in April 1991. The social role of the researcher conducting interviews and observations was that of an *insider* (Jorgensen, 1989). This author possessed knowledge about Emma's experiences in the community and had established a trusting relationship with staff by serving as a volunteer behavioral consultant for the "Carol and Emma" house for 7 months prior to the initiation of the study.

Qualitative Interviews

Semistructured interviews were conducted with six key informants: Emma's mother and father; a brother and a sister-in-law who were strong advocates for Emma; a staff person who had worked with Emma in the community for more than 2 years; and one of Emma's closest friends, a former part-time community staff person and current relief staff person for Emma. The interviewer presented participants with open-ended questions about Emma's quality of life in the institution and/or the community and about changes in Emma's behavior since her move to the community. An interview guide ensured that each question was included in all of the interviews. Specific interview questions are presented in Table 2. Interviews lasted from 2 to 5 hours and were completed across one to five sessions. A total of 17 hours of interviews were completed. All interviews were tape recorded and transcribed verbatim.

Participant Observations

Participant observations were completed with Emma and her staff and friends as they interacted and participated in a wide range of activities. Experiences sampled included the following: 1) typical home and community activities, 2) interactions with staff and friends, and 3) different times of day and days of the week. A total of nine observations were completed. Observations lasted from 1 to 5 hours; a total of 16 hours were spent in the field. Immediately following an observation session, detailed field notes were written describing the environments, activities, and interactions between Emma and others, including the observing researcher. Subjective impressions, analysis, and contextual information based on insider knowledge were written in observer comments.

Data Analysis Procedures

Qualitative data analysis occurred throughout data collection as new field notes and interview transcripts were analyzed for preliminary descriptive and conceptual categories (i.e., themes). After all field notes were written and all interviews were transcribed, the data were entered into the *Ethnograph* qualitative data management software program (Seidel, Kjolseth, & Seymour, 1985) in the form of individual files for each observation or interview. This resulted in 18 files consisting of 325 pages of interview data and 233 pages of participant observation data. Data first were sorted into 12 descriptive categories drawn from the interview questions (e.g., community life, changes). The basic characteristics of these categories were defined, and these definitions guided the initial coding of all files.

Following this initial organization of the data, the *grounded theory method of open coding* described by Strauss and Corbin (1990) was used to identify 43 additional descriptive and conceptual categories (e.g., "demandingness," staff relationship). Questions asked about the data included the following: 1) What are people doing? 2) Why are the people doing this? 3) To what class of phenomenon do these concepts relate? As each new category was identified, its

---

Table 2. Qualitative interview guide for careprovider/friend and family members

Questions for Careprovider/Friend
1. Tell me about Emma. What is she like?
2. Tell me about Emma's life in the community. What is it like?
3. What kind of things does she do? Where does she go? Whom does she see?
4. What makes her happy? What tends to set her off?
5. Describe a good day. Describe a bad day.
6. How does Emma make her preferences known? What does she express an interest in doing or not doing?
7. How do careproviders typically respond to Emma's preferences?
8. How happy do you believe Emma is living in the community?
9. From the time you first met her until now, how has she changed, if at all?
10. Why do you think she has changed?

Questions for Family Members
1. Tell me about Emma. What is she like?
2. What was her life like at the institution from your perspective?
3. Describe your experience with visiting Emma at the institution.
4. How often do you see Emma now?
5. What is Emma's life like in the community from your perspective?
6. Describe your experience with visiting Emma in the community.
7. From the time she entered the community until now, how has she changed, if at all?
8. Why do you think she has changed?

characteristics were defined, and these definitions guided further coding of the data.

Finally, axial coding (Strauss & Corbin, 1990) was employed to organize the content of major categories (i.e., phenomena) into a set of descriptive relationships. During this analysis, one or more of the following questions were asked about the data:

1. What are the properties and dimensions of the category (e.g., what are the properties and dimensions of the changes that Emma experienced)?
2. Which contexts or intervening conditions promote or inhibit the phenomenon?
3. What are the interactional strategies by which the phenomenon is managed or carried out?
4. What are the consequences of the phenomenon's promotion or inhibition?

Through the process of inductive and deductive analysis, properties and relationships within each category were proposed and were checked for their presence in the data. Theories about Emma's life in the community emerged from an analysis of the data. With the use of the constant comparative method (Bogdan & Biklen, 1982), coding categories, the properties of coding categories, and the relationships among coding categories that continually reappeared in the data were retained for theory development. These theories, grounded and verified in the actual data collected, then were organized into an analytical description and interpretation of Emma and her life in the community.

Procedures to Ensure Data Credibility and Consistency

Several procedures were used to enhance the credibility and consistency of the qualitative data (Merriam, 1988; Patton, 1990). First, triangulation across research methods was employed. Quantitative behavioral and lifestyle data served to support interpretations of Emma's experience from the participant observations and interviews. Second, triangulation across qualitative sources of data was used to compare and cross-check the consistency of information derived at

different times and by different means. Third, member checks were completed with interview informants and observation participants throughout the course of the study. After the analytical descriptions of Emma's life were completed, a draft was submitted to four key informants, who were asked to evaluate the accuracy of the interpretations. Informants, for the most part, affirmed the researchers' interpretations and suggested improvements in accuracy, emphasis, or completeness. These recommendations then were incorporated into the final interpretation.

To minimize the bias inherent in the researcher's insider role, the chapter's second author, a qualitative researcher with no association to the support program, provided guidance and feedback on the analysis and interpretation of the data and evaluated the congruence between the emerging findings and the data. In addition, two other qualitative researchers each reviewed 3 randomly selected files (6 of 18 files) and assessed the degree to which the defined categories reflected what they saw in the data. Both researchers reported that the categories accurately represented the data and were coded with a high degree of consistency.

RESULTS

Quantitative and qualitative results were juxtaposed and merged to provide an overview of Emma's community and social integration while living in the institution and the community, a summary of her problem behavior levels, and an interpretation of the pattern and complexity of her community participation and social relationships.

Community Participation

Figure 1 indicates the number of physically integrated activities performed per week from April 1989 through September 1991. During Emma's first 2 months in the community, she engaged in an average of 19.4 community activities per week. During the next year, she gradually increased her frequency of community activities to a peak of more than 40 activities per week. Between August 1990 and January 1991, her rate of community activities returned to approx-

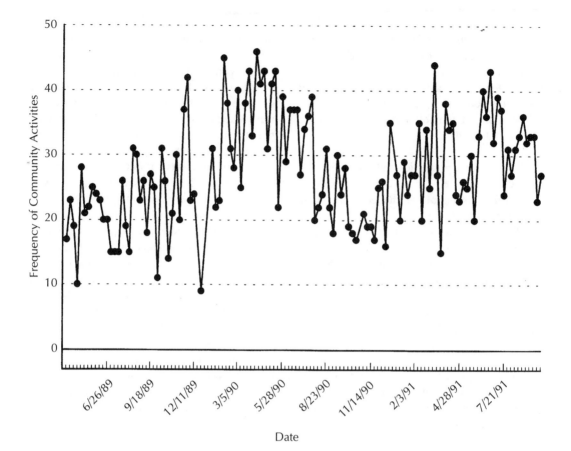

Figure 1. Frequency of community activities across 131 weeks.

imately 20 per week and then increased again during 1991 to a rate of 30.6 activities per week (range of 20–44). Qualitative interviews suggest that the initial growth in Emma's activity patterns was related to both staff and Emma's coming to understand her preferences and becoming more comfortable with activities and support strategies in the community. Later growth seemed to be related to staff members' introducing Emma to less preferred and more challenging activities and encouraging and supporting her participation. Cyclical decreases in community participation were attributed by staff to cold weather, multiple staff changes, and accompanying increases in Emma's frequency of problem behaviors.

Table 3 presents RLI data for Emma before and after her move to the community. These data demonstrate a high frequency of community use

(a mean of 171 community activities per month). Together, these data indicate that Emma engaged in more activities in the community, more varied activities in the community, and more preferred activities in the community after her move from the institutional setting.

Qualitative analysis of Emma's activities reveals three major patterns: relaxing activities, lively pursuits, and physically demanding activities. Each is described in turn in the following sections.

Relaxing Activities

Many of Emma's activities in the community reflected her preference for sitting with a staff person or friend and enjoying a beverage, food, music, or an interesting view. These activities included "hanging out" at a local coffee shop, having dinner at a Thai restaurant, and watch-

Table 3. Summary of Emma's RLI community participation scores while living in the institution and in community environments

Measures (number during assessed month)	Institution		Community		
	8/88	3/89	6/89	1/90	5/91
Number of community activities	22	4	171	178	166
Number of different community activities	8	1	16	25	21
Number of different activities identified as "preferred" community activities	3	1	9	8	20
Mean number of community activities per day	.71	.13	5.7	5.7	5.4

ing rock climbers scale the walls of a cliff in the early evening. During these activities, Emma usually expressed contentment punctuated with anxious worries or simple demands (e.g., "Melissa's coming on Tuesday?" "Fix the arm guard"). When staff skillfully offered Emma reassurance, honored reasonable preferences, negotiated compromises, or communicated limits, Emma typically returned to a calm disposition.

Lively Pursuits

Emma regularly participated in a smaller set of more lively activities in the community. These included going on walks, purchasing preferred items at discount stores, and dancing at a local nightclub. Some of these activities began as staff preferences but over time developed into Emma's preferences as well. These activities typically generated expressions of enthusiasm, as can be seen in the following description from an interview with a staff member:

On the way [to the coffee shop] she was skipping . . . laughing . . . I would say euphoric. It was a pretty somber band, but Emma was dancing. No one else was. Everybody just looked at her, adored her. She was making it a better experience for everybody. Her happiness was contagious. People smiled at her a lot.

Sometimes, however, anxious comments and multiple demands accompanied the activity. Staff reported, for example, a shopping trip during which Emma anxiously worried about what to buy. After finally making her purchase, she demanded to buy a different item. In situations such as this, the skillful use of support strategies (e.g., communicating limits, providing reassur-

ance) typically was necessary to prevent escalation into problem behaviors.

Physically Demanding Activities

Emma also participated in physically demanding activities that represented the preferences of veteran staff. These staff, having successfully integrated Emma into many typical activities, attempted to expand her experiences and interests further. In some cases, Emma quickly overcame some initial anxiety and developed an interest in the new activity. Examples included a t'ai chi class one year and wading in a river one summer. For other activities, such as hiking, Emma's initial participation was associated with both anxiety and problem behaviors. After repeated outings and staff persistence, however, Emma gradually developed an interest in the activity. Field notes from a hike up a small butte near Emma's house illustrate this experience:

As we began hiking up the steep trail on the west side of the butte, Emma demanded, "Go home now." Sarah [staff person] ignored her pleas and encouraged Emma to continue to hike the short distance to the top. Emma marched up the trail, punctuating her assent with demands to "go home now." Three quarters of the way to the top, she stopped, looked back at the cars driving by on a highway in the distance, and became transfixed. Enthusiastically she demanded, "Come back next Friday." . . . After the hike, Sarah asked, "Did you like the hike?" Emma replied, "Yes way." Sarah continued, "Do you want to do it again next week?" Emma, with much animation, replied, "Yes!"

In other cases (e.g., an overnight camping trip), staff honored Emma's anxiety and protests by ending the activity and not trying to do it again. These activities appeared to represent the limits of Emma's interest in challenging, physical activities.

Social Relationships

The weekly frequency of Emma's socially integrated activities is presented in Figure 2. These data indicate that Emma interacted with people who were not paid to provide support an average of 6.2 times per week, with high variability (standard deviation = 3.9) across individual weeks. Qualitative interviews suggest that staff turnover, high levels of problem behaviors, and limited transportation funds for visits to family members contributed to the variability in Emma's social contacts.

Social network data from the SNAF are presented in Table 4 and document an increase in the size and complexity of Emma's social net-work after she moved to the community. Prior to her move, there were from six to nine people who were actively involved in Emma's social life. All of these people were family members or people who were paid to provide support. While Emma was living in the community, more of her family became involved in her life, and she developed relationships with friends and co-workers without disabilities. In fact, for the first time in her adult life, Emma developed relationships with people who were typical members of her community. A qualitative understanding of Emma's social life emerges from four descriptive or conceptual categories in the data: staff, family members, friends, and acquaintances.

Staff

While working with Emma, staff experienced her charm and energy, as well as her anxiety, de-

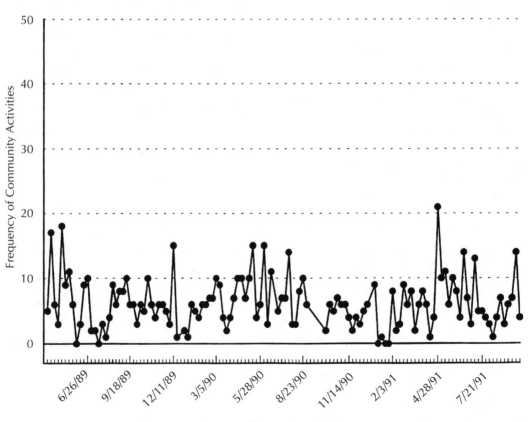

Figure 2. Frequency of socially integrated activities across 131 weeks.

Table 4. Summary of Emma's Social Network Analysis (SNAF) scores while living in the institution and in community environments

Measures (number during assessed month)	Environment					
	Institution		Community			
	8/88	3/89	6/89	1/90	9/90	7/91
Number of people paid to provide services	3	5	5	7	6	11
Number of friends	0	0	1	1	11[a]	3
Number of family members	3	4	4	4	7	5
Number of co-workers/roommates	0	0	0	0	2	1
Total social network size	6	9	10	12	26	20

[a]Six of the people were friends of staff members and were identified as part of Emma's social network.

mands, and problem behaviors. Interviews and observations stressed the importance of Emma's relationships with several direct care staff. Her sister-in-law reflected this when she commented, "I think what motivates her is people. With certain people, when she's established [a positive relationship], she is fine. She'll do wonderful things." Our analysis of contextual factors and consequences observed in the data suggests that the continuity of these core relationships and the quality of these interactions often determined Emma's level of problem behavior and happiness as perceived by others.

One pattern that emerged from the data on relationships with staff was the mutual effort of Emma and a few veteran staff to develop a friendship that went beyond the boundaries of a typical staff–client relationship. Several factors seemed to promote this process of friendship development. First, working in Emma's home created a context of informality. Second, staff and Emma had much freedom to plan their day and often engaged in enjoyable activities together. Third, the effective use of positive behavioral support strategies was associated with successful experiences in the community and with increases in Emma's positive communications and expressions of affection. These factors appeared to encourage a trust and mutual regard between Emma and some veteran staff that evolved into friendships. There were positive benefits associated with these friendships: Staff taught Emma additional social and conversation skills and did activities with Emma during their free time, and Emma willingly participated in

new activities with staff. Associated negative outcomes included the anxiety and problem behaviors that ensued when beloved staff reduced their work hours or terminated employment.

Family Members

Emma's family included parents, three older brothers, and one older sister. Family members lived in the suburbs of a large city 120 miles north of her home. Interviews with family members suggest that Emma's relationship with them improved considerably after Emma moved to the community. Her parents, brother, and sister-in-law reported that when Emma lived in the institution they were not permitted to take her off campus, and she was not allowed to visit them at their homes because of safety and liability concerns. When they visited Emma at her cottage, she often was "out of it" because of high levels of medication; consequently, she did not engage in meaningful conversation or activity.

In contrast, informants indicated that Emma saw her family more often and developed a more active and affectionate set of relationships while living in the community. She was perceived as looking forward to seeing family members with a mixture of enthusiasm and anxiety. During family visits to Emma's home, trips by Emma to see family members, or telephone contacts, Emma typically engaged in animated greetings and simple conversations. When family members visited Emma, they took her shopping or out to a movie without incident. Visits with family often were associated with receiving presents and favorite foods or sweets and with outings to purchase preferred items or treats. A visit by Emma to her parents' house, as described by her mother, illustrates this finding:

She was so excited. When she came here she wanted a cold drink, and then she was ready to go shopping. Glenn [Emma's brother] and Sarah were going to take her to [a shopping center]. I said, "How much money do you have?" Well, she didn't tell me, so I said, "Take another 10 dollars, and you can really have some fun buying things" [laughter]. . . . She was so happy. She took that and put it in her purse.

Friends

Qualitative analysis suggests the central role that staff played as a source of potential friends, as a resource for contacts with community members, and in the maintenance of friendships with community members. For example, two former staff members maintained a close relationship with Emma after leaving the agency. One of these was Teresa, who was regarded as Emma's best friend. Teresa occasionally worked relief shifts and continued to see Emma once per week during her free time, usually for dinner. Another former staff member, Melissa, continued to see Emma a few times each month.

Staff members were a resource for new friends when they introduced Emma to their own friends. Heather, for example, was a close friend of a staff member named Sarah. She occasionally accompanied Emma and Sarah on day hikes or sometimes invited them to her country home for dinner.

The importance of the role of staff in Emma's development of friendships can be seen in the friendships that faltered because the community member was not a member of the staff's social network. For example, Meredith, who lived in Emma's new community, was an acquaintance of Emma's sister-in-law. Meredith attempted to establish a relationship with Emma during her first 2 years in the community. Eventually, however, Meredith stopped contacting Emma, and the relationship faded because Emma did not ask to see Meredith and staff did not remember to arrange contacts with her because, unlike Heather, she was not one of *their* friends.

Acquaintances

Interviews and observations indicated that Emma developed a large number of acquaintances while living in the community. These individuals included friends of staff, employees of small businesses, and co-workers at a supported employment jobsite.

Problem Behaviors

While Emma lived in the institution, the frequency and intensity of her problem behaviors had placed her at major physical risk and had been perceived as a fundamental barrier to community placement. The weekly rate of problem behaviors in the institution was difficult to assess reliably because of variation in measurement procedures. In the community, Emma continued to engage in problem behaviors throughout the 30 months of this analysis. Frequency counts of Emma's self-injury and aggression per week are presented in the first two graphs of Figure 3. The quantitative results indicate periods with very low rates of problem behaviors punctuated by two periods of major regression. Qualitative accounts suggest changes in the topography and intensity of problem behavior across these regressions. These perceived changes were in the direction of less intense and less physically harmful topographies.

The first 4 months of community life were associated with low levels of self-injury and aggression. There was a modest and gradual increase in problem behaviors between September and December of 1989. In the last 2 weeks of 1989, there were very high rates of very intense self-injury and aggression (e.g., biting wrists and arms, scratching others). The next 9 months were associated with sustained reductions in most problem behaviors. The final months of 1990 were associated with an increase in novel, low-intensity (e.g., knocking knuckles) and moderate intensity (e.g., hitting self, kicking self) self-injurious behavior. Across 1991, there was another decrease in the frequency of problem behaviors.

These results are purely evaluative and are not part of a design that allows discussion of controlling variables. Covariation of problem be-

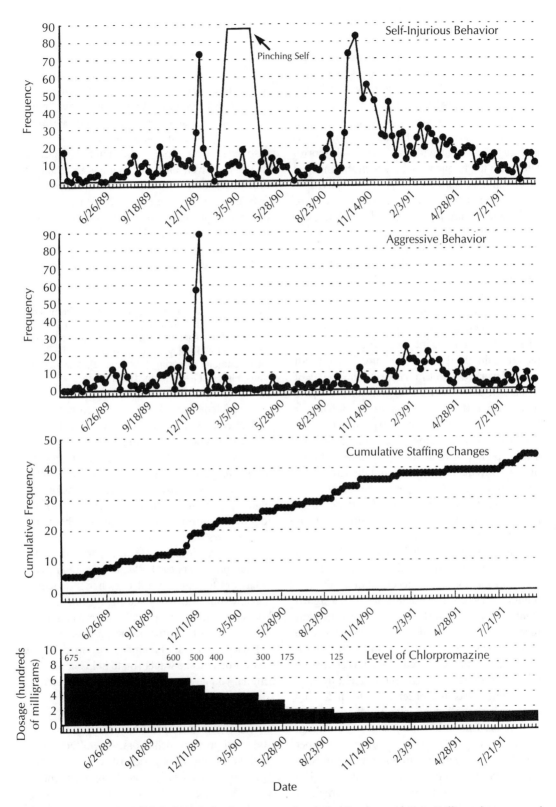

Figure 3. Emma's self-injurious behaviors, aggressive behaviors, cumulative staffing changes, and chlorpromazine levels across 131 weeks.

haviors, however, was looked at with physical and social integration, staff changes, and medication levels. In addition, qualitative data about contextual factors that appeared to escalate problem behaviors contributed to the analysis.

The frequency of Emma's self-injurious and aggressive behavior was negatively correlated with the frequency with which she engaged in community activities (r [131] = $-.21$, $p < .05$), although less correlated with the level of social integration. In general, very high rates of problem behaviors were associated with reductions in integration. Emma continued to be involved in community activities and socially integrated activities during weeks when she had low to moderate elevations in problem behaviors.

Staff changes were perceived to be associated with increased levels of problem behavior. The cumulative frequency of staff changes is depicted in the third graph of Figure 3. A total of 23 staff worked with Emma during the course of this study. Self-injury and aggression were positively correlated with changes in staffing (r [131] = $.21$, $p < .05$). Visual inspection of these data suggests that multiple staff changes during a brief period of time were associated with an increased frequency of problem behaviors. This covariation was most apparent during the two major regressions in behavior in December 1989 and September–October 1990. Qualitative interviews support the view that Emma's intense acceleration in problem behaviors in December 1989 was associated with the departure of several staff members. The acceleration in the last months of 1990 was attributed partly to a significant reduction in work hours of a favorite staff member. A second contextual factor related to these regressions was the temporary loss of program fidelity that occurred when new staff were hired and trained. A final factor, noted by staff and family, was the onset of cold and rainy weather in the fall and winter months.

When Emma left the institutional setting, she was taking 675 mg of chlorpromazine per day. This was decreased to 600 mg/day in September 1989 and dropped progressively to 125 mg/day by August 1990 (see fourth graph of Figure 3). No clear link between medication reduction and rates of problem behavior was ob-

served across the 30 months of quantitative data, and no such perceived association was reported during interviews with staff or family members.

Analysis of the qualitative categories "problem behavior" and "dislikes" suggests several additional contextual and antecedent variables associated with problem behavior. In addition to the perceived effect of major staff changes, other disruptions in Emma's contact with staff or friends were perceived as related to self-injury or aggression, including staff members' going on vacation, unexpected schedule changes, and friends' leaving after a visit. During one observation, a staff member described a particularly difficult week:

> Rebecca went on vacation and didn't tell Emma until 2 days before she left. On Monday, Jake got sick and had to call in a substitute staff person. Emma became very anxious Monday through Wednesday. She did a lot of anxious repeating [about staff], knocked her shins a lot, and had a major fit on Wednesday.

Problem behaviors also occurred when staff attempted to assert control over Emma. Examples included controlling Emma's access to her passive restraints (e.g., helmet, arm and ankle guards) and demanding that she do nonpreferred tasks or activities. Other predictors included lapses in attention from staff and failures to provide information or reassurance about anxious worries.

A final finding was the perception that Emma did not appear to "enjoy" using problem behaviors to gain control over her interactions and environment. When she engaged in problem behaviors, staff often perceived her as an active participant in the effort to de-escalate her own behavior. As one staff member described, "If she has a problem, she wants you to help her . . . with Emma, you go through the problem together."

Additional Positive Changes

Concurrent with improvements in Emma's lifestyle and problem behaviors, several additional positive changes were described or observed. Qualitative analysis indicated improvements in Emma's physical well-being, active engagement, level of security, communication and social skills, level of independence, ability to contribute to her support, and level of happiness. These changes were attributed to a number of factors: the reduction in Emma's medication levels, Emma's participation in community activities and social relationships, staff continuity, and the implementation of a wide array of positive behavioral support strategies.

Improvements in Emma's physical well-being and activity level were among the first changes noticed by family and staff. After chlorpromazine levels were reduced, the improved health of her skin and gums was noted. Although the quantitative data did not reveal a link between reductions in chlorpromazine levels and behavioral improvement, family members and staff viewed Emma as more alert and more responsive to attempts at interaction and support. Improvements in Emma's active participation in activities also were reported. In addition, efforts by staff to give Emma information about her day and to assuage her worries were viewed as more successful. She was reported to make eye contact and to listen to information more often and to escalate to problem behaviors less often.

Emma's verbal communication and social skills also were perceived as improving. She was reported to communicate a wider variety of wants, needs, and worries (e.g., "Go dancing," "Go to the bathroom," "Buy a new chin guard if this one breaks"). She expressed affection more often, more successfully engaged in simple as well as abstract conversations with staff (e.g., "When you go to heaven, you can bring your arm guards?"), and began to initiate and prompt greetings with acquaintances and friends in the community.

Emma also was observed making several positive contributions to her own support. She sometimes praised herself or prompted staff to praise her (e.g., "Great hiking!" "You worked hard?"), prompted staff to use positive support strategies (e.g., "Write a promise card," "Look at the schedule"), or offered words of encouragement to staff after enjoyable activities together (e.g., "Had fun with you at Wenneker's Butte!"). During preferred activities with staff and friends, Emma engaged in numerous expressions that suggested contentment or happiness. As her sister-in-law observed, "If you

could have seen her at [the institution] and now . . . what is obvious is that she is happy, that she is enjoying herself, and she likes it here."

Support Strategies and Continued Adaptations

Interview and participant observation data reveal several categories of support used by staff:

1. Increasing predictability by providing information about the daily schedule and contingencies many times and in many different forms throughout the day
2. Providing many opportunities for clear choices among desirable alternatives and then honoring Emma's decision
3. Teaching new skills that made preferred activities easier to perform
4. Providing high rates of verbal praise and reassurance
5. Communicating limits clearly and consistently
6. Blocking attempts at self-injury or aggression
7. Using physical restraint when problem behaviors escalated in intensity

When we analyzed the process by which support strategies were introduced and revised, we found a pattern of continued adaptation by staff to changes in Emma's behavior and to contextual events affecting her behavior. Adaptations included performing new functional analyses of persistent problem behaviors, improving implementation fidelity, temporarily decreasing Emma's participation in community activities during major regressions, and developing and implementing new support strategies to ameliorate recurring or new problem behaviors. Contextual factors that appeared to facilitate these adaptations included weekly staff meetings, consensual decision making, leadership by direct services staff, and flexibility in the organization of Emma's daily schedule.

When Emma first arrived in the community, staff implemented a set of positive support strategies based on an initial understanding of the functions of her problem behavior and the conditions that appeared likely to promote adaptive behavior. Staff helped Emma develop an individualized lifestyle that matched her interests by offering her a variety of choices and by honoring many of her preferences. For example, she decorated her room to her personal taste, bought preferred items such as toy cars, and engaged in preferred activities such as going out for coffee.

Staff also provided Emma with information and reassurance to help her overcome her worries about keeping possessions and to help her predict valued future events, such as staff schedules, family visits, and community activities. When verbal information was not sufficient, they wrote "promise cards" that included a pictorial representation of the promise. Staff used positive contingencies, instruction, and frequent praise to build Emma's capacity to complete home routines, participate in activities, and express her wants and needs using language instead of problem behavior. When Emma engaged in self-injurious or aggressive behavior, staff physically blocked the attempts and positively redirected her to adaptive alternative behavior. When problem behaviors escalated, staff used physical restraint procedures to prevent injury to herself and others—not as a programmed consequence.

Staff use of positive support strategies first faltered, however, when several staff changes occurred and Emma's frequency and intensity of problem behavior increased. The potential for mortal danger compelled staff to understand better the reasons for Emma's problem behavior and to use support strategies that would prevent or minimize these behaviors. A new functional assessment was completed with the support of a behavior specialist, and increased efforts were made to

1. Offer clear and timely information and reassurance when Emma expressed a worry
2. Teach Emma to express her wants and to ask for help when she was feeling unsafe
3. Teach Emma self-managed de-escalation tactics (e.g., deep breathing relaxation)

During Emma's second year in the community, the success of staff at teaching Emma to communicate verbally her wants and needs contributed to a new set of problems that required new support strategies. Emma's new-found assertiveness often escalated into incessant demands. Sometimes these demands were unreasonable for the time, place, or resources available; disrespectful to others; or harmful to herself. This new problem reemphasized that Emma's aggression and self-injury were used in some situations to escape nonpreferred activities and/or to obtain preferred items or activities. The support plan was revised to include strategies for negotiating compromises, communicating limits on choice, and preventing aggression and self-injury from being rewarded.

The second regression in problem behaviors, although not as serious as the first, prompted staff to develop strategies to minimize problem behaviors associated with staff changes. Staff developed a package of interventions that included providing advance notice of staffing changes, having a going-away party for terminating staff, and arranging multiple positive experiences with new staff. This strategy was implemented during staff changes in the summer of 1991 and was associated with low to moderate accelerations in problem behaviors at that time.

DISCUSSION

We have combined quantitative and qualitative methods to provide a portrait of Emma and her life in the community. Together, these data reveal a young woman striving to build a lifestyle that is safe; predictable; and filled with trusted people, favorite possessions, and preferred activities. This effort was mediated by and shared with a core staff who were committed to Emma's success, skilled in the use of a variety of support strategies, and tolerant of the stresses inherent in supporting her. This mutual endeavor was associated with substantial improvements in Emma's behavior, community participation, and social relationships as compared with her life in the institution and even her first year in the community. After 2½ years of support, Emma was perceived as more alert, verbally assertive, conversational, and affectionate. She was viewed as being more independent, socially competent, and happy. Although problem behaviors continued to occur, the intensity of her self-injurious behavior was viewed as significantly reduced. The overall pattern of problem behaviors, however, was a caution to view these improvements as fragile and contextually bound. Because major disruptions in staffing patterns were associated with increases in problem behaviors, problem behaviors are predicted to rise again when Emma experiences major staff changes in the future—a situation not unlike that experienced by many typical people who experience major changes in the people who participate in their lives.

These data suggest that although there were long periods during which problem behaviors were of low frequency and intensity, there was no indication that Emma was "cured" of these problem behaviors. It is likely that significant efforts will be needed during the remainder of her life to adjust her environment continually in response to her problem behaviors. The results also suggest, however, that these behaviors need not be viewed as a barrier to a reasonable life in the community. Emma's problem behaviors may require continual adjustment of the type and quality of support that she receives but not elimination of her opportunity to work, play, and learn in the community.

Qualitative analysis of the factors associated with the development of a safe, active, and valued lifestyle suggested the presence of a complex ecology of support. First, several organizational features of the residential program supported staff efforts to involve Emma in community activities, facilitate social relationships, and use positive support strategies. These features included the following:

1. An individualized planning process that identified community participation, social integration, behavioral support, and health and safety goals
2. Staff's daily use of the VOIS lifestyle outcome monitoring system (Newton et al., 1988) and a functional assessment data collection system (O'Neill et al., 1997)
3. Control by staff and Emma over the schedule of daily activities and how goals were to be achieved
4. Weekly meetings led by a program manager who reviewed lifestyle and behavioral data and facilitated problem-solving discussions
5. Staff participation in the design of positive behavioral support strategies

Second, several conditions involving staff mediated the development and effective implementation of positive behavioral support strategies. These included the following:

1. Staff continuity
2. Staff members' achieving a consensus about the reasons for Emma's problem behaviors
3. Leadership in the use of positive support strategies by at least one staff member
4. Commitment by several staff members to a relationship with Emma
5. Mentorship by a behavioral consultant who was knowledgeable in positive behavioral support technology

The skillful use of positive support strategies subsequently was associated with the improvements in Emma's behavior and lifestyle, as previously described. In addition, positive relationships with staff appeared to enhance further Emma's social skills, positive contributions to her support, and development of friendships and acquaintanceships. This broad ecology of support also appeared to promote the development of a staff culture that was, for the most part, committed to Emma and to the mission and the goals of her support program.

This ecology, however, also contained obstacles to Emma's continued progress and to the fulfillment of the organization's mission. These obstacles included significant staff turnover and staff error in the implementation of Emma's positive behavioral support plan.

The story of Emma's life in the community resonates deeply with the larger context of the supported living movement (Taylor, Bogdan, & Racino, 1991) and the emerging technology of positive behavioral support (Horner et al., 1990; Koegel et al., 1996). Emma's life with its setbacks, successes, and continued challenges provides an in-depth illustration of how people with severe disabilities and severe problem behaviors can live and prosper when adequate support is provided in the community. Emma's experiences with core staff illustrate the highly personalized relationships that can develop when staff are employed as educators and facilitators of social relationships and community participation (Knoll & Ford, 1987; Newton,

Olson, & Horner, 1995)—not just as custodians (see Chapter 22).

The support methods used in this study are responsive to the frequent call for comprehensive positive behavioral support programming (Carr, Robinson, Taylor, & Carlson, 1990; Durand, 1990a; Horner & Carr, 1997). This chapter also addressed a need to employ multiple methodologies to reveal the complexities of current service delivery systems and to measure meaningful outcomes of positive behavioral interventions (Kaiser, 1993; Meyer & Evans, 1993a; Vaughn, Dunlap, Fox, Clarke, & Bucy, 1997). Emma's case study is an example of how clinical time-series data, empirically validated assessment instruments, participant observations, and semistructured interviews can be combined to describe comprehensively the life of people with severe disabilities who live in the community. Quantitative methods revealed longitudinal patterns of behavioral and lifestyle changes and contributed to predictions about the future course of individual progress. Qualitative methods organized the complex phenomena of community living, offered an understanding of the social processes that operate in the community, and contributed to the generation of grounded theory (Bercovici, 1981, 1983).

Despite the breadth of the results, the report of these often dramatic findings is limited by the methodologies employed. The nonexperimental nature of the methods do not permit any firm conclusions about causal relationships among contextual conditions, support strategies, and Emma's behavior or lifestyle. The qualitative interpretations provided hypotheses about the relationships among categories, rather than causal associations. Quantitative results described covariation among contextual variables, interventions, and behavioral or lifestyle outcomes. Functional relationships were not identified. Also, the external validity of the results— the ability to generalize these procedures to other people and situations—is limited because of the focus on a single individual.

The methods also contained shortcomings that may limit the reliability or credibility of the results. The clinical data do not include reliability measures, so the reader must view the quantitative results with caution. However, triangulation across multiple methods and multiple data sources was employed to increase the overall credibility of the data. In addition, program managers for Emma's house made efforts to maintain the accuracy of the data through staff training activities, weekly data reviews, and the omission of suspect data.

CONCLUSION

This study adds to a modest body of descriptive and experimental research that empirically examines the use of multicomponent support plans to promote behavioral and lifestyle improvement for people with severe disabilities and severe problem behaviors (Berkman & Meyer, 1988; Carr & Carlson, 1993; Dunlap, Kern-Dunlap, Clarke, & Robbins, 1991; Foxx, 1993; Lucyshyn, Albin, & Nixon, 1997; Malette et al., 1992). A central message that these studies offer is that we must go beyond the use of single interventions and develop comprehensive, multicomponent plans of support that are responsive to the unique demands of each person and setting and that are continually guided by functional assessment data (Mace, Lalli, Lalli, & Shea, 1993). The study contributes two additional messages. First, if we are to serve people with severe disabilities and problem behaviors in the community, we need to design service environments that promote durable lifestyle changes. Multicomponent positive support plans are only one feature of this larger ecology of support. Organizational structures that promote community participation, social relationships, and the use of positive support strategies are necessary elements of effective service environments (Baker, 1998; Carr, Robinson, Taylor, & Carlson, 1990; Emerson, McGill, & Mansell, 1994; Foster-Johnson & Dunlap, 1993; Reichle & Wacker, 1993; Van Houten & Axelrod, 1993). Second, if we are truly to understand the richness, depth, and complexity of the lives of people with severe disabilities who live in the community and the environments that are designed for their benefit, we will benefit from the creative use of multiple research methods (Kaiser, 1993; Meyer & Evans, 1993a, 1993b; Tharp, 1981). We believe that when quantitative and qualitative researchers work together and honor each other's unique contribution to knowledge development, they can enhance their capacity to influence the effectiveness and quality of community-based services for people with severe disabilities and severe problem behaviors. Emma and all people who share her history and promise deserve nothing less.

REFERENCES

Baker, D.J. (1998). Outcomes of behavior support training to an agency providing residential and vocational support to persons with developmental disabilities. *Journal of The Association for Persons with Severe Handicaps, 23,* 144–148.

Bercovici, S. (1981). Qualitative methods and cultural perspectives in the study of deinstitutionalization. In R.H. Bruininks, C.E. Meyers, B.B. Sigford, & K.C. Lakin (Eds.), *Deinstitutionalization and community adjustment of mentally retarded people* (pp. 133–144). Washington, DC: American Association on Mental Deficiency.

Bercovici, S.M. (1983). *Barriers to normalization: The restrictive management of retarded persons.* Baltimore: University Park Press.

Berkman, K.A., & Meyer, L.H. (1988). Alternative strategies and multiple outcomes in the remediation of severe self-injury: Going "all out" nonaversively. *Journal of The Association for Persons with Severe Handicaps, 13,* 76–86.

Bogdan, R.C., & Biklen, S.K. (1982). *Qualitative research for education: An introduction to theory and methods.* Needham Heights, MA: Allyn & Bacon.

Boles, S., Horner, R.H., & Bellamy, G.T. (1988). Implementing transitions: Programs for supported living. In B.L. Ludow, A.P. Turnbull, & R. Luckasson (Eds.), *Transitions to adult life for people with mental retardation: Principles and practices* (pp. 101–118). Baltimore: Paul H. Brookes Publishing Co.

Bromley, B.E., & Blacher, J. (1991). Parental reasons for out-of-home placement of children with severe handicaps. *Mental Retardation, 29,* 275–280.

Campbell, D.T., & Fiske, D.W. (1959). Convergent and discriminant validation by the multitrait-multimethod matrix. *Psychological Bulletin, 56,* 81–105.

Carr, E.G., & Carlson, J.I. (1993). Reduction of severe behavior problems in the community using a multicomponent treatment approach. *Journal of Applied Behavior Analysis, 26,* 157–172.

Carr, E.G., Robinson, S., & Palumbo, L.W. (1990). The wrong issue: Aversive vs. nonaversive treatment. The right issue: Functional vs. nonfunctional treatment. In A.C. Repp & N.N. Singh (Eds.), *Perspectives on the use of nonaversive and aversive interventions for persons with developmental disabilities* (pp. 361–379). Sycamore, IL: Sycamore Press.

Carr, E.G., Robinson, S., Taylor, J.C., & Carlson, J.I. (1990). Positive approaches to the treatment of severe behavior problems in persons with developmental disabilities: A review and analysis of reinforcement and stimulus-based procedures. *The Association for Persons with Severe Handicaps, Monograph 4.*

Cunningham, P.J., & Mueller, C.D. (1991). Individuals with mental retardation in residential facilities: Findings from the 1987 National Medical Expenditure Survey. *American Journal of Mental Retardation, 96,* 109–117.

Dunlap, G., Kern-Dunlap, L., Clarke, S., & Robbins, F.R. (1991). Functional assessment, curricular revision, and severe behavior problems. *Journal of Applied Behavior Analysis, 24,* 387–397.

Durand, V.M. (1990a). Reader response: The "Aversives" debate is over: And now the work begins. *Journal of The Association for Persons with Severe Handicaps, 15,* 140–141.

Durand, V.M. (1990b). *Severe behavior problems: A functional communication training approach.* New York: Guilford Press.

Emerson, E., McGill, P., & Mansell, J. (Eds.). (1994). *Severe learning disabilities and challenging behaviours: Designing high quality services.* London: Chapman and Hall.

Foster-Johnson, L., & Dunlap, G. (1993). Using functional assessment to develop effective, individualized interventions for challenging behaviors. *Teaching Exceptional Children, 25,* 44–57.

Foxx, R.M. (1993, May). *Confluence therapy for highly dangerous aggressive and self-injurious behavior: Producing lasting effectiveness.* Paper presented at the 19th annual meeting of the Association for Behavior Analysis, Chicago.

Foxx, R.M., Bechtel, D.R., Bird, J.R., Livesay, J.R., & Bittle, R.G. (1986). A comprehensive institutional treatment program for aggressive-disruptive high functioning mentally retarded persons. *Behavioral Residential Treatment, 1,* 39–56.

Hill, B.K., & Bruininks, R.H. (1984). Maladaptive behavior of mentally retarded individuals in residential facilities. *American Journal of Mental Deficiency, 88,* 380–387.

Hill, B.K., Lakin, K.C., & Bruininks, R.H. (1988). Characteristics of residential facilities. In L.W. Heal, J.I. Haney, & A.R. Novak Amado (Eds.), *Integration of developmentally disabled individuals into the community* (2nd ed., pp. 89–124). Baltimore: Paul H. Brookes Publishing Co.

Horner, R.H., & Carr, E.G. (1997). Behavioral support for students with severe disabilities: Functional assessment and comprehensive intervention. *Journal of Special Education, 31,* 84–104.

Horner, R.H., Close, D.W., Fredericks, H.D.B., O'Neill, R.E., Albin, R.W., Sprague, J.R., Kennedy,

C., Flannery, K.B., & Tuesday-Heathfield, L. (1996). Supported living for people with profound disabilities and severe problem behaviors. In D.H. Lehr & F. Brown (Eds.), *People with disabilities who challenge the system* (pp. 209–240). Baltimore: Paul H. Brookes Publishing Co.

Horner, R.H., Dunlap, G., Koegel, R.L., Carr, E.G., Sailor, W., Anderson, J., Albin, R.W., & O'Neill, R.E. (1990). Toward a technology of "nonaversive" behavioral support. *Journal of The Association for Persons with Severe Handicaps, 15,* 125–132.

Howe, J., Horner, R.H., & Newton, J.S. (1998). Comparison of supported living and traditional residential services in the state of Oregon. *Mental Retardation, 36,* 1–11.

Jorgensen, D.L. (1989). *Participant observation: A methodology for human studies.* Thousand Oaks, CA: Sage Publications.

Kaiser, A.P. (1993). Understanding human behavior: Problems of science and practice. *Journal of The Association for Persons with Severe Handicaps, 18,* 240–242.

Kennedy, C.H., Horner, R.H., & Newton, J.S. (1990). The social networks and activity patterns of adults with severe disabilities: A correlational analysis. *Journal of The Association for Persons with Severe Handicaps, 15,* 86–90.

Kennedy, C.H., Horner, R.H., Newton, J.S., & Kanda, E. (1990). Measuring the activity patterns of adults with severe disabilities using the resident lifestyle inventory. *Journal of The Association for Persons with Severe Handicaps, 15,* 79–85.

Kincaid, D. (1996). Person-centered planning. In L.K. Koegel, R.L. Koegel, & G. Dunlap (Eds.), *Positive behavioral support: Including people with difficult behavior in the community* (pp. 439–465). Baltimore: Paul H. Brookes Publishing Co.

Knoll, J., & Ford, A. (1987). Beyond caregiving: A reconceptualization of the role of the residential service provider. In S.J. Taylor, D. Biklen, & J. Knoll (Eds.), *Community integration for people with severe disabilities* (pp. 129–146). New York: Teachers College Press.

Koegel, L.K., Koegel, R.L., & Dunlap, G. (Eds.). (1996). *Positive behavioral support: Including people with difficult behavior in the community.* Baltimore: Paul H. Brookes Publishing Co.

Lakin, K.C., & Bruininks, R.H. (1985). Contemporary services for handicapped children and youth. In R.H. Bruininks & K.C. Lakin (Eds.), *Living and learning in the least restrictive environment* (pp. 3–22). Baltimore: Paul H. Brookes Publishing Co.

Lucyshyn, J.M., Albin, R.W., & Nixon, C.D. (1997). Embedding comprehensive behavioral support in family ecology: An experimental, single-case analysis. *Journal of Consulting and Clinical Psychology, 65,* 241–251.

Mace, F.C., Lalli, J.S., Lalli, E.P., & Shea, M.C. (1993). Functional analysis and treatment of aberrant behavior. In R. Van Houten & S. Axelrod (Eds.), *Behavior analysis and treatment* (pp. 75–99). New York: Plenum.

Malette, P., Mirenda, P., Kandborg, T., Jones, P., Bunz, T., & Rogow, S. (1992). Application of a lifestyle development process for persons with severe intellectual disabilities: A case study report. *Journal of The Association for Persons with Severe Handicaps, 17,* 179–191.

McGee, J.J., Menousek, F.J., Hobbs, D.C., & Menousek, P.E. (1987). *Gentle teaching: A nonaversive approach to helping persons with mental retardation.* New York: Human Sciences Press.

McGrew, K.S., & Bruininks, R.H. (1994). A multidimensional approach to the measurement of community adjustment. In M.F. Hayden & B.H. Abery (Eds.), *Challenges for a service system in transition: Ensuring quality community experiences for persons with developmental disabilities* (pp. 65–79). Baltimore: Paul H. Brookes Publishing Co.

Merriam, S.B. (1988). *Case study research in education: A qualitative approach.* San Francisco: Jossey-Bass.

Meyer, L.H., & Evans, I.M. (1989). *Nonaversive interventions for behavior problems: A manual for home and community.* Baltimore: Paul H. Brookes Publishing Co.

Meyer, L.H., & Evans, I.M. (1993a). Meaningful outcomes in behavioral intervention: Evaluating positive approaches to the remediation of challenging behavior. In J. Reichle & D.P. Wacker (Eds.), *Communication and language intervention series: Vol. 4: Communicative alternatives to challenging behavior: Integrating functional assessment and intervention strategies* (pp. 407–428). Baltimore: Paul H. Brookes Publishing Co.

Meyer, L.H., & Evans, I.M. (1993b). Science and practice in behavioral intervention: Meaningful outcomes, research validity, and usable knowledge. *Journal of The Association for Persons with Severe Handicaps, 18,* 224–234.

Newton, J.S., Ard, W.R., & Horner, R.H. (1993). Validating predicted activity preferences of individuals with severe disabilities. *Journal of Applied Behavior Analysis, 26,* 239–245.

Newton, J.S., Olson, D., & Horner, R.H. (1995). Factors contributing to the stability of social relationships between individuals with disabilities and other community members. *Mental Retardation, 33,* 383–393.

Newton, J.S., Stoner, S.K., Bellamy, G.T., Boles, S.M., Horner, R.H., LeBaron, N., Moskowitz, D., Romer, L., Romer, M., & Schlesinger, D. (1988). *Valued Outcomes Information System (VOIS) operations manual.* Eugene: University of Oregon, Center on Human Development.

Nisbet, J., Clark, M., & Covert, S. (1991). Living it up! An analysis of research on community living. In L.H. Meyer, C.A. Peck, & L. Brown (Eds.), *Critical issues in the lives of people with severe disabilities* (pp. 115–144). Baltimore: Paul H. Brookes Publishing Co.

O'Brien, J. (1987). A guide to life-style planning: Using *The Activities Catalog* to integrate services and natural support systems. In B. Wilcox & G.T. Bellamy, *A comprehensive guide to* The Activities Catalog: *An alternative curriculum for youth and adults with severe disabilities* (pp. 175–189). Baltimore: Paul H. Brookes Publishing Co.

O'Neill, R.E., Horner, R.H., Albin, R.W., Sprague, J.R., Storey, K., & Newton, J.S. (1997). *Functional assessment and program development for problem behavior: A practical assessment guide* (2nd ed.). Pacific Grove, CA: Brooks/Cole.

Patton, M.Q. (1990). *Qualitative evaluation and research methods* (2nd ed.). Thousand Oaks, CA: Sage Publications.

Reichle, J., & Wacker, D.P. (Eds.). (1993). *Communication and language intervention series: Vol. 4. Communicative alternatives to challenging behavior: Integrating functional assessment and intervention strategies.* Baltimore: Paul H. Brookes Publishing Co.

Repp, A.C., & Singh, N.N. (Eds.). (1990). *Perspectives on the use of nonaversive and aversive interventions for persons with developmental disabilities.* Sycamore, IL: Sycamore Publishing.

Seidel, J., Kjolseth, R., & Seymour, E. (1985). *The ethnograph.* Littleton, CO: Qualis Research Associates.

Skodak-Crissey, M., & Rosen, M. (1986). *Institutions for the mentally retarded: A changing role in changing times.* Austin, TX: PRO-ED.

Strauss, A., & Corbin, J. (1990). *Basics of qualitative research: Grounded theory procedures and techniques.* Thousand Oaks, CA: Sage Publications.

Taylor, S.J., Biklen, D., & Knoll, J. (Eds.). (1987). *Community integration for people with severe disabilities.* New York: Teachers College Press.

Taylor, S.J., & Bogdan, R. (1981). Qualitative methods and cultural perspectives in the study of community adjustment. In R.H. Bruininks, C.E. Meyers, B.B. Sigford, & K.C. Lakin (Eds.), *Deinstitutionalization and community adjustment of mentally retarded people* (pp. 133–144). Washington, DC: American Association on Mental Deficiency.

Taylor, S.J., Bogdan, R., & Racino, J.A. (Eds.). (1991). *Life in the community: Case studies of organizations supporting people with disabilities.* Baltimore: Paul H. Brookes Publishing Co.

Tharp, R.G. (1981). The metamethodology of research and development. *Educational Perspectives, 20,* 42–48.

Van Houten, R., & Axelrod, S. (1993). *Behavior analysis and treatment.* New York: Plenum.

Vaughn, B.J., Dunlap, G., Fox, L., Clarke, S., & Bucy, M. (1997). Parent–professional partnership in behavioral support: A case study of community-based intervention. *Journal of The Association for Persons with Severe Handicaps, 22,* 186–197.

Widaman, K.F., Stacy, A.W., & Borthwick-Duffy, S.A. (1993). Construct validity of dimensions of adaptive behavior: A multitrait-multimethod evaluation. *American Journal of Mental Retardation, 98,* 219–234.

Zigler, E., Hodapp, R.M., & Edison, M.R. (1990). From theory to practice in the care and education of mentally retarded individuals. *American Journal of Mental Retardation, 95,* 1–12.

Chapter 14

Michel's Story

We Needed Only to Listen to Him

Denise Fraser & Lucien Labbé

This chapter presents the story of Michel, who displayed excessive behaviors. Michel's story illustrates the critical importance of integrating values with the science of behavior. The framework for the program described in this chapter is grounded in a set of fundamental human and professional ethical values; day-to-day implementation of the program was driven by the procedural rigor needed to demonstrate effectiveness of positive approach. Michel's story is representative of an approach used by Florès Rehabilitation Center (formerly Le Contrefort) since 1986. The next section summarizes two of the principal parameters that are essential components in the center's approach.

HISTORICAL CONTEXT

In the 1970s, there were numerous restrictions on people with disabilities, and the environments available to them were highly constrained. Restrictions existed not only in larger institutions but also in smaller residential homes that proliferated in the community in the 1980s. The per-petuation of those restrictions regardless of environments illustrates that a change in a physical environment is no guarantee of change in living conditions and in the attitudes of others toward people with disabilities. Some of the more particularly disturbing restrictions included the following:

1. The life of the student or individual was organized around learning programs. Everything was supervised and structured to address rules dictated by those learning programs, and the individuals themselves were perceived as "objects of learning." Often, the only tokens of attention and affection that an individual received were dependent on how well he or she performed relative to the many learning objectives that he or she was to meet. There was no unconditional positive regard, despite the fact that the positive reinforcements were decided by the staff.

2. Any guarantee of increased access to a more typical life was dependent on an indi-

Michel's story is based on Drouin and Labbé (1989) and is included here with permission.

The authors thank Robert Drouin, Serge Lachance, Madeleine and Guy Letourneau, Mario Levesque, Jeannine Racine, Hans Renaud, and Claudette Wilkes for their collaboration. Their provision of useful data assisted in the telling of Michel's story. The authors also express their appreciation to Lovechild Ermentrout and Corinne Loisy at Syracuse University, who translated the chapter from French to English.

vidual's capacity to meet all of the objectives of the continuum of services. That is, to live in an apartment rather than in a more segregated congregate-care facility, a person was required first to prove that he or she could be successful in a group home. An individual had to earn his or her way through virtually the entire services continuum to prove that he or she could live outside it.

3. In the contexts provided by the continuum of living environments, all aspects of daily life—schedules, clothing, food and drink, and the people with whom a person spends his or her time—were imposed by staff. The person with a developmental disability never experienced what it is like to "be at home" and to own possessions that could be used at one's convenience rather than according to formal rules imposed by someone else.

4. Daily life was full of activities that were not meaningful, fulfilling, or even interesting. The daily schedule instead comprised therapeutic, occupational, or routine tasks. Most were not useful, and even those said to be "rehabilitative" evidenced only an abstract connection to anything practical, sensible, or functional in typical daily life. Stringing beads, practicing psychomotor skills as an adult, looking at catalogs, taking a daily scheduled nap at 30 years of age, being involved in a "zoo-therapy program" (rather than simply having a cat or a bird for a pet), going to "music therapy" (rather than listening to favorite music on the radio), and having to change into pajamas at 5 P.M. because of staffing difficulties are just a few of the less than edifying activities that are sometimes forced on people with disabilities.

5. Services did not adapt to meet the evolving needs of individuals. For example, even when an individual was judged by professionals to be "ready" to move to another level of the continuum, the move often was delayed because of administrative or resource problems.

6. People who displayed several problems, such as autism, mental disorders, and excess behaviors, were grouped together; services were organized around controlling their behavior and meeting their needs in segregated "problem" environments.

7. People who lived in institution-style environments had no choice other than to comply with staff directives. Individuals were assigned a passive role and given few, if any, opportunities for self-determination. The decisions that concerned individuals' own lives—no matter how intimate or how great the impact on their lives—were made by others.

The preceding observations and the reactions of individuals to institutional restrictions led the chapter authors to question the methods of intervention and the nature of the center's services; both authors made the attitude and cognitive shifts necessary to return the focus of concern to the real needs of the individuals for whom they provided care. The deinstitutionalization movement in the mid-1980s provided the center with the physical and program structures that allowed it to organize the service delivery options and put these ideas into action.[1] Even as this shift was occurring from the institution to the community, however, individuals did not yet play an active role in their own lives and had few social interactions with other people.

INTERVENTION FROM A DUAL PERSPECTIVE

In the organization of the center, the function of the clinical consultant is to provide support to the aides and to the service supervisors who were working in community environments. Most consultation requests have as their goal the resolu-

---

[1]In 1985, the deinstitutionalization movement in Québec resulted in planning for approximately 350 people with cognitive disabilities in the Basses-Laurentides to move from congregate-care environments to a range of residential services and supports that were integrated into the community and managed by the Rehabilitation Centers of Le Contrefort.

tion of problem, excessive, or challenging behavior. The clinical consultants' analyses quickly led supervisors to question the factors responsible for these consultation requests. It soon was realized that most causal factors were linked to an individual's unsatisfying quality of life. The introduction of new intervention strategies that allowed lifestyle enrichment, improvement in the quality of relationships between aides and individuals, decreased environmental constraints, and increased social interactions within the community has led to some rather dramatic outcomes. Following are the principal strategies that are considered to be associated with improved outcomes:

1. The individual should be offered the opportunity to have a home that corresponds to his or her aspirations and for which he or she has a feeling of ownership.
2. Irritations (e.g., useless rules, institutional routines, group-life habits) must be eliminated.
3. Self-determination must be a priority, and services must be a catalyst for greater involvement in decision making and for increased opportunities for individuals with disabilities to make choices.
4. Individuals must encounter new situations and a variety of social interaction opportunities with different people to expose them to a wide range of experiences and lifestyle options.
5. Daily life must be filled with useful activities that are meaningful and interesting for the individual.
6. Positive social interactions, more egalitarian social relationships, and opportunities for social recognition must become a part of daily life.
7. Staff must strive to develop a reciprocal bond with the individual—not a hierarchical, caregiving relationship—and must help each individual create or maintain more reciprocal bonds with those who are close to him or her.
8. The individual needs support in the creation and maintenance of a satisfying and personalized social network.

9. When assistance is needed, the individual should be helped to acquire skills that can replace certain inappropriate behaviors.

As the preceding strategies have been more widely applied, the center has become increasingly convinced that excessive behaviors are likely to fade or disappear quickly as the individual's quality of life improves. Rather than focus on the elimination of behavior, staff initially should emphasize a meaningful and typical lifestyle to provide a more global view of the individual's actual needs and to permit staff to get a closer look and a better understanding of the individual's aspirations and wishes. The center's global approach to the issue of quality of life is to ask what can satisfy and contribute to the improved well-being of every individual.

To translate this more global approach into practice for an individual and to design an appropriate intervention, it is necessary to go beyond simply pursuing traditional learning and behavior modification objectives. Figures 1 and 2 illustrate the dual perspective on the elements of quality of life and provide an analysis of the factors that are responsible for excessive behavior that must be addressed for prevention and intervention to be successful. Note in these figures that prevention and improving quality of life are considered as two central and interrelated features of this approach. These features are shown in Figure 1 by the links among aspects of typical or "ordinary" (see Emerson, McGill, & Mansell, 1994) lives (e.g., living in a typical home, having a valued social role, being physically healthy) and by how these features both are central to quality of life and can alter the environment and thereby better meet an individual's needs—thus *preventing* the need for certain excessive or challenging behaviors. This point is demonstrated in another manner in Figure 2, in which the intervention *process* is shown to describe and analyze the problem, formulate viable hypotheses, and then intervene and use the evaluation to monitor the outcome of intervention. Then, as necessary, feedback is provided for the revision of the analyses, hypotheses, and intervention, as necessary. At all points, however, the focus is on evaluating and addressing quality-of-life issues and

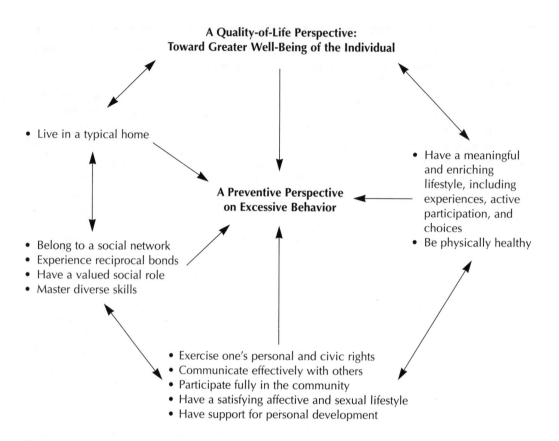

Figure 1. A conceptual model of intervention with a focus on quality of life and prevention of excessive behavior. (Translated and adapted from Fraser & Labbé, 1993.)

how enhancing these aspects influences—and potentially prevents—the exhibition of excessive behavior.

During the intervention process, the center's staff also have become increasingly persuaded by their analyses of problematic situations and environments that *all* behavior is a message. The attempt to understand these messages elicits a series of factors that can explain the manifestation of behaviors judged by others to be problematic. Again, many of these factors are connected to quality-of-life issues. Table 1 provides a list of the variables that the chapter authors have identified in case after case that seemed to covary with severe challenging behavior in the individuals who were referred to the center. Each of these factors, the chapter authors believe, can be related directly to issues of quality of life that should be as legitimate an in-

tervention target as, historically, targeted excessive behaviors have been (see also Meyer & Evans, 1989).

MICHEL

The chapter authors chose Michel's story for discussion because it provides a dramatic example of the elements that underlie the positive approach used at the center. First, the authors' contact with Michel extended over a substantial period of time and enabled them to document clinically convincing results. Second, the hypotheses formulated to explain Michel's excessive behavior can be generalized to many institutional environments. Third, the interventions established for Michel clearly had beneficial effects not only on *his* lifestyle but also on all of the other individuals who lived with him, as well

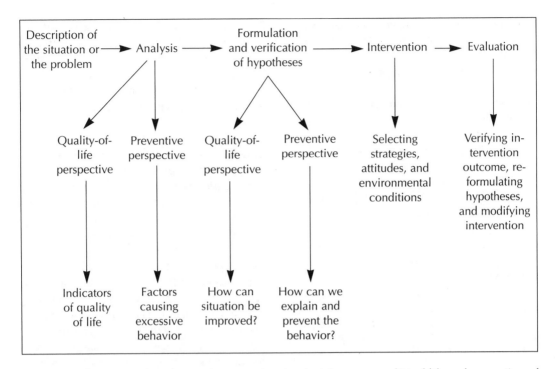

Figure 2. The intervention process incorporating the dual focus on quality of life and prevention of excessive behavior.

as on the staff responsible for providing Michel's support. Finally, the program plan both permitted and required a change in the perceptions of others about Michel and his life. The authors believe that a great part of their success is attributable to the fact that others were able to see Michel from a fresh viewpoint, adopting new attitudes and asking themselves what Michel (and others with disabilities) were trying to "say" with their behaviors.

Some Information from Michel's Past

Michel was a 33-year-old man who lived in an apartment with two housemates. He received 24-hour support from a group of paid staff members (aides). He had entered an institution at the age of 9 years. Based on the little information available about Michel's early life, it is clear that his condition deteriorated over the years, which the authors interpreted as a child's difficulties in adapting to institutional life. In 1961, Michel was diagnosed as "educable mentally retarded"

and described as having "lively eyes" and "good manners." In the record, a health professional recommended against institutionalizing Michel, arguing that to do so would provoke an affective deficit and a slowing down of his cognitive abilities occasioned by depression. Unfortunately, for reasons unknown, this recommendation was not followed, and a subsequent report from 1973 classified Michel as "severely mentally retarded" and recommended lifetime care.

In 1977, the reports began to include behavior problems, such as physical aggression toward other residents, and noted that his personal hygiene needed improvement. In 1979, another evaluation echoed the 1977 evaluation. By age 20, Michel was described as a passive, isolated, timid, fearful individual, who was indifferent toward others except to ask them for cigarettes; cigarettes apparently had become a strong reinforcer for Michel, who seemed to have few other interests. He did not initiate activities and did not act unless a teacher asked him to do so. He occasionally exhibited self-

Table 1. Personal and quality-of-life factors that may influence the emergence and maintenance of excessive behavior

Overly controlling environment

Poor social relationships

Unsatisfying affective life and personal gratification

Communication problems

Unpleasant environmental circumstances

Physical and mental health problems

Unsatisfactory lifestyle

Few opportunities to play worthwhile roles

Lack of cognitive understanding

Lack of useful skills

Inappropriate teaching and learning models

Negative social perceptions

Inappropriate support

From Fraser, D., & Labbé, L. (1993). *L'approche positive de la personne . . . une conception globale de l'intervention.* Laval, Québec, Canada: Editions Agence D'ARC, Edifice Educalivres; translated and reprinted by permission.

injurious behavior, such as picking at the skin on his hands.

In 1984, at the time of the deinstitutionalization movement in Québec, Canada, Michel was placed in an apartment in the community and began working in a sheltered workshop. Reports began to describe Michel's strengths and needs rather than his problems and disabilities. The focus shifted to various functional curricula—self-medicating, using adequate hygiene, preparing a simple meal, and wiping after using the toilet. He participated in only one leisure activity—bowling—and there was little progress noted for an objective to help Michel express his preferences.

Initial Description of Michel's Excess Behavior

In January 1988, when the center's program for Michel was to begin, the authors observed the following about Michel:

1. Michel refused to participate in many activities of daily life, had left his job at the workshop, and angrily opposed all requests. He refused to take a bath.

2. Nothing seemed to interest Michel, with the exception of watching television, sitting in his armchair, smoking, and drinking coffee.
3. Michel's feet had begun to swell, probably because he spent so much time sitting in his armchair—often for the entire night.

Aides described Michel as passive, even lazy, inclined to isolation, and withdrawn. He was believed to be afraid of water and possibly of the dark because he refused to go to sleep until he collapsed from exhaustion. He did not express his needs and sometimes became aggressive; he often repeated that he wanted to leave and was uncomfortable living in the apartment. Some of the aides wondered whether Michel should still be entitled to the same privileges as the other individuals (e.g., watching television) when he did nothing to deserve them. Reinforcement programs had begun using cigarettes, money, and car trips to elicit some cooperation from Michel, but he was beginning to refuse even these. When he refused reinforcers, there would be a confrontation between Michel and the staff; one aide later wrote, "I don't intend to let myself be imposed on about this point, even if it means using radical methods against [Michel's] will." Michel's situation had become a vicious power play between him and staff, a cycle of punishments and rewards. Staff wanted him to move out of the apartment and believed that none of the methods that they knew worked any longer.

Analyzing the Problem: An Open Door to a Better Understanding

Members of the team, the service manager, and the first author, who was acting as a clinical consultant, carried out the first analysis of Michel's situation and developed three principal hypotheses related to personal and quality-of-life issues at the beginning of the intervention in 1988. The hypotheses were as follows:

1. *Could Michel's refusal to move when asked to carry out a task actually be his way of objecting to being controlled by others?* Michel's entire life had been controlled by others. The institutional environment in

which he had been living did not offer him opportunities to express his own preferences and share his strengths. The group interpreted Michel's resistance to requests as his way of trying to express himself. Expression was something that he thought he would be able to do in the apartment (in contrast to the institution that he had left behind). As he did not know how to express himself in a way to which staff could respond, he had decided to assert his right to make a place for himself in his home and to make his own decisions even if all he could do was say "no." It was noted, for example, that when participation in an activity was phrased as a suggestion rather than as a direct order, he was more likely to agree to participate. It also was observed that when the aide did the activity with Michel, on a friendly basis, Michel completed the entire task. Perhaps what needed to be done with Michel was to propose things to him rather than impose things on him, suggest rather than command, and give him space to begin to show his own initiative as opportunities for activities occurred. By being more egalitarian and friendly with Michel, aides would be respecting his capacity to make his own decisions and would be changing Michel's perceptions that staff wanted only to give him orders.

2. *Could Michel have become withdrawn and inactive because he was actually tired of never responding to expectations of those around him and therefore having nothing to do?* Michel seemed to have fallen into a "vicious cycle." His "low level of initiative" was actually rarely satisfying, only led the aides to demand more, and thus virtually guaranteed that he almost never met the expectations that others had of him. In many ways, his behavior seemed symptomatic of severe depression. His level of self-determination led the group to believe that if Michel wanted, he could achieve much more. The group decided to envision a form of intervention that would have as its major goal the reinforcement of each of Michel's initiatives as a strategy to increase

his feelings of self-efficacy and then, in turn, increase those initiatives—creating a new cycle of behavior.

3. *Could Michel's refusal to go to bed actually be an assertion of his adult status and right to stay up as late as the night aide did?* The group observed that one of the aides behaved in a very natural way: She opened the sofa bed and went to bed at the same time as did the residents of the apartment. When this aide was on duty, Michel did not resist going to bed. The group asked another question: *Who would go to bed when a guest was at his or her home?* Perhaps Michel, considering himself at home, did not want to go to bed leaving an outsider still awake and "in charge" of the household.

Our new approach to Michel, which began with these questions in 1988, continues to this day, with new hypotheses continually arising. As aides looked at Michel through these new "lenses" and Michel responded positively to the aides' changed perceptions and behavior, everyone became increasingly motivated to pursue new directions and ask new questions. As these are not artificial "treatment contingencies" but are very real and appropriate issues in daily life, a new golden rule emerged that sustained our efforts. What was needed was continuity and persistence in continuing to expand Michel's access to more opportunities and experiences.

The authors' analysis of the problem from a preventive perspective and by looking at possible causes for the problems in conditions that the group had created moved the group increasingly toward a quality-of-life perspective. The group asked how Michel's well-being could be improved and began to ask how he could be happier. (Refer to Figures 1 and 2 for the application of this process.)

Priority Interventions and Strategies

To implement a positive approach, the group focused on four principal intervention *components:* the individual, the staff, the organization, and the environment. The group began with the premise that in any analysis of an individual's situation, consideration must be given to the people who surround the individual. The intervention team needs to know these people's values and to understand an individual's potential for social interaction with the people in his or her life. Finally, the intervention team must consider the support and framework needed by the team if members are to invest themselves in a positive approach based on the four components of successful interventions.

Individual Component

Two interventions initially were formulated to test the hypotheses established for Michel: 1) The intervention team prepared a list of situations or actions (no matter how small) initiated by Michel; and 2) the team observed Michel's behaviors and attitudes following suggestions versus commands, and this comparison was done during different activities. After approximately 2 weeks, the team knew the following:

1. Aides generally must initiate activities (only 6 of 26 activities were initiated by Michel).
2. When a request to participate was framed as a suggestion rather than as a directive, Michel's acceptance rate was higher (14 of 26).
3. "Taking a bath" was an exception to this pattern (bathing was never initiated by Michel, and he was willing to take a bath only 3 of 10 times that it was suggested to him).

These data provided the intervention team with a new direction. The team would pursue earlier observations but, parallel to that, attempt another goal of inviting Michel to take a bath in a more favorable context. The team was not going to focus on teaching him to wash himself; instead, the focus would be on finding some way to make him want to wash. Aides would run the bath, put bubble bath in the tub, put candles in the room, play music, and stay and talk with him if he wished, while respecting his privacy. In addition, any initiation of bathing by Michel would be praised so as to increase his interest in participation. Results were clear: When the bath was made agreeable and the opportunity to bathe was presented in a nondirective manner, Michel's

participation increased. For the first 2 weeks of the "program," he took a bath on 33% of the opportunities, and by that same time a month later, he was taking a bath 74% of the time.

Staff observations increasingly convinced everyone that Michel did not want to be controlled and wanted to participate in activities. He especially enjoyed meal preparation. Across time, situations that had been defined as "problems" previously (i.e., taking a bath, going to bed) were no longer seen as problems because they were reframed as Michel's *choices* as an adult. In turn, he choose to do these activities at a level typical of adults. The team also believed, however, that the new approach to Michel needed to be generalized throughout his lifestyle. Thus, in addition to the "programs" for bathing and other specific activities, each of his aides was required, at least twice daily, to offer Michel a choice of three different activities. The team continued to operate with the hypothesis that the more opportunities Michel had to make choices, the less he would feel the need to oppose or resist activities that must be done. The team's observations of Michel's choices also allowed the team to learn more about his particular "likes."

The choice report format that the team used was completed by an aide, including information such as the date, what was said to Michel, and how he responded. Staff recorded their own words verbatim and were to note Michel's behaviors (i.e., whether he did one of the activities offered as a choice) as well as anything else that they noticed (e.g., mood, affect).

After several weeks, personnel had offered Michel a choice from among three activities a total of 35 times. Not only did the team know more about Michel's varied choices, but also the observations recorded by aides clearly revealed that they viewed him differently. Their comments noted that Michel was capable of making choices, was happy with the choices that he had made (demonstrated by smiling and/or doing something without hesitation), was more active with far less time spent watching television, and was open to doing new things. Furthermore, staff began to question whether the choices offered included enough variety, so they decided to add new activities and new choices. By October 1988, aides had recorded offering Michel 172 choices from among 17 different activities; Michel showed high rates of selecting activities (e.g., going to the bank, going shopping, making coffee, renting a video, going to the garage, washing the car, going for a ride, making a meal). He never once chose to watch television when given that option as one of the choices. This was, of course, in stark contrast to the beginning of the program when television was Michel's major activity.

Faced with these increasingly positive results, the team's next steps involved continuing to offer Michel choices but introducing as much novelty as possible. The team made a list of new situations or ones that Michel previously had few opportunities to experience. The team hypothesized that if Michel continued to have greater control over his life, then he could get more enjoyment out of experimenting and expanding his lifestyle. Staff members encouraged one another to support certain attitudes toward Michel (see Figure 3 for specific examples). As Michel continued to expand his repertoire of interests and choices, his individual program goals were rewritten to resemble more closely the kinds of aspirations that any typical person might have. Rather than goals that were focused on the remediation of "deficits" or "problem behaviors," Michel's two principal objectives for the coming year became the following: 1) Michel will have the opportunity to make choices about activities in his daily life, and 2) Michel will continue to experience many new activities.

Michel's progress was measured with the Adaptive Functioning Index (AFI; Marlett, 1973). The AFI is a three-section evaluation instrument comprising a social assessment, a vocational checklist, and a residential checklist. The measure was validated in Canada by the Calgary Vocational and Rehabilitation Research Institute, a research organization affiliated with Calgary University, and the standardized version was published in 1973. The residential checklist section was used directly in the design of Michel's intervention plan. This section contains 150 skills that are organized into categories, including 1) Personal Routines (including

cleanliness, appearance, eating, room management, time management, and health/hygiene), 2) Community Awareness (including transportation, shopping, leisure, budgeting, cooking, and home management), and 3) Social Maturity (which evaluated communication, consideration, making friends, keeping friends, and handling problems). The program supervisor and the counselor believed that the AFI was a good choice for assessing Michel's community living skills, particularly because the residential checklist section of the measure was familiar to Michel's aides. The checklist was completed before and during the intervention to assess Michel's progress in the checklist's categories. As can be seen in Table 2, Michel's scores on each of these AFI scales consistently improved during the first 3 years of data reported and then stabilized for community awareness and social maturity.

Staff Component

Three essential values constitute the basis of the center's personal positive approach. First, there is the belief that to assist people with disabilities to achieve a rich and valued lifestyle, it is necessary to acknowledge that the individual should play an active role in decisions concerning different aspects of his or her life; the individual should (and does!) make choices. Second, to succeed in establishing a respectful and warm relationship with someone with disabilities—an interdependent and reciprocal relationship—people without disabilities must respect the person with disabilities as a valued interlocutor who has the ability to influence others. Finally, to respect his or her rights and to provide the needed support for the exercise of those rights, staff must recognize a person with disabilities as a full and complete individual who is not defined by his or her disability. Thus, staff were actively involved in supporting Michel so that he could establish and maintain a social network to meet his affective and social needs; this is quite different from teaching "social skills" to Michel. Participation in community life and different activities was a condition for the quality of Michel's life, not something he had to "earn" or for which he had to demonstrate any "readiness level." New activ-

Name: __Michel__ Short-term objective: __Each week, Michel will participate in five activities of his choice.__

Intervening staff: __Serge__ Week from: _____ to: _____

Possible situation	Date	Choice situation	By aide	By Michel	Interaction done to suggest an activity	Michel's reaction to the situation	Interaction with Michel throughout the activity
Go to the library Go to the Nautilus Play a game of pool Write to Michel's family Woodworking Organize a party Eat supper in a new restaurant Collect something Go to church Go to a show Hand out pamphlets Bake a new recipe (e.g., cakes, doughnuts) Other:		What is Michel's or staff's choice in the possible situations?	This choice is initiated by aides.	Michel made this choice.	What was my approach? What did I tell Michel?	How did Michel react during the activities?	What kinds of social interactions? What happened during the activity? Describe what Michel did and what the intervening aide did.

Figure 3. Sample observation chart. (Translated and adapted from Fraser & Labbé, 1993.)

Table 2. Michel's progress in three areas of the Adaptive Functioning Index

Year	Personal routines	Community awareness	Social maturity
1988	32	26	28
1989	59	42	57
1990	63	53	76
1991	53	47	79
1992	55	49	78

ities were *not* selected as something that staff predicted that Michel would be able to do; instead, staff brainstormed to develop a far broader range of new activities and saw Michel's participation in those activities as part of an experimentation in lifestyle that would enable him to make more and better choices in the future.

Throughout this whole process, center staff were encouraged to reflect on their own attitudes in relation to the principles of the positive approach. In contrast to previous, more pessimistic comments, the aides who worked with Michel at this stage commented,

"Michel is interested in doing new things."
"Michel is very happy; he has changed a lot."
"Michel likes to learn when he is motivated and supported."
"Michel participates in everything; he takes initiative."
"Michel belongs fully in his environment."
"Michel can make choices."
"He's a nice guy; it is a pleasure to work with him."
"He has more interactions with staff as well as the people around him; he is affectionate."
"Looking at the past, you would never think that he would be where he is now."

Organization Component

The positive approach that the center uses involves both preventing excess behavior and providing continuous evaluation of the quality of life of each individual who is receiving services. This evaluation focuses not so much on the behavior of the individual who is receiving services as it does on all of the people who are providing those services and the context or the environment for those services. Thus, it is im-

portant to put into place systems that will permit each staff member to be part of this process and adapt to needed changes. For Michel, the attitude of staff was critical, requiring a conscious awakening and reevaluating each step along the way. At the center, supervision by a service supervisor is a primary vehicle for encouraging and supporting staff as they learn and implement new skills.

The service supervisor provides responsive but demanding support for the staff. The supervisor must ensure that decisions about implementation of the intervention process are followed through, that observation tools are used as planned, and that everyone involved respects the selected intervention direction and plan. The service supervisor also functions as a counselor for one key staff member for each individual with challenging behavior. In Michel's case, a close relationship developed with one particular member of the team; a link of reciprocity was established between this staff member and Michel, and he became a major advocate for Michel's interests on the team. The supervisor used the link between Michel and the staff member to emphasize the natural and positive aspects of their relationship to all team members, and the supervisor encouraged everyone to realize new experiences and to further develop such links of reciprocity to get to know Michel better. By using relatively simple but rigorous data collection procedures, the supervisor also was able to monitor the development of reciprocal relationships continuously and share ongoing developments with team members.

Meetings were held between the counselor and Michel's service supervisor approximately once per month. The supervisor also met with each staff member for an individual session every

2 weeks; a team supervision conference occurred monthly. At the beginning of the process, the individual meetings were needed to monitor closely whether service implementation followed the intervention plans made by the team; these meetings were also the context for not only evaluating but also supporting staff members' involvement in the intervention process.

Over time, staff members seemed to internalize the new principles of positive approach, whereas the positive results also reinforced the direction that the center was taking as well as made the group supervision process easier and more enjoyable. Thus, the team evolved toward the realization of the principal objective—the well-being of Michel. When asked to summarize the actions taken toward Michel, the supervisor used the following words: coherence within the intervention staff, belief, implication, conviction, involvement, and adherence by everyone. Those values facilitated success of the process.

Environment Component

Through the activities that he performed, Michel was able to establish linkages with various aides over the years. Both friendship and reciprocity were developed with some of them. Because staff "lived" the different situations with Michel, they got closer to Michel and he learned to approach others socially. The introverted and perhaps depressed individual described at the beginning of this chapter became someone who smiled and increasingly expressed himself. As the intervention progressed, Michel was invited by some staff into their families' activities and to other social events. This has enabled Michel to connect with other individuals and begin to establish a social network that goes beyond paid staff. Thus, the center included the following additional objectives in his plan: 1) Michel will go out with his relatives; and 2) Michel will cultivate social contacts with other people, these being *nonpaid* friendships.

Staff looked for activities that involved using the services and infrastructure of the surrounding community. Michel's choices reflect these opportunities, as can be seen by some of his favorite social activities: going to a local restaurant for coffee or a beer, traveling, going to the flea market, going to theater plays or shows, selecting books at the library, participating in local festivals, and going ice skating.

Other Outcomes and a Look Toward the Future

The chapter authors believe that the most significant measure of Michel's progress is his willingness to take many initiatives in his daily life. His smiles and occasional singing show that he considers himself at home in his environment and in control of his own life. What should be most striking about the activities in which Michel has engaged and the choices that he has made is how typical and ordinary they are. These are the same kinds of activities that many people without disabilities do in their daily lives (e.g., take a bath, rent a movie, shave, make coffee). The real measure of Michel's success was that the data no longer looked like the program for the person with disabilities described at the beginning of this chapter.

What was equally striking about Michel's story and the many others experienced by the center was the change in the behavior of staff and others in Michel's environment. The center's approach to Michel and his needs was grounded in rearranging his lifestyle from that of a restrictive program for a "problem individual" to treating him with respect and attempting to determine what he needed and wanted. Evans (see Chapter 22) discusses how training staff in contingency management has not always yielded positive results. Staff aides in particular often are described as having a difficult time with mastering the data collection requirements as well as delivering the appropriate contingencies on the appropriate schedule. The directors of the center also found that learning more about contingency management made it increasingly difficult for staff to interact socially with individuals in a positive way. Recall how staff in Michel's group home believed that he should somehow "deserve" or "earn" the right to watch television through his behavior. Few of us would accept that, as adults, another person in our household—no matter how close that person was to us—would have the power to tell us that because our behavior was unacceptable we could not watch television! But once the center shifted the approach to encouraging the staff to examine Michel's lifestyle—comparing it with their own, in fact—the aides were empowered to use knowledge that was familiar to them. Although aides are paid staff, they also are "peers" of the individuals with whom they work in the sense that they share important personal characteristics as adults living within a particular community. As the aides were empowered to draw on the community resources that they already knew about to expand choices for Michel, they enjoyed the natural social reinforcement of seeing Michel respond as any other adult might. Both Michel and the staff then were released from the "vicious cycle" and established a new cycle—a cycle in which a typical lifestyle provides the necessary motivation to engage people in meaningful activities without artificial reinforcers as part of a formal contingency management program.

As Michel's connections to his community expanded, his social network also expanded. The staff and the directors at the center continue to challenge themselves, in their work, to see new social networks and social interactions with other people as the central elements in Michel's new lifestyle. Michel still needs support from staff, but this support is minimal. Michel makes choices in his lifestyle like everyone else in the community.

REFERENCES

Drouin, R., & Labbé, L. (1989, November). *"Moi aussi je veux choisir"* ["I want a choice, too!"]. Paper presented at the annual convention of the American Association on Mental Retardation, Montréal, Québec, Canada.

Emerson, E., McGill, P., & Mansell, J. (Eds.). (1994). *Severe learning disabilities and challenging behaviours: Designing high quality services.* London: Chapman and Hall.

Fraser, D., & Labbé, L. (1993). *L'approche positive de la personne . . . une conception globale de l'intervention.* Laval, Québec, Canada: Editions Agence D'ARC, Edifice Educalivres.

Marlett, N.J. (1973). *The Adaptive Functioning Index.* Calgary, Alberta, Canada: The Vocational and Rehabilitation Research Institute Publication (translated into French and adapted with permission by Palombo, E. [1977], Canadian Association on Mental Retardation Publishing Co.).

Meyer, L.H., & Evans, I.M. (1989). *Nonaversive intervention for behavior problems: A manual for home and community.* Baltimore: Paul H. Brookes Publishing Co.

Chapter 15

Creating Multiple Support Strategies for an Individual with Serious Challenging Behavior

Karen A. Berkman

When I first met "Eric" in 1992, he was 33 years old. He was living in a locked forensic unit of a state developmental center with several other men who exhibited serious violent behavior. I had made a point *not* to familiarize myself with Eric's history before meeting him so that I would have an open mind and see the man, not his reputation. Given the context of our meeting, I was surprised to find a very charming and personable man.

WHO IS ERIC?

Eric is a 39-year-old man who has severe speech apraxia, which makes communication difficult for him. Because of his strong desire to connect with people, however, Eric uses all possible strategies to get his message across to his listener. He uses sign language, gestures, and speech, and—if all else fails—he will show the listener what he wants. Eric has a strong need to tell his story to others. When given the opportunity, he tells about his years growing up in institutional

environments; the pain of those years is still very present and real to him.

There are many ways to interpret the characteristics that are seen in other people. I have heard Eric described by others as "obsessive," "controlling," "self-centered," and "selfish." I have noticed these characteristics described by others but have interpreted them in a different way. When faced with new situations, Eric becomes anxious and tends to focus on a topic. I believe that this is an effort to create something concrete out of ambiguity. Eric sees the world in black-and-white terms, and he likes stability and predictability in his life. He is a very determined man. He will pursue something that he wants until he obtains it. He also has the need to make decisions for his own future, but he has had limited freedom to make choices. I have come to understand that when Eric is given positive opportunities within a supportive environment, he can make good choices for himself.

Eric has a great need to feel like an important person. Having been neglected by his family

---

In creating this personal portrait, I have relied on information transcribed from actual documents from Eric's past residences as well as from my own detailed journal notes written from the time of my first meeting with Eric through 1998.

and having learned to obtain attention through his negative behavior within several institutional placements, Eric had to learn how to feel important. These congregate care facilities did not teach residents about taking into account the feelings of others or how to make friends. To say that Eric was "selfish" criticizes him for learning the values of the environments in which he resided. He learned to survive against all odds. Eric understood that if he did not make his own needs a priority, no one else would.

This chapter tells the story of how Eric achieved a new life over the course of 6 years. There are many signs to indicate that he does, in fact, care deeply for family and friends. Although old habits are hard to break, Eric has been learning new values, within both his home and his community. Eric has shown that he is a generous man who has a desire for a happy, successful life.

EARLY HISTORY

Eric was born in March 1959, one of nine children in his family. It was a chaotic family situation; Eric's mother was overwhelmed and unable to care for all of the children. His father had been in prison at an early age but managed to hold a consistent job to support his family. Two of Eric's siblings also had disabilities. Because of the nature of the household, Eric lived with his maternal grandmother during his first year of life and established a very close relationship with her. When his grandmother died in 1960, Eric returned to his mother's home and had difficulty bonding with her.

During his preschool years, Eric attended a nursery school that was operated by a local group for children with disabilities. This was the first of many times that Eric was given IQ tests and found to be mentally retarded. At age 7, at his mother's request, Eric was admitted to his first institution. The actual admission papers state, "The boy has no understanding, cannot talk properly, cannot dress himself completely and because of a big family, he is unable to have proper supervision at home . . . . Long-term care and supervision appear indicated." The psychiatrist's report after his examination added,

This 7-year-old boy does not talk. Sometimes he mumbles and according to the attendants, no one can understand him. Usually he is quiet and cooperative and does not cause any serious problems on his ward. He seems to be friendly and takes care of his personal habits quite well. He does not mingle with other patients on the ward, probably because of his inability to talk.

Eric had been in the institution for only 2 months when the following progress report was written:

Fights all the time, will not stay dressed, refuses to keep shoes on, throws shoes constantly as fast as we can put them on. Throws toys at other children. In the dining room, very poor eating habits, throws food on the floor. Cries most of the time. Also soils. ["Soils" was written in big red letters at the top of each page.] He does not appear to be adjusting to the ward and activities.

It was at this time that Eric was placed on the first of many medications; he received various medications for "behavior control" between November 1966 and 1978. Little else is known about specific behavioral issues during this period because daily notes were not written until the 1970s. Other notes found from this period indicate that Eric had chronic ear infections, rashes, injuries, and childhood illnesses. It was not addressed whether there was a relationship between Eric's medical condition and behavioral incidents.

In 1972, when Eric was 13, a progress report stated,

Received from 049 [a living unit at the institution] as one of their behavior problems. Although Eric can dress himself, he has a difficult time looking neat. Table manners are terrible. Although Eric can understand, he refuses to speak. Eric is usually the center of trouble and is not liked by the other boys.

During July 1974, Eric was transferred to a developmental center in his community of origin. From June 1979 through June 1980, Eric was moved into community environments such as group homes, family care, and so forth. Eric was involved in 28 incidents of assault and property destruction of varying degrees during this 1-year period. He was arrested on three occasions for violent behavior. After these unsuccessful attempts at community living, Eric was moved into a group home specifically designed for people with behavior difficulties. While at this residence, Eric set a fire and was convicted of second-degree arson. Then, in June 1980, the director of the developmental services office recommended that Eric be placed in a locked forensic unit of another developmental center, citing as justification Eric's unmanageable behavior in even the most restrictive environments.

Reports indicate that Eric had behaved very well in the locked unit, and he was released in August 1981 to the same group residence where he had previously been unsuccessful. Eric responded to the token economy system of the group home and began showing interest in moving to a "less restrictive setting." In 1982, he moved to another group home and lived there for 6 months without incident, but then his behavior began to deteriorate. He was arrested again for harassment, assault, and disorderly conduct on three occasions and was sent to jail. Eric was moved back to his previous residence until a decision could be made as to where he should live. Eric subsequently moved to a room-and-board home located in a poor neighborhood in October 1983. He received case management services from the local state agency in the areas of money management, recreation, transportation, and so forth. Within 1 week, this situation fell apart and culminated in another arrest as a result of Eric's destructive and assaultive behavior.

From 1984 to 1987, Eric's history was marked by similar scenarios of placements in group homes and three correctional facilities. Upon his readiness for release from the last correctional facility, a psychologist from the state services office where Eric had resided wrote a report that stated,

It was my recommendation not to offer Eric services at any of our residential settings while his long history of physically aggressive, assaultive, and violent behavior places him at high risk of returning to the criminal justice system. His violent tendencies place anyone who comes into contact with him at risk of serious bodily injury.

Thus, Eric returned to the secure unit of the aforementioned developmental center. He remained there for the next 5 years.

LIFE IN A LOCKED FORENSIC UNIT

From 1987 to 1992, Eric was part of a highly structured environment on a locked unit. He had to earn all privileges, including the opportunity to work, leave the unit, make purchases and telephone calls, and have visitors. Eric took part in classes centering on academic skills and social skills and had specific goals in each area. These goals included

- Participation in a lifestyles training class to address displaying inappropriate sexual behavior
- Social skills training to reinforce taking turns and not being the focus of attention in group situations
- Vocational skills class to improve work skills
- Speech-language therapy to increase use of sign language skills and use of a picture communication book
- Goals in reading and math
- Behavioral goals

Despite his aggressive behavior, Eric was a man who also had many areas of strength. According to the annual and quarterly reviews at the institution, Eric was capable of all self-help and personal care skills. He enjoyed a wide array of social and recreational activities and exhibited positive community behavior. He had good vocational skills, specifically being capable of completing multistep assembly tasks, collating, and packaging tasks, and he was interested in working. Eric had limited academic skills but could read some words. He knew the alphabet and could add single digits. He had a good working vocabulary of sign language; however, most staff did not understand sign language. It was during this placement that Eric was diagnosed with severe speech apraxia. As Eric was unwilling to use an augmentative communication system, sign language was the one communication option available to him.

During this time, Eric received a diagnosis of intermittent explosive disorder. According to the *Diagnostic and Statistical Manual of Mental Disorders, Third Edition–Revised* (DSM-III-R; American Psychiatric Association, 1987), three main criteria must be met for this diagnosis. First, he had to display several episodes of failure to resist impulses to engage in serious assaultive or destructive acts. Second, these acts of aggression had to be grossly out of proportion to the precipitating stressor. Last, these aggressive acts could not be better accounted for by another mental disorder or medical condition. Eric did have a long history of explosive behavior. He had been described as becoming upset, turning red in the face, beginning to sweat and shake, and then becoming violent. Many people who had witnessed these incidents said that Eric was "uncontrollable" in this state. It took several large men to contain him when he exploded into a rage.

Beginning in July 1988, Eric started receiving thioridazine (50 milligrams [mg] total per day), a medication intended to help subdue this impulsive aggressive behavior; however, Eric continued to have outbursts and assaultive behavior. He attempted to hit people and throw objects, as well as destroy unit property. At times, he was self-abusive and punched his legs. Reports said that Eric required almost constant attention from staff and was demanding of their time and attention. When he did not receive these things, he would strike out at others. Because of an increase in assaultive behavior at the end of 1990, the dosage of thioridazine was increased to 75 mg per day, and it has remained relatively constant at this level as of this writing.

In the latter part of 1992, the multidisciplinary team at the forensic unit started discussing the possibility of moving Eric back to his area of origin and into a community environment. The social worker and team began to connect with administrators from the receiving team. Both teams discussed creating a group home environment that would include Eric and several other individuals who had lived with Eric in the institution.

MEETING ERIC

In August 1992, I was asked by my supervisor to meet Eric. All that I knew was that Eric had been institutionalized within developmental centers, group homes, and prisons since age 7 years. Because he had been free of serious violent behavior for 2 years, the administrator of

the unit had decided that Eric was prepared to live in a less restrictive environment. The plan was to have him return to a community group home, despite Eric's failure on more than one occasion in this type of environment.

As a psychologist for a state-operated agency, I was to develop a plan for Eric. Knowing that I had successfully assisted another individual with challenging needs to move into his own home (Berkman & Meyer, 1988), my supervisor encouraged me to become involved with Eric. Given what I knew of Eric's failed attempts at living in the community, I understood that the challenge was to create unique options for living and working that had not been previously attempted. My goal was to involve Eric directly in all stages of decision making as he moved from the locked forensic unit to his own home.

I first met Eric in August 1992 at the locked forensic unit of the developmental center. Accompanying me to this appointment were my supervisor and a consultant from the local university who specialized in positive approaches for individuals with challenging behavior. My supervisor already knew Eric from previous experiences with him and introduced us. We all found a corner of the large, open room containing tables and chairs. Eric arrived with a staff person who had known him for several years. She assisted us in understanding Eric's speech, as it was difficult to decipher at times. We made small talk with Eric about how he was doing and about the types of activities in which he was involved. He told us that he enjoyed all kinds of sports, he liked going to work, and he was involved in classes for reading and math. Eric periodically would use sign language to augment his speech. When I noticed this, I, too, began using sign language. He was surprised but increased his use of sign during the conversation. We asked Eric, "Where do you want to live when you move from here?" He stated, "In a group home with. . . ," naming three men with whom he lived at the institution. We found out later that he was reiterating the plan that he had heard from the staff about his future move, as defined by the administrators of the sending and receiving teams. We tried to describe other types of places where people live, but he seemed to understand only the "group home" concept. It became clear that one task would be to show Eric what his residential options were so that he could make informed choices. Our visit lasted approximately 1 hour. Before leaving, I explained to Eric that I wanted to help him by developing a home and a job around what *he* wanted. We also stressed to him that we needed him to be involved in all parts of that development and that that would mean visiting with him regularly.

After this initial visit, we formulated preliminary ideas on the tasks needing completion and how we would implement them. The first concern was to create *real* choices for Eric to make. This meant having him see how other people lived and the types of jobs that they held.

DESIGNING A NEW LIFESTYLE

It was necessary for me to obtain more information about Eric, such as his daily routines, likes and dislikes, and challenges, before proceeding further. I attended a review meeting at the secure unit and met all of the staff involved with Eric. The staff reviewed the activities and responsibilities in which Eric was involved but mostly what his need areas were. These areas included social skills, work skills, and, to a great extent, Eric's behavior.

My goal was to develop a *multiple support strategy* that would improve the quality of Eric's life while promoting positive alternatives to challenging behavior. The plan would include several components. The primary focus would be on creating a home that would support Eric in all aspects of his life and help him to become a member of his community. The second focus was to develop a job opportunity around Eric's interests and skills and to find an environment that would include Eric within the team of employees. The third component involved a network of support people from a variety of agencies, Eric's family, and friends and acquaintances of Eric's choosing. Last, we had to evaluate the best funding streams to support such a plan financially.

The Planning Process

To begin the process of developing a list of options from which Eric could choose, we needed to expose him to an array of reasonable choices for a home and a job. During initial visits over a 4-month period, I showed Eric a variety of situations in which people lived and worked. He saw supervised apartments; homes shared by two or three housemates; and jobs at a local college, a parcel delivery service, and a grocery store. With each visit, Eric expressed his interests and dislikes.

I noted several things about Eric during these initial visits. He could use a picture schedule well and referred to it often throughout the day, but he was always anxious to move on to the next activity. Eric had difficulty remaining on a topic, and he would impulsively bring up a new topic, even when everyone was still on the previous discussion. He did ask good questions when seeing the worksites, such as the hours people worked, their salaries, the job tasks, and so forth; however, he did not seem to be able to weigh the pros and cons of a job or a housing situation without assistance.

In January 1993, the social worker where Eric lived informed me that Eric was beginning to "deteriorate." Eric was having increased tantrums when he did not "get his own way." The staff at the institution discussed the idea of having Eric's visits with me be contingent on his nonassaultive behavior. I expressed concern with this idea because I understood Eric's anxiety and frustration from living between two sets of expectations; I also believed strongly that my relationship with Eric should not be contingent on his behavior in an institutional environment. The social worker was to discuss the issues further with Eric. Staff decided to continue monitoring Eric's behavior without making our monthly visits contingent on his behavior.

Finding a Job

During January 1993, Eric met with me for the purpose of going on a job interview with "Mr. Harvey," the manager of several grocery stores in the area where Eric was to reside and a personal resource of mine. Eric and I went for the job interview with Mr. Harvey. Upon our arrival, we learned that Mr. Harvey was ill that day and that "Mr. Granger" would interview Eric instead. Mr. Granger seemed quite confused about

Eric's disability and thought that Eric was hearing impaired, although I explained that he had a speech problem. Mr. Granger was very cautious about Eric's ability to fit in, and he suggested that Eric work in the back warehouse where customers would not interact with him. This type of discrimination was only the first that we encountered during this project. I told Mr. Granger that Eric's desire was to work as a bagger and that he would have a job coach with him to negotiate the language barrier. It was apparent that Mr. Granger was unprepared to accept Eric as a typical employee who required extra help.

I contacted Mr. Harvey the following week. Mr. Granger had given him erroneous information about Eric and his skills and his disability. Mr. Harvey was willing to reschedule an interview on another day when he was available; however, he was unable to see Eric until the beginning of March. This gave us 2 months to work on resolving the living arrangements and support network.

During this 2-month period, Eric continued to meet with me. We outlined a variety of tasks that required completion. Eric began filling out job applications at various locations. This prompted a referral to a state-operated agency that would provide support monies to hire a job coach for Eric. We made a request for a counselor who was proficient in sign language to ensure accurate and complete communication.

In March, Eric had his job interview with Mr. Harvey; Mr. Granger also was present. Mr. Harvey took the lead by asking Eric questions. I clarified information and acted as an interpreter when needed. Once Mr. Harvey had seen Eric's smile and his eagerness to work, he hired him. He wanted Eric to work in the front of the store, where all other employees start. Mr. Harvey assigned Eric to bagging groceries; if he did well, Eric would be assigned to other tasks. Mr. Granger attempted to convince Mr. Harvey that Eric should be in the back warehouse, but Mr. Harvey disagreed and felt that Eric's way with people would make Eric an asset out front. Mr. Harvey told Eric what his uniform would be, how he was expected to look each day, and what was appropriate behavior on the job. He offered Eric 30 hours of work per week, at minimum wage, on Monday through Friday. Mr. Harvey gave Eric a start date of May 3, 1993. This date was then set as the goal for all services and the new home situation to be in place.

Search for Housemates

To identify possible candidates for Eric's housemates, I initially used my contacts through my job. I asked people whether they knew of anyone who might be interested in living and working with Eric. I introduced Eric to a few possible housemates and one family with whom he might live. He spent half of a day with each potential housemate, and they got to know each other. With each visit to his new community, Eric also spent longer periods of time with the family. He felt very positive about living with them and was hoping that they would accept him into their home.

To ensure that there were choices for Eric, I placed an advertisement for the position of housemate, offering free room and board in exchange for supporting a man with a disability in the areas of daily living, recreation, and socialization. Two men responded to the advertisement; I interviewed each man, and Eric deemed them potential housemates. Eric also spent increasing amounts of time with them with each visit. It had appeared that significant relationships were forming with the two men and Eric. Although these two people were quite different from each other, we felt that this was positive. We hoped that it would give Eric a greater variety of opportunities through each man's personal interests. It was not clear, however, how these two men would get along with each other.

To begin considering the support network, we needed a sense of the types of activities in which Eric wanted to participate with others. The recreation therapist generated a list of ideas and a communication book containing specific recreational choices. This became a positive beginning for Eric to make real choices based on his expressed interests.

The family that Eric had been visiting decided that they were not prepared to have Eric live with them. During the month of March, many telephone calls and meetings took place with the two potential housemates to discuss their involvement with Eric and how best to arrange for a successful situation. Many negotiations followed about who would assume primary responsibility for Eric and the running of the house and who would be the support person. The paperwork chain began to certify one man as the family care provider through the local state-operated agency. This created a financial arrangement by which the family care provider received a monthly check for room and board costs, bills, and a personal allowance for Eric.

During the next 2 weeks, I worked on developing a mechanism for hiring the second man as a support staff person through a local private agency of Eric's choosing. We expected that he would draw a salary for a 40-hours-per-week position and live with Eric and his new housemate. He also agreed to contribute an equal portion toward the household expenses. Both housemates then received the standard training appropriate to their positions as family care provider and residential habilitation specialist. In addition, I discussed with them aspects of Eric's history, how we had reached the present situation, and what we all hoped the future held for Eric—as well as their roles in that future.

Finding a House

With the job now in place, Eric expressed his desire to live within walking distance of work. Although this was a primary concern, we did look at a variety of houses on all sides of town. All three men viewed each location and discussed the pros and cons of each. Using a personal resource, I found an apartment in walking distance of Eric's new job. All three men agreed that this would be a good location in which to start. Arrangements were made to have Eric sign his first lease during his April visit with the family care provider.

Organizing Supports

In March 1993, options for securing needed support services were discussed with Eric. I explained the various agencies that provided the support services so that Eric could make his preliminary choices. He expressed a preference for a small agency that would give him the individualized attention that he wanted. Eric and I chose

an agency whose philosophy was *person centered*. I arranged an initial meeting with the agency staff to discuss Eric's needs and their ability to provide for him.

The initial meeting took place without Eric. I provided an overview of Eric's background and areas in which he required assistance. We discussed the necessary hours of services for residential habilitation and a budget for these services. We also requested a budget for training, recreation, and respite funds. I explained that two men had already been selected as housemates. One man was to be the family care provider; the other would function as the residential habilitation support staff that the agency could hire to provide services and live in the home.

I then contacted another agency to provide a job coach who was proficient in sign language. We also requested a sign language instructor to work with all involved parties to enhance their skills and assist Eric with augmenting his communication. To purchase these services, I contacted a local state agency that provided vocational and educational supports to individuals with disabilities.

During the remainder of March 1993, I arranged for psychiatric services for Eric. In addition, a nurse from the state agency was assigned the task of securing medical services for Eric, based on his needs. I completed the procedure for enrolling Eric in the Medicaid waiver program and certifying the family care provider. I also started the process for securing the start-up costs, such as rent, food, and utilities. To accomplish this, I wrote a letter of justification to the central office of the state agency requesting monies for initial needs as there would be a 2-month lag before the scheduled monthly payments started.

Eric had a move date of April 30, 1993. I was still concerned about several problems:

1. Signing a lease
2. Obtaining money to pay for monthly expenditures for a 2-month period
3. Acquiring household items and furniture
4. Getting a commitment for job coach services
5. Introducing Eric to all involved people

During April 1993, Eric met the people at the small agency who would be providing residential habilitation. He also met with the counselor from the state agency that provided funding for job coach services, as well as a representative from the agency that provided the job coach. Eric asked relevant questions pertaining to the job coach's responsibilities and the hours that the person would be working.

It was mid-April before I had a method for purchasing furniture for Eric's new home. The paperwork was completed for the state agency to issue vouchers to a variety of stores in the area. Eric, his housemates, and I shopped for furniture and necessary household items, and Eric chose the larger items in the colors and styles that reflected his taste.

Relocation Meeting

A large meeting to plan Eric's relocation took place on April 15, 1993. Staff and clinicians from the institutional residence, as well as clinicians and representatives from the various agencies in the new location, met with Eric and his sister. This was the second opportunity for Eric's sister to meet the new people in Eric's life. She was pleased that Eric would be moving back to the area but made it clear that she was only able to do "just so much" because of her own problems. Eric attempted to gain from his sister a concrete response of how often she would see him. She agreed to a schedule of every other week.

Participants then discussed all aspects of Eric's life, including his housemates, job, recreation options, social network, finances, and relationships with family, and then considered ways for Eric to be included in his community and educational opportunities. Although the issue of behavior was superficially discussed, I did not want it to become the sole focus of the meeting. It was our contention that with the correct supports and more opportunities for Eric to control his decisions and outcomes, Eric's behavior would not be the primary area of concern.

LIVING IN A NEW COMMUNITY: THE FIRST YEAR

Eric moved into his new apartment on April 30, 1993, with his housemates. The first 3 days included arranging the house, putting items together, and purchasing necessary items. This time also was spent familiarizing Eric with his new neighborhood, including the location of his job, and choosing a bank and a pharmacy within proximity.

Providing Structure

Knowing that Eric required structure to his days, we developed a picture calendar system. Eric's housemate took sign language pictures that depicted recreational options, household tasks, responsibilities, and other relevant photos and mounted them on small cardboard squares with magnets attached on the backs. Eric used these with his housemates to plan the schedule for the week. This picture schedule system has proved to be useful not only to provide structure to the week but also to make specific events more concrete. Examples included visits with family, appointments with doctors, and meetings with other involved parties. It did not take Eric long to learn how to schedule his week with activities using the picture calendar system.

During a typical week, Eric woke between 7 A.M. and 8 A.M. and independently prepared for work. Once the expectations for his morning routine were reviewed, Eric could make his own breakfast, prepare a lunch for work, and clean his room.

During the first several months of his new living arrangement, I visited Eric three times per week for 2 hours each visit and provided counseling as needed to assist Eric with his transition. Eric, the family care provider, the residential habilitation provider, and I met weekly at Eric's home. We reviewed the activities for that week, assessed the needs and issues of housemates, and problem-solved as a collaborative group. Over time, we changed our meeting schedule from weekly to biweekly to monthly, with periodic meetings as needed. This helped to keep continuity among group members and ensured that we had the same information.

Worksite

Eric left for work at 10:30 A.M., initially walking to and from work with a housemate. After several months, Eric asked to walk part of the way home by himself. Over time, Eric built up his level of confidence and walked to and from work independently.

Eric met his job coach at the worksite. They established a routine of punching in on a time clock, putting away his personal items, and checking in with a manager for the day's instructions. Eric started bagging groceries and taking them to the customers' cars. He learned to smile and to act friendly and helpful toward customers. Eric quickly learned that this paid off, as he began earning big tips from his customers. This was the best natural positive reinforcement that Eric could have received to provide feedback for a job well done. The grocery store personnel liked Eric, and I frequently observed him getting the "high-five" from job peers as he entered the store. Eric had become an included team member at work.

Eric began showing independent initiative at work by running to clean spills and helping people as needed. During the month of June, his manager paired him with a co-worker who started teaching Eric how to stock the frozen food section. This was a major challenge as Eric could not read beyond basic survival words. Between the co-worker and the job coach, Eric learned one small section at a time and how to match items by certain features of their labels. Over time, Eric stocked the frozen food section with minimal assistance and on 3 days assisted with bagging groceries.

Friendships

The development of relationships has been the most challenging area. Eric has had access to his housemates, their friends and families, his own family (but only on a limited basis, per their request), acquaintances through work, and paid staff. He has had opportunities to meet people through a variety of activities, such as bowling, pool, parties, a running club, and classes. Eric did not show an interest in pursuing anyone for a friendship until many months after he had moved to his new home. He also began expressing a desire to meet a woman to date, although he had never had such a social experience. He did attend two parties, one through the private agency and one through work. Eric met people whom he was interested in seeing again, and we helped him with making those arrangements.

The greatest deterrent to the development of relationships was twofold. First, Eric was unsure of how to proceed with getting to know someone as a friend or a partner. Second, a staff person accompanied him everywhere he went. We looked at ways to have the staff person become "part of the background" yet still remain as a support, if needed. In addition, Eric was embarrassed by his speech, and he tried to have other people speak for him. Toward the latter part of the first year, Eric was driven to activities and met up with his peers for class or recreation; he then called home after the activity to be picked up.

Changing Supports

Throughout the course of this first year and a half, many changes and modifications occurred. One month after Eric's move, the second housemate (residential habilitation support staff) decided not to live with Eric but to continue to work with him 40 hours per week. The reason for his decision was a conflict with the primary housemate. Through many attempts to resolve these issues, we were unsuccessful in finding a solution. The situation changed again in November 1993 when the residential habilitation support person was fired from his position for questionable conduct on the job. This caused the private agency to attempt to fill the 40 hours weekly with several staff. Eric enjoyed meeting and working with a variety of people, but he needed more stability. With each staff person's own interests, Eric gained new experiences and met new people. In February 1994, a new housemate moved in with Eric, providing his first experience with living with a female. It was a positive experience for all three people—for a time. Conflicts soon arose between the two housemates over the equity of time spent with Eric and job responsibilities.

The second major change was with the original job coach. Although he and Eric had a good relationship, the job coach was not responsibly fulfilling his obligations to be at work during scheduled times. He was replaced by two temporary people until a new job coach could take the position. By the end of the first year, there was little need for a full-time job coach, and she was phased out of daily contact with

Eric. The job coach taught the managers of the store the system that she and Eric had developed for stocking shelves, and the store managers then began to take over direct supervision of Eric.

Given Eric's need for a wide assortment of activities, there was ongoing development of new ideas. Eric and his housemate and support staff looked at all of their resources for information and attempted to keep their options fresh and novel. For example, Eric had the opportunity to take a trip to Washington, D.C., for his first vacation. He chose this location because he wanted—in his words—to meet "the big boss." When I was unsuccessful in contacting the President, I was able to arrange for Eric to meet the director of the administration on developmental disabilities. It was seeing such results from his own hard work that motivated Eric to look forward to his future.

A NEW LIFESTYLE: THE SECOND YEAR

During Eric's first year, he had met a variety of people as friends and workers. I was approached by a man who had become friendly with Eric through his job at the small private agency. He asked about having Eric join him and his roommate in sharing a house. Eric had been expressing a desire for a change in living arrangements. I had the men speak directly with Eric so that he could make his own decision about this invitation.

Eric decided to move in with three typical men, who were living in a house in the outer university area of the town. One housemate was the certified family care provider through the state-operated agency. A second housemate was a residential habilitation staff person hired by a local private agency. This person worked 25 hours per week with Eric. A second residential habilitation staff person came in 15 hours per week to teach Eric new recreational, community, and home skills. The third housemate was Eric's friend. He and Eric planned activities together or spent time at the house. During the summer of 1995, Eric and his friend went on a 1-week vacation to DisneyWorld. All of these support people worked with Eric on learning the

values and responsibilities necessary to live successfully in the community.

Eric continued to work in a local grocery store as a stock person and bagger with periodic visits from a job coach. He walked to and from work on his own and became known in his community. His reputation was no longer built on the negative aspects of his behavior but on his hard work as an employee and his friendly gestures toward people in his community. Eric loved being active in a wide array of activities. He enjoyed sports, music, participating in group recreational activities, joining his housemate at the local health club, dining out, movies, and family activities.

Since Eric returned to community living, he has had the opportunity to rekindle former relationships with certain family members. There are still dysfunctional aspects to these relationships; however, Eric needs to have this connection, feeling that he is a part of something special as a member of a family. Eric enjoys visiting his family on holidays, buying gifts and cards for relatives, and inviting them to his house for parties. Eric has several new nieces and nephews, and he loves being an uncle. This is another opportunity for Eric to feel important in a positive way.

Personal and Situational Changes

There have been many changes, both in Eric and in the circumstances surrounding him, since 1992. The most obvious change that Eric's friends and support staff have noted is that Eric is happy most of the time. He speaks frequently about his previous life in institutions, crying about his painful experiences. He sees the benefits of his new life and reminds himself that he never wants to return to an institution or a correctional facility.

Eric has been afforded more opportunities for recreation and entertainment than ever before. These opportunities do not have to be earned by "good behavior" but are given parts of his life. He has experienced having control over his life through choice making. Eric also has shown that he can ask for help when he needs guidance to make decisions on issues with which he is not familiar. He is encouraged to take some risks with new activities or learning experiences. Although he initially preferred his house-mate to be with him for all "first-time" experiences, Eric has become independent in familiar activities within a short period of time.

Behavior Changes

Eric has not had one incident of assault or a serious tantrum since he began living in his own home. We did note a change in Eric's mood during the fall of his first and second years. He became depressed, vacillating between crying often and being angry. As his emotional status worsened during those few months each year, we decided to have a consultation with a psychiatrist. Eric agreed to try an antidepressant medication, fluoxetine (20 mg daily), in combination with the thioridazine (75 mg daily) that he was already taking. Within a few weeks, Eric seemed to feel somewhat better, but he did not return to his typical demeanor.

After Eric returned from his first vacation in May 1994, his residential habilitation support staff person told him that she was leaving her job. This seemed to affect Eric quietly at first but over time escalated into a major upset. On one occasion during this second summer of community living, Eric threw his deodorant through his bedroom window. According to Eric, this incident was related to being angry at his housemate and feeling like he was always being told what to do. It was more likely, however, that this incident, as well as other minor upsets, arose out of an accumulation of frustrations and disappointments. He paid to have his window repaired, and after discussing other ways of expressing his feelings, Eric requested more structure. He asked that I develop a chart, similar to the one that he had when he lived on the forensic unit. He wanted daily feedback and a visual reminder of how he was doing. We also decided to have the psychiatrist consult with Eric about his emotions and behavior. They agreed to increase temporarily the thioridazine to 100 mg per day to assist Eric with regaining control of his behavior. This combination of efforts did help, and Eric began to feel and act better. The thioridazine was then reduced to its original dosage of 75 mg per day, remaining at that level until the fall of 1996.

In September 1994, Eric moved to a new residence with two of his current housemates, and his life seemed novel to him again. He was excited about all of the new activities and people. As the winter season came on, however, his mood again changed to depressed and angry. This was the same pattern displayed in the previous year. Eric agreed to try temporarily increasing the dosage of fluoxetine to 40 mg (daily) to see whether it was possible to bypass this depressive period. It appears that this was successful in positively changing Eric's affect.

As of September 1996, Eric continued to take fluoxetine (40 mg per day) but with a lower dosage of thioridazine (50 mg daily). The thioridazine was further reduced to 25 mg daily in February 1997, with a subsequent increase to 35 mg daily in April 1997. Although all previous attempts to lower the dosage of thioridazine had been unsuccessful, it seems that there has been a positive management of cyclical moods with the use of fluoxetine.

Support Changes

During the second and third years of Eric's community living, he had two consistent housemates. This was positive in light of several changes in residential habilitation support staff. After much discussion about recommended practices for supporting Eric, the team decided that Eric enjoyed working with a variety of people. Eric made the transition from a model of live-in residential habilitation support by one consistent person to a schedule of rotating staff. This decreased staff "burn-out" and gave Eric an opportunity to meet new people and be exposed to novel activities.

During the summer of 1996, one of his housemates moved to a new home but remained in the same community as Eric. This left Eric's friend as the primary care provider. They found a new person to share the house with them, and they received residential habilitation supports on a rotating schedule.

After 3 successful years of community living, I approached the private agency from which Eric received his residential support staff and requested that they assign a service coordinator to manage Eric's case. I had filled this role for

Eric—in part—because I had been a consistent person in his transition to the community but also to prove that with the right arrangement he could flourish. In fact, Eric far exceeded my expectations. I continued to advocate for Eric and serve as his psychologist until May 1997, when I took a new job out of state. Our relationship has continued for several years through good and bad times. During the fall of 1998, Eric and a support staff member visited me. Our friendship remains important to both of us. We continue to write to each other, exchange gifts on special occasions, and express our mutual gratitude for having shared such a rich history.

Family

Eric has experienced many disappointments from his family since his move, and this has made him upset. Eric has repeatedly discussed his frustration about his family's inaccessibility or their inability to follow through with plans. During the first 2 years, he raised his voice or cried out of frustration. Other times, he might go to his room and talk to himself and listen to music until he is calmed. Eric has difficulty seeing his family in a realistic manner. He wants his family to be kind, loving, and stable. He wants family members to act like the families that he saw on television in the 1970s. Eric makes many gestures of gifts and time for his family. Only on occasion is this reciprocated, but it is enough to keep him wishing for the day that his dream family becomes a reality. His perceptions and tolerance have improved over the years.

Independence

Eric has shown an increase in his ability to be independent in various areas. Eric has learned to budget $50 weekly for spending money. He independently goes to the bank and completes his weekly transactions after his housemate has written out the paperwork.

Eric wakes up in the morning and prepares for his day. When he first moved in with his three housemates, he tended to wake everyone else, but he has learned to complete his routine independently. He is alone from the time he awakens until he leaves for work in the latter part of the morning. He walks to and from work, crossing one major street. Eric is basically independent in most work tasks but requires some supervision when stocking the freezer section. Eric was complimented for work when he was given the employee of the year award in 1994 for supportive work after his first year on the job.

Eric has had opportunities to learn cooking skills for the first time after moving to his own apartment. Each night, he helped his housemate prepare one part of the meal. His repertoire expanded, and he can now meet his basic needs in this area.

Eric made his greatest step toward independence when he learned of his father's death. Eric made the trip to Florida in 1995 to be with his family for the funeral—without the supervision of a staff person. This was a major step for a man who was characterized as so dangerous that he should not be without a staff person to monitor him at all times.

One major area of change has been choice making. I have attempted to provide Eric with many opportunities for making his own decisions after looking at all of the issues involved. At times, it is difficult for Eric to see beyond the moment to the consequences of his decisions. He has learned from some mistakes, but he continues to repeat others. One example is when Eric elects to spend all of his weekly money on snacks and then has no money left to participate in activities later that week—a recurrent problem, even though it results in his being unable to engage in a preferred activity.

Social Relationships

Eric has shown improvements in his social skills. He is frequently out in the community with staff and peers participating in social functions. He has been learning to consider the feelings of other people, although he still likes to be the focus of attention—which has interfered with his making friends or getting involved in a relationship. However, 1998 was filled with great strides. Eric met a woman in whom he became interested, and they dated for 8 months. They went to social functions together, participated in family planning counseling for safe sex practices, and enjoyed special occasions together.

Eric decided to end this relationship as he was not prepared to consider marriage.

I have also noticed a major change in Eric's ability to have a two-way conversation. Eric used to provide his listener with a litany of his interests. He did not ask questions of others or seem to have any interest in the other person. Today, Eric does want to know what is happening to other people and what they are doing. He can carry on a more typical conversation because his life is more typical. He has many more things that he can talk about, and this has normalized the content of his conversations.

Finances

On a larger scale, another positive change is finances. In reviewing the budget for maintaining Eric in the forensic institutional environment, I noted a rate of approximately $650 per day ($237,250 per year). Currently, Eric is living in his own home for approximately $212 per day ($77,380 per year), which includes all living costs (rent, food, utilities), the cost of the residential habilitation person, and the family care income. This is *one third* of the cost of living in an institutional environment where—as Eric has stated—the quality of life was less than acceptable for him.

Eric has had several raises in pay since he started working at the grocery store. This has allowed him to remove himself from the Social Security rolls and function without additional income from the state. This has been a source of pride for him, and he enjoys being financially secure.

Attitude Changes

One important area of change has been the attitude of others toward Eric. Eric is keenly aware that the staff people whom he knew from his last attempt at community living did not see him as any different from his prior reputation. In spite of all of the positive changes that have occurred in his life, some staff people were waiting for "the other shoe to drop." They expected that Eric's success was going to be short lived and that he would fail again, as he had done so many times in the past. This was a great disappointment to Eric. He had tried to make a new beginning with those who had treated him poorly. I had made a serious attempt to protect Eric from these types of negative expectations and attitudes by surrounding him with people who felt positive about him and were willing to make an investment in his future.

It would be hard for even the greatest of cynics to deny Eric's success. He has proved himself many times over and has earned a new level of self-respect. As one example of the respect that Eric has begun to earn from others, Mr. Granger, the manager who originally wanted Eric to work in the warehouse away from customers, has told me, "Send me five more workers like Eric . . . he's the best."

FIVE-YEAR FOLLOW-UP

The opportunity to be Eric's case manager, advocate, and friend has given me a new perspective on the difficulties of taking a journey with an individual who has a disability. Establishing consistent supports is a major task when lives (both of the focus person and of those around him or her) are constantly changing. Eric has expressed different preferences for whom to live and work with. He has experienced the pain of having important people move on with their lives and the relief of moving away from people whom he found difficult. Finding the right balance of supports without imposing on Eric's freedom to make life choices was a juggling act.

Observing Eric for 5 years has allowed me to see the patterns in his affective state and his behavior. Given this information, Eric was able to avoid the emotional upheaval observed in the first 2 years by proactively prescribing antidepressant medication. In addition, Eric has established trusting relationships with a core group of people. This has allowed him to express himself in more positive ways without having to resort to negative behavior. Eric knows that his friends and support staff will listen and that they will help him resolve his problems. He does not have to yell or act out to capture their attention. Eric knows that all he has to do is ask.

It has been a unique experience to combine efforts from a large state agency and a small private agency. We have successfully come together around one person, creating a cohesive support network. The collaboration among all involved people has proved to be a positive method of providing the benefits of a large support system with an individualized approach.

Eric remains thankful for his opportunity to live independently and to have people care about him. He is, in fact, aware of this chapter about his life and wanted to indicate his excitement about it, as well as his satisfaction with his new life—his job, his home, his activities, and reuniting with family. Eric is a man who continually shows great potential to be successful. With the support and structure from caring people, the possibilities are endless. The challenge is to allow flexibility in the structure so that Eric can grow and experience his own freedom.

In response to the many ways in which Eric has grown, become integrated into his community, and displayed independence, I nominated him for a statewide achievement award. This award, which recognizes achievements in community integration and independence, is given annually through the state developmental disabilities planning council, by the vote of fellow consumers. Eric, one of two 1997 recipients of this award, was honored at a luncheon in the state capitol by the commissioner of services for people with developmental disabilities. Eric's achievement was that he refused to recognize his developmental disabilities as a barrier to a full and productive life.

REFERENCES

American Psychiatric Association. (1987). *Diagnostic and statistical manual of mental disorders* (3rd ed., rev.). Washington, DC: Author.

Berkman, K.A., & Meyer, L.H. (1988). Alternative strategies and multiple outcomes in the remediation of severe self-injury: Going "all out" nonaversively. *Journal of The Association for Persons with Severe Handicaps, 13,* 76–86.

Chapter 16

The School Consultation Project

Functional Assessment and
Educative Intervention for Excess Behavior in
Various Community Environments

Cynthia M. Anderson, Kurt A. Freeman,
Kimberly B. Mullen, & Joseph R. Scotti

An emerging theme in the developmental disabilities literature is the provision of educative, community-referenced interventions for the habilitation of individuals with challenging behaviors (e.g., Carr, Robinson, Taylor, & Carlson, 1990; Dunlap, Kern-Dunlap, Clarke, & Robbins, 1991). A major focus of these intervention strategies is to replace challenging excess behaviors that inhibit successful community integration with acceptable alternative skills, thus producing meaningful lifestyle changes (Horner et al., 1990; Meyer & Evans, 1989).

The educative, or constructional (Goldiamond, 1974), approach to behavior change is characterized by an emphasis on 1) identifying the environmental conditions that are maintaining repertoires of excess behavior, 2) decreasing or eliminating these reinforcing environmental influences, and 3) *establishing* or *strengthening* repertoires of *functionally equivalent* appropriate skills (Meyer & Evans, 1989). This approach focuses on arranging or rearranging the environmental variables that are associated with an excess behavior to reduce its necessity. Thus, if reinforcement is delivered contingently on the functionally equivalent behavior rather than on the excess behavior, then the rates of the excess behavior will decrease (Meyer & Evans, 1989; Scotti, Evans, Meyer, & DiBenedetto, 1991).

OVERVIEW OF THE EDUCATIVE APPROACH

There are five central philosophical assumptions of the educative approach to behavioral intervention:

Support for this work was provided through a grant to Joseph R. Scotti from the West Virginia Developmental Disabilities Planning Council, Charleston, West Virginia, and the Division of Special Education of the Monongalia County Schools. The authors acknowledge the efforts of numerous individuals in implementing the School Consultation Project since 1992, especially Doug Nangle, Glenda Vittimberga, Jim Ellis, Karen Weigle, Karen Kirk, Rachel Bowman, Michelle Robertson, Estelle Lombardi, Frank Kirkland, and Don Kincaid, as well as the numerous undergraduate assistants who performed an invaluable service to the project and the people whom we served.

1. Behavior is maintained by environmental consequences that reinforce it.
2. Environmental variables serve as antecedents that set the occasion for the behavior to occur.
3. A functional assessment that identifies environmental variables (e.g., antecedents, consequences) that are related to the excess behavior should be conducted prior to developing an intervention.
4. The hypotheses generated from the functional assessment should be used to guide the design of intervention strategies.
5. Intervention should focus not just on decreasing excess behavior but also on increasing an individual's competency in active community participation.

Each of these assumptions is examined in turn.

The Functional Nature of Behavior

Identifying the function of behavior has primarily involved the examination of two types of relations: 1) that of a behavior and the environmental consequences with which it is associated and 2) the stimulus conditions associated with the occurrence *and* nonoccurrence of behavior (Dunlap & Kern, 1993).

Functional Relations Based on Consequences

The first type of functional relation considers the environmental consequences that are associated with a behavior. When a particular consequence follows a response and that response is then more likely to occur in the future, that consequence is assumed to maintain (through reinforcement) the preceding behavior. In layperson's terms, the behavior is said to be "motivated" by its reinforcing consequence.

Excess behaviors may be maintained through either positive or negative reinforcement (Carr, 1977; Dunlap & Kern, 1993; Iwata, Dorsey, Slifer, Bauman, & Richman, 1982/1994). Excess behaviors may be maintained by positive reinforcement through attention from others or through access to preferred items or activities (e.g., Day, Rea, Schussler, Larsen, & Johnson, 1988; Hagopian, Fisher, & Legacy, 1994; Vollmer, Iwata, Smith, & Rodgers, 1992).

For example, to obtain a favorite picture book in a classroom, a child may have a tantrum until her teacher gives it to her. Thus, the child's tantrum behavior is positively reinforced by obtaining access to a preferred tangible, namely the picture book.

Negative reinforcement involves the removal of an unpleasant stimulus contingent on the exhibition of a particular behavior. Negative reinforcement also has been shown to maintain excess behaviors (Carr, Newsom, & Binkoff, 1980; Weeks & Gaylord-Ross, 1981). For example, a child who does not enjoy writing tasks may bang his head on the desk when his teacher puts a worksheet in front of him because, in the past, the teacher has removed the worksheet when he banged his head.

In addition to positive and negative reinforcement, internal factors may maintain excess behaviors (Carr, 1977; Iwata et al., 1982) and thus may constitute a third contingency class. This class of reinforcement often is referred to as automatic, perceptual, or sensory reinforcement. Behaviors maintained by this type of reinforcement also may be either positively or negatively reinforced. A child may slap his ears because it sounds good (positive reinforcement) or because it stops his ears from ringing (negative reinforcement).

Although the previous examples serve to illustrate the ways in which excess behavior can be reinforced, it is important to note that a single behavior may serve multiple functions for an individual (e.g., Day, Horner, & O'Neill, 1994; Iwata, Vollmer, & Zarcone, 1990). For example, an individual may hit her head to gain attention from others and to avoid cleaning her room. Furthermore, investigation of response interrelations has highlighted that several topographically different behaviors may serve a single function (e.g., Parrish, Cataldo, Kolko, Neef, & Egel, 1986; Sprague & Horner, 1992). Thus, it may occur that a person both hits others and engages in head banging to gain attention.

Functional Relations Based on Stimulus Conditions

A second class of functional relations involving the antecedent events and contextual stimuli associated with behavior is receiving increased attention in the literature (Dunlap et al., 1991; Haring & Kennedy, 1990). *Antecedents* may be conceptualized as stimuli that reliably predict that a particular stimulus will be delivered contingent on a behavior. Antecedents that reliably predict that a reinforcing consequence will follow a behavior come to serve as *discriminative stimuli* that set the occasion for the occurrence of previously reinforced behaviors (Wahler & Hann, 1986). Examples of antecedents to particular behavior might include the presentation of a demand, the presence of a particular individual, a time of day, or the interruption of an activity.

Researchers and clinicians also have been examining the effects of broader antecedent events, often referred to as *setting events,* on excess behavior. Setting events are influential events that are temporally distal from the target behavior. Halle and Spradlin (1993) categorized setting events into two types: 1) durational or concurrent events, including physiologic conditions (e.g., establishing conditions such as deprivation, satiation, physical discomfort) and discrete or complex events that occur concurrently with the target behavior (e.g., the difficulty of a task, the amount of space in a room), and 2) historical events separate in time and space from current stimulus conditions but that still affect present conditions (e.g., an argument with a family member that later affects performance at work).

Understanding the relation between antecedent stimuli and the occurrence of a target behavior is important because it enables caregivers to predict the situations in which a behavior will and will *not* occur, which leads to the implementation of preventive measures (Meyer & Evans, 1989).

Functional Assessment of Excess Behavior

Given the assumption that behavior is functional, the task for behavioral clinicians and researchers then becomes primarily to identify the function(s) of excess behavior and use the resulting information to design functionally based interventions (see Repp, Felce, & Barton, 1988). To achieve this task, it is necessary to conduct a functional assessment. A functional assessment attempts to determine the environmental variables that are associated with a behavior. Specifically, it aims to identify the environmental setting events, antecedents, and consequences that influence the occurrence of a response (Baer, Wolf, & Risley, 1968). Information about the environmental variables associated with a target behavior allows interventionists to form hypotheses about the functional relations between environmental variables and the exhibited target behavior.

A variety of techniques have been developed to assist with gathering functional analysis information. Methods frequently utilized include *indirect* methods, such as interviews and rating scales, and *direct* methods, such as descriptive analyses and analog assessments.

Indirect Methods

Indirect methods of functional assessment allow for the assessment of the targeted behavior from the perspective of a person who works closely with the individual who is being assessed. The Functional Analysis Interview Form (FAIF), developed by O'Neill, Horner, Albin, Storey, and Sprague (1990), for example, provides a semistructured format that assists the interviewer with gathering information about the following: the targeted behavior's topography, frequency, intensity, and duration; antecedent events (in terms of both setting events and establishing operations); and consequences of the behavior. The interview also allows for the assessment of a variety of adaptive behaviors (e.g., communication, daily living skills), and it may help the clinician identify possible reinforcers.

Rating scales are another indirect strategy commonly used to develop hypotheses about the function(s) of excess behaviors. The Motivation Assessment Scale (MAS), developed by Durand and Crimmins (1988, 1992), for example, assesses whether the targeted behavior is being maintained by positive reinforcement from gaining access to tangibles or attention, by negative reinforcement through escape from tasks, or by automatic reinforcement.

Direct Methods

When indirect assessment methodologies do not provide sufficiently clear clinical support for particular hypotheses regarding environmental variables that affect excess behaviors, more direct methods of assessment that require direct observation or manipulation of the targeted behavior may be used. Two commonly used direct methods are *descriptive analyses* and *analog assessments*.

Descriptive analyses (Bijou, Peterson, & Ault, 1973) typically take place in the natural environment (i.e., the environment in which the individual lives, works, or goes to school) and involve recording each occurrence of the target behavior, as well as the antecedent and consequent events. An example of a descriptive analysis methodology is the antecedent-behavior-consequence (A-B-C) or sequence analysis chart (Sulzer-Azaroff & Mayer, 1977) in which the observer records the events that occur prior to and subsequent to the behavior of interest. This method may reveal the consistency with which antecedent and consequent events are associated with the occurrence of the targeted behavior. A less data-based but no less useful approach to the same ends is to generate alternative hypotheses about the function of the behavior during team "brainstorming" sessions; hypotheses then may be evaluated through "mini-experiments" in which relevant factors are manipulated. It is this less formal cross between descriptive and analog assessments that Meyer and Evans (1989; see also Evans & Meyer, 1985) suggested for laypersons or professionals who are less familiar with formal data-based procedures.

A final way that the function of a targeted behavior may be ascertained is through the use of analog methodology. An analog functional assessment is conducted in a controlled environment and utilizes analog experimental conditions that are designed to model the student's environment and to demonstrate control. The analog assessment allows the therapist to manipulate experimentally both antecedent conditions that may occasion the target behavior and consequent events that may maintain the behavior.

A frequently used example of this methodology is based on the work of Iwata, Dorsey, Slifer, Bauman, and Richman (1982/1994). This procedure involves manipulating environmental events in four different analog conditions:

1. *Social attention,* designed to assess the hypothesis that positive reinforcement in the form of attention from others is a motivating factor
2. *Demand,* designed to assess the hypothesis that negative reinforcement in the form of escape from an aversive situation affects the behavior
3. *Unstructured play,* a control condition designed to provide an enriched environment
4. *Alone,* designed to test whether positive reinforcement in the form of automatic or sensory reinforcement is a motivating factor

Since Iwata, Dorsey, et al., research (e.g., Iwata, Pace, et al., 1994) has demonstrated the utility of including a fifth condition, referred to as the *tangible* condition, during the analog assessment. The tangible condition is used to assess whether reinforcement in the form of gaining access to preferred stimuli affects the behavior. Other analog conditions also may be designed on an individual basis, depending on the question to be addressed (Scotti, Schulman, & Hojnacki, 1994).

Intervention Implications of Understanding Function

Identifying behavioral functional relations through a functional assessment is only worthwhile to the extent that the acquired information is used to guide the design of functional interventions (Dunlap & Kern, 1993; Evans & Meyer, 1985; Meyer & Evans, 1989; Scotti, Evans, Meyer, & DiBenedetto, 1991). A functional intervention does not simply *eliminate* the maintaining variables of a behavior but instead focuses on teaching acceptable, alternative skills that are *functionally equivalent* to the excess behavior and that are more *efficient* and *effective* for the individual than the excess behavior (Carr et al., 1994; Durand, 1990; Horner & Day, 1991). In contrast to the "cookbook," or packaged, approach so characteristic of eliminative programs (e.g., Barkley, 1987; Forehand & McMahon, 1981; see also Scotti, Mullen, & Hawkins, 1998), intervention becomes individualized based on the person's unique history of reinforcement—not simply on the structural or topographic aspects of the behavior (Scotti, Morris, McNeil, & Hawkins, 1996).

Desirable Intervention Outcomes: Quality Lifestyles

An overriding outcome goal of an educative intervention is a quality-of-life improvement, partially determined by the person's engaging in more appropriate and *effective* behavior and having greater access to typical settings and social roles and by the improved perceptions of significant others in the person's life (Evans & Scotti, 1989; Meyer & Evans, 1989; see Chapter 22). Meaningful lifestyle change is almost always directly tied to maintained improvements in the targeted excess behavior, but—although traditional behavioral approaches have sought deceleration of the excess behavior as the primary and often the sole outcome of interest—this is almost a secondary goal of educative interventions. Table 1 lists a variety of other outcomes that may be more important contributors to quality of life than the simple reduction of excess behavior. We must always ask ourselves the question, "Now that the problem behavior has decreased or ceased, what does this individual have that he or she did not have before?" The answer to this question will point us toward quality-of-life improvements and a focus on constructional (i.e., skill-building and opportunity-enhancing) interventions. Accomplishing constructional interventions requires an approach to behavior reduction that depends on intervention strategies that are as minimally intrusive as possible and that respect the human dignity of the individual—a third goal of educative interventions. Finally, the educative approach to intervention recognizes that quality-of-life improvements will be sustained only to the extent that the excess behavior remains decreased across all environments, thus making behavioral generalization and maintenance necessary intervention goals.

Meyer and Evans (1989) proposed four components of educative interventions that are able to address collectively the previously stated goals. These include implementation of the following:

1. Short-term, individualized strategies (e.g., environmental manipulations, distraction and interruption techniques) to prevent the occurrence of excess behavior while other intervention components are put in place

Table 1. Levels of outcome that are important in evaluating educative interventions

- Deceleration or cessation of the targeted excess behavior (the traditional focus of behavioral interventions)
- Acquisition of alternative behaviors that are incompatible with the targeted excess behavior
- Acquisition of alternative behaviors that are functionally equivalent to the targeted excess behavior (often a form of communicative behavior)
- Absence of negative side effects of an intervention
- Occurrence of positive collateral effects, both in the repertoire of the individual and in the response of the social system
- Acquisition of long-term self-control, self-monitoring, or self-management strategies
- Decreased need for medical intervention and crisis management that had previously resulted from the targeted excess behavior
- Expanded environments (i.e., less restrictive placements) through movement to typical home, work, school, and leisure environments
- Increased quality of life, as noted by subjective report (or corresponding nonverbal behaviors) and increased opportunity to make choices and have those choices honored (even when they may be viewed as the "wrong" choice by others)
- Perceptions of significant others in the person's life (e.g., family, spouse, friend) that favorable changes have occurred—including changes in their own lives
- Expanded social contexts through friendships (especially with "nonpaid friends"), family, dating and partners, and community participation

Adapted from Meyer & Evans (1989, 1993).

2. Planned immediate consequences (e.g., reinforcement of desirable, alternative behaviors; interruption and redirection of excess behavior; crisis management procedures) when needed

3. The teaching of acceptable, functionally equivalent alternative skills—especially communication strategies

4. Long-term prevention through lifestyle enhancement (e.g., planning for community integration, moving to a typical residence) and the development of skills (e.g., teaching self-regulation strategies, learning job skills) that either remediate or obviate the "need" for the excess behavior

An effective and complete intervention plan that contains these four components can create a meaningful and lasting change in a person's behavioral repertoire and quality of life. It is predicated, however, on recognizing that both the individual and the social contexts within which an individual lives are complex, interrelated, and dynamic *systems* (Evans & Meyer, 1985; Evans, Meyer, Kurkjian, & Kishi, 1988; Meyer & Evans, 1989; Scotti, Evans, Meyer, & DiBenedetto, 1991; Voeltz & Evans, 1982). The systems are complex in that the individual is not just the sum of his or her targeted excess behaviors but is a person with a variety of skills, interests, preferences, and goals—no matter how limited or limiting these may appear to other people. The systems are interrelated in that changes in the rates of one behavior—such as through consequence-oriented procedures—affect the rates of other behaviors (see Evans & Meyer, 1985; Evans et al., 1988; Voeltz & Evans, 1982; Chapter 3). In addition, changes in the environment result in changes in the person, and vice versa—an aspect we often forget. And finally, dynamic in that both systems—the individual and the social context—are constantly in a state of change (behavior is movement not stasis).

SCHOOL CONSULTATION PROJECT

Many programs and agencies have adopted the educative approach to behavior change. In West Virginia, the School Consultation Project (SCP),

housed in the Quin Curtis Center of the Department of Psychology at West Virginia University, uses this approach. The SCP provides services to students and adults with developmental disabilities who display excess behavior and to parents, teachers, and staff who need assistance with addressing these behaviors. The project title is a bit of a misnomer in that, over time, services were expanded to include group home and residential environments, preschoolers, and adults, along with students who are attending public school programs.

The target individuals served by the SCP typically have cognitive impairments in the severe to profound range of mental retardation and exhibit a range of behavioral excesses and deficits. Services are provided throughout West Virginia (including rural, underserved areas) at minimal or no charge to the referring agency. The goals of the SCP are twofold: 1) to provide intensive intervention with students and adults based on a functional assessment of behavioral skills and deficits and 2) to educate parents, teachers, and mental health professionals in functional assessment and educative intervention techniques through consultation, workshops, and undergraduate- and graduate-level courses.

The remainder of this chapter provides a discussion of the process used by the SCP to implement an educative approach to the treatment of excess behaviors. First, a discussion of the assessment phase of consultation is provided. Second, intervention strategies that typically are used with the individuals served are outlined. Third, specific case examples provide a description of the application of the educative approach to behavioral change in the natural environment using a consultative model.

Assessment

As discussed previously, research (e.g., Carr, 1977; Carr et al., 1980; Iwata et al., 1982) has shown that often environmental, rather than organic, factors maintain excess behaviors that are displayed by people with developmental disabilities. Thus, prior to developing and implementing treatment recommendations, a thorough analysis of potential antecedent and consequent events that are associated with the occurrence of excess behaviors is completed. SCP personnel employ pretreatment functional assessment methodologies to develop hypotheses regarding maintaining events both for the identified excess behavior and for potential, functionally equivalent replacement skills.

The SCP considers several factors when determining the functional assessment strategies best suited for use with each individual. First, the accessibility of the individual and the individual's caregivers is considered. Conducting analog functional analyses can be very time consuming (often many hours over several days or more) and thus may not be appropriate for individuals to whom there is limited access because of distance or time constraints. In contrast, completing an MAS takes approximately 10–15 minutes and thus may be an appropriate measure to use in cases with limited access.

A second, related consideration is the location of the individual. Following the guidelines stipulated by the funding agency, the SCP provides services throughout West Virginia. Staff limitations, however, necessitate changes in the type of consultative services provided for individuals who live a considerable distance away (as far as 250 miles in some cases). Except for the project director (author JRS), all SCP personnel are either graduate or undergraduate students. Thus, most of the direct consultation is completed by students who have other significant time commitments.

Finally, the severity, intensity, and frequency of excess behaviors displayed are important factors in determining the type of assessment used. Methods such as the experimental analog analysis (e.g., Iwata, Dorsey, et al., 1982/ 1994) are designed to elicit excess behaviors through the systematic manipulation of different environmental events. For participants with intense self-injurious behavior, the implementation of such an assessment may not always be appropriate because of the possibility of irreparable tissue damage resulting from an increased rate of self-injury. In addition, for individuals who exhibit targeted excess behaviors at a low frequency (e.g., once per day, once per week), unstructured direct observation may not be a useful procedure because there may be little opportunity to witness the occurrence of the excess behavior.

Conducting a functional analysis of excess behavior is only part of a complete assessment of an SCP case. Identifying socially appropriate behaviors in the same response class as the targeted excess behavior is also an integral component of the pretreatment analysis (see Scotti, Evans, Meyer, & DiBenedetto, 1991). The method of analysis used to identify these "alternative" behaviors depends on the same factors outlined previously. Typically, the same functional analysis methods used with the excess behaviors are used with the alternative responses. The purpose of conducting an analysis of socially appropriate responses is to detect whether the individual currently engages in functional skills that may be incorporated into the intervention plan. Such an analysis determines whether these alternative behaviors are functionally equivalent to the excess behaviors (e.g., are maintained by the same consequences).

Often, the alternative behaviors identified for analysis are responses that are exhibited prior to the occurrence of the excess behavior— that is, earlier in a chain of responses. Take, for example, a 3-year-old child who has tantrums when his father will not buy him a candy bar. The child might first ask for the candy bar. If that behavior does not result in his obtaining the candy bar, then the child may point to the candy and stomp his feet. After still not getting what he wants, the child may begin to cry and scream, at which point his father gives him the candy bar to quiet him. In this example, several more appropriate behaviors (i.e., asking appropriately and pointing) occurred well *before* the child exhibited tantrum behavior. These behaviors are likely to be in the same response class as tantrum responses and are thus under the control of the same environmental events. The intervention implications of finding functionally equivalent, socially appropriate alternative behaviors are discussed more fully next. It should be clear, however, that the chain of escalating behavior can be averted by intervening at an early point—such as allowing candy when it is asked for politely but not when the child has a tantrum.

When completing a functional analysis, clinicians use multiple methods to gain the most accurate representation of the individual's behavior. The analysis process usually begins with a thorough review of the individual's available records (e.g., institutional progress notes, individualized education programs, school records). This allows for a better understanding of the individual's social and educational history and of his or her excess behavior. Perhaps what is most important is that reviewing records typically provides information regarding previously completed assessments as well as attempted intervention plans. Previous intervention failures and successes often can point to maintaining variables and viable intervention options. For example, one child with whom the SCP worked frequently engaged in aggressive behavior during task demands. Although the teacher dutifully put this individual in a time-out room following aggression, the behavior escalated rapidly, suggesting that aggression served an escape function and was being negatively reinforced by cessation of task demands while he was in time-out. Thus, this information added to our understanding of the function of the behavior and suggested which intervention strategies to avoid.

Conducting semistructured interviews with several different caregivers (e.g., parents, teachers, group home staff) also is an essential component of the analysis process. The SCP uses the FAIF when conducting formal interviews. Because the FAIF is so comprehensive, conducting a complete FAIF may be overly time consuming in certain instances. Thus, typically SCP personnel either will complete the FAIF with one caregiver or will administer only portions of the FAIF to two or more caregivers from the same situation (e.g., a teacher and a teacher's aide).

The functional analysis typically also involves having caregivers complete the MAS. A separate MAS is completed for each targeted excess behavior, as well as for potential alternative behaviors. Completing separate questionnaires helps to determine whether topographically distinct targeted behaviors serve similar functions (e.g., does the individual gain attention when exhibiting both head banging and biting of others or only when he bites others?). In

addition, because perceptions of a situation may vary across individuals and because individuals often behave in a distinct manner with different people, several people from the same environment (e.g., two parents, a teacher and the classroom aide) each complete an MAS. This helps with gaining the most accurate representation of the individual's behaviors. Finally, because behavior can be situation specific (e.g., self-injury may result in attention at home but in escape from academic demands at school), separate MAS questionnaires are completed by people from all situations in which the excess behavior occurs (e.g., school, child care). This provides information regarding whether similar or different environmental events maintain the targeted behaviors in different situations.

The data from interviews and questionnaires do not always provide unambiguous support for hypotheses regarding potential function(s) of excess and alternative behaviors. When this occurs, more direct methods of analysis are used if time and distance allow. One direct observation method employed is the A-B-C analysis. Preferably, this form of observation is completed across several days and in the different environments in which the excess behaviors are being displayed (e.g., at home, at school). Varying the time and the place of the observations increases the likelihood of observing a representative sample of the individual's behaviors and of maintaining environmental events. Because of the time and distance limitations often encountered, however, the A-B-C analysis may need to be completed in only 1 day.

The final method used by the SCP is the experimental analog analysis. All analog sessions are completed with a member of the SCP who is trained in the procedure present to ensure accurate and safe implementation. Generally, SCP staff are the therapists in an analog evaluation; however, staff from the individual's treatment environment also may serve the therapist role with intense monitoring and prompting by SCP personnel.

The analysis conducted with each individual may involve from one to all of the different procedures described previously. After completing the appropriate procedures, the project staff look for consistencies and discrepancies in the hypotheses developed from each assessment procedure. Through continued analysis, attempts are then made to resolve significantly ambiguous findings and conflicting interpretations.

Intervention

To develop an effective intervention plan, it may be necessary to implement short-term preventive measures as well as long-term intervention plans. Preventive measures taken by the SCP involve environmental manipulations that are designed to arrange or rearrange events so that situations that are likely to elicit excess behaviors cease to occur. Environmental manipulations may involve allowing the individual to avoid the situations that are likely to occasion the excess behavior. For example, if the functional analysis suggests that the presentation of difficult demands elicits an individual's self-injury, then the initial recommendation may be to reduce or eliminate such demands. Thus, the situation resulting in self-injury is no longer present in the individual's daily schedule, and self-injury should decline in frequency. Conversely, the manipulation simply may involve minor alterations to a situation so that it no longer occasions the excess behavior. Examples of this may include providing toys to children during long trips so that boredom does not occur or interspersing fun activities with demands for individuals who have difficulty in task situations. The troublesome situations are still present; however, slight modifications reduce the likelihood that they will result in excess behaviors.

Some environmental manipulations may create atypical situations that, over time, are not beneficial for the individual. Take, for instance, the first example in the previous paragraph (difficult demands elicit self-injury). It is neither plausible nor beneficial for the individual to avoid difficult demands for a significant period of time (e.g., months, years). Thus, environmental manipulations rarely constitute the complete intervention recommendations; rather, their benefit lies in decreasing the frequency of the excess behaviors, thereby allowing service providers more time to implement proactive, educative strategies to assist the individual in dealing

effectively with the problematic situations. Such a strategy also removes or reduces the stress that results from the excess behavior on everyone in the situation—staff and target individual. This reduction of excess behavior can both give time for adequate intervention planning and implementation and reduce interfering reactions of staff to the individual.

After implementing necessary environmental manipulations, the next stage of intervention involves capitalizing on more socially appropriate communicative responses that are currently in the individual's repertoire and that serve the same function as the excess behaviors. As described previously, functionally alternative behaviors are identified during the preintervention analysis. Thus, intervention recommendations during this step involve manipulating reinforcement contingencies for the excess and alternative behaviors (Scotti, Evans, Meyer, & DiBenedetto, 1991).

Prior to intervention, excess behavior was the most efficient means that the individual had of receiving reinforcers. To eliminate the need for the excess behavior, the alternative behavior must become more efficient in gaining the desired reinforcer. To this end, the alternative behavior that is chosen must be as easy or easier to emit than the excess behavior. For example, if a child throws herself to the floor and screams to get attention, then the alternative behavior must involve less effort than throwing herself to the floor—such as raising her hand. It is also important that the alternative behavior result in more immediate reinforcement than the excess behavior: If the raised hand fails to get the teacher's attention, then the excess behavior likely will follow. Therefore, it typically is recommended that service providers and caregivers reinforce each occurrence of the alternative responses while initiating the following changes.

Using appropriate responses that are currently displayed by the individual as the focus of intervention is beneficial for two main reasons. First, because the behavior is already in the person's repertoire, it is not necessary to teach a new response. A person does not have an extensive learning history with newly acquired skills; thus, he or she may be less likely to exhibit them.

Capitalizing on behaviors that are already in the person's behavioral repertoire alleviates this problem because they usually have been displayed as long as, if not longer than, the excess behaviors. Second, as described previously, the targeted alternative responses are precursors to the excess behaviors. As such, they are likely to occur fairly consistently when the problematic situation is reintroduced into the person's daily schedule. Because the alternative response generally occurs *before* the excess behavior, reinforcing it should interrupt the chain of behaviors, decreasing the likelihood that the excess behavior will occur.

Most individuals who receive services from the SCP emit alternative responses that can be incorporated easily into an intervention. It occasionally is difficult, however, to identify consistently occurring appropriate behaviors that serve the same function as the excess behaviors. In addition, individuals may emit alternative behaviors that are not easily understood by people who do not regularly interact with the individual. In cases such as this, a shaping procedure may be used whereby the alternative behavior is gradually shaped into a more widely recognized response. For example, fist clenching that precedes punching other students may be shaped into signing STOP.

In addition to ensuring that the individual gain the desired reinforcement for exhibiting the alternative responses, it is important that he or she no longer receive the same reinforcement for the excess behavior. Although reinforcing precursor behaviors often results in reduced occurrences of the excess behavior, it is perhaps overly optimistic to believe that the excess behavior will never occur again: Behaviors are not removed from repertoires; it is their probability in certain contexts that is altered by intervention. Thus, an additional component to most interventions that are recommended by the SCP is the use of extinction when the excess behavior occurs.

CASE VIGNETTES

The remainder of the chapter explores use of the educative approach through three case vignettes. The first two vignettes discuss intervention options that are available for individuals who live close to the service providers, whereas the third vignette discusses some of the difficulties with serving individuals at a distance.

Serving Individuals Locally

Many of the individuals who are seen by the SCP reside within a 1-hour drive of Morgantown, West Virginia. Because the individuals are easily accessible, a wide variety of assessment techniques may be considered. In addition, assessment of intervention efficacy often is possible. Finally, with individuals who live locally, the SCP is more involved in staff training and in monitoring intervention implementation. This allows for "fine-tuning" intervention packages when difficulties arise. To illustrate these points further, two cases are presented next. The first case history, Arnold, provides an example of the assessment procedure used when an individual presents with a wide variety of excess behaviors that occur across many situations. Also illustrated is how an intervention package may be modified to accommodate "real-world" problems such as budget cuts and staffing difficulties. The second case history presents an individual who exhibited less severe problem behaviors in a more limited environment. This second case, Barney, also illustrates how the development of an intervention package can result in major life-enhancing changes for an individual.

Arnold

Arnold was a 7-year-old boy with moderate to severe mental retardation who was referred to the SCP for the assessment of multiple excess behaviors, particularly aggressive and destructive behaviors. His aggression toward other children was of special concern as he had already hurt several classmates. Because of the severity and intensity of his excess behaviors, Arnold attended school for only half of the day and was in a classroom for students with behavior disorders and emotional disturbances. His only exposure to general education peers occurred during approximately 10–15 minutes each of homeroom and lunchtime.

Assessment

As is the first step in virtually all assessments conducted by the SCP, interviews and rating scales were completed by Arnold's general education and special education teachers. Arnold's general education teacher, Ms. Nisbet, reported having significant difficulties with managing Arnold. Ms. Nisbet stated that Arnold engaged in excess behaviors whenever she could not devote her complete attention to him. These behaviors also occurred when Arnold was required to do his schoolwork or quietly participate in a group activity. As a result of the severity and intensity of Arnold's behaviors, Ms. Nisbet reported spending the vast majority of her time attempting to keep Arnold from physically injuring other students or from being destructive. Because of these difficulties with managing Arnold's excess behaviors and because of repeated complaints from the parents of other children in the classroom, Ms. Nisbet was attempting to have Arnold completely removed from her classroom and from the lunchroom.

The rating scales completed by Ms. Nisbet provided information that was similar to what her interview provided. Specifically, Ms. Nisbet's responses suggested that Arnold engaged in aggressive and destructive behaviors to gain attention or to avoid doing schoolwork.

The interviews with and the rating scales completed by Ms. Cunningham, Arnold's special education teacher, provided a markedly different picture of Arnold. According to Ms. Cunningham's report, Arnold rarely was aggressive toward other children in the classroom and had not attempted to hurt her in more than a month. Although Arnold was occasionally disruptive, these outbursts generally were short-lived and infrequent. The MAS that Ms. Cunningham completed suggested that Arnold's behaviors might occur to gain attention or to gain access to preferred toys or activities. She also believed that some of Arnold's behaviors (in particular, his destructive behaviors) might be self-stimulatory in nature.

The discrepancies between the reports provided by Ms. Nisbet and Ms. Cunningham strongly suggested that Arnold's behaviors were maintained at least partially by environmental factors. As a result, observations of Arnold in Ms. Nisbet's and Ms. Cunningham's classrooms, as well as in the lunchroom, were conducted to generate clearer hypotheses regarding maintaining variables. During the observations, Arnold exhibited excess behaviors only during the times when he was supervised by Ms. Nisbet. It is interesting to note that Arnold was most likely to exhibit excess behaviors after repeated verbal requests for attention were ignored. Arnold occasionally would exhibit excess behavior after Ms. Nisbet had given him a task on which to work. When this occurred, Ms. Nisbet generally had the aide return Arnold to his special education classroom.

From both brief observations of Arnold and conversations with his teacher and his mother, it was clear that Arnold had many more appropriate behaviors in his repertoire. He was verbal and could request objects and attention. He also frequently would tell the teacher to "stop" or "go away" during work situations.

The combined results of the assessment indicated that adult attention played a large role in maintaining Arnold's excess behaviors. It seemed feasible that other factors might be responsible, as well. In particular, Arnold's behaviors might be maintained by escape or by gaining access to tangibles. An analog functional assessment was conducted to provide empirical support for these hypotheses regarding maintaining variables.

Two analog assessments were conducted with Arnold: one targeting his excess behaviors and one targeting his alternative skills (verbal communication). The assessment was conducted utilizing an ABAB (reversal) design to demonstrate functional control. Figure 1 presents a graphical representation of the analog assessment results for the excess behaviors under four analog conditions (attention, tangible, demand, and control) across two types of phases. The first type of phase (A and A') was the standard procedure in which the analog conditions were implemented such that the targeted excess behavior was positively (attention, tangible) or negatively (demand) reinforced and all other behaviors were ignored. During the second type of phase (B and B'), contingency reversal was implemented such that the alternative, appropriate behaviors (verbal communication) were reinforced (negatively or positively according to the condition) and the excess behaviors were ignored.

The results of the analog assessment suggested that Arnold exhibited excess behavior

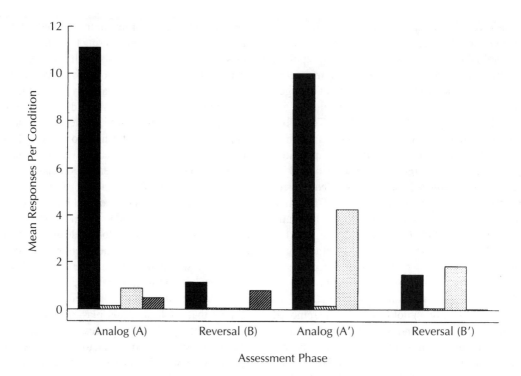

Figure 1. Mean responses per condition for excess behavior during the analog functional assessment with Arnold. Phases A and A′ represent the analog assessment targeting excess behaviors (alternative behaviors were ignored). Phases B and B′ represent a contingency reversal in which the excess behaviors were ignored and the alternative skills received positive or negative reinforcement, according to the condition. (Key: ■ = Attention, ▨ = Tangible, ▨ = Demand, ▨ = Control.)

primarily for attention (as seen in phases A and A′) but also to escape task demands (seen most clearly in phase A′). It was much less likely that Arnold engaged in excess behaviors to gain access to preferred objects. Perhaps most important, the assessments demonstrated that when Arnold's verbalizations were reinforced (i.e., verbalization resulted in attention, a break from work, or gaining access to preferred toys, depending on the analog condition), he was much less likely to exhibit the excess behaviors. This is demonstrated clearly in phases B and B′ in which the contingency reversal was in effect and access to reinforcement was contingent on verbalizations and not excess behavior.

The results of the analog assessment were congruent with the results of the unstructured observations. Specifically, Ms. Cunningham had very few problems with Arnold because she attended to Arnold's verbal requests. In Ms. Nis-

bet's classroom and in the lunchroom, Arnold's verbalizations were not effective, so Arnold resorted to the more effective—and bothersome— excess behaviors.

Intervention Recommendations

Recommendations for intervention for Arnold consisted of a behavioral component and an inclusion component. The behavioral component focused on reducing Arnold's excess behaviors by increasing his more appropriate communicative behaviors. Specifically, it was recommended that teachers provide Arnold with what he requested verbally. So, if Arnold said "stop" while working, then teachers were instructed to allow a brief break from work. If he requested attention, then teachers were to interact briefly with Arnold. The goal was to make verbalizing more effective in obtaining reinforcers than the excess behavior, thus both preventing the excess behavior and strengthening an existing positive skill. In addition, it was recommended that any excess behaviors that did occur be ignored.

The inclusion component focused on increasing the amount of time that Arnold spent in general education classes. By increasing Arnold's involvement with peers who were developing typically, Arnold would have the opportunity to learn more appropriate social skills as well as be able to learn academic skills in a more natural environment. The plan initially was developed during the winter break and was to be implemented in the spring semester of the school year.

Because of Ms. Nisbet's history with Arnold, Ms. Nisbet understandably was concerned about having Arnold in her classroom for an entire day without any additional assistance. For this reason and because it was likely that Arnold would need extra help with his school work, the SCP recommended that an aide be placed in the classroom. Unfortunately, the county board of education was unable to hire an aide for Arnold at that time, thus putting the plan on hold. During a meeting at the end of the academic year, the board of education committed to hiring an aide so that the plan could be implemented during the upcoming school year. To ensure that the behavioral intervention was carried out consistently, the SCP worked intensively with the aide in the beginning of the year and then provided consultation on an as-needed basis.

Barney

Barney was a 10-year-old boy with severe mental retardation who was referred to the SCP for the assessment and treatment of aggression. Barney reportedly was exhibiting high rates of intense aggression toward his teachers and other students. In addition, the school had requested assistance with developing an appropriate educational plan for Barney.

At the time of the assessment, Barney was in the first year of his current academic placement. Prior to this, he was in a segregated classroom for students with multiple disabilities. His parents had requested that he be removed from this classroom because they believed that Barney was not receiving appropriate academic or

social skills training in such an exclusionary environment. At the time of the SCP's evaluation, Barney had been attending a new classroom for students with mild mental retardation or behavior disorders for approximately 6 months.

Assessment

MAS rating forms were completed by Barney's teacher, Ms. Shelly, and by both classroom aides. In addition, the SCP conducted approximately 4 hours of unstructured observations.

The results of the MAS suggested that Barney was exhibiting excess behaviors primarily to gain attention from others, although he seemed also to exhibit these behaviors to gain access to preferred objects and to avoid work (see Figure 2). During the unstructured observations, Barney rarely received any attention from an adult unless he "misbehaved." Barney spent the majority of the school day sitting at a desk in the corner of the room completing connect-the-dot pictures. During the observations, Barney did not exhibit any aggressive behaviors. Whenever Barney went near another student, he was sharply reprimanded by either Ms. Shelly or an aide. It is interesting to note that Barney seemed to enjoy the reprimands as he would laugh and smile while the teachers were scolding him.

Intervention Recommendations

Based on observations of Barney, it was clear that he engaged in problem behaviors to gain attention from others. It also was likely that he was bored with his required work. Because both of these areas were related to poor academic planning, this was the major focus of the intervention plan. The goal of intervention was to involve Barney in more stimulating and age-appropriate activities and to increase his involvement with typically developing peers of similar age. Unfortunately, Barney's teachers believed that they were unable to make the necessary curriculum changes without compromising the education of the other children in the classroom; therefore, arrangements were made for Barney to attend a new school program in the upcoming year. As per the intervention plan, Barney would spend 45 minutes in the morning and 1 hour in the afternoon in a classroom with

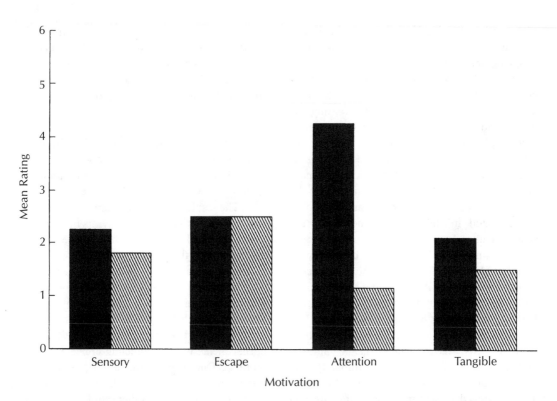

Figure 2. Results of the Motivation Assessment Scale completed by Barney's teachers and the residential staff who worked with Donald. The bars represent mean ratings across respondents. (Key: ■ = Barney, ▨ = Donald.)

general education peers, attending either physical education or art classes. For the remainder of the day, Barney would attend a vocational training program that would focus on teaching basic self-help and job preparation skills.

The next area addressed by the SCP was Barney's lack of any formal system of communication. Although Barney tapped people on the arm to get their attention, this was occasionally misconstrued by his teachers as aggression. In addition, it was unlikely that other people with whom Barney interacted recognized this as a request for attention; therefore, it was recommended that Barney be provided with a picture communication system. A detailed plan was developed by the SCP to teach Barney how to communicate using this system. A conversation with his mother approximately 4 months after the implementation of this system revealed that Barney was doing well with it.

Discussion

The stories about Arnold and Barney demonstrate how information from a functional assessment leads naturally to a functionally based, educative intervention. In both cases, the students were taught alternative, more appropriate ways to communicate their wants and preferences. In addition, each intervention plan contained a lifestyle-enhancing component. For both students, this involved increasing the amount of time spent with typically developing peers. To accomplish this with Barney, it was necessary to move him to a new school, where he is able to spend time in a general education environment.

Serving Distant Individuals

The grant under which the SCP is funded requires that service be provided throughout West Virginia. When working with individuals who are more than 1 hour away from Morgantown, the SCP often is required to make many modifications to the consultation process. First, assessment length typically is shortened to only 1–2 days, 4–5 hours each day. In addition, fewer SCP staff are available to assist with individuals who live far away, reducing the feasibility of conducting analog assessments. Third, after intervention plans are developed, the SCP often does not have the time or the resources to evaluate empirically the intervention plans. Finally, although the SCP does provide caregivers with initial training in the plan and is available through telephone contact, extensive follow-up services with distant individuals often are difficult to arrange. The following case example highlights some of the difficulties encountered when working with individuals who reside a fair distance from Morgantown.

Donald

Donald was a middle-age man who displayed severe self-injurious behavior (SIB) and had resided in institutional environments for the majority of his life. The facility in which he resided was in the process of moving individuals into the community and had contracted with the SCP to develop an intervention plan to reduce the rates of Donald's SIB before he moved into the community. In addition to exhibiting multiple forms of SIB (e.g., head banging, eye gouging, hair pulling), Donald exhibited aggressive behavior when caregivers attempted to block his self-injury.

Assessment

Initial assessments completed by the SCP staff included conducting semistructured interviews (e.g., FAIF) and MAS forms with staff members who worked closely with Donald. The results of the MAS are depicted in Figure 2 and show inconsistent information as to possible functions of Donald's SIB. Some staff suggested that his self-injury occurred to get attention or to avoid unpleasant situations, whereas others believed that it was self-stimulatory. The semistructured interviews revealed that Donald's day already had been completely restructured in an attempt to avoid situations in which Donald was more

likely to engage in SIB. Donald was no longer required to work on tasks that he did not appear to enjoy. Instead, he was allowed to spend a great deal of time sitting by himself (a time when SIB was rarely exhibited).

To gather further functional assessment information, approximately 3 hours of unstructured observations were made. Donald was observed in his day program (a workshop environment), at lunch, and in his residential building. During these observations, no SIB was observed; however, very few demands had been placed on Donald. Most of the time, Donald was observed to be sitting alone, playing with a piece of cloth (reported to be a favorite activity).

The results of the assessments suggested that Donald's SIB might be maintained by escape from unpleasant situations or tasks. Because some staff had suggested that Donald's SIB might be maintained by attention or self-stimulation, it was decided that an analog assessment would be conducted to test empirically these various hypotheses. However, the analog assessment had to be terminated during the second 15-minute session—a demand session—because Donald's SIB was occurring at such a high rate and intensity that the SCP staff believed that they could not keep him safe from injury. Fortunately, the high rates of SIB exhibited by Donald during the terminated demand session provided further support for the hypothesis that these behaviors occurred to avoid unpleasant tasks or situations. Although staff suggested that Donald's behaviors might be maintained by attention, this seemed unlikely as Donald rarely engaged in self-injurious behaviors when he was left alone. It was also unlikely that his SIB was self-stimulatory in nature as it most often occurred under distinct stimulus conditions (i.e., the presence of nonpreferred tasks or activities).

Intervention Recommendations

Because of the severity of Donald's SIB (in particular, his eye gouging), the SCP staff believed that they should continue to physically block this behavior when it did occur. To reduce the likelihood that Donald would exhibit SIB, the SCP staff recommended that Donald be taught rudimentary sign language, beginning with the sign for STOP, and that the sign be taught in a manner that was noninvasive. This was so that Donald did not construe prompts to sign as task demands and thus engage in SIB. The SCP staff also recommended that Donald be provided with a variety of functional and stimulating activities in which to engage.

Facility Policies

All residents at this particular facility had a "team" of individuals (e.g., social worker, behavior therapist, communication specialist, physical therapist) involved in planning and overseeing all aspects of their lives. Before the recommended intervention plan could be implemented, it first had to be approved by Donald's team. According to facility policy, all intervention plans for a resident were to be developed by the relevant team member and were to be oriented toward a single intervention goal. For example, the communication specialist could develop an intervention to increase use of sign language, whereas the behavior specialist could develop a plan to decrease the rates of SIB. Intervention plans, however, were not allowed to have goals in multiple areas. Thus, the team found the plan that was developed by the SCP to cover multiple areas: a behavioral area (blocking self-injury), a communication area (teaching sign language), and a vocational/leisure area (providing a variety of functional activities). Facility policy therefore required that the SCP plan be broken down into individual intervention plans with goals specific to each area.

The overall intervention plan developed by the SCP was designed to incorporate overall lifestyle-enhancing changes. The modifications made by Donald's team effectively removed the intended effects and naturalistic context by breaking down the plan into specific components to be completed at a particular time. For example, communication training was to be completed at 2:00 in the afternoon, not throughout the day during situations in which it would be functional to sign—thus avoiding SIB and teaching a functionally equivalent response/skill. When the modified plan was put into place, many caregivers stated that it was not markedly different from what they had been doing—and

they were correct in this belief as the facility policy had successfully counteracted the context into which the plan was to be embedded. Thus, staff were disinclined to follow the plan.

CONCLUSION

The SCP has been active in a variety of other activities largely designed to develop and evaluate methods of functional assessment (e.g., Freeman, Anderson, & Scotti, in press). The SCP has investigated the agreement among various methods of functional assessment (i.e., MAS, A-B-C, analogs), as well as evaluating the reliability (of the procedure and its interpretation), validity, and generalizability of these procedures (e.g., Anderson, Freeman, & Scotti, in press; Freeman, Anderson, Mullen, Boccio, & Scotti, 1995; Scotti, Kirk, et al., 1993; Scotti et al., 1994; Scotti, Weigle, et al., 1993). The use of functional analysis strategies has been a continuing area of concern in the published literature on developmental disabilities (Scotti, Evans, Meyer, & Walker, 1991; Scotti, Ujcich, Weigle, Holland, & Kirk, 1996), chronic psychiatric disorders (Scotti, McMorrow, & Trawitzki, 1993), and child behavior therapy (Scotti et al., 1998; see Chapter 4). Finally, the SCP has expended a great deal of effort to provide and evaluate the effects of training programs on functional assessment and educative approaches to intervention. For instance, the SCP has evaluated the effects of providing information to special educators and other intervention staff about the function of an excess behavior on 1) ratings of intervention acceptability, 2) choices of intervention strategy, and 3) perceptions of the causes or functions of behavior (Anderson et al., 1995; Weigle & Scotti, 1995; Weigle, Scotti, et al., 1995).

It is with investigations such as those listed in the previous paragraph that the staff of the SCP hope to increase the effectiveness of direct clinical intervention efforts. As has been seen time and again—and as is evident in some of the vignettes presented here—it is insufficient to attempt behavioral change with an individual when the context within which that individual resides does not also adapt, change, and grow with him or her. The SCP's greatest clinical successes for individuals have been in environments in which the staff have taken the time to be trained in the educative approach, have understood the approach's validity and implications, and have allowed individuals to develop new repertoires of skills in an environment that provides choices rather than limits. Environments in which staff approach the SCP's interventions and consultation as "old-style" behavior modification (i.e., the consultant "fixes" the individual with a consequence-based procedure, and the staff do not need to change their own behavior) have resulted in the SCP's greatest frustration and failures. This chapter closes with a reminder that the context and not the person is the "client." Interrelated systems must be modified through a combination of strategies targeting multiple individuals.

REFERENCES

Anderson, C.M., Freeman, K.A., & Scotti, J.R. (in press). Evaluation of the generalizability (reliability and validity) of analog functional assessment methodology. *Behavior Therapy.*

Anderson, C.M., Mullen, K.B., Freeman, K.A., Lewis, J., Weigle, K., Kirk, K., & Scotti, J.R. (1995, May). *Assessment of a course designed to increase educators' understanding of behavioral principles and functional assessment methodologies.* Poster presented at the 21st annual convention of the Association for Behavior Analysis, Washington, DC.

Baer, D.M., Wolf, M.M., & Risley, R.R. (1968). Some current dimensions of applied behavior analysis. *Journal of Applied Behavior Analysis, 1,* 91–97.

Barkley, R.A. (1987). *Defiant children: A clinician's manual for parent training.* New York: Guilford Press.

Bijou, S.W., Peterson, R.F., & Ault, M.H. (1973). A method to integrate descriptive and experimental field studies at the level of data and empirical concept. In R.D. Klein, W.G. Hapkiewicz, & A.H. Roden (Eds.), *Behavior modification in educational settings* (pp. 44–77). Springfield, IL: Charles C Thomas. (Reprinted from *Journal of Applied Behavior Analysis, 2,* 175–191, 1968)

Carr, E.G. (1977). The motivation of self-injurious behavior: A review of some hypotheses. *Psychological Bulletin, 84,* 800–816.

Carr, E.G., Levin, L., McConnachie, G., Carlson, J.I., Kemp, D.C., & Smith, C.E. (1994). *Communication-based intervention for problem behavior: A user's guide for producing positive change.* Baltimore: Paul H. Brookes Publishing Co.

Carr, E.G., Newsom, C.D., & Binkoff, J.A. (1980). Escape as a factor in the aggressive behavior of two retarded children. *Journal of Applied Behavior Analysis, 13,* 101–117.

Carr, E.G., Robinson, S., Taylor, J.C., & Carlson, J.I. (1990). Positive approaches to the treatment of severe behavior problems in persons with developmental disabilities: A review and analysis of reinforcement and stimulus-based procedures. *Monographs of The Association for Persons with Severe Handicaps, 4.*

Day, M.H., Horner, R.H., & O'Neill, R.E. (1994). Multiple functions of problem behavior: Assessment and intervention. *Journal of Applied Behavior Analysis, 27,* 279–289.

Day, R.M., Rea, J.A., Schussler, N.G., Larsen, S.E., & Johnson, W.L. (1988). A functionally based approach to the treatment of self-injurious behavior. *Behavior Modification, 12,* 565–589.

Dunlap, G., & Kern, L. (1993). Assessment and intervention for children within the instructional curriculum. In J. Reichle & D.P. Wacker (Eds.), *Communication and language intervention series: Vol. 3. Communicative alternatives to challenging behavior: Integrating functional assessment and intervention strategies* (pp. 177–203). Baltimore: Paul H. Brookes Publishing Co.

Dunlap, G., Kern-Dunlap, L., Clarke, S., & Robbins, F.R. (1991). Functional assessment, curricular revision, and severe behavior problems. *Journal of Applied Behavior Analysis, 24,* 387–397.

Durand, V.M. (1990). *Severe behavior problems: A functional communication training approach.* New York: Guilford Press.

Durand, V.M., & Crimmins, D.B. (1988). Identifying variables maintaining self-injurious behavior. *Journal of Autism and Developmental Disorders, 18,* 99–117.

Durand, V.M., & Crimmins, D.B. (1992). *The Motivation Assessment Scale (MAS) administration guide.* Topeka, KS: Monaco & Associates.

Evans, I.M., & Meyer, L.H. (1985). *An educative approach to behavior problems: A practical decision model for interventions with severely handicapped learners.* Baltimore: Paul H. Brookes Publishing Co.

Evans, I.M., Meyer, L.H., Kurkjian, J.A., & Kishi, G.S. (1988). An evaluation of behavioral interrelationships in child behavior therapy. In J.C. Witt, S.N. Elliot, & F.M. Gresham (Eds.), *Handbook of behavior therapy in education* (pp. 189–216). New York: Plenum.

Evans, I.M., & Scotti, J.R. (1989). Defining meaningful outcomes for persons with profound disabilities. In F. Brown & D.H. Lehr (Eds.), *Persons with profound disabilities: Issues and practices* (pp. 83–107). Baltimore: Paul H. Brookes Publishing Co.

Forehand, R., & McMahon, R.J. (1981). *Helping the noncompliant child: A clinician's guide to effective parent training.* New York: Guilford Press.

Freeman, K.A., Anderson, C.M., Mullen, K.B., Boccio, K., & Scotti, J.R. (1995, May). *A comparison of three forms of graphical representations of functional assessment data on ability to identify maintaining variables.* Poster presented at the 21st annual convention of the Association for Behavior Analysis, Washington, DC.

Freeman, K.A., Anderson, C.M., & Scotti, J.R. (in press). A structured descriptive methodology: Increasing agreement between descriptive and experimental analyses. *Education and Training in Mental Retardation and Developmental Disabilities.*

Goldiamond, I. (1974). Toward a constructional approach to social problems: Ethical and constitutional issues raised by applied behavioral analysis. *Behaviorism, 2,* 1–85.

Hagopian, L.P., Fisher, W.W., & Legacy, S.M. (1994). Schedule effects of noncontingent reinforcement on attention-maintained destructive behavior in identical quadruplets. *Journal of Applied Behavior Analysis, 27,* 317–325.

Halle, J.W., & Spradlin, J.E. (1993). Identifying stimulus control of challenging behavior: Extending the analysis. In J. Reichle & D.P. Wacker (Eds.), *Communication and language intervention series: Vol. 3. Communicative alternatives to challenging behavior: Integrating functional assessment and intervention strategies* (pp. 83–109). Baltimore: Paul H. Brookes Publishing Co.

Haring, T.G., & Kennedy, C.H. (1990). Contextual control of problem behavior with students with severe disabilities. *Journal of Applied Behavior Analysis, 23,* 235–243.

Horner, R.H., & Day, M.H. (1991). The effects of response efficiency on functionally equivalent competing behaviors. *Journal of Applied Behavior Analysis, 24,* 719–732.

Horner, R.H., Dunlap, G., Koegel, R.L., Carr, E.G., Sailor, W., Anderson, J., Albin, R.W., & O'Neill, R.E. (1990). Toward a technology of nonaversive behavior support. *Journal of The Association for Persons with Severe Handicaps, 15,* 125–132.

Iwata, B.A., Dorsey, M.F., Slifer, K.J., Bauman, K.E., & Richman, G.S. (1994). Toward a functional analysis of self-injury. *Journal of Applied Behavior Analysis, 27,* 197–209. (Reprinted from *Analysis and Intervention in Developmental Disabilities, 2,* 3–20, 1982)

Iwata, B.A., Pace, G.M., Dorsey, M.F., Zarcone, J.R., Vollmer, T.R., Smith, R.G., Rodgers, T.A., Lerman, D.C., Shore, B.A., Mazaleski, J.L., Goh, H., Cowdery, G.E., Kalsher, M.J., McCosh, K.C., & Willis, K.D. (1994). The functions of self-injurious behavior: An experimental-epidemiological analysis. *Journal of Applied Behavior Analysis, 27,* 215–240.

Iwata, B.A., Vollmer, T.R., & Zarcone, J.R. (1990). The experimental (functional) analysis of behavior disorders: Methodology, applications, and limitations. In A.C. Repp & N.N. Singh (Eds.), *Perspectives on the use of nonaversive and aversive intervention for persons with developmental disabilities* (pp. 301–330). Sycamore, IL: Sycamore Publishing.

Meyer, L.H., & Evans, I.M. (1989). *Nonaversive intervention for behavior problems: A manual for home and community.* Baltimore: Paul H. Brookes Publishing Co.

Meyer, L.H., & Evans, I.M. (1993). Meaningful outcomes in behavioral intervention: Evaluating positive approaches to the remediation of challenging behaviors. In J. Reichle & D.P. Wacker (Eds.), *Communication and language intervention series: Vol. 3. Communicative alternatives to challenging behavior: Integrating functional assessment and intervention strategies* (pp. 407–428). Baltimore: Paul H. Brookes Publishing Co.

O'Neill, R.E., Horner, R.H., Albin, R.W., Storey, K., & Sprague, J.R. (1990). *Functional analysis: A practical assessment guide.* Sycamore, IL: Sycamore Publishing.

Parrish, J.M., Cataldo, M.F., Kolko, D.J., Neef, N.A., & Egel, A.L. (1986). Experimental analysis of response covariation among compliant and inappropriate behaviors. *Journal of Applied Behavior Analysis, 19,* 241–254.

Repp, A.C., Felce, D., & Barton, L.E. (1988). Basing the treatment of stereotypic and self-injurious behaviors on hypotheses of their causes. *Journal of Applied Behavior Analysis, 21,* 281–289.

Scotti, J.R., Evans, I.M., Meyer, L.H., & DiBenedetto, A. (1991). Individual repertoires as behavioral systems: Implications for program design and evaluation. In B. Remington (Ed.), *The challenge of severe mental handicap: A behaviour analytic approach* (pp. 139–163). London: John Wiley & Sons.

Scotti, J.R., Evans, I.M., Meyer, L.H., & Walker, P. (1991). A meta-analysis of intervention research with problem behavior: Treatment validity and standards of practice. *American Journal on Mental Retardation, 96,* 233–256.

Scotti, J.R., Kirk, K.S., Weigle, K.L., Cuddihy, K., Lumley, V., Magruda, A., Rasheed, S., & Cohen, T. (1993, May). *Analog functional assessments and nonaversive interventions in special education classrooms: A comparison of brief versus extended assessments.* Poster presented at the 19th annual convention of the Association for Behavior Analysis, Chicago, IL.

Scotti, J.R., McMorrow, M.J., & Trawitzki, A.L. (1993). Behavioral treatment of chronic psychiatric disorders: Publication trends and future directions. *Behavior Therapy, 24,* 527–550.

Scotti, J.R., Morris, T.L., McNeil, C.B., & Hawkins, R.P. (1996). DSM-IV and disorders of childhood and adolescence: Can structural criteria be functional? In W. Follette (Ed.), The DSM-IV [Special issue]. *Journal of Consulting and Clinical Psychology, 64,* 1177–1191.

Scotti, J.R., Mullen, K.B., & Hawkins, R.P. (1998). From theory to practice in the treatment of excess behaviors in child conduct disorders and developmental disabilities. In J.J. Plaud & G.H. Eifert (Eds.), *From behavior theory to behavior therapy* (pp. 172–202). Needham Heights, MA: Allyn & Bacon.

Scotti, J.R., Schulman, D.E., & Hojnacki, R.M. (1994). Functional analysis and unsuccessful treatment of Tourette's syndrome in a man with profound mental retardation. *Behavior Therapy, 25,* 721–738.

Scotti, J.R., Ujcich, K.J., Weigle, K.L., Holland, C.M., & Kirk, K.S. (1996). Interventions with challenging behavior of persons with developmental disabilities: A review of current research practices. *Journal of The Association for Persons with Severe Handicaps, 21,* 123–134.

Scotti, J.R., Weigle, K.L., Kirk, K.S., Ellis, J.T., Jackson, S., Kennedy, C., & Schreiber, R. (1993, May). *A comparison of three functional assessment strategies with the excess and positive behaviors of students with developmental disabilities.* Poster presented at the 19th annual convention of the Association for Behavior Analysis, Chicago.

Sprague, J.R., & Horner, R.H. (1992). Covariation within functional response classes: Implications for treatment of severe problem behavior. *Journal of Applied Behavior Analysis, 25,* 735–745.

Sulzer-Azaroff, B., & Mayer, G.R. (1977). *Applying behavior analysis procedures with children and youth.* Austin, TX: Holt, Rinehart & Winston.

Voeltz, L.M., & Evans, I.M. (1982). The assessment of behavioral interrelationships in child behavior therapy. *Behavioral Assessment, 4,* 131–165.

Vollmer, T.R., Iwata, B.A., Smith, R.G., & Rodgers, T.A. (1992). Reduction of multiple aberrant behaviors and concurrent development of self-care skills with differential reinforcement. *Research in Developmental Disabilities, 13,* 287–299.

Wahler, R.G., & Hann, D.M. (1986). A behavioral systems perspective in childhood psychopathology: Expanding the three-term operant contingency. In N.A. Krasnegor, J.D. Arasteh, & M.F. Cataldo (Eds.), *Child health behavior: A behavioral pediatrics perspective* (pp. 146–166). New York: John Wiley & Sons.

Weeks, M., & Gaylord-Ross, R. (1981). Task difficulty and aberrant behavior in severely handicapped students. *Journal of Applied Behavior Analysis, 14,* 449–463.

Weigle, K.L., & Scotti, J.R. (1995, May). *The effects of functional analysis information on ratings of treatment acceptability and effectiveness.* Poster presented at the 21st annual convention of the Association for Behavior Analysis, Washington, DC.

Weigle, K.L., Scotti, J.R., Kirk, K.S., Bowman, R., Robertson, M., & Kincaid, D. (1995, May). *Explanations of the excess behavior of students with developmental disabilities: A validation study.* Poster presented at the 21st annual convention of the Association for Behavior Analysis, Washington, DC.

Chapter 17

Communication-Based Interventions

Denise Berotti & V. Mark Durand

In the late 1990s, many interventions are available for severe challenging behavior displayed by individuals with developmental disabilities (Evans & Meyer, 1985; Meyer & Evans, 1989). One major component of such interventions is *functional communication training* (Carr et al., 1994; Durand, 1990). Functional communication training is a widely researched intervention that consists of assessing the function of the targeted behavior and teaching individuals alternative ways to elicit the variables that are maintaining their problem behavior (e.g., Carr & Durand, 1985; Durand & Carr, 1991; Wacker et al., 1990).

A large-scale investigation of the effects of functional communication training with students with multiple disabilities and sensory impairments was conducted from 1990 to 1993. (See Chapter 11 for the details of this program.) To illustrate the procedures of functional communication training, this chapter presents a detailed case study on work done with one student who was involved in this program.

Each of the steps of the intervention is described, including training teachers, conducting a functional assessment, selecting and teaching

the communicative response, creating a positive context to avoid eliciting problem behaviors during sessions, training for a delay of reinforcement, and responding to challenging behavior. In addition, obstacles that were encountered during training are discussed, including working with limited resources, working with a student whom most teachers feared, and working with a skeptical teacher.

BACKGROUND

Teri was an 18-year-old student who attended a public school. She is legally blind and had been diagnosed with mental retardation requiring pervasive supports. Teri attended a special education class with nine other students who have developmental disabilities.

Teri lives with her mother and her younger sister, both of whom visited the school frequently to be involved in Teri's education. Teri's family reported that while at home Teri enjoyed being by herself or playing catch with her sister. At school, she also appeared to prefer spending time by herself. In addition, she enjoyed holding var-

This chapter was supported in part by the U.S. Department of Education Office of Special Education and Rehabilitative Services (Grant No. H086G00005); however, the opinions expressed here do not necessarily reflect the policy of the U.S. Department of Education, and no official endorsement should be inferred.

ious items (a newspaper and her pocketbook) and playing catch, but she appeared to dislike classroom tasks. In fact, she typically became visibly upset when any demands were placed on her (e.g., "come here," "sit down").

Prior to intervention, Teri's ability to communicate with others was severely limited. On rare occasions, she used a limited number of single-word sentences (e.g., "hi," "ball"). Despite numerous efforts by her teacher and teacher aides to teach Teri to use picture books and miniature items, she had not successfully used an augmentative communication system.

Teri engaged in several forms of challenging behavior, including frequent tantrums (e.g., jumping up and down in her seat and screaming), occasional yet severe aggression (e.g., biting, head butting, scratching), and self-injury (e.g., knee biting). Teri's teacher was most concerned with her aggression and tantrums. Teri had seriously hurt two teacher aides during the previous school year, and most staff were afraid to work with her. Teri's teacher was also concerned with the tantrums because they were very disruptive and reliably preceded aggression, but she was not very concerned with Teri's knee biting because she noticed that Teri never left any type of mark on her knee from biting.

Teri's mother also reported that Teri engaged in aggression, tantrums, and mild self-injury. She agreed with the teacher that Teri did not appear to hurt herself when she bit her knee. She indicated that Teri began to engage in the various forms of challenging behavior as a very young child. She admitted that she and her other daughter were at times somewhat afraid of Teri and that they generally let her do what she wanted to avoid problem behavior.

FUNCTIONAL ASSESSMENT

A functional assessment was conducted with Teri to identify the variables that were controlling her targeted behavior: tantrums and occasional severe aggression. The functional assessment consisted of interviews, observations, the Motivation Assessment Scale (MAS; Durand & Crimmins, 1992), and a functional analysis. The interviews were conducted to generate hypothe-

ses concerning the function of the targeted behavior. Teri's teacher and assistant teachers were questioned about the antecedents to and consequences of Teri's challenging behavior. Teri's teacher reported that the behavior problems were random. The teacher could not identify any situation that seemed reliably to precede the targeted behaviors. The teacher believed that Teri simply "woke up on the wrong side of the bed some mornings" and that this resulted in frequent challenging behavior for that day. Because Teri's teacher believed that the challenging behavior was random, she did not think that there was anything that anyone could do to help Teri. Upon further questioning, however, a clearer picture of the antecedents to and consequences of Teri's challenging behavior began to emerge.

A teacher aide, who spent a great deal of time with Teri, had more insight into the possible function of the challenging behavior. He noted that Teri was most likely to exhibit a targeted behavior when demands were placed on her and that her challenging behavior almost always was successful in ending the demands to perform a task. He reported that most staff were aware that Teri had seriously hurt various staff in the past and were afraid to continue to work with her once she began to scream; therefore, she typically was left alone. For example, when the students were called on to sit at one table for a group lesson, Teri was the only student who was allowed to remain in her seat alone. When Teri screamed when a teacher asked her to sit down, she typically was allowed to remain standing.

Teri's teacher aide reported that a second variable occasionally was associated with Teri's challenging behavior. Teri was also likely to display problem behavior when she saw one of her favorite items, namely a ball, a newspaper, or her pocketbook (she had some residual vision). The challenging behavior would terminate when Teri was given the object that she wanted. Teri's mother's comments concerning the possible purpose of Teri's problem behavior were consistent with those of school personnel.

Teri was observed in her classroom on several occasions. The antecedents to and consequences of the targeted behavior appeared obvious and reliable. Typically, the teacher's demands on Teri resulted in tantrums. When staff persisted in trying to get Teri to work, she often tried to bite or scratch them. Teri also screamed when she saw a favorite item, but Teri was quiet when left alone. The only interaction with others that she appeared to enjoy was playing catch.

The MAS also was administered to Teri's teacher and teacher aide to help identify the variables that were maintaining the challenging behavior. (See Chapter 11 for a detailed description of the MAS.) The results of the MAS were consistent with those of the interviews and observations. The Escape scale was scored the highest, and the Tangible scale also was high. A consistent picture suggesting that Teri's tantrums and aggression were multiply motivated began to emerge. Teri appeared to display challenging behavior most often to escape from demands, but sometimes she engaged in these behaviors to gain access to favorite items.

During the final phase of the functional assessment, the hypothesis that was based on the initial evaluation was supported by the results of a brief functional analysis. Although the results of the first three forms of the functional assessment were the same, errors can occur when an evaluation does not include direct manipulation of variables that are thought to be influencing the challenging behavior. In Teri's case, the initial assessment suggested that demands were the most important influence on the problem behavior; however, there may have been another variable that was closely associated in time with the presentation of demands and that might actually have been responsible for eliciting challenging behavior. For example, Teri's class worked primarily in a group, with all of the students sitting at one table. Typically, when Teri was asked to do something, the first demand that she heard was, "Teri, come to the table," or, "Teri, sit here with the other students." Perhaps Teri's problem behaviors were maintained by avoidance of proximity to other students and not the demands per se.

To rule out the possibility (and others similar to it) that her problem behaviors were maintained as a function of proximity, the effects of demands on Teri's challenging behavior were isolated. She was presented with two nearly identical conditions during which the only variable manipulated was the presence or absence of the demands. During the first condition, Teri sat at her desk with a teacher aide sitting next to her; however, no one interacted with her. Any occurrence of challenging behavior was ignored; that is, the teacher aide continued to do whatever he was doing before the challenging behavior occurred. During the second condition, Teri sat at her desk and the teacher aide continually asked her to engage in a classroom task. Problem behavior was once again ignored. A specific teacher aide who was not afraid to work with Teri was chosen for these sessions because he was able to continue working with her even when Teri began to scream, hit, or scratch.

Each session was 10 minutes long and was presented three times across several visits to the classroom. All sessions were videotaped and divided into 10-second intervals. Undergraduate students scored the videotapes for the percentage of intervals of challenging behavior (e.g., tantrums, aggression). During the three sessions in which Teri received no demands, she engaged in no (0%) disruptive behavior; when directed to work, Teri engaged in challenging behavior during 20% of the intervals.

PREVIOUS INTERVENTIONS

Teri had been receiving her instruction in the same class with the same teacher and teacher aides for 2 years. To reduce the likelihood that Teri would exhibit challenging behavior, the staff in the class rarely asked her to work or to join group activities. The teacher indicated that this did result in a substantial reduction in problem behavior but that the behavior was still frequent. This "intervention" probably achieved only moderate success because it was difficult to avoid presenting certain demands to Teri (e.g., "Take off your coat," "It's time to go to the cafeteria"). Another obvious problem was that Teri was *not* receiving an education; she rarely engaged in work, and most of her day was spent sitting by herself or playing catch. It seemed clear that for Teri to progress in her education, it was time to alter her pattern of avoiding demands.

As noted previously, staff knew that Teri would occasionally display problem behavior when she saw certain items (a newspaper, a ball, her pocketbook). To prevent problem behavior that was associated with these items, they had tried to keep these items out of sight. According to Teri's teachers, keeping newspapers out of the class and asking Teri's mother not to let Teri bring her pocketbook to school appeared to be successful in eliminating problem behavior that was associated with these items. Teachers had not been able to prevent Teri from seeing balls because the other students enjoyed playing catch during their breaks and in physical education class. Teri continued to display problem behavior when she saw other students playing ball.

INTERVENTION: FUNCTIONAL COMMUNICATION TRAINING

Functional communication training was implemented as the intervention for Teri's challenging behavior (Durand, 1990). Because the results of Teri's functional assessment suggested that escape from demands was the most important variable that was maintaining her challenging behavior, the intervention consisted of teaching Teri a new way to escape from tasks.

An important goal of the intervention was to prepare the staff who were working with Teri to implement functional communication training themselves. It was believed that Teri would need frequent communication sessions to teach her to make requests independently. Having staff, instead of outside consultants, implement the intervention increased the likelihood that Teri would have an adequate amount of communication training. Staff also could maintain this intervention long after consultants would have left. In addition, it was hoped that once the staff gained skills in functional communication training they would use the skills when they worked with other students who also engaged in challenging behavior.

Staff who were working with Teri were provided with a full-day workshop on the assessment of and intervention for severe behavior problems. They learned about common influences on problem behavior, including stimulus events (e.g., social attention, escape from demands, access to tangibles, sensory feedback) and setting events (e.g., crowding, hunger, illness). The staff were taught how to identify which variables might be influencing the challenging behavior of a given student using various functional assessment methods, including the MAS and scatter plots (Touchette, MacDonald, & Langer, 1985). The staff also were taught to use the information generated from a functional assessment to provide the student with an alternative means of obtaining the variables that maintain challenging behavior. Topics discussed during this phase of the workshop included deciding which communicative response to teach, how to teach the response, determining which form of communication should be taught (e.g., verbal language, sign language, augmentative communication), and how to respond to problem behavior.

Although Teri's teachers primarily were responsible for implementing the intervention, they did receive regular consultation visits (approximately once per month) for more than 1 year following the start of the intervention. During the first consultation visit following the functional assessment, the consultants—who were advanced doctoral students—modeled the procedures of functional communication training. Staff then were provided with a detailed step-by-step description of how to teach Teri to make a request. During the consultation visits, Teri's progress was monitored. The staff were observed while they worked with Teri, and they were provided with feedback. In addition, Teri's communication plan was modified often in response to difficulties that arose.

The first consideration when developing the functional communication program for Teri was to decide which communicative response she needed to learn. As escape from demands was the most important maintaining variable of her challenging behavior, the goal of the intervention was to teach Teri a *functionally equivalent response* that would allow her to escape from work when she used it. Therefore, it was decided by the team (including school personnel and the consultants) to teach Teri first to request a break from work.

The next consideration for Teri's intervention was to decide which form of communication Teri would be taught. Teri's teachers and family indicated that she had a history of limited success with both vocal communication and sign language and believed that she might have more success if she were provided with a vocal-output device. In fact, Teri initially was chosen for the program because her team believed that she would benefit from a communication program involving a vocal-output device. Teri was provided with a vocal-output device (Wolf Board) that was programmed to emit the phrase, "May I take a break, please?" Because Teri had visual impairments, her device was covered with a thin piece of sandpaper to inform Teri where the device needed to be pressed to be activated. Teri was to be taught to activate the message when she wanted to stop working. It was hoped that once Teri had a simple and reliable way to escape from work, she would no longer rely on challenging behavior for this escape.

The next consideration was how to teach Teri to request a break from work. Initially, it was decided that intervention sessions would begin by requesting that Teri complete a small amount of work and then by prompting her physically and verbally to request a break by activating the device. Immediately following the message, teachers were to pull the task materials away from Teri and allow her to sit alone for several minutes. This would provide Teri with a simple way to escape instantly from work so that she would no longer need to rely on tantrums and aggression. As Teri began to activate the device on her own, the physical and verbal prompts would be faded until she communicated independently.

Another important consideration was how to respond to Teri's challenging behavior. The results of the assessment suggested that Teri had learned that challenging behavior was an effective means of avoiding demands. To break the association between challenging behavior and avoiding work, staff were advised to avoid reinforcing Teri's challenging behavior with a break. This was done in two ways. First, staff were to avoid eliciting Teri's challenging behavior by not presenting her with large demands. During the initial training sessions, they were to present Teri with small, brief tasks, and they were to prompt her to request a break before she exhib-

ited any signs of distress. This way, they would not have to worry about accidentally reinforcing the challenging behavior with a break from work. Second, staff were to ignore any problem behavior that Teri did exhibit. More specific, they were to avoid letting the behavior problems change their own behavior. This often meant continuing to work with Teri once she began to have a tantrum or to become aggressive. Such a response-independent consequence is an important component of functional communication that teaches individuals that their behavior problems will no longer have an effect on the environment (Durand, 1990). Only one teacher aide felt comfortable with the idea of continuing to work with Teri once she became disruptive; therefore, it was decided that he would be the only one to work with her for the first several weeks of the communication training.

At this point, a major impediment to beginning functional communication training with Teri became apparent. Teri's teacher already felt overwhelmed by her job and did not think that she could afford to have one of her teacher aides spend individual time with Teri each day. She continued to believe that Teri's problem behaviors were random, and she had little confidence that communication training would result in a significant reduction in these behaviors. Fortunately, the administration in Teri's school was very supportive and, like the one teacher aide, was willing to work with Teri. The assistant principal (who was a special educator) was very eager to gain experience in functional communication training and attended all training sessions. The assistant principal agreed to come into Teri's class for 15 minutes twice per day to work with Teri. The teacher agreed to assign the teacher aide to work with Teri once she began to communicate independently. In addition, Teri's speech-language therapist and her physical education teacher both agreed to conduct daily sessions with Teri.

The first day of communication training was designed to determine how long Teri would be able to work without engaging in challenging behavior. This information would be used to decide how much work Teri would be expected to complete before she was prompted to ask for a break with her vocal-output device. It was quickly determined that Teri rarely was willing to complete any work without screaming. In fact, she typically began screaming the moment she perceived that someone was approaching her with task materials.

To address this problem, training sessions were made easier for Teri. Instead of beginning sessions by presenting work materials to Teri, sessions were begun by engaging in some preferred activity with her (Carr et al., 1994; Meyer & Evans, 1989). The only activity that the staff agreed that Teri enjoyed was playing catch; therefore, sessions began by spending 2 minutes playing catch with Teri. After a couple of minutes of play, a small amount of work materials were placed in her view and she was quickly prompted to request a break with the device. The materials then were removed from her sight, and the teachers once again engaged Teri in playing catch.

During this phase of the training, Teri was not asked to work. She was simply expected to tolerate briefly the sight of the materials and to use the communication device to request a break. Introducing catch into the communication training served two purposes. First, it resulted in Teri's tolerating the presence of work material without engaging in challenging behavior. Second, because ball playing was now associated with Teri's tolerating work, Teri's teacher agreed to allow Teri to engage in this preferred activity. As a result, the sight of the ball no longer elicited challenging behavior because Teri knew that she would now be allowed to use it. It was agreed that no one in the class would play catch unless one of Teri's communication trainers was in the classroom (i.e., assistant principal, physical education teacher, speech-language therapist, or teacher aide). Teri's teacher was not willing to reintroduce Teri's other favorite items (newspaper and pocketbook) into the communication sessions because success was achieved by simply eliminating their presence from the classroom.

Once Teri began to tolerate the presence of work materials without exhibiting challenging behavior, small demands were embedded into trials. Communication trainers began to request that Teri complete a small amount of work as soon as they placed the materials in her view. For example, after 2 weeks of training, teachers played catch with Teri for 1 minute and then directed her to fold a towel in half. She then was quickly prompted to request a break. Over time, the size of the demands placed on her were systematically increased, and the amount of time that the teachers spent playing catch with her during sessions was decreased.

While the teachers were concentrating on increasing the amount of work that Teri completed by directing her to complete larger tasks, they were fading the prompts that they gave her to activate the device. This was done by always providing Teri with as little prompting as she needed to activate the device successfully. The prompts began, for example, by placing Teri's hand on the device and pressing her hand down to activate it. After several sessions, Teri began to put her hand on the device herself but did not activate it. At that point, the teachers helped her apply pressure to the device. During each session, they applied less and less pressure until Teri was activating the device independently.

Once Teri was communicating independently, she began to request breaks after completing only a small amount of work. At this point, a delay of reinforcement was introduced (Carr et al., 1994). She was taught that she could have a break each time she activated her vocal-output device but that she would have to complete a little more work first. For example, initially the teachers played catch with her for 30 seconds and asked her to fold a towel. Typically, she folded the towel in half once and quickly activated her device. Teachers told Teri that she could have the break as soon as she finished folding the towel. Fortunately, this change in the communication training did not result in an increase in challenging behavior. The teachers requested that Teri complete larger amounts of work before they would grant her request.

INTERVENTION RESULTS AND MAINTENANCE

After 2 months of training, Teri learned to activate her device without any verbal or physical prompts. At this time, all classroom personnel were working with Teri, and she was working for 20–25 minutes at a time, several times per day, with only a few brief breaks. It is important to note that Teri's progress was monitored for more than 1 year, and her problem behavior was rare. During the baseline sessions, Teri engaged in problem behavior during 20% of the intervals. Following intervention, she engaged in the behaviors during fewer than 4% of the trials. Moreover, because Teri's mother and sister attended many of the training sessions, Teri was able to take her device home, where she was able to communicate with her family.

IMPLEMENTATION ISSUES

Teri's case study illustrates the details of conducting functional communication training with a student with multiple disabilities. During the course of the intervention, many obstacles could have compromised the success of the intervention. The obstacles included working with a teacher who had witnessed failed attempts to teach Teri to communicate and was therefore skeptical that the intervention would be successful, classroom staff who were afraid to work with Teri (with one exception), and a student who would not often tolerate the presence of work materials. Each of these obstacles could have resulted in a decision to exclude Teri from the program. However, experience with working with individuals such as Teri and her teachers has suggested that functional communication training often can be successful even in less than ideal environments, as long as those who work with the students are willing to work around potential obstacles and to reconsider their initial hesitation.

Because significant support had been gained from the administration at Teri's school, school administrators were willing to assist when problems arose. The administration agreed that functional communication training with Teri likely would fail without additional support. As mentioned previously, the assistant principal agreed to conduct the initial sessions with Teri, and others (e.g., speech-language therapist, physical education teacher) offered their support. If the administration had not given this type of support, then work with Teri probably would not have been so successful.

Furthermore, as expected, when Teri began to communicate independently and to work without engaging in frequent challenging behavior, the primary teacher realized that communication was having a positive effect with Teri and facilitated the process by assigning teacher aides to work with Teri. In addition, once the teacher aides saw others working successfully with Teri, they indicated that they were less afraid to work with her themselves.

Another potentially serious problem was Teri's exhibiting challenging behavior almost immediately before any work even began. This made it very difficult to prompt her to request a break before she became distressed. This problem was solved by creating a work situation that Teri could tolerate. For individuals who display challenging behavior immediately upon seeing tasks, embedding the demands in a positive context is essential (Carr et al., 1994; Meyer & Evans, 1989). Once staff began functional communication sessions by playing catch with Teri, Teri was able to tolerate reliably the presence of the materials without displaying challenging behavior. It is important to note that staff then were able to prompt Teri to request a break from work before she became visibly distressed. By gradually decreasing the length of time that staff would play catch with Teri between each trial of work, staff were able to fade out playing catch completely after 2 months of communication training.

The final obstacle faced while working with Teri was a problem that is fairly common when conducting functional communication training. Once Teri learned to communicate independently, she began to request many breaks, so that she was working for only short periods of time before receiving a break. During the early stage of functional communication training, individuals initially request the variables that are maintaining their problem behavior at a high rate (e.g., Bird, Dores, Moniz, & Robinson, 1989). The rate of requesting, however, often decreases to a tolerable rate without any intervention (Durand, 1990). For individuals who continue to make requests at a high rate, a delay of reinforcement usually is introduced (Durand, 1990; Meyer & Evans, 1989), as was done with Teri.

CONCLUSION

Overall, several important outcomes resulted from the functional communication training that Teri received. First, as mentioned previously, Teri displayed a substantial decrease in challenging behavior that maintained for more than 1 year. Teri engaged in a variety of tasks with minimal problem behavior. A second important effect was that Teri was—for the first time—participating in classroom activities on a regular basis. She no longer spent the day in the corner by herself. Instead, she began engaging in educational tasks. Staff were no longer afraid to work with her. Adults who previously avoided Teri because of fear of getting hurt began to work with her and to interact with her socially. In a similar fashion, for the first time, Teri joined her classmates at the group table without displaying challenging behavior, and she appeared to begin to develop friendships. Overall, Teri became less isolated and became a more involved member of her classroom.

In sum, this case study illustrates that functional communication training can succeed in less than ideal situations. This work was conducted with a student who had a long history of severe aggression and who exhibited multiple severe disabilities, including sensory impairments. In addition, a consultation model was used in a public school classroom that had limited resources. Many obstacles did arise during training, which could have resulted in termination of this approach. However, as this chapter illustrates, when a problem-solving approach is used and program modifications are an ongoing component, functional communication training can succeed in even the most difficult situations.

REFERENCES

Bird, F., Dores, P.A., Moniz, D., & Robinson, J. (1989). Reducing severe aggressive and self-injurious behaviors with functional communication training: Direct, collateral and generalized results. *American Journal on Mental Retardation, 94,* 37–48.

Carr, E.G., & Durand, V.M. (1985). Reducing behavior problems through functional communication training. *Journal of Applied Behavior Analysis, 18,* 111–126.

Carr, E.G., Levin, L., McConnachie, G., Carlson, J.I., Kemp, D.C., & Smith, C.E. (1994). *Communication-based intervention for problem behavior: A user's guide for producing positive change.* Baltimore: Paul H. Brookes Publishing Co.

Durand, V.M. (1990). *Severe behavior problems: A functional communication approach.* New York: Guilford Press.

Durand, V.M., & Carr, E.G. (1991). Functional communication training to reduce challenging behavior: Maintenance and application in new settings. *Journal of Applied Behavior Analysis, 24,* 251–264.

Durand, V.M., & Crimmins, D.B. (1992). *The Motivation Assessment Scale (MAS) administration guide.* Topeka KS: Monaco & Associates.

Evans, I.M., & Meyer, L.H. (1985). *An educative approach to behavior problems: A practical decision model for interventions with severely handicapped learners.* Baltimore: Paul H. Brookes Publishing Co.

Meyer, L.H., & Evans, I.M. (1989). *Nonaversive intervention for behavior problems: A manual for home and community.* Baltimore: Paul H. Brookes Publishing Co.

Touchette, P.W., MacDonald, R.F., & Langer, S.N. (1985). A scatter plot for identifying stimulus control of problem behavior. *Journal of Applied Behavior Analysis, 18,* 343–351.

Wacker, D.P., Steege, M.W., Northup, J., Sasso, G., Berg, W., Reimers, T., Cooper, L., Cigrand, K., & Donn, L. (1990). A component analysis of functional communication training across three topographies of severe behavior problems. *Journal of Applied Behavior Analysis, 23,* 417–429.

Chapter 18

Applying Behavioral Assessment and Intervention Procedures in Home Environments

A 2-Year Evaluation of Behavior Problems and Social Interactions for a Young Girl

Wendy K. Berg, David P. Wacker,
Jay W. Harding, & Jennifer M. Asmus

This chapter presents an overview of a series of assessment procedures and the resultant intervention package that was developed for a young girl, Sharon, who engaged in severe problem behavior and actively avoided social contact. Each phase of the assessment and intervention process was conducted in Sharon's home; her mother served as the therapist and used the tasks and materials that were common to Sharon's daily routine. We describe each phase of the assessment process and explain how the results of the assessment were used to develop an intervention for Sharon's problem behavior. We also describe how we addressed multiple intervention objectives and how those objectives were evaluated over a 2-year period. The focus of this chapter is on the practical aspects of conducting these procedures in the child's home.

Sharon was 3 years old when we started working with her and her mother. She lived at home with her mother and two brothers in a large midwestern city. Sharon was diagnosed with mental retardation requiring limited to extensive supports and a visual impairment, and she was nonambulatory. She repeated a few words, such as her name, but did not use language in a functional manner. Sharon engaged in self-injurious behavior and often screamed and had tantrums during daily activities, such as completing self-care routines, participating in activities recommended by her early intervention teacher, and responding to her mother's attempts to play with her. Sharon spent much of her time waving items in front of her face or bouncing on her knees in front of a reflective surface, such as a mirror or a blank television screen.

Sharon was enrolled in a clinical research project,[1] the purpose of which was threefold. The first goal was to apply assessment and intervention procedures that had been developed

[1]This research project was funded by a grant through the National Institute of Child Health and Human Development of the National Institutes of Health and the Iowa Department of Education (Grant No. RO1 HD29402-01).

within controlled environments, such as hospitals, to the homes of very young children who engaged in severe problem behavior. Preliminary research (Cooper, Wacker, Sasso, Reimers, & Donn, 1990; Derby et al., 1997; Northup et al., 1991) indicated that both antecedent-based (Carr & Durand, 1985) and consequence-based (Iwata, Dorsey, Slifer, Bauman, & Richman, 1982) experimental analyses of problem behavior could be conducted by a target child's parent with coaching by trained staff. We believed that by conducting the assessment and intervention procedures within the child's home—and including the people who reside there—we could minimize problems associated with generalization. For example, an evaluation of outpatient clinic assessments (Derby et al., 1992) revealed that approximately 30% of the people referred because of self-injurious behavior did not display any problem behavior during the outpatient evaluation. Conducting the assessments in the home with people and activities that were associated with problem behavior increased the likelihood that we would see the behavior of concern as it typically occurred.

The second goal was to evaluate the durability of intervention effects that occurred with functional communication training (FCT). The children who participated in this project were followed for up to 2 years to determine whether decreases in the occurrence of problem behavior and increases in adaptive responding were maintained over time.

The third goal was to examine the long-term side effects, both positive and negative, of the FCT intervention. Specifically, we wanted to determine whether the extended use of FCT resulted in an increase in additional adaptive behaviors, such as social interactions, toy play, and compliance, and whether there were any negative side effects, such as an increase of problem behavior during nonintervention times.

We conducted weekly assessment and intervention sessions in the homes of 12 children for 1 year. Six of these children were followed for an additional 12 months via monthly and trimonthly in-home probes. Direct observation data were collected by recording the in-home assessment (experimental analyses) and intervention sessions with a video camcorder. Video re-cordings of these sessions were later scored by project staff using a 6-second partial-interval scoring system. Child behaviors included self-injury, aggression, destruction, social interactions, and appropriate forms of communication. Parent behavior was scored to measure the integrity with which parents conducted assessment and intervention sessions. Parent behaviors included positive social interactions (e.g., praise), negative social interactions (e.g., reprimands), task prompts, and the use of mild punishment (e.g., guided compliance).

GOAL 1: CONDUCTING ASSESSMENTS AND INTERVENTIONS IN THE HOME

Assessment

Sharon was referred to our project for intervention for her self-injurious behavior. Prior to designing an intervention, we used behavioral assessment procedures to identify the environmental events associated with problem behavior and to identify the function or purpose that the problem behavior served for Sharon.

Carr (1977) proposed that severe problem behavior may be social in nature. Behavior often occurs in response to events in the child's environment, and, as discussed by Iwata et al. (1982), problem behavior may function to facilitate the occurrence of desired events or to terminate undesired events. Carr discussed three classes of environmental events that may be associated with severe problem behavior. The first event is gaining social attention. If problem behavior is associated with situations that are characterized by an absence of attention or relatively low levels of attention, then problem behavior may function to gain more attention. The second event is obtaining preferred items. Problem behavior may be associated with the presence of preferred versus nonpreferred materials and may function to obtain preferred items. The third event is escaping difficult tasks. For example, some children engage in problem behavior when they are required to perform a task that is difficult for them. Problem behavior may function to terminate the task or reduce its difficulty by obtaining assistance from another person. Identifying the function of behavior is critical for designing effective interventions and is often more important than information regarding the specific topography (i.e., form) of behavior or demographics (e.g., diagnosis) of the child.

A multiphase assessment process was used to evaluate the effect of environmental events on the occurrence of problem behavior for Sharon (see Table 1). Phase 1 was a descriptive assessment. The descriptive assessment included a parent interview, a record of child behavior, and a description of the activities in which Sharon engaged on a daily basis. This information was used to generate initial hypotheses regarding the events that might be maintaining Sharon's problem behavior. For example, task demands appeared to be related to problem behavior.

The second phase of assessment was an experimental analysis of the effects of specific antecedent events on behavior (structural analysis). This phase was conducted to identify situations and activities that preceded or set the occasion for self-injury. The results were used to confirm or modify initial hypotheses that were generated from the descriptive assessment. In the third phase, these hypotheses were tested further via an experimental analysis of the effects of different consequences (e.g., escape from demands) on the occurrence of problem behavior (functional analysis). Thus, the process was one of repeated hypothesis generation and the testing of those hypotheses by gathering data from addi-

tional relevant assessment conditions and intervention probes (see Repp, Karsh, Munk, & Dahlquist, 1995; Scotti, Schulman, & Hojnacki, 1994).

Finally, a preference assessment was conducted to identify toys and activities that Karen preferred and that could be used to supplement the basic intervention procedures. Again, Karen's mother served as the therapist (with our coaching) throughout the assessment and intervention process.

Descriptive Assessment

The assessment process began with a brief interview with Sharon's mother to determine the specific behaviors of concern and to obtain a description of the situations in which problem behavior was likely to occur. Sharon bit her arm and pulled her hair. These behaviors usually were accompanied by screaming and having a tantrum. According to Sharon's mother, these behaviors occurred whenever she tried to interact with Sharon.

Daily Time Sheet

After the specific target behaviors were identified, we wanted to determine their approximate daily frequency and to obtain more specific information regarding the activities associated with their occurrence. During the first week of assessment, Sharon's mother completed a daily time sheet similar to the one developed by Touchette,

Table 1. Assessment process

Phase	Procedure	Purpose
Phase 1	Descriptive assessment	Identify the specific behaviors of concern and the environmental events associated with the occurrence of those behaviors
	Daily time sheet	Identify times of day associated with the target behavior
	Task list and description	Describe activities associated with occurrences of target behavior
Phase 2	Experimental analysis of antecedent events (structural analysis)	Directly evaluate the effects of antecedent variables, such as task demands, on the target behavior
Phase 3	Experimental analysis of consequence events (functional analysis)	Directly evaluate the effects of consequences, such as escaping demands, on the target behavior
Phase 4	Preference assessment	Identify toys and activities that might serve as reinforcers for adaptive behavior

MacDonald, and Langer (1985). Sharon's day was divided into 30-minute intervals, beginning with the time when she woke up each day and ending with the time when she fell asleep for the night. Whenever problem behavior occurred, Sharon's mother placed a checkmark in the appropriate time slot and provided a brief description of the events surrounding that episode of problem behavior.

The daily time sheet revealed that between one and six episodes (mean of three) of self-injurious behavior and screaming occurred each day during the hours that Sharon was at home. These behaviors typically occurred while Sharon's mother was assisting Sharon with dressing and grooming, while her mother attempted to implement with Sharon the activities that were recommended by an early childhood teacher (e.g., fine motor activities, using a walker), when the school bus or family car pulled up to her house, or immediately before meals. Sharon's mother attributed most instances of problem behavior to Sharon's being tired or hungry.

Task List and Description

We asked Sharon's mother to list the toys with which Sharon played and the activities in which Sharon engaged on a daily basis. When the list was completed, we asked her mother to describe each toy or activity in terms of whether it had a high or a low degree of preference, was difficult or easy for Sharon to perform, and was an activity that Sharon engaged in alone or with other people. This resulted in an initial list of activities that were rated with respect to three antecedent variables often associated with problem behavior:

1. Amount of adult attention (low or high)
2. Preference for activity (low or high)
3. Level of difficulty (low or high)

The daily time sheet provided a list of activities that were associated with episodes of problem behavior. For example, according to the daily time sheet, Sharon frequently engaged in self-injury and screaming while stacking blocks (an activity recommended by Sharon's early in-

tervention teacher). On the task list, Sharon's mother described stacking blocks as a nonpreferred activity that was difficult for Sharon to perform and that was accompanied by high levels of adult attention in the form of verbal encouragement and physical assistance. In contrast, playing with dolls was not listed on the daily time sheet as being associated with problem behavior, but it was included on the task list as a frequently performed activity. Sharon's mother described playing with dolls (i.e., waving the dolls in front of her face) as a highly preferred activity in which Sharon engaged by herself.

The descriptions of tasks associated with episodes of problem behavior were compared with tasks not associated with problem behavior to develop initial hypotheses regarding the effects of environmental events on the occurrence of problem behavior. As mentioned previously, Sharon's mother attributed problem behavior to hunger or fatigue. These are reasonable hypotheses, but we noted that the activities associated with problem behavior usually included tasks that were difficult for Sharon to perform and that were accompanied by adult attention. Self-injury occurred across tasks that were described as preferred, as well as tasks that were nonpreferred. Based on this information, three additional hypotheses appeared to be tenable.

First, the presentation of difficult tasks resulted in self-injurious behavior, suggesting that Sharon was attempting to terminate the demands associated with performing those tasks. Second, Sharon engaged in problem behavior during activities that were accompanied by high levels of parental attention but not during times when she was left alone. Thus, problem behavior may have functioned as a way to escape adult attention. Finally, Sharon may have been attempting to escape both task demands and adult attention; that is, the behavior was multiply determined.

Experimental Analysis of Antecedent Events

Carr and Durand (1985) developed an assessment procedure to evaluate directly the impact of antecedent events on behavior. This assessment procedure is referred to as a *structural analysis* (Axelrod, 1987). In a structural analysis, antecedent events such as attention, task difficulty, or task preference are directly manipulated to determine which events occasion problem behavior. For example, some children engage in problem behavior only when parent attention is not available. For these children, the structural analysis would focus on the impact of the presence or absence of parent attention. The presence or absence of preferred toys or task demands can also be manipulated to determine whether these variables are related to problem behavior.

In Sharon's case, problem behavior occurred in situations with high levels of task demands and high levels of parent attention and across both preferred and nonpreferred activities. Therefore, we evaluated the impact of all three of these variables on Sharon's behavior. To evaluate whether difficult tasks were associated with problem behavior, we compared Sharon's behavior across brief sessions (5 minutes) in which she was given a difficult task to perform versus sessions in which she was given an easy task. Task preference was evaluated by comparing Sharon's behavior during sessions in which she had a preferred activity with sessions in which she had a nonpreferred activity. Finally, the impact of attention was evaluated by pairing tasks that required high levels of parental attention and comparing Sharon's behavior during these sessions with sessions that required very little parental attention. A minimum of three sessions were conducted per condition, but more were conducted when it was necessary to provide stability in the data and thus a less ambiguous interpretation of the results.

To control partially for the impact of Sharon's physical state (tired, hungry), we conducted all assessment sessions at the same time each day: immediately after Sharon arrived home from the afternoon preschool program but before snack. If either fatigue or hunger were related to self-injury, then problem behavior would occur at high frequencies throughout the antecedent manipulations described previously (across demands, preference, and attention conditions). However, if behavior increased or decreased with changes in these antecedent variables, then environmental influences on behavior would be identified.

The preliminary results of the structural analysis revealed that Sharon engaged in problem behavior at very low levels (a mean of 8% of observation intervals) when she was allowed to play with a toy (preferred or nonpreferred) by herself. In contrast, severe problem behavior occurred at high rates (a mean of 60% of observation intervals) during sessions that included high levels of parent attention, regardless of the activity. On the basis of these results, we hypothesized that Sharon's behavior functioned to escape demands, adult attention, or both.

To assess these hypotheses further, activities that had been identified as highly preferred were presented without any task demands but with high levels of parent attention. During this condition, Sharon's mother sat near Sharon and made positive comments to her as she played (low demand, high preference, high attention). In a comparison condition, the same task was presented to Sharon, but her mother directed the play situation, telling Sharon how to play with the toy (high demand, high preference, high attention). For example, as Sharon played with her doll, her mother handed her a comb and said, "Let's comb the doll's hair. I'll help you." The same comparison was conducted with tasks that were considered to be of low preference.

The results revealed that Sharon did best (little or no self-injury, screaming, or having a tantrum) during sessions with a preferred activity, no demands, and little or no adult attention; problem behavior occurred during an average of 6% of the intervals for these sessions. In contrast, problem behavior occurred during an average of 50% of the intervals during sessions with high levels of adult attention. The sessions with the highest frequency of problem behavior were those that included high levels of attention combined with a low-preference task (mean of 73% of intervals) and during high-attention conditions with high levels of task demands (mean of 69% of intervals).

The overall results failed to support the hypothesis that problem behavior was due mostly to fatigue or hunger. Instead, problem behavior appeared to occur in response to attention and to demands. Furthermore, the structural analysis revealed that the use of nonpreferred tasks aggravated the occurrence of problem behavior during the sessions with high levels of attention.

Experimental Analysis of Consequence Events

The structural analysis allowed us to identify, in a controlled, systematic fashion, the effect of different *antecedent events* on behavior. This information can be used to infer the function that the behavior serves for the child. For example, a child who engages in problem behavior during difficult tasks presumably is attempting to escape from performing the task. An experimental analysis of *consequence events,* or a *functional analysis* (Iwata et al., 1982), reduces the level of inference that one makes when testing hypotheses because it allows for a direct evaluation of the effects of different consequences on behavior. For this reason, we followed the structural analysis with a functional analysis.

A functional analysis is similar to a structural analysis in that it consists of a series of brief analog conditions. It differs from a structural analysis in that different consequences are applied to the target behavior across analog conditions. For example, to test the role of adult attention in problem behavior, attention is withheld from the child until he or she engages in the target behavior. When the behavior occurs, it is immediately followed by adult attention, such as a mild reprimand (e.g., "Don't do that, you might hurt yourself") or a soothing statement (e.g., "Now, now, everything is OK").

The impact of preferred items on the occurrence of behavior is assessed in much the same way. The preferred item is withheld from the child and delivered contingent on the occurrence of the target behavior. To determine whether problem behavior occurs to reduce or to terminate task demands, a demand situation is initiated, but as soon as the child engages in the target behavior, the task is terminated and the child is allowed to take a brief break (e.g., 30 seconds). The functional analysis continues until a distinct pattern of behavior is clear.

Four conditions were conducted within the functional analysis for Sharon. The purpose of the first two conditions was to determine whether gaining either parent attention (contingent attention condition) or preferred objects (contingent tangible condition) increased the occurrence of problem behavior. During the contingent attention condition, Sharon was given several toys with which to play while her mother visited with one of the investigators. Sharon's mother was instructed to attend to Sharon *only* if Sharon engaged in self-injury, screaming, or having a tantrum. For example, if Sharon bit her arm, then her mother would approach her and say, "Don't bite your arm—you might hurt yourself." This attention would continue as long as Sharon engaged in the problem behavior. During this condition, Sharon did not engage in any of the problem behaviors when she was left alone to play with toys, thus ruling out attention as a maintaining consequence for her self-injurious behavior.

During the contingent tangible condition, the toys were removed and Sharon was left sitting on the floor with nothing with which to play. In this condition, Sharon's mother was instructed to offer Sharon a toy if she engaged in problem behavior. The purpose of this condition was to determine whether having access to preferred objects reinforced problem behavior. Once again, Sharon did not engage in any of the targeted behaviors during this condition.

The remaining sessions of the functional analysis were conducted to confirm the hypothesis that problem behavior occurred to terminate both task demands and social interactions. A contingent escape condition was conducted to test whether escaping task demands negatively reinforced the occurrence of problem behavior. In this condition, Sharon's mother assisted Sharon as she performed a difficult, nonpreferred task. Each time that Sharon screamed, had a tantrum, or engaged in self-injury, her mother removed the task materials and allowed Sharon to take a brief break (30 seconds) from the work task. At the end of 30 seconds, her mother brought Sharon back to the work task to start again. Sharon engaged in problem behavior during an average of 29% of the intervals under this condition.

The final condition, free play, was conducted as a contrast condition to contingent escape. In this condition, Sharon was allowed to play with toys while her mother sat near her and talked to her, but the mother did not attempt to direct Sharon's play. As typically conducted, the free-play condition includes high levels of adult attention, preferred toys, and no task demands. This condition serves as a control condition by providing the child with noncontingent access to adult attention and preferred items and by eliminating task demands. For Sharon, however, the results of the structural analysis had already indicated that high levels of adult attention triggered problem behavior. Therefore, the free-play condition for Sharon was altered to include low levels of adult attention. Her mother sat near Sharon and spoke to her softly but did not attempt to interact physically with Sharon or with her toys. Sharon engaged in problem behavior during an average of 7% of the intervals in this condition, suggesting that even low levels of adult attention resulted in some problem behavior.

Overall, the results of the functional analysis supported the hypothesis that Sharon's self-injury, screaming, and tantrums functioned primarily to escape difficult tasks and/or adult attention. The assessment outcomes suggested that breaks from nonpreferred tasks might be used to reinforce desired behaviors. The combined results of the assessment procedures were then used to guide our selection of an intervention strategy.

Preference Assessment

To identify toys and activities that Sharon preferred and that could be used during her requested "breaks," we conducted an assessment of toy preference. During the descriptive assessment, Sharon's mother had completed a task list in which she described frequently used toys and activities as either preferred or nonpreferred. Although this list was useful as a starting point, we did not rely on it exclusively because previous researchers (Green et al., 1988) have demonstrated that caregivers may not reliably predict which toys will reinforce a child's behavior.

We began the preference assessment with a forced-choice procedure similar to the one developed by Fisher and his colleagues (1992). The items identified by Sharon's mother as preferred toys and activities were selected for the forced-choice procedure. These toys were presented to Sharon in pairs. The investigator held two toys approximately 40 centimeters in front of Sharon and asked, "What do you want to play with?" Each pair of toys was presented to Sharon until she selected one toy or 30 seconds had elapsed, at which point a different pair of toys was presented. Presentations were counterbalanced across toys so that each toy was presented in the left and right positions and paired with every other toy an equal number of times. If Sharon selected a toy, then she was allowed to play with it for the remainder of the 30-second period, at which point a new pair of toys was presented. We recorded the number of 6-second intervals during which Sharon interacted with each toy.

The results of the forced-choice assessment demonstrated that Sharon would select toys when presented with a choice. However, Sharon frequently cried when her play was disrupted so that a new pair of toys could be presented. To reduce the problems associated with taking the toys from Sharon, we switched from a forced-choice to a group presentation format to identify preferred toys and activities (Windsor, Piché, & Locke, 1994). The group presentation assessment was conducted by presenting a set of toys that Sharon's mother had identified as "most preferred." The investigator placed the group of toys on the floor in front of Sharon and asked, "What do you want to play with?" The toys remained available to Sharon during the 5-minute assessment condition, and she was allowed to play with whichever toy she chose for the duration of the session. When Sharon discarded a toy or wandered away from the toys, she was returned to her original position and was asked, "What do want to play with?" The toy that she played with for the longest amount of time was identified as the most preferred. This procedure eliminated the need to take toys from Sharon, but it still required that she choose between toys. The results of this procedure indicated that two toys, a fashion doll and a top, were selected almost exclusively during the initial preference assessment sessions utilizing the group presentation format.

Typically, when intervention sessions are conducted in a child's home, the toys utilized in the intervention sessions are available to the child during nonintervention times, as well. As a result, it is not uncommon to find that the child has spent a good deal of time playing with the preferred toys just prior to the intervention session. When this happens, the child may tire of the toy, reducing its effectiveness as a reinforcer for that day's intervention session. Also, because toys are available to the child and his or her siblings throughout the week, it is not uncommon for toys to be missing or broken when it is time to conduct intervention sessions. For these reasons, we always attempt to identify several toys that can serve as reinforcers for engaging in the desired behavior during intervention.

The descriptive assessment, the structural and functional analyses, and the initial preference assessments all were conducted within the first month of our evaluation of Sharon. The preference assessment was repeated monthly throughout intervention to ensure that the toys used as a consequence for complying with task demands were still preferred. Although the assessment time might be considered lengthy, particularly given the severity of Sharon's behavior problems, we believe that the time spent in assessment was crucial to the success of intervention. Given the consistency of the results from the descriptive, structural, and functional assessments, we were confident that problem behavior served an escape function for Sharon. Furthermore, the occurrences of problem behavior during the free-play condition—but not during conditions with little or no attention—suggested that Sharon was escaping social attention, as well as task demands. Finally, we knew with which toys Sharon preferred to play.

An additional benefit of this assessment methodology was its efficacy in engaging Sharon's mother as an active participant in the process. We made it clear from the beginning of the project that we could provide technical expertise but that Sharon's mother was the "expert" with respect to Sharon. Her involvement during each phase improved the utility of our analyses. It also enabled her to observe firsthand how seemingly minor changes in her behavior had a substantial impact on Sharon's behavior. Ultimately, we believe that establishing a collaborative relationship with Sharon's mother was instrumental to the success of the intervention program. This assessment also permitted Sharon's mother to become comfortable with us, an important aspect of ongoing consultation.

Intervention

Although teaching Sharon appropriate ways to request a break from undesired activities was important, we did not want to teach Sharon to escape all task demands or her mother's attention. Therefore, intervention objectives focused on 1) teaching Sharon to comply briefly to task demands before requesting a break and 2) increasing the occurrence of positive social interactions between Sharon and her mother.

Compliance and Communication Training

The first objective for intervention was to teach Sharon to obtain breaks from undesired activities by engaging in adaptive behavior—that is, appropriate communication. Teaching Sharon to engage in the new, adaptive behavior rather than in problem behavior required two components: 1) teaching Sharon the new, adaptive response and 2) extinguishing the problem behavior.

Teaching New, Adaptive Responses to Replace Self-Injury

Sharon had a history of avoiding or escaping any activity that involved physical assistance by screaming and biting her arm. Therefore, we decided to use compliance to brief task demands (stacking blocks) as the adaptive response based on the recommendations of the early intervention teacher and our assessments showing active resistance to this task. This was an easy task for Sharon's mother to conduct and did not require a lengthy amount of time or unusual resources. Finally, stacking blocks provided a discrete activity during which Sharon's mother could practice the intervention procedures. Sharon initially was required to stack only a few blocks, with or without parent assistance, prior to receiving a brief break.

In addition to promoting compliance to task demands, we wanted to teach Sharon to use appropriate communicative behaviors to indicate when she wanted a brief break. We selected the word *done,* accompanied by the manual sign, as a way for Sharon to request a break. The sign for "done" was included because it appeared to be an easy sign for Sharon to imitate, and it was easy for Sharon's mother to prompt physically if Sharon did not say, "Done."

Training sessions typically were conducted for 5–10 minutes daily; they were brief so as to avoid their becoming aversive to Sharon, to ensure that they ended with a period of appropriate behavior, and to make them easier for Sharon's mother to fit into her schedule and thus complete. Sharon's mother set one block on the floor in front of Sharon. Holding a second block in her hand, her mother said, "Sharon, put this block on," and held out the block to Sharon. If Sharon did not immediately reach for the block, then her mother would place the block in Sharon's hand and guide her hand to place the second block on top of the first. When the second block was in place, her mother held out a third block and repeated the procedure of verbally and, if necessary, physically prompting Sharon to stack the blocks. When the third block was in place, Sharon's mother said, "Sharon, say, 'Done.'" She then physically guided Sharon's hands through the DONE sign. Sharon then was allowed to leave the area for a 1-minute break. After 1 minute had elapsed, the process was repeated.

Extinguishing Problem Behavior

The first intervention component focused on teaching Sharon appropriate, adaptive responses. However, it was unlikely that Sharon would attempt these new responses if the previously learned responses of screaming, having a tantrum, and self-injury continued to terminate task demands. Horner and Day (1991) demonstrated that responses that result in more immediate access to reinforcement or to greater amounts of reinforcement or that are easier to perform will be selected over alternative responses that are less efficient in gaining access to reinforcement. When compared with compliance and signing, which were new behaviors, problem behaviors resulted in quicker access to a break and were easier for Sharon to perform because they did not require new skills. From this comparison, it is clear that if Sharon were

allowed breaks from tasks by engaging in problem behavior, then she would engage in problem behavior. For this reason, a second intervention component, escape extinction (Iwata, 1987), was included in the intervention package. This intervention component consisted of not allowing a break from the task if problem behavior was occurring.

When Sharon engaged in screaming, a tantrum, or self-injury while her mother presented task prompts to her, every attempt was made to continue the task prompt procedure. When problem behavior occurred immediately after the final block was stacked or following signing for a break, another block was presented to Sharon. When problem behavior occurred while Sharon was on break, her mother immediately initiated the block stacking routine. In this way, the reinforcing consequences for engaging in problem behavior were reduced.

Increasing Positive Social Interactions

Teaching Sharon to engage in appropriate behaviors to gain breaks from task demands was one objective of intervention. Increasing positive social interactions between Sharon and her mother was the second objective, which was accomplished by pairing her mother's attention with identified reinforcers. The results of the functional analysis and preference assessment identified two categories of reinforcers for Sharon. The first category was escape from task demands. Sharon engaged in problem behavior most frequently when that behavior resulted in a brief break from task demands. The second category of reinforcers was preferred toys. These two reinforcers were paired with attention from Sharon's mother during all breaks.

Immediately following the sign DONE, whether emitted independently or following a prompt, Sharon's mother offered Sharon a choice of two highly preferred toys. When Sharon reached for one of the toys, her mother handed the toy to her. When Sharon did not reach for a toy, her mother selected a toy for her. When the toy was given to Sharon, her mother spoke to Sharon about the toy and attempted to remain close to Sharon throughout the break. By pairing the mother's attention with both the break from task demands and access to preferred toys, we hoped to increase the value of the mother's attention as a reinforcer for Sharon.

Results of Intervention

Intervention follow-up probes were conducted over a 2-year period. For the first year of intervention, the probes were conducted weekly. During the first 2 months of intervention, Sharon engaged in problem behavior (noncompliance with tasks, screaming, having tantrums, and self-injury) during an average of 23% of the intervals for each intervention session. However, by the third month, the incidence of problem behavior (primarily noncompliance) had declined to 11% of the intervals. By the sixth month of intervention, problem behavior was occurring during fewer than 5% of the intervals for each session. At the end of the first year of intervention, Sharon no longer engaged in self-injury, and even mild inappropriate behaviors (noncompliance) were at low levels of occurrence.

The second objective for intervention was to increase Sharon's positive social interactions with her mother. Positive social interactions for Sharon were defined as active, appropriate verbal and nonverbal behaviors directed toward her mother, including verbalizations (e.g., laughing, babbling, words), touching her mother with her hand, and mutual physical contact through a toy or an activity (e.g., holding a doll or a book together). By active, we mean that the behavior involved some action. This ruled out several positive behaviors. For example, a common form of physical interaction between a parent and a child is when the child sits in the parent's lap. Although this occurred with increasing frequency during the course of Sharon's intervention, we did not score this as a social interaction. We were interested in recording interactions that reflected an increasing repertoire of prosocial behaviors and that included an *active exchange* between Sharon and her mother. Thus, our measurement of social interactions was deliberately conservative.

During the first few months of intervention, Sharon crawled away from her mother as soon as she was allowed a break from the block task. Sharon ignored the toys that her mother offered her and, instead, bounced on her knees in front of the blank television screen. To increase the opportunities for social interactions, Sharon's mother followed Sharon around the room during the break periods and continued to offer her the two preferred toys. We hoped that, over time, this procedure would increase Sharon's social interactions with her mother and her time spent playing appropriately with toys.

During the first 2 months of intervention, Sharon accepted a toy from her mother or participated in a physical or vocal exchange with her mother during an average of 6% of the intervals. Over time, her mother's attempts to engage Sharon in toy play began to show beneficial effects. By the sixth month, Sharon engaged in social interactions with her mother during an average of 17% of the intervals; this increased to 51% by the end of the first year of intervention.

In addition to reducing the occurrence of problem behavior and increasing social interactions, we had hoped to increase adaptive communicative behaviors. The communication training component of Sharon's intervention included a chain of behaviors: completing the block stacking task and then signing DONE. This approach was only partially successful for Sharon. Sharon began complying with the task demands during the first few months of intervention; however, she did not say or make the sign DONE without being prompted until the last intervention session. Initially, we attempted to increase Sharon's motivation to initiate the sign DONE by increasing the task demands. Following the third month of intervention, we increased Sharon's task demand to stacking first three and then five blocks. Sharon complied with each of these changes in demands. As there are practical limits on how many small blocks a child can effectively stack, when Sharon consistently complied with requests to stack several blocks, we added a second task demand: putting away the blocks in the toy box. We initially required Sharon to put away two or three blocks before she was prompted to request a break. Sharon complied with these demands, but she still did not independently initiate the sign DONE. In an attempt to increase signing, we placed a large group of blocks on the floor for Sharon to pick up and eliminated her mother's prompt to sign DONE. Sharon responded to these demands by putting away each of the blocks in the toy box without any occurrence of self-injury, screaming, or having a tantrum. At the end of the final intervention session, Sharon put away the blocks, shut the lid of the toy box, and said, "Done." Sharon seemed to have learned the relation between complying with task demands and gaining a brief break from the task; however, it appeared that the sign DONE was an extraneous step in the behavioral chain.

GOAL 2: EVALUATING THE DURABILITY OF INTERVENTION

The second goal of the project was to evaluate the durability of the intervention effects over time. For the purposes of this project, durability referred to both the maintenance of the intervention effects on Sharon's behavior and the continued use of the intervention package by Sharon's mother.

Maintenance of Intervention Effects

We followed Sharon and her mother for 2 years to evaluate the long-term effects of the intervention package on Sharon's behavior. Sharon did not engage in any instances of self-injury during the intervention probes for the second year. Inappropriate behavior during the second year was very mild and consisted of holding the block in her hand for longer than 12 seconds before completing the task demand or knocking over the block tower. (*Note:* Continuation of the block task allowed for a consistent context for data collection—variation of tasks would be recommended under other circumstances.) Although Sharon became adept at creating a tower of five blocks, she occasionally hit the tower with her hand or foot and yelled, "Ka-boom!" while laughing. Even though this misbehavior was very minor in comparison with the original behaviors of self-injury and screaming (and it might have been considered an appropriate play behavior in another context), Sharon's mother was consistent in requiring her to complete the task appropriately before she was allowed to take a break. These mild inappropriate behaviors occurred during 7% or fewer of the intervals during the trimonthly probes. Social interactions maintained at a level of 50% or more of the intervals for the second year of the project.

Treatment Acceptability

In addition to directly observing Sharon's mother as she implemented the intervention, we asked her monthly to complete an intervention acceptability rating form based on the Treatment Acceptability Rating Form–Revised (Reimers & Wacker, 1988). This form asks caregivers to rate intervention procedures with regard to overall acceptability, effectiveness, and negative side effects (e.g., disruption to family routine). Responses to 10 items are scored using a Likert-type scale. For example, regarding the question, "How acceptable do you find the intervention to be regarding your concerns about your child?" possible responses ranged from 1 ("Not at all acceptable") to 7 ("Very acceptable"). The rating by Sharon's mother of the overall acceptability of the program during the 2-year period was uniformly high, ranging from 6 to 7, with a mean of 6.4.

GOAL 3: EVALUATING THE SIDE EFFECTS OF INTERVENTION

Behavior Checklist

The first set of data used to evaluate the side effects of the intervention package was a behavior checklist. The behavior checklist is a brief report completed by the parents weekly to reflect overall occurrences of the problem behavior throughout the week. Sharon's mother was asked to rate Sharon's behavior across three categories of activities. The first category included the daily intervention sessions that her mother conducted throughout the week. The second category included activities that had been listed as problems according to the daily time sheets completed during the first week of assessment. For Sharon, the activities listed within the second category included getting dressed and getting off the school bus. The final category consisted of activities that typically were associated with good behavior. Sharon's mother listed in this category bath time and listening to music.

For each activity, Sharon's mother rated Sharon's behavior for that week as including 1) major behavior problems that were severe and required sustained verbal and physical prompting and redirection, 2) minor behavior problems that were mild and required only brief redirection, or 3) no behavior problems and no intervention. This checklist was completed once per week for each week of intervention. The purpose of the checklist was to determine whether behavior problems were occurring throughout the week and whether the effects of the intervention package were generalizing to other problematic activities. We also wanted to determine whether the intervention package produced any negative side effects for times that had not been problematic at the start of intervention.

During the first 4 months of intervention, Sharon's mother rated Sharon's behavior during the daily intervention sessions as including minor behavior problems. Sharon's behavior during the activities listed for the other problematic times (dressing and getting off the school bus) was also rated as including minor behavior problems. During the fifth month, the ratings for these three activities changed to no occurrence of problem behavior for most weeks. Sharon's behavior for the final category, bath time and listening to music, reflected no behavior problems throughout the 2-year period. These results indicate that the intervention effects observed during the weekly probes were reflective of Sharon's overall behavior throughout the remainder of the week. Furthermore, the positive effects of intervention—increased compliance to task demands and decreased episodes of problem behavior—generalized from the intervention sessions to other problematic times. This was also true for the preschool environment, where compliance increased.

Weekly Probes

In addition to using the behavior checklist, we conducted two types of weekly probes of Sharon's behavior during nonproblematic activities to determine whether implementing the intervention package produced any negative

side effects across nonproblematic situations. During each of our weekly visits to Sharon's home, we observed Sharon and her mother interacting during a 10-minute free-play condition and during a 10-minute low-attention condition. Based on the results of the structural and functional analyses, the free-play and low-attention conditions represented situations in which Sharon engaged in little or no problem behavior. An increase in problem behavior during these situations would suggest that the intervention package was producing negative side effects.

A second reason for conducting these probes was to determine whether any gains observed in social interactions during the intervention sessions generalized to other situations. The free-play and low-attention conditions provided Sharon with multiple opportunities to engage in social interactions with her mother. Increases in social interactions during these probes would suggest that the second part of our intervention package—pairing mother's attention with preferred objects—was having the desired effect of increasing the value of the mother's attention as a reinforcer for Sharon.

In the free-play condition, Sharon was allowed to play with a group of preferred toys while her mother provided attention to her. Inappropriate behavior was ignored. During this condition, we encouraged Sharon's mother to interact with Sharon, even when Sharon attempted to crawl away or engage in stereotypic behavior. For example, when Sharon crawled toward the television screen, her mother was encouraged to follow her and attempt to engage her in toy play. During the initial months, Sharon typically ignored her mother and the toys. Over time, Sharon spent more time interacting with her mother and less time engaging in stereotypic behavior. During the weekly free-play probes, the incidence of problem behavior averaged 3% of the intervals for the entire first year. The incidence of social interactions averaged 9% of the intervals for the first 2 months of intervention, increasing to 70% of the intervals by the end of 1 year of intervention.

The social interactions between Sharon and her mother increased not only in frequency but also in quality. For example, during the first few months of intervention, Sharon frequently selected a fashion doll with which to play. However, Sharon's "play" behaviors typically consisted of waving the doll in front of her face and putting the doll's head into her mouth. Sharon's mother persisted in introducing different ways to play with the doll. She showed Sharon how to brush the doll's hair and to dress the doll. She pointed out the doll's eyes, nose, mouth, and other body parts. She showed Sharon how to take the doll for a walk and how to position the doll's body. Over time, Sharon's mother introduced a baby doll during the free-play probes. She modeled rocking, feeding, and singing to the baby doll. Each time that Sharon attempted to initiate stereotypic behavior with the doll, her mother redirected her to more appropriate play behaviors. As these stereotypic behaviors occurred at a low rate and were not considered to be a problem, a formal functional analysis and intervention (other than redirection to appropriate play) were not implemented.

As Sharon became more responsive to her mother's attempts at play, her mother engaged her in a broader array of play activities. For example, Sharon's mother learned the songs and fingerplays that were used at Sharon's preschool. At first, Sharon watched her mother perform the fingerplay activities for brief periods of time. Eventually, she began to imitate her mother and approximate the words to the songs. At the end of the first year of intervention, Sharon independently completed verses to the songs and guided her mother's hands through the fingerplay movements. Thus, her interactions changed from avoidance to passive attending to initiating and sustaining interactions with her mother. These types of shared activities were an important aspect of increasing the positive social interactions between Sharon and her mother throughout intervention.

During a weekly probe designed to be a low-attention condition—which would reflect situations in which Sharon's mother was busy and could not be interrupted to play with her—Sharon was allowed to play with preferred toys while her mother sat in a chair across the room from Sharon and conversed with the project staff or with one of Sharon's brothers. Sharon's mother was instructed to ignore Sharon with the exception of neutrally blocking any potentially dangerous or destructive behavior. When Sharon approached her mother and attempted to initiate an appropriate interaction (e.g., touch her mother's hand), she was directed to play with her toys. During this low-attention condition, Sharon engaged in problem behavior during an average of 5% of the intervals across the first year of the project. Her engagement in social interactions remained at an average of 2% of the intervals throughout the first year. These results demonstrated that although Sharon's engagement in appropriate social interactions increased in response to her mother's initiations of play, she did not actively solicit her mother's attention during the low social conditions during the first year. These results caused concern for us because they suggested that if left alone, Sharon would choose to remain alone and would be dependent on others to initiate social exchanges.

Although Sharon's behavior did not change significantly during the low social conditions conducted throughout the second year of the project, her behavior at times other than during the probes suggested that she had begun to initiate social interactions with her mother. When an intervention session ended and Sharon's mother and project staff were reviewing the sessions, Sharon would sometimes drop to the floor and cry. Her mother typically responded to this behavior by picking her up and rocking her or offering juice or food items; Sharon's brother also indicated responding to Sharon by offering her toys and snacks. It appeared that gaining social attention and preferred items maintained these behaviors. To take advantage of this positive development, we suggested to Sharon's mother and brothers that they delay approaching Sharon until she stopped crying and, at that point, present her with a choice of two items. The project investigator taught Sharon's family the manual signs for the food and toys typically offered to Sharon and encouraged her family to model using the signs (accompanied by the oral presentation of the word) when prompting Sharon to make a choice between items. This approach was effective. During the second year of the project, Sharon began using manual signs and spoken words to request activities (e.g., bath, outside) and food items (e.g., juice, cracker) and to label objects in the environment.

CONCLUSION

As demonstrated by our evaluation of Sharon, conducting behavioral assessments in the home of a very young child is a reasonable and effective approach for addressing severe behavior problems. The information provided by Sharon's mother throughout the descriptive assessment process allowed us to focus on the types of activities that were most likely to occasion self-injury, tantrums, and screaming. Furthermore, conducting the assessments in Sharon's home allowed us to use the times, toys, and activities that typically were associated with episodes of problem behavior, thus increasing our opportunities to observe directly the behavior and the environmental events surrounding the behavior.

Conducting the assessment procedures in Sharon's home may have improved our ability to identify the specific stimuli affecting Sharon's behavior. Of equal importance, it allowed us to establish with Sharon's mother a collaborative relationship that may not have been possible in a clinic or a school. Sharon's mother conducted all assessment and intervention procedures, which allowed us to observe directly the interactions between parent and child. Of equal importance, it allowed Sharon's mother to demonstrate the types of problems that she was experiencing with Sharon and to observe directly the way that changes in her own behavior affected Sharon's behavior.

Having Sharon's mother conduct the intervention sessions with our coaching alleviated problems associated with transferring control from a professional to a parent. Sharon's mother was able to implement daily intervention sessions, thus providing multiple training opportunities for Sharon. Our weekly outreach visits allowed us to provide immediate feedback to Sharon's mother and provided a forum for Sharon's mother to discuss difficulties that she experienced with the procedures. We believe that this type of collaborative arrangement was directly responsible for the generalization and maintenance achieved with intervention.

Although there are advantages associated with implementing experimental analyses of behavior and intervention packages in the home, there also are disadvantages. The primary disadvantages are threats to experimental control during the assessment process and disruptions during intervention sessions. All of the assessment and intervention sessions for Sharon were conducted in the living room of her home. It was not uncommon for one or both of her brothers to be present in the immediate area as we conducted the assessment and intervention sessions. In addition to the disruptions provided by other children who also required their mother's attention, there were frequent visits by neighbors and other family members and telephone calls that needed to be answered. As problematic as these disruptions may be to establishing consistent experimental conditions, they also reflect the events of Sharon's daily life—events that may surround the occurrence of severe problem behaviors and events that will, in all likelihood, continue throughout intervention. In our opinion, it is best to observe these ongoing environmental events directly and to adjust the intervention package so that it can be delivered effectively in conjunction with these routine events. An intervention that can withstand the rigors of daily living has an increased probability of promoting long-term intervention gains.

REFERENCES

Axelrod, S. (1987). Functional and structural analyses of behavior: Approaches leading to reduced use of punishment procedures? *Research in Developmental Disabilities, 8,* 165–178.

Carr, E. (1977). The motivation of self-injurious behavior: A review of some hypotheses. *Psychological Bulletin, 84,* 800–816.

Carr, E., & Durand, V.M. (1985). Reducing behavior problems through functional communication training. *Journal of Applied Behavior Analysis, 18,* 111–126.

Cooper, L.J., Wacker, D.P., Sasso, G.M., Reimers, T.M., & Donn, L. (1990). Using parents as therapists to evaluate appropriate behavior of their children: Application to a tertiary diagnostic clinic. *Journal of Applied Behavior Analysis, 23,* 285–296.

Derby, K.M., Wacker, D.P., Berg, W., DeRaad, A., Ulrich, S., Asmus, J., Harding, J., Prouty, A., Laffey, P., & Stoner, E.A. (1997). The long-term

effects of functional communication training in home settings. *Journal of Applied Behavior Analysis, 30,* 507–531.

Derby, K.M., Wacker, D.P., Sasso, G., Steege, M., Northup, J., Cigrand, K., & Asmus, J. (1992). Brief functional assessment techniques to evaluate aberrant behavior in an outpatient setting: A summary of 79 cases. *Journal of Applied Behavior Analysis, 25,* 713–721.

Fisher, W., Piazza, C.C., Bowman, L.G., Hagopian, L.P., Owens, J.C., & Slevin, I. (1992). A comparison of two approaches for identifying reinforcers for persons with severe and profound disabilities. *Journal of Applied Behavior Analysis, 25,* 491–498.

Green, C.W., Reid, D.H., White, L.K., Halford, R.C., Brittain, D.P., & Gardner, S.M. (1988). Identifying reinforcers for persons with profound handicaps: Staff opinion versus systematic assessment of preferences. *Journal of Applied Behavior Analysis, 21,* 31–43.

Horner, R., & Day, M. (1991). The effects of response efficiency on functionally equivalent competing behaviors. *Journal of Applied Behavior Analysis, 24,* 719–732.

Iwata, B.A. (1987). Negative reinforcement in applied behavior analysis: An emerging technology. *Journal of Applied Behavior Analysis, 20,* 361–378.

Iwata, B., Dorsey, M., Slifer, K., Bauman, K., & Richman, G. (1982). Toward a functional analysis of self-injury. *Analysis and Intervention in Developmental Disabilities, 2,* 3–20.

Northup, J., Wacker, D., Sasso, G., Steege, M., Cigrand, K., Cook, J., & DeRaad, A. (1991). A brief functional analysis of aggressive and alternative behavior in an outclinic setting. *Journal of Applied Behavior Analysis, 24,* 509–522.

Reimers, T., & Wacker, D. (1988). Parents' ratings of the acceptability of behavioral intervention recommendations made in an outpatient clinic: A preliminary analysis of the influence of intervention effectiveness. *Behavioral Disorders, 14,* 7–15.

Repp, A.C., Karsh, K.G., Munk, D., & Dahlquist, C.M. (1995). Hypothesis-based interventions: A theory of clinical decision making. In W. O'Donohue & L. Krasner (Eds.), *Theories of behavior therapy: Exploring behavior change* (pp. 585–608). Washington, DC: American Psychological Association.

Scotti, J.R., Schulman, D.E., & Hojnacki, R.M. (1994). Functional analysis and unsuccessful treatment of Tourette's syndrome in a man with profound mental retardation. *Behavior Therapy, 25,* 721–738.

Touchette, P.E., MacDonald, R.F., & Langer, S.N. (1985). A scatter plot for identifying stimulus control of problem behavior. *Journal of Applied Behavior Analysis, 18,* 343–351.

Windsor, J., Piché, L.M., & Locke, P.A. (1994). Preference testing: A comparison of two presentation methods. *Research in Developmental Disabilities, 15,* 439–455.

Chapter 19

Issues and Challenges in Implementing Community-Based Behavioral Support for Two Boys with Severe Behavioral Difficulties

Meme Hieneman & Glen Dunlap

The enterprise of behavioral support has experienced tremendous maturation since the mid-1980s (e.g., Horner et al., 1990; Koegel, Koegel, & Dunlap, 1996; Meyer & Evans, 1989, 1993), but important challenges need to be resolved before beneficial outcomes can be promised in all circumstances. Some of the most significant challenges pertain to the intricacies and impediments that occur in the process of developing and implementing support plans in complex community contexts. This chapter addresses some of these issues through two case studies. The cases illustrate a model of assessment-based, positive behavioral support (e.g., Dunlap & Kern, 1993; Koegel et al., 1996) and emphasize important features of a team approach for building and maintaining a coordinated structure of support in a person's key environments.

POSITIVE BEHAVIORAL SUPPORT

As the chapters in this book demonstrate, approaches to seriously destructive and disruptive behaviors have developed substantially from the practices of behavior management that were promoted in previous decades. Earlier practices consisted essentially of a dominant core technology of contingency manipulation in which interventions primarily were in the form of recommended schedules of rewards and punishments, which were augmented occasionally by instructional or other auxiliary procedures. Concerted efforts by advocates, researchers, and practitioners have broadened perspectives on behavioral intervention extensively such that contingency management is appreciated as only one component of a much broader support process.

Preparation of this chapter and the authors' roles in the case studies were supported by Cooperative Agreement No. H133B2004 and Grant No. H133B980005 from the U.S. Department of Education (National Institute on Disability and Rehabilitation Research) and by the Center for Autism and Related Disabilities and the Florida Mental Health Institute at the University of South Florida. The opinions expressed in this chapter, however, are those of the authors, and no official endorsement by any agency should be inferred. The authors acknowledge with appreciation the children, families, and support providers whose efforts are described herein.

The approach to positive behavioral support that this chapter's authors endorse (and that serves as the framework for the case studies described in this chapter) is consistent with perspectives that have been articulated in the literature (e.g., Carr et al., 1994; Horner et al., 1990; Koegel et al., 1996) and applied with people who experience a variety of cognitive, emotional, and behavioral challenges (e.g., Dunlap & Kern, 1993; Horner, Sprague, & Flannery, 1993; Kern & Dunlap, 1999). Some of the key features of the approach include the following:

1. *A commitment to effectiveness* that is evaluated in terms of outcomes that are meaningful from the perspectives of the person, the person's family and friends, and support providers

2. *An educational orientation* that includes interventions designed to enhance the person's abilities to control his or her environment (Evans & Meyer, 1985; Meyer & Evans, 1989)

3. *An appreciation for the influence of contextual factors* and a determination to modify antecedent and setting variables in support of a person's preferences and predilections (Dunlap & Kern, 1993; Turnbull & Turnbull, 1990)

4. *An applied pragmatism* that is open to diverse and idiosyncratic strategies, as long as they are demonstrably useful for an individual's support

5. *A reliance on a functional assessment process* that produces individualized information about the reciprocal influences between a person's behavior and the (external and internal) environment (Dunlap & Kern, 1993; Repp & Horner, 1999)

The central process for developing and implementing a behavioral support plan has been described in several sources (e.g., Dunlap & Fox, 1996; Dunlap & Kern, 1993). The process begins with a comprehensive functional assessment during which the support team seeks to gain sensitivity for the person, understanding of the value of the problematic behaviors, and comprehension of the ways in which the behaviors interrelate with environmental events. Multiple methods for gathering information are used, including direct observations and systematic data collection, interviews, record reviews, and, sometimes, direct manipulations (Foster-Johnson & Dunlap, 1993; Kern, Dunlap, Clarke, & Childs, 1994; O'Neill, Horner, Albin, Storey, & Sprague, 1990; Repp & Horner, 1999). The initial assessment process culminates with the formation of hypothesis statements that present the support team's best understanding of the relation between the environment and the person's problem behavior. These statements should indicate the functions that are served by the behaviors as well as the specific contextual variables, or circumstances, that are associated with both high rates and very low rates (or an absence) of the behavior (Meyer & Evans, 1989).

Hypothesis statements then are translated into components of a comprehensive plan of positive behavioral support. For example, a statement that implicates escape from a noxious stimulus as the motivational function of a person's aggression should operate as a trigger to develop the following plan: 1) a program of communication training that provides a more effective, efficient, and socially acceptable means for the person to elude offensive stimuli (e.g., Carr et al., 1994; Durand, 1990) and, perhaps, 2) a preventive rearrangement of the environment to remove or ameliorate the noxious stimulus (Dunlap & Kern, 1993, 1996). The hypothesis statements supply the focal elements of the behavioral support plan, whereas other ingredients are included to address broader quality-of-life issues and promote positive longitudinal outcomes (e.g., Kincaid, 1996). Finally, the model maintains a process of evaluation and ongoing assessment to refine hypotheses, adjust interventions, and continue the advancement of comprehensive support.

CHALLENGES IN COMMUNITY-BASED IMPLEMENTATION

Although there is an impressive and growing database that testifies for positive behavioral support, there also are substantial challenges that frequently plague efforts to develop and provide effective support in community environments.

One set of challenges pertains to severe problem behaviors that have persisted for many years despite numerous and complicated histories of intervention. Such situations can be exacerbated when a person has cognitive and/or physical disabilities that require extensive support services. Circumstances such as these often require a highly focused, individualized plan and an infusion of special expertise to identify appropriate and effective interventions. The processes that are involved in arranging, coordinating, and deploying needed levels of individualization and expertise have not been investigated in the context of community-based intervention for very severe behavioral challenges. These processes, however, are crucial if effective support programs are to be accomplished in typical community contexts.

Not all of the difficulties in developing effective support programs come from the individual with challenging behavior. Indeed, a second and related challenge is that people often participate in a number of complicated environments with support from a variety of service systems. There usually are a number of staff, family members, friends, and other individuals who influence a person's activities and behavioral repertoire. The agencies and individuals who are involved in work with salient behavioral challenges maintain varying perspectives based on diverse experiences; philosophies; disciplinary orientations; and cultural, ethical, and spiritual frameworks. Furthermore, service systems typically offer limited options for support providers and placements. Coordinating the participation of the network of key support providers is a tremendous challenge in developing and implementing an effective program of comprehensive behavioral support. If severe behavioral challenges are to be resolved for the long term, then building and maintaining a milieu of effective support may be a vital (but underappreciated) feature of community-based, behavioral support endeavors.

The approach that the chapter authors have adopted for addressing behavioral challenges involves developing a cohesive *team* of support providers. Although outside consultants introduce the framework of the support model and provide technical assistance, the community support team is empowered as the vehicle through which assessments are conducted, hypotheses are developed, and support plans are produced. The team includes members who represent the chief entities responsible for the person's support (e.g., family, residential support, educational support). The team concept has the potential to offer numerous advantages, including group investment in the process and the shared objectives, a sense of accountability, reciprocal support of a technical and/or a social nature, a multiplicity of contributors and problem solvers, and increased awareness of and increased access to resources. In addition, the development and operation of a support team can serve to increase the capacity of the local support providers to assist in future efforts.

The remainder of this chapter is devoted to the presentation of two case studies, both of which concern children with very significant support needs and extensive histories of severe destructive behavior. The support efforts for both children began with and were defined by the formation of support teams that included their families. The following pages describe the steps in each of the children's support programs, with an emphasis on those features that hindered or contributed to progress.

JOEY AND ROLAND

The cases of Joey and Roland are presented together because they offer both similarities in their challenges and complexities and contrasts in their processes of assessment and intervention, as well as in the initial outcomes that resulted from the support efforts. Both Joey and Roland had been given a primary diagnosis of autism, exhibited an array of serious behavioral challenges, and had extensive deficits in the performance of adaptive skills. Both children had such high rates of aggressive and self-injurious behavior that attempts were under way to move them to more restrictive placements. Previous attempts at intervention had been ineffective in managing their behavior, and some of the children's support providers had resorted to intrusive intervention strategies.

The children's physical and social environments were highly complex. Both families were extremely committed and involved; however, the severity of the children's destructive behaviors led to residential placements outside the home in the local community. These placements expanded the children's support and service networks considerably, and, thus, the process of comprehensive behavioral support required coordination of resources and communication among families, schools, and residences.

Joey

Joey was 6 years old at the beginning of the assessment and intervention process. He had dark, straight hair and brown eyes and was extremely small for his age. Joey was a cute child; however, his face was scarred from many years of self-injury. He enjoyed listening to music, looking at books, and being held by adults.

Joey had experienced medical problems since infancy. He had numerous allergies, a hearing loss, and significant dietary and digestive problems. He frequently had flu-like symptoms. Joey was taking three different medications for behavioral regulation; the dosages of these medications were adjusted frequently.

Joey was described as having profound developmental delays. The strength and range of motion in his arms were limited, possibly because of the prolonged use of protective equipment to prevent his ongoing self-abuse. His motor limitations made it difficult for him to perform self-care and daily living skills. Joey's most severe needs were in the area of communication. He did not speak, sign, or use any augmentative systems to express his needs effectively. For the most part, Joey communicated through gross gestures, expressions of pleasure and distaste, and self-injury.

Joey's family was a powerful resource for him and for his professional staff. Joey lived at home until just over a year before the support team was assembled. Throughout his infancy and early childhood, Joey had required constant supervision to prevent damaging self-injury. Although creative devices had been provided for his protection, Joey still managed to bang his head on furniture and other fixtures. Finally,

after painful deliberation, Joey's family decided to arrange for residential placement.

At the initiation of the comprehensive support process, Joey was living in a residential program for children with developmental disabilities and severe behavioral challenges and attending a center school for children with disabilities. As a result of the frequency and severity of his self-injurious behavior, he wore protective equipment almost 80% of the time. Joey's family made regular visits to the residence and had brought him home on weekends until shortly before the chapter authors became involved, when Joey's problem behavior had escalated to unmanageable levels. Joey's support providers were extremely concerned about Joey's level of self-injury, the extensive use of restraints, and his failure to develop adaptive skills. However, there were no plans for addressing these concerns in a systematic manner. There was considerable pressure from the state agency that monitors behavior programs to address Joey's behavior more effectively or to consider more restrictive placement options.

Roland

Roland was 11 years old at the time of his referral to the program. He was an attractive boy with big blue eyes and reddish-brown hair. His preferred activities included playing in water, collecting and manipulating small objects, and exploring his environment (e.g., walking outside, visiting new places). He tended to become obsessively immersed in a variety of sensations, including smells, tastes, and textures (often making it difficult to redirect him to other activities). Roland generally was healthy, with the exception of inconsistent sleep patterns and unusual food preferences. He was taking two medications for behavioral control; both were well monitored and regulated.

Roland's options for communicating his needs were severely restricted. Initially, his teacher and the staff at his group home were using facilitated communication (FC; Biklen, 1990), sometimes to the exclusion of other methods. Roland also was able to communicate by making sounds, pointing, and leading. Although he was able to verbalize, he spoke only when he was under duress. Roland lacked many of the skills that he needed to interact and function independently in his surroundings. Although he had been taught some self-care and daily living skills, he was unable to generalize these skills adequately. Roland's ability to self-initiate was poor. He tended to wait for an adult to tell him what to do.

Roland's parents were deeply concerned for his welfare, but they often had difficulty with obtaining appropriate supports. As a young child, Roland was very resistant to limits imposed by his parents and teachers (e.g., having to wait for items that he wanted). His difficulties in communication, lack of independence in self-care, and increasing aggression caused great turmoil for his family. When Roland's behavior became progressively more disruptive and dangerous in the home and at school, his family sought residential placement. Roland had been living in programs outside his family's local community for 2 years before his referral. In those programs, he had received services from some skilled practitioners. There was also considerable evidence, however, that he had experienced mistreatment; the most serious incident resulted in Roland's sustaining bruises and a broken arm as an inexperienced staff member tried to restrain him. In response to these abuses and to inadequate responsiveness from system officials, Roland's father worked hard to become an increasingly active and knowledgeable advocate for his child.

When the comprehensive support process was initiated, Roland's father had just succeeded in securing a small, community-based group home placement for Roland. He was attending a special education program at a general school. Still, Roland continued to engage in severely disruptive behaviors, such as head butting, hitting, and feces smearing, both in the residence and at school. His teacher and her assistant were on leave from school as a result of injuries that they sustained while restraining Roland. The other students had been removed from his classroom and placed elsewhere on parental request. Roland rarely participated in educational activities and had missed all but 10 days of school as a result of the school's difficulty in managing

him. The restraint and overcorrection procedures used in the school and residence seemed only to intensify his aggression. Representatives of the school system were questioning the appropriateness of his placement.

A TEAM-BASED APPROACH TO BEHAVIORAL SUPPORT

In both Joey's and Roland's cases, the communication among the key individuals in these children's lives was strained and limited. The families and service providers typically met only as required by the programs' planning processes and in response to crises, and these meetings often were unproductive in terms of developing proactive supports. Discrepancies in philosophies regarding how to interpret the children's challenging behaviors led to inconsistent practices across environments. A more comprehensive and coordinated approach was urgently needed. To address the severe and complex challenges presented by Joey's and Roland's problem behaviors, a team approach was deemed appropriate and necessary. The behavioral support team, composed of the most significant people in a child's life, would offer a collaborative and transdisciplinary stratagem (Rainforth & York-Barr, 1997) in which assessment and intervention could be addressed within and across multiple environments and circumstances (e.g., Carr et al., 1994) to create and implement individualized, proactive, and continuing supports for a person who exhibits challenging behavior.

Rationale for Team-Based Support

Children with significant disabilities invariably have needs for many support and intervention programs (e.g., medical, educational), and these programs are engineered and implemented by different providers representing various disciplines. The programs are, invariably, interdependent and, to be implemented holistically and with any degree of integrity, must be coordinated. The arrangement of comprehensive and longitudinal behavioral support, which often is necessary for intransigent behavioral challenges, requires that coordination be continued over a period of time. The development and maintenance of a working team of support providers is essential, and it provides a number of supplementary advantages. First, team support provides *multiple perspectives* in the assessment process and leads to holistic, integrated intervention approaches. Second, a team approach increases the sense of *accountability* and *commitment* that individual support providers bring to the behavioral support effort. Third, teams can create a social and emotional *support system* for families and support providers. Fourth, a team process *builds new capacities* for team members to exchange knowledge and to generalize to other circumstances through each member's involvement in all aspects of the assessment, plan development, and implementation.

Principles of Team Functioning

Simply convening a group of individuals does not constitute a team. An effective team approach adheres to principles of interaction that emphasize basic values (Rainforth & York-Barr, 1997):

1. There must be recognition that each member is important and should be valued.
2. The team must be willing to operate from a consensus model of decision making, which promotes shared responsibility in the intervention.
3. Although team members will have competing priorities, the emphasis must remain on the unique needs of the child as a family member, a friend, a student, or an employee and as a part of the community.
4. Teams must learn to operate creatively to overcome the barriers posed by systems with limited resources.
5. To promote learning, team members must be willing to transfer their knowledge and skills through a collaborative process. They also must be capable of abandoning an expert, or hierarchical, model in favor of a more integrated and participatory process of decision making.

An effective behavioral support team provides an open forum for exchanging information and ideas and developing comprehensive interventions within a child's and a family's community.

Functions of Behavioral Support Teams

A behavioral support team should include representatives of the environments in which the child interacts and the various disciplines or perspectives involved in supporting him or her (Rainforth & York-Barr, 1997). The individuals who know the child best are critical members of the team. A child's family may have the clearest perception of the child's needs and is, therefore, an essential part of the team. Professional support providers, however, typically are aware of the resources and services that may be available. Families and practitioners must come together to ensure that services are matched to the child's needs. It is also important that those who are in the position to allocate time and resources be included and that all key decision makers be included for the team to be productive. Although there may be core members (e.g., family members, teacher) who participate consistently on the team, other members may be included when a specific need dictates their involvement. Individuals who are important to the child but cannot be engaged in the team process because of unavoidable conflicts must be kept abreast of developments in the assessment and intervention process by the team members.

For the team to function well, important roles need to be filled. Parker (1990) referred to the roles as collaborator, communicator, contributor, and challenger. These roles have been applied in early intervention (Briggs, 1991) and also may provide a useful framework in community-based behavioral support.

Collaborators help to retain the vision and goal-directedness of the team to retain the "big picture" and must have familiarity with functional assessment and be receptive to all suggestions. In contentious circumstances, sometimes it is helpful to have individuals who are not involved in the daily intervention to occupy this role. *Communicators,* possessing strong social skills and sensitivity, observe and enhance the process of interaction among the members of the team by building consensus, addressing conflicts, and solving problems. *Contributors* implement the team's ideas by collecting data, trying environmental manipulations, and implementing the behavioral support plan. Given the variety of environments in which children with severe disabilities function, it may be necessary to have active contributors from each environment (e.g., school, home, residential program) involved in the team process. *Challengers* help the team members to produce innovative solutions and to think critically about their ideas before putting them into practice.

Team members can change roles and, sometimes, assume multiple roles. Each role, however, is key to the team's success. A primary goal is to maintain an appropriate balance in roles and to ensure that members feel supported and encouraged in their participation. Consultants, therefore, should be familiar with these group dynamics and be capable of filling certain roles as needed.

Team Building for Joey and Roland

The organization of behavioral support teams for Joey and Roland involved collaborative efforts among the schools, families, and residential programs in which each child participated. The teams convened on a regular basis, approximately every 2 weeks; each meeting took approximately 2 hours. The teams were asked to adopt a guiding philosophy and shared responsibility in the process of assessment and intervention. For both teams, this meant open communication, contribution of time and resources, and commitment to assessment-based intervention. The teams, therefore, spent time during the initial meeting and throughout the process discussing the foundations of functional assessment, positive behavioral support strategies, and members' own belief systems. The process of building a support plan was reviewed as were expectations for data collection and commitment to consistency in intervention.

Joey

Members of Joey's team included Joey's mother (and, when possible, his father), teacher, a teacher assistant, occupational therapists, the administrator and staff members from the residential facility, and a behavior analyst. Other individuals participated in the team activities by attending a single meeting and maintaining contact with members via telephone. Two representatives from the university program, a doctoral student (the first author) and a research coordinator, were involved as facilitators. Both of these individuals had several years of experience with working in a consulting capacity with individuals with severe disabilities. The doctoral student organized and facilitated the team meetings (later transferring this responsibility to direct support providers) and provided oversight for the assessment and intervention processes. The research coordinator took primary responsibility for data collection and analysis in Joey's case but was not involved with Roland. The university personnel presented their roles to the teams as facilitators and providers of technical assistance.

During the initial meeting, Joey's team identified general goals. The first concern was Joey's safety. Many members of the team were concerned about the length of time that Joey was in protective equipment and believed strongly that they should be removed. The residential personnel, however, were concerned that they would be unable to protect Joey from injury. The team, therefore, developed crisis management procedures for the interim. The other primary concern was the limited benefits that Joey was deriving from his education and therapeutic programs because of the frequency and intensity of his self-injury. The team agreed that other important goals would include improving Joey's ability to respond adaptively and communicatively and for him to remain in his current placement. The team agreed at the first meeting that change would not come quickly and that they would need to commit a great deal of time and resources to developing and implementing a support plan.

Although many aspects of the team process progressed well, there were some problems. One major concern was that a number of key staff from the residential facility were not included. In addition, no single representative of that program was able to accept the commitment and responsibility for organizing the data collection, data synthesis, or intervention. Although there was regular participation at the team meetings, the commitment to allocate needed resources frequently appeared ambiguous.

Also, disagreements between the school and residential programs occurred throughout the process and became more apparent as time passed. As communication deteriorated, some team members began to express frustration with the prolonged nature of the process and began to question the feasibility of the interventions and the likelihood of their implementation in the residential facility. Although each of the individuals in Joey's life was very concerned about his welfare, the team experienced difficulties in developing fully equitable and respectful interactions and did not achieve the cohesiveness necessary for optimal outcomes.[1]

Roland

Although Roland's team had fewer core members than Joey's, there was excellent representation. The people who had the most contact with Roland and the people who controlled the available resources were consistently involved. The team included Roland's father and mother, the owners/operators of the group home, and representatives of the school and the school district. When a new teacher was hired (to replace the teacher who was on leave because of injury), she joined the team. In addition, Roland's case manager and other service providers maintained participation through occasional attendance, contact with members, and regular exchanges by telephone. A special education coordinator at his school assisted in the process, and, later, a behavior analyst affiliated with the group home provided coordination in the residential program.

Roland's team developed foundations for the assessment and intervention related to four primary goals:

1. To modify the environment to promote more adaptive behavior
2. To provide communicative alternatives to problem behavior

3. To improve independence through functional skills instruction
4. To reduce the salience of the variables that were maintaining his problem behavior

To achieve these goals, Roland's team agreed to pursue a process of functional assessment and intervention within natural environments. Because acceptable crisis procedures were already in place to deal with emergencies, the team was able to make progress toward developing consensus among the members.

Roland's team offered an excellent example of how communication can and should improve over time. Although there was a history of adversarial interactions, the team members who gathered together in this support process were committed to a constructive approach. Roland's father took steps to develop his ability to advocate in constructive ways, and, in general, the team members learned to deal with conflict more effectively and to address issues in a positive manner. Roland's team had contributors from all three environments—family, school, and group home. His teacher, father, and staff at the group home left each team meeting with a list of responsibilities that they put in place. Not only were these individuals able to implement strategies, but they also ensured that other support staff in both locations were capable of doing so.

FUNCTIONAL ASSESSMENT AND HYPOTHESIS DEVELOPMENT

Functional assessments were conducted within the children's natural environments to identify the specific factors that were contributing to the problem behavior. The process required gathering information about the children's behavior across a variety of circumstances, analyzing this information, developing hypotheses about the functions of the behavior, and, in some cases, conducting manipulations for the purpose of test-

---

[1]It is important to point out that perfect team unity and mutual respect can be difficult to achieve and may be especially difficult when the problems are very severe, when solutions are difficult to envision, and when there are histories of distrust among individuals and/or agencies. In Joey's team, important progress was accomplished despite such obstacles; however, it is possible that a team that operated with more complete collaboration may have achieved even more impressive results.

ing those hypotheses. The purpose of the assessment process was to identify the functional relations that governed the behavior within particular contexts so that appropriate, individualized interventions could be developed. Information was obtained through reviewing records, interviewing people who lived and worked with the children, and conducting direct observations of the children in a variety of situations. Record reviews tapped into a variety of sources including medical, psychological, and educational assessments. These data helped the teams to identify factors that were not readily apparent but that could be influencing the children's behavior and to include the perspectives of individuals who were not currently involved in the child's support.

The interviews were based on the Functional Analysis Interview Form (FAIF) developed by O'Neill and colleagues (1990). This interview process defines the specific behaviors, helps to identify when and where they are likely to occur (or not to occur), surveys the communication skills of the individual, and provides information that is useful in delineating operant and antecedent functions. Interviews were conducted with a number of relevant people in each child's life. In some cases, an abbreviated form or a less structured presentation of the interview questions was used (e.g., Dunlap & Kern, 1993; Kern & Dunlap, 1999).

The information obtained from the interviews and file reviews was clarified and verified through direct observation. With both children, the data collection included a scatter plot (Touchette, MacDonald, & Langer, 1985) to estimate the frequency of the children's problem behaviors across activities, as well as recordings of the specific antecedents, behaviors, and consequences (Bijou, Peterson, & Ault, 1968). The observational data were collected by staff from the university program and by the support providers who worked directly with the children on a daily basis. The aggregated data were synthesized so that the teams could generate hypotheses regarding the precipitating factors and communicative functions of the children's behavior (Repp, Felce, & Barton, 1988). This included identifying the circumstances in which the behavior was most desirable and most problematic and

then trying to isolate the key variables within those contexts to explain the variations in the frequency of the children's behavior across activities, people, environments, and times of day.

In cases in which the functions of the problem behaviors were less than clear, the team opted to test certain hypotheses through direct manipulations prior to integrating them into the support plan (Dunlap, Kern-Dunlap, Clarke, & Robbins, 1991; Iwata, Dorsey, Slifer, Bauman, & Richman, 1994; Iwata, Vollmer, & Zarcone, 1990; O'Neill et al., 1990).

Joey

As anticipated, the functional assessment process for Joey was difficult because Joey had displayed severe self-injury consistently since he was an infant and because relatively high rates of the behavior were reported in every identified circumstance. It appeared as though multiple functions were governing the behavior, and, because self-injury occurred even when Joey was alone, at least one function seemed to be a type of self-stimulation. A significant complication in the assessment process was the variety of physiological and medical disturbances that affected Joey's composure, attitude, and, understandably, problem behaviors. As noted previously, Joey was ill frequently and, as a result, missed a good deal of school. Many staff members believed that his self-injury, tantrums, and other problem behaviors increased when he was ailing; however, his physiological status was not easy to assess. The extent to which physiological variables influenced Joey's behavior from day to day and moment to moment was almost impossible to evaluate, but these certainly were factors and, unfortunately, obscured the presence of other variables.

The assessment process included detailed interviews with many individuals, including Joey's parents, sister, extended family, teacher and other education personnel, occupational therapists, several people at the residential program, and the behavior analyst. Direct observation data were collected in a variety of ways, ranging from informal to highly systematic methods. Activities that team participants described as the most and the least problematic were recorded on videotape. Data were obtained from the videotapes to estimate Joey's rate of self-injury, appropriate engagement in activities, and positive affect (e.g., smiling, making faces). At the school, the teacher recorded data on the same three behaviors every 10 minutes, but the staff at the residential program were able to record data only on the application and removal of Joey's splints; these were data mandated by regulations.

As data were collected and as the team reviewed their observations, attempts were made to test preliminary hypotheses through probe sessions conducted within the context of reversal and alternating treatment designs (Iwata et al., 1990; O'Neill et al., 1990). The hypothesis tests were conducted within the context of Joey's typical routine by his regular staff. Unfortunately, the data from these sessions were confounded by the influence of numerous ecological and physiological disturbances, including medication changes, illness and related discomforts, and sudden schedule changes and absences from school. These variables interfered frequently and unpredictably and reduced substantially the precision and heuristic value of the systematic-testing phase of the assessment process.

Other evidence showed that the frequency of Joey's self-injury was very high in every circumstance that was recorded. Data from the videotapes showed that Joey was engaging in self-injurious behavior in approximately 50% of the intervals; the teacher's data gave a rate of at least five to six times per minute. Unfortunately, the quantifiable data did not present clear patterns, except that self-injury occurred at a lower rate when Joey was left alone. Although the data patterns were disappointingly obscure, the interviews and the syntheses of historical and anecdotal observations provided some assistance. For example, the people who were interviewed generally believed that elevated rates and intensities of self-injury were associated with a number of ecological, instructional, and physiological variables.

The following variables seemed to be affecting Joey's behavior:

1. Joey's self-injury increases and task performance decreases with extremely high (i.e., increased noise level and commotion, dis-

tracting sensory properties) and extremely low (i.e., "down times") levels of stimulation present in his surroundings.
2. Increased predictability in Joey's environment (i.e., degree of preparation for transitions between settings and activities) may reduce the occurrence of self-injury.
3. Joey's self-injury increases when specific characteristics of tasks are present, including increased length or difficulty and inconsistent pacing of instructions.
4. The proximity of adults and the degree to which rapport has been established may reduce Joey's rate of self-injury and increase his independent performance in activities.
5. Joey's self-injury meets multiple social functions, including requesting attention and physical contact from adults; initiating activities; indicating hunger, thirst, or discomfort; and attempting to avoid task conditions, for which he lacks communicative alternatives that are discernible to adults.

Certain ecological aspects of Joey's surroundings appeared to be contributing to his behavior. First, a great deal of noise, commotion, or inconsistent movements appeared to exacerbate Joey's self-injury and interfere with his ability to concentrate on tasks. In contrast, Joey also engaged in self-injury when the level of stimulation was extremely low. When he had access to toys or magazines during these solitary periods, his self-injury was reduced. These observations suggest that some self-injury was serving a self-regulatory function. This speculation may be further supported by observations that the restraint devices seemed to be reinforcing; for example, he would occasionally reach for his protective equipment and resist their removal.

Second, certain routines or breakdowns in routines seemed to be problematic. Joey's self-injury appeared highest during transitions between activities, particularly when those transitions occurred unexpectedly. He also seemed to have difficulty when he was aware that an expected transition did not occur and he was required to wait. When adults used objects and/or verbal reminders to signal the promise of upcoming events, his self-injury often subsided.

Third, there were task characteristics that appeared to be related to Joey's self-injury and engagement. There appeared to be low expectations for his independence in all environments. People assumed that Joey could not or would not perform most activities; therefore, he was restricted to a limited range of tasks. Yet on some occasions when the activities were designed in particular ways, he exhibited superior performance when higher levels were requested. Instructional and task characteristics that seemed to be most crucial were the level of difficulty, length, and pacing of instructions (Munk & Repp, 1994). Joey was challenged by the physical requirements of some tasks, particularly activities that required extensive fine motor control, upper-arm strength, and balance. When he was required to perform activities that had these characteristics, his self-injury seemed to be more prevalent. The pacing within activities also appeared to be a critical issue. When Joey was rushed to respond or when there were long hesitations during tasks, he would hit himself more intensely. He was able to remain actively engaged only for short periods of time. Joey's self-injury appeared to escalate as activities progressed, suggesting that self-injury served to communicate frustration and to terminate tasks.

Fourth, Joey was drawn to particular adults, and when these adults were present, Joey appeared to want them close to him. When they moved away or stopped interacting with him, Joey would hit himself intensely. Joey also performed more independently when working with individuals with whom he apparently had rapport. His most positive relationships seemed to be with people who talked to him and showed a great deal of affection. These were individuals who knew Joey well and were capable of anticipating and responding to his needs.

Finally, depending on the circumstances and Joey's current needs, his behavior appeared to have multiple communicative functions. These included gaining attention and physical contact from adults, gaining access to tangible reinforcers, and escaping conditions that he found to be highly demanding or unstimulating. When Joey engaged in self-injury, there was a great deal of inconsistency in how the adults in his life

responded. In some cases, staff and family members provided immediate attention. In others, they accepted his behavior as a cue to change or to terminate the activity. In still other cases, the adults simply ignored him. The attention and physical contact required to block his self-injury, and the environmental changes, whether contingent on self-injury or not, often seemed to be reinforcing. Joey had very few ways, other than self-injury, to express his needs and gain access to these types of reinforcement.

Roland

The assessment process for Roland was much easier than it was for Joey. Roland's destructive behaviors, although very serious, occurred at a much lower rate, and they were easy to detect in his typical environments. In addition, there were fewer professionals involved in Roland's support (especially in the residential program), and the team members communicated more effectively, reducing the time required to obtain and integrate their perspectives. Finally, the support providers had the knowledge and resources to collect their own data and to analyze patterns with minimal support from members of the university staff.

Roland's interviews were conducted with his parents, the couple who managed the group home, and the special education coordinator. As new team members (e.g., the teacher) joined the process, their perceptions also were solicited and, when appropriate, incorporated into Roland's support plan. Roland's parents were interviewed in the context of a discussion focused around the major questions of interest (e.g., Why does he engage in the behavior? What do the behaviors help him to get or to avoid? What relevant communication skills does he have, and what does he need to learn?). During this discussion, Roland's family provided extensive historical detail that was useful in constructing hypotheses.

Roland's teacher maintained data that correlated with her daily schedule so that she could analyze patterns of behavior within and across activities. She also recorded antecedent-behavior-consequence (A-B-C) data describing the specific conditions and consequences that surrounded incidents of Roland's serious problem behavior. She later included a communication log (e.g., to document when Roland initiated requests) and data sheets to track the occurrence of developing academic, leisure, and self-care skills. The group home providers kept frequency data on Roland's problem behavior (e.g., aggression, running, fecal play). At a later point, they added an activity log to record skills that were being taught to Roland at home. In addition, university program staff observed Roland's behavior in both environments at least weekly during the first 2 months, with observations gradually diminishing in frequency thereafter. The observations ranged from 30 minutes to 3 hours.

At the outset, Roland's serious aggression was occurring daily at the group home and several times per day at school. In addition, he periodically hit himself, threw food, smeared feces, disrobed, and ran out of the building or area. Although there was consistent one-to-one supervision and varied activities in both environments, the data showed that certain events were likely to be precipitating Roland's aggression and disruptive behavior. Roland appeared to have great difficulty when transitions and interruptions occurred in the environment. The lack of consistent routines and parameters within and across environments was troublesome. His aggression and running seemed to be more prevalent when it was unclear what was coming next, when there were rapid changes in routines, when his options were unclear, and when he had to wait for prolonged periods.

His curriculum also seemed to lack predictability and consistency. From Roland's perspective, some of the tasks that he was asked to perform had no clear relevance or meaning. For example, as part of a vocabulary lesson, he was required to label things that he was not using or even observing in his surroundings (e.g., naming colors and types of vehicles). In contrast, Roland performed better when he could see the product of his work (e.g., Dunlap, Foster-Johnson, Clarke, Kern, & Childs, 1995). He did best when the tasks involved physical manipulations, were defined in terms of discrete steps, and had obvious and relevant outcomes. In addition, Roland seemed to require time to process and respond to adult

directives. When staff issued several requests simultaneously, he often became aggressive. Roland also was likely to become disruptive or aggressive during unpleasant tasks (Foster-Johnson, Ferro, & Dunlap, 1994) and when preferred items or attention was withheld. His aggression served obvious communicative functions, and aggression occurred because he lacked an equally effective and efficient alternative. Although he was engaged in a process of FC, the validity of this form of expression for Roland was in doubt. Even if the FC were accurate, it was not sufficiently accessible for spontaneous requests in all circumstances.

The assessments for Roland yielded strong hypotheses that, in sum, indicated that his aggression and disruptive behavior were functionally related to challenges and confusion present in his environment and served as his most powerful means of controlling the environment and, especially, escaping unpleasant task circumstances. Following are the hypotheses that were developed for Roland:

1. Aggression occurs most frequently during unsignaled transitions (e.g., abrupt changes, deviations in routine) between activities and environments.
2. Aggression occurs in response to being told "no" or to wait, particularly when Roland has no clear understanding of when the items or activities that he is requesting will become accessible to him.
3. Roland becomes aggressive when the complexity of task demands is too great and the expectations for performance are not made clear to him.
4. Aggression is less likely to occur when Roland is given time (a few seconds) to respond to instructions before repeating the instruction or guiding him through the activity.
5. Roland becomes aggressive when he wants access to certain activities or people and cannot communicate these needs.
6. Roland becomes aggressive when he finds a task, activity, or situation to be aversive (because of a high rate of instructions, unclear expectations, or prolonged engagement in the same activity) because his be-

havior results in escape or avoidance of these circumstances.

BUILDING A SUPPORT PLAN

Comprehensive support plans were developed on the basis of the information obtained during the assessment process for each of the children. The plans reflected an integration of the observations and recommendations of team members and the data obtained through direct observation. The strategies included in the plans were designed to be realistic and to fit within the context of the resources available in each environment (Albin, Lucyshyn, Horner, & Flannery, 1996). While providing consistency in the approaches across environments, the plans allowed flexibility in their application across people and environments.

Comprehensive behavioral support plans incorporate multiple components (Berkman & Meyer, 1988; Dunlap, Ferro, & dePerczel, 1994; Horner et al., 1990). In contrast to traditional, single-procedure strategies, positive behavioral support includes environmental and curricular changes, goals and strategies for building useful skills, methods for responding to the children's problem behavior, generalization and maintenance procedures, and systems for the ongoing monitoring of the children's progress. Modifications to the physical and social environment and in schedules of activities and curriculum are generated by identifying the setting events and antecedent stimuli that precipitate relevant behaviors (Eno-Hieneman, Dunlap, & Reed, 1995; Halle & Spradlin, 1993). When such antecedent and contextual variables are identified, they can be entered into a support plan by increasing the presence of stimuli that are associated with desirable behaviors and removing or ameliorating stimuli that are associated with problems (Dunlap & Kern, 1993).

Comprehensive behavioral support plans also include strategies for the adults to prompt and reinforce skills in the children's behavioral repertoire, as well as methods for teaching more adaptive skills (Carr et al., 1994; Durand, 1990; LaVigna, Willis, & Donnellan, 1990). Providing effective and efficient replacement skills for the

problem behavior allows the children to adapt to their environmental circumstances in more productive ways. This approach often involves modifying curricula to include more functional skills. The behavioral support plans also are designed to promote effective use of consequences based on the hypothesized communicative functions of the children's behaviors (Carr & Durand, 1985; Carr et al., 1994; Donnellan, Mirenda, Mesaros, & Fassbender, 1984; Durand & Carr, 1988). The plans should include the most positive and natural contingencies for intervening with problem behavior and for prompting appropriate replacement skills (e.g., choice making). The reinforcers that appear to be maintaining the child's behaviors should be given contingent on more appropriate behavior and withheld in the presence of problem behavior.

Finally, comprehensive support plans include mechanisms to build generalization and maintenance of skills (Dunlap, 1993; Horner, Dunlap, & Koegel, 1988). This involves goals for teaching self-management skills and implementing the plan across contexts. It may also add procedures to facilitate interaction and support of the team. Sustaining the team is likely to ensure that ongoing communication among the team members occurs and that the interventions are monitored and revised as needed.

Behavioral Support Plans for Joey and Roland

Behavioral support plans for Joey and Roland were developed primarily from the hypotheses generated about their behavior. In addition, other elements were incorporated (e.g., techniques for establishing communicative alternatives [Carr et al., 1994; Durand, 1990]) because they enhanced the quality of interaction and improved supports in ways that were expected to add to the children's quality of life and development. The plans were constructed in a team context, and staff in the different environments adapted the recommended strategies to their own circumstances. The authors' program, in association with the team members, offered training on implementation of intervention components, including techniques for establishing communicative alternatives (Carr et al., 1994; Durand, 1990).

Joey

Joey's plan included environmental modifications that would help regulate Joey's sensory environment in response to his needs. These changes involved 1) reducing noise level, commotion, and extraneous stimuli in high-demand circumstances and 2) enhancing the sensory properties inherent within low-demand environments. For example, it was recommended that Joey be encouraged to sit on the periphery of groups, rather than in the middle, to reduce the amount of commotion to which he was exposed. Also, he was provided with an assortment of materials with which he could interact during "down times."

The predictability of Joey's environment was enhanced by providing explanations of upcoming events and pairing these explanations with object cues. His family initiated each outing by describing their agenda for the day. The staff at the residence were encouraged to warn Joey about doctor visits or changes in staff, and his school staff maintained a picture schedule that allowed Joey to anticipate the sequencing of major daily activities. This preparation was particularly important for Joey when his regular routines were disrupted or when he was required to wait for any period of time.

The team's occupational therapists noted that Joey had particular needs in mobility, strength, and balance that seemed to be related to his level of independence in activities and to his rate of self-injury. The occupational therapists taught other members how to design activities that could be performed with regard to his physiological limitations. Joey's support plan included certain modifications in the presentation of instructional sessions. The staff who worked with him were encouraged to limit activities, when possible, to no more than a few minutes. In addition, the team suggested adjusting their pacing of prompts and physical guidance in response to Joey's rate of engagement, rather than forcing his compliance. Staff also were taught to provide breaks or changes when Joey signaled a request (initially by whining or pushing materials).

Joey's support plan also included an emphasis on building rapport with adults. Prior to initiating tasks and during leisure times, the sup-

port providers interacted with Joey in a positive, demand-free context (Carr et al., 1994). During these times, they engaged in Joey's favorite activities, allowing him to take the lead. New staff at the facility and school were given the opportunity to get to know Joey prior to working with him. Although it may have been preferable to restrict the staff who worked with Joey to those who had previously developed a good rapport, this was not completely feasible within the constraints of scheduling and staffing patterns.

Measures were taken to make staff more aware of Joey's communicative repertoire of gestures and expressions and to encourage more standardized forms of communication. His team developed a gesture dictionary that helped staff to interpret and to respond to his whining, pushing, and reaching (Beukelman & Mirenda, 1998). For example, Joey had a little dance that indicated that he wanted to interact with adults. When adults saw this dance, they were encouraged to prompt Joey to touch their arm, thereby initiating contact. Although Joey had access to picture communication symbols and they made sense within the context of routines, he did not use them to express his immediate needs. A goal of the plan was to expand his communication options by interpreting his behavior as communication, then substituting more formalized (and easily interpreted) gestures or pictures.

Both Joey's school and residential programs emphasized and promoted skills needed for independence in self-care and daily living; however, implementing the support plan required changes to the school and residential programs in which he participated. At school, additional toys were purchased and the classroom was adapted in a variety of ways to encourage independence in performing activities. Such modifications were more difficult for the residential program. For example, to allow Joey to take brief naps in the afternoon or to exit the dining area after meals, typical routines and staff assignments had to be modified. For Joey's school, such adaptations were more feasible and, therefore, more readily implemented.

Roland

Because Roland appeared to have difficulty with unsignaled transitions, his support providers at the school and residence developed picture schedules that listed his daily activities (e.g., meals, academic tasks, self-care routines, leisure activities, chores) in temporal sequence. Between each activity, Roland was prompted to go to his schedule, obtain the relevant picture, complete the activity, and then discard the picture in a box next to his schedule. The schedule was referred to and altered when changes had to be made in his routines. In addition, the staff and his family began to use reminders, or safety signals (O'Neill & Reichle, 1993), to cue Roland that changes were coming (e.g., "You're almost done here, and then we'll do ____") and to indicate how long he would have to wait (e.g., for items that he wanted, for attention from preferred adults). As Roland became more consistent with his schedule, the staff added clock faces to the schedule and began teaching him that when the clock face matched the actual time, he would be allowed to do the activity depicted in the picture.

Roland's support providers performed a major overhaul with regard to his education goals at school and in the residence to enhance the functional value of activities and to clarify the expectations within the activities. Both programs instituted more activities involving community-based instruction, such as trips to the post office, local restaurants, and softball games. These activities had more meaningful outcomes for Roland, and they had clearer performance criteria. Roland also was given additional responsibility in caring for himself and his environment, especially at the group home. The staff required Roland to complete chores, clean up after meals, and perform his self-care routines more independently. The goals for each of these activities were made explicit by sequencing the skills consistently and providing visible outcomes (e.g., having him follow a regular sequence for clearing his place setting). In addition, his academic tasks were modified to reduce unnecessary repetition.

Roland's plan, similar to Joey's, had a strong emphasis on communicative alternatives to problem behavior. In conjunction with Roland's picture activity schedules, he was given opportunities to make choices within his schedule (e.g., pictures of staff so that he could select with whom to work) and a separate but accessible choice menu that included all of his favorite activities, toys, and people. Initially, the choice menu was restricted to items that were immediately available. When Roland indicated that he wanted something through reaching, grunting, or minor problem behaviors, the staff were asked to prompt him to select something from the choice menu or to use another mode of communication. He also was taught a BREAK sign that could be used to remove him from an unpleasant circumstance. When staff saw that he was becoming anxious (e.g., looking around, increasing activity) or had been engaged in the same activity for a prolonged period, they modeled this sign and, if he repeated it, allowed him to exit the situation. His picture cards, available gestures, FC, and vocal expressions all were integrated into a multimodal system of communication. These communication-based measures were designed to replace the use of punitive consequences. Therefore, restrictive procedures such as overcorrection and excessive use of manual guidance were eliminated from his intervention program.

Explicit mechanisms for generalizing and maintaining Roland's skills were included within his plan. He was encouraged to practice his skills, particularly his communicative alternatives to challenging behavior, across environments. For example, he often had difficulty on the softball field when required to play with other children. The group home staff began prompting him to use his BREAK sign rather than aggression to exit the field. He also was taught to tolerate gradually increasing periods of waiting in naturally occurring circumstances across environments.

In addition to the issues related directly to the hypotheses, other supports were included in Roland's plan. Roland benefited from consistency in his physical environment and the availability of clear cues for behavioral expectations. His teacher and, later, the residential staff identified zones related to specific types of activities so that Roland would come to recognize that one set of expectations was in place for a particular area of the classroom but that expectations were quite different for other areas. In the classroom, particular areas were off limits to students, whereas others were intended for group interaction and free access to materials. In this way, Roland could anticipate more successfully the operative rules of conduct. The team believed that in some circumstances Roland was running from the classroom not to avoid activities but rather because he was curious about aspects of his surroundings. Therefore, he was given regularly scheduled opportunities to walk around campus and explore his surroundings and, in essence, to orient himself to the school grounds.

Initially, there was a significant discrepancy in the level of expectations and structure for Roland between the residence and the school. In contrast to the regimen of activities at the school, the group homeowners wanted to maintain a relaxed, "homey" milieu. Therefore, Roland's support plan had to be adjusted based on the characteristics of each environment and the characteristics of the support providers in his home, community, and school environments. Although all of Roland's support providers embraced similar principles (e.g., need to enhance predictability, communication-based intervention) and sought to improve the consistency among them, the actual applications of the support plan differed across contexts. For example, whereas the school activity schedule was based on a 15- to 30-minute time frame, chores at the group home were interspersed across longer periods. The data systems used to monitor Roland's progress and the specific strategies and activities were selected on the basis of support provider preference as well as by the nature of the environments in which Roland participated.

INITIAL OUTCOMES AND ONGOING SUPPORT

The support teams for Joey and Roland were assembled less than 1 year prior to the writing of this chapter. The process of comprehensive behavioral support in complex community environments involves many considerations, and it must be viewed as an ongoing endeavor. Substantial behavior change and lifestyle enhancement are not achieved simply; their accomplishment requires diligence, tenacity, and, often, patience. Although some procedures (e.g., punishment, stimulus change) can produce rapid decreases in the rate of problem behavior in particular environments, these reductions are nei-

ther enduring nor generalized. Comprehensive behavioral support is a longitudinal enterprise in which assessment and intervention are ongoing, interactive processes and in which support teams evolve and change membership, but it is hoped that they retain their focus and commitment.

The outcomes for Joey and Roland—and other children who share their circumstances—need to be viewed from a broad perspective. Important objectives include decreases in the rates of problem behavior and increases in the rates of targeted skills as well as enhancements in the child's relationships; increased access to preferred activities; and numerous manifestations of emotional, cognitive, social, and physical development.

The support plans were introduced in various stages in the children's different environments. For both children, intervention strategies were introduced earlier and easier in the school environments. The residential programs have taken somewhat longer to institute the changes fully. Substantial efforts have now occurred in all contexts. At the time of this writing, the teams for Joey and Roland are continuing the process of implementing components of their respective plans, monitoring initial progress (and lack of progress), analyzing new circumstances, and adding and modifying goals and strategies. This status can be expected to continue for some time. Nevertheless, initial outcomes can be summarized for both boys.

Joey

The initial outcomes for Joey have been inconsistent, with some positive indications and some disappointments. First, there were favorable trends in the percentage of time that Joey was attentive to and engaged in scheduled activities. The data collected at school indicated an increase in Joey's engagement in daily activities from about 50% to more than 90% of the intervals during the first 5 months of assessment and intervention. Figure 1 depicts these data collected at school by Joey's teacher. The increase in daily activity engagement was considered an important gain because low levels of engagement had been implicated in Joey's relatively slow pace of skill development.

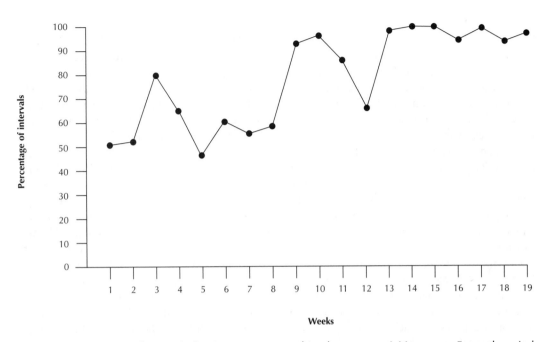

Figure 1. Percentage of intervals that Joey was engaged in classroom activities over a 5-month period spanning the assessment and initial intervention. Engagement refers to the average number of intervals in which Joey manipulated materials associated with task or leisure activities.

Another desirable change occurred in the amount of time that Joey participated in activities without wearing his protective equipment. Following intervention, the equipment was removed almost constantly at school and for steadily increasing periods at home and in the residential program. This trend seemed to be related to the adults' ability to block and redirect his self-injurious behavior. Furthermore, with the behavioral support plan in place, Joey's family resumed home visits on the weekend, including overnight stays (which had been stopped because of the severity of his self-injury). The data on Joey's self-injurious behavior, however, have not reflected noticeable improvements. The evidence suggests that his self-hitting has continued at the same rate as before the support plan was initiated. Reports on the intensity of his hitting do not indicate improvements either.

The cohesiveness and synergy of Joey's support team did not develop to the full extent that the program had hoped. Because of internal conflicts and problems in communication, the team decided to discontinue meetings, planning to regroup at a later point. The individual members continued support efforts within their separate programs, but the attempts to coordinate and participate in joint problem solving declined. Despite these disappointments, it is important to note that the team process *did* appear to produce some favorable results in regard to attitudes toward Joey and toward the whole issue of behavioral support. Interviews conducted with Joey's primary support providers after 3 months of involvement reflected higher expectations for progress, greater (more sensitive) recognition of Joey's subtle communication, and an acknowledgment of the importance of collaboration. Joey's parents also reported greater expectations for Joey's independence in self-care routines around their home and greater optimism with regard to his treatment.

Roland

In contrast to Joey's outcomes, in which problem behaviors did not show an initial or rapid decline, the early outcomes for Roland were highly encouraging, and they continue to show very positive trends. Roland's participation in activities both at school and in the community improved such that he rarely declined to participate. His escape-motivated disruptive behavior was reduced sharply in these circumstances, and he even began to refrain from using his legitimate sign to request a break. At this writing, Roland was engaging in the full range of social, functional, and academic skills required of him at school (activities included on his picture schedule), participating at church and in softball games, and performing chores at the residence. His aggression has decreased to near zero in all environments. For example, Figure 2 depicts Roland's rate of aggressive behavior and running out of the classroom. The baseline data were from the first 3 weeks with his new teacher.

After a short period, Roland's aggression escalated to levels similar to those experienced by Roland's previous teaching staff. Once the staff initiated the BREAK sign, his aggression and running diminished substantially, and they gradually dropped to near-zero levels after imple-

mentation of his picture schedule. His aggression has decreased to near zero in all environments.

When Roland does have an incident of hitting, it is much milder in severity and the staff tend to interpret it as his way of saying no. The staff at both home and school have become more competent at anticipating problems and promoting communication as a productive alternative to aggression, and they have eliminated all punitive measures to control his behavior. Roland's range of communication options and consistency in utilizing these options also have improved. He is beginning to request breaks or items from his choice menu without being prompted. He also has been included in a classroom context with peers again. At the end of the school year, two students had been placed back in the classroom, and Roland is scheduled soon to be in a class with six other children. Although his history of injuring other people has been an obstacle to inclusion, he is participating in a school program with peer tutors without disabilities, and he is included in grade-level field trips and assemblies.

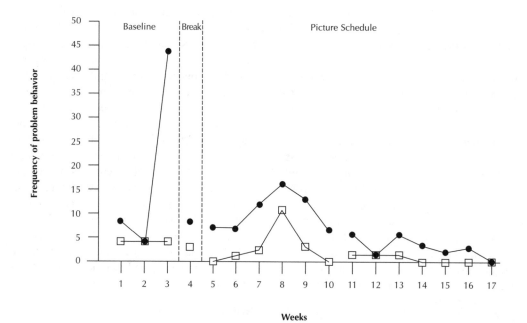

Figure 2. Frequency of Roland's problem behaviors per week during a 3-week baseline period, after initiation of the BREAK sign, and then following implementation of the picture schedule. Problem behaviors include aggression (hitting, kicking, head butting, biting) toward others and exiting the classroom or designated area without permission, labeled "running." (–●– = aggression, –⊟– = running.)

The team continues to meet, although less frequently than during the initial assessment and intervention. During monthly meetings, members share stories of frustration and success and suggest strategies to enhance the behavioral support plan. Roland was in his last year of elementary school during the assessment and intervention process. An important objective for the upcoming year was to make a smooth transition to middle school. Roland's team planned this transition carefully and integrated him gradually into his new environment, which ensured his success.

STATUS AND FUTURE CONSIDERATIONS

Joey and Roland continue to live in their community-based residential programs, participate with their families, attend local schools, and engage in a variety of community activities. Their families, educators, and caregivers report that the children are progressing and that their status in the community is stable. For both children, this represents a great improvement over their previous situations, which were dominated by increasing hazardous, destructive behaviors and impending danger of expulsion from their residential and/or school placements.

Although the circumstances for the two children had many similarities, the vicissitudes of the support process and the quality of the initial outcomes had some differences. Joey's case presented some very severe challenges that were not experienced as deeply by Roland. For example, Joey's physiological status presented a substantial set of questions and influences that could not be resolved adequately by medical diagnosis or intervention. Joey experienced a variety of illnesses and allergies, and he experienced physical disabilities that impeded his ability to gain access to and benefit from his environment. His physiological uncertainty, compounded by frequent changes in medications, interfered with his team's efforts to detect patterns of environmental influence. It is likely that the assessment process was complicated further by the ongoing interactions of multiple functions governing the occurrence of self-injury (e.g., Guess & Carr, 1991). Although the functions of Roland's aggression and other disruptive behaviors were intricate, they seemed to be much more accessible than Joey's.

Another difference was in the team composition and operations. Joey's team was larger (yet it did not include some key caregivers) and never seemed to develop an integrated perspective from which to operate. Although the team was united in its purpose, there were discrepancies in philosophy among some of the team members. Some members had difficulty using shared decision making and extending their roles. There were occasional instances in which one member would make a unilateral decision without consulting the others. As the process was drawn out by Joey's medical status and logistical problems, members of the team became frustrated. They seemed to want from the members of the university program clear and rapid prescriptions to use in response to Joey's behavior, an expectation that was not realistic given the complexity of his needs and environmental circumstances. The residential providers and teacher are working hard to overcome certain logistical barriers to the implementation of the support plan. Although the suggested interventions may be appropriate for Joey's needs, making them work in large systems is difficult, even for people who are committed to making the changes. Such barriers are likely to influence the efficacy of Joey's behavioral support plan now and in the future.

The team process worked very well for Roland. Even though the team began with histories of contentious interactions, the relationships among his family, the school, and the residential program have become productive and positive. Although discrepancies of opinion still emerge, they are dealt with more tactfully and constructively. The members of Roland's team appear to have recognized that consensus building strengthens rather than diminishes the role of individuals. All key members of Roland's team committed time and energy to the process, and their perseverance appears to have been rewarded.

For Joey and Roland to show continued progress, their current and future support teams will need to demonstrate vigilance and a continuous drive to improve the status of the children's surroundings. Both children have long histories of severe behavioral challenges. Such challenges require a concerted program of support over an extended time span, and they need to be addressed comprehensively. Similar to all other people, Joey and Roland will experience good days and bad days, and the course of their two lives will be uniquely theirs, but the quality of their lives will depend, to some extent, on the caliber of support that committed and caring providers are able to deliver in the complex environments that they inhabit.

CONCLUSION

This chapter discussed the process of team building, assessment, and intervention for two children who exhibited significant disabilities and very serious problem behaviors. The chapter illustrated some of the complications that affect implementation of positive behavioral support in complex community environments.

The two cases raise numerous questions about how to deliver behavioral support most effectively. Many of the most pressing questions seem to be related to the logistics of and necessary ingredients in developing coordinated and consistent supports. Almost no research has looked at these issues. However, the authors are confident that efficacy and desirable outcomes can be achieved if inclusive communities continue to be encouraged and increasingly solid teams and partnerships are developed on behalf of families and children with disabilities.

REFERENCES

Albin, R.W., Lucyshyn, J.M., Horner, R.H., & Flannery, K.B. (1996). Contextual fit for behavioral support plans: A model for "goodness of fit." In L.K. Koegel, R.L. Koegel, & G. Dunlap (Eds.), *Positive behavioral support: Including people with difficult behavior in the community* (pp. 81–98). Baltimore: Paul H. Brookes Publishing Co.

Berkman, K., & Meyer, L.H. (1988). Alternative strategies and multiple outcomes in the remediation of severe self-injury: Going "all out" nonaversively. *Journal of The Association for Persons with Severe Handicaps, 13,* 76–86.

Beukelman, D.R., & Mirenda, P. (1998). *Augmentative and alternative communication: Management of severe communication disorders in children and adults* (2nd ed.). Baltimore: Paul H. Brookes Publishing Co.

Bijou, S., Peterson, R., & Ault, M. (1968). A method to integrate descriptive and experimental field studies at the level of data and empirical concepts. *Journal of Applied Behavior Analysis, 18,* 111–126.

Biklen, D. (1990). Communication unbound: Autism and praxis. *Harvard Educational Review, 60,* 291–314.

Briggs, M. (1991). Team development: Decision-making for early intervention. *The Transdisciplinary Journal, 1,* 1–9.

Carr, E.G., & Durand, V.M. (1985). Reducing behavior problems through functional communication training. *Journal of Applied Behavior Analysis, 11,* 459–501.

Carr, E.G., Levin, L., McConnachie, G., Carlson, J.I., Kemp, D.C., & Smith, C.E. (1994). *Communication-based intervention for problem behavior: A user's guide for producing positive change.* Baltimore: Paul H. Brookes Publishing Co.

Donnellan, A., Mirenda, P., Mesaros, R., & Fassbender, L. (1984). Analyzing the communicative functions of aberrant behavior. *Journal of The Association for Persons with Severe Handicaps, 9,* 201–212.

Dunlap, G. (1993). Promoting generalization: Current status and functional considerations. In R. Van Houten & S. Axelrod (Eds.), *Behavior analysis and treatment* (pp. 269–296). New York: Plenum.

Dunlap, G., Ferro, J., & dePerczel, M. (1994). Nonaversive behavioral intervention in the community. In E. Cipani & F. Spooner (Eds.), *Curricular and instructional approaches for persons with severe handicaps* (pp. 117–146). Needham Heights, MA: Allyn & Bacon.

Dunlap, G., Foster-Johnson, L., Clarke, S., Kern, L., & Childs, K.E. (1995). Modifying activities to produce functional outcomes: Effects on the disruptive behaviors of students with disabilities. *Journal of The Association for Persons with Severe Handicaps, 20,* 248–258.

Dunlap, G., & Fox, L. (1996). Early intervention and serious problem behaviors: A comprehensive approach. In L.K. Koegel, R.L. Koegel, & G. Dunlap (Eds.), *Positive behavioral support: Including people with difficult behavior in the community* (pp. 31–50). Baltimore: Paul H. Brookes Publishing Co.

Dunlap, G., & Kern, L. (1993). Assessment and intervention for children within the instructional curriculum. In J. Reichle & D.P. Wacker (Eds.), *Communication and language intervention series: Vol. 3. Communicative alternatives to challenging behavior: Integrating functional assessment and intervention strategies* (pp. 177–203). Baltimore: Paul H. Brookes Publishing Co.

Dunlap, G., & Kern, L. (1996). Modifying instructional activities to promote desirable behavior: A conceptual and practical framework. *School Psychology Quarterly, 11,* 297–312.

Dunlap, G., Kern-Dunlap, L., Clarke, S., & Robbins, F. (1991). Functional assessment, curricular revision, and severe behavior problems. *Journal of Applied Behavior Analysis, 24,* 387–397.

Durand, V.M. (1990). *Severe behavior problems: A functional communication approach.* New York: Guilford Press.

Durand, V.M., & Carr, E.G. (1988). Functional communication training to reduce challenging behavior: Maintenance and application in new settings. *Journal of Applied Behavior Analysis, 21,* 251–264.

Eno-Hieneman, M., Dunlap, G., & Reed, M. (1995). Predictability, structure, and personal control. *Network, 4,* 23–29.

Evans, I.M., & Meyer, L.H. (1985). *An educative approach to behavior problems: A practical decision model for interventions with severely handicapped learners.* Baltimore: Paul H. Brookes Publishing Co.

Foster-Johnson, L., & Dunlap, G. (1993). Using functional assessment to develop effective, individualized interventions for challenging behaviors. *Teaching Exceptional Children, 25*(3), 44–50.

Foster-Johnson, L., Ferro, J., & Dunlap, G. (1994). Preferred curricular activities and reduced problem behaviors in students with intellectual disabilities. *Journal of Applied Behavior Analysis, 27,* 493–504.

Guess, D., & Carr, E.G. (1991). Emergence and maintenance of stereotypy and self-injury. *American Journal of Mental Retardation, 96,* 335–344.

Halle, J.W., & Spradlin, J.E. (1993). Identifying stimulus control of challenging behavior: Extending the analysis. In J. Reichle & D.P. Wacker (Eds.), *Communication and language intervention series: Vol. 3. Communicative alternatives to challenging behavior: Integrating functional assessment and intervention strategies* (pp. 83–109). Baltimore: Paul H. Brookes Publishing Co.

Horner, R.H., Dunlap, G., & Koegel, R.L. (Eds.). (1988). *Generalization and maintenance: Lifestyle changes in applied settings.* Baltimore: Paul H. Brookes Publishing Co.

Horner, R., Dunlap, G., Koegel, R., Carr, E., Sailor, W., Anderson, J., Albin, R.W., & O'Neill, R. (1990). Toward a technology of "nonaversive" behavioral support. *Journal of The Association for Persons with Severe Handicaps, 15,* 125–132.

Horner, R., Sprague, J., & Flannery, B. (1993). Building functional curriculum for students with severe intellectual disabilities and severe problem behaviors. In R. Van Houton & S. Axelrod (Eds.), *Behavior analysis and treatment* (pp. 47–71). New York: Plenum.

Iwata, B., Dorsey, M., Slifer, K., Bauman, K., & Richman, G. (1994). Toward a functional analysis of self-injury. *Journal of Applied Behavior Analysis, 27,* 197–209.

Iwata, B.A., Vollmer, T.R., & Zarcone, J.R. (1990). The experimental (functional) analysis of behavior disorders: Methodology, applications, and limitations. In A.C. Repp & N.N. Singh (Eds.), *Perspectives on the use of nonaversive and aversive interventions for persons with developmental disabilities* (pp. 301–330). Sycamore, IL: Sycamore Press.

Kern, L., & Dunlap, G. (1999). Assessment-based interventions for children with emotional and behavioral disorders. In A.C. Repp & R.H. Horner (Eds.), *Functional analysis of problem behavior: From effective assessment to effective support.* Pacific Grove, CA: Brooks/Cole.

Kern, L., Dunlap, G., Clarke, S., & Childs, K. (1994). Student assisted functional assessment interview. *Diagnostique, 19,* 29–39.

Kincaid, D. (1996). Person-centered planning. In L.K. Koegel, R.L. Koegel, & G. Dunlap (Eds.), *Positive behavioral support: Including people with difficult behavior in the community* (pp. 439–466). Baltimore: Paul H. Brookes Publishing Co.

Koegel, L.K., Koegel, R.L., & Dunlap, G. (Eds.). (1996). *Positive behavioral support: Including people with difficult behavior in the community.* Baltimore: Paul H. Brookes Publishing Co.

LaVigna, G., Willis, G., & Donnellan, A. (1990). The role of positive programming in behavioral treatment. In E. Cipani (Ed.), The treatment of severe behavior disorders: Behavior analysis approaches. *Monographs of the American Association on Mental Retardation, 12,* 59–83.

Meyer, L.H., & Evans, I.M. (1989). *Nonaversive intervention for behavior problems: A manual for home and community.* Baltimore: Paul H. Brookes Publishing Co.

Meyer, L.H., & Evans, I.M. (1993). Science and practice in behavioral intervention: Meaningful outcomes, research validity, and usable knowledge. *Journal of The Association for Persons with Severe Handicaps, 18,* 224–234.

Munk, D.D., & Repp, A.C. (1994). The relationship between instructional variables and problem behavior: A review. *Exceptional Children, 60,* 390–401.

O'Neill, R., Horner, R., Albin, R., Storey, K., & Sprague, J. (1990). *Functional analysis of problem behavior: A practical assessment guide.* Sycamore, IL: Sycamore Publishing.

O'Neill, R., & Reichle, J. (1993). Addressing socially motivated challenging behaviors by establishing communicative alternatives: Basics of a general-case approach. In J. Reichle & D.P. Wacker (Eds.), *Communication and language intervention series: Vol. 3. Communicative alternatives to challenging behavior: Integrating functional assessment and intervention strategies* (pp. 205–235). Baltimore: Paul H. Brookes Publishing Co.

Parker, G. (1990). *Team players and teamwork.* San Francisco: Jossey-Bass.

Rainforth, B., York, J., & Macdonald, C. (with Salisbury, C., & Dunn, W.). (1992). *Collaborative teams for students with severe disabilities: Integrating therapy and educational services.* Baltimore: Paul H. Brookes Publishing Co.

Repp, A., Felce, D., & Barton, L. (1988). Basing the treatment of stereotypic and self-injurious behaviors on hypotheses of their causes. *Journal of Applied Behavior Analysis, 21,* 281–289.

Repp, A.C., & Horner, R.H. (1999). *Functional analysis of problem behavior: From effective assessment to effective support.* Pacific Grove, CA: Brooks/Cole.

Touchette, P., MacDonald, R., & Langer, S. (1985). A scatter plot for identifying stimulus control of problem behavior. *Journal of Applied Behavior Analysis, 18,* 343–351.

Turnbull, A., & Turnbull, R. (1990). A tale about lifestyle change: Comments on toward a technology of "nonaversive" behavioral support. *Journal of The Association for Persons with Severe Handicaps, 15,* 142–144.

Chapter 20

A Person-Centered Approach to Providing Support to an Adolescent with a History of Parental Abuse

Cynthia M. Anderson, Alisa B. Bahl, & Donald W. Kincaid

Behavior analysis has served to further the conceptualization and treatment of challenging behavior. Specifically, applied behavior analysis emphasizes the importance of considering not only the topography or form of a given behavior but also the function of that response—that is, the reason that the behavior is occurring. Behavior analysis also has provided effective techniques for reducing challenging behavior and increasing more appropriate behavior, and the efficacy of such techniques has been well established for such behaviors as self-injury (e.g., Coman & Houghton, 1991; Day, Rea, Schussler, Larsen, & Johnson, 1988; Iwata, Dorsey, Slifer, Bauman, & Richman, 1982; Iwata et al., 1994), aggression (e.g., Carr, Newsom, & Binkoff, 1980; Vollmer, Iwata, Smith, & Rodgers, 1992), disruption (e.g., Vollmer et al., 1992), and tantrums (e.g., Carr & Newsom, 1985). Building on this established research, new approaches, collectively termed *positive behavioral support,* have emerged. These approaches generally have a broader focus and use a wider variety of strategies than was typical within "traditional" behavioral approaches.

Behavior analytic approaches have focused on discrete responses, such as rate of swearing or latency to compliance. Although assessing such responses admittedly is important, these approaches often have neglected to consider more global "quality of life" issues, such as where a person lives, with whom a person lives, and how a person spends his or her time. In contrast, positive behavioral support recognizes the importance of examining all aspects of an individual's life, not just his or her challenging behavior. As was noted by Anderson, Russo, Dunlap, and Albin (1996), positive behavioral support programs focus on such outcomes as increasing an individual's skills and competencies, building more satisfying relationships with others, and increasing participation in community activities (see also Meyer & Evans, 1989).

A second distinction between traditional approaches and positive behavioral support concerns the intervention strategies used. Traditional approaches to behavior management typically emphasize the use of consequence-based procedures to reduce challenging behavior. Although such procedures may result in reductions in challenging behavior, these reductions often are not sustained or more severe behavior emerges (Meyer & Evans, 1989; Scotti, Evans, Meyer, & Walker, 1991). Although positive behavioral support does not rule out the use of consequences, interventions are based on the results of a functional analysis to determine the reason that behavior is occurring. The functional analysis leads to an intervention that focuses on

1. Rearranging situational variables to reduce the probability that a challenging behavior will occur
2. Teaching the individual new, more appropriate responses that serve the same function as the challenging behavior
3. Changing the consequences so that the challenging behavior is no longer being reinforced

Therefore, rather than emphasizing structural, consequence-based approaches, the emphasis is placed on making environmental changes and on teaching the individual new skills so that he or she can function more independently.

A final characteristic of traditional approaches to behavior management is that they often emphasize the role of an "expert" in determining what is best for a given individual. This person typically is charged with determining why a challenging behavior is occurring, as well as how to treat it. Although positive behavioral support recognizes the importance of including on a team individuals who specialize in certain areas (e.g., behavior analysis, occupational therapy) when their services might be required, professionals are not the center of the team. As increased emphasis has been placed on measuring more global issues, it has become apparent to some practitioners that the real "experts" often are the focus individual and his or her friends and family. These individuals are most likely to know what the focus individual likes and values or does not like or value and will be in a position to support the focus person in achieving meaningful outcomes, such as living in the community and participating in meaningful employment. This recognition has led to the development of techniques and practices

that encourage individuals to take leading roles in making decisions about their life. This approach (embedded within positive behavioral support) has been called *person-centered planning,* and it involves "not only a change in the philosophies and values about people . . . but . . . a range of new techniques for identifying and pursuing what a person wants and needs" (Kincaid, 1996, pp. 439–440). A variety of person-centered methodologies have been developed, including Life Style Planning (O'Brien, 1987; O'Brien & Lyle, 1987), Personal Profile and Futures Planning (Kincaid, 1996), Planning Alternative Tomorrows with Hope (PATH; Pearpoint, O'Brien, & Forest, 1995), and Personal Futures Planning (Mount, 1987; Mount & Zwernick, 1988). This chapter delineates the goals and characteristics of person-centered planning and illustrates the use of one person-centered methodology, PATH.

GOALS OF A PERSON-CENTERED APPROACH

Although a variety of person-centered approaches have been developed, they exhibit many similar goals. For example, most of these approaches use graphic techniques and include as part of the team the people who are important in the life of the focus person. Also, most person-centered approaches are committed to the following five essential goals or outcomes for the person's life (Kincaid, 1996).

First, person-centered approaches emphasize that the individual should be present and participating in community life. That is, the person not only should be living in the community with others but also should be able to participate in "normal" routines, such as going shopping, going out to eat, or taking a walk in the park.

The second goal is to help the individual gain and maintain satisfying relationships. Individuals who exhibit challenging behavior often have limited relationships with individuals beyond those who are paid to be with them. For example, an adolescent who frequently lies, skips school, and sets fires may have very few friends. His or her primary interactions (other than with immediate family members) are likely to be with teachers, administrators, or the police. Because satisfying relationships with others fulfill a number of important roles, such as providing peer models of appropriate behavior and increasing opportunities for reinforcement, person-centered approaches recognize the necessity of helping an individual acquire the skills needed to develop and maintain meaningful personal relationships with others.

The third goal is to help the individual express preferences and make choices in everyday life. Typically, individuals who work in human services assume the role of "expert" when working with people who exhibit challenging behavior. They may determine the goals and type of treatment, where a person should work and live, and with whom the person should associate. For example, school administrators working with an adolescent who often is truant may decide that the student should be placed in vocational classes rather than in college preparatory classes. This decision is likely to be made without consulting the adolescent to determine why he or she is skipping school, what the child wants to do after graduation, or which classes he or she prefers. In contrast, person-centered approaches emphasize providing opportunities for the individual to express preferences and emphasize the importance of hearing and respecting those choices.

The fourth goal is to ensure that the focus individual has opportunities to fulfill respected roles and to live with dignity. As with several of the previously mentioned goals, this is something that often is taken for granted by most of us in our daily lives but frequently is overlooked by those providing support to individuals with challenging behavior. Often, these individuals are forced into demeaning roles. For example, individuals with developmental disabilities who exhibit challenging behavior may be provided with ill-fitting clothing or "placed" in demeaning jobs. Person-centered approaches recognize that everyone can contribute something to the community and should be allowed to do so—with dignity.

The final goal of person-centered approaches is to help the individual continue to develop personal competencies; these approaches focus on helping the individual to develop new skills and areas of expertise. Rather than focus

exclusively on reducing challenging behavior, person-centered approaches emphasize providing the individual with opportunities to grow and develop and to control one's life and future (Meyer & Evans, 1989).

CHARACTERISTICS OF A PERSON-CENTERED APPROACH

In addition to specific goals or outcomes to be achieved, there are a number of characteristics that many person-centered approaches share. Each characteristic is related to at least one of the five essential goals.

One characteristic of person-centered planning approaches is that they *include and focus on the person.* In other words, these approaches are driven by the individual's needs and goals rather than by the goals of an agency or a professional. This can be difficult when the goals of the individual are different from those envisioned by others. For example, an adolescent may express the desire to become an automobile mechanic after graduating from high school. If his or her parents had hoped for their child to go to college and become a surgeon, then it may be difficult for them to accept their child's goal and help him or her achieve it.

Another characteristic of person-centered approaches is *respect.* Person-centered approaches recognize that the person has something valuable to contribute to society, and they focus on helping the individual achieve his or her potential. In addition to recognizing that the individual is a valued member of society, person-centered approaches recognize the importance of respecting a person's culture and heritage. For example, the first author recently worked with an adolescent who did not want to go to college upon graduating from high school. Further discussion with this individual and with his family revealed that nobody in his family or even in his town had ever gone to college and that they did not see any reason for education to continue beyond high school. Based on this information, several team members had to learn to respect cultural values that were different from their own and allow this adolescent to develop and work toward his own goals, not those of the team.

Person-centered approaches *encourage the focus individual to express choices,* and those choices must be respected by other team members. This is in contrast to more traditional approaches that focus on telling an individual what is best for him or her rather than asking the person what he or she prefers. For example, rather than tell an individual with disabilities that she should live in a group home with four other people, a person-centered approach would involve presenting the individual with several options (e.g., a group home, an apartment with one other person, living alone) and supporting the individual in choosing where she wanted to live.

Another characteristic of person-centered approaches concerns the focus of the intervention. When using a person-centered approach, *the focus is not on an individual's deficits or problems but rather on his or her strengths, abilities, and capacities.* Focusing on an individual's strengths and abilities provides the team with specific skills on which to build. For example, an individual who frequently loiters outside buildings and yells obscenities at passersby might be exhibiting such behaviors because he does not have a meaningful activity in which to engage and because such behavior often results in attention from others. However, this individual might also have good carpentry skills. One component of a treatment plan might involve helping the individual become involved with an organization that builds houses for homeless people. Such involvement likely would result in more attention (or more positive attention) from others than did yelling at passersby.

In addition to emphasizing the abilities of the individual, person-centered approaches emphasize the abilities of community and team members. For example, during a recent team meeting, it became evident that the focus individual was very interested in horses. Instead of stating that the individual could not be around horses because of her "bad temper," the team began to explore available options. One of the team members stated that she had a friend who had horses and who was looking for someone to help out at the farm in exchange for riding lessons. The team pursued this option, and the focus person began working at the farm and riding.

Person-centered approaches also are characterized by an *emphasis on gaining access to typical resources within the community.* These approaches focus on accomplishing goals that are considered valuable to the individual by using approaches that are acceptable and used by typical people in the community. As an example, instead of sending an individual with a disability to a "special school" in another district, a person-centered approach might focus on developing supports so that the individual can attend the school in his or her own community.

Another attribute of person-centered approaches is that they *create an environment where everyone involved is a learner.* Person-centered approaches recognize that the focus person and everyone who knows him or her all have something valuable to add to the process. Therefore, the "experts" are the focus individual and his or her family and friends. Often, this focus results in team members' learning valuable information about the focus person. To illustrate, group home staff who worked with a man with disabilities were surprised to learn that the man had been severely abused by several men when he was younger. This information had not been included in any of his reports and came out only when the team members (and especially his family) were discussing the man's history. As a result of this information, staff were able to understand better why the focus person did not like to be escorted to the bathroom by male staff and why he seemed happier when working with female staff. The team developed a support plan that included strategies that would allow the focus person to work primarily with female staff. Also, the team began to investigate ways in which the focus person might be able to participate in a support group that dealt with abuse issues.

Another characteristic of person-centered approaches is that they are *idiographic;* that is, they focus on the strengths and needs of that individual. In contrast, traditional approaches often provide very rigid, set supports for everyone, overlooking the fact that they are serving many different individuals with very different needs. For example, an agency may provide 10 hours of respite per week to all families of children with autism. The agency may specify that these respite hours can be used only between the hours of 3:00 P.M. and 7:00 P.M. In contrast, a person-centered approach would examine the needs of the family to determine when respite is needed. Perhaps one family needs respite only in the mornings when the parents are busy getting the older children ready for school, whereas another family needs respite all day every Saturday.

Most person-centered approaches can also be characterized as working toward a similar goal: *creating a positive future for the focus person.* This future should be possible and realistic, but it also must be the best that can be accomplished. These approaches do not accept mediocre outcomes or the status quo. Also, the focus is not simply on solving an immediate crisis; rather, person-centered planning seeks to affect all areas of a person's life so that the quality of his or her life can be improved.

In addition, person-centered approaches work to *empower the focus person and the team.* Person-centered approaches usually improve communication among team members and result in all members' working toward a common goal. Team members and the focus person typically begin to work actively toward changing their lives (and perhaps changing the system). As the process progresses, a focus person may take charge of his or her team and begin to plan his or her life. One focus person with whom we worked actually carried his plan with him wherever he went. When someone proposed some change in the plan or a new strategy, he would ask, "How does what you're saying help me get what is listed here?"

Finally, because person-centered approaches encourage team members to try new strategies and to consider new ways to provide support, they often result in solutions that might not otherwise have been identified. An emphasis on new approaches to providing support seems especially critical today, as there appears to be an ever-decreasing amount of funds available for supporting individuals with challenging behavior.

As was noted previously, several person-centered strategies have been developed. Although these approaches may vary along such dimensions as the length of time required to complete the process or the amount and type of information gleaned, they all share the previously mentioned goals and characteristics. To delineate further a person-centered approach, the remainder of this chapter is devoted to a specific person-centered strategy, PATH. A case study illustrates how PATH can be used to guide teams toward positive and possible futures.

PLANNING ALTERNATIVE TOMORROWS WITH HOPE

PATH is a person-centered planning technique that allows individuals to express their long-term goals ("dreams") as well as to delineate goals that they would like to achieve within a particular time frame. This time frame is determined by the focus person and often is approximately 1–2 years into the future. PATH is especially useful because in addition to allowing the focus person to identify dreams and goals, it breaks down the larger goal into manageable steps. The responsibility for each step of PATH is assigned to team members who are willing to commit to the chosen goals. This process brings together people from all aspects of an individual's life (e.g., family, teachers, case manager, friends, people from the community). These individuals work together toward achieving goals that are determined by the focus person, and group collaboration toward these common goals is promoted.

PATH is divided into eight steps that follow a specified sequence. The sequence is important for two reasons. First, upon its completion, PATH provides the team with a detailed "map" of how to get from where they are to where they want to be at a specified future date. Second, it provides a logical and organized sequence of steps to follow to achieve the goal. Often, the first step is the most difficult to envision when the goal is dramatically different from the present situation. Thus, steps are broken down and organized in a reverse sequence from the desired goal, leaving the first step as the final step of PATH to be outlined. The steps to be completed in PATH are

1. Touching the dream
2. Sensing the goal

3. Grounding in the now
4. Identifying people to enroll
5. Recognizing ways to build strength
6. Charting action for the next few months
7. Next month's work
8. Committing to the first step

To illustrate how each of the steps in PATH combine to result in a "road map" that describes how to support an individual in getting from where he or she is to achieving his or her dreams, a case study is presented.

Case Background

The individual who participated in the PATH described here was 14 years old at the time that PATH was completed. Beth, a typically developing adolescent, had been living in a residential group home with six other adolescent girls for about 10 months. Beth and her younger sister, Lucy, had been removed from their natural home because of extensive verbal and physical abuse by their parents. Upon removal from their home, both children had been placed in foster care. Lucy had remained with one family, who had recently expressed interest in adopting her; however, Beth, as a result of her challenging behavior, had been removed from multiple foster homes before being placed in the group home.

Although Beth's challenging behavior decreased somewhat after admission to the group home, she continued to exhibit significant problems. For example, she frequently was argumentative and defiant, and she was often truant from school. She also seemed to have few friends, and the group home staff reported that she displayed a restricted range of interests.

Staff at the group home learned about PATH during a semester-long course taught by the three authors on positive behavioral support. These staff were interested in completing a PATH with Beth to develop a plan to decrease her challenging behavior. In addition, they wanted to improve Beth's quality of life in terms of her attitude about school, school performance, and peer relationships.

Several people assisted Beth in developing her PATH. In addition to the first two authors, who facilitated the PATH, four staff from the group home who regularly worked with Beth were present. Although in this case the facilitators did not know Beth and so were involved primarily in drawing the PATH and in keeping the team focused, the process seems to go the most smoothly when the facilitators have met the focus person before beginning the process. The PATH took approximately 3 hours to complete and is displayed in Figure 1. We began the PATH by explaining the process to everyone present. We then asked the team to decide on a time frame within which to develop a plan. One team member suggested that we focus on 1 year, but Beth immediately stated that 1 year was much too far in the future for her to think about. We then suggested that we focus on developing goals that might be met by the end of the school year (approximately 8 months away); Beth agreed that this was a manageable time frame.

Touching the Dream

The first step of PATH involves helping the individual to describe the things that he or she values and enjoys, as well as his or her dreams about the future. Therefore, this component is both an expression of the identity of the focus person and a description of the things that he or she wants to work toward. The dream elucidates values that support choices that are made along the PATH. During the dream step of PATH, only the focus person is allowed to speak. This ensures that the dream is that of the focus person and not of a team member. Also, it keeps other members of the team from interjecting negative comments indicating their belief that the focus person will be unable to reach these dreams. It is important to listen to what is underlying the words of the dream. The dream may sound impossible, but the underlying notion may not be, and it may be realistic in another form. For example, an individual who cannot see may state that she would like to fly planes. Instead of assuming that the goal is unattainable, a team might further explore why she wants to fly. Perhaps she believes that flying would allow her to feel independent and free from constraints. With this information, the team might explore other options that would increase her independence.

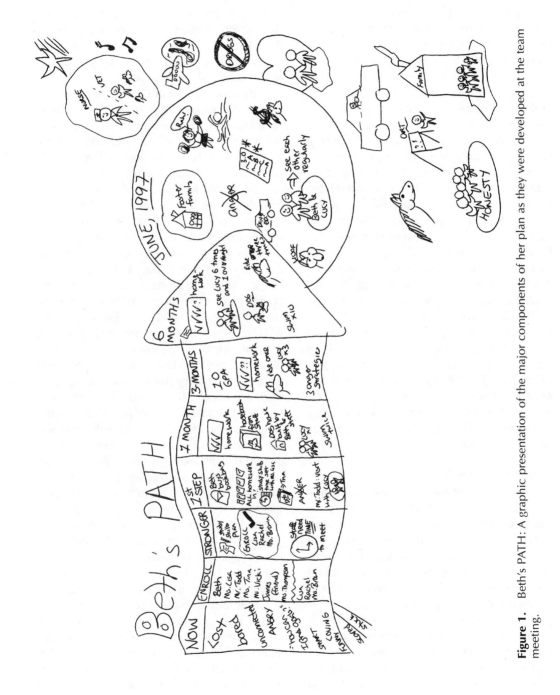

Figure 1. Beth's PATH: A graphic presentation of the major components of her plan as they were developed at the team meeting.

Beth's dream is depicted at the far end of the PATH in Figure 1. We were initially somewhat worried about completing a PATH with Beth as she appeared rather sullen during the initial part of the team meeting. However, as the process progressed and she saw that people were genuinely interested in what she had to say, she began to speak more openly. In fact, about half of the way through the dream, she began drawing the PATH herself! In articulating her dream, Beth talked about what she wants when she is an adult (e.g., to travel and become either a veterinarian or a nurse); however, the majority of her dream focused on things that were important to her in the present. For example, Beth stated that she would like to be able to ride horses and that she would like to draw and paint (represented in Figure 1 by the person painting at the easel). Beth also stated that she would like to get her driver's license as soon as possible and that she wanted to own a dog. She also stated that she would like to have honest friends and be reunited with her family. Related to being reunited with her family, Beth said that she would like to spend more time with her sister, Lucy (represented in Figure 1 by the drawing of Beth and her sister holding hands inside the heart). Finally, Beth noted that staying away from drugs or people who were involved with drugs was very important to her.

Sensing the Goal

The second step of the PATH process involves delineating several goals that the focus person and the team believe are attainable within a specified time frame. It is important that the goals be positive and that they be possible; that is, that they can be accomplished within the allotted time. The time frame is decided on by the focus person and his or her team. For some people, a good time frame is 1 year. For others, 1 year is too long. Yet other individuals may need a longer period, such as 18 months or 2 years, to accomplish significant results. Often, teams will focus on an upcoming transition as the goal date. In Beth's case, the team chose to set goals that could be met by the end of Beth's school year. During this and subsequent steps, the entire team is encouraged to express their thoughts and ideas;

however, it is important that the focus person continue to "own" the process. Therefore, we typically encourage the focus person to be the first person to speak when each step is begun. After the focus person has expressed his or her thoughts, other team members are encouraged to add ideas and information.

After completion of Beth's dream, the team moved on to sensing the goal. At this point, other team members were encouraged to help Beth develop positive and possible goals to be achieved by the end of the school year in June. Several goals were delineated, a number of which were directly related to Beth's dream. As we began this phase, one team member noted that Beth had expressed interest in having a dog, so the team member asked Beth whether she would like to own a dog. Beth's eyes lit up, and she said that she would love to have a dog but that she had not believed that she could have one in the group home. When staff confirmed that she could, Beth became even more interested in the PATH process, perhaps because she realized that it was already helping her to achieve her dreams. A second goal was that Beth wanted to spend more time with Lucy. Another goal was that Beth wanted to live in a foster home. Recall that Beth said that she would like to live with her family. Unfortunately, several staff noted that this was not possible as Beth's natural family life was quite turbulent and significant abuse had occurred. Therefore, we took time to talk with Beth about what it meant to her to be in a family. Beth said that a family involved living with the same people and having a mother and a father to take care of her. We asked Beth whether these outcomes might be met in foster care, and she said that they could. Therefore, a goal was to help Beth move in with a foster family by June.

Beth also delineated several goals involving extracurricular activities, such as cheerleading, swimming, gymnastics, playing music, and taking driver's education. One staff member noted that children could participate in extracurricular activities only when their grade point average (GPA) was 2.0 (on a 4-point scale) or better. Beth immediately stated that she could have a 3.0 GPA by June, and so that was added to the goal. At this point, a team member returned to the issue of living with a foster family and said that such arrangements had not worked well in the past because Beth had difficulty with controlling her anger. The team then suggested that Beth be provided with anger control strategies so that she could cope with her anger more effectively and acceptably. Beth agreed that this was a good plan. Beth also expressed interest in earning money over the summer. Because she had expressed interest in horses during the dream step, a team member told Beth that she knew of a "riding for the handicapped" program where Beth might be able to work. Beth was very interested in this, so it was added to the goal.

Grounding in the Now

The third step of PATH is called grounding in the now. This step is important because for PATH to work, the focus person and the team must recognize the difference between the hopeful direction of the goal and the reality of the present—the "now." Therefore, during this step everyone contributes his or her ideas about the present. Often, a sense of being "stuck," "bored," or "not altogether well" is conveyed. The words that are used are added to the PATH in the now section. To contrast this, the facilitator returns to the goal and asks the team how they felt during the goal section, and these words are added to the PATH. Enough difference between these two sections must exist to create a "pull" from one to the other. The tension generated between the now and the goal can be likened to a stretched rubber band. There must be enough distance between the two points to create tension so that the team will move forward, like a rubber band being shot across the room. If the difference is too great, however, then the rubber band will break. The same is true for PATH. It is important that enough difference exist between the goal and the now, but if the difference is too great—and perhaps unrealistic—then forward movement will not occur.

Team members were asked to suggest words to describe Beth's current life. Beth immediately said that she felt lost and bored. Other team members suggested that Beth was uncommitted and angry; however, they also noted that she was compassionate, smart, and loving. After completing grounding in the now, the team was asked to describe briefly how they felt about Beth's current situation. These words were recorded outside the "now" box and included such descriptions as scared, frustrated, and stuck. After completion of grounding in the now, team members returned to the goal and were asked to describe how they felt about the goal. Descriptors were recorded on the perimeter of the "goal" area; these included excited, nervous, optimistic, and organized.

Identifying People to Enroll

The fourth step involves identifying people who will be important throughout the realization of the goals delineated by the PATH. People who are integral to offering support for the focus person and the attainment of the PATH are people who can be asked to commit to the achievement of the dream. Often, the people identified are those who already share a commitment to the focus person's life. For each person identified, his or her specific role and contribution to the PATH should be stated. Also, each person must commit to the PATH, thus acknowledging his or her role in the ongoing process.

To begin the enroll step, we asked Beth whether she was committed; when she confirmed that she was, she came up and signed her name. Then, we asked Beth whom she wanted to be involved, and the names of those people were recorded. If the people were present at the team meeting, then we asked them whether they were willing to help Beth prior to recording their name. Those individuals who were not present were recorded at the bottom of the enroll section to indicate that Beth needed to contact them about enrollment on her PATH. Beth wanted to enroll nine people, six of whom were at the PATH meeting and agreed to participate.

Recognizing Ways to Build Strength

Movement and change are difficult, and obstacles are likely to be encountered as the focus person and the team work toward their goals. Thus, it is important to identify characteristics that will strengthen the team. These strengths could be in the form of skills to be learned, relationships to be maintained, and increased knowledge in particular areas. For example, after completion of the initial part of a PATH, one team realized that although team members shared goals, it often had not appeared that way because everyone was attempting to accomplish things in different orders or through different strategies. Therefore, one component of the ways to build strength step involved improving communication among the teachers, school administrators, and family members who were participating in the PATH.

Beth's team identified several ways in which they could build strength. Team members immediately noted that Beth would need a study skills plan to achieve many of her goals. Also, those individuals who were identified in the enroll phase but who were not present had to be enlisted. Finally, staff needed to set aside time to meet.

Charting Action for the Next Few Months

The time frame to determine actions for the next few months depends on the time allotted to accomplish the goals. Also, this section can be broken down into two or three sections, as determined by the team, to maximize success. For example, a 1-year PATH might be broken into steps for 6 months, 3 months, 1 month, and first step. Or a 1-year PATH could be broken into fewer steps, eliminating the 3-month step. Similarly, a PATH for a longer or shorter time period would be adapted as appropriate.

It is important that most, if not all, of the aspects of the goal be accounted for in the steps outlined in the actions. This ensures that movement toward change in those areas is being continually addressed and acted on. In addition, it is important that individuals who are needed to help facilitate the accomplishment of the steps be considered and identified. After the actions have been delineated, it is important for the focus person and the team to verify that these actions are consistent with the values articulated in the dream.

After completing the ways to build strength component with Beth's team, we moved forward to identify goals that would be achieved in 6 months. These goals were directly related to the outcomes identified in the goals component ("June 1997" in Figure 1). Because many of the identified goals depended on Beth's improving her GPA, the team decided that within 6 months Beth would be turning in her homework four of five times each week for each class. Beth suggested that when she met this goal she could have a candy bar, and other team members agreed with this plan. It was also decided that Beth would have begun music classes and that she would be signed up for gymnastics. Also, she would have been horseback riding three times and have gone swimming once per week. Perhaps most important to Beth, she would have seen her sister six times—one of which would have been an overnight visit—and she would have a dog.

The next step in the PATH process involved determining goals to be met within 3 months. First, Beth indicated that she could attain at least a 1.0 GPA within 3 months. Also, Beth would be turning in three of five homework assignments every week in each class. Over the next 3 months, Beth would have seen Lucy 3 times, learned three anger control strategies, been horseback riding once, and been swimming 10 times.

The next step involved identifying goals to be met within 1 month of completion of the PATH. The team identified several steps to be taken within 1 month so that Beth would meet her 3-month goals. The first goal that the team considered was Beth's homework. Beth said that by 1 month she would already be turning in three of five assignments, so this was placed in the "1 month" phase. Second, because Beth was going to begin riding, a team member would have given Beth a book on riding for Beth to read within the month. Another goal was that Beth and a team member would have built a doghouse and acquired dog care supplies. Also, Beth would have seen Lucy once and been swimming twice.

Committing to the First Step

One of the most difficult steps to take when attempting to make changes is the first step. Thus, this step is carefully outlined on the PATH, explicitly identifying each action that needs to be taken by each individual enrolled in the PATH. This serves as an accountability check because each person is clearly responsible for a certain step. The first step must be taken within the first week following the development of the PATH.

Earlier in the development of her PATH, Beth said that she always had her homework completed but did not always turn it in because she frequently left it in her locker. Therefore, during the first step, a team member suggested that Beth buy a backpack so that she could carry all of her materials to every class. Beth said that this would not be possible because students at her school were not allowed to carry closed packs because of safety concerns; however, she said that she would be allowed to carry a book-bag and that she would buy an acceptable bag within the week. Second, because Beth said that she was going to improve her GPA, the team decided that Beth and another team member would set a time for weekly study skills meetings. Also, Beth was to begin regular appointments with her therapist to learn anger control strategies. Fourth, a team member was to give Beth a book about dogs so that she could begin to learn how to care for the dog that she was going to get. Finally, a team member was going to arrange for Beth to visit Lucy.

After the PATH was completed, team members arranged specific dates for team meetings. Meetings were set to correspond with each of the time periods in the PATH. Therefore, meetings were scheduled for 1 week, 1 month, 3 months, and 6 months from the date of the initial PATH meeting. In addition, the staff at the group home identified times when they could meet on a more regular basis, as was identified in the ways to build strength component. Then, each team member reviewed his or her goals and responsibilities. Finally, we reminded team members that the PATH is not a rigid and inflexible process but rather just one of many possible ways to support Beth in achieving her goals. Therefore, the PATH might change in upcoming months as new information becomes available. For example, if Beth were turning in only one of five homework assignments at the 1-month goal, then the 3-month goal might be changed to two of five assignments. In addition, consideration would be given to the reasons that Beth and the team were having trouble meeting certain goals.

CONCLUSION

The way that behavioral health providers support individuals with challenging behavior has changed markedly. The growth of positive behavioral support has resulted in an increased focus on broader "quality of life" outcomes and on more individualized, person-centered support. This chapter presented a case study that illustrated how a person-centered approach (PATH) can lead to the development of positive and possible goals in which the focus person is invested.

In this case study, team members initially were interested in reducing rates of Beth's challenging behavior. Because the PATH focused on helping Beth to delineate her dreams and goals for the future, team members were able to help Beth realize that controlling her anger and doing better in school were directly related to her achieving the future that she wanted for herself.

The PATH process also was useful in uniting the team. Prior to completing the PATH, Beth viewed many of the group home staff as people who were trying to control her and force her to participate in activities in which she was not interested. Similarly, group home staff reported that Beth never talked to them about what she wanted to do or expressed interest in any activities. Because the PATH provided a means for Beth to express her dreams and for the team to develop specific plans to achieve a positive and possible future, Beth began to view team members as individuals who were "on her side," working toward goals in which she was interested and invested. Also, for the first time, those who worked with Beth were clear about Beth's interests and goals.

Person-centered planning approaches, such as PATH, provide a framework that is useful in helping individuals and the people who are important in their lives to develop strategies to achieve a positive and possible future. These procedures are especially useful because they can be tailored to meet the individual needs of each focus person and his or her team. Although person-centered processes are extremely useful when working with individuals who exhibit challenging behavior, we hope that readers will recognize the potential to facilitate change in the lives of anyone who desires a more positive future.

REFERENCES

Anderson, J.L., Russo, A., Dunlap, G., & Albin, R. (1996). A team training model for building the capacity to provide positive behavioral supports in inclusive settings. In L.K. Koegel, R.L. Koegel, & G. Dunlap (Eds.), *Positive behavioral support: Including people with difficult behavior in the community* (pp. 467–490). Baltimore: Paul H. Brookes Publishing Co.

Carr, E.G., & Newsom, C. (1985). Demand-related tantrums. *Behavior Modification, 9,* 403–426.

Carr, E.G., Newsom, C.D., & Binkoff, J.A. (1980). Escape as a factor in the aggressive behavior of two retarded children. *Journal of Applied Behavior Analysis, 13,* 101–117.

Coman, P., & Houghton, S.J. (1991). A functional analysis of self-injurious behavior. *Educational Psychology in Practice, 7,* 111–116.

Day, H.M., Rea, J.A., Schussler, N.G., Larsen, S.E., & Johnson, W.L. (1988). A functionally based approach to the treatment of self-injurious behavior. *Behavior Modification, 12,* 565–589.

Iwata, B.A., Dorsey, M.F., Slifer, K.J., Bauman, K.E., & Richman, G.S. (1982). Toward a functional analysis of self injury. *Analysis and Intervention in Developmental Disabilities, 2,* 3–20.

Iwata, B.A., Pace, G.M., Dorsey, M.F., Zarcone, J.R., Vollmer, T.R., Smith, R.G., Rodgers, T.A., Lerman, D.C., Shore, B.A., Mazaleski, J.L., Goh, H., Cowdery, G.E., Kalsher, M.J., McCosh, K.C., & Willis, K.D. (1994). The functions of self-injurious behavior: An experimental-epidemiological analysis. *Journal of Applied Behavior Analysis, 27,* 215–240.

Kincaid, D. (1996). Person-centered planning. In L.K. Koegel, R.L. Koegel, & G. Dunlap (Eds.), *Positive behavioral support: Including people with difficult behavior in the community* (pp. 439–465). Baltimore: Paul H. Brookes Publishing Co.

Meyer, L.H., & Evans, I.M. (1989). *Nonaversive intervention for behavior problems: A manual for home and community.* Baltimore: Paul H. Brookes Publishing Co.

Mount, B. (1987). *Personal futures planning: Finding directions for change* (Doctoral dissertation, University of Georgia). Ann Arbor, MI: UMI Dissertation Information Service.

Mount, B., & Zwernick, K. (1988). *It's never to early, it's never to late* (Publication No. 421-88-109). St. Paul, MN: Metropolitan Council.

O'Brien, J. (1987). A guide to lifestyle planning: Using *The Activities Catalog* to integrate services and natural support systems. In B. Wilcox & G.T. Bellamy (Eds.), *A comprehensive guide to* The Activities Catalog: *An alternative curriculum for youth and adults with severe disabilities* (pp. 175–189). Baltimore: Paul H. Brookes Publishing Co.

O'Brien, J., & Lyle, C. (1987). *Framework for accomplishment.* Decatur, GA: Responsive Systems Associates.

Pearpoint, J., O'Brien, J., & Forest, M. (1995). PATH: *A workbook for Planning Positive Possible Futures and Planning Alternative Tomorrows with Hope for schools, organizations, businesses, families.* Toronto, Ontario, Canada: Inclusion Press.

Scotti, J.R., Evans, I.M., Meyer, L.H., & Walker, P. (1991). A meta-analysis of intervention research with problem behavior: Treatment validity and standards of practice. *American Journal on Mental Retardation, 96,* 233–256.

Vollmer, T.R., Iwata, B.A., Smith, R.G., & Rodgers, T.A. (1992). Reduction of multiple aberrant behaviors and concurrent development of self-care skills with differential reinforcement. *Research in Developmental Disabilities, 13,* 287–299.

Section IV

ISSUES AND FUTURE DIRECTIONS

In the closing section of this book, the authors discuss several untapped issues and help to point out several courses for future work. The section opens with a personal perspective in Chapter 21 by Ervin, with commentary by Scotti. Ervin uses a wheelchair as a result of his severe cerebral palsy, and he spent several years as a consumer living in a residential facility. He is now active in positive behavioral support, and he brings a unique—and often appropriately jaded—perspective to bear on the field.

Evans's chapter (Chapter 22) on the consumer model of services for individuals with challenging behavior is a fine follow-up to Ervin's comments. If, as Evans suggests, we can allow ourselves to view the person with a disability as a true consumer of services, then this has important implications for consumer–staff relationships, staff training, and community supports. Staff training is a central issue of Chapter 23 by Hastings. In this chapter, basic research is brought to bear on the behavior of staff (is it rule governed or contingency shaped?), and Hastings offers a functional analysis of staff, in terms of their implementation of programs and perceptions and understanding of problem behaviors. The chapters by Evans and Hastings provide the same complementary views as in Section I with respect to a social system versus behavior analytic perspective. Taken together, they cover both sides of the issue.

The concluding chapter (Chapter 24) by Webb-Johnson brings us to an issue not touched on by any other chapters in this volume. Webb-Johnson discusses the overrepresentation of African American learners in special education, making us aware of a context for behavior—both a cultural context and a racist context—that often is not acknowledged, confronted, or included in our analyses. The reader should finish this chapter with not only a broader appreciation for the contexts of behavior but also, more fundamental, an understanding that behavioral intervention cannot be a monocultural affair. Clinicians and researchers alike need to evaluate their work in multicultural contexts.

Chapter 21

I Get By with
a Little Help from My Friends

A Personal Perspective on Behavioral Support

Kenneth Ervin & Joseph R. Scotti

I first met Kenneth Ervin (Ken) around 1991, during a visit to the University Affiliated Center for Developmental Disabilities (UACDD) at West Virginia University. I frankly admit that upon first meeting him, I thought that he was a client of the agency: wheelchair-bound with severe cerebral palsy (CP) and speech that was difficult to understand. My world view tilted a few degrees to one side when I learned that he was an employee at the UACDD; it nearly fell off its axis when I later found out that Ken had acquired master's degrees in both rehabilitation counseling and severe/profound special education. Once you become accustomed to his speech patterns, you find that Ken is extremely articulate and has a clear (and appropriately cynical) view of the disabilities field. As a person dedicated to advocacy for individuals with disabilities, he brings a unique perspective to his work: that of "having been there" and having directly experienced the shortcomings of the system.

The first part of this chapter provides the reader with edited extracts from an autobiographical account completed by Ken through the Oral History Project sponsored by the West Virginia Developmental Disabilities Planning Council. With these comments on his early life as a backdrop, Ken then provides his perspective on behavioral support in a conversation with myself. I hope that his comments tilt your world view as they did mine. (JRS)

BACKGROUND

I was born in Buckhannon, West Virginia. A lot of the reason that I wound up where I wound up and a lot of the things that influenced my life came directly from where I was born and the kind of family I was born into. There's not many resources in Buckhannon, and my parents went through high school and that's it. My mom works in a grocery store, and my dad's a barber. My original birth weight was 3 pounds, and I dropped down to $1\frac{1}{2}$ pounds. I was 3 months premature.

I'm an only child. My parents didn't get along. I'm not really tight with my parents. I get

Portions of this chapter are abstracted and edited from an interview conducted by Missy Woolverton on January 14, 1994, in Charleston, West Virginia, as part of the Oral History Project sponsored by the West Virginia Developmental Disabilities Planning Council and are used with permission. The opinions expressed herein, however, do not necessarily reflect the opinions or policy of that agency.

along with my mother from a distance. If I need something, she'll help me out, but we're not close. I wouldn't talk to her about anything. My grandmother told me, "Your mother was told to bring you home and put you in bed and feed you." My grandma is a bright, perceptive lady, but even though she knew that I had memorized every animal in the World Book and that I loved books and would sit with them for hours and that I could tell you what I saw on the news, even with all that, she still saw this disability. My parents didn't know what to do with me. My dad took my disability really hard. He's never dealt with me at all. To this day. He made the remark to somebody that he feels cheated because I'm the way that I am. I don't understand that. Why does he feel cheated? God, I've got two master's degrees. I've trained 4,000 people on the Americans with Disabilities Act alone—not to mention the other workshops that I'm doing. I write articles for monthly newsletters. But I try to get around that by blaming it on the times—the way things were back then—and their lack of sophistication.

My mother loves me dearly—to the point that it almost suffocates me—but she's the queen of negative images. I call her up and say, "Mom, I just did a class of 100 people today," and she'll say, "Well, are you getting yourself shaved?" or, "Is that guy you're living with holding up his end of the rent?" My parents said really insensitive stuff when I was a little boy. At least now they try to cloak it. But when I was a little boy, they figured, what the hell, he doesn't know what we're talking about anyway, so we can just say whatever we feel like: "What are we going to do with him?" Stuff like that.

Cerebral Palsy

You've got to remember at the time when I was born (1962), if you had CP, it was automatically assumed that a mental impairment went hand in hand with that. CP is a brain injury, either pre- or postnatal. It can manifest itself in a variety of ways. You could have slurred speech. It can be as simple as walking with a limp. It can be on one side of your body. Both sides of your body. One limb. All of your limbs. There's different kinds. There's spastic—that's me. The legs go out. Sometimes if I'm startled, my head will go

back. I tend to get really tight, especially in cold weather. It makes transfers to and from my chair and things like that a lot harder. You could have a mental impairment or you couldn't. You could be very, very, very disabled, or you could be like me, or a lot less.

The Methany School for the Handicapped

I was institutionalized 2 days before my ninth birthday, January 5, 1971. My parents did it in desperation. My home was its usual anarchy. They were calling all over the place. They didn't want to put me in some little pre-fab trailer out away from the rest of the kids. My dad blamed the fact that he was so miserable on my disability. And my mom, as silly as that may be, was trying to save her marriage. The Ph.D. who oversaw the kindergarten gave them the name of this place in New Jersey. It wasn't out of any malice. My parents didn't realize what kind of place it was, and not even that—*for that time* it wasn't that hideous a place. The school was the classic medical model: take-em-out-and-sit-em-in-the-sunshine kind of place. And we'll do everything for you. My parents were just desperate, and somebody threw them this bone, and they grabbed onto it. They didn't get a second opinion. They didn't do anything.

I remember feeling really clueless. Of course, my parents didn't talk to me about it because they didn't think I had any . . . you know what I mean. Yes, we did go to visit, and, yes, I saw it, but it wasn't like I had any choice—"Ken, do you like it?" "Ken, do you think this is a good place for you?" To be quite honest, I think the most attractive aspect to them was that it was a boarding school. Out of sight, out of mind.

There wasn't a lot of pomp and circumstance. You drive there. You pull up. You grab your suitcases. You go through the doors. And there's the head of housing. They tell you where to go, and you get to the door and there's the attendant. There's five of us in a room. They introduce you and unpack your stuff, and you're on your own.

Peapack, New Jersey, where the school was located, was a resort town for rich folks. They used to farm out all the cute kids whom they knew weren't going to spit on people or hit somebody or something like that to the rich folks for holidays. We'd get church groups coming through every other Sunday, and they'd push us around and talk to us, talking about how good they feel about themselves. I felt kind of ambivalent. At one level, it was good to see people who had all of their faculties and didn't have to use metal to get around. And talked normally. And it wasn't the same old people I saw every day. On another level, I was really pissed because they don't know me—they don't really wanna know me. They're just here to massage their ego and their sense of good will. And then by Wednesday, they'll even forget my name. But on the other hand, I wanted to sit down and tell them everything about me. "Well hey, are you going to come back again? And will you hang out with me when you do come?"

Everything was in one place. If those church people didn't come through every once in a while, you'd never see a stranger. You had your little schedule that they'd stick to your crutch or stick to the back of your chair, and somebody would come by and read it once in a while to see that you weren't watching TV when you weren't supposed to.

When you hear about institutions, you're going to hear about physical abuse. Maybe sexual abuse even. I can never say that kind of thing happened to me, with the exception of maybe once. But there were all kinds of human rights violations at the Methany School. Listening in on phone calls. Getting my mail. I used to know where the mail room was, and I'd go in and get my mail and leave everybody else's. They even took our Tooth Fairy money. They would tape it to a part of your bed, and then they would take it. I knew where the money was kept. I would go in when nobody was around when I knew it was unlocked. I knew how big a quarter was, and I knew how many they owed me—even though I didn't know how much a quarter was worth. In a lot of ways, my institutionalization, although it confined what was inside of me, wasn't as bad in a lot of ways—environmentally—as some of the stories you hear. But it was a miserable way to exist when you felt like there were other places you needed to go.

Resident Friends

I knew two people through all 4 years. They were Keith and Mike. They were two African American guys. I was pretty tight with them. I got really immersed in all of their habits because they were city kids and had all this ethnicity going on. And I was new to them, and I thought it was neat. Even then I was really inquisitive, and if I saw somebody really different, I wanted to investigate what they were doing and why they did it. And a lot of times I picked up their habits just because they were different.

Both Mike and Keith were from foster homes, and I remember that I wanted to know why my family couldn't adopt them and they could live at home with me—which was kind of idiotic because none of the houses I've ever lived in with my mother has ever been accessible to me. They never even thought about putting a ramp on the house. I lived with my grandmother, and she doesn't have a ramp. I have to walk up steps to this day. My mom's trailer had a ramp for a couple of years, and that's only because she was breaking her back, and at my insistence, she built it. None of the bathrooms had ever been set up for me. Nothing has ever been put in my reach. If you ask for something to drink, it's not set up so that you can get your own; but somebody bitches if you ask for help.

There was another guy named John, and he was an educated, little wimpy kid—really skinny and really defenseless. There was a kid in our room who'd known him from somewhere else and who didn't like him, who always picked on him and made it hard for him and did physical things to him. And I got where I would beat up the other kid. I was a little guy, and I'm pretty slow, but when you're in a place where everybody's slow, the person with a little bit of reflexes is king. I would take up for him, and I thrashed this other kid a bunch of times. John's parents liked me because I looked out for him.

The Attendants

The people who were our attendants—and this was like in the 1970s—were like hippies: "I'm tired of school. I'm going to drop out. I'm going to help the handicapped people." A lot of them didn't know jack-diddle about developmental disabilities. But they thought it was cool, and they wanted to do it, and they liked it. They had an intense personal interest. They had a commitment that maybe the people who were the professionals, because of the mind-set toward people with developmental disabilities, didn't have.

Bob, Dave, and Bernadette were like that. They used to sneak over. They weren't allowed to come over after they were done with work. That was fraternizing with the residents. You had to get permission. Those three people meant a lot to me. They made me see myself different. I was miserable, and while I knew there was other stuff in me that needed to get out, if it weren't for those two or three people, who knows what I'd be or what I'd be doing. They changed the whole course of my existence. They made me see myself as somebody totally different. They made me see myself as somebody beyond someone who was going to get the same level of care as his mother's house plants for the rest of my life.

I remember one time Bob had come back to read me *The Last of the Mohicans* because I wanted to get through it, and I was getting real tired because I was just learning. I was teaching myself, but I was struggling. And they brought around medications at a certain time at night. We'd hear the wheels on the med cart. And Bob would jump into the closet, which had this cotton curtain. He would line himself up with everybody's shoes and pull the curtain while the nurse was giving everybody their meds. I would look down at the shoes and hope that she wouldn't realize that one of us had suddenly acquired size 12 feet!

Dave had his master's and was getting his Ph.D. in philosophy. He worked nights, and all he did was walk around in circles and punch this little clock that he carried around on his arm—and make sure that none of us had aspirated or that something wacky didn't happen. He used to stop and wake me up and tell me about shit he'd learned in class. And I said, "Dave, why are you telling me? There's the high school guys up the hall who would probably appreciate what you're saying a whole lot more." And he said, "No, I'm telling you because you're the most intelligent person here and you don't know it yet. But one of these days you're going to find it out. And I know you're real excited about what I'm telling you. I'm telling you because I think you need to know. You may not know you need to know, but you need to know."

I got attached to a lot of attendants. As you can tell, and as I said, I kind of make my family where I can find it. But I remember at one point Bob told me that he wanted to leave. He said, "Maybe I expend a lot more energy at this job than some people, and I'm getting burned out, and I can't go on." And I was miserable. I cried and I cried. I went into a frenzy. They couldn't even reason with me. That was my most miserable day. So, finally what happened is he wound up staying until it was almost the time for me to be released because he said he didn't want to leave me. I think he even stayed until after my release. It really meant a lot to me because he and these other people took somebody who was basically a nonreader and opened up a whole new world to me. Then just as I was getting my feet on the ground, he was considering leaving. And I thought, "Oh, man, what's going to happen to me?"

Quality of Education

In the educational classes, there wasn't a whole lot of emphasis on *individualized education.* They had certain niches. There was the high school people. And all of the people who could kind of read went in one class. All of the people who were real low functioning went in another class. It was very much labels and niches and pigeonholes. I'm sitting there reading *Dick and Jane* and learning how to count by putting beads on a string. *That's real functional!* It was very boring. At one time, they had me tested for seizures because I would drift off, or I would be walking down the hall on my crutches and I would go splat. When they sent me home for vacation, they told my mom that I needed to have a brain scan because they thought I was having seizures. But what I was really doing was getting sleepy because I was bored. Now they let people read things that they like, to teach them how to read. They were giving me things that I didn't want to read. I was just bored.

The physical and the occupational therapy wasn't geared toward functionality, either. It wasn't geared toward my being independent. It wasn't a functional curriculum. It was subject based.

What the discharge summary said was that I had "plateaued." I think it was basically that they were just tired of me. They were tired of my instigating stuff. They were tired of my talking about my human rights—even though I really don't think I understood what those were at that time. It was just something I heard on television, and I thought it was kinda cool. They were tired of my getting mail from the mail room and organizing movements to write Congressmen. They just got tired of it.

Wanna know how I found out I was going to be discharged? I had gotten these two other guys to write a letter with me to my Congressman. One of the attendants found out—one of the "walk-in-line" attendants—and he told the administration. They called me in to the office, and I said, "A—you listen to our phone calls. B—you read our mail. C—you don't give us the right education. And D—the food here is terrible. So there." And finally old Mrs. Methany stood up and got in my face and screamed at me, "What do you care? You're leaving in 6 months anyway." That was how I got official notification of my discharge.

My mom was told that I would never make it past the fourth grade and I would never read for pleasure. In 4 years, all that the school could generate on me was *one paragraph*—that was my discharge summary. And what it said is that I "should be given access to educational opportunities as they occur sequentially." Whatever the hell that means. I think what it meant was if I got to second grade, I go to second grade, and if I never make it out, that's cool.

Four and a half years of my life, being one of their little "show kids" because I was semi-articulate. I was the kid who got to go thank the candy man for the Easter bunny, and I was the kid who got to go down and say thanks to the state representatives for Thanksgiving dinner—yet, I was retarded. And all they can generate on me is one little measly paragraph. These are the kind of professionals you're dealing with. And I'm getting to read "see Spot run" in education,

and the people who are giving me a bath are having to teach me how to read.

That last year I was learning a lot, and I was growing a lot. But also as I grew and I got to understand more words and I knew more of what was going on, I got more pissed off. I think the people who were closest to me had a lot of concern. They wanted to make sure that I got out, and yet they didn't want to see me go because they didn't know what I was walking into—and I didn't either. And once again, my mom's still got this mind-set, and to this day it's somewhat true, that I'm somebody to be moved wherever. My mom's carrying baggage from doctors and from what reports said and what Ph.D.s said. She doesn't realize that in a couple of years I could very easily be a Ph.D.

Then it was like, "God, I'm out. And holy shit, what's going to happen?" I'm trying to get adjusted. Basically, I went back into myself and just read. I spent more time with Frodo than I did with Reality. While I'm reading these highly complicated fantasies, my mom's telling me, "Now we should really start in the fourth grade 'cause we don't know what's going to happen." When I went for my interview, the principal said, "Well, let's start him in sixth. But he doesn't really belong there either."

With the exception of kindergarten, I'd never spent that much time with "normal" kids. I'm like a novelty. I got along with the kids. My world in a way has been a lot broader because I've tried to read and make myself bigger. My integration experience in public schools was great for me. I did everything that anybody in my class did. The principal said I couldn't go on the senior trip and I said, "Oh, think again, Frank. Think again. Think again. Think again."

There was nothing remarkable about junior high. I wasn't really that good a student because I was busy integrating. C's and B's were good enough. My mom was so strange about that, and she's still strange to this day. She didn't think I could do it. Once I did it in sixth grade, I remember her sitting me down and saying, "If you keep getting C's, I'm going to take you out of school." And I'm saying, "Well, 5 years ago you were telling me if I didn't make it out of fourth grade I was all right."

What can I say about my high school years except that they were like everybody else's? A little bit more raucous because I wanted to experience everything. I never want to look back on my life and say that I didn't try something because my disability limited me, or gee, I couldn't do that or I wouldn't have fit in there because of my disability. I wanted to do everything that an average teenager would do.

My high school graduation was significant because nobody even expected me to be there. There's a picture of me at graduation. I was trying not to look goofy, but I guess I was pretty happy with the mortarboard sliding off my head, looking like I was going to be *real* happy to get out of there. My best friend at the time got to push me across the stage because they didn't want to hold up the line. I've got this silly picture of myself confusing this poor administrator because he didn't realize that because of my CP I'm totally only left-handed. At this point, all I want is my diploma. Give it to me *now.* The administrator's trying to figure out, "OK, I'm supposed to hand him this with this . . . this isn't working. All the other 300 kids did it the right way. This is confusing me. I hope they're not going to alternate." I did the whole thing. I got the presents and stuff. And then I started getting ready for college. Since my sophomore year in high school, I'd been getting ready for college.

THERE AND BACK AGAIN

As noted previously, Ken went on to get master's degrees in rehabilitation counseling and severe/ profound special education, after completing his undergraduate degree at West Virginia Wesleyan College in Buckhannon, West Virginia. He then worked in a number of environments from which he has further observations to share. The remainder of this chapter is edited from a conversation with myself on June 27, 1997, in Morgantown, West Virginia. (JRS)

Scotti: Ken, in a way, you built your own support system—once you got a start from your three friends at Methany School—by being so adamant about not being left out . . . to always experience what anyone else could experience. From your unique viewpoint, where are we now,

and what still has to change? What is the status of positive behavioral support?

Ken: The residential staff is thinking, "What am I going to do *to* him? What about when he does this or that?" You know what I mean? "How does this—positive behavioral support— relate to me, and how does this protect me?" I think that [positive behavioral support] requires a certain amount of personal and professional investment, which I don't see when I'm hanging out in a group home or something.

Scotti: So, you're saying that at the direct care level, things have to change in terms of knowledge and commitment.

Ken: Yeah. While I think that maybe the parents and the caregivers might not articulate it very well, they're coming at it from a different perspective. The parents and caregivers are people who may be 50 or 60 years old or have little education or are from lower socioeconomic backgrounds. They are thinking, "Well, you know, Billy does have a disability and we just have to do what we can." So there's not that commitment, unless the consumers can vocalize and articulate it for themselves. For example, in a Life Quilters [a positive behavioral support project] situation—you're only there on a consulting basis— there and gone. You do some follow-up, but not a lot—who knows what happens afterward.

Scotti: With so many people on a caseload, you can't follow up on them all . . . you don't always know what happens after you leave.

Ken: Right, but that is why it is imperative that we leave somebody who works with the team on a regular basis with the skills to bring the team together to help with maintenance and follow-up. Let's face it, *it's not rocket science.*

Scotti: Let me ask you some more about that. I think what you are saying is that we're going in the right direction. A lot of professionals have internalized things, like the Life Quilters model— in which you have to plan for people's futures, you can't set limits on them, you have to give them supports—and we talk a good talk. But when we leave, are the direct care staff or the family members—the people who have to care for the person with a disability every day—still walking that walk?

Ken: Right, but as the "professionals," it's our job to teach them to walk. Caregivers haven't spent 10 years in college, and most direct care staff took their jobs because it pays better than McDonald's. I deal with people with disabilities every day. My fiancée is going to be out here in a minute. She's a wheelchair user. She is 28 years old, and she was in special education all her life. And it's obvious that she didn't belong there. It just astounds me that these things still happen. I was a witness recently for a due process hearing, and I read a report by somebody who claimed that they did a functional analysis with this person. But when I read the report, all I saw was a bunch of charts that indicated that he engaged in this behavior for attention—he bites his thumb because it's attention seeking. All these really pretty graphs and charts . . . but there was no talk of replacement behavior. The one recommendation that I did agree with is that he be given a communication device— which he still doesn't have 3 years later. Which is one reason that we were there. I was just astounded. If you do a functional analysis, *do it right!* I didn't find the word *antecedent* one place in there. If you did a functional analysis . . . show me that you did a *real* functional analysis.

Scotti: So here is this professional psychologist in 1997, who has done a functional analysis, and says, "It's attention motivated." The report doesn't talk about the conditions under which the behavior occurs, doesn't talk about what else we should be teaching this person . . .

Ken: No talk of replacement behaviors.

Scotti: . . . and he is far from talking about getting this person a life where this behavior isn't even necessary.

Ken: Yeah. And the person was 5 years old and sitting in the back of a kindergarten class. If it's "attention seeking," why not pair him with a peer and let him do activities?

Scotti: Have a friend . . . learn some behaviors . . . build repertoires . . . etc. When you were back in Methany School, in New Jersey, what were you seeing—if you were even seeing it— in terms of treatment? You told us some of the conditions in your paper [the first half of this chapter].

Ken: I was at that time in the country club of institutions. It wasn't like they were walking around with spray bottles and spraying us in the eyes. It's just that we were totally disregarded. I remember once in a sixth-grade math class— after I got out of Methany—that I couldn't do a problem and I bit my arm because that's what I had seen people do at Methany. I'm frustrated . . . ahhh . . . [makes biting movement toward arm] . . . and I looked around and thought, "Wow, other people must be getting this wrong too, but they're not biting their arms." I benefited from the models in my natural environment. So many of us professionals set up these elaborate interventions when the natural variables are right in front of us. Of course, I didn't know that in the sixth grade. Did anyone in 1974?

Scotti: Well, we certainly weren't doing functional analyses as we do them now. And if we had treated that behavior—if you had kept doing that and we treated it—it could have been the spray bottle in the face.

Ken: Right. Or 10 minutes on a mat and a leg sweep. At Methany, they didn't use the classic punishments, they more or less ignored these behaviors. "Oh, their parents are paying good money for them to be here. We gotta make sure they don't fall or anything. It's OK 'cause they're not going to get out anyway. What does it matter?"

Scotti: From that regard, it was neglectful.

Ken: Oh yeah. It was very neglectful. I've told you this, that my discharge summary—after 4½ years—was a paragraph long. "Ken has plateaued and should be presented with educational opportunities as they occur, sequentially." What does that mean? These weren't specific recommendations. My parents were told, "He couldn't read for pleasure . . . he'll never make it past the fourth grade . . . problems interacting socially." Well, that's still debatable! It was very neglectful. We both know how harsh treatment was in most institutions. To tell you the truth, when I first got my master's and started working in the training center in Buckhannon, West Virginia, I knew this wasn't right in the core of my being. But, I had a rehab degree . . .

Scotti: When did you get that degree?

Ken: In 1986–1987.

Scotti: And you started working in this vocational center . . .

Ken: A year after I got my degree—it took a year for me to get a job. The day program was very old-style, sitting at tables and stacking blocks; there was no functional curriculum. If an individual exhibited "inappropriate" behavior, the behavior plan consisted of being restrained on the mat or placed in time-out. Punishment. Put them on the mat. Time-out where somebody would almost stand over you and berate you while you were in time-out. And I'm thinking, "This isn't time-out the way that I read it." I know functional analysis was a concept at that time, and people were actually using it. But where I was working, we definitely hadn't caught up. And like I just said, I knew instinctually that it wasn't right. I had a good psychology background. Maybe if we did this a different way—but I didn't have the knowledge of functional analysis until I came back to get my special education degree and started working at UACDD. Down in Buckhannon it was like the stone age—we hadn't caught up.

Scotti: What do you think you would see if you went back there now?

Ken: Well, of course they have closed it down because the Medicaid well ran dry. But, to tell you the truth, I think I would see pretty much the same thing because these entities tend to hire people who aren't qualified. One group home manager had a degree in broadcasting, the other had a degree in theater arts. I asked her what her qualifications were, and she said that she used to type for a QMRP [Qualified Mental Retardation Professional]. What qualifications are those? To place people like that in positions of power is a disservice to those we are paid to work for.

Scotti: So there you were, you are talking about the late 1980s. You hadn't learned much about functional analysis at that time—despite a master's in rehabilitation—and it certainly wasn't learned previously in that setting. My impression is that's how we were as a field in general at that time. Of course, we had been talking about it as a concept since Skinner in 1953, but had we been applying it? No. We had been talking about it, and our idea of a functional analysis was, "Oh, he is self-injurious and we put him

in time-out and the behavior stopped." That's a functional *relation:* behavior–time-out–no behavior. We really didn't start getting into doing a serious functional analysis that says, "This is what maintains behavior," until the mid-1980s, and even now it still hasn't caught on in a lot of places. But even when it does occur, there is something lacking.

You don't know about a lot of the chapters in this book, but what we have been trying to do is take people who have been working in this field and doing good functional analyses and good behavior analytic treatment—but who are also providing positive behavioral support. In some camps, it's almost like these are two different things. You can do a functional analysis, you can do a behaviorally oriented treatment, or you can be over here doing positive behavioral support—getting people out and getting them a life. It's almost like they are different strategies. That's what I see.

Ken: I guess because I had influences from here and so on and so forth . . . when I went out to Illinois, I was so excited. This was going to be cutting edge. This is going to be so cool. And I walked in and basically they were doing canned curriculum because they had some students for whom English was their third language, and it's easier to just do a canned curriculum. And I'm going back to the department saying, "Doesn't that offend you guys?" And they said, "Well, we are just doing what we can." And I said, "This is not what I came here for . . . this is not what I expected." I found that most people who consider themselves "behavior analysts" think, "I'm a scientist . . . I step back from it." You know what I mean? And if you are a "human services person," there is a degree of something that is hard to operationalize because it means something different to everybody else. There is a degree of humanity involved and a degree of commitment that you don't have if you are a "scientist." I see you, I take my data, I go home. So I don't know what the solution is, but I think that's what we are dealing with.

Scotti: Do you think they can be integrated? I think they can, and what we are trying to show in this book is that you can do both. They are almost different levels of analysis. Here's a problem: Let's solve this particular behavior. Why does it occur, what is the context within which it happens? But once you start talking about a context, that's positive behavioral support.

Ken: Yeah, I think it all can work. But it's almost a two-tiered thing. The behavior analyst gives it to somebody who actually does the hands-on positive behavioral support.

Scotti: That is kind of the way it is starting to happen. Back to what you were saying, when it first started, a lot of people out there didn't have the philosophy of support. The expert came in and told them all this good stuff, and then they left. The staff were left with a plan, and if they didn't buy the philosophy of the plan, they were not going to do *support*—they would just do *programs*.

Ken: Yeah. I think it's possible, but yet I don't know. I'm not convinced that creating another tier of the system is going solve the problem. My experience is that the more layers you put on it, the harder it is to get to the real reason that we are here, which is the person.

Scotti: Right. Well, given what you saw growing up, firsthand from the consumer side, and where you are now, what do you think are some of the most important things that have changed about how we are dealing with 1) persons with disabilities and 2) challenging behavior?

Ken: You know, it's really cool that you ask me that question now because if you had asked me that question when you first asked me to do this . . . well, my life has almost come full circle since then. I would have given you a totally different answer. I think we are dealing much better with people who have challenging behaviors, because if you have a challenging behavior, you are a danger to the community, you are a danger to staff. So we are going to focus every bit of our human service "know-how" on you. And because we want to make sure this is going to work—and now we have figured out a way to bill it all—so that's really cool! But I'll tell you, since I've been seeing Darla [Ken's fiancée] for awhile, I have been coming out of the office and just hanging out with people. And man, if you only have a severe disability [without challenging behavior], you are poorly case-managed and you don't have the staffing that you need. Darla

has a friend who has staffing, who has her own apartment . . . but she stays in those three rooms *all the time.*

Scotti: So if you have a behavior that is crying out for attention, mostly because it is affecting the people around you, you get support.

Ken: So if I'm somebody with even a glimmer of intelligence, who wants to have good services, I'm going to develop some kind of challenging behavior because then people will want to build me "bridges to the community." It's like, "We have these challenging behaviors and we don't have time to deal with this other stuff." I can understand that . . .

Scotti: . . . but it leaves the person who just needs some support.

Ken: Yeah, they fall between the cracks.

Scotti: So, we haven't gone where we need to go.

Ken: Oh, no. There is not an even distribution. I understand that if somebody is starting fires or hitting the people who work with them or their caregivers or whatever, and they are a danger. I understand that. Or if they are not safe. Or they walk down Main Street in the winter, naked in sub-zero weather. You have got to take care of that. But, yet, there is a whole population, I've got to tell you, just in this town, that is *not* being served. And I can't really extrapolate how to study it, but I would assume that you could find that pattern almost anywhere.

Scotti: Well, what are your thoughts on what that group needs in terms of support?

Ken: Well, I think the same process can be done. You just don't focus it on a challenging behavior. I mean, that's what we all need, and that's what we all want. All of us—I mean you; me; Darla; my buddy and personal assistant Dave who helps me with daily living activities, transportation, cooking, cleaning, and also has a learning disability. Dave, who was told by DRS [the Department of Rehabilitation Services] that he can only be a barber. If he wasn't going to be a barber, they weren't going to help him. And who was told a couple of years ago by an agency where he was getting services that if they saw him out around town, they couldn't say "hello" to him because that would breach confidentiality. That's ridiculous, the concept of "professional distance" is someone's excuse for not working very hard! I know it's a long and involved process. All people need to have certain things to have a rewarding life. Everybody wants friends, everybody wants a sense of purpose, everybody wants places to go and to have a myriad of life experiences. People with disabilities are no different. For these people [with disabilities but without challenging behavior], you don't need to know an antecedent or a consequence or any of that stuff. All you have to do is understand the basic processes and what kind of people belong in a circle—and that's it.

Scotti: And you can do that for anybody.

Ken: Yeah. You can teach that to case managers, to group home managers. You can teach that to group home staff. It's just a simple matter of learning how to move people along and cut people off. You can teach somebody to teach your basic positive behavioral support workshop or a counseling class, and I think they would pretty much be ready to go. I think this is something that everybody who doesn't have a strong network of friends—which is just about everybody with a disability—needs to have done.

Scotti: It's the people with a challenging behavior who, in a sense, are advocating for themselves because they engage in this extreme behavior and everybody around them says, "We have got to do something, and we have got to do it quick and we have got to do it big-time." But if you don't have a "voice" like that, how do you advocate, how do you get that service, how do you get that network of support around you?

[Darla has entered the room from getting dressed and joins us.]

Darla: That's kind of hard because a lot of people use communication devices, but a lot of people don't want to sit down and pay attention to them.

Ken: So, I guess your question was how do you do that if you can't communicate?

Scotti: Yes, how do you do that? How do you advocate for yourself? Is there really a movement for people to do that, which says, "Look, we want a full life, too"?

Ken: Well, there is a movement nationally, which I have been lucky enough to hook up with. But here in West Virginia, I would say it doesn't

exist. Here in West Virginia, and I said this on the advocacy tape that I did for the DDPC [Developmental Disabilities Planning Council], and I don't think it was very well received. I said that, in West Virginia, it's that whole Appalachian mentality that we have—and I think this extends to other rural areas, as well. "Well, you know, if we don't have it, we don't want to say anything. We don't want to rock the boat because then they'll take away what we do have."

Scotti: So, you just take the "stiff upper lip" approach, do without, and fend for yourself.

Ken: Yeah. And I think nationally there is a sense of anger, and anger is something that is nonexistent here. But nationally there is a sense of anger that, "Hey, our brothers and sisters are dying in nursing homes, pay attention!" That's not coming from here. I mean I have struggled to get three or four people to go to an ADAPT [a national disability rights organization] meeting with me. "Oh no, oh no, that's not good. We don't want to make waves, now." See, we suffer under this fallacy here in West Virginia that we are an institution-free state. That's not true. Obviously people aren't looking at the group homes that I have seen with a critical eye. And nursing homes aren't even an issue here. Like, somebody who works for the Center for Independent Living, which nationally is the real voice for persons with disabilities, here in the state calls me and says, "There is this 13-year-old boy in a nursing home and it's awful. What should we do?" Why don't you go to the paper? One, it will get the kid's face out there . . . he may get services. The other thing is it will bring attention. You know, I have got a personal assistance bill that has died in the legislature 2 years in a row because people don't see the need for it. Because if you don't apply for Medicaid waiver and you don't work, you don't have any options to receive personal assistance services here in West Virginia.

Scotti: What you are saying is that part of where we need to go is advocacy.

Ken: Yeah.

Scotti: Self-advocacy.

Ken: I think it starts with that. You have to decide, "This is what I want, and I'm going to move forward." Yet there may be some consequences, but I've got to take those. Because as people with disabilities, many times you haven't had any experiences with consequences—natural consequences. So, many times you are afraid of the unknown. It's not so much that you are afraid of the consequences, it's that you don't know what they are. And many times you build up all this self-talk in your head, "This is going to happen . . ."

Since I have been living here with Darla, for example, a lot of times she'll ask me, "Well, what if this happens?" Well, last night, for example, we went over to the career college and did an interview. She had been accepted to the career college, and we meet this career counselor, who immediately says, "Well, you know. . . ."

Darla: My test scores are really low.

Ken: ". . . that costs a lot of money and your test scores are really low." And I broke in and I said, "Look, I've got a buddy who used to live across the road from me, who is like a high-quad who has no use of his extremities, that was told to sort bolts. And he says, 'How am I supposed to do that, with my nose?' " So, I said, "I know where you are going with this, and I won't allow it."

Darla: They're telling me that they want all this testing just for me to go to computer school.

Ken: Basically, I told them that I would be able to meet with them to talk about her accommodations, because that's an eligibility criterion that they are creating for her that isn't for everybody else. So, to get to the point of what you asked me, Darla is saying that they will make those tests say whatever they want, and so I say then we'll ask for an independent evaluation, and then we'll call CAP [Client Assistance Program], which protects the rights of individuals who have active rehabilitation cases. So it's that voice in my head that says why should I bother because the system has beat me down so many times.

Darla: I know why I bother. I've never gotten anywhere before, so it's kind of scary.

Ken: Yeah, but I have! [We all laugh.]

Darla: Yeah, I know. (Hey Dave, whenever you get a chance, I need my shoes on.)

Ken: It's that fear of the unknown, it's that fear that, "Hey, nobody's ever given me any help before, so why should I pursue this?"

Scotti: Why do you pursue it? That may sound naive, but just to hear you say it, why do you pursue it?

Ken: I think people with disabilities throughout history—and I don't mean to climb up on my soapbox because that is really hard for me to do [physically]. [We all chuckle.] But people with disabilities throughout history . . . it's been, "You can't do it, you can't do it, you can't do it. Touch me again like that and I'm going to tie you up. I'm going to stand you in the corner. I'm going to mist you. I'm going to throw the net over you." In my case, "You can't read your mail. You'll never make it past the fourth grade." Before you can move forward, you have to develop—you have to have a core . . . you have to have some self-respect. And that's what we as professionals are doing by engaging in this process of support for everybody, whether it's just linking them up with a bunch of people to go to the movies or helping them quit banging themselves on the head. Well, I guess we are getting away from behavioral support now.

Scotti: No, I think you are right on track there.

Ken: Support is so vital. Because you know how you get self-respect? It's when you go out in the community and people go, "Wow, he is really fun to be with. This was like our structured time to be with him, but let's invite him to the picnic." Or, "Maybe he can come to our house for Christmas." Or, "Gee, I notice you like to paint. Do you want to come to my craft store? Do you want to display some of your stuff in the craft store?" I'll tell you, Scotti, if it wasn't for those three or four people back in the institution, I don't know where I would be. Because—I think I mentioned the guy who used to get me up—the guy who was working on his Ph.D. in philosophy. He would sit and tell me things, and I would say, "The high school kids are down the hall, why are you coming to me and telling me stuff?" And he is like, " 'Cause you are really smart. You are smarter than you think you are right now, and one of these days hopefully you'll find out."

Scotti: Have you found that out?

Ken: Well, I don't know whether I found it out or not. We base so much on "plans" and what we *have to do.* It's just a matter of reaching out. All that stuff I got wasn't "planned." None of those people ever sat down and said, "I bet if we sit and teach Ken Ervin how to read the *Last of the Mohicans* whether we're supposed to or not, he's going to get two master's degrees, and these are going to be his long-term and short-term goals." You know what I mean?

Scotti: Yeah. The guy just did it because he saw something and he wanted to do it.

Ken: Right. I know we all work 8-hour jobs and we have to go home and we have our other shit to do—but if you get people out in the community where they can be seen, they are going to build their own relationships. There's no task analysis for a friendship. Just get them out there!

Scotti: That's an interesting point because back in April, I was on a panel at the West Virginia Autism Society conference, and a woman in the audience asked, "How do I get my son with autism beyond having *paid* friends? He has no friends. The only people who interact with him are paid to do so." What you are saying is just get him out there in the world.

Ken: Right.

Scotti: Let him build a network by being out there.

Ken: I think it is crucial that staff appear that this is not a burden to them. "Oh my god, we have 20 minutes left in the park . . . this is active treatment." I think it is inherent that staff do that. I don't care if you have the commitment. But it's just like when I hire somebody to do a job for me. When I was on Medicaid waiver, they were going to pick the person to assist me. I wasn't allowed to interview. I wasn't allowed to choose the person. I told them what I wanted, but what I wanted isn't what they sent through the door. So the way that I picked what I wanted is that I kicked them all back out. And I didn't ask them to like me. If you don't like me, you don't have to be my friend. But no matter what, if you are hired to be my staff, you should do your job and do it relatively pleasantly. If I'm not doing something to you—and even if I am, and that's part of my disability—then you are supposed to handle it *professionally,* not go home and pout about it, because that's what we're working on. That's what you're there to work on. So get over it. If you work in a quarry busting rocks and a

rock falls on your foot, you don't go, "Ooh, I'm mad at that rock!" It's part of the game. So I just think, when we're out in the community, staff shouldn't be like, "Come on everybody, walk in a line," and treat everybody like herd animals. If people are going to be put—and I assume they are going to be when we are both dead and gone—if people are going to be put in a congregative setting, then when people are hired they need to be told this is *their* house, and when you walk in this door, you're in *their* house. This is their house, and they are all individuals. They're not herd animals.

Scotti: But something about that setting, particularly for folks who can't verbalize and advocate for themselves, just fosters that.

Ken: I totally agree. That's why I hated doing projects when I was in special ed, because I had to go back into those kinds of settings, and that was unsettling for me. It caused a lot of memories to come back up for me that I didn't want to deal with. So, I agree; but yet, I think it's a matter of people. I still think it is. Because look, I've had three or four people in this house with a disability for overnights for a couple of days at a time, and people aren't paid to be here. Well, I mean Dave is paid to be here. But Chris [another roommate], whom you've met before, is over there on the couch sacked out—he isn't paid. And Darla is here, and I think she feels more like she has a home here than she has ever had.

Darla: I've gotten out more in the past several months. I didn't know there was so much out there to do. I've been out to restaurants, I'm trying to get into school, and I'm working on getting custody of my little boy.

Ken: So I really think it's about people. I don't know how to legislate that, but it just seems like the further people get removed from their own humanity, the less effective we are in providing quality services. Behavioral science will only take you so far.

Scotti: It seems that you could do positive behavioral support the wrong way, if you feel like, "We're the team coming in and we're going to do this *for* them." Instead of *with* them. So, where do you think we need to go from here?

Ken: I just think there needs to be more emphasis on *friends.* More emphasis on gathering people. Even if they're just people who live in this person's community or around this person, who would consent to come and be part of a positive behavioral support circle. "Do you think you would be interested in providing any . . . ?" Or even if we didn't want to share that much confidentiality, we could say, "So and so, who lives next to you, has a disability and has expressed an interest in doing this. Would you be willing to take him down to the Dairy Queen or let him come over and rake your yard?"

And I think it's the way we are socialized as professionals. Because when I got out of school. . . . Well, one time I was sitting in a meeting at a mental health center and I was toeing the company line. A buddy of mine from West Virginia Advocates took me outside and was wanting a cigarette. And he said, "Where did you come from?" And I said, "What do you mean?" He said, "That story you told me . . . did you make it up, or did you actually live it?" And I said, "Yeah, I lived it." And he said, "Well, act like you lived it." And I walked back in and really that was the turning point in my career. Or I would have just been like a stupid little schmuck working for a mental health center, because I was *Kenneth Ervin, M.S., and I had gotten out!* But because I had gotten out, I've got a responsibility to make sure that other people have the same opportunities. That's why these people who are poorly case-managed—because so and so has 40 people on his caseload—that's why I'm willing to expend a little extra effort. Because as an individual, it's important to me because I have been there. And that's why—even though I'm going to be relatively poor and back on assistance—if I am going to tell people, "Man, you've got to get services, and you've got to stand up for yourselves," if I believe that I'm getting shafted and I don't step out there and let people know . . . then how am I supposed to go back and tell people to use their voice? I have to look at myself in the mirror.

Scotti: I don't see a lot of that either: knocking on the neighbor's door and saying, "Hey, your neighbor has a disability. Can you do this one thing for him or her?"

Darla: Some of them think that we've got the plague.

Ken: Oh yeah! Have you ever read the book *Interdependence: The Route to Community* by Al Condeluci? He's got this really cool story, and I think West Virginia—a rural environment—is the perfect place to do this. He tells this story about his cousin who had some form of mental impairment. And his cousin didn't have an IEP [individualized education program], and she didn't have related services. She was just their cousin and everybody looked out for her because that is what was expected of society—within the context of their family. It's not like it's a big deal. For example, Dave drives for me, and Dave cooks for me. There are things I can do for Dave, like, "They gave me this stuff to read and I really don't understand it . . . can you tell me what it says?" I mean, we're all interdependent, you know. There are things Darla can't do. I can't tie my shoes, so she can tie my shoes. It was kind of funny, we went to the PATHS [Partnerships in Assistive TecHnology Systems] conference, and someone said to me, "Are you going to need attendant care for the PATHS conference?" I said, "Darla is my attendant care." I think we need to get back to that. Everybody is interdependent. There are things you can't do that maybe your neighbor can. "Well, I can't cook, but if you come over and cook for me, I'll fix your car for you." And I think here in West Virginia we are sitting on a gold mine because that's how this culture works. In a big city, if you try that, you might get knocked over the head. But I think here, that is something . . . because people relate to that.

Scotti: It's like that's a philosophy that has taken us all these years to come up with that we are now calling "positive behavioral support," which is really saying that, "OK, this person needs a life, this is what they want, this is what they have said they want . . . how do we help them get it?" And different people help them do different things, and they get help in return.

Ken: They do help in return, which I think people miss. I've had people with disabilities out in the community—who were able-bodied—come in and clean my house and I gave them a couple bucks. Or I took them out to dinner, or whatever.

Darla: Just saying, "Thank you."

Ken: Yeah. Having someone just treat them with a little dignity, instead of putting a checkmark by their name and saying you don't have to do that anymore . . . like a task analysis.

Scotti: I was called in on a case recently. A young man who lives in a two-story, two-bedroom house. He is very aggressive, and he is living in this house by himself with one-on-one staffing around the clock. They have bolted every door. They have actual *chicken wire* on every window. He is a young adult, but his favorite thing to do is watch "Looney Toons" on TV and sit around in this room with all these Sesame Street characters. The guy reads, but they don't let him have books because he rips them to pieces. I thought this was 1997, and I walked into this house and I thought it was *1967*.

Ken: And if he is acting aggressively, it's no wonder. Give him something age appropriate to do.

Scotti: Not only age appropriate but something . . .

Ken: . . . purposeful.

Scotti: Yes. He spends his whole day . . .

Ken: . . . hanging out with Cookie Monster.

Scotti: The only thing we need to do for this guy. . . . We don't need to fix his aggression—he needs a life!

Darla: Give him something to do and let him do it.

Scotti: And this man actually says, "I'd like to have a job. I'd like to have friends."

Darla: I was the same way until about 3 months ago. I met Ken through one of my best friends I knew for 15 years. She asked me to spend the night with her and I did, and on the way she stopped by here and picked up Kenny. And I was like . . . OK . . . now everything has changed for me.

Ken: Scotti, I've heard you say a couple of times during our conversation that we need to help people make a purposeful life for themselves. While I think that should be the aim of all human services professionals, I think the more important lesson we need to learn is how to get out of the way. So many of our regulations and so much of the system has been created for our own benefit and our own convenience. They don't really have anything to do with improving the quality of life of persons with disabilities. Many times the system creates hurdles to getting a life. The only way that all people can grow and develop self-esteem is through achievement and opportunity. As professionals, our aim should be to build bridges to opportunity and then get out of the way.

Scotti: You have been on both sides of the line here, and that's an important perspective to bring to this book. Thank you, Ken.

Chapter 22

Staff Development, Caring, and Community

Ian M. Evans

One of the first and most important insights in behavior modification (therapy) was the recognition of the critical role of caregivers in shaping an individual's behavior (see Chapter 1). People with significant cognitive or emotional disabilities are, ipso facto, going to be in somewhat dependent relationships with adults who are designated as their caregivers. As a result, the way in which caregivers respond to these individuals has a very significant effect on how the individuals behave. Because caregiving staff are employees—and the individuals who are receiving care are the employers (albeit, indirectly)—one might expect the direction of the influence to be the other way around. However, because of the individual's disability and the oblique nature of the employer–employee relationship, it is the influence of the caregiver on the consumer that typically has been the focus of research and training in behavior analysis.

When people who were in need of support were being served mostly in formal institutions, caregivers were exclusively paid staff. In community contexts, caregivers are still, of course, paid staff, but their role can be defined somewhat differently. There also are opportunities for people with developmental or psychiatric disabilities to come into contact with a wide range of other adults—those who typically provide people without disabilities with paid or professional services: bus drivers, plumbers, social welfare agency staff, bank clerks, and so forth (Segal & Aviram, 1978). Although this second group of service providers is not paid specifically or exclusively to provide services for people with disabilities, their fiduciary role is similar to that of direct caregiving staff in that the individual is a customer, not a friend, a partner, or a relative; and the way in which customers are treated has considerable influence on their quality of life and degree of independence. Furthermore, a person who lives in a more typical domicile has greater credence as a customer if he or she also participates in valued roles, such as renter, home handy-person, or avid gardener (Berkman & Meyer, 1988; Horner, Sprague, & Flannery, 1993; O'Brien, 1994). This chapter, therefore, is about the support roles of paid professionals, ranging from those who have regular and specific caregiving functions to those who have only sporadic and occasional contact with their customers.

Support for the preparation of this chapter was provided in part by the School of Social Sciences Research Fund, University of Waikato, which is acknowledged with thanks.

The unifying presumption of the client-as-customer creates four conditions for community services. First, the services should benefit the customer, or at least the customer's use of the services should be based on his or her own desires. Second, the services need to be of recognizable quality. Third, they need to be provided without creating a dependency relationship (exploiting the customer's vulnerabilities). Finally, the individuals providing these services may require special training in how to serve this particular group of customers appropriately and thus be able to meet the other three criteria.

Much of what this chapter discusses typically might be subsumed under the title of "staff training." To place the discussion in context, the chapter begins with a brief history and critique of some earlier perspectives in behavioral approaches to staff development. It then elaborates on an alternative conceptual model of the caregiving role, emphasizing the client-as-customer and articulating certain values and presumptions of the interpersonal relationship that should guide caregiver behavior. The chapter then examines the implications for training support staff and the skills and performance criteria that might be emphasized within this alternative conceptualization. Finally, the concepts are extended to the training needs of other professionals who provide services to customers with cognitive disabilities, and that direction is linked to the general topic of community support.

BRIEF HISTORY AND CRITIQUE OF "STAFF TRAINING"

Among the most influential articles in the early behavior analysis literature was a paper by Ayllon and Michael (1959), provocatively titled "The Psychiatric Nurse as a Behavioral Engineer." This and a number of other early papers were extremely important in revealing the significance of institution staff in shaping and controlling residents' behavior (Kazdin, 1984). The influence, it was thought, could be summarized within three broad categories: spontaneous behavior management, explicit behavior management, and skill development.

Spontaneous Behavior Management

One of the strongest arguments that evolved from the original insights was that staff in institutions inadvertently maintained negative behavior through selective attention (i.e., unplanned social reinforcement). Thus, a major concern became to reduce the iatrogenic tendencies of the institutional environment and to limit its tendency to shape undesirable behaviors. Principles of applied behavior analysis could not, of course, generate a completely different insight: namely, that people did not belong in institutions that took total control over their lives.

Because there were typically low rates (densities) of available reinforcement, social attention could be positively reinforcing even when the attention was perceived as negative or punitive by the person delivering it. Thus, criticisms, reprimands, yelling of commands, threats of punishment, and similar angry, hostile verbal behaviors from staff often seemed to increase undesirable behaviors among residents. It became very important to point out during staff training that any degree of attention might be reinforcing, even if the attention typically would be thought to be aversive. A related observation was that an aversive social event (e.g., a rebuke, a cross look, a slap, a yell) might cause a short-term suppression or cessation of the behavior of concern but that the general attention from staff would serve to reinforce the behavior in the future. Less consideration was given in the literature to the fact that the residents also represented a community of sorts. Thus, a staff member's use of negative attention might suppress behavior, but the reaction (e.g., laughter, admiration, respect, cohesion) from other individuals who were receiving care would maintain the behavior, particularly behaviors that were designed to irritate or retaliate against a disliked staff member. This phenomenon has been portrayed poignantly in popular descriptions of institutional life, such as in the novel and movie *One Flew over the Cuckoo's Nest.*

For staff training, recognition of such contingencies usually resulted in two types of recommendations. The least sophisticated—and probably the least effective—was to encourage extinction through the removal of social reinforcers such as attention, whether positive or negative. A problem was that if the individual's undesired behavior was being maintained because it evoked a reaction in otherwise relatively unresponsive staff, then efforts by staff to react even less would merely increase the motivation of the person to provoke a reaction. Thus, an individual would engage in increasingly undesirable or dangerous behavior until the staff simply could no longer inhibit their response. Planned extinction, unless superbly regulated, often broke down under sufficient duress, and more extreme behavior was actually being shaped by such contingencies.

The second variant of the general plan was to try to place the undesired behavior under extinction but simultaneously to maintain high levels of positive social behavior and attention, either by delivering it noncontingently or contingently on some other behavior that was considered acceptable. This often would be explained to staff as "catch the person being good." Technically, this is differential reinforcement of other behavior (DRO), a contingency usually defined as reinforcing the nonoccurrence of the undesired behavior, with a co-contingency that the more desirable behavior also must occur.

These contingencies are difficult to explain to care staff who are not steeped in principles of operant behavior and practically impossible for anyone to implement. The staff member essentially has to be programmed in a manner similar to an operant control panel, such that any response on lever A delays the delivery of noncontingent reinforcement or that any response on lever A delays the opportunity for the reinforcement of a response on lever B. In the lab, the length of the delay, whether the delay accumulates, and the positive contingency on lever B all can be easily regulated with timers. For the staff member, however, not only is it very difficult to define and time the contingency, but also the behavior to be extinguished (the A lever press) often is an entire class of behaviors (e.g., being disruptive, breaking institution rules) judged undesirable by someone. In addition, the

behavior(s) reinforced in the DRO contingency may not be functionally related to the target behavior (see Chapter 3).

Explicit Behavior Management

A different feature in staff training evolved from a second very important insight in early behavior modification. Most treatment plans, which were designed by a therapist, usually involved the careful orchestration of planned consequences by a clinician who might have only a few hours per week available for their implementation. Why not, therefore, teach other individuals who have more time and more access to implement the contingencies? In some environments, this became known as *pyramid therapy* because the sophisticated behavior analyst would design the program and teach it to nurses, for example, who in turn would train aides, who in turn might encourage higher functioning individuals to implement the conditions (Page, Iwata, & Reid, 1982). Instructing parents or teachers to deliver and, sometimes, to design these behavioral conditions became one of the cornerstones of behavior modification (Kazdin, 1978). A strong argument was not just that these "behavior change agents" would have more time but that they also would be much more socially reinforcing because they would have already established a meaningful relationship (e.g., a sibling, a peer) with the individual (Cash & Evans, 1975). The pioneering program developed by Tharp and Wetzel (1968) was called "behavior modification in the natural environment."

In institutional environments, nonclinically trained therapists (or clinicians from other disciplines [e.g., nurses]) inevitably were the direct care staff for individuals with cognitive disabilities. Thus, staff members with few formal educational qualifications were given the responsibility of implementing planned behavior management programs to reduce negative behaviors. Staff training manuals and workshops blossomed into a substantial industry. Many critics (e.g., Evans, 1990) have pointed out a number of concerns with the approach. First, however carefully behavior management programs are presented, it is difficult to avoid conveying to staff that their job is to *control* individuals' behaviors. Self-regulation techniques never received from professionals anything similar to the enthusiasm that was accorded to the extraordinary collection of control methods (e.g., overcorrection, time-out, response cost, token economy, Self Injurious Behavior Inhibiting System). Second, the language and the terminology of applied behavior analysis is not easy to master without the necessary university-level background in principles and theory. Finally, staff who already might be good "natural" therapists have to learn an alternative, sometimes artificial, set of concepts to guide their decision making and interactions with the people for whom they provide care.

Skill Development

A third way that staff were considered to have a large impact on the individuals under their care was the rapid realization in applied behavior analysis that instructional programs designed to teach people new skills, particularly self-help, could and should be implemented by direct care staff. Staff members were not in these environments simply to care for the individual or, indeed, to be doing things for an individual that he or she might eventually be capable of doing independently. The importance of this was highlighted by a number of dramatic civil rights cases in which it was successfully argued that if an institution were not actually providing for the rehabilitation and greater future independence of the individual, then the institution had no right to keep the individual in that environment (Scheerenberger, 1983). This important judicial trend placed considerable pressure on institutions to implement habilitative programming.

There is little doubt that the development of a teaching technology for basic skills that used simple but sound principles of operant conditioning (reinforcement, shaping, chaining, discriminative stimulus control, planned generalization, maintenance) was a major contribution by behavior analysis to the welfare of individuals with disabilities. One indirect benefit was that when learning opportunities were consistently and properly structured, it soon became apparent that individuals with mental retardation could be taught to do things that many considered them

incapable of doing. Another was that it greatly improved staff morale. Direct care staff could now see themselves as "teachers" or coaches and not just as babysitters whose only responsibility was physical care. A third benefit was that individuals did indeed learn these new skills at a surprising rate, which enabled movement from highly restrictive total care units to wards in which greater responsibility was placed on individuals. From these wards, individuals then were able to move to semi-independent living situations and eventually from the institution altogether. Behavior modification thus made a major contribution to the possibility and the reality of deinstitutionalization.

There were some limitations to behavior skills development: Most of them were technical, and some of them were procedural. A procedural concern was that staff members sometimes saw it as their duty to introduce programs, thus forcing individuals to learn skills all of the time, without breaks, time off, or holidays as would happen for any other, more typical student. The skills taught tended to be self-help skills, which were important but should not have been taught in the absence of other equally important skills, such as social and leisure skills. The various individual habilitation plans (IHPs), therefore, lacked balance. In some environments, quality assurance rules led to staff members' being cued to initiate a program according to a clock or a schedule, regardless of whether the recipient of the program wanted it, was ready, or was doing something else of greater interest.

The technical problems arose because the methods of instruction relied on an overzealous or literal generalization from the animal operant laboratory. These problems have been described many times before, but the following can be considered the major limitations:

1. The institution is an unnatural environment; many important functional skills (e.g., shopping) cannot be taught in it unless under artificial conditions (e.g., using the ward "store").
2. Many of the things that individuals should learn to do (e.g., making meals, washing clothes, performing basic house mainte-

nance) are not available to residents because these tasks are carried out in bulk by paid hospital staff (e.g., janitors, cooks).

3. Staff members have to rely heavily on external and often artificial rewards (e.g., reinforcers). Thus, the skilled behaviors were maintained not by intrinsic factors such as pride of accomplishment but by material reinforcements and tokens that, when removed, would result in decreases in performance.

4. Skills often were taught out of context and in a repetitive fashion. Even in the mid-1990s it was still possible to read behavioral training manuals in which repetitive practice of a basic skill was encouraged, rather than distribution of learning opportunities throughout the day in accordance with appropriate environments.

Repetitive, trial-by-trial instruction, occurring out of natural contexts and using artificial cues, materials, and rewards, has been one of the most consistently criticized aspects of poorly conceived and implemented behavior modification. Yet practices often continued because some of the developers of these methods thought that they somehow represented good behavioral principles (for a case study, see Leduc, Dumais, & Evans, 1990). This appears to have been a chronic problem throughout the history of behavior modification for developmental disabilities (Meyer & Evans, 1993; Voeltz & Evans, 1983) and is, indeed, partly the motivation for this book. Standard laboratory procedures and operant technology became confused with the clinically and socially sensitive application of sound behavioral and other psychological principles.

REEXAMINING THE CONSUMER–STAFF RELATIONSHIP

The implication of all three facets—spontaneous behavior management, explicit behavior management, and skill development—of nonprofessionals' roles as intervention agents was that staff would require even more intensive training in behavior modification. Performance standards for staff members were based on the assumption that slippage resulted from lack of

monitoring and reinforcement for correct performance. In retrospect, it can be argued that very little careful thought was given to the exact contents of this training: Were staff to be taught to implement programs designed for them by clinically trained professionals, or were staff actually to learn how to be behavior modification experts themselves? As in other aspects of behavior therapy, did the relationship between staff and individual matter (Wilson, Hannon, & Evans, 1968)? When behavior therapy is implemented with other individuals, therapists must spend considerable time in supervised training to learn a balance between caring for the client and being able to set sensitive personal boundaries and limits (e.g., Persons & Burns, 1985). Direct care staff spend much more time with particular individuals than do therapists. Who helps *the direct care staff* deal with feelings of overprotectiveness, disappointment with slow progress, and becoming too emotionally attached (Evans & Berryman, 1995)?

Should Staff Members Be Trained as Behavior Analysts?

Because a significant part of behavior therapy is the use of research methodology, the formulation of problems, and the application of scientific principles, teaching staff to be behavior analysts would involve such assessment and monitoring skills as being able to chart behaviors, to carry out functional analyses, and even to understand single-participant research designs. If, however, the staff members' roles are to implement a well-designed program, then they do not need to know any behavioral principles.

In addition, staff often have been expected to embrace the basic principles of behaviorism and to accept the general validity of this perspective on behavior and humanity. Staff who resisted certain aspects of the behavioral perspective, such as thinking of it as punitive or mechanistic, often were subjected to more intensive training or reassigned to other programs and agencies. No mechanism was developed whereby the staff could become better skilled at their tasks while maintaining some of their beliefs about care for individuals and the nature of their own roles. Often, these beliefs were based on humanistic principles that were not at all incompatible with behavioral perspectives, but staff would have a difficult time reconciling their new training with what they perceived to be an alternative perspective.

The upshot of these conflicting pressures was that staff members often did not implement behavioral procedures particularly well: They were quite poor at charting behaviors, and they did not understand the complexity of many principles and thus had no way of dealing with unexpected situations and crises. Perhaps most troublesome is that a certain number who already saw their role as that of controlling individuals under their care were encouraged by the language and style of behavior modification to adopt highly structured and frankly punitive programs. These programs, apparently, then were justified in the name of applied behavior analysis. It is not uncommon to hear staff members say that they cannot be sympathetic to an individual who is upset, whose feelings might be hurt, or who might be feeling rejected or jealous because to do so would just reinforce bad behavior. Such a fundamental misunderstanding of behavioral and psychological principles suggests that there could be negative consequences of teaching traditional behavior analysis principles to staff. There is a small but growing body of literature indicating that it is particularly helpful to teach staff to think about the causes of problem behavior rather than to focus on its modification (Berryman, Evans, & Kalbag, 1994). And, of course, there is nothing intrinsically controlling about behavioral principles, which can just as readily be used to promote the empowerment of individuals who are receiving care (Fawcett et al., 1994).

Should Caregivers Be Teachers or Facilitators of Learning?

At first glance, there may seem to be little difference between the two conceptualizations of staff as teachers and staff as facilitators of learning. There is, however, an important distinction between formal instruction and arranging conditions so that positive learning is facilitated. If caregivers see their role as similar to that of a teacher, then there will be pressure to impart particular skills to individuals, whether individuals want them or not. With this comes a related need for discipline and control (as in a school classroom), with the caregivers as authority figures. If, though, staff members create a responsive environment in which learning is possible, then considerable incidental learning will take place.

An analogy might be useful. If Kate decides that she wants to learn a new skill, such as carpentry or home repair, then she might choose to enroll in an adult education course at the local high school. Kate, as a consumer, would be selecting and buying, often at very little cost, a structured learning opportunity to provide her with a new skill. She probably would not like having a housemate or a landlord or a paid assistant insisting that she acquire home repair skills every 15 minutes when she is at home relaxing, not particularly wanting to learn anything. Similarly, if her housemate automatically repairs everything in the house as soon as it needs fixing, then Kate will have no opportunity to pick up some simple skills through watching and participating. Instead, her housemate might use a simple fix-it project to teach Kate new skills by inviting her to participate. For example, her housemate could ask Kate to hold the ladder or to get the glue. Individuals with cognitive disabilities need a responsive environment, but if formal teaching is to take place, then they need a choice of topics, tutors, locations, and times through or at which learning can take place. Many extension and adult night courses cater to the needs of individuals with mental retardation by providing brief courses in money management, nutritious cooking, growing vegetables, and so forth.

How Much Caring Is Needed in the Caregiver Role?

Training staff to be more potent agents of behavior change (the "engineers" in Ayllon and Michael's [1959] words) represented a paternalistic philosophy of staff roles (Kahn, 1985). The philosophy has become implicit in much of behavior modification, but it is not intrinsic to a behavior analysis. With community-based services, the concept of caregiving's providing *support* (Brown & Gothelf, 1996) has become much clearer, especially with the American Association on Mental Retardation's (1992) important and dramatic redefinition of mental retardation in terms of support systems needed. If a support concept is added to the essential realization that the individual is a customer who purchases support services, then the engineer metaphor for staff becomes even less apt.

In conventional behavior therapy, in which the contractual nature of the therapist as paid provider has been obvious from the beginning, it is still recognized that the nature of the relationship between client and therapist is of fundamental importance (Rosenfarb, 1992; Wilson & Evans, 1977). Caring becomes a parallel phenomenon and superordinate to the customer–provider contractual relationship. This is because, unlike commercial or business transactions, the service cannot be delivered without the caring element. To illustrate this assertion, consider the issue of the relationship simply within the educative function of staff.

SOCIAL CONTEXT AND LEARNING FACILITATION

The implication of the previous discussion is that the formal instructional role of caregivers should be clarified. Also, it may not be suitable for caregivers to be in a formal teaching role at all. Nevertheless, learning will take place in any positive environment—in the same sense that people come back from a trip to a foreign country and say, "I learned a lot," or go on an adventure experience and say, "I learned about myself," or share a dorm room in college and say later, "I learned how to live with others." Thus a caregiver's task is probably still to ensure that living environments foster positive learning and prosocial skill development (Favell & McGimsey, 1993). This section briefly considers some ways that social relationships and behavioral knowledge can assist in the design of positive living and learning environments.

Incidental Learning

Although applied behavior analysis has not used the term *incidental learning,* a similar construct has been part of behavioral theory. Incidental

teaching has been particularly well developed in the context of language learning (Hart & Risley, 1975; Warren & Kaiser, 1988). Favell and her colleagues (e.g., Favell & McGimsey, 1993; Favell, Favell, Riddle, & Risley, 1984) emphasized the response class construct of consumer *engagement,* defined as the active participation of individuals in the activities provided in the living environment. (Note how the word *provided* sustains the paternalism model.) Engagement sets the occasion for exploration, play, and practice.

Some of the conditions that promote engagement seem to be available menus of age-appropriate, fun, and useful activities that are not forced on residents. This is similar to the conditions at a holiday resort. Just as there are (presumably) at a resort facility shy people or depressed guests who might need some encouragement to select activities that they later find they enjoy, so, too, is it often the case that individuals who are receiving care—particularly those with long institutional histories—may need ways to facilitate their initial contact with an activity so that its intrinsic reinforcement value can then sustain the engagement. When to encourage someone to try something new and when to require him or her to participate is a complex discrimination requiring sensitivity and good judgment; however, it is presumed that staff who understand the importance of individual choice can learn the distinction.

One way that people who are not in institutions are prodded into new activities is through the energies of friends, who insist that they play tennis or visit an art exhibit or start a pottery class, even when they do not feel much like doing so at the time. It is difficult to imagine paid caregivers being able to fill this role. Therefore, an individual's access to friends with different and varied interests from his or her own would seem to be another essential condition to facilitating engagement. Caregivers could suggest that an individual contact a friend and then help him or her arrange a novel activity, which seems to be a more naturalistic way of promoting activities than having the staff be the organizers. Technically, this suggestion seems similar to the construct of peers as functional mediators (Fowler, 1988).

Learning that Is Generalizable

Generalization is an important issue: If an individual's living situation is to facilitate learning, then it also should assist the individual with coping with the more erratic contingencies of the everyday world. If the group home or community residence does not foster learning of useful community competencies, then it is difficult to argue that it is much better than the institutional environment. If the learning conditions created by staff are too consistent or too much under staff stimulus control, then the individual is not going to be able to function in the highly varied and inconsistent conditions of the real world.

There are some good strategies in applied behavior analysis to respond to this problem. One of the better known ones, general case instruction, has been described extensively and studied by Horner and his associates (e.g., Horner, McDonnell, & Bellamy, 1986). Essentially, the strategy involves providing the student with training opportunities that vary according to the range of actual variance that will be found in everyday tasks; training also can include negative examples of what not to do or what to avoid. If staff understand the need for variety in activities, events, and places, then general case instruction will occur naturally. At the same time, of course, an individual might have a preferred way of doing things, which must be respected. Staff need to understand that there is no need for general case instruction when the individual has mastered a skill that he or she likes in an environment that he or she most prefers.

A somewhat related problem exists when an individual is taught in a highly structured context and becomes dependent on the presence of a particular instructional cue or prompt. Because staff are used to being in charge of a situation, they often will provide the cue to begin a particular routine rather than encourage an individual to initiate the behavior. In work done on breaking down complex living tasks into separate, *meaningful* elements (Evans, Brown, Weed, Spry, & Owen, 1987), certain patterns have been noticed. An individual might, for example, be capable of going to the corner store and buying milk. This usually would be precipitated by a staff member's saying, "We're low on milk. Ruth, would you like to go out and get half a gallon of 2%?" Without the request by staff, Ruth would not have initiated this behavior on her own and might have waited until the milk had run out. This, in turn, would have confirmed staff perceptions that Ruth needed to be prompted to do things—"If she isn't reminded, then she just ignores it until it is too late," they would say.

Staff need to understand the importance of fading cues and using strategies to dilute instructional control. In the example given, for instance, a staff member can prompt by saying, "Let's look around and see whether there is anything that we need before the store closes." The formal procedure is to introduce a time delay between the natural cue (milk is getting low) and the prompt ("We need to get more milk"; Halle, Baer, & Spradlin, 1981). In practice, however, it has proved easier to coach staff in the general principle that individuals need to initiate behavior routines. From this, staff can derive a number of procedures for prompt/cue fading; alternating; or making more subtle or encouraging use of mnemonics, lists, and "duty" rosters (similar to any household with different people, such as college students, sharing responsibilities). Notice that for individuals with the most severe cognitive or motor impairments, initiation as *responsibility* is critical; it would be the correct consumer–caregiver role if staff approached the individual and said, "We are low on milk. Can you give me $2 from the household fund so that I can go and get some?" The actual task is fully supported (even initiated and certainly done entirely by the caregiver), but the individual retains the authority (by approving the purchase).

Social Context for Learning

From many different research areas is an enormous convergence of findings that indicate that children are most likely to participate actively in their own development when certain conditions of adult–child interaction are met. These have been reviewed and integrated skillfully by MacDonald (1990). There are four sets of conditions that might be thought of as ecobehavior patterns or supercontingencies, which does not mean setting events but setting interactional contingency rules that go beyond the traditional three-term contingency of antecedent-behavior-consequence.

Reciprocal Partnership

Hundreds of child development studies have demonstrated that child learning is influenced by the degree to which the adult–child interaction is give and take rather than one-sided control (Bronfenbrenner, 1979). In such interactions, both members of the partnership perceive themselves as doing something together. This is a criterion that can be taught to staff relatively easily. Turn taking is an easily understood rule or condition to which staff can adhere. Similar to any partnership, a necessary condition is that child and adult—or, for the purposes of this chapter, individual and supportive adult—reinforce each other equally so that each partner experiences success in influencing the other and thus gains a sense of competency. This, of course, means that both staff and individual will enjoy the interactions.

Matching

A staff member always understands that if he or she is playing a game with an opponent who is far more skilled than he or she is, then the resulting activity is neither enjoyable nor beneficial. In tennis, for example, a person cannot improve his or her game by playing with a world champion who overpowers him or her with every stroke. Because, by definition, staff will be more skilled in many domains than clients, effective learning requires that staff be attuned to an individual's motivational and cognitive state. Community environments that are unbalanced (consisting of cognitively typical "staff" on one side of the net and individuals with disabilities on the other) produce unusual, unbalanced conversations. For example, staff sometimes treat individuals under their care as though they were children, with high levels of teasing, joshing, and patronizing styles. Conversely, individuals under care often engage in a wheedling, bantering interaction that is insensitive to audience interests. When these unbalanced conversations dominate in a living environment, they do not teach the conversational styles necessary for a workplace, a café, or a quiet evening with friends.

Behavior analysts have investigated in some detail these communication patterns and the social conditions that shape them (see Guerin, 1997), but the implications for support service design in applied contexts have yet to be drawn.

Consumer-Centeredness

In the parent–child interaction literature, being sensitive usually is described as the adult's having some knowledge of the child's developmental pathways. In teaching, the comparable concept is that the learning situation needs to be oriented toward the child's level of knowledge and meaningful life experiences (Tharp & Gallimore, 1988). For staff, the task is complicated when individuals have been in restrictive environments: Their developmental steps may have been infantilized and distorted, and the individuals may be interested in juvenile things. This requires staff to make a very fine discrimination in which an adult-oriented, age-appropriate activity is presented in a manner that fits the developmental level of the individual. The concept of supports needed might be a more promising way of expressing developmental stage than is the *age*-normed concept of IQ score, which implies, erroneously, that a person with mental retardation is somehow similar to a young person.

Another important skill for staff that might sustain this developmental understanding is to explain that individuals need to express themselves. This serves to reduce the percentage of directives, commands, and staff-oriented rather than individual-oriented questions. One of the intriguing features of the procedure called Facilitated Communication—a skill that staff can develop to assist individuals to express themselves—is that the contingencies are such that the individual can never do wrong (i.e., the individual is errorless because he or she is never contradicted or told to type something out again) and that it typically seems to be directing the interaction (a bit similar to Gentle Teaching). This in turn may reduce the presence of inappropriate behavior to the extent that "negative" behavior is designed to be assertive and resistive of staff/ teacher control. As Green and Shane (1994) indicated, however, one of the weaknesses of Facilitated Communication is that if the communications do not in fact emanate from the individual, then the method essentially strips the person of self-expression entirely. This dilemma perhaps underlies much of the controversy about the procedure. For staff, the lesson is that ultimately they have to believe that the individual has something worthwhile of his or her own to offer, to say, or to contribute. This perception reduces the tendency to consider staff standards and opinions paramount. Similarly, managers need to respond in the same fashion to *staff* ideas and accept that they, too, have good ideas when allowed self-expression.

Emotional Attachment

The quality of the emotional attachment between parent and child is the fourth of the generalized contingency rules. The degree to which there is a positive affective (affectionate) bond between adult and child appears to influence the kinds of specific social and learning interactions that are possible. The quality of the attachment can be considered a setting event for a wide range of adult/staff behaviors. By observing that isolated, stressed mothers were unable to maintain the parenting skills that they had been taught, Wahler (1980) was able to conceptualize quality of attachment in behavior analytic terms. There is a difference, however, between a setting event that sets the occasion for a response or even a class of responses and a setting event that sets the occasion for a class of contingencies. Because paid staff are not similar to parents in role or function, a more suitable parallel to the latter type of setting event has been elaborated within the context of behavioral psychotherapy.

The best example of these generalized contingency rules being based on a relationship-derived setting condition is the dialectical behavior therapy developed by Linehan (1993) for treating people with borderline personality disorder. Simply put, the setting condition is one of acceptance: Rules, contracts, reinforcement schedules, or conditions stated in the treatment must first conform to the general criterion that the client is accepted by the therapist and will not be rejected or abandoned. Very difficult individuals with cognitive impairments often have

been moved from residence to residence or from service to service. Rejection, not the formation of positive emotional attachments, becomes the general rule, and staff may need to alter this global contingency, just as Linehan requires her trainee therapists to understand that once they have engaged an individual in treatment they may not act in a rejecting manner.

These topics have not previously been seen as relevant to the arena of staff training and development. They are so important that they are addressed again in a later section devoted specifically to the issue of emotional attachment, under the general rubric of the individual's "need to belong." It is expressed as general belonging because *attachment* is a construct that really applies specifically to early child–*parent* emotional bonding. It is important to recognize that staff are not parents, while at the same time realizing that a person who has not formed secure attachments is very difficult to integrate into a reciprocal and fair social world.

Developing New Performance Criteria for Staff

The four facets of social interaction that seem to be most effective for enhancing an individual's development and personal growth could be translated into specific competencies to be looked for in staff. The facets can, to a certain extent, be taught as well. They certainly are incorporated in some of the values that have emerged in educational and residential services for people with disabilities. Recognizing that staff–consumer interactions must be partnerships—responsively matched to developmental level, permitting self-expression, in the context of a positive affective relationship—is a clear set of verbal criteria or values (Meyer & Evans, 1989). Achieving the requisite behavior is a more complex task.

Staff can easily learn, for example, the approach developed by Durand (1990) regarding the value of teaching an alternative communication skill with the same function as the challenging behavior. If, however, they see this approach as a *treatment* for challenging behavior rather than as the importance of permitting individual self-expression, then they will continue to exert control over individuals, even if staff are focused on positive skill development rather than on negative contingencies. This is a situation in which a reorientation in perceived role might help make the distinctions clearer. But even if staff cannot articulate these concepts verbally, basing their performance evaluation on individual satisfaction might be a useful approach.

It has frequently been noted in the field of disability services that the daily per capita cost of maintaining large residential institutions is comparable to the price of a room in a 5-star hotel. But the question of why institutional employees do not behave like the *staff* of a 5-star hotel has not really been posed. The answer, of course, seems obvious—the contingencies are wrong. It is true that behavior analysts have managed to arrange salaries contingent on staff performance but have themselves (rather than the individuals who are receiving care) been the arbitrators of what the desired performance should be. Such an approach would be similar to running a hotel in which staff's conduct and compensation were not a function of the wishes of the guests but, instead, of some other management team who never stayed in the hotel.

A slight shift in orientation would result in a few simple standards and criteria for formally evaluating direct care staff. Customer satisfaction would be an important one. Personal evaluations (e.g., of staff by individuals who are receiving care) can be inconsistent as measures of consumer satisfaction, so it would be important to ensure that evaluations were not *just* a popularity measure, although assessing the degree to which individuals feel that staff care about them as people seems fundamental. Thus, a valuable and related measure is one that assesses the degree to which individuals spontaneously engage in various activities in the environment. In other words, the criterion would not be the correct implementation of a specific behavioral technique but the degree to which the customer actually benefited and valued the way in which progress was achieved. If a community support program has goals such as teaching self-advocacy, teaching individuals to recruit help to attain their own goals, and becoming more aware consumers—

all teachable repertoires (Balcazar, Fawcett, & Seekins, 1991)—then empowerment of individuals under their care is a legitimate standard for staff performance.

IMPLICATIONS FOR PURCHASE OF OTHER SERVICES

There often is a wide array of services offered to individuals in large residential institutions (e.g., a dentist who visits occasionally, a hairdresser, a small shop at which sundries can be bought, a librarian, an art therapist, a recreational therapist). People who live in the community, however, have to find their own dentist, their own hairdresser, and their own library. Thus, deinstitutionalization is one of the ultimate forms of privatization for people with disabilities, and with it comes the advantages (e.g., choice, competition) and disadvantages (e.g., deregulation, lack of protection for the public) of that business trend.

Evaluation by Consumer Reports

Just as some service companies find a market niche (e.g., youth, older adults, wealthy people, bargain hunters), many have found the economic benefits of being able to attract customers who have mental retardation. Quite a few behavior analysts have done very well in this market, and the family practitioner, dentist, or hairdresser who is able to provide a good service to people with disabilities soon discovers that he or she can be in considerable demand. As long as they are not expected to provide their services at a reduced price for people with disabilities, it may be reasonably assumed that the contingencies of the marketplace will soon shape the behavior of such providers.

The process can be facilitated. People with disabilities can be taught skills about how to select a service, how to judge its quality, and what is expected. Or they can be helped to make these judgments and arrangements. A comparable model from everyday life is provided by publications such as *Consumer Reports*. It is possible to subject various service providers to simple tests to ascertain the quality of the service as it is provided to people with disabilities.

Consumer Obligations: Being a Paying Customer Is Not Enough

Just as information about competent service providers can be provided to consumers with disabilities, additional information can be provided to the professional and service groups themselves. Unfortunately, prejudice or anxiety and fear can overcome the desire to make a sale. Thus, the emphasis on people with disabilities as reliable, paying customers should perhaps be promoted along with simple strategies for serving customers whose communication skills might be impaired.

There are few examples of such community-based efforts in the literature because the dominant model has been that people with disabilities have to be taught the functional skills that will make them indistinguishable as customers. A poignant example is how the person with a disability who flashes an American Express card is treated as opposed to how he or she is treated if he or she laboriously counts the correct change out of a little purse.

In a nice example of how practical such skills can be, Daysh (1995) taught people with significant cognitive disabilities and psychiatric problems to use an electronic bank card. In New Zealand, this technology is so widespread that it has all but replaced the writing of checks. All one needs is a card and a personal identification number (PIN), but one has to key some information into a small, handheld gadget that the storekeeper hands you. To make sure that the learners would be able to master all of the steps of this procedure (including the important one of not telling the PIN to someone else), Daysh obtained cooperation from the banks to set up some dummy accounts that could be used during the training.

Whereas much of the previous discussion in this chapter focuses on professional services, community living also requires contact with many other people on a less frequent basis. Staff members usually act as the point of contact for such services: It is staff who will telephone the electrician, the agency that will pay the property taxes, or the parent support group that will build the picnic table in the backyard. The principle that the individual, not the service provider, needs to be in charge, however indirectly, is worth maintaining. It has always been claimed that a primary reason for ensuring school-level integration (i.e., inclusion) is that children without disabilities will grow up to be the electricians, the government clerks, the hairdressers, the police, and so forth for people with cognitive disabilities. Thus, it is important that the people without disabilities learn to accept and respect people with disabilities—in school, on the job, and in the community. It is now time to test that assertion. Direct care staff are the mediators of community interactions for people who require extensive supports to have their needs and desires known, recognized, and objectively represented.

COMMUNITY CARE AND RISK

Perhaps the primary task of any caregiver is to reduce an individual's risks of living without sacrificing essential autonomy and civil liberties. As in any other area of social or medical services, there are rights and duties that have to be sustained in some sort of balance.

Rights and Duties

One of the interesting implications of the conceptual model presented is that *competence*—the state of having mental retardation or having a psychiatric disability—should have little effect on what people are allowed to do. People who have an income should pay taxes on it and support (e.g., vote against, campaign for) the political representatives who will spend those taxes. Certainly the idea that people with severe disabilities have civil rights is not a new one. And yet such appeals usually have contained a strong element of paternalism because they emphasize the rights without equally emphasizing the responsibilities that accompany them. Thus, a person might have the right to obtain a driver's license, regardless of being classified as having mental retardation; but with that right comes the responsibility to drive safely and not place other motorists at risk. The point can be generalized across the entire spectrum of civic and community behaviors (Winkler, 1986).

There are special implications of the relation between rights and responsibilities for the selection and targeting of problem behaviors. Behavior analysts tend to be especially interested in self-injurious behaviors and often refer to individuals as being a danger to themselves. Yet this emphasis contains a sense of the practitioners' professional and social culpability for the individual's being self-injurious. For example, if the self-injurious behaviors can be thought even partially to be caused by inappropriate treatments or residential environments, then indeed there is a special responsibility to change the treatments or environments. But if self-injurious behaviors are the product of (relatively) free choice (e.g., smoking, being tattooed, putting a stud in one's nose), then practitioners are less likely to interfere, which is how it should be.

The extension of this argument is that the behaviors that are most serious are those that harm other people. This does not refer to activities that are annoying or inconvenient to other people but to those that violate the rights and safety of others: crimes against property and people. Anyone who works in community-based services knows that the "last frontier"—the really difficult and challenging problems—are those problems that are caused by people with cognitive and psychiatric disabilities who break the law and commit serious offenses, especially aggressive acts. Again, statutory offenses are not included here: It is the chapter author's opinion that if someone with mental retardation wants to take illicit drugs, it should not be a major concern of the service provider unless the irresponsible use of drugs results in loss of control, psychotic states, or disinhibition that leads to violent crime.

As it is very difficult to remediate aggressive or even illegal behavior in community environments, it would seem to follow that people with severe disabilities must accept the same consequences for crime as any other citizen, *provided* that he or she also has been afforded all of the other civil rights of citizens. The only justification for not subjecting people with mental retardation to the natural contingencies of the justice system is if paternalistic control has been retained over the individual. It is simply that the incompetence argument (i.e., person did not know right from wrong) cannot be applied to void duties (i.e., responsibilities) and at the same time be used to validate rights. These arguments will shift the criteria for judging the change-worthiness of behavior toward the elimination of risk for society and the reduction of risk for the individual.

Risk Reduction

Community living involves risk for anyone, and the risks are two-way: There are opportunities in the community for people with severe disabilities to be hurt, exploited, and victimized; and there are opportunities for people with diminished levels of socialization, responsibility, self-knowledge, and coping ability to commit distressing antisocial acts of disruption and annoyance.

Staff members should not have to make decisions about these issues on their own. It should not be their sole responsibility to decide whether an individual is sufficiently safe to be allowed to exercise choice in activities, relationships, and so forth. Similarly, as staff members begin to make riskier decisions to reduce controls and restraints on individuals, they cannot be held solely accountable for the accidents that might happen or for the other harms that might befall individuals in the "big bad world." Supports for staff should, therefore, include clarification of the risk–benefit decisions that must be made in programming.

The consumer model is another element in this decision-making process. By clarifying the role of staff as the employees of the individual with the disability, the discussion can move away from the language, metaphors, and images that sustain other, less functional models. Calling individuals who were receiving care "kids" was common in agency consultation not that long ago; a bit further back, staff members would carry a large bundle of keys on a coiled, plastic-covered wire hanging from their belts. The implicit model of service conveyed by such icons is quite clear; it is certainly not that of the individual as employer. The word "staff" itself fits the consumer model quite well, as long as the image is of the staff at the baronial hall: Lords and millionaires probably do not really need an army of chambermaids, chauffeurs, butlers, and cooks to take care of their needs, but they are able to purchase these services. By a rapidly coalescing sense of social justice, society has decided that people with disabilities also may purchase such services, from funds provided by others. The next goal should be to help people with disabilities to actually live similar to lords and ladies—but perhaps less parasitically, returning to the community something of themselves, their labor, and their talents.

COMMUNITY SUPPORT: BELONGING

The previous discussion uses the language and metaphors of business to emphasize the responsibilities of staff members and other service providers toward individuals as their customers. Many concerned professionals, however, resist the analogy of the marketplace as the model for human services. There also are certain limits to the parallels that can be drawn, even though they do help reorient the nature of the professional–consumer relationship. A move away from obvious commercial service providers (e.g., taxi drivers, store clerks, podiatrists) to paid caregivers and professional consultants and finally toward totally nonreimbursed community and neighborhood supports shifts the nature of the exchange considerably toward concepts of reciprocity, belonging to a group, and acceptance. Thus, the discussion returns to the topic of emotional attachment but at the level of adult social interaction rather than in the context of parent–child relationships.

Social supports for most people come from a variety of sources: family and friends; neighbors; and special groups such as church (or other religious organization) membership, sports and clubs, even bars and coffee shops. The social support from staff cannot replace such communities. Generalizations can be made from the rest of the behavior therapy literature; for example, staff–individual relationships can provide a facilitative learning opportunity that permits a wider range of social opportunities. Community participation, therefore, may require both opportunity (physical integration within the community across roles—customer, contributor, friend, relative) and desire.

Need to Belong

There is a great deal of evidence that the desire for interpersonal attachments is a fundamental human motivation (Baumeister & Leary, 1995). This can be thought of as a basic need to belong,

to make social bonds. Challenging behavior in individuals with cognitive disabilities has been interpreted within behavior analysis as having a primary communicative function (see Chapter 11); however, it is possible to imagine that the function runs deeper, to the desire to connect, to affirm a social bond.

People whose social attachments are limited by their diagnostic status will have to satisfy this fundamental need by forming social bonds that are less than ideal. Mental retardation, for instance, is used as an excuse to restrict people's opportunities for sexual intimacy, for marriage, or for having (and thus loving and connecting to) children. It is ironic that larger residential institutions, which potentially *increased* a person's opportunity to make social attachments with others of similar abilities, self-perceptions, and interests, made serious efforts to *restrict* intimacies such as courtship, dating, and sexual exchanges. Relationships (nonsexual) with staff, however, often were tolerated, and anyone who has worked in such environments knows the status and importance attached to a special relationship with a staff member. This gave the resident access not only to various privileges and perks but also, perhaps more critical, to an affirmation that he or she was someone and belonged to something more than a devalued group.

The obvious problem, of course, is that the relationships with staff members are extremely uneven and nonreciprocal. Some of them, in fact, are genuine; one of the most prominent experiences of professional helpers is the formation of sometimes intense relationships with clients, perhaps similar to what in the psychoanalytic literature is called *countertransference*. But, at the end of the day, professional staff retire, resign, graduate, move away, lose interest, and thus break off contacts that might well have been meaningful to both parties. Presumably, staff have other family and social attachments or make new ones in new employment. But individuals in residential programs are stuck. They have to start over with a new employee, a new shift, new foibles, new rules, new nuances of social interaction. Even if the individual is in community-based services, surveys have revealed that social integration cannot be guaranteed, especially for people with psychiatric diagnoses. Former patients' contacts with family and friends are limited, and social networks largely consist of professional contacts (Brugha et al., 1988; Francis, Vesey, & Lowe, 1994). A New Zealand study of individuals with chronic mental illness conducted after 18 months in community programs found them to have little contact with neighbors, more than half had no contact with outside friends, and one third had no contact with family or relatives (Macmillan, Hornblow, & Baird, 1992).

Caring Relationships

If there is validity to this analysis of relationships between staff members and the individuals under their care, then no amount of staff training, however focused on social relationships rather than on management skills, can help meet the needs of people with disabilities unless such people have or can forge their own nonemployee, close personal relationships. Surely, one cannot guarantee that a friendship will last any longer than the staffperson's employment contract (see Chapter 13). Break up of relationships is known to be highly disruptive to all people, and individuals cope in various ways—many of them mediated by supportive family and friends. Thus, the person with a disability must have the same range of social supports, with their multiple functions and availability. This connects the analysis of this chapter with those research and policy directions that emphasize friendships but takes it perhaps further in terms of romantic (e.g., lovers, sex partners, spouses) and family ties that are intergenerational (e.g., one's parents and one's children). Without these opportunities, the burden on staff as substitutes is simply too great.

As caring helpers, caregiving staff—similar to a psychotherapist—can assist in the mediation and development of relationships, but they cannot—and should not—provide relationships themselves. They can facilitate, using the self-same strategies as a therapist. These include but are not limited to some of the following strategies:

Unconditional positive regard: providing noncontingent acceptance for an individual in times of need and difficulty so that his or her willingness to rely on and trust others is reaffirmed

Social reality testing: by responding honestly and expressing feelings about interactions (giving social feedback), providing a nonthreatening or relatively neutral opportunity to learn how one's behavior is likely to be received by others

Facilitation of social opportunities: providing information and guidance for an individual on how to meet new people, how to gain access to a social group

Reducing emotional barriers: working to overcome emotional barriers to social activities, often in the form of desensitizing fears and anxieties about social contact, and cognitive restructuring of self-defeating attitudes and perceptions about one's acceptability to others

If the relationship-facilitation effect of caring support staff is recognized, then the emotional quality of attitude toward people under staff's care is only part of a complex set of interpersonal behaviors that dictate the nature of the interaction between staff and individual. One might presume that staff mood, stress levels, and acceptance of their task all affect the quality of caregiving. The caregiving task itself can be a stressful one. A study has shown that African American caregivers coped better with the stress of supporting people with Alzheimer's disease; the authors speculated that there are aspects of the African American culture that allow for better coping with the demands of the caring role (Haley et al., 1996). Very little is really known about the cultural expectations, personal beliefs, environmental pressures, and internal mood changes that determine the day-to-day behavior of staff, who often are poorly paid and recruited from many walks of life.

Culture of Support Environments

Every social organization, be it a business, office, school, or social service, has a distinctive atmosphere. The "feel" of a social environment is related to management practices and policies and the values inherent to and articulated for the participants. No matter how they are trained or what the management philosophies might be, direct care staff are able to make countless decisions every day regarding individuals and staff expectations for them, from the general to the specific: Which behaviors are going to be allowed; how much autonomy will be permitted; is teasing acceptable; who should answer the door; should I tell her that her sweater doesn't match her skirt and if I should, how should I do it without hurting her feelings?

These decisions rarely can be anticipated by management rules, especially when, as already argued, the staff bring their own unique set of values and expectations to the task. In a study of teaching empathy skills to care staff, McLees and Evans (1996) noted that the deeply religious background of many employees in a particular region influenced the atmosphere of the residences. Assessing the homes using the Community-Oriented Programs Environment Scale (Moos, 1988), the study found that although the staff created an atmosphere that was highly supportive and that encouraged individual involvement, the program emphasized order, program clarity, and staff control, thus reducing the degree of individual autonomy, expression of feelings, and the identification of the individuals' personal problems. Although staff learned the empathy skills that they were taught, they tended not to apply them, arguing that such a stance would give individuals the message that staff agreed with their feelings, when in actuality they thought that the individuals' behaviors were wrong. Staff also found it difficult to abandon their well-rehearsed tactics of threatening and cajoling the individuals under their care. After the empathy training, one staff member was heard to combine empathy and coercion: "I know you're angry, but if you don't cool down you will lose your privileges."

The culture (i.e., climate, atmosphere, social environment) of support environments is fascinating to observe and often hard to change. Small, independent fiefdoms always have seemed to be the most resistive to consultative influence, whether it be the teacher who is sole master of his or her classroom, a parent advocacy group that is influenced by a strong leader,

or a group home that is cut off from the interactional demands of the neighborhood. Therefore, paradoxically, it may be the nonexpert, "untrained" service providers, who deliver the mail, read the meter, or tint the hair, who may provide a normative community standard for the treatment of customers.

CONCLUSION

The consumer model, although an extended metaphor, does represent what can be called a generalized contingency. If an individual who receives care is the customer who purchases services, then the contingencies that are put into effect by such a conceptualization are powerful ones. At least they have been considered to have influence in many other areas of public and social services in which privatization has redefined the public as the direct purchasers of services. In New Zealand, for example, this business service ethic was introduced in the Department of Social Welfare. Clerical staff who determine welfare payments are now titled "customer service representatives," and people who are seeking welfare (or visiting the offices for any reason) may not be kept waiting more than 2 minutes prior to being helped. Staff have training in such areas as cultural practices, how to respond to angry customers, and how to pronounce the names of members of minority groups. The difference in atmosphere between such offices and the typical social welfare office in the United States is palpable. Effectiveness notwithstanding, it demonstrates that management practices and standards can alter support services. Brown and Gothelf (1996) and Fredericks (1996) provided interesting examples of the management philosophies that affect the living conditions of people with multiple disabilities.

Conversely, it is apparent that the consumer model has limitations with respect to human services. Once a service contract is purchased from government, subsequent choice is restricted. It is ironic that the term "choice" has become almost synonymous with the new values and yet for individuals it is almost always choice within a range offered or provided by those who have the service contract for a given region. The consumer model also is influenced heavily by conservative, market-economy ideologies. University faculty recognize that it is because of relationships with students that the activity is different from that between customer and storekeeper. Universities do not "sell" degrees, but they produce better informed, more knowledgeable minds. Educated students are the products of the university, not the customers; and agreed-on (not exploitative) social interaction makes the development of these minds possible.

The relationships between therapist and client, doctor and patient, teacher and pupil *are* different from commercial transactions, and they involve specific values, ethical principles, and contractual understanding that go beyond the purchase of a service. Thus, do not take the metaphor of the consumer too far and too literally. At the same time, however, the consumer model provides a useful reorientation and provides an alternative to various forms of paternalism that have characterized models of caregiving in the past—from those that are autocratic (into which much of behavior analysis readily fits) to those that are benevolent (into which some of the recent foci on values seem to fit). Services are purchased for individuals by a benevolent society. It has not always been so and perhaps will not be so again in the future. The model of the individual as consumer who *also* enters into a social and trusting relationship with caregivers (to the mutual benefit of the individual and society), however, still provides a more precise framework for judging staff and their competence.

REFERENCES

American Association on Mental Retardation. (1992). *Mental retardation: Definition, classification, and systems of supports.* Washington, DC: Author.

Ayllon, T., & Michael, J. (1959). The psychiatric nurse as a behavioral engineer. *Journal of the Experimental Analysis of Behavior, 2,* 323–334.

Balcazar, F.E., Fawcett, S.B., & Seekins, T. (1991). Teaching people with disabilities to recruit help to attain personal goals. *Rehabilitation Psychology, 36,* 31–42.

Baumeister, R.F., & Leary, M.R. (1995). The need to belong: Desire for interpersonal attachments as a fundamental human motivation. *Psychological Bulletin, 117,* 497–529.

Berkman, K.A., & Meyer, L.H. (1988). Alternative strategies and multiple outcomes in the remediation of severe self-injury: Going all out nonaversively. *Journal of The Association for Persons with Severe Handicaps, 13,* 76–86.

Berryman, J., Evans, I.M., & Kalbag, A. (1994). The effects of training in nonaversive behavior management on the attitudes and understanding of direct care staff. *Journal of Behavior Therapy and Experimental Psychiatry, 25,* 241–250.

Bronfenbrenner, U. (1979). *The ecology of human development.* Cambridge, MA: Harvard University Press.

Brown, F., & Gothelf, C.R. (1996). Community life for all individuals. In D.H. Lehr & F. Brown (Eds.), *People with disabilities who challenge the system* (pp. 175–188). Baltimore: Paul H. Brookes Publishing Co.

Brugha, T.S., Wing, J.K., Brewin, C.R., MacCarthy, B., Mangen, S., Lesage, A., & Mumford, J. (1988). The problems of people in long-term psychiatric day care: An introduction to the Camberwell High Contact Survey. *Psychological Medicine, 18,* 443–456.

Cash, W.N., & Evans, I.M. (1975). Training pre-school children in the modification of their retarded siblings' behavior. *Journal of Behavior Therapy and Experimental Psychiatry, 6,* 13–16.

Daysh, R.C. (1995). *Training people with an intellectual disability to utilize the EFTPOS system to enhance community independence.* Unpublished master's thesis, University of Waikato, Hamilton, New Zealand.

Durand, V.M. (1990). *Severe behavior problems: A functional communication training approach.* New York: Guilford Press.

Evans, I.M. (1990). Teaching personnel to use state-of-the-art nonaversive alternatives for dealing with problem behavior. In A.P. Kaiser & C.M. McWhorter (Eds.), *Preparing personnel to work with persons with severe disabilities* (pp. 181–201). Baltimore: Paul H. Brookes Publishing Co.

Evans, I.M., & Berryman, J.S. (1995). Naturalistic strategies for modifying and preventing challenging behaviors. In W.W. Woolcock & J.W. Domaracki (Eds.), *Instructional strategies in the community: A resource guide for community instruction for persons with disabilities* (pp. 157–184). Austin, TX: PRO-ED.

Evans, I.M., Brown, F.A., Weed, K.A., Spry, K.M., & Owen, V. (1987). The assessment of functional competencies: A behavioral approach to the evaluation of programs for children with disabilities. In R.J. Prinz (Ed.), *Advances in behavioral assessment of children and families* (Vol. 3, pp. 93–121). Greenwich, CT: JAI Press.

Favell, J.E., & McGimsey, J.E. (1993). Defining an acceptable treatment environment. In R. Van Houten & S. Axelrod (Eds.), *Behavior analysis and treatment* (pp. 25–45). New York: Plenum.

Favell, J.E., Favell, J., Riddle, J.I., & Risley, T.R. (1984). Promoting change in mental retardation facilities: Getting services from the paper to the people. In W.P. Christian, G.T. Hannah, & T.J. Glahn (Eds.), *Programming effective human services: Strategies for institutional change and client transition* (pp. 83–97). New York: Plenum.

Fawcett, S.B., White, G.W., Balcazar, F.E., Suarez-Balcazar, Y., Mathews, R.M., Paine-Andrews, A., Seekins, T., & Smith, J.F. (1994). A contextual-behavioral model of empowerment: Case studies involving people with physical disabilities. *American Journal of Community Psychology, 22,* 471–496.

Fowler, S.A. (1988). The effects of peer-mediated interventions on establishing, maintaining, and generalizing children's behavior changes. In R.H. Horner, G. Dunlap, & R.L. Koegel (Eds.), *Generalization and maintenance: Life-style changes in applied settings* (pp. 143–170). Baltimore: Paul H. Brookes Publishing Co.

Francis, V.M., Vesey, P., & Lowe, G. (1994). The closure of a long-stay psychiatric hospital: A longitudinal study of patients' behaviour. *Social Psychiatry and Psychiatric Epidemiology, 29,* 184–189.

Fredericks, H.D.B. (1996). Residential living for individuals with profound disabilities who are deaf-blind. In D.H. Lehr & F. Brown (Eds.), *People with disabilities who challenge the system* (pp. 189–208). Baltimore: Paul H. Brookes Publishing Co.

Green, G., & Shane, H.C. (1994). Science, reason, and facilitated communication. *Journal of The Association for Persons with Severe Handicaps, 19,* 151–172.

Guerin, B. (1997). Social contexts for communication: Communicative power as past and present social consequences. In J.L. Owen (Ed.), *Context and communication behavior* (pp. 133–179). Reno, NV: Context Press.

Haley, W.E., Roth, D.L., Coleton, M.I., Ford, G.R., West, C.A.C., Collins, R.P., & Isobe, T.L. (1996). Appraisal, coping, and social support as mediators of well-being in Black and White family caregivers of patients with Alzheimer's disease. *Journal of Consulting and Clinical Psychology, 64,* 121–129.

Halle, J.W., Baer, D.M., & Spradlin, J.E. (1981). Teachers' generalized use of delay as a stimulus control procedure to increase language use in handicapped children. *Journal of Applied Behavior Analysis, 14,* 389–409.

Hart, B., & Risley, T.R. (1975). Incidental teaching of language in the preschool. *Journal of Applied Behavior Analysis, 8,* 411–420.

Horner, R.H., McDonnell, J.J., & Bellamy, G.T. (1986). Teaching generalized skills: General case instruction in simulation and community settings. In R.H. Horner, L.H. Meyer, & H.D.B. Fredericks (Eds.), *Education of learners with severe handicaps: Exemplary service strategies* (pp. 289–314). Baltimore: Paul H. Brookes Publishing Co.

Horner, R.H., Sprague, J.R., & Flannery, K.B. (1993). Building functional curricula for students with severe intellectual disabilities and severe problem behaviors. In R. Van Houten & S. Axelrod (Eds.), *Behavior analysis and treatment* (pp. 47–71). New York: Plenum.

Kahn, R.F. (1985). Mental retardation and paternalistic control. In R.S. Laura & A.F. Ashman (Eds.), *Moral issues in mental retardation* (pp. 57–68). London: Croom Helm.

Kazdin, A.E. (1978). *History of behavior modification.* Baltimore: University Park Press.

Kazdin, A.E. (1984). *Behavior modification in applied settings* (3rd ed.). Homewood, IL: Dorsey.

Leduc, A., Dumais, A., & Evans, I.M. (1990). Social behaviorism, rehabilitation, and ethics: Applications for people with severe disabilities. In G.H. Eifert & I.M. Evans (Eds.), *Unifying behavior therapy: Contributions of paradigmatic behaviorism* (pp. 268–289). New York: Springer.

Linehan, M.M. (1993). *Cognitive behavioral treatment of borderline personality disorder: The dialectics of effective treatment.* New York: Guilford Press.

MacDonald, J. (1990). An ecological model for social and communicative partnerships. In S.R. Schroeder (Ed.), *Ecobehavioral analysis and developmental disabilities: The twenty-first century* (pp. 154–181). New York: Springer-Verlag.

Macmillan, M., Hornblow, A., & Baird, K. (1992). From hospital to community: A follow-up of community placement of the long term mentally ill. *New Zealand Medical Journal, 9,* 348–350.

McLees, E.E., & Evans, I.M. (1996). *The effects of empathy skills training: Groups interventions with adults with mild mental retardation and their direct care staff.* Unpublished manuscript, State University of New York at Binghamton.

Meyer, L.H., & Evans, I.M. (1989). *Nonaversive intervention for behavior problems: A manual for home and community.* Baltimore: Paul H. Brookes Publishing Co.

Meyer, L.H., & Evans, I.M. (1993). Science and practice in behavioral intervention: Meaningful outcomes, research validity, and usable knowledge. *Journal of The Association for Persons with Severe Handicaps, 18,* 224–234.

Moos, R.H. (1988). *Community-Oriented Programs Environment Scale* (2nd ed.). Palo Alto, CA: Consulting Psychologists Press.

O'Brien, J. (1994). Down stairs that are never your own: Supporting people with developmental disabilities in their own homes. *Mental Retardation, 32,* 1–6.

Page, T.J., Iwata, B.A., & Reid, D.H. (1982). Pyramidal training: A large scale application with institutional staff. *Journal of Applied Behavior Analysis, 15,* 338–351.

Persons, J.B., & Burns, D.D. (1985). Mechanism of action of cognitive therapy: Relative contribution of technical and interpersonal intervention. *Cognitive Therapy and Research, 9,* 539–551.

Rosenfarb, I.S. (1992). A behavior analytic interpretation of the therapeutic relationship. *The Psychological Record, 42,* 341–354.

Scheerenberger, R.C. (1983). *A history of mental retardation: A quarter century of promise.* Baltimore: Paul H. Brookes Publishing Co.

Segal, S.P., & Aviram, U. (1978). *The mentally ill in community-based sheltered care: A study of community care and integration.* New York: John Wiley & Sons.

Tharp, R.G., & Gallimore, R. (1988). *Rousing minds to life: Teaching, learning, and schooling in social context.* Cambridge, England: Cambridge University Press.

Tharp, R.G., & Wetzel, B. (1968). *Behavior modification in the natural environment.* New York: Academic Press.

Voeltz, L.M., & Evans, I.M. (1983). Educational validity: Procedures to evaluate outcomes in programs for severely handicapped learners. *Journal of The Association for the Severely Handicapped, 8,* 3–15.

Wahler, R.G. (1980). The insular mother: Her problem in parent–child treatment. *Journal of Applied Behavior Analysis, 13,* 207–217.

Warren, S.F., & Kaiser, A.P. (1988). Research in early language intervention. In S.L. Odom & M.B. Karnes (Eds.), *Early intervention for infants and children with handicaps: An empirical base* (pp. 89–108). Baltimore: Paul H. Brookes Publishing Co.

Wilson, G.T., & Evans, I.M. (1977). The therapist–client relationship in behavior therapy. In A.S. Gurman & A.M. Razin (Eds.), *The therapist's contribution to effective psychotherapy: An empirical approach* (pp. 335–355). New York: Pergamon.

Wilson, G.T., Hannon, A.E., & Evans, I.M. (1968). Behavior therapy and the therapist–patient relationship. *Journal of Consulting and Clinical Psychology, 32,* 103–109.

Winkler, R.C. (1986). Rights and duty: The need for a social model. In N.J. King & A. Remenyi (Eds.), *Health care: A behavioural approach* (pp. 265–276). Sydney, Australia: Grune & Stratton.

Chapter 23

The Dialogue Between Research and Application

A Focus on Practical Issues in Behavioral Intervention

Richard P. Hastings

In the late 1970s, behavior analysts began analyzing the apparent lack of impact of basic research in the applied field and called for closer links between the basic and applied domains (e.g., Deitz, 1978; Hayes, Rincover, & Solnick, 1980; Michael, 1980; Poling, Picker, Grossett, Hall-Johnson, & Holbrook, 1981). These pleas resulted in a number of reviews of basic research findings that had clear clinical implications (e.g., Epling & Pierce, 1983, 1990; McDowell, 1982, 1988; Myerson & Hale, 1984; Remington, 1991). Despite laudable attempts to facilitate connections between research and application, and the clear relevance of basic research findings to human behavior problems, commentaries have suggested that much still remains to be done (e.g., Mace, 1994).

Although this paints a rather negative picture, there are a growing number of examples of applied studies that have drawn on principles derived from basic research with humans and animals. For example, a special issue of the *Journal of Applied Behavior Analysis* (JABA; Mace & Wacker, 1994) was devoted to papers that used basic research findings in the analysis of human behavior. A study in that special issue by

Lerman, Iwata, Zarcone, and Ringdahl (1994) illustrated the nature of this kind of research. These researchers sought to apply the concept of adjunctive behavior (schedule-induced behavior) to the analysis of problem behaviors of people with developmental disabilities. Basic research has shown that some responses in nonhuman subjects increase in frequency when exposed to intermittent reinforcement. For example, intermittent food delivery to rats can result in polydipsia (Falk, 1961). In the applied study of people with developmental disabilities, Lerman et al. (1994) exposed participants who engaged in stereotyped behaviors to a variety of fixed-time schedules of noncontingent food delivery. The results confirmed previous applied research findings (e.g., Emerson & Howard, 1992) by demonstrating schedule induction of stereotypies in some participants. Thus, the basic phenomenon of schedule induction may be a useful model to consider in the analysis of human behavior problems.

A further development in the same journal is a series of essays in which a basic and an applied researcher analyzed the applied significance of research published in an issue of the

Journal of the Experimental Analysis of Behavior (JEAB; see JABA, Winter 1993). These essays contain a wealth of information and ideas that are relevant to the design and implementation of behavioral interventions. The basic research issues addressed in these essays include delayed reinforcement (Hayes & Hayes, 1993; Hineline & Wacker, 1993); instructions, rule-governed behavior, and self-reports (Cataldo & Brady, 1994; Hineline & Wacker, 1993; Kirby & Bickel, 1995; Shull & Fuqua, 1993); the collateral effects of behavior change (Shull & Fuqua, 1993); choice and the matching law (Pierce & Epling, 1995; Shull & Fuqua, 1993); response effort (Friman & Poling, 1995); stimulus classes (Stromer, Mackay, & Remington, 1996); and reinforcement schedules (Lattal & Neef, 1996). JABA has also begun publishing the JEAB table of contents and selected abstracts for papers of applied relevance.

All of the areas of basic research just mentioned are crucial for those involved with the implementation of behavioral interventions. Research on delayed reinforcement can inform interventions when reinforcers cannot be applied immediately. Clearly, clinicians are asking staff to follow rules and instructions: How can clinicians ensure that staff do as they ask? There are a number of other questions that can be informed by developments in basic research: What are the side effects or collateral effects of interventions? How can clinicians select effective reinforcers and devise appropriate schedules of reinforcement for intervention?

Given these developing resources in the main behavior analytic journals, the aim of this chapter is not to provide another detailed summary of basic research findings and their implications for applied work but rather to discuss in some detail two issues that have immediate implications for the planning and implementation of behavioral interventions. These issues are central to the design and implementation of behavioral interventions, but they have often been given little if any attention in the literature—even in the essays cited previously.

The first issue is the development of problem behavior. Although the methods used to identify the *current functions* of problem behaviors

are well developed (e.g., Neef & Iwata, 1994; JABA special issue; see, e.g., Chapters 3, 13, 16, and 18), there has been little work of a behavior analytic nature that has examined the *development* of such behavior. Research of this nature would have implications for preventive intervention. The second issue is a framework for the analysis of the behavior of those who implement behavioral interventions in applied environments. This analysis draws on a number of concepts from the basic literature, including rule-governed behavior. Despite a growing awareness of the importance of developing appropriate support for intervention staff and of the central role that these staff play in determining the success of behavioral intervention in community environments (e.g., Chapters 5, 6, 14, 15 and 22; Weigle, 1997), there is no established behavioral research literature to inform this aspect of intervention.

DEVELOPMENT OF PROBLEM BEHAVIORS

The contributions to this book demonstrate that complex analytical and multicomponent intervention strategies have become established in the treatment of human behavior problems. Such state-of-the-art behavioral interventions are concerned primarily with a consideration of the *current* functions of a particular behavior or behaviors (i.e., the maintaining conditions for the behavior). Implicit in behavior analytic accounts of problem behaviors is the notion that these responses developed as a result of the same basic behavioral processes that currently maintain the behavior. However, there is a paucity of research that directly addresses this issue.

This apparent lack of attention is understandable given that interventionists typically are not asked to assist individuals until their behavior has reached a threshold of possible harm to the person or to others or is interfering seriously with the person's enjoyment of an "ordinary life" (Emerson, Felce, McGill, & Mansell, 1994). However, behavior analysts would also be able to contribute to the prevention of serious behavior disorders if the development of such behaviors were better understood.

Development of Self-Injurious Behavior

There are a small number of relevant studies and hypotheses in the literature that provide a useful starting point for understanding the development of self-injurious actions. Self-injurious behaviors, as brought to the attention of behavior analysts in clinical practice, appear to develop in one of two ways.

First, self-injurious behaviors may evolve from existing stereotyped responses (Guess & Carr, 1991). A large proportion of individuals with developmental disabilities engage in stereotyped behaviors (e.g., up to 70% of those living in residential facilities [Rojahn, 1986]). These behaviors may arise in the course of typical human development (Thelen, 1981) but simply persist in individuals with developmental disabilities (perhaps because their behavioral repertoires are limited or because of the relatively impoverished environments in which they live). Exactly how stereotypies evolve into self-injurious actions remains a topic for debate and investigation.

Guess and Carr (1991) suggested that repetitive actions can be understood at three levels. At Level I, repetitive behaviors are viewed as a behavior-state condition in the same way as being asleep, awake, alert, or inactive (cf. Guess et al., 1990). Thus, engagement in repetitive actions is regulated internally (i.e., via biological processes of some kind). At Level II, people with disabilities may regulate their arousal levels through the use of stereotyped behaviors. For example, individuals may engage in more stereotypy to maintain arousal levels when little else is going on in their living environment. This functional use of repetitive behaviors may emerge alongside development of awareness of the physical environment. At Level III, repetitive behaviors (particularly those labeled as self-injurious) come to manipulate the social environment. It is hypothesized that a large proportion of repetitive self-injury develops through these three stages (i.e., control of the physical environment leads to control of the social environment). Essentially, this model suggests that self-injurious behaviors move from Level II to Level III through the same basic shaping process that is responsible for the development of other human behavior.

Second, the establishment of some self-injurious responses may be more dramatic than that of gradual shaping processes. According to this model, certain apparently self-injurious topographies of behavior may develop originally for one purpose and be maintained as a result of associated effects. For example, Carr and McDowell (1980) worked with a young boy who began hitting the side of his head as a result of an irritating and painful ear infection. When the ear infection cleared up, however, the boy continued to injure himself. This self-injury had been reliably associated with attention from caregivers, who were concerned about the ear infection, and persisted because it continued to be a reliable way of obtaining attention from others.

This second model of the emergence of self-injury probably leaves little room for behavioral intervention as a preventive measure. Of course, clinicians can make sure that medical problems are identified and treated quickly in people with developmental disabilities. Other than that, it is difficult to predict who will be at risk for developing self-injurious responses. The first model—emphasizing a gradual shaping process—may offer many more opportunities for preventive behavioral intervention. The challenge, however, is to identify the early stages of that process of response evolution.

A project that is being conducted by researchers in London aims to take up that challenge. Hall, Oliver, and Murphy (e.g., Hall, 1997; Murphy & Hall, 1995) have been observing young children with developmental disabilities who display stereotypies that may be considered very mild versions of potentially damaging self-injurious responses. These children engage in behaviors such as light head tapping, very mild eye poking, and contact between body parts and teeth—all without causing any injury. Following a survey of schools for children with developmental disabilities, 17 children who were younger than 10 years and who were identified by teachers as exhibiting these "early self-injury" behaviors were selected for study. This was not an epidemiological study; therefore, it is not clear what proportion of children in these schools displayed the target behaviors.

The methodology used in this study is similar to that developed in a case study of a young adult male living in a residential facility (Hall & Oliver, 1992). Approximately 16 hours of real-time observations of the man's typical interactions in his living environment revealed a characteristic pattern repeated several times during the day. The man began to self-injure when the probability of care staff's attending to him was very low. As he continued to injure himself, the probability of staff's attending to him increased dramatically. Self-injury was then likely to cease. After the cessation of self-injury, the probability of the man's receiving attention from staff gradually returned to pre–self-injury levels. Thus, low attention acted as an establishing operation for self-injury, and high attention acted as an abolishing operation. Similarly, self-injury was an establishing operation for staff attention, and cessation of self-injury was an abolishing operation (Hall & Oliver, 1992; Oliver, 1995). An escape-motivated behavior would simply have a mirror-image profile to that just described for an attention-motivated behavior.

The Hall and Oliver (1992) study identified the processes that were maintaining the self-injurious behavior of the young man. The rationale for observing young children who display *potentially* self-injurious responses is that if the same behavioral processes are responsible for the development and maintenance of problem behaviors, then the characteristic interaction patterns obtained in the pilot study are likely to be found for some of these children (the Guess & Carr, 1991, model makes a similar prediction). Preliminary analyses of the data from Hall's (1997) study have shown that 4 of the 17 children observed have either the escape- or the attention-motivated behavior profiles described previously. Behavior theory would predict that these children are most likely to develop serious self-injurious behaviors in the future; however, this will not be known until these children are followed in a longitudinal fashion over several years. At the time of observation, these children were not injuring themselves in a manner that led to tissue damage. Research comparing children treated at this stage with a no-treatment control would be very revealing (although, ethically, this would be inappropriate when children who are at risk have been identified).

Prevention of Behavior Problems

Studies that examine in detail the processes responsible for the development of problem behaviors are very much in their infancy, and research in this area is a priority for the future. However, some implications can be drawn from this work for the possibility of preventive behavioral intervention. The observational methodology used appears to aid the identification of children who are at risk for developing self-injurious behaviors. Of course, there are already a number of well-established risk factors for self-injury, such as sensory impairment and nonambulation (Oliver, 1995). However, identification of certain socially mediated behavioral profiles intuitively seems to be more likely to have predictive validity. In addition, many individuals who have a number of characteristics that are risk factors for self-injury do not develop self-injurious behaviors. It might be expected that children with the attention-seeking and escape behavior profiles for precursors of damaging, self-injurious responses will develop full-blown self-injurious responses unless an intervention is established.

Once identified, children who are at risk could be treated according to intervention models described elsewhere in this book. In brief, the target behavior would be prevented from achieving its current function, and an educational component would be incorporated to teach the child a socially acceptable way of achieving the same function. Thus, preventive intervention for self-injurious behavior in children with developmental disabilities may involve periodic observations of possible precursors to self-injurious responses (certain stereotypic topographies) to identify the beginning of the developmental process and the application of established intervention models.

The previous discussions are based only on preliminary data and on logical extensions of theories of behavioral development. More research is needed before the goal of preventive interventions for human behavior problems can be realized.

An alternative strategy for preventing behavior problems is to devise interventions that are aimed at other people in care environments. Taking the example of self-injury, data collected in the clinical environment might be used to identify to their caregivers children who are at risk. The caregivers then can be encouraged to interact with the identified children and others in a manner that is unlikely to contribute to the development of problem behavior. However, such an intervention could not, at present, be based on adequate research data addressing the behavioral processes that are responsible for the way in which caregivers behave toward children and adults who engage in problem behaviors. Just as intervention with problem behaviors should be based on functional analyses (cf. Repp, Felce, & Barton, 1988; Chapter 3), so should interventions involving caregivers or others be based on functional analyses.

FUNCTIONAL ANALYSIS OF THE BEHAVIOR OF IMPLEMENTATION STAFF

There are at least three important reasons for having an interest in analyzing the behavior of

people who ordinarily are required to implement behavioral intervention programs. First, many problem behaviors occur in social contexts and serve social functions. In the field of developmental disabilities, epidemiological research that is based on clinically referred samples (Derby et al., 1992; Iwata et al., 1994) has suggested that approximately 70% of problem behaviors may serve one or more social functions (e.g., attention, escape from demands or social contact).

Therefore, to analyze and remediate behavior problems, there must be an understanding of the behavior of other people in the environment in which the problem behavior occurs. In essence, the behaviors of other people are often the antecedents and consequences for an incident of a problem behavior. Thus, an extended model of problem behaviors would consider the antecedents and consequences of those behaviors of other people that in turn are antecedents and consequences for problem behaviors. This can be illustrated by Figure 1, which represents the H model (so called because of its characteristic shape) of problem behavior in developmental disabilities.

This model is not intended to be all-inclusive; rather, it is presented in a simple form

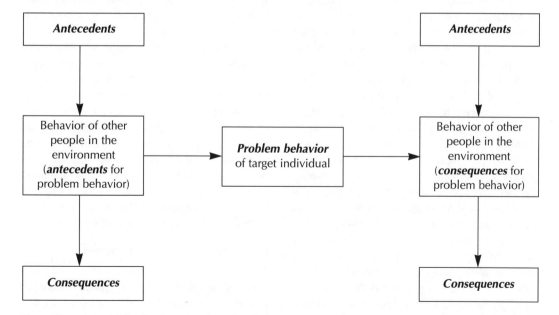

Figure 1. A model for the functional analysis of the behavior of implementation staff as it relates to the problem behavior of a target individual.

to emphasize the importance of focusing on an analysis of the behavior of other people in the environment of individuals who engage in problem behavior. The key aspect that is missing from the model is the dynamic nature of the relation between the problem behaviors and the behavior of other people; that is, these behaviors occur within a cyclical system (cf. Oliver, 1995; Taylor & Carr, 1992). Not only do the actions of other people act as antecedents and consequences for problem behavior, but also problem behavior often acts as antecedent and consequent conditions for the behavior of others.

The second reason for having an interest in the behavior of program implementers is that behavioral interventions require a person to behave in a particular way; usually in a way that is somewhat different from his or her typical responses. Thus, behavioral programs *intervene* with the behavior of program implementers at the same time that they constitute interventions for target problems. All behavioral interventions should be rooted in functional analysis; however, it is very rare for behavioral programmers to consider the behavior of implementation staff at all—let alone to attempt some kind of functional analysis of their behavior.

The literature in this area has focused on how to ensure that program staff actually implement behavioral interventions. This has been accomplished through the use of such methods as supervisor feedback; public posting of performance (either staff behavior or client progress); and various reward systems, such as increased pay (see Reid, Parsons, & Green, 1989, for a review). Earlier interventions for behavior problems have been criticized as behavior *modification* rather than behavior *analysis;* that is, powerful reinforcement and punishment contingencies were applied to problem behavior without a functional analysis. An identical criticism can be made about procedures that focus on the behavior of implementation staff. However, a functional approach to staff behavior has failed to materialize alongside the emphasis on the functional analysis of problem behavior.

The result of this neglect of implementation staff is parallel to that experienced when behavior problems themselves are not subject to a functional analysis. When the issue of function is not addressed, behavioral interventions often fail to remediate problem behaviors, fail to maintain any effects, or result in increases in other undesirable responses. Similarly, behavioral interventions often are not carried out by staff at all or are implemented in an inconsistent fashion (Hastings & Remington, 1993).

The third reason for having an interest in an analysis of staff behavior is that staff behavior can be the explicit target of behavioral intervention. In addition to not implementing intervention programs, staff who provide services for people with developmental disabilities behave in a number of other ways that could contribute to the maintenance or development of problem behaviors (see previous discussion and Hastings & Remington, 1994b). For example, staff may give an occasional "encouraging" response to a problem behavior (e.g., Felce et al., 1987) or may spend little time developing the skills of individuals in their care (Hile & Walbran, 1991), thus increasing the chances that problem behaviors will become effective strategies for attaining socially mediated reinforcement. Behavioral staff management interventions often have been applied to improve staff behavior (see Cullen, 1992, for a review). Once more, however, these interventions are not based on a functional analysis of staff behavior.

Hastings and Remington (1994a) have begun to develop a framework for the functional analysis of implementation staff behavior in the field of developmental disabilities. This framework and preliminary research addressing parts of the model are outlined next. Although the model was constructed with reference to one particular applied field, it is likely that many of the issues raised are relevant to implementation staff in other areas. The analysis has implications for the design of interventions for problem behaviors, both of clients and of care staff.

Behavior Analytic Framework

The foundation for analyzing staff responses to behavior problems is the distinction between *contingency-shaped* and *rule-governed* behavior. Both contingencies and rules contribute to a functional analysis of staff behavior (Hastings &

Remington, 1994a). The process of contingency shaping is what immediately comes to mind when one thinks of behavioral psychology. The relation between a behavior and its consequences can be described as a two-term contingency (Sidman, 1986). A cornerstone of operant psychology is the understanding that behavior is modified by such contingencies through the processes of reinforcement and punishment. In general, behavior can be shaped and maintained through either positive or negative reinforcement. Consider the case of severe problem behavior in individuals with developmental disabilities. Carr (1977) proposed that both positive and negative reinforcement processes often may be responsible for the development and maintenance of challenging behaviors. People may engage in self-injury, for example, because as a consequence of such action, staff 1) attend to them (attention as a positive reinforcer), 2) give them preferred items (tangible items as positive reinforcers), or 3) cease to make demands on them (demands as an aversive stimulus, the removal of which is negative reinforcement).

Staff Behavior as Contingency Shaped

A growing body of evidence suggests that staff responses to problem behaviors are related directly to aspects of those behaviors themselves. A previous section described how self-injurious behavior may act as an establishing operation for staff behavior (Hall & Oliver, 1992). Further research by Taylor and her colleagues (e.g., Carr, Taylor, & Robinson, 1991; Taylor & Carr, 1992) also supported the thesis that staff behavior may be shaped by contingencies that involve problem behavior. In one study, for example, naive adults were asked to interact with two children who engaged in problem behaviors. In the situation in which one child's behavior was maintained by attention and the other's by escape from social contact, the adults attended most to the "attention seeker" (Taylor & Carr, 1992). In the short term, this would have led to the lowest rates of problem behavior in both of the children. One proposition that is heuristically useful here is that caregivers find problem behaviors aversive. Thus, caregivers quickly learn to behave in ways that lead to escape or avoidance of problem behaviors.

The question remains, "What is it that caregivers find aversive about problem behaviors?" The only hypothesis discussed in the literature through 1998 is that problem behaviors elicit negative emotions that act as establishing operations for caregiver escape behavior (i.e., actions that reduce or remove the negative emotion). A small number of self-report studies lend support to this hypothesis. In interviews with 19 staff who were working with people with developmental disabilities and severe problem behaviors, Hastings (1995) found that self-injury led to staff feelings of sadness and anger, aggression led to feelings of fear and anger, and stereotypy occasionally was viewed as annoying. In another study, staff were asked to estimate the proportion of other staff who would experience a range of emotions when dealing with problem behaviors. These staff also identified as salient negative emotions such as sadness, anger, despair, and fear (Bromley & Emerson, 1995). Finally, Hastings (1994) compared 148 experienced and 98 inexperienced health care workers' self-rated emotions in response to a hypothetical incident of problem behavior. The results confirmed the pattern found in the other studies: Staff found self-injury to be the most disturbing and saddening, and aggression toward staff and other clients was associated with fear.

Staff Behavior as Rule Governed

Following Skinner (1957), several operant researchers (e.g., Catania, Matthews, & Shimoff, 1990; Hayes, 1989; Lowe, 1983) argued that verbal behavior, in particular the use of verbal rules, explains the characteristic differences between human and animal behavior in laboratory environments. There is indeed extensive evidence from laboratory research concerning performance on schedules of reinforcement that testifies to the distinctiveness of human behavior (Holland, 1958; Lowe, 1979; Weiner, 1969, 1970). In fact, some researchers (e.g., Catania, Shimoff, & Matthews, 1989) have argued that human practical (i.e., nonverbal) behavior is most often rule governed rather than directly shaped by contingencies. Given this burgeoning literature, it is timely to consider the clinical relevance of the analysis of rule-governed behavior, and several operant researchers have begun that process in relation to the behavior of clinical groups (e.g., Hayes, Kohlenberg, & Melancon, 1989; Lowe, Horne, & Higson, 1987; Poppen, 1989; Whitman, 1990; Zettle & Hayes, 1982). Remington (1991) argued that such an analysis could also be extended to the actions of caregivers. Given the many efforts to instruct the behavior of care staff, the concept of rule governance should be of great relevance to understanding the ways in which they interact with the individuals who are in their care. Despite this, however, there has been no conceptual analysis of the question of how verbal formulations may affect the way that staff respond to incidents of challenging behavior.

Types of Rule-Governed Behavior

The concept of rule governance needs some further explication. Rules are verbal formulations of contingencies. They describe relations between behavioral and environmental events that normally would need to be learned through direct experience. For example, the rule, "When reinforcement is withdrawn, the to-be-extinguished behavior increases, then decreases," describes a relation between behavior and its consequences that is not immediately obvious. A person who is told the rule and uses it can thereby operate as if he or she had experienced many extinction procedures. In Skinner's (1957) analysis of verbal behavior, the "speaker" is the source of a rule, and the "listener" is the person whose behavior may be modified by hearing the rule. In fact, rules do not need to be voiced; verbal behavior may appear in other forms, such as signs or text. In this case, speakers may be managers; psychologists; other staff; or the authors of guidelines, textbooks, or other written sources; and the listeners are the staff. In fact, as described later, it is also possible for the speaker and the listener to "inhabit the same skin" (Skinner, 1953, p. 410).

According to Zettle and Hayes (1982), there are two main types of rule-governed behavior: pliance and tracking. *Pliance* on the part of a listener is rule-governed behavior that is primarily under the control of consequences that are apparently mediated by the speaker. These consequences relate to the correspondence (or noncorrespondence) between the speaker's rule and the listener's behavior. For example, a manager of a service for people with challenging behaviors may tell staff, "When John engages in stereotypic behavior, you must restrain him." If this instruction occasions restraining activity from staff under the control of consequences that are mediated by the manager (e.g., praise, bonus payments, withholding or terminating criticism), then such behavior can be described as pliance. Staff would be engaging in pliance if they restrained John when he engaged in stereotypy because they had previously enjoyed the praise or avoided the anger of the manager by acting in ways that accorded with his or her requests.

Tracking is rule-governed behavior under the control of the apparent correspondence between the rule and the part of the world that is the subject of the rule, rather than controlled by speaker-mediated consequences. For example, a psychologist may say, "The way to stop John from hurting himself is to ignore him when he self-injures." If this utterance reduces the probability that staff will attend to John when he bites himself, then they may be said to be tracking the psychologist's rule—provided that their behavior is attributable to their previously experiencing environmentally mediated reinforcing outcomes as a result of acting in ways specified by the psychologist (or similar others).

It should be clear from the previous examples that the verbally specified contingencies often generate behavior that mitigates against that reinforced by more immediate nonverbal contingencies. Thus, before these rules were uttered, staff may have ignored stereotypic behavior and intervened to restrain self-injurious behavior—actions that were under the control of consequences other than those specified by the rule. These dual contingencies distinguish rule-governed behavior from behavior that is directly shaped by contingencies. In fact, rule-governed behavior has been defined on this basis as "behavior in contact with two sets of contingencies, one of which includes a verbal antecedent" (Zettle & Hayes, 1982, p. 78).

Implicit in the previous discussion is an acknowledgment of the distinction between the function of rules in determining listener behavior and the apparent form of rules. For example, a manager may say, "When John is left alone, he is likely to self-injure." Although this rule has a form that suggests tracking, the fact that staff ensure that John is never left alone may be the result of prior experience with manager-mediated consequences. If so, then such rule following is functionally pliance, not tracking. So far, the only case considered is when the speaker and the listener are different people; that is, rules are supplied by someone other than the listener (externally supplied rules). However, individuals may also construct rules to govern their own behavior; that is, the speaker and the listener may be the same person. Zettle (1990) called rules of this kind *self-rules*. He argued that the social psychological concepts of "attitude" and "belief" can be conceptualized as forms of self-generated rules.

Rules that Influence Staff Behavior

Hastings and Remington (1994a) suggested that the rules that influence staff behavior can be classified along two dimensions. First, a staff member's own rules (beliefs, perceptions, attributions) and the rules of other staff (informal culture) and the service in which staff work (formal culture) all are important in determining responses to problem behaviors. Second, the rules with which staff may act in accordance may be about *why* problem behaviors occur (hypotheses about causes) or *what to do* about it (performance-related rules). Hastings and Remington have begun a program of research aimed at addressing each of these categories of rules relevant to the care of people with developmental disabilities and problem behaviors. The results of this work through 1998 are summarized next.

The first study (Hastings, 1995) was an interview-based exploration with a small group of care staff working in two residential establishments for people with severe problem behaviors. These staff were asked to talk about why problem behaviors occur, what to do about them, and the way in which problem behaviors are dealt with by professionals and at the service

level. Analysis of the interview transcripts revealed a number of interesting findings. First, staff concurred with the main hypotheses in the research literature about the causes of problem behaviors. They cited attention, environmental conditions such as noise and illness, and especially the idea that problem behaviors may be a form of communication. Second, when describing their interventions for problem behaviors, they outlined strategies such as restraint for self-injury and for aggression and talking in a calming manner. These reports are not inconsistent with observational studies of staff behavior that have found staff responses to problem behaviors to be those likely to maintain such behaviors (Hastings & Remington, 1994b).

Third, these staff identified a number of aspects of the formal and informal service culture that may help others to understand their behavior. In particular, a number of staff comments suggested that the informal staff culture may have more influence over them than the formal service culture. For example, approximately half of the staff interviewed said that they had received no formal training on problem behaviors but had learned on the job and from other staff. In addition, 25% of the staff described "informal" programs developed by the staff group to deal with incidents of problem behaviors.

In the second study, 250 health care workers were asked to complete a questionnaire that asked them to read a description of a problem behavior and to rate each of 25 possible causes of that behavior on a seven-point scale (Hastings, Remington, & Hopper, 1995). Factor analysis of the ratings of care staff showed that, again, they appeared to view the causes of problem behaviors in a similar manner to dominant models in the literature. Staff beliefs about intervention for problem behaviors were elicited in another questionnaire study (Hastings, 1996). Open-ended questions asked staff to describe how they would intervene with a problem behavior described in a short vignette. The responses given by the staff confirmed the findings of the pilot interview study. Interventions often were of a kind that would lead to the maintenance of large proportions of problem behaviors (consistent with the high proportion of severe problem behavior that has been found to be maintained by attention or escape contingencies [e.g., Derby et al., 1992; Iwata et al., 1994]). For example, self-injury and aggression often were associated with restraint, exclusion of the person or others in the vicinity, and attempts to calm the person or communicate with him or her. The pattern of these results has been replicated in research on staff working in community rather than institutional environments (Hastings, Reed, & Watts, 1997; Watts, Reed, & Hastings, 1997).

The results of these studies are somewhat surprising. Staff beliefs about the causes of problem behaviors appear to be appropriate and, therefore, may not have a significant impact on the way in which staff respond to problem behaviors. However, staff beliefs about what to do about problem behaviors do seem to correspond with the results of observational studies suggesting that they will respond in a manner that is likely to maintain many problem behaviors. Returning to the distinction between contingency-shaped and rule-governed behavior, two hypotheses explain staff responses to problem behaviors. First, staff behavior is influenced by aversive contingencies that involve problem behaviors themselves. Second, staff may have inappropriate beliefs about how to deal with problem behaviors.

The second hypothesis was explored by asking staff to distinguish between how they would deal with problem behaviors immediately and what their longer-term strategies would be (Hastings, 1996; Watts et al., 1997). The results described previously were what staff said when asked to report their immediate responses. For the longer term, however, staff described approaches to intervention that most professionals would consider to be fairly appropriate (e.g., completing antecedent-behavior-consequence [A-B-C] analyses, agreeing on a consistent management response with other staff, changing aspects of the person's lifestyle). One interpretation of this finding is that there is something about the immediate situation when dealing with problem behaviors (perhaps because these behaviors are aversive) that leads staff *not* to act in accordance with appropriate intervention knowledge that they actually have. We might conclude

cautiously that staff behavior in the immediate situation is indeed contingency shaped, whereas outside this context it may be more likely to be rule governed. However, what is needed is a way to compare directly the impact of both rules and contingencies on the behavior of staff to assess this tentative hypothesis.

Staff Behavior: Rule Governed or Contingency Shaped?

One attempt to conduct a research study in which rules given to staff could be pitted against the contingencies involving problem behaviors was a computer simulation of a care situation with two young people who engaged in self-injury (Hastings, Remington, & Hall, 1995). To achieve the level of experimental control necessary to investigate this question, a methodology that did not rely on a natural care environment was needed. In addition, one of the experimental manipulations that would be required to demonstrate the relative effects of contingencies and rules was to assess the impact of inaccurate rules given to staff. In the natural environment, where problem behaviors could increase in frequency or severity as a result, this strategy is unethical. Therefore, the essential aspects of a care situation were simulated and the participants were asked to interact with the computer program as if they were responding in a real-life situation.

Two figures on the screen could be seen self-injuring at various points, and sound accompanied incidents of self-injury. One of the two simulated people was an "attention seeker" (self-injury was maintained by attention from others), and the other was a "social avoider" (self-injury was maintained by escape/avoidance of social contact). Participants in the experiment could "attend" to either one or the other of the people by moving a mouse pointer between the two of them. In addition, participants carried out a vigilance task (analogous to engaging the person in educational activities) on the side of the computer screen adjacent to the person to whom they were attending at the time.

The "attention seeker" engaged in high rates of self-injury when not being attended to and low rates when being attended to. The "social avoider" "behaved" in the opposite fashion.

The schedule determining the occurrence of self-injury was switched between high and low rates immediately after a participant shifted his or her attention from one person to the other. In addition to the contingencies generated by this pattern of self-injurious responding, some groups of participants were given advice from a psychologist before beginning the task. Some groups were told the results of an assessment of the self-injury (hypotheses about the causes of the behavior), and some were advised to spend more or less of the time with one or the other of the two people (performance-related rules). (A full description of the simulation and of the experimental procedure can be found in Hastings, Remington, & Hall, 1995.)

The results of this study showed that all of the participants in the groups that were given performance-related information behaved in accordance with the advice that they were given— even when this advice was incorrect and did not lead to low rates of self-injury. The groups that were given information about the causes of the self-injury appeared not to know how to translate this into attending behavior and mostly divided their time equally between the two people. Those who were given no additional information from a psychologist also spent equal amounts of time with each of the two people on screen. There was little evidence to suggest that the different schedules of contingencies in operation within the simulation had any impact on the participants' behavior. Leaving aside the thorny issue of ecological validity, these findings were interpreted as supporting a position that staff responses to problem behaviors, like the majority of human behavior (Catania et al., 1989), are rule governed.

Implications and Future Research

Although there are several studies that are relevant to an analysis of the behavior of program implementation staff and a growing recognition of the importance of care staff in the development and maintenance of problem behavior (e.g., Emerson, Remington, Hatton, & Hastings, 1995), there remain a large number of unanswered questions. The conceptual model (Hastings & Remington, 1994a) was an attempt to

stimulate research into this issue, but there may be other models that could contribute to an analysis of staff behavior. The results of the studies outlined previously suggest a number of research questions for the future.

First, there still is very little known about how and when staff beliefs influence their behavior in the care environment. Second, it is important to understand how staff beliefs about problem behaviors develop. This is likely to involve analysis of the societal context in which people develop beliefs and ways of intervening with difficult behaviors (Hastings, Remington, & Hatton, 1995). Third, there is very little understanding of the informal culture of services in which programs often are implemented. Given that such cultures appear to be more salient to care staff than formal aspects of service cultures, research in this area is an urgent priority. Finally, researchers should address how and when staff utilize information and skills that are presented in staff training courses. This would have implications for the content and process of staff training on problem behaviors and behavioral intervention programs.

Evidence that has a direct bearing on the analysis of staff behavior is relatively scarce. However, to illustrate the salience of such an analysis for the work in this book, it is worth highlighting some of the implications of these preliminary findings for the design of behavioral interventions. For example, although staff may have similar beliefs about why problem behaviors occur, they are likely to have very different views from those espoused in a behavioral program about how to intervene when those behaviors occur. This requires some additional planning, preparatory work, and careful monitoring on the part of program designers.

In addition, staff may have already developed an informal way of dealing with a particular problem behavior. In situations in which staff perceive this to be an effective strategy, the job of convincing staff to adhere to a program introduced by an outside agent is particularly complex. Finally, staff behavior may be shaped by the occurrence of problem behaviors themselves. Thus, even when staff perceive an intervention program in a positive manner, they may not implement it when they have to deal with an incident of problem behavior. The challenge for program designers here is to recognize staff needs in this situation. One particularly relevant factor here may be the extent to which one equally effective type of intervention will lead to a more pronounced extinction burst than another. Research has shown that treatment fidelity is more easily maintained when interventions that lead to less pronounced extinction bursts are used (McConnachie & Carr, 1997).

CONCLUSIONS

The dialogue between research and application in the field of behavioral psychology remains at an early stage. Great advances have been made in the application of basic theory to research focusing on the current functions and maintenance of human behavior problems. However, even basic considerations, such as functional analysis and the collateral effects of interventions, are taking some time to be incorporated into published research on behavioral intervention (e.g., Scotti, Ujcich, Weigle, Holland, & Kirk, 1996). The extent to which these factors and others are addressed in applied environments on a day-to-day basis is unknown.

There are also a number of areas of basic research that have not yet received significant attention in terms of their application to human problem behaviors. In particular, interventions generally apply carefully planned contingencies to ameliorate behavior difficulties. One factor that may explain the failure of many interventions is that problem behavior often is rule governed and "insensitive" to environmental contingencies. Only in populations in which severe communication impairments abound is behavior likely to be purely contingency shaped. Even in these groups, however, large numbers of individuals are likely to reach a developmental level that is commensurate with the emergence of rule-governed behavior. Basic experimental research has shown that children as young as 18 months fail to show patterns of behavior characteristic of laboratory animals exposed to similar reinforcement schedules (Bentall & Lowe, 1987; Bentall, Lowe, & Beasty, 1985; Lowe, Beasty, &

Bentall, 1983). This finding has important implications for analysis and intervention with problem behavior.

Two other issues that are crucial for the design and implementation of behavioral intervention have received little or no attention in the literature. These issues have been the focus of this chapter: the development of problem behavior and the behavior of program implementers. In terms of the development of problem behavior, there are a large number of unanswered questions. For example, what is the relation between problem behavior and language ability (i.e., does behavior that was originally contingency shaped become rule governed as a child develops)? In addition, there are few data available to inform an understanding of how behaviors serving the same underlying function might develop together (cf. Scotti, Evans, Meyer, & DiBenedetto, 1991).

Although an emphasis on the current functions of behavior clearly is important for intervention, an understanding of the processes underlying the development of problem behavior is crucial for prevention. As of 1998, there were no directly supporting data, but some authors have argued that intensive skill-based education may prevent the emergence of problem behavior (Dunlap, Foster Johnson, & Robbins, 1990). The basic assumption is that if people with developmental disabilities have been taught basic skills to communicate with others, they will have much less need to engage in problem behavior when they can achieve the same ends more efficiently in a socially acceptable (and presumably effective) manner. Research on the development of problem behavior may lead to a refinement of the nature of intensive early support programs. In addition, problem behaviors will not all be prevented by these inclusive strategies. Following the rationale of Hall, Oliver, and Murphy, it may be possible to develop a number of methods for identifying children who are at risk for developing problem behavior and to intervene early to prevent the emergence of serious difficulties.

Finally, although there has been some attempt to build a behaviorally based framework for understanding processes that maintain patterns of implementation staff behavior, this research is also at a very early stage. No research has focused directly on the behavior of staff in their day-to-day interactions with those who engage in problem behaviors. Furthermore, the concept of a staff culture that may be a powerful determinant of staff behavior has received no research attention. Behavior analysts have argued that the same processes that are responsible for the selection of behavior (selection by consequences) are responsible for the selection of cultural practices (Malagodi, 1986; Malott, 1988; Vargas, 1985). Some research methods for investigating the nature of cultures have also been suggested (see Lamal, 1991). The application of a behavioral analysis of cultures to the informal and formal cultures of implementation staff would be a valuable step forward.

The central message of this chapter is that, from the perspective of behavioral intervention, there are three areas in which a dialogue between research and application would be fruitful: 1) the current functions of problem behavior, 2) the development of problem behavior, and 3) the behavior of program implementation staff. There has been considerable advance in the first of these areas, and this can be seen clearly in this book. However, little attention has been given to the second and third areas, and these should inform the focus of the future dialogue between research and application.

REFERENCES

Bentall, R.P., & Lowe, C.F. (1987). The role of verbal behavior in human learning: III. Instructional effects in children. *Journal of the Experimental Analysis of Behavior, 47,* 177–190.

Bentall, R.P., Lowe, C.F., & Beasty, A. (1985). The role of verbal behavior in human learning: II. Developmental differences. *Journal of the Experimental Analysis of Behavior, 43,* 165–181.

Bromley, J., & Emerson, E. (1995). Beliefs and emotional reactions of care staff working with people with challenging behaviour. *Journal of Intellectual Disability Research, 39,* 341–352.

Carr, E.G. (1977). The motivation of self-injurious behavior: A review of some hypotheses. *Psychological Bulletin, 84,* 800–816.

Carr, E.G., & McDowell, J.J. (1980). Social control of self-injurious behavior of organic etiology. *Behavior Therapy, 11,* 402–409.

Carr, E.G., Taylor, J.C., & Robinson, S. (1991). The effects of severe behavior problems in children on

the teaching behavior of adults. *Journal of Applied Behavior Analysis, 24,* 523–535.

Cataldo, M.F., & Brady, J.V. (1994). Deriving relations from the experimental analysis of behavior. *Journal of Applied Behavior Analysis, 27,* 763–770.

Catania, A.C., Matthews, B.A., & Shimoff, E.H. (1990). Properties of rule-governed behavior and their implications. In D.E. Blackman & H. Lejeune (Eds.), *Behavior analysis in theory and practice: Contributions and controversies* (pp. 215–230). Mahwah, NJ: Lawrence Erlbaum Associates.

Catania, A.C., Shimoff, E.H., & Matthews, B.A. (1989). An experimental analysis of rule-governed behavior. In S.C. Hayes (Ed.), *Rule-governed behavior: Cognition, contingencies and instructional control* (pp. 119–150). New York: Plenum.

Cullen, C. (1992). Staff training and management for intellectual disability services. *International Review of Research in Mental Retardation, 18,* 225–245.

Deitz, S.M. (1978). Current status of applied behavior analysis: Science versus technology. *American Psychologist, 33,* 805–814.

Derby, K.M., Wacker, D.P., Sasso, G., Steege, M., Northup, J., Cigrand, K., & Asmus, J. (1992). Brief functional assessment techniques to evaluate aberrant behavior in an outpatient setting: A summary of 79 cases. *Journal of Applied Behavior Analysis, 25,* 713–721.

Dunlap, G., Foster Johnson, L., & Robbins, F.R. (1990). Preventing serious behavior problems through skill development and early intervention. In A.C. Repp & N.N. Singh (Eds.), *Perspectives on the use of nonaversive and aversive interventions for persons with developmental disabilities* (pp. 273–286). Sycamore, IL: Sycamore Publishing.

Emerson, E., Felce, D., McGill, P., & Mansell, J. (1994). Introduction. In E. Emerson, P. McGill, & J. Mansell (Eds.), *Severe learning disabilities and challenging behaviours: Designing high quality services* (pp. 3–16). London: Chapman and Hall.

Emerson, E., & Howard, D. (1992). Schedule-induced stereotypy. *Research in Developmental Disabilities, 13,* 335–361.

Emerson, E., Remington, B., Hatton, C., & Hastings, R.P. (1995). Staffing issues in learning disability services [Special issue]. *Mental Handicap Research, 8,* 215–339.

Epling, W.F., & Pierce, W.D. (1983). Applied behavior analysis: New directions from the laboratory. *The Behavior Analyst, 6,* 27–37.

Epling, W.F., & Pierce, W.D. (1990). Laboratory to application: An experimental analysis of severe problem behaviors. In A.C. Repp & N.N. Singh (Eds.), *Perspectives on the use of nonaversive and aversive interventions for persons with developmental disabilities* (pp. 451–464). Sycamore, IL: Sycamore Publishing.

Falk, J.L. (1961). Production of polydipsia in normal rats by an intermittent food schedule. *Science, 133,* 195–196.

Felce, D., Saxby, H., de Kock, U., Repp, A.C., Ager, A., & Blunden, R. (1987). To what behaviors do attending adults respond? A replication. *American Journal of Mental Deficiency, 91,* 496–504.

Friman, P.C., & Poling, A. (1995). Making life easier with effort: Basic findings and applied research on response effort. *Journal of Applied Behavior Analysis, 28,* 583–590.

Guess, D., & Carr, E.G. (1991). Emergence and maintenance of stereotypy and self-injury. *American Journal on Mental Retardation, 96,* 299–319.

Guess, D., Siegel-Causey, E., Roberts, S., Rues, J., Thompson, B., & Siegel-Causey, D. (1990). Assessment and analysis of behavior state and related variables among students with profoundly handicapping conditions. *Journal of The Association for Persons with Severe Handicaps, 15,* 211–230.

Hall, S.S. (1997). *The early development of self-injurious behaviour in children with developmental disabilities.* Unpublished doctoral dissertation, University of London.

Hall, S., & Oliver, C. (1992). Differential effects of self-injurious behaviour on the behaviour of others. *Behavioural Psychotherapy, 20,* 355–366.

Hastings, R.P. (1994). *A functional approach to care staff behaviour.* Unpublished doctoral dissertation, University of Southampton, Southampton, England.

Hastings, R.P. (1995). Understanding factors that influence staff responses to challenging behaviours: An exploratory interview study. *Mental Handicap Research, 8,* 296–320.

Hastings, R.P. (1996). Staff strategies and explanations for intervening with challenging behaviours. *Journal of Intellectual Disability Research, 40,* 166–175.

Hastings, R.P., Reed, T.S., & Watts, M.W. (1997). Community staff causal attributions about challenging behaviours in people with intellectual disabilities. *Journal of Applied Research in Intellectual Disabilities, 10,* 238–249.

Hastings, R.P., & Remington, B. (1993). "Is there anything on. . . . Why 'good' behavioural programmes fail?" A brief review. *Clinical Psychology Forum, 55,* 9–11.

Hastings, R.P., & Remington, B. (1994a). Rules of engagement: Toward an analysis of staff responses to challenging behavior. *Research in Developmental Disabilities, 15,* 279–298.

Hastings, R.P., & Remington, B. (1994b). Staff behaviour and its implications for people with learning disabilities and challenging behaviours. *British Journal of Clinical Psychology, 33,* 423–438.

Hastings, R.P., Remington, B., & Hall, M. (1995). Adults' responses to self-injurious behavior: An experimental analysis utilizing a computer simulation paradigm. *Behavior Modification, 19,* 425–450.

Hastings, R.P., Remington, B., & Hatton, C. (1995). Future directions for research on staff performance in services for people with learning disabilities. *Mental Handicap Research, 8,* 333–339.

Hastings, R.P., Remington, B., & Hopper, G.M. (1995). Experienced and inexperienced health care workers' beliefs about challenging behaviours. *Journal of Intellectual Disability Research, 39,* 474–483.

Hayes, S.C. (1989). *Rule-governed behavior: Cognition, contingencies and instructional control.* New York: Plenum.

Hayes, S.C., & Hayes, L.J. (1993). Applied implications of current JEAB research on derived relations and delayed reinforcement. *Journal of Applied Behavior Analysis, 26,* 507–511.

Hayes, S.C., Kohlenberg, B.S., & Melancon, S.M. (1989). Avoiding and altering rule control as a strategy of clinical intervention. In S.C. Hayes (Ed.), *Rule-governed behavior: Cognition, contingencies and instructional control* (pp. 359–385). New York: Plenum.

Hayes, S.C., Rincover, A., & Solnick, J.V. (1980). The technical drift of applied behavior analysis. *Journal of Applied Behavior Analysis, 13,* 275–285.

Hile, M.G., & Walbran, B.B. (1991). Observing staff–resident interactions: What staff do, what residents receive. *Mental Retardation, 29,* 35–41.

Hineline, P.N., & Wacker, D.P. (1993). JEAB November '92: What's in it for the JABA reader? *Journal of Applied Behavior Analysis, 26,* 269–274.

Holland, J.G. (1958). Human vigilance. *Science, 128,* 61–67.

Iwata, B.A., Pace, G.M., Dorsey, M.F., Zarcone, J.R., Vollmer, T.R., Smith, R.G., Rodgers, T.A., Lerman, D.C., Shore, B.A., Mazaleski, J.L., Goh, H.L., Cowdrey, G.E., Kalsher, M.J., McCosh, K.C., & Willis, K.D. (1994). The functions of self-injurious behavior: An experimental-epidemiological analysis. *Journal of Applied Behavior Analysis, 27,* 215–240.

Kirby, K.C., & Bickel, W.K. (1995). Implications of behavioral pharmacology research for applied behavior analysis: JEAB's special issue celebrating the contributions of Joseph V. Brady (March 1994). *Journal of Applied Behavior Analysis, 28,* 105–112.

Lamal, P.A. (1991). *Behavioral analysis of societies and cultural practices.* New York: Hemisphere Publishing.

Lattal, K.A., & Neef, N.A. (1996). Recent reinforcement-schedule research and applied behavior analysis. *Journal of Applied Behavior Analysis, 29,* 213–230.

Lerman, D.C., Iwata, B.A., Zarcone, J.R., & Ringdahl, J. (1994). Assessment of stereotypic and self-injurious behavior as adjunctive responses. *Journal of Applied Behavior Analysis, 27,* 715–728.

Lowe, C.F. (1979). Determinants of human operant behavior. In M.D. Zeiler & P. Harzem (Eds.), *Advances in analysis of behavior: Vol. 1. Reinforce-*

ment and the organization of behavior (pp. 159–192). Chichester, UK: Wiley.

Lowe, C.F. (1983). Radical behaviourism and human psychology. In G.C.L. Davey (Ed.), *Animal models of human behavior: Conceptual, evolutionary and neurobiological perspectives* (pp. 71–93). Chichester, UK: Wiley.

Lowe, C.F., Beasty, A., & Bentall, R.P. (1983). The role of verbal behavior in human learning: Infant performance on fixed-interval schedules. *Journal of the Experimental Analysis of Behavior, 39,* 157–164.

Lowe, C.F., Horne, P.J., & Higson, P.J. (1987). Operant conditioning: The hiatus between theory and practice in clinical psychology. In H.J. Eysenck & I. Martin (Eds.), *Theoretical foundations of behavior therapy* (pp. 153–165). New York: Plenum.

Mace, F.C. (1994). Basic research needed for stimulating the development of behavioral technologies. *Journal of the Experimental Analysis of Behavior, 61,* 529–550.

Mace, F.C., & Wacker, D.P. (1994). Toward greater integration of basic and applied behavioral research: An introduction. *Journal of Applied Behavior Analysis, 27,* 569–574.

Malagodi, E.F. (1986). On radicalizing behaviorism: A call for cultural analysis. *The Behavior Analyst, 9,* 1–17.

Malott, R.W. (1988). Rule-governed behavior and behavioral anthropology. *The Behavior Analyst, 11,* 181–203.

McConnachie, G., & Carr, E.G. (1997). The effects of child behavior problems on the maintenance of intervention fidelity. *Behavior Modification, 21,* 123–158.

McDowell, J.J. (1982). The importance of Herrnstein's mathematical statement of the law of effect for behavior therapy. *American Psychologist, 37,* 771–779.

McDowell, J.J. (1988). Matching theory in natural human environments. *The Behavior Analyst, 11,* 95–108.

Michael, J. (1980). Flight from behavior analysis. *The Behavior Analyst, 3,* 1–22.

Murphy, G., & Hall, S. (1995, September). *Early development of self-injurious behavior in young children with learning disabilities.* Paper presented at the BILD International Conference on Challenging Behavior, Oxford, UK.

Myerson, J., & Hale, S. (1984). Practical applications of the matching law. *Journal of Applied Behavior Analysis, 17,* 367–380.

Neef, N.A., & Iwata, B.A. (1994). Current research on functional analysis methodologies: An introduction. *Journal of Applied Behavior Analysis, 27,* 211–214.

Oliver, C. (1995). Self-injurious behaviour in children with learning disabilities: Recent advances in assessment and intervention. *Journal of Child Psychology and Psychiatry, 36,* 909–927.

Pierce, W.D., & Epling, W.F. (1995). The applied importance of research on the matching law. *Journal of Applied Behavior Analysis, 28,* 237–241.

Poling, A., Picker, M., Grossett, D., Hall-Johnson, E., & Holbrook, M. (1981). The schism between experimental and applied behavior analysis: Is it real and who cares? *The Behavior Analyst, 4,* 93–102.

Poppen, R.L. (1989). Some clinical implications of rule-governed behavior. In S.C. Hayes (Ed.), *Rule-governed behavior: Cognition, contingencies and instructional control* (pp. 325–357). New York: Plenum.

Reid, D.H., Parsons, M.B., & Green, C.W. (1989). Treating aberrant behavior through effective staff management: A developing technology. In E. Cipani (Ed.), *The treatment of severe behavior disorders: Behavior analysis approaches* (pp. 175–190).Washington, DC: American Association on Mental Retardation.

Remington, B. (1991). Behaviour analysis and severe mental handicap: The dialogue between research and application. In B. Remington (Ed.), *The challenge of severe mental handicap: A behaviour analytic approach* (pp. 1–22). Chichester, UK: Wiley.

Repp, A.C., Felce, D., & Barton, L.E. (1988). Basing the treatment of stereotypic and self-injurious behaviors on hypotheses of their causes. *Journal of Applied Behavior Analysis, 21,* 281–289.

Rojahn, J. (1986). Self-injurious and stereotypic behavior of non-institutionalized mentally retarded people: Prevalence and classification. *American Journal of Mental Deficiency, 91,* 268–276.

Scotti, J.R., Evans, I.M., Meyer, L.H., & DiBenedetto, A. (1991). Individual repertoires as behavioral systems: Implications for program design and evaluation. In B. Remington (Ed.), *The challenge of severe mental handicap: A behavior analytic approach* (pp. 139–163). Chichester, UK: Wiley.

Scotti, J.R., Ujcich, K.J., Weigle, K.L., Holland, C.M., & Kirk, K.S. (1996). Interventions with challenging behavior of persons with developmental disabilities: A review of current research practices. *Journal of The Association for Persons with Severe Handicaps, 21,* 123–134.

Shull, R.L., & Fuqua, W.R. (1993). The collateral effects of behavioral interventions: Applied implications from JEAB, January 1993. *Journal of Applied Behavior Analysis, 26,* 409–415.

Sidman, M. (1986). Functional analysis of emergent verbal classes. In T. Thompson & M.D. Zeiler (Eds.), *Analysis and integration of behavioral units* (pp. 213–245). Mahwah, NJ: Lawrence Erlbaum Associates.

Skinner, B.F. (1953). *Science and human behavior.* New York: Macmillan.

Skinner, B.F. (1957). *Verbal behavior.* New York: Appleton-Century-Crofts.

Stromer, R., Mackay, H.A., & Remington, B. (1996). Naming, the formation of stimulus classes, and applied behavior analysis. *Journal of Applied Behavior Analysis, 29,* 409–431.

Taylor, J.C., & Carr, E.G. (1992). Severe problem behaviors related to social interaction 2: A systems analysis. *Behavior Modification, 16,* 336–371.

Thelen, E. (1981). Rhythmical behavior in infancy: An ethological perspective. *Developmental Psychology, 17,* 237–257.

Vargas, E.A. (1985). Cultural contingencies: A review of Marvin Harris' Cannibals and Kings. *Journal of the Experimental Analysis of Behavior, 43,* 419–428.

Watts, M.J., Reed, T.S., & Hastings, R.P. (1997). Staff strategies and explanations for intervening with challenging behaviours: A replication in a community sample. *Journal of Intellectual Disability Research, 41,* 258–263.

Weigle, K.L. (1997). Positive behavior support as a model for promoting educational inclusion. *Journal of The Association for Persons with Severe Handicaps, 22,* 36–48.

Weiner, H. (1969). Controlling human fixed-interval performance. *Journal of the Experimental Analysis of Behavior, 12,* 349–373.

Weiner, H. (1970). Human behavioral persistence. *The Psychological Record, 20,* 445–456.

Whitman, T.L. (1990). Self-regulation and mental retardation. *American Journal on Mental Retardation, 94,* 347–362.

Zettle, R.D. (1990). Rule-governed behavior: A radical behavioral answer to the cognitive challenge. *The Psychological Record, 40,* 41–49.

Zettle, R.D., & Hayes, S.C. (1982). Rule-governed behavior: A potential framework for cognitive-behavior therapy. In P.C. Kendall (Ed.), *Advances in cognitive-behavioral research and therapy* (pp. 73–118). New York: Academic Press.

Chapter 24

Cultural Contexts

Confronting the Overrepresentation of African American Learners in Special Education

Gwendolyn C. Webb-Johnson

Joshua is 9 years old. As a fourth grader, he is exhibiting behaviors that have become of consistent concern in school. Questions about his constant movement during work periods, his talkative nature, and his challenging authority when he perceives that he is being treated unfairly cause his teachers and his parents great concern. Should he be referred for testing to determine special education eligibility? Because Joshua was born to a teenage mother and an unemployed father, many educators might have the opinion that his life chances are limited. Some educators may further examine the plight of African American male children like Joshua by "mainstream" standards that often dictate predictable outcomes within the school context. For example, Joshua will be more likely to develop poor reading and math skills. He will more than likely present behavior problems in classroom and community contexts. In fact, if he is labeled as "behaviorally disordered" and drops out of school, then he will probably be arrested within 5 years of leaving school. The results of such a deficit paradigm would be incomplete school success for Joshua. However, if educators reconstruct the knowledge base by acknowledging and embracing Joshua's cultural frameworks and realize that his circumstances of birth include, among other realities, his being a vibrant part of an extended family that is deeply socialized in the dimensions of African American culture (Boykin, 1986), then an integrity/strength model (Webb-Johnson & Albert, 1995) can emerge. For example, Joshua then will be viewed as part of a family that loves him dearly. An entire community will support and facilitate his school success, even if it means looking to the school system and service providers for direction. His verve (propensity toward high levels of activity; Boykin, 1986) will be challenged and encouraged within the reading and math skills development context. He will more than likely be identified as gifted and talented because his socially reinforced creativity is rewarded with academic challenge and rigor. He will be more likely to go to college and study to become a physician, especially because he will have greater opportunities to study science than he will to shoot a basketball as a professional athlete.

THE DILEMMA

Joshua is in a general education environment, but fourth grade presents new academic and social skills challenges. He is progressing in math, but his science and language arts skills are lacking. He is talking to peers more than he is working. He completes his homework, but he complains that his teacher never calls on him. She constantly tells him to be quiet. She wants him to behave appropriately; then she will be more likely to call on him. Joshua never receives any positive feedback on his writing, so he prefers not to complete writing assignments. He loves science but often complains of being bored.

Evidence supports the possibility that educators and policy makers are *not* prepared to teach effectively the Joshuas of the world. The overrepresentation of African American learners in special education programs has persisted in spite of Dunn's (1968) warning that students of color would too readily become a part of the special education system for some very inappropriate reasons. Twenty-five years later, Artiles and Trent (1994) demonstrated that a more comprehensive knowledge base was necessary for understanding the challenges that educators who work in diverse environments face. Systematic research is needed to promote teacher efficacy that embraces, confronts, and designs outcomes that have an impact on the effective education of culturally diverse students in the school context. In fact, the placement of African American learners in special education and in lower academically tracked programs has steadily increased since the Supreme Court's decision in 1954 regarding *Brown v. Board of Education.* General education, by definition, is designed to be capable of educating *all* children. However, general education historically has found ways to avoid or pass on this responsibility. In turn, special education, suffering from the same dilemma, along with its failure to embrace cultural contexts, has found ways to avoid or pass on this responsibility. This premise is demonstrated by the high dropout rates among African American learners with identified disabilities.

This chapter explores the overrepresentation of African American students in special education and offers suggestions for the research agenda necessary to have a positive impact on and to reverse this negative trend in education, especially among those who are labeled "emo-tionally disturbed" or "behaviorally disordered." Embracing this issue does not mean that *some* African American learners do not and will not benefit from special education services. Embracing this issue does, however, mean that a more comprehensive awareness and understanding of African American culture from integrity, sociopolitical, and pedagogical contexts may assist service providers in implementing more effective and culturally responsive teaching practices in the school context (Boykin, 1986, 1994; Boykin & Ellison, 1993; Delpit, 1995; Gay, 1997; Ladson-Billings, 1994; Nieto, 1996).

ISSUES IN THE EDUCATION OF AFRICAN AMERICAN YOUTH

What is ironic is that since *Brown v. Board of Education* (1954)—the intended proviso for a more equitable education—considerable educational damage has occurred among African American children. Many have fallen prey to *tracking,* and overrepresentation in special education and underrepresentation in gifted and talented programs have been observed (Hilliard, 1991; Patton, 1995). According to the U.S. Department of Education (1998), youth who are identified as having a disability are *twice* as likely to be of African American descent. In fact, 21% of all children and youth who receive special education services are African American (U.S. Department of Education, 1998). The Individuals with Disabilities Education Act Amendments of 1997 (PL 105-17) required that states, beginning in the 1998–1999 school year, submit their special education count, environment, exit, and discipline data by race and ethnicity. This decision was greatly influenced by the growing overrepresentation data shared by the U.S. Department of Education's Office of Civil Rights (1994). This data indicated that African American youth are overrepresented in all special education categories except gifted and talented and speech impairment (see Table 1).

Deficit Modes of Intervention

Joshua's teacher has sent four letters home in the past 2 weeks. She is concerned; she cannot seem to get through to Joshua. He seems to be upset all of the time. The teacher has placed him in the

Table 1. African American public school adjusted enrollment status

Population	Number of African American students	Percentage of total school enrollment
General school population	6,616,308	16.85%
Gifted and talented	190,127	8.0%
Educable mental handicap	138,963	35.0%
Trainable mental handicap	47,253	32.0%
Speech impairment	171,540	16.0%
Emotional disturbance	59,190	22.0%
Learning disability	327,799	17.0%

Source: U.S. Department of Education, Office of Civil Rights (1994).

hallway during class on several occasions because she cannot convince him to remain on task. She appears to focus a great deal on what he is not doing.

Research has addressed the life and education of African American youth in several ways. However, data often suggest that the cause of achievement problems resides *within* African American youth. Millions of African American youth have entered classrooms where teachers' expectations have been based on interpretations of IQ scores that are believed to define student ability (Jensen, 1969). Instructional intervention often is based on what students cannot do academically and socially within the context of the school arena rather than on the integrity and the strength that they bring with them to that arena (Boykin & Ellison, 1993).

Researchers have attempted to respond to continued inequities in education. Through the *universal model,* African Americans were studied in relation to the problems that they posed for the larger society. Studies tended to focus on controlling attitudes and behaviors rather than on empowering learners through academic skills development (Franklin, 1985). Environmentalists believed that African American underachievement was due to a lack of cognitive, linguistic, motivational, and social competencies because African American parents did not use the same child-rearing practices as Caucasian, middle-class parents. Developmentalists contended that African American underachievement might be due to a lack of the cognitive competencies necessary for achievement (Jensen,

1969). Each of these components of the universal model has been rejected by researchers, including Hale-Benson (1986), Heath (1981, 1991), Holliday (1985), and Tatum (1997). Components of the universal model do not embrace the reality that populations within the same society differ in cognitive, linguistic, motivational, and social competencies. Even within these populations, the same differences can and do occur.

Alternatives to Deficit Models

Joshua's mother has had several conferences with the teacher. She shares the teacher's belief that Joshua is deeply steeped in an oral tradition. She questions the teacher about providing opportunities for Joshua to have academic outlets that allow him to use his dynamic strengths, especially in science. The adults have a conference with Joshua and share with him the expectations of classroom behavior and their ideas on how he can become more productive during class. They welcome his ideas and thoughts.

The *difference model* contended that "minority" groups have their own distinct cultural patterns of child-rearing practices and learning competencies (Boykin, 1983; Hale, 1980; Hale-Benson, 1986). This model also suggested that children fail in school because "schools do not recognize and utilize their unique competencies for teaching, learning, and testing" (Ogbu, 1986, p. 49). Although the difference model was not rejected, at least one researcher pointed out that the model did not explain why children of other minority groups, who also have distinctive cultural frames of reference, were not "turned off" by the same educational process (Ogbu, 1985, 1986, 1992).

Ogbu suggested the development of a *cultural ecology* that "enables us to discover distinctive black competencies and the relationship of the instrumental competencies to black child-rearing competencies as well as to black school experiences" (1985, p. 49). Such a posture may allow research to be based on the study of different populations *contextually,* not from studying one population as a standard (Boykin, 1983, 1986, 1994; Boykin & Ellison, 1993; Jones, 1991).

This cultural ecological model of child rearing and development includes an affective environment, subsistence tasks, and survival strategies that lead to child-rearing techniques in various environments (Spencer, Brookins, & Allen, 1985). The dominant adult categories generate the process to produce dominant child/adolescent types and competencies. The secondary cultural differences (culture that is in opposition to European American culture) require programs that are designed to deal with the discontinuities.

Holliday (1985), in a study examining competence and ecology, found that the expectations of parents were quite different from expectations of teachers as they related to African American children. She found nonsignificant relations between academic performance and competence at home:

Mother's perceptions of the children's skills bear no relationship to the children's academic achievement. But teacher's perceptions of the children's skills are highly predictive of children's academic achievement. In the home and neighborhood, children's roles most frequently demand problem-solving skills. But at school, children's interpersonal skills, as well as academic excellence, are in great demand. (Holliday, 1985, p. 63)

Holliday's findings suggest that, although they were competent in their roles at home and in the community, African American children were experiencing problems in school. Ogbu (1985) suggested that help will be needed in separating behaviors and skills that facilitate school and later socioeconomic success from behaviors and skills that imply assimilation and threaten cultural identity.

Research supports and develops Ogbu's suggestion by demonstrating that cultural identity development is an important tenet in constructing academic success among youth of color (Tatum, 1997), even when their behavior suggests the presence of a disability and possible need for special education services. For example, teachers often are alarmed when African Americans, especially those in predominantly European American school environments, congregate in the cafeteria. When this congregating is highlighted by culturally sanctioned movement, supported by verve, powerful conversation, expressive individualism (Boykin, 1983, 1994), and proximity, teachers often ask, "Why are all of the Black kids sitting together in the cafeteria?" Rather than merely succumb to negative explanations in answer to this question, a suburban Massachusetts middle school introduced a program called Student Efficacy Training. A special class was organized to create a forum whereby African American students could discuss their academic challenges, encounters with racism in school, and other social issues. Students initially resented having to attend this class; they did not understand why only African American students from the city were required to attend. However, when the class began to highlight the reality of low academic achievement among African American youth and the challenges of functioning in an environment where teachers and other students were not affirming of differences that they brought to the school environment, significant changes occurred. Drawing support from one another became an important coping strategy. Their academic success increased, and these students began to feel and become more of an integral part of the school environment.

The opportunity to come together in the company of supportive adults allowed these young Black students to talk about the issues that hindered their performance—racial encounters, feelings of isolation, test anxiety, homework dilemmas—in the psychological safety of their own group. In the process, the peer culture changed to one that supported academic performances rather than undermined it. (Tatum, 1997, p. 72)

Embracing Dimensions
of African American Culture

Joshua and his teacher and parents have had discussions about how to provide avenues for Joshua to highlight his verve and expressive individualism. He is excited about joining the Science Club; he welcomes the opportunity to share his experiments. He is encouraged to study and practice during transition times and when he has completed assignments before the next class period begins. He is also given options of visiting other classrooms to share his new and developing science skills.

Understanding the history of African American culture is important to understanding culture and its application to the cultural frameworks of teaching African American children in public schools (Asante, 1991, 1992; Boykin, 1991, 1994; Boykin & Ellison, 1993; Delpit, 1988, 1995; Hilliard, 1991; Tatum, 1997). With little surprise, the acknowledgment and acceptance of African American cultural existence continues to meet with resistance in educational arenas. Teachers must be knowledgeable of the nine dimensions of African American culture (see Table 2) and the "mediation techniques" (Spencer et al., 1985) that are exercised in the continued survival strategy of African American youth in public schools. These nine cultural dimensions highlight the essence of African American interactions and are linked to traditional West African cultural ethos (Boykin, 1986). Although African culture has not remained fully intact with the "intrusions of racism and oppression and the necessity to function for 300 years within the American social context" (Ogbu, 1985, p. 40), researchers have suggested that evidence of behavioral practices that are consistent with West African traditions do abound and are witnessed within African American family life and do have an impact on school life (Boykin, 1991; Boykin & Ellison, 1993; Boykin & Toms, 1985; Hale-Benson, 1986; Shade & Edwards, 1987).

Boykin and Toms (1985) contended that African American culture was not overly socialized in the conventional teaching of its components. African American cultural socialization was not pragmatic, it was culturally conditioned. "The cultural motifs are passed on through a 'tacit' cultural process. Children pick up modes, sequences, and styles of behavior through day-to-day encounters with significant others. These habitual forms are acquired through an unarticulated process" (Boykin & Toms, 1985, p. 42).

In a study designed to assess the orientation of African American and European American youth, Shade and Edwards (1987) found that because of the social preference of African American youth (member to member), the modal orientation of African American youth was toward extroversion. They were drawn more toward people than were European American youth. African American youth also developed different recognition patterns. They were more capable of discerning faces and facial emotions and paid more attention to the affective characteristics of pictures. They appeared to be more adept at detecting social reactions and nuances. Although there were individual differences within both groups, the modal orientation of European American youth was toward introversion; they preferred to concentrate on self, ideas, tasks, and things (member to object).

Shade and Edwards (1987) identified the visual mode, play behavior, and family interactions as important environmental correlates to the strength that African American children bring to the classroom. The homes of African Americans tended to display more pictures of people, family, and famous people (member to member), whereas the homes of European Americans displayed more objects, landscapes, and abstract pictures (member to object). The play of African American children was highly structured and physical; group games were intricate in design, movement, rhythm, and timing.

Because public schools seldom have been prepared to embrace the "realities" necessary to teach effectively from a culturally responsive perspective (Gay, 1997; Ladson-Billings, 1994), many special education programs have grown significantly since the *Brown v. Board of Education* desegregation mandate of 1954. However, the problem of effectively educating African American youth has not been consistently embraced, despite a warning by Dunn (1968). He

Table 2. Nine dimensions of African American culture

Dimension	Example	Considerations
Spirituality	Jamal acts on his curiosity and accepts his own convictions.	Approach to life is vitalistic; nonmaterial forces influence life.
Harmony	Ashanti is linked to her surroundings in class, at home, and in her versatile community.	Fate interrelated with other elements/schemes; human kind and nature are harmonically joined.
Movement	Dahliya prefers moving from and through several locations frequently.	Emphasis on interweaving of movement, rhythm, percussion, music, dance; central to psychological health.
Verve	Joshua is immersed in a variety of activities and diunital interactions. He glories in constant activity.	Propensity for high levels of stimulation, energetic and lively action.
Affect	Imani is emotionally tied to everything that happens in her school life.	Emphasis on emotion and feelings; sensitivity to emotional cues; tendency to be emotionally expressive.
Communalism	Omarr is tied to family and community allegiance. He feels responsible to peers.	Commitment to social connectedness; social bonds and responsibility transcend individual privileges.
Expressive Individualism	Ashanti expresses her unique self while sharing community ties with peers. She often seeks ways to affirm her differences.	Cultivation of distinctive personality and a proclivity for spontaneous, genuine personal expression.
Oral Tradition	Jody thrives in dialogue with others. She has creative command of language.	Preference for oral/aural modes of communication; speaking and listening are treated as performances.
Social Time Perspective	Ayinde is bound by his commitment to activity. He is often reluctant to make the transition into other activities when he wants to complete a project.	Orientation in which time is treated as passing through social space; recurring, personal, and phenomenological.

From Boykin, A.W. (1983). The academic performance of Afro-American children. In J. Spence (Ed.), *Achievement and achievement motives* (pp. 344–346). San Francisco: W.H. Freeman & Company; adapted by permission.

clearly stated that the trend (which was initiated prior to the passing of the Education for All Handicapped Children Act of 1975 [PL 94-142]) "in special education appeared to be the inappropriate labeling and placement of significant numbers of low income status children" (Dunn, 1968, p. 6). A significant number of African Americans, Native Americans, Mexican Americans, and Puerto Rican Americans were represented in this low-income status, labeling, and placement process. The continued problem has merely embedded itself across several educational environments.

Chenault asserted that this trend was an example of a macroscopic psychological and educational construct that may have "provided the theoretical foundation for questionable educational diagnosis and inappropriate placement of vast numbers" of African American children (1975, p. 93). He further asserted that the two theoretical models applied to research in special education—medical and psychometric—had utilized "quantitative statistical techniques to generate qualitative conclusions" (p. 94). As a result, theorists and practitioners of special education are to be challenged because the results of education research have not consistently reflected this violation of research methodology in the education of African American youth. These "traditional approaches to meeting the academic and social skill needs of these learners often focus on perceived individual weaknesses and lowered expectations. Such instructional approaches may limit African American student choices and problem-solving abilities" (Brooks, 1985, p. 6). Educators may be charged to teach the explicit rules of "the culture of power" (Delpit, 1988, 1993, 1995) within the context of school environments and also "tap" the academic potential of students (Brooks, 1985).

Coping Strategies Among African American Youth

Many African American children who experience challenges within the educational context accept their school situation and do the best that they can in the classroom. Some children learn to "play the game" and are passed on from grade to grade. Other children learn various coping strategies, and some children consistently resist what they perceive to be unfair treatment as it relates to their language and their personhood. Many of these children withdraw intellectually and emotionally from the learning environment. As a result, they often fail and do not acquire adequate reading and other academic skills.

The case of *Martin Luther King Junior Elementary School v. Ann Arbor School District* highlights this point. The plaintiffs claimed that "intelligibility can be affected by the lack of familiarity with the rhetorical and semantic strategies of black English" (Smitherman, 1985, p. 46). Smitherman contended that the court case was built on nonstructural barriers. Within the context of the school environment, negative linguistic attitudes, reflected in institutional policies and practices, were partially responsible for African American children's becoming educationally dysfunctional. Although the court con-

cluded that if language barriers existed they existed because the process of attempting to teach African American children to speak standard English made them feel inferior and, thereby, turned them off to the learning process, Smitherman believed that the conflict remained unresolved. The teachers involved in the case denied that the children talked differently. The teachers did not acknowledge the existence of a language difference even after taped conversations with the children were shared in court. The original case charged, on behalf of 15 African American children, that the school had failed to educate the children properly. This allegation included charges that the children 1) were improperly placed in special education classes and 2) had been suspended, disciplined, and repeatedly retained without taking into account the ecological differences that they brought with them to the classroom. Although the school's attitude suggested that "perhaps the children were uneducable" (Smitherman, 1985, p. 42), the final disposition of the case was based on the language provision of the Equal Educational Opportunity Act of 1974 (PL 93-380). The judge ruled that "there is no constitutional provision guaranteeing the right to educational services based on cultural, social, or economic background" (Smitherman, 1985, p. 43).

Embracing language and differences in language styles is an important issue for educators. Understanding the cultural references and inferences of language usage may be instrumental in the development of curricula and instructional strategies for African American learners. Such "realities" rest impatiently on the thresholds of schools, homes, neighborhoods, and society as service providers attempt to educate effectively all youth in public school environments. The problem demands an empirical and qualitative examination that will lead to treatment models that have an impact on the educational, ecological, and personal environmental frameworks in which African American youth interact (Asante, 1991; Comer & Poussaint, 1992; DuBois, 1903; Hilliard, 1991; Holliday, 1989; Hopson & Hopson, 1990; Jones, 1991; Obiakor, Algozzine, & Ford, 1993; Spencer et al., 1985; Woodson, 1933).

Educational Realities
Among African American Youth

The quality of educational life is at risk for African American youth. These youth continue to experience disproportionate poverty, ill health, inadequate education, and high unemployment. African American underachievement in public schools is more the rule than the exception (Ford, 1992; Hale-Benson, 1986; Kunjufu, 1993; Murray & Fairchild, 1989; Nichols, 1976; Obiakor et al., 1993; Patton, 1995). Classrooms for students who demonstrate behavior disorders, emotional disturbances, and learning problems, especially in metropolitan areas, are heavily populated with African American youth. "Teachers' attitudes and perceptions both affect and moderate children's academic achievements" (Holliday, 1989, p. 32). Students who are placed in special education classes might be at greater risk for failure because in many cases it is the attitude and the perception of teachers that have initiated and led to the recommendation of special education placement (Anderson, 1992, 1994; Grant, 1992; Pine & Hilliard, 1991). Placement and intervention often are based on models that do not embrace the cultural and societal realities experienced by African American youth (Anderson, 1992; Anderson & Webb-Johnson, 1995). Such placement decisions may result from prejudice, discrimination, and racist behavior under the guise of compliance to the provisions of the Individuals with Disabilities Education Act (IDEA) of 1990 (PL 101-476) and its amendments of 1997 (PL 105-17).

Overrepresentation

Joshua's semester report card shows As and Bs. His behavior grade was a B, and the teacher has noted significant progress. Joshua appears happier at school; he now enjoys assisting peers with their academic assignments, and he has convinced two other boys to join the Science Club. The teacher is not sure about special education referral now. Although Joshua's talking and challenging of authority still occasionally are of concern to the teacher, she realizes that she has learned a great deal as she has continued to read about the culture of African Americans and the problems associated with increased special education referrals in her school.

African American learners constitute 16.85% of the general school-age population (U.S. Department of Education, National Center for Education Statistics, 1995). According to the U.S. Department of Education's Office of Civil Rights (1998), however, they represent only 8% of those youth identified as gifted and talented. In sharp contrast, they represent 24% of all youth identified as demonstrating serious emotional disturbances (SED) or behavior disorders (BD). According to Chinn and Hughes (1987), a disproportionate range of placement exists in special education if such decisions fall outside a 10% difference, positive or negative, in a total student population. As a result, one could assume that the percentage of special education placements for African American learners should fall between 15.17% and 18.53% (16.85% ± 1.68%). Furthermore, African American learners compose 35% of all youth identified as demonstrating educable cognitive disabilities (ECD) and 32% of all youth identified as demonstrating trainable cognitive disabilities (TCD; U.S. Department of Education, Office of Civil Rights, 1994).

According to Harry and Anderson (1994), this overrepresentation is even more startling among African American males. African American males compose 8.2% of the total school-age population. However, African American males are identified more often as exhibiting ECD, TCD, and SED, at the rates of 19%, 17%, and 19%, respectively, *more than double* their proportion of the school-age population (Harry & Anderson, 1994). Similarly, these males receive 30% of the instances of corporal punishment and 23% of the suspensions (Harry & Anderson, 1994). In fact, African American males are overrepresented in *all* disability areas. Such disproportionate distribution clearly is problematic (Anderson & Webb-Johnson, 1995; Artiles & Trent, 1994; Chenault, 1975; Harry & Anderson, 1994).

Problematic Implications

Because of the limited scope of this chapter, the following discussion focuses only on the SED category in an effort to explore and analyze the

need for developing a cultural context to assist service providers in reversing the trend toward incomplete school success among African American learners. Children are expected to learn and comply with the rules established by the school and the classroom teacher. Cultural orientations seldom are addressed in this context. For example, few teachers are aware of the nine dimensions of African American culture identified by Boykin (1983; see Table 2). Spirituality, harmony, movement, verve, affect, communalism, expressive individualism, oral tradition, and social time perspective are tenets that may assist teachers in embracing the integrity and the strength that African American learners bring to classrooms (Boykin, 1983, 1986; Boykin & Ellison, 1993; Webb-Johnson & Albert, 1995). In schools, a single culturally given body of knowledge, values, and behaviors based on mainstream-validated beliefs often defines appropriate and inappropriate behavior among children. Deviation from such norms often is perceived as inappropriate. In fact, many SED placements are based on very subjective decisions often in direct contrast to the perceptions and support offered by family and community members. The current federal definition and the proposed revised definition of SED are void of culturally legitimate and responsive integrity as it relates to African American youth (Anderson & Webb-Johnson, 1995).

Racism and Special Education

"Race has been a central issue in American life" (Comer, 1989, p. 93). As a result, "racism, prejudice, and discrimination are shamefully sabotaging our nation's efforts to provide a high-quality education for all children" (Pine & Hilliard, 1991, p. 79). Pine and Hilliard asserted the importance of educators' prizing and valuing different views that cultural orientations create and present as resources for learning. These authors also posited that the low-level demands of the special education system cause culturally diverse learners to miss exposure to higher levels of educational action because the differences that they present to the education system and its personnel are not valued.

There has been a long history of discriminatory acts in the special education placement of African American children (Grant, 1992; Kunjufu, 1984; *Larry P. v. Riles* 1972, 1979, 1984; Mercer, 1973; Mercer, 1982; Pine & Hilliard, 1991). *Larry P. v. Riles* prohibited California from using any individualized intelligence tests to identify African American children as cognitively disabled unless the state could prove that the tests were not racially or culturally discriminatory. The case also demanded that tests be administered in a way that was nondiscriminatory; any tests used were to be validated for use with culturally diverse students. The ruling also mandated that data collection address the overrepresentation of African Americans in placements for youth with mild cognitive disabilities. Although the ruling was overturned in 1992, the *Larry P. v. Riles* case is responsible for initiating a reform in the status quo or accepted assessment practices by challenging the special education concept of "mild mental retardation" and for stimulating a noncategorical movement in the field.

Mercer's (1973) comprehensive study of "mental retardation" labeling in Riverside, California, revealed that 86% of the African Americans labeled as "mentally retarded" were between the ages of 5 and 19. In comparison with European and Latino Americans, the labeling of African Americans was more school-age specific. African Americans from low socioeconomic levels were not likely to perceive their children as cognitively disabled during preschool years. In contrast, European Americans were labeled intellectually subnormal at earlier ages than were culturally diverse individuals. "For persons from minority groups, labeled retardation is more age specific and more closely tied to the statistical model of normal and performance on an intelligence test than for Anglos" (Mercer, 1973, p. 82). She further concluded that there was a clear overrepresentation of African American school-age children assessed, identified, and placed in classes for children with cognitive disabilities. African Americans represented 7.9% of the school-age population in Riverside; however, they represented 19.8% of children found eligible, 21.2% of children recommended, and 22.6% of children actually placed in special education.

Anderson identified four specific relations that influenced the nature and consequences of the educational treatment that African American children experienced within public school environments as a result of being labeled behaviorally disordered: "definitions of disorder and community consensus, identification and intervention, shared educational commitment and the imposition of professional perceptions, and expectations for compliance and professional competition" (1992, p. 93). She asserted that the current terminology and definition were not clear regarding identification and placement procedures for any youth who may be considered for or placed in an environment for individuals with behavior disorders. Subjective judgments often led to the labeling of individuals. This judgment often was focused on disturbing behaviors demonstrated by students rather than on their academic difficulties. Anderson further asserted that

Prior to the 1954 *Brown v. Board of Education* litigation, the separation of Black American children from the mainstream population of public school classrooms was perceived by Black parents as another example of racial prejudice which Black children would have to learn to conquer. Gaining educational experiences in separate classrooms or separate facilities was not viewed as detrimental to the general welfare of the child. Due to the unique history of Black Americans in this country, any educational experience an individual received was highly valued. The quality and consequence of the educational experience was not devalued because of the location in which the experience took place. . . . After 1954 the relationship between the school and the community was active and ongoing . . . the parents and the community trusted the wisdom of the teacher to do "what was best for the child." (1992, pp. 94–95)

PL 94-142 mandated due process. Although its intent has been to protect the rights of individuals with disabilities, it had a significant impact on the testing and labeling of African American youth. There often is disagreement between the school and the community when school personnel label African American children "disordered" or "cognitively disabled" (Anderson, 1992; Harry, 1992; Holliday, 1985; Mercer, 1973). As a result, "the lack of consensus between the school community and the African American commu-

nity has contributed to the creation of a separate educational 'way of life' or 'culture' for African American children labeled BD and their families" (Anderson, 1992, p. 96).

The second factor that Anderson (1992) identified as influencing the educational treatment of African American youth is the practice of identification and intervention. IDEA and Section 504 of the Rehabilitation Act of 1973 (PL 93-112) acknowledge the discriminatory effects of educational assessment and practices as they potentially relate to youth and individuals from culturally and linguistically diverse populations. States such as California and Illinois have addressed such effects in combating the systematic overrepresentation of African American youth in the category of individuals with cognitive disabilities. If federal and state practices have embraced real and potential discriminatory actions in identification as suspect or

Fundamentally flawed, then intervention models become less believable and, in actuality, less effective as treatment approaches. Nevertheless, the reality of special education identification and placement for African American children labeled BD continues to be based on flawed and psychometrically unsound practices. (Anderson, 1992, p. 97)

The third factor identified by Anderson (1992) as influencing the educational treatment of African American youth is shared educational commitment and professional perceptions. She posited that the African American and public school communities share a commitment to teach children; however, the perception of all children is not shared. Some professionals in school systems often seek to highlight the differences in such a way that differences help "to sustain an inadequate and inappropriate basis for communication. . . . Simply, when differences between people rather than commonalities among people are emphasized, perceptions of 'sameness' become the yardstick by which all 'others' are judged" (Anderson, 1992, p. 98). As a result, professional misinterpretations or perceptions of behavior potentially have an impact on the educational treatment of African American youth who are perceived as having a behavioral or emotional problem.

The last factor identified by Anderson (1992) as influencing the educational treatment of African American youth is expectations for compliance and professional competition. Special educators of youth who allegedly present behavioral or emotional challenges often rely on non-education professionals to define education phenomena and design educational intervention methodologies based on a medical model. Anderson asserted that this reality is evinced by recommended treatment practices that often are inconsistent among non-education personnel who "diagnosis" the disorder.

Professional imposition rather than individual responsibility remains the basis of current special educational classification schemes. The temptation to rely on non-educational ways for understanding educational phenomena is proving to be a devastating practice affecting African American children, their families, their communities, and the larger society to which we all contribute. (Anderson, 1992, p. 101)

Such school practices may be perceived as racist as they relate to African American learners (Grant, 1992; Pine & Hilliard, 1991). Historically, African American youth have been assessed, taught, and evaluated in public schools based on the social value system of middle-income European Americans (Akbar, 1985; Delpit, 1988, 1993; Hilliard, 1991). These values define differences as deficits, and deficits as problems. African American learners are considered problematic or "difficult to teach" (U.S. Department of Education, 1992, p. 48). Children perceived by professionals as "difficult" often are devalued, defined as deficit learners, and, thereby, expected to fail.

Special Education and Multicultural Education

Further problematic implications appear inherent because few researchers embrace the similarity of issues within the field of special education and multicultural education. Services provided in both arenas champion efforts to provide equitable education outcomes for youth with identified disabilities and those from culturally different environments. However, each arena falls short in reaching those goals because systematic efforts to provide the services necessary do not exist in many classrooms throughout the United States. More inclusive general and special education environments are needed. Service providers in both environments must be educated to embrace *all* children. Therefore, preservice and in-service development must be transformed to prepare educators better to embrace and teach those who are different and demonstrate behavioral differences. Cultural diversity is not new; however, the response to the rich diversity presented by youth who once were denied access to public education in the United States must be transformed and reconstructed.

EMBRACING SOLUTIONS

The deficit-remedial structure of intervention in education has persisted in reflecting and expecting learning and behavior representations from youth perceived as demonstrating behavior disorders. Reversing the trend toward academic and social failure among African American youth will involve a comprehensive and dynamic research agenda that requires the entire village (home, school, and community) to come together to bring about change. First, the village will have to embrace the historical and deeply embedded racist structure of general and special education. Educators must remember that schooling in the United States was not designed for African American youth. If a group is not a part of the initial problematic design, then they have little chance of being included in any successful part of solutions or reconstruction of that design. The historical and political construction of savagery and racialization is, unfortunately, deeply rooted in the history of education in the United States (Takaki, 1993).

The reconstruction and reform of special education within a multicultural paradigm will demand embracing a dynamic process of change. Leadership and inclusion of scholars of color and those who are culturally conscious is paramount. This scholarship should be rooted in the historical and deep structural tenets of African American culture (Boykin & Ellison, 1993) as it relates to education reform for African American youth. As the field seeks to assert further special education *as a service and not a place,* it also is challenged to redefine behavior disorders as a disability and to broaden the knowledge base necessary to create culturally responsive educators.

Research Agenda

The research agenda that is needed to reverse the trend toward school failure among African American learners requires multifaceted, dynamic, and innovative tenets (Spencer et al., 1985). If educators are to be ready for Joshua and all who demonstrate similar strengths and needs, then quantitative and qualitative methodology may prove beneficial in action research arenas. For example, with the findings in the literature regarding *cooperative learning* (Slavin, 1995), the agenda is compelled to expand the research of Allen and Boykin (1992) and to explore further *communal learning:* academic contexts in which students are encouraged to work together and assist one another because it is the expectation within the community. Cooperative learning appears to be an effective intervention for most youth; however, academic gains by children of color, especially those who are African American, appear to be even more significant. Allen and Boykin (1992) supported this notion but also found that African American youth preferred and demonstrated more academic growth when given the opportunity to work in communal groups. Such a classroom context supported both cultural and home contexts so that students began with educational tenets that were familiar and affirming. Their academic development prospered in such an arena. As a result, such research-supported interventions may be duplicated to increase and improve the academic achievement among African American youth in general, special, and inclusive education environments.

THE FUTURE

Joshua's verve will be challenged to explore his interest in science and math beyond merely regurgitating facts. At a very early age, he will be socialized to explore the scientific method and look forward to solving mathematical equations because he is constantly expected to demonstrate excellence. His school socialization will focus on building on the strengths that he brings to the classroom arena. Teachers study and participate in frequent staff development that assists them in addressing dysconscious bias (King, 1991) resulting from a lack of a cultural knowledge base about diversity. Integrity/strength models (Webb-Johnson & Albert, 1995), based on the dimensions of African American culture (Boykin, 1983), will be utilized to assist in the development, design, and implementation of culturally responsive pedagogy throughout Joshua's education. Homework will be a natural part of his daily life. Teachers will not become discouraged because it may sometimes be difficult to convince students to complete homework assignments. Joshua's teachers will support standards of excellence and then teach Joshua how to work toward those academic goals that often prove to be challenging. He will look forward to reading every day. He will not have to wait on a teacher assignment; in fact, he will begin to develop his own assignments. He will critically approach problems and dilemmas. He will be socialized to implement social action agendas (Banks, 1996). Teachers will embrace paradigms that empower Joshua and other African American children and youth.

The overrepresentation of African American youth in special education remains a phenomenon that requires the entire village to seek solutions. However, the collaborative village first must be built (P. Norwood, personal communication, February 1996); researchers can be initiators in that challenge. Researchers are challenged first to embrace the reality that masses of African American youth are inappropriately referred to and placed in special education because of a lack of understanding and knowledge of cultural contexts (Anderson, 1994; Anderson & Webb-Johnson, 1995).

Children from diverse backgrounds often receive little consistent exposure to academic challenges (Pine & Hilliard, 1991; Stevens & Grymes, 1993). As a result, educators are further challenged to assist in the construction of culturally responsive curriculum and instruction. Such an empowerment agenda is necessary to make a positive impact on the Joshuas in classrooms (see Table 3). Just as the multicultural movement found its roots and direction in the African American Civil Rights movement (Banks, 1996), systematically addressing the strengths and needs of African American youth in special and general education may well become the catalyst and standard for better meeting the educational needs of *all* children.

CONCLUSION

This chapter has explored the dilemma in effectively educating African American youth, especially those who are overrepresented in special education environments. The pervasive overrepresentation in special education with few positive outcomes is of concern to teachers, ad- ministrators, families, and state and federal legislatures. A research agenda altering the negative trend toward labeling and school failure must be constructed. Strength models of intervention that highlight culturally relevant and responsive pedagogy are needed to replace deficit modes of thinking and intervention. A renewed research agenda, assisting service providers in understanding and developing strategies that are steeped in cultural identity development and the dimensions of African American culture, is necessary. Research paradigms that include qualitative as well as quantitative methodology will yield more productive outcomes in assessment and intervention strategies. General, special, and multicultural education communities will benefit from collaborative action plans to construct improved academic environments for African American youth.

Table 3. Ten standards toward empowerment among African American youth

1. *Embrace cultural frameworks.* Study the cultural frameworks of African American youth. Affirm the continued development of their identity. Do not make assumptions. Get to *know* who they are and who they perceive themselves to be.

2. *Assessment and labeling alert.* Understand the implications attached to the assessment and labeling of African American youth.

3. *Explicit/implicit.* Remain aware that some African American children may not be familiar with many of the school practices that some educators take for granted. Orchestrate experiences that explicitly and implicitly teach certain skills. Remember that many African American students have learned to "work" the system as a defense mechanism for survival. Remember also that some African American students have not learned the system and as a result are vulnerable to racist propaganda.

4. *Cultivate the intrinsic.* Use every possible means for motivating African American youth to do well in school. Create and encourage communication with the home and the community. Such strategies can be based on the strengths demonstrated by African American youth.

5. *Teach how to learn.* Teach study and test-taking skills. Provide experiences that are rich in the academic "tricks of the trade." Use "person-to-person" orientations to promote peer and group learning based on communal, kinship, and cooperative practices.

6. *Feedback alert.* Use teaching techniques that provide constant, appropriate, challenging, and realistic feedback. Make homework and continued study a part of the very fabric of their academic existence.

7. *Standards of excellence.* Encourage African American youth to identify with people from the African American community and people from the community at large who have achieved success through establishing and maintaining standards of excellence.

8. *Cognitive behavioral empowerment.* Combine classroom management with elements of choice based on class standards, critical thinking, self-direction, and problem-solving skills.

9. *Talent development.* Encourage talent and skill *development.* Rely less on talent *assessment.*

10. *Orchestrate effective outcomes.* Encourage and assist African American youth in applying principles and ideas learned in the academic environment. Provide an arena where those experiences can be assessed and improved on in the context of the school, family, and community.

Adapted from Webb-Johnson & Albert (1995).

REFERENCES

Akbar, N. (1985). Our destiny: Authors of a scientific revolution. In H.P. McAdoo & J.L. McAdoo (Eds.), *Black children: Social, educational, and parental environments* (pp. 17–31). Thousand Oaks, CA: Sage Publications.

Allen, B.A., & Boykin, A.W. (1992). African-American children and the education process: Alleviating cultural discontinuity through prescriptive pedagogy. *School Psychology Review, 21,* 586–596.

Anderson, M.G. (1992). The use of selected theatre rehearsal technique activities with African-American adolescents labeled "behavior disordered." *Exceptional Children, 59,* 132–140.

Anderson, M.G. (1994). Perceptions about behavioral disorders in African-American cultures and communities. In R. Peterson & S. Ishii-Jordan (Eds.), *Multi-cultural issues in the education of students with behavioral disorders* (pp. 93–104). Cambridge, MA: Brookline Books.

Anderson, M.G., & Webb-Johnson, G.C. (1995). Cultural contexts, the seriously emotionally disturbed classification and African American learners. In B.A. Ford, F.E. Obiakor, & J.M. Patton (Eds.), *Effective education of African American exceptional learners* (pp. 153–188). Austin, TX: PRO-ED.

Artiles, A.J., & Trent, S.C. (1994). Over-representation of minority students in special education: A continuous debate. *The Journal of Special Education, 27,* 410–437.

Asante, M.K. (1991). The Afrocentric idea in education. *Journal of Negro Education, 60,* 170–180.

Asante, M.K. (1992). Afrocentric curriculum. *Educational Leadership, 49*(4), 28–31.

Banks, J.A. (1996). *Multi-cultural education: Transformative knowledge and action.* New York: Teachers College Press.

Boykin, A.W. (1983). The academic performance of Afro-American children. In J. Spence (Ed.), *Achievement and achievement motives: Psychological and sociological approaches* (pp. 324–371). New York: W.H. Freeman & Company.

Boykin, A.W. (1986). The triple quandary and the schooling of Afro-American children. In U. Neisser (Ed.), *The school achievement of minority children* (pp. 57–92). Mahwah, NJ: Lawrence Erlbaum Associates.

Boykin, A.W. (1991). Black psychology and experimental psychology: A functional confluence. In R.L. Jones (Ed.), *Black psychology* (3rd ed., pp. 481–507). Berkeley, CA: Cobb & Henry.

Boykin, A.W. (1994). The sociocultural context of schooling for African American children: A proactive deep structural analysis. In E. Hollins (Ed.), *Formulating a knowledge base for teaching culturally diverse learners* (pp. 233–245). Philadelphia: Association for Curriculum and Supervision Development.

Boykin, A.W., & Ellison, C. (1993). The multiple ecologies of Black youth socialization: An Afrographic analysis. In R. Taylor (Ed.), *Black youth* (pp. 76–99). Thousand Oaks, CA: Sage Publications.

Boykin, A.W., & Toms, F.D. (1985). Black child socialization: A cultural framework. In H.P. McAdoo & J.L. McAdoo (Eds.), *Black children: Social, educational, and parental environments* (pp. 33–51). Thousand Oaks, CA: Sage Publications.

Brooks, C.K. (Ed.). (1985). *Tapping potential.* Champaign, IL: National Council of Teachers of English.

Brown v. Board of Education of Topeka, Kansas, 347 US 483 (1954).

Chenault, J. (1975). Special education and the black community. In L.A. Gary & A. Favor (Eds.), *Restructuring the educational process: A black perspective* (pp. 93–78). Washington, DC: Institute for Urban Affairs and Research.

Chinn, P.C., & Hughes, S. (1987). Representation of minority students in special education classes. *Remedial and Special Education, 8*(4), 41–46.

Comer, J.P. (1989). Racism and the education of young children. *Teachers College Record, 90,* 352–361.

Comer, J.P., & Poussaint, A.F. (1992). *Raising Black children.* New York: Plume.

Delpit, L.D. (1988). The silenced dialogue: Power and pedagogy in educating other people's children. *Harvard Educational Review, 58,* 280–298.

Delpit, L.D. (1993). The politics of teaching literate discourse. In T. Perry & J.W. Fraser (Eds.), *Freedom's plow: Teaching in the multi-cultural classroom* (pp. 285–295). New York: Routledge.

Delpit, L.D. (1995). *Other people's children: Cultural conflict in the classroom.* New York: The New Press.

DuBois, W.E.B. (1903). *The souls of black folk.* Greenwich, CT: Fawcett.

Dunn, L.M. (1968). Special education for the mildly retarded: Is much of it justifiable? *Exceptional Children, 35,* 5–22.

Education for All Handicapped Children Act of 1975, PL 94-142, 20 U.S.C. §§ 1400 *et seq.*

Equal Education Opportunity Act of 1974, PL 93-380, 20 U.S.C. §§ 1221 *et seq.*

Ford, B.A. (1992). Multi-cultural education training for special educators working with African-American youth. *Exceptional Children, 59,* 107–114.

Franklin, V.P. (1985). From integration to Black self-determination: Changing social science perspectives on Afro-American life and culture. In M.B. Spencer, G.K. Brookins, & W.R. Allen (Eds.), *Beginnings: The social and affective development of Black children* (pp. 19–28). Mahwah, NJ: Lawrence Erlbaum Associates.

Gay, G. (1997). Educational equality for students of color. In J.A. Banks & C.A. Banks (Eds.), *Multi-cultural education: Issues and perspectives* (3rd ed., pp. 195–228). Needham Heights, MA: Allyn & Bacon.

Grant, P. (1992). Using special education to destroy black boys. *The Negro Educational Review, 43*(1–2), 17–21.

Hale, J. (1980). De-mythicizing the education of Black children. In R. Jones (Ed.), *Toward a Black psychology* (pp. 221–230). New York: Harper & Row.

Hale-Benson, J.E. (1986). *Black children: Their roots, culture and learning styles* (Rev. ed.). Baltimore: The Johns Hopkins University Press.

Harry, B. (1992). *Cultural diversity, families, and the special education system: Communication and empowerment.* New York: Teachers College Press.

Harry, B., & Anderson, M.G. (1994). The disproportionate placement of African American males in special education programs: A critique of the process. *Journal of Negro Education, 63,* 602–619.

Heath, S.B. (1981). Questioning at home and at school: A comparative study. In G. Spindler (Ed.), *Doing ethnography: Educational anthropology in action* (pp. 120–131). Austin, TX: Holt, Rinehart & Winston.

Heath, S.B. (1991). *Children of promise: Literate activity in linguistically and culturally diverse classrooms.* Washington, DC: National Education Association.

Hilliard, A.G. (1991). Do we have the will to educate all children? *Education Leadership, 24,* 18–25.

Holliday, B.G. (1985). Towards a model of teacher–child transactional processes affecting black children's academic achievement. In M.B. Spencer, G.K. Brookins, & W.R. Allen (Eds.), *Beginnings: The social and affective development of black children* (pp. 117–130). Mahwah, NJ: Lawrence Erlbaum Associates.

Holliday, B.G. (1989). Trailblazers in black adolescent research: The American Council on Education's studies on Negro youth personality development. In R.L. Jones (Ed.), *Black adolescents* (pp. 29–48). Berkeley, CA: Cobb & Henry.

Hopson, D.P., & Hopson, D.S. (1990). *Different and wonderful: Raising black children in a race conscious society.* New York: Simon & Schuster.

Individuals with Disabilities Education Act (IDEA) of 1990, PL 101-476, 20 U.S.C. §§ 1400 *et seq.*

Individuals with Disabilities Education Act Amendments of 1997, PL 105-17, 20 U.S.C. §§ 1400 *et seq.*

Jensen, A.R. (1969). How much can we boost I.Q. and scholastic achievement? *Harvard Educational Review, 39,* 1–117.

Jones, R.L. (Ed.). (1991). *Black psychology* (3rd ed.). Berkeley, CA: Cobb & Henry.

King, J.E. (1991). Dysconscious racism: Ideology, identity, and the miseducation of teachers. *Journal of Negro Education, 60,* 135–146.

Kunjufu, J. (1984). *Developing positive self images and discipline in Black children.* Chicago: African American Images.

Kunjufu, J. (1993). *Hip-Hop v. MAAT.* Chicago: African American Images.

Ladson-Billings, G. (1994). *The dreamkeepers: Successful teachers of African American children.* San Francisco: Jossey-Bass.

Larry P. v. Riles, C-71-2270-RFP (N. D. Cal. 1972), 495, F. Supp. 96 (N. D. Cal 1979) Aff'r (9th Cir. 1984), 1983-84 EHLR DEC. 556:304.

McLoughlin, J.A., & Lewis, R.B. (1994). *Assessing special students* (4th ed.). Columbus, OH: Merrill.

Mercer, J.R. (1973). *Labeling the mentally retarded: Clinical and social system perspectives on mental retardation.* Berkeley: University of California Press.

Mercer, M.M. (1982). Reassessing the larger number of Black children in special education classes: A challenge for the 80's. *The Negro Educational Review, 32,* 28–33.

Murray, C.B., & Fairchild, H.H. (1989). Models of Black adolescent underachievement. In R.L. Jones (Ed.), *Black adolescents* (pp. 29–48). Berkeley, CA: Cobb & Henry.

Nichols, E.J. (1976, August). *Cultural foundations for teaching black children.* Paper presented at the Conference of the World Psychiatric Association and Association of Psychiatrists, University of Ibadab, Nigeria.

Nieto, S. (1996). *Affirming diversity* (2nd ed.). New York: Longman Publishers.

Obiakor, F.E., Algozzine, B., & Ford, B.A. (1993). Urban education, the general education initiative, and service delivery to African-American students. *Urban Education, 28,* 313–325.

Ogbu, J.U. (1985). A cultural ecology of competence among inner-city blacks. In M.B. Spender, G.K. Brookins, & W.R. Allen (Eds.), *Beginnings: The social and affective development of Black children* (pp. 45–66). Mahwah, NJ: Lawrence Erlbaum Associates.

Ogbu, J.U. (1986). The consequences of the American caste system. In U. Neisser (Ed.), *The school achievement of minority children* (pp. 19–56). Mahwah, NJ: Lawrence Erlbaum Associates.

Ogbu, J.U. (1992). Understanding cultural diversity and learning. *Educational Researcher, 21*(8), 5–14.

Patton, J.M. (1995). The education of African American males: Frameworks for developing authenticity. *Journal of African American Men, 1,* 5–27.

Pine, G.J., & Hilliard, A.G. (1991). Schools should emphasize their ethnicity. In D.L. Bender & B. Leone (Eds.), *Racism in America: Opposing viewpoints* (pp. 193–200). San Diego: Greenhaven Press.

Rehabilitation Act of 1973, PL 93-112, 29 U.S.C. §§ 701 *et seq.*

Shade, B., & Edwards, P.A. (1987). Ecological correlates of educative style of Afro-American children. *Journal of Negro Education, 56,* 88–99.

Slavin, R.E. (1995). *Cooperative learning: Theory, research, and practice* (2nd ed.). Needham Heights, MA: Allyn & Bacon.

Smitherman, G. (1985). What go round come round: King in perspective. In C.K. Brooks (Ed.), *Tapping potential* (pp. 41–62). Champaign, IL: National Council of Teachers of English.

Spencer, M.B., Brookins, G.K., & Allen, W.R. (Eds.). (1985). *Beginnings: The social development of black children.* Mahwah, NJ: Lawrence Erlbaum Associates.

Stevens, F.I., & Grymes, J. (1993). *Opportunity to learn: Issues of equity for poor and minority students.* Washington, DC: National Center for Education Statistics.

Takaki, R. (1993). *A different mirror: A history of multi-cultural America.* Boston: Little, Brown.

Tatum, B.D. (1997). *"Why are all the Black kids sitting together in the cafeteria?"* New York: Basic Books.

U.S. Department of Education. (1998). *To assure the free and appropriate public education of all handicapped children: 20th Annual Report to Congress on the Implementation of the Handicapped Act.* Washington, DC: Author.

U.S. Department of Education, National Center for Education Statistics. (1995). *The conditions of education, 1995* (NCES No. 95-273). Washington, DC: U.S. Government Printing Office.

U.S. Department of Education, Office of Civil Rights. (1994). *Elementary and secondary school civil rights compliance report: Projected values for the nation.* Washington, DC: Author.

Webb-Johnson, G.C., & Albert, H. (1995). Integrity/strength models: Empowering African American youth through culturally based curricular, instructional and counseling strategies. In *Proceedings of the 4th Biennial International Special Education Conference* (pp. 75–79). Brighton, England: International Special Education Association.

Woodson, C.G. (1933). *The mis-education of the Negro.* New York: Amsterdam Press.

Author Index

Subject Index

Page numbers followed by "f" indicate figures; those followed by "t" indicate tables.